LECTURES ON THE RAMAYANA

LECTURES ON THE RAMAYANA

V S SRINIVASA SASTRI

GYAN

Published by

Gyan Publishing House
5, Ansari Road
Daryaganj, New Delhi-110002
Phone: 011-47034999, 9811692060
E-mail: books@gyanbooks.com

Distribution Network
gyanbooks.com
India, USA, Canada, UK, Australia

ISBN: 978-93-7225-415-0 (PB)
First Published, 1949

2nd Impression 2025

Printed at: Gyan Press, Delhi.

LECTURES ON THE RAMAYANA
Author: V S SRINIVASA SASTRI

LECTURES ON THE
RAMAYANA

BY

the Rt. Hon.
V. S. SRINIVASA SASTRI

With a Foreword
BY
SRI T. R. VENKATARAMA SASTRI

CONTENTS

PREFACE

The thirty lectures on the Ramayana which are published here were delivered by the late Rt. Hon. V. S. Srinivasa Sastri under the auspices of the Madras Samskrit Academy, in the Madras Sanskrit College grounds. The series began on 5-4-'44 and concluded on 8-11-'44, and the Academy had made special arrangements for taking shorthand reports of these lectures with a view to publish them eventually in book-form.

The concluding function was celebrated in traditional manner: the then President of the Academy, Sir P. S. Sivaswami Aiyar who was in the chair, observed that by delivering these lectures on the national epic of India, the distinguished lecturer had added one more to the manifold and valuable services rendered by him to the country; the Academy and the enthusiastic audience which had, in large numbers, attended these lectures every Wednesday, presented the lecturer, in grateful admiration, with a shawl, an address and a silver plate inscribed with the verse

संस्कारक्रमसंपन्नामद्रुतामविलम्बिताम् ।
उच्चारयसि कल्याणीं वाचं हृदयहारिणीम् ॥

(Ramayana, IV. 3. 32)

and subscribed to the fund for the publication of these lectures.

The Executive Committee of the Academy appointed a sub-committee consisting of Sri T. R. Venkatarama Sastri (Chairman), Sri. K. Balasubrahmanya Aiyar, Sri. R. S. Venkatarama Sastri and Dr. V. Raghavan to arrange for the printing of the lectures. It was decided to entrust the publication to Sri S. Viswanathan of the Central Art Press, Chetput, Madras, and create with the proceeds an endowment in the Academy for a lecture in the name of the late revered Sastriar to be delivered on the Ramayana on the Valmiki Day celebrated by the Academy every year on Sri Rama Navami.

Sri R. Narayana Aiyar, I.C.S. (Retd.), was kind enough to help Sri K. Balasubrahmanya Aiyar and Dr. V. Raghavan in preparing the typescripts of these lectures for the press and in reading the proofs. For these and for the Errata, Index, cross-references and analytical summary of the lectures given here, which were prepared by him, the Academy tenders to Sri R. Narayana Aiyar its profound thanks. The thanks of the Academy are also due to Sri V. Doraswami for assistance in the preparation of the shorthand notes of the lectures.

A word of explanation is due for the delay that has been unavoidably caused in publishing these lectures. The Academy desired very much that the lecturer himself should revise the typescripts of the lectures and made arrangements for it. But the illness of the lecturer prevented him from undertaking the revision. The large number of verses quoted in the lectures had to be written out with their references and the preparation of the matter for the press took some time. This and the difficult conditions in printing presses had caused the delay in placing this book in the hands of the public who were making frequent and anxious enquiries about it.

March 27, '49,
Madras.

V. V. Srinivasa Ayyangar,
President,
Madras Samskrit Academy.

FOREWORD

This volume is a collection of thirty discourses on the Ramayana by the Right Honourable Srinivasa Sastri delivered at the Samskrit Academy in 1944. They evoked great interest and were attended by a large number of persons from all parts of the City. There was keen desire that they should be published in book-form and funds were contributed on the very day that these discourses were brought to a close. Publication was unavoidably delayed. There have been inquiries even from outside the Presidency as to when they will be published. Now at last they are published in this volume.

Mahatma Gandhi, when he was last in Madras, saw Mr. Sastri at the General Hospital and at the end of an interesting talk which turned on the Ramayana asked Mr. Sastri to put down his ideas in writing for the instruction of the public. When last I saw Gandhiji at Delhi he inquired when these lectures would be published. If he had been alive to-day, he would have gladly undertaken to write a Foreword to this volume. Now that neither he nor the author is alive, this volume may well go forth and deliver its message without Foreword or Introduction. But usage will not be denied and I have been asked to write a Foreword to the Volume and I have undertaken this supererogatory task, persuading myself that it would be an act of piety towards one whom I held in great respect and not without a desire to attain this lightly-won immortality of association with a book embodying so eminently pious a series of discourses on our Immortal Epic.

Having ventured to call these discourses pious, I am reminded of the hurt that they caused to some devout persons by their professed object of presenting Sri Rama in a purely human aspect, ignoring His place among the Great Avatars or Incarnations. I hope I shall not be deemed repeating the offence by putting the question whether there is nothing to be gained by studying the Epic as a human document rather than as a religious text book. The author of the Ramayana puts in the mouth of his Divine Hero the words "Atmanam manusham manye," suggesting that according to himself his conduct was that of a human being desirous of acting conformably to the highest ideals of Dharma or the best traditions of his time. His example is of value to common men, not to be put aside as that of one who stood on a plane all his own and to be judged by other than human standards. The lessons of his life are available as much to those who do not accept his Divinity as to those who accept him as such.

To those who were present at these discourses and watched the lecturer's emotional breakdowns on occasions, it must have been obvious that Sastri was not without the reverence that is of the substance of religion, though it might not have satisfied orthodox standards of faith.

The Commentators have struggled with the texts which pulled them one way and their own conception of what would be appropriate in an omniscient Divinity which pulled them another way, the conception of Godhead every time prevailing over the obvious meaning of the texts. It is worth noticing that Valmiki's sense of piety was not shocked by making the Hero say that he could not distinguish Vali from Sugriva at their first encounter or that he considered himself only as a human being. Orthodoxy might also reflect that if Divinity could exercise its omnipotence without employing human agency for its ends, incarnations would be unnecessary and we should not have had an Epic of heroic life to instruct and chasten the hearts of men. It is by assuming the human form and associating with erring humanity that God confers the choicest benefits on the world of men by precept and by example. It may also be added that the boon secured by Ravana that he should receive no hurt from all others than mere mortals of whom he was not afraid had to be upheld by the Highest taking the human form before the Evil that was Ravana could be destroyed.

It is well known that particular incidents in the story of his life have been subjected to criticism as not coming up to the highest standards as conceived by the critics and the commentators have laboured to answer all such criticisms in their commentaries. To my mind even these criticisms are not wholly purposeless. Even orthodoxy at times is inclined to agree with the critics. To give but one illustration, there is the treatment by Rama of Sita which no pious person has approved and I have seen tears roll down the cheeks of devotees of Rama at the cruel words of Rama addressed to her in the Yuddha Kanda.

While Rama's divine nature is to all devout Hindus an unquestionable fact, the chastening effect of the Epic on the minds of men comes out of the study of it as the unfolding of the drama of the highest human life. So at any rate it seems to me.

I daresay these discourses will be subjected to criticism, even as the Ramayana itself has been even before the age of the most ancient commentators. I should welcome all such discussions as educative and useful.

T. R. VENKATARAMA SASTRI

ANALYTICAL SUMMARY OF THE LECTURES

LECTURE I

EXORDIUM

1-13 No summary is attempted as none can do justice to such ideas as the essentially human aspect of Rama's character as apart from his divinity that to many is a just article of faith; the evolution that is discernible of Rama's personality in his particular **milieu,** through trials, temptations, and weaknesses, as contrasted with the notion of his incarnation as a perfected being; the supreme instructional value of the Ramayana read as an epic pure and simple rather than conned over as a form of devotional exercise—ideas which are pivotal to the talks, and which, for a proper appreciation of the series of character-studies, must be imbibed in the entirety of their eloquent expression.

LECTURE II

LANDMARKS IN THE MAIN STORY OF BALAKANDA

14-15 Rama's superiority, from the beginning, to his brothers, younger than he only by a few hours.

Their two outstanding qualities—reverence towards elders, particularly towards their parents; brotherliness.

15-18 I. Viswamitra carries off Rama and Lakshmana with him to guard his sacrifice from Maricha and Subahu.

Lakshmana is treated throughout the story as if he were in physical body as in functions and characteristics only a part of Sri Rama. We have evidence of this unique bond between them here in their first public appearance. Visvamitra did not ask Dasaratha for Lakshmana, but Lakshmana was inseparable from Rama, and it was taken for granted that he was to go with Rama. He seems hardly to be noticed by the rishi, but this simply means that in his eyes Lakshmana and Rama were one. The sentiment occurs frequently—'Lakshmana is like a second life to Rama, only he functions outside Rama's body'; 'Lakshmana is Rama's right arm'.

18-22 II. The young heroes' baptism of fire in Tatakavana.

Though Tataka equally with her brood was a source of torment in sacrifices, Visvamitra kept her name back from Dasaratha as he might have jibbed at Rama killing a woman to win his spurs.

Visvamitra warned Rama that Tataka was not only a she-devil but a tricky one at that, and that no softness should be shown to her on the ground of her sex. Rama without thinking of it promised that he would **without doubt** kill her straightway; but when she appeared before him, somehow his conscience smote him, and he thought he would just mutilate her and put her

hors de combat. Only when he found himself harassed and his shafts going rather wide of the mark and the rishi reminded him that time was all but up, did Rama dispatch her. Rama's hesitation and doubt were natural; he had no intention of going back on his plighted word.

As for the duty of sparing the sex, Visvamitra enunciated a good rule and sound law—if a woman is a confirmed enemy to social order her sex ought to be no protection to her. The killing of Tataka is no blot on Rama's escutcheon.

22-27 III. The quadruple wedding in Mithila.

When Visvamitra led his young charges to Janaka's great sacrifice, he told them about the famous bow of Siva at Mithila which none could lift, let alone string, and whetted their appetite, but with muni-like reticence he stopped short of telling the lads that Sita was to be the glittering prize of the champion!

Sita narrating her svayamvara to Anasuya in Ayodhyakanda says—and it must be correct of course, though it is not mentioned in Balakanda —that when Rama broke the bow, Janaka offered her there and then to Rama, but that Rama refused to take her without knowing his father's wish.

As regards the wedding of Rama's brothers, it is noteworthy that it was not the fathers of the brides that offered them, but Vasishtha and Visvamitra respectively that solicited their hand, on behalf of Dasaratha.

The phrase 'pitrkrta' in 1.77.27 discussed. The meaning of the Poet, who probably had in mind Sita's words to Anasuya, is that though Rama won Sita by bending the bow, she was dear to him because his father had heartily consented to his wedding her. That is one of the great virtues of Rama—that he never forgot or underweighed the importance of having the full consent and approval of his father before doing great things in his life.

LECTURE III

LAKSHMANA

28-31 Rama's love for Lakshmana exceeded his love for Sita. It was **sui generis.** What does Rama himself say? That Sita was not so high in his estimation as Lakshmana! Vide his lament when Lakshmana was prostrated by Indrajit's serpent-arrows, and again when he was transfixed to the ground by Ravana's 'sakti'. And Sita, who judged unerringly by her innate womanly perception, told Hanuman that Lakshmana was dearer to Rama than herself!

31-33 Contrast between Rama and Lakshmana—

Rama's passion was for Dharma; his greatest love was Right, Honour, Truthfulness, vide his emphatic declaration to Kaikeyi when he was told to give up the yauvarajya in favour of Bharata, and to Sita when she remonstrated with him for bearing arms in the forest.

To Lakshmana, on the other hand, Rama's dharma is an abstraction and makes no appeal. Rama was all in all to him, he did not look beyond Rama, vide his message sent through Sumantra.

33-34 Chief points in Lakshmana's character—'kainkaryalakshmi'; a watchful guard, suspicious of visitors; utter devotion to Rama; vigilance at post of duty—twice he was tried hard; efficiency in work; reticence; proneness to anger, but quick repentance, and generosity; shyness before women.

34 Sumitra's injunction to him to look upon Rama as his father and upon Sita as his mother. Sita's testimony on this point to Hanuman.

34-37 Extraordinary display of Rama's affection to Lakshmana—when Lakshmana had built the hermitage at Panchavati; when he had killed Indrajit.

37-38 Lakshmana's shyness before women—

his wrath abated at sight of Tara;

he could not identify any of Sita's jewels cast off at Rishyamuka except the nupura as he had never raised his eyes to look at her;

his distress and extreme misery when Sita whom Rama had abandoned asked him to be witness to her pregnancy!

39 Reflections on this last scene of woe between Sita and Lakshmana—in comparison to the sufferings of the great and good what are those of ordinary mortals?

LECTURE IV

LAKSHMANA CONCLUDED

40 Sita's characterization of Lakshmana as one who is strong and one who does not speak much.

40-43 But Lakshmana could explode and explode violently too when Rama's interests were at stake. In Kausalya's apartments we see him pouring scorn on Rama's "dharma". He suspects a well-laid plot between his father and Kaikeyi, and declares that he will put the old man in chains or put him to death.

As may be expected, his twin brother Satrughna, later, utters a similar violent sentiment.

43-45 Rama's 'fatalism' makes little impression on Lakshmana, but he will not take the field without Rama's orders.

45 Rama bids Lakshmana remain behind to look after Kausalya and Sumitra; Lakshmana says that Rama has already given him leave to accompany him to the forest and easily wins the point.

45-47 Lakshmana's strong denunciation of the Dharma ideal in the presence of Kausalya was no mere accident. Strange as it may seem in a brother of Rama, he goes the whole hog when after Indrajit's murder of the counterfeit Sita in the battlefield he despises Dharma and preaches Artha to Rama!

47 Get angry quickly, get gently quickly too—a remarkable quality in Lakshmana's transparent nature, well illustrated in two cases:

47-49 (a) in the preliminary scene in Chitrakuta where Lakshmana suspects Bharata's intentions in coming with his army. Rama convinces him of his impatience and folly in a noteworthy speech pitched in a lofty tone. Lakshmana is repentant and blushes with shame.

Rama on this occasion half playfully says that if Lakshmana is after the kingdom there is nothing easier for him than to get Bharata to transfer it. This speculation came to the test of fact at Rama's coronation. Rama offered the coronet to Lakshmana and Bharata pressed it earnestly on him. But Lakshmana was firm in refusing.

49-53 (b) In the scene in Sugriva's palace where Lakshmana who is in a mighty rage is pacified by Tara, and he magnanimously apologises to Sugriva.

53 Rama a martinet. Departure from the rule of obedience must be punished. Lakshmana was twice in a great difficulty—

53-55 (i) when Sita drove him from Panchavati hermitage to go to Rama's assistance;

55-57 (ii) when Durvasas threatened to curse everybody and everything if not admitted to see Rama who was then closeted with Kala.

Lakshmana had to choose the lesser of two evils, but wasn't let off. For the first act of disobedience Rama solemnly censured him. For the second Rama banished him.

56-57 Moral—the penalty of a wrong must be paid.

LECTURE V

RAMA

58-65 **Introduction:—**

58 Unlike Lakshmana who is a simple character, Rama has a somewhat complex character. There are conflicting elements in it, and some of his doings have given room for criticism and have been subjects of controversy.

58-59 Valmiki did not create Rama. He found him already in being and gave him body and being. Even the events were given him. He was not free to discard episodes which seem inconsistent with the received character of his hero. In spite of this, there is a remarkable consistency, coherence, and firmness of conception which ranks Valmiki with the great authors of the world.

59-61 What does Rama stand for today?

He stands for the highest in man—as son, husband, king and ally or friend of the oppressed.

Take his act of self-sacrifice, for instance. When only five or six and twenty he accepted exile without a demur and without visible sign of disappointment. Did not listen to prayers, entreaties, counsel. Asserted the sanctity of promise and the virtue of obedience. So unquestioned was his moral authority that he lectured **dharma** to father, mother, brother, wife and subjects. All who came into contact with him bowed to him in reverence.

62 The most striking proof of his moral supremacy is his repudiation of Sita. The world was shocked, but durst not protest. Their attitude was one of awe as to a god; they accepted Sita's ordeal as some doom of fate.

63 Or take these incidents—

In spite of the advice of eminent counsellors including Lakshmana, he granted protection to Vibhishana.

63-64 Having beaten Ravana in the first encounter, he magnanimously let him off, refusing to pursue his advantage.

When Vibhishana refused to perform Ravana's obsequies, he offered to do them himself and brought Vibhishana to a sense of right.

64 Such were the heights of moral purity and grandeur reached by Rama. No wonder that the world bowed deeply and devoutly to him. He was almost immaculate.

Almost, because he yet exhibited the common qualities of human nature with its emotions and infirmities; He gave way to anger, grief, despair like any of us; he said harsh things of people; he suspected; occasionally he declined from his own highest level and did and said things which perhaps his own higher nature would not approve. These however do not detract from the sublimity of Rama's character, never a whit. We raise ourselves rather to kinship with him by contemplation of them. If we cannot aspire to the great altitudes that he attained, may we not subdue our nature to some extent by his lofty example?

65-72 Incidents in Rama's life which show his human qualities as distinguished from his superhuman virtues—

65-66 With Sita he looks forward with pleasurable anticipation to his coronation as yuvaraja.

66 When that hope is dashed to the ground, he shows no trace of disappointment in his outward bearing, but he is unhappy all the same, the Poet saying that he controlled the feeling within his own heart as he went to his mother to tell her.

67 Breaking the news to Sita he can hardly control his grief.

67-69 His human weakness is shown particularly in his speech to Lakshmana whom he asks to stay behind to protect his mother and Lakshmana's from Kaikeyi's ill-treatment and from Bharata's possible hostility. Under the stroke of adversity he suspects like us.

Then there are little peccadillos which make us feel that Rama is after all of flesh and blood with us.

69-70 He is not above enjoying a little innocent fun at the expense of that holy mendicant Trijata.

70-71 He asks Sumantra to tell Dasaratha a white lie, that he did not hear the old king shouting to him to stop the chariot.

71 He adopts a ruse to get away from the importunate people who follow him.

72 Valmiki in other words presents Rama to us in a way we can understand him.

"Was Rama the ideal always and every moment, in big matters and in small, to the great ones and the little ones? If so, he was a bloodless robot, an impossible prig, mounted on stilts and hardly visible in perspective".*

LECTURE VI

RAMA CONTINUED

73-74 Rama tells Sumantra that the reason why he could not have Sumantra share his exile is that if he did not return to the city immediately, Kaikeyi would not be sure that Rama had come to the forest and would make life a hell for his father. This shows how unerringly Rama was able to read the heart even of one who was so out of sympathy with his as Kaikeyi.

74-75 The first night after Sumantra's return when Rama was left free to commune with himself as it were, we see him giving strange vent to long-repressed inner feelings, without any restraint, in what is really a soliloquy, though the words are addressed to Lakshmana.

75-78 Running commentary on the passage (II. 53) in which Rama discharges as it were the smaller and the lower part of his nature.

78-80 An interesting point—was there a lower part in Rama's nature? There was. And it is no blasphemy to utter it. Nor does it mean that Rama was just a hypocrite who deceived the world by putting on an appearance of goodness and noble-mindedness. The higher element was his real nature, not only the one which the world saw, but the one which he actually and habitually practised. The lower nature in his case was not only hidden, but put down, conquered—and this is what makes a world of difference between him and us.

80 In common with us Rama had a taste for enjoying a little fun, occasionally. We noticed this trait in connection with the Brahman, Trijata. A more hilarious occasion was the advent of Surpanakha.

80-87 The episode related in detail and commented on.

82-87 Discussion of Rama's description of Lakshmana as 'akrtadarah', the plain meaning of which pace commentators, is that Lakshmana was unmarried. A terminological inexactitude, but why should we regard it as anything other than what it was—a pure jest?

* Reproduced from the Lecturer's own notes of his talk.

LECTURE VII

RAMA CONTINUED

88-89 Lamentation of bereaved rakshasa women (VI. 95) after the wholesale destruction of Ravana's army by Rama with the gandharva weapon. As is natural, they revile one of their own sex as the author of all the woe; Surpanakha's humiliation the seed-plot of the whole story.

Incidentally we note one of Rama's "contradictions" here. Opposed as he was to maya yuddha, we find him playing a marvellous trick himself in this gandharvastra battle, assuming myriad forms and appearing separately to each enemy warrior!

89-92 Rama was not above the frailties of ordinary human beings who are cast down by great misfortunes. Overcome by a paroxysm of grief at the loss of Sita, Rama loses his balance of mind, becomes unhinged, and is thrown into a mad fit of anger against the gods; it falls to Lakshmana's lot to calm him down and comfort him.

92-93 The human element in his character comes out again in intensity during the time of enforced inactivity in Prasravana cave. We see him working himself up to a pitch of anger, impatience, and jealousy against Sugriva.

Subtleness with which the Poet, an unsurpassed student of human nature, depicts this side of Rama's character brought out in a close study of sargas 27 to 39 of Kishkindhakanda.

Sugriva's orgy of sensual passion. Rama who was pining notices it.

Lakshmana consoles him and begs him to wait patiently till saradrtu comes on. But Rama shows signs of impatience. Lakshmana counsels him.

93-94 The curious similes in Rama's description of the rains show the way his mind was going; in describing natural objects he mentions Sita as the standard of comparison. The rainy season becomes unendurable. Rama's chagrin.

94-95 Meanwhile, Hanuman, servant of Rama by desire and of Sugriva by profession, warns the latter of the expiry of the time fixed for the search of Sita to begin. Sugriva's orders.

95-96 Rama however without inquiry is angered by Sugriva's indulgence.

From uncontrolled passion Rama goes on by a natural transition to an outburst of anger and threat; he did not inquire about what had been done.

96-97 Lakshmana threatens to kill Sugriva. Rama calms him and asks him to use soft language when he goes to Sugriva with his message. But Lakshmana makes the threat of death, though he hears of the plan of Sugriva.

97-98 Then Tara talks Lakshmana round. Lakshmana is satisfied and apologises.

98 Rama's gentle speech to Sugriva when he comes with Lakshmana and makes submission.

98-99 We see here how Rama's higher nature asserts itself.

Time after time Sri Rama curses his lower self and continually moves in action on the higher.

LECTURE VIII
RAMA CONTINUED

100-101 Rama's characteristic generosity further illustrated in a later instance. In the council of war which debated the question of Vibhishana's acceptance or rejection.

Sugriva, backed by Lakshmana and others, Hanuman alone excepted, expresses himself strongly against Vibhishana on the ground that the rakshasa having proved a traitor to his brother in dire extremity cannot be trusted. Rama's reply is notable, and the verse (VI. 18. 15-16) is worth expatiating on.

Giving examples of excellence in certain relationships, Rama says to Sugriva: 'there are few allies and friends so trustworthy as you'. This acknowledgment of Sugriva as the **ideal friend** is Rama's repentance for his former harshness to him.

The Poet here teaches the lesson that the falling out of faithful friends is a renewing of affection.

101-102 Of the **ideal brother,** Bharata is the outstanding example cited by Rama in the verse. That is of course because Bharata surrendered to his elder brother in an extraordinary way the kingdom that had fallen to him by every right. Lakshmana had no such opportunity.

103-104 Of the **ideal son,** Rama gives himself as the example. This is not a boast but a true statement, because he stood faithful to his father and renounced the kingdom, not once but twice—at Ayodhya and again at Chitrakuta.

104 While for every single relationship one person can thus be taken as a pattern—for brotherliness, for filial duty, and for faithful friendship—**Rama was a model of all these relationships.**

104-107 The **ideal brother**—that was Sri Rama, not even Bharata! In the conversation at Chitrakuta he pointed out to Bharata what no other body has mentioned, not even Kaikeyi, that at her marriage their father had promised the succession to her offspring, and that that promise was still binding. Dasaratha of course remembered it, and remembering it suspected that there might be trouble from Bharata and was therefore anxious to crown Rama heir-apparent while Bharata still tarried at Rajagriha. Rama did not gainsay his father at the time, but this element of suspicion was not wholly off his heart. He sent Hanuman from Bharadvaja's seat to ascertain Bharata's real feelings towards him. But what was a real and malignant suspicion in Dasaratha's case was in Rama's case sublimated. He was ready to give up his right to the kingdom if Bharata who had deputised for fourteen years wished to continue to rule. There can be no greater proof of brotherliness.

107-108 Rama was not an **ideal friend** only, he was an **ideal enemy too.** 'You who love even your enemies' said Garuda justly.

LECTURE IX

RAMA CONTINUED

'Vanavaso mahodayah'. "Most glorious is forest life!" See outline sketch of this talk at pp. 109-120 below.

LECTURE X

RAMA CONTINUED

121-143 Detailed study of the debate between Rama and Bharata in Chitrakuta in which Rama's character is brought out in high colours, sargas 103-112 of Ayodhyakanda.

121 The principals were only Rama and Bharata. Lakshmana is mentioned, curiously enough Satrughna is not.

The debate begins on a certain night, and the skirmish lasts most of the night.

122 Bharata makes three points to begin with—

(1) In the Ikshvaku line the eldest son has always succeeded to the throne.

(2) The misconduct of Kaikeyi—whom Bharata denounces in unmeasured terms—ought not to prevail.

(3) People, high and low, unanimously want Rama.

122-123 Rama won't allow Bharata to abuse his mother. "Mother is as good as Father", he says, and he pointedly refers to both as dharmasilas.

124 Next morning Bharata opens with a legal issue. 'Granted that the kingdom is mine, my mother has been satisfied by my taking it. Having taken it I dispose of it now by offering it to you. Take it'.

124-127 In reply we have a dissertation from Rama on Fate—sixteen aphoristic slokas embodying moral truths and emphasising life's impermanence, translated.

127-128 Bharata praises Rama's teaching and professes to be edified. But his heart is untouched. He won't for instance relent towards Kaikeyi; as for Dasaratha, he was senile and doted on her. He ventures on an exhortation on the duty of a good son. 'Be a good apatya to our father,' he says to Rama, 'save him from the wrong he has done'.

128-132 Then he fastens on a speciality of Rama, a pet notion—that dharma must be followed with suffering and sacrifice—the idea being that when Rama elected to carry out his father's promise to Kaikeyi, although there was a prior promise to the king's feudatories and subjects to give the yauvarajya to Rama (which as a matter of fact was no 'promise' but a mere arrangement), he showed a preference for a course which involved a sacrifice and entailed suffering. Bharata says, "You prefer a painful duty. Take upon yourself the burden of the kingdom, which I but a callow youth am, altogether unequal to. Let Vasishtha anoint you here and now". The great assembly had a mixed feeling, satisfaction and grief at once, but they loyally seconded Bharata's prayers.

131-133 But Rama was firm and unyielding. 'Father's promise,' he points out to Bharata, 'is binding on you as well as on me. You asked me to be an **apatya**. I ask you **to be a 'putra'**, and he adduces the ancient saying about **Gaya**.

133-134 As to Bharata's commiseration that forest life with its hardships must be intolerable, Rama says, 'Nothing of the kind. Don't you fret about it. I am no worse than you. There is perfect parity between us. You are lord over Ayodhya. I am going to be king of the wild beasts, and Sita and I are going to be perfectly happy in the forest.'

134-135 Jabali interposes with his false doctrine of materialism, the hollowness of which Rama exposes, with some vigour.

Vasishtha intervenes with a long enumeration of the Ikshvaku kings to prove that the crown has always descended to the eldest son, and he seconds Bharata's petition.

Also, Vasishtha claims for the guru as great authority as for father. Rama won't grant the claim.

135-136 Remarks on the curious and ineffective part played by Vasishtha throughout the transaction. The very fountain of Dharma as he was, he did not once raise his voice in support of Rama's resolve to go to the forest. When Bharata came, Vasishtha advised him to crown himself, for which Bharata actually chid him in the assembly in Ayodhya.

136 Bharata now threatens 'prayopavesa', brings the grass himself and settles down to it. Rama disapproves; 'it is not the province of a kshatriya to resort to it'.

136-138 Remarks on prayopavesa. It was considered the proper thing in those days, but the Ramayana shows its futility. Bharata tried it and failed. Rama himself attempted it against Samudra—this being another of Rama's "contradictions"—and he failed of course; he had to use force. Angada's prayopavesa amusingly enough was cut short by Sampati turning up and offering to make a meal of the monkeys. The idea occurred also to Hanuman when he had not yet seen Sita.

Bharata from his bed of grass appeals to the assembly. They approve of Rama's action, and Rama bids Bharata get up and purge himself of the offence.

138-139 Bharata obeys, but he is by no means at the end of his resources. He broaches the proxy idea, and says that he will pass the fourteen years in the forest in place of Rama. 'No,' says Rama, 'that's not done!', and in his turn he appeals to the assembly. Carried away by the vehemence of his own argument, Rama not merely acquiesces in Kaikeyi's course, but justifies it saying that she and Dasaratha had done no wrong, and that he having saved father for his part, Bharata must do his part.

The celestials who had listened to the debate with a sense of edification now intervene and declare that Rama is right and that his action has saved Dasaratha from naraka.

139-140 Bharata weakens, but does not bow to the inevitable. He pleads incompetence.

140-141 Rama is glad of this humility. He thinks it proves genuine capacity. 'It is impossible that I should neglect father's promise,' he says, and he closes the debate by addressing a strong plea to Bharata on Kaikeyi's behalf.

141-142 Whereupon, Bharata produced a pair of gold sandals, and at Vasishtha's instance begged Rama to stand once on the sandals and step down. This done, mystic power passed!

Bharata put the sandals on his head and carried them home. He installed them, reported to them, and took orders from them.

142-143 Who won? Both won and both lost. Rama won in fact; Bharata won in law and in form, and at the same time derived his power to govern from Rama's sandals.

143 Observations on the finished literary excellence of the debate—exalted sentiments, concentration of thought, directness, simplicity and beauty of the speeches—in a word, language and matter married together with rare skill.

LECTURE XI

RAMA CONTINUED — THE VALI EPISODE

144-146 Main points for discussion.

146-148 (i) (a) Was Rama concealed? The text leaves no room for doubt. Rama himself does not deny it but answers Vali's charge from the analogy of the chase in which much is allowed to princes.

Govindaraja whose Ramabhakti is unquestionable expressly admits and defends it.

148-149 (b) Was this proper? Hanuman did not deem it chivalrous to attack Ravana when the latter was engaged with Nila. Vali not only was engaged with Sugriva, but also was not aware of Rama's existence on the spot; so it is a greatly aggravated form of unworthy combat.

149-159 (ii) Why did Rama avoid a straight fight? It was Rama that first mentioned the **killing** of Vali, without any suggestion from Sugriva; and he seems to have contemplated many arrows, using the **plural**, which shows that he was thinking only of an open battle. Then when with **one** arrow Rama pierced the **seven** sal trees, and Sugriva, convinced and exultant, lauded the miraculous feat, the idea first came into Rama's mind, 'why not kill Vali with a single arrow?' This **one-arrow idea** is confirmed in his mind when Sugriva beaten hard in the first encounter had to flee for his life and accused Rama gently. Rama says, 'Challenge Vali again and I will with a **single arrow** kill him **at once**! The idea of having a straight fight and the necessity of using many arrows has gone from Rama's mind. Why? Because Vali would have given immense trouble in open fight, the battle might be prolonged to seven or eight days like the battle with Ravana, everything would be left in doubt, Sugriva's patience might be exhausted, and he might lose faith in Rama. Some extraordinary importance was attached to the idea of killing Vali by a **single arrow**, and killing him that very day. So Rama avoided a straight face to face encounter as he originally thought of, and decided to despatch Vali from his concealed position.

159-161 (iii) Why was Vali not killed at the first encounter? Rama told Sugriva that he could not distinguish the brothers from each other when they were locked in single combat. It was a false excuse. But there is no reason whatever to doubt Rama's good faith—unless, and this is not at all unlikely, he hesitated between an open fight and concealment, finally coming down on the side of the latter!

159 (iv) Why was Vali not chosen for ally? Because Danukabandha had mentioned Sugriva and advised Rama to strike a pact with him. Rama and Sugriva had a subtle bond of sympathy. Their wives had been taken away by force. Only distressed people come together. Each had something to give and something to expect. Vali was at the very height of his power and he was in no trouble. He was also a sworn friend of Ravana.

161-162 (v) Rama's imperialistic claims—advanced in his justification to Vali—obnoxious to modern advanced notions. We must judge Rama not by the light of modern theory or modern aspiration but by the standards of his time. **'La gloire'** was a kshatriya's creed and he was expected to extend his dominion.

By a sort of extension of his naked imperialist doctrine, Rama claimed jurisdiction over Vali; had he Bharata's commission or authorization? · Govindaraja and Tilaka on the point. We may justify Rama's assumption of power and authority on the ground that as under the arrangement come to at Chitrakuta, Bharata was only regent for Rama, Rama whenever he liked could resume the authority which he had delegated.

145-146 (vi) Was death the penalty for Vali's offence in respect of Rama? Was it not something against the course of natural justice for Rama to have killed him? Compare the judicial murder of Nuncomar; "I am afraid that in punishing Vali with death Sri Rama was guilty of some such extension."

162-164 (vii) Rama's apparent inconsistency—his strange and misplaced feeling of sympathy with Ruma contrasting with his attitude to Sita. Rama who was so considerate to Ruma who had lived with Vali as his wife, and so considerate to Sugriva who was not very scrupulous about taking her back, "had not an iota of compassion when he came to consider his own wife whose innocence was blazoned forth to all the world."

LECTURE XII

RAMA CONTINUED—THE REPUDIATION OF SITA

165-166 Two preliminary points:—

(1) The legend that when Ravana turned up in Panchavati Sita disappeared entering Agni, and that the Sita who figures thereafter till the death of Ravana

is a Maya Sita, must be discarded as entirely unfounded and as robbing the epic of all interest.

166-167 (2) The idea that Sita brought all her woes upon herself by her 'apachara', the extravagance of her behaviour to Lakshmana in Panchavati, can hardly command our respect and must be dismissed.

The state of mind of Rama and Sita during the tragic scene.

167-168 Rama's direction to Vibhishana to bring Sita bathed and adorned seems to show that there was trouble in his breast already. When she appears before him he is agitated by strong feelings, and though he speaks sternly his head is bent and turned in one direction.

As she approaches him she is alarmed by the severity of his look. His opening speech to her is not calculated to allay it.

(a) He says that he has wiped out the disgrace, but that what he did was for the sake of honour and of his family, not for her.

168-170 (b) Then follows his harsh and unfeeling abandonment of her. 'There is a stain on your character. I have no attachment, no desire for you. You can go where you like'. And then, by way of shutting out any remonstrance or protest on her part, he adds, 'You may fix your affections on Lakshmana, Bharata, Sugriva, or Vibhishana.'

170-171 Commentators are anxious that no sinister construction should be put on this. My opinion is that there is no need to soften the language here. Rama meant harsh things. He was angry. He was dissatisfied. He suspected her fidelity without a doubt. Sri Rama was just a human being, and when he was angry he said foolish things. There is no doubt about it.

173-174 Sita upbraids him in strong language. Rama is unmoved. Sita says to Lakshmana, 'Set up a pyre, let it blaze. That is the only remedy.'

174 Not a voice was heard in protest. Rama had imposed himself so completely on all by his moral supremacy.

172 Now, after Sita had been handed back by Agni thoroughly purified, Rama was satisfied and protested hard, "I didn't suspect her. I never had a doubt about her conduct." This was simply boast of foreknowledge after the event. If you give cent per cent value to these subsequent protestations, you must convict Rama of some insincerity and pretended harshness in the speech in which he actually repudiated Sita.

172-173 The true way of interpreting it however is that Rama swayed this way and that. He was in two minds about Sita's fidelity. At first the worse feeling prevailed, he lent himself entirely to sinister thoughts and under their influence repudiated his wife. The repudiation was sincere. Equally sincere was the subsequent repentance when she was restored on the highest possible authority, and the contrary feeling prevailed.

174 The fire ordeal was Sita's thought. Rama did not demand proof. The proof he had already constructed for himself, and he acted upon it. He had condemned her in spite of Hanuman's most unimpeachable testimony.

174-175 After the tragedy had been gone through each person of course was anxious to put the best face on it. Dasaratha's comfort to Sita coming as it did after the event can only be viewed in this light.

175 Rama's conduct on this occasion then has to be explained by his suspicion of infidelity. Unfounded as it was, it was still there rankling in his bosom.

175-177 For the later act of abandonment of Sita by Rama related in the Uttarakanda there was no such heavy justification.

Rama hears ugly gossip and slander. He hesitates: 'I myself had a little suspicion. Sita took the fire ordeal. The devas testified to her purity. My heart tells me that she is pure'.

But there is a tussle in his mind—Good name versus Ill name. Ill fame, there's the rub!

So what does he do? He calls his brothers together and says to them that he would rather kill them and kill himself than have his name covered with infamy. As for Sita, she simply didn't count! 'A man who has lost his fame on earth,' he says, 'is condemned by the gods.' Apparently according to Rama, certain persons have only to take it into their wicked heads to slander a person, and that person is damned in the next world as well!

177-179 To understand Rama's viewpoint about Sita, it must be remembered that in the old days any woman was only the private property of the husband, completely at his disposal; her independent existence was not recognised. Where a kshatriya's honour was at stake, his wife, however worthy she may be, when weighed in the balance of real values, sinks into the position of 'indriyartha'. In Rama's eyes Sita was only a means of gratifying the sexual passion. So he decrees that she shall incontinently be banished.

179-180 This time Rama sinks lower and lower. Not only does he against the testimony of his conscience agree to banish Sita, but he does it secretly. And he will have no pleading, no contradiction, from his brothers; he binds them down by an oath upon his legs—a very extraordinary thing, though it occurs elsewhere also in the Ramayana.

180-181 Rama's conduct in abandoning Sita, then, must be put down to the influence of jealousy, one of the worst passions known to men, and worst of all where the canker appears in a man of genuine greatness. It is the noblest man who, when he is torn by feelings of jealousy and suspicion against his wife, is capable of doing the worst things.

181-183 Rama and Othello compared. Both noble minds and hearts. Both are led to an unjust suspicion; Othello poisoned by Iago; Rama poisoned by self! Both take extreme steps. Both repent.

183-186 King Arthur and Guinevere. The charge of sin in this case was just; Guinevere's misconduct had led to "red ruin, and the breaking up of laws." But, unlike Rama, unlike Othello, King Arthur who partook of divinity to some extent, instead of pronouncing harsh judgment upon her, extended truly Christian forgiveness to her.

186 True repentance followed by a pure life must lead to forgiveness. The Ramayana has a parallel to King Arthur's act in Sage Gautama's forgiveness of Ahalya.

Forgiveness though practised by a human mind is divine in its quality.

LECTURE XIII

BHARATA

187-191 In the pages of the Ramayana all the three great kingdoms change hands; in each the elder brother is ousted, and the younger gets the kingdom. But while Sugriva and Vibhishana, both good and without overweening ambition, eagerly desired the kingdom, and were not unwilling that their elder brothers should be killed in order that they might succeed to them, Bharata did not care for the kingdom that fell to him. He offered it to Rama, and when Rama refused it, held it in trust for him, and yielded it back to him out of the gladness of his heart, enhanced tenfold in value all round. The display of saubhratra (good-brotherliness) drew tears from monkey and Rakshasa alike. Bharata thus stands on a pedestal of his own.

191-192 What are his chief characteristics?

Persistence and strength of will. Untamed youth. Spoilt uncle's pet.

Lakshmana wouldn't stand up to Rama; there would be an outburst of temper, and then surrender and collapse.

But where Lakshmana, evokes our love, Bharata evokes our respect and admiration rather than love.

Bharata's character marked by a strong individuality, a deal of courage, self-confidence, and resource, witness his changing tactic after tactic to persuade Rama at Chitrakuta. He censured even Vasishtha!

193-195 It was a hard, thrust when Kausalya accused Bharata of having hankered after the kingdom, and, remembering Dasaratha's curses, added that she would carry the agnihotra away to prevent him from performing the king's obsequies. Bharata invokes terrible curses on his own head if he had any share in banishing Rama. The whole sarga, by the way, is really intended by the Poet to describe the round of a man's duties and virtues in life. Kausalya relents and forgives.

196-197 The proxy idea started by Bharata in Chitrakuta (vide Lec. X, p. 138) was not new. He had already told his mother that he would take Rama's place in the forest; that was his form of vengeance for the wrong she had done.

197-200 Guha who suspected Bharata's good faith is satisfied.

Bharata's grief on seeing the place where Rama and Sita slept, and the gold particles that had come off her jewels. (Remarks on primitive jeweller's art.)

Bharata takes a vow of asceticism, but does not change dress immediately. He wears silk when he pays his respects to Bharadvaja; when he saw Rama later he is in ascetic garb.

He pours his heart to Satrughna: "My soul will know no rest till I see the feet of Rama", and so on.

200-202 Rama's unbounded confidence in Bharata expressed on various occasions—to grieving subjects, to Lakshmana on their first night out of Ayodhya, to Lakshmana again when the latter says a harsh word about Kaikeyi, to Vibhishana when he pressed Rama to stay as his guest in Lanka for a day or two.

202-207 Bharata unfilial. This is an aspect of his character that is not pleasing to dwell upon. His abuse of his mother to the messengers from Ayodhya before he knew anything of the happenings there is scandalous. When he returns to Ayodhya, he heaps abuse, curses, taunts upon her in most unpardonable language. When Manthara is maltreated by Satrughna, he says that but for fear of Rama's displeasure he would kill his mother. He describes her to Bharadvaja in such strain that the sage is shocked. Even after Kaikeyi had, by coming with Kausalya and Sumantra to Chitrakuta, given proof of her repentance, Bharata is not mollified. He says to Rama himself that she was wicked, sinful, and that if he was not afraid of Rama he would kill her!

207-209 Rama pleads for Kaikeyi earnestly. His behaviour towards her at parting was both a lesson and a rebuke to Bharata. Rama prostrated himself before her as before the other queens. He would have done it in any case whether Kaikeyi was repentant or not; but Bharata must have a practical object-lesson in filial duty, and that was his object in making pranamams to Kaikeyi.

LECTURE XIV

SUGRIVA

210-211 Sugriva in the earlier and lesser part of his life overshadowed, overawed, by Vali; at a disadvantage; mistrustful of himself; cautious to a degree. In the later and greater part of his life when he had come into his own, he becomes stronger and more like his own self.

Hanuman is represented as laughing at Sugriva for his dread of Rama and Lakshmana whom Sugriva first mistakes for emissaries of Vali, though the derisory expression 'sakhamrgatva', we fancy, is rather the poet's gibe than noble Hanuman's.

211-212 Charges usually brought against Sugriva—

(i) Affront to the greatness of Rama. At the beginning of his friendship with Rama we see that in semi-official talk and courtesies like offering seats, the personages pair off, Rama and Sugriva, Lakshmana and Hanuman. This has led commentators to imagine that Sugriva was guilty of disrespect to Lakshmana, and that some of his troubles later were due to this 'bhagavad-apachara'. The pairing off was natural and it is difficult to believe that any insult could have been intended by Sugriva.

212-213 (ii) Falsehood with regard to his knowledge of Ravana. Sugriva's statement that he was not in full possession of details concerning Ravana is certainly too wide, as he could not have been so ignorant as he makes out. And if we take the Uttarakanda story of Ravana's stay for a month with Vali as the latter's honoured guest into account, Sugriva's statement is certainly false. But Rama did not suspect him, and Sugriva was not able to talk clearly for grief, and he is not to be lightly accused of any subterfuge at the very beginning of his friendship. There appears to have been complete understanding between him and Rama.

213 (iii) Neglect of Rama's business. This charge is superficial. Sugriva had given orders in good time for the search for Sita to be started, and had ordered Hanuman or Nila or perhaps both together to attend to the business. His only mistake was that he lived his riotous life a little too ostentatiously for the comfort of Rama.

213-215 Sugriva's excessive caution is shown in his objection to Rama accepting Vibhishana; but when Rama declares that any one who just comes and says 'please protect me' is entitled to his protection, Sugriva shows his good nature by heartily welcoming Vibhishana.

215-217 Sugriva's greatness of soul—

Before ever the bridge is constructed, Sugriva promises that he will kill Ravana as soon as he sets eyes on him.

He sends a spirited answer to Ravana's appeal through Suka.

He flies impulsively from Suvela before regular hostilities begin, engages Ravana in a remarkable single combat, and knocks off his diadem. When Rama remonstrates with him on this piece of recklessness, Sugriva says: 'When I saw the fellow who took your wife away by force, how could I keep quiet?'

217-218 Kumbhakarna seizes Sugriva in battle and walks off with him into Lanka thinking that he had done for Rama; Sugriva bit off his nose, tore off his ears with nails, and escaped from his clutches.

218 Among his great exploits were the killing of Kumbha, Virupaksha and Mahodara.

218-219 The odium that attaches to Sugriva-ajna undeserved. There is no instance of Sugriva having inflicted death or other cruel punishment. The monkeys who played havoc with the Madhuvana in the exuberance of their joy were let off because of the great deed they had performed in finding Sita.

219-222 Brilliant as Sugriva was, a certain shadow rests on his reputation. Of the various counts on which Angada indicted his uncle to Hanuman, some were unjust; but one charge was not altogether groundless. Sugriva closed the cave into which Vali had gone in pursuit of Mayavi, imagining from the blood that issued that Mayavi had killed Vali; and he allowed himself to be hustled by the ministers into the kingship! He was certainly hasty in this; his choice of the easier and more advantageous course shows a weak trait in his character at that time.

LECTURE XV

VIBHISHANA

223-229 Was Vibhishana a traitor? No. He was a bhakta of the first order and a noble example of devotion to dharma.

It is a melancholy fact that Vibhishana is held up to odium by a certain class of people, especially in North India. It is necessary to place his character in a correct light.

Then follows a disquisition on the debasement of politics in India at the present day, and on the origin and true nature of patriotism.

229-232 Vibhishana was drawn to Rama knowing how Rama was the exemplar of human virtue in the world and how he was there to save humanity. He deserted Ravana because Ravana combined all the wickedness of the worst kind with actions that degrade mankind utterly.

'Well,' say Vibhishana's detractors, 'if Ravana was bad, Vibhishana might have severed his connection with him, but why should he have gone over to his enemy?' Because as between dharma and adharma one has simply no right to be neutral.

'All right,' they say, 'but why should he have given active help, highly valued advice and assistance to Rama?' Joining Rama, Vibhishana was quite right in doing his best to ensure the triumph of virtue over wickedness.

Finally they ask, 'Why should he make himself king?' We should ask rather 'How could Vibhishana renounce the kingdom?' Lanka lay desolated. Vibhishana was the sole surviving member of the ruling family. If he took Lanka it was not because he was an ambitious, grasping man, but because the stricken land wanted a wise, righteous ruler. It was in the highest sense of duty and service that he accepted the crown of Lanka; far from being a proof of his selfish ambition, it was a proof of unselfishness!

Vibhishana was not betraying his country to a conqueror to fasten his yoke on; Rama was not going to annex Lanka to his dominions but restore it to a son of the soil. To call Vibhishana a traitor therefore is wrong.

LECTURE XVI

VIBHISHANA CONTINUED

233-236 A problem propounded, the consideration of which brings out the contrast between Sugriva and Vibhishana—"Why was Vibhishana crowned in anticipation and by way of token while Sugriva was not?"

Sugriva was an ally of Rama and was sought as 'saranam', that is, Rama sought the protection of Sugriva. Vibhishana sought Rama as 'saranam'. The closeness of affinity between Sugriva and Rama attested by Bharata's greeting of Sugriva as their fifth brother.

Sugriva brought a mighty army into the field, including such persons as Hanuman, Jambavan, Angada, Nala, Nila. Vibhishana brought four ministers who played no big part, though Vibhishana brought himself and that was a great thing to bring.

Sugriva was indispensable to the conquest of Lanka. Vibhishana wasn't even expected.

Sugriva did not know Rama and even tested him. Vibhishana knew all about Rama and worshipped him.

Sugriva was crowned after a sudden and swift stroke, the killing of Vali—the very day, 'adyaiva'. Vibhishana could be crowned only after a terrible war; so, to show that he was in earnest, Rama ordered a token abhisheka, to be converted into a real one after Ravana was destroyed.

Sugriva hadn't to live on hopes and promises. Vibhishana lived on a promise and hope occasionally sank.

Sugriva's services were subsequent to the coronation, Vibhishana's preliminary.

May be Sugriva had a higher status and was considered to be of the same rank as Rama, though he with due modesty styles himself 'dasa' in preference to 'ally'. Perhaps the status was not on the same footing in Vibhishana's case, but he enjoyed the greater love and the greater confidence of the Ayodhya brothers and became a 'chiranjivin'.

236-238 Rama when he received Vibhishana's request to be taken seemed to be unaware of his identity. As a matter of fact, Surpanakha had mentioned him, distinguishing him as a dharmatma and not a rakshasa in spirit. Hanuman also must have communicated to Rama how Vibhishana's womenfolk had befriended Sita, and how on Vibhishana's intercession Ravana had spared his own life, though Hanuman forgot to mention this in the council of war.

238-240 Between Indrajit and Vibhishana there was the greatest antipathy, as seen in the debate in Ravana's great assembly which ended in Ravana's rejection of Vibhishana. Indrajit's praise of patriotism, his self-laudation, and his flouting of Vibhishana and of his 'dharma'.

241-243 Indrajit's witchcraft at the nagapasabandha seen through by Vibhishana, who gives comfort to Sugriva. Presently when Rama sets up a wail for Lakshmana, repining at not having crowned Vibhishana according to his promise, Vibhishana, down-hearted, sets up a wail, and it is Sugriva's turn to comfort him.

243-244 Kumbhakarna and Ravana. Kumbhakarna having spoken his mind to Ravana is faced with a dilemma, and decides that blood is thicker than water. No more blame to him than to Bhishma. In a conflict of duties different people choose differently.

244-246 Signal service rendered by Vibhishana in the war—he points out the nyagrodha tree under which Indrajit is to perform sorcery before becoming absolutely invisible and invincible; Lakshmana is enabled to give Indrajit battle in time and kill him.

In this battle occurs another great altercation between Indrajit and Vibhishana. The patriotic point of view forcibly put by Indrajit, who indeed is stronger in his vilification and denunciation than Vibhishana in his rather tame defence; compare Vali's indictment of Rama and Rama's defence.

When however Vibhishana takes his bow and arrow to aim at his nephew, his eyes are bedimmed with tears. He owns to the natural affection which paralyses his arm. Behold the conflict, 'dharmasankata', in a nutshell!

LECTURE XVII

VIBHISHANA CONCLUDED—HANUMAN

247-248 Vibhishana's services—his devotion to Rama, timely warnings, timely and helpful suggestions.

In particular, his knowledge of magic arts enabled him to pierce through Indrajit's murder of Maya Sita and to reassure Rama of her safety.

248-249 His active participation in battle along with Lakshmana—unhorsing of Ravana's chariot and its sequel.

249-252 His remorse at the death of Ravana and lament.

He seeks and obtains Rama's consent to perform Ravana's obsequies and then is visited with a compunction. Rama settles his doubts.

252 **To sum up,** Vibhishana was no traitor. He has his rightful place among the chiranjivis.

HANUMAN CONTINUED

Hanuman's greatness.

253-254 The curse laid on him by the rishis in early childhood, viz., that he shall not remember his strength till at the right moment he is reminded of it.

The curse evidently had other implications. Hanuman's loss or failure of memory was not in respect of his strength only, but of necessary particulars at time of need.

This AMNESIA was a source of weakness in him.

Instances of Hanuman's amnesia:—

255 Forgot Matanga's asrama being a sanctuary.

255-256 Forgot that Sugriva had done his duty and that he himself (Hanuman) was at fault.

256-258 Forgot Rama's promise to Sugriva to bestow Vali's kingdom on him, and suggested Angada's accession to the throne to Tara.

LECTURE XVIII

HANUMAN CONTINUED

259 Hanuman's lapses further illustrated.

His lapse of memory in regard to Sugriva's supposed failure in his duty to Rama.

260 Forgot the description of the herbs which he had to fetch to revive Lakshmana.

261 Failed to return to Rama from Nandigrama and report about Bharata's attitude.

262 Omitted Sita's ordeal in his narrative to Bharata.

Among Hanuman's **Failures,** two were conspicuous:—

263 (1) Failed to get Tara to countenance Angada's coronation;

263-264 (2) Failed to turn Angada away from his resolve not to return to Kishkindha but remain behind in the vicinity of Svayamprabha's cave.

LECTURE XIX

HANUMAN CONTINUED—THE EXPLOITS OF HANUMAN

LECTURE XX

HANUMAN CONTINUED

LECTURE XXI

HANUMAN CONCLUDED

LECTURE XXII

RAVANA

LECTURE XXIII

RAVANA CONTINUED—HIS ABILITY

told. Maricha is over-bold; in reply to his claim to give candid counsel to his king, Ravana speaks sharply to him.

During the discussion which goes on through seven sargas, Ravana improves upon his original plan and adds the detail that Maricha was to cry out "O Sita, O Lakshmana."

Enunciation of a great truth by Maricha, that the innocent suffer by a wicked man's wrong; this is true of all men in high positions of authority; and it is not only their faults but their mistakes cost society dear.

After giving a solemn warning Maricha yields to Ravana's threat and Ravana is pleased.

LECTURE XXIV

RAVANA CONTINUED—HIS RELATIONS WITH WOMEN

334-335 Ravana captured women, killed their protectors, and violated them. They once cursed him and the gods rejoiced.

Rambha, decked out for a rendezvous with Nalakubara, was ravished on the way by Ravana. He cursed Ravana.

335-336 Ravana himself tells in Council that owing to a curse of Brahma that his head would split into a thousand pieces if he raped a woman, he durst not use violence towards Sita.

These curses apparently led to a change in Ravana's ways to women. He became a gentle and affable lover.

336-337 Hanuman testifies that the women in Ravana's harem were contented and happy. Ravana was no monster. He was a good lover and was loved well.

337-338 The grief of the women at his death was genuine.

338-339 Mandodari's wail which reaches heights of eloquence in places.

Notwithstanding this change in his ways to women, Ravana by no means became good.

His cruelty and cunning—

339-341 At his first entry on the stage he performs an act of infamy, planned with low trickery and in defiance of honour's code. The abduction of Sita begins a drama of wickedness which hurries forward through scenes of tense anxiety and suffering to an end which holds the soul in an exquisite thrill. Fifty times he is taxed with its meanness and cowardice, but he gives no proof that he was ashamed of it.

341-342 Despicable deceit practised by him on Sita with Vidyujjihva's counterfeit head of Rama.

342-343 A second act of malicious cruelty was when he had Sita brought in the Pushpaka to see Rama and Lakshmana in the toils of Indrajit's nagastra.

A third act, one of demoniac fury, was when Indrajit had fallen, and Ravana losing self-control rushed to kill Sita himself.

343-344 The Sita infatuation—the root-cause.

It was Akampana and Surpanakha that put the poison into Ravana. Aranya 31 regarded as spurious contains fine verses of description by Akampana, of Rama's prowess, Sita's charm, and Rama's boundless affection for her.

Surpanakha wanted Ravana to kill Rama and Lakshmana and then carry Sita off, though Akampana thought that it was beyond Ravana's strength. Ravana preferred stealth to a straight fight—not cowardice, but a natural taste for that sort of adventure.

The scene between Ravana and Sita—

344-346 Ravana was skilled in observing women's charms and could pay chivalrous compliments.

His long amatory address, in parts very vulgar and too direct.

This elicits no rebuke from Sita, she fearing the holy guest's curse.

To her inquiry he discloses himself and not having enough time goes straight to the point and declares his passion for her. 'I have dames of high degree from all parts of the world, shoals of them. My love for them is dead and cold. Come, be you my chiefest queen of them all!'

In those days there was no rule against polygamy (sic). What Ravana offered to Sita was, according to the notions of the time, fair and honourable marriage.

Sita's rejection was unreserved. She provoked him to such an extent by her reproaches that he assumed his ten-headed form and threatened her.

The rule amongst voluptuous people. If there is real love offered, there ought to be no repudiation.

Ravana carries her off by force. In his palace he renews his overtures in high style, but when rejected again in unyielding fashion, he is rendered abject by his infatuation, and falls at her feet with all his ten heads. Cajolery and threats alternately, all unavailing. But no final breach or abandonment. Woos her again in a scene of which Hanuman was witness from the tree.

LECTURE XXV

RAVANA CONCLUDED—SITA

347-352 Ravana's wooing in the asoka grove continued. How his infatuation for Sita overmastered him.

Certain noteworthy sayings from the scene—

348-349 Sita to Ravana—"Are there no good people in Lanka or do you not heed their advice?" Moral—In any community it is the duty of good elderly people to give a timely warning to persistent wrong-doers.

349-350 Ravana to Sita, stung by her harsh speech—'My love for you restrains my just anger. Such is love's vagary that when it is fixed upon some person, it induces compassion and affection towards its object where sternness and coldness would be more in place.'

351 At the close of the scene, Dhanyamalini throwing herself on Ravana to prevent him from striking Sita, speaks a great truth: 'Pining after a woman who does not return your love, you only mortify yourself; why not gratify yourself by returning the love of a woman who longs for you?'

352-353 Ravana in Council declares his infatuation openly, justifying his capture of Sita as it were on the ground that she was on Rakshasa territory and was lawful prey. He pretends to seek advice of his ministers but tells them that he will not give up Sita on any account, and that their business is to advise him how Rama and Lakshmana could be disposed of.

353-354 Vibhishana who knew Ravana's infatuation assures Rama after the murder of the counterfeit Sita by Indrajit that Ravana would never kill Sita as he would not lose hope of her.

354 When after Indrajit's death Ravana made up his mind to kill her himself, he desisted from the attempt on Suparsva's advice that he should kill her husband first, as this would leave some hope still of his winning Sita's compliance.

SITA CONTINUED

354-355 Valmiki's conception of Sita as the paragon of virtue, the nonpareil of her sex.

355-357 A preliminary point—The sentiments about the unhappy fathers of girls (kanyapitrtva) uttered by Sita to Anasuya cannot be hers, but are Valmiki's own reflecting ideas prevalent in his own time, which the Poet indeed was rather fond of ascribing to generations long anterior to himself, e.g. Sumali, father of Kaikasi, and Maya, father of Mandodari.

Janaka was not so terribly anxious about Sita, or he would not have instituted so hard a test for her suitors.

357-362 Discussion between Rama and Sita regarding her going to the forest with him.

357 Rama paints the terrors of the forest and says it is not fit for her. She pooh-poohs the dangers and says beasts will fear him and she is safe in his company. A sojourn in the forest has been predicted for her, and she has always longed for it.

358-359 For the many maxims of worldly wisdom and of duty to elders which Rama imparts to her she has no ear. She says that her dharma is to follow her husband. Pushed to an extremity she says she will rather end her life than live in the city without Rama.

359 Seeing that Rama is unmoved by her entreaties and her threat, she has recourse to taunts. 'My father mated me with a woman in a man's form.' 'To think of your handing me over to Bharata's care! Why, it's the sort of thing a dancer (sailusha) does!

359-361 That Sita should be found fault with, as she has been by learned commentators, for her bold speech to her husband on this occasions, betrays narrow-mindedness. She was a kshatriya, high-born and noble, and was entitled to say these things, which the Poet with marvellous skill has brought together in one sarga (*II*. 30) and put into her mouth. And seeing how women are usually kept down, repressed, all honour to her, we say, for having given utterance to her high sentiments!

361-362 Why, what did Rama himself say? He gave way to her wholly, gracefully. No trace of reluctance or of disapprobation of Sita's taunts and reproaches! 'I know now what high courage you possess. I go to the forest because of my parents' order which may not be neglected. I have made up my mind that you shall go with me. Be my partner in all that I have to do in the forest.'

362 Whereupon Sita got ready for the forest, giving away her possessions.

LECTURE XXVI

SITA CONTINUED

363 The happiest period of Sita's life was her first twelve or thirteen years' sojourn in the forest.

365-366 We take up the tale after Sumantra's departure. With Guha's assistance the exiles cross the broad Ganges. When (after a visit to Bharadvaja) they come to the swift-flowing Jumna, Rama and Lakshmana improvise a craft for themselves. We are not to suppose that to Lakshmana fell all the drudgery; Rama had his fair share of the toil too in the forest.

369 Sita salutes Syama, the great banyan tree, and they march on to Chitrakuta.

365-368 Pretty and pleasing touches by the Poet regarding Sita and regarding Lakshmana's solicitude for her comfort and enjoyment. The zest with which Sita entered into her new life.

364-368 Rama's devout ways—utterance of sacred mantras ('sutramana' and 'devim navam') at the crossing of the Ganges; punctilious performance of purificatory ceremonies on completion of the hut at Chitrakuta ('vastu homa' and 'vaisvadeva').

367 The popular fallacy that Lakshmana went without food and sleep for fourteen years (and thereby fulfilled the condition required for killing Indrajit) exposed.

368-369 Sita vowing offerings to the river-goddesses would seem to have had the weakness of her sex in this respect.

369-370 Glimpses of forest life. Meat-eating. Perfect happiness in Chitrakuta.

Then after Bharata had come and gone, and when the exiles entered Dandaka,

370 Viradha seizes the brothers and carries them off; Sita offers herself as a ransom as it were, which shows her complete self-effacement.

Then follow visits to holy hermitages.

371-378 On the eve of the departure from Sutikshna's, Sita, handing their respective weapons to the brothers, takes occasion to remonstrate with Rama on the incompatibility of his following kshatriya dharma in the forest whither he had come to lead an ascetic's life, and voices her misgivings. Sita is often blamed for this, but the censure is due to ignorance. What is Rama's reaction? He not only takes her admonition in good part, but commends her for it.

Would that wives were fit to advise and admonish us, and that we were willing to listen!

Sita's story of 'The Rishi and his Sword' has a moral for these latter days: if you want peace, disarm all the nations!

378-380 Another important incident in connection with which Sita's conduct is called in question is when Maricha, simulating Rama's voice, cried 'O Sita, O Lakshmana,' and Sita drove Lakshmana away from Panchavati hermitage. Now, in the extremity in which Sita found herself any woman would act as she did in asking Lakshmana to go to his brother's help. Her fears, and her anger when Lakshmana refused to go, were natural. All that we can say is that it would have been worthy of Sita if she had refrained from saying harsh things to Lakshmana.

380-381 Rama, it must be remembered, blamed Lakshmana for leaving his post of duty, not Sita for driving him away from it.

LECTURE XXVII

SITA CONCLUDED

382 Exit Lakshmana. Enter Ravana, in sanyasi garb. Sita receives the guest in due form. He praises her. She is uneasy, both because she has to do the honours all by herself and because she is anxious about Rama and Lakshmana.

383 Ravana asks her about herself. In the account she gives she refers incidentally to Lakshmana as a 'dharmachari' and a 'dridhavrata,' which shows that in speaking harshly to Lakshmana she had no thought other than to force him to obey her.

384-385 Ravana declares himself and announces his evil intention. Stung by his wicked sentiments, she answers without hesitation or doubt. Her words were hot with anger and contempt. Translation of her speech (III. 47). Remarks on its rhetorical and vituperative tone. Not dramatic in form. Effect jejune.

385 Ravana carries her off. Her presence of mind in casting off her ornaments among the monkeys in Risyamuka.

386-388 The torments to which Sita was subjected in captivity in the asoka grove. Translation of her soliloquy in V. 28; literary merits of the passage as contrasted with III. 47.

Some tit-bits—

388-389 'Fire of chastity'—self-acting or to be directed? Hanuman's remarks. Sita's own statement is that as she had no order from Rama to defend herself she did not reduce Ravana to ashes.

389 Tender as she was in the extreme, we see her breathing revenge on Lanka and cursing it.

390-393 Again, we see her telling the rakshasa women that she did not know Hanuman and that he must be a rakshasa. Patent falsehood this! Why did she utter it? Because she thought Hanuman was in danger from Ravana. Had not Hanuman risked his life for her already? Who could blame Sita? Only, Sita might have spared herself, because presently Hanuman proclaimed himself openly to all whom it concerned that he was Rama's messenger.

393 While her falsehood was thus of no particular avail, her prayers certainly saved his burning tail!

Trijata's dream, followed by Sita's promise of protection to the rakshasa women if the dream came true.

394 How she actually protected them from Hanuman's wrath after Ravana was killed. Translation of her beautiful reply to Hanuman.

The "tragedy" of Sita—

395-396 Scene i—the most impressive and solemn in all the first six kandas. Rama's repudiation of Sita on the charge of infidelity. Sita's reply translated.

396-399 Scene ii—After the ordeal by fire and the re-union, and after an all too brief period of perfect bliss, Rama's final abandonment of Sita to placate a censorious world. Sita's touching farewell to Lakshmana in Uttara 48 translated.

399-400 Scene iii—Twelve years pass, and we have the final scene, not less tragic but transcending our experience. Sita is called upon to take an oath of purity. She calls upon Mother Earth to vindicate it. Mother Earth opens and receives Sita into her bosom.

400-401 The key to Rama's action seems to be his unflinching and inexorable pursuit of the highest ideals of his **DHARMA** in all circumstances whatsoever, the particular dictate of that dharma in this case being the maintenance of the honour of his family, however harsh and inhuman it might appear.

LECTURE XXVIII

KAIKEYI

This talk deals at length with

(1) the unscrupulous use by Kaikeyi of her power over Dasaratha to wring from him a two-fold promise, to banish Rama to the forest forthwith for fourteen years, and in his room to crown Bharata yuvaraja;

(2) the staggering renunciation by Bharata of these wicked works of hers.

The main points made are:—

402 Kaikeyi a most unlovely character, her name a by-word for iniquity.

The only redeeming feature was the affection that she bore to Rama and the affection that she drew from him.

402-403 Like mother, like daughter—Sumantra's story of her mother's repudiation by Asvapati.

403-407 Her haughty and contemptuous treatment of the senior queen and the other wives of the king.

407-410 The devilish cunning and cruelty with which she ensnared the old king in her toils.

410-419 A rehabilitation of Dasaratha—

But the common belief, voiced at the time, and prevalent through the ages, that Dasaratha was wrought upon by Kaikeyi's spells and charms, and that in yielding to her demands he was a slave to Kama, is a fallacy. In this respect, the opinion expressed by Rama in II. 53, where he refers to his father as a 'kamatma' and holds him up as a warning, has moulded the judgment of posterity. The verdict is quite wrong all the same. What held the old king as in a vice was not his infatuation for Kaikeyi, but the promise that he had made to her in days gone by. The Poet makes this abundantly clear. Dasaratha himself for instance dreaded that what as a satyavrata he could in no way escape doing would be censured by the world as a dotard's doing, so notorious was his uxoriousness. His out and out repudiation of Kaikeyi when once he discovered her wickedness and her treachery to Rama is irrefragable proof that it was not to please her or under charm that he decreed Rama's banishment.

413-415 Her calculated lie to Sumantra; her lie to Rama.

420 Why she did nothing to send for Bharata as promised by her to Rama is a puzzle.

420-423 Remarkable interview between her and Bharata.
Strikes one as not perfectly natural. What its inner meaning may be is a puzzle again.

423-426 Two changes noticeable in Kaikeyi as we study her character:—

i. Her affection for Rama was genuine and steady. It was not easily dislodged from the mind, not till Manthara painted to her in lurid colours the fate that would overtake
   (a) Bharata—banishment, nay death, at the hands of Rama;
   (b) herself—whom Kausalya would not be slow to revenge herself upon for past insults.

ii. When Bharata disowned her doings and condemned her outright and she saw how her works had turned to bitterness and ashes, she was truly and deeply humbled. The Poet does not say in so many words that Kaikeyi repented, but her actions show a contrite spirit.
   (a) She who had proudly defied the whole world and driven Rama to the forest, meekly, nay gladly, joined Kausalya and Sumitra when they went with Bharata to Chitrakuta to fetch Rama back from the forest
   (b) She on whose face there was not the slightest change of hue or softening of look when the exiles were departing was in choking sobs with the other queens when Rama refused to return to the city.
   (c) When Rama returned from his exile and her son made rendition of the kingdom to him, she was sincerely delighted.

One likes to think of this reformation in Kaikeyi as a proof of the tremendous power of Rama's character.

427 As between Kausalya and Sumitra to be dealt with next, Sumitra is developed spiritually better, and her sayings and sentiments challenge our notice.

LECTURE XXIX

KAUSALYA AND SUMITRA

428-432 Rama tells his mother of his banishment. She complains of Kaikeyi and her oppression and asks Rama to take her with him. Lakshmana offers to fight for Rama, but Kausalya, good woman, does not approve. She asks Rama to remain behind and protect her, and threatens prayopavesana. Rama charges her upon oath to give him leave. She still forbids, and there ensues an altercation between Rama and Lakshmana upon Fate. When Kausalya insists that she will go to the forest with him, Rama in the plenitude of his faith in Dharma takes it upon himself to preach it on a high level. When he teaches his mother her duty, she is brought to her senses somewhat, and says she will stay behind. When Rama drives his lesson home, she again rebels, the poor lady in her distressed condition swinging this way and that. It is not till after another sermon from Rama that she learns her duty and yields.

432-433 Her elaborate ceremonies in which she is well versed, and the famous benediction she pronounces on Rama.

433-434 Rama taking leave of his father commends his mother to him.

434-435 When Sita takes leave of Kausalya, the latter praises pativratya to her daughter-in-law, and condemns women generally.

Reference to a tirade against women by Agastya in III. 13.

Remarks on the uncharitable and unwarranted imputations against the sex in the Ramayana.

436-439 It is refreshing to turn to Sumitra. Her injunction to Lakshmana. Kausalya's miserable wail, and Sumitra's grand consolation to her, both translated.

The great difference between Kausalya and Sumitra. The younger queen more self-possessed, more understanding, is seen at the very peak of her wisdom in these scenes.

439-440 When Sumantra returns and delivers the message of the exiles, we have a distressing scene; Kausalya taunts the old and stricken monarch; rubs salt into his wound.

440-442 Again we see her reproaching Dasaratha. Her speech and Dasaratha's reply both translated.

442-443 Then when the poor old king made anjali to her, Kausalya realised how wrong and thoughtless she had been, caught his joined palms, placed them on her head with reverence, and became thoroughly penitent.

443 Midnight. Dasaratha recalls a past misdeed of his—the killing of a boy of blind aged hermits. Kausalya and Sumitra fall asleep, and the king passes away.

443-444 When Bharata arrives, Kausalya at once accuses him. Contrast Kaikeyi's fencing and beating about the bush.

Bharata invokes the most awful curses on himself in vindication of his innocence.

Once more we see Kausalya penitent.

Pathetic and tender scenes witnessed in Chitrakuta.

445-446 Kausalya speaks to Sumitra of her son's devotion to Rama and says that Lakshmana will no longer have menial duty to perform as Rama will return to the city.

Her grief at sight of the offerings of ingudi cake made by Rama and Lakshmana to their departed father.

Her fond and touching greeting of Sita.

LECTURE XXX

PATTABHISHEKA

447 A coronation ceremony is mentioned four times in the Ramayana—Rama's coronation as heir-apparent, which miscarried; Sugriva's; Vibhishana's double coronation, symbolical on this side of the ocean, real in Lanka after Ravana's death; and the grand coronation of Rama.

Certain features that distinguish these—

447-448 Waters were brought from seas and rivers and sacred places for all. Monkeys available for this service fetched them at short notice in all but the first case. That they were ready for the abortive coronation shows that the cunning old king must have had them brought in advance of the public announcement he made of his intention. Query: what became of these waters?

Sixteen radiant maidens in attendance at Sugriva's coronation as adhiraja of the monkeys. We notice that only eight were provided for Rama's coronation as yuvaraja.

Sugriva was bathed by friends of his own race, the great monkey-chiefs; whereas Lakshmana took the leading part in Vibhishana's double coronation.

Brahmans would appear to have been called in to officiate at Sugriva's coronation.

Neither Sugriva nor Vibhishana had a queen crowned along with him. Sita was the only one to be crowned with her husband, and that only when he was crowned in full sovereignty.

449-455 The grand coronation of Rama and Sita—

449-452 Remarkable parallelism in the circumstances in which Bharata offered the throne to Rama in Chitrakuta (II. 105) and those in which he invited Rama to occupy it after the latter's return from exile (VI. 131): translation of Bharata's address on the later occasion.

452 Rama resumes 'civilization'; the poet's curious silence about Satrughna's bath; similar omission of his name in the Chitrakuta parleys (II. 103. 32).

452-453 Rama's monkey allies all assume human form for the occasion; in the war in Lanka, by express command of Rama they had retained their own monkey form.

453-454 Description of the actual ceremonies of the coronation.

454 Descrepancy between the accounts in Yuddhakanda and in Uttarakanda touching the termination of the festivities. In Yuddha Sita presents a garland to Hanuman; in Uttara Rama does this. Which is better, Sita's hand giving the 'hara', or Rama binding it on the neck?

454 No warrant in the text for the traditional belief that the 'kuladhana' given to Vibhishana at the leave-taking was the image of Ranganatha worshipped by the Ikshvaku family; it refers simply to the kingdom of Lanka.

455 The captains and the kings depart. Each goes to his several home—as a body is sorry to part!

Epilogue

455-456 May Rama and Sita sit for ever enthroned in our hearts!

FIRST LECTURE*

Ladies and Gentlemen,—Never before in my life have I felt so nervous at the beginning of a talk as I do today. The causes are many. One or two of them I must indicate. The first is my sense of utter diffidence for the task I have undertaken. The second is the nature of the audience that I have which frightens me out of my wits. The third is the exalted nature of the subject matter upon which it is difficult even for the most original minds to say anything like what may be new. But, I am upheld by the traditional reflection that when a man talks of subjects like the Ramayana, it does not matter how inadequate his ability may be; those that come to listen come with hearts ready to be influenced, willing to be touched and, therefore, always in a condition to overlook deficiencies and errors, however serious they be. Besides, there is the thought that I am talking to Mylapore, to people who are known to me very well and from whom I am entitled to expect not only sympathy but unstinted indulgence.

I am not going to deal with the Ramayana in the spirit of a critical scholar. Questions of its date, questions of the historicity of Sri Rama, questions of the nature of the authorship, single or multiple, questions of the various forms that the story has taken where it has travelled—and it has travelled widely, questions how far Valmiki was indebted to others for the outline and the details, questions whether the version as we have it today is authentic and may be considered as his in the main or whether, as some students maintain, we should reject as spurious considerable parts of the story as it has come down to us, questions of these kinds are beyond my scope. And, there is a further limitation which I should, at the outset, bring before you by way of a confession, a limitation which many may consider inimical to the interest of my talks and absolutely cancelling any claim that I may have to your attention. Just listen to me in this part with all your charity alive and fully active. I shall not deal except today and by way of allusion to Sri Rama as a God. That is because not merely by my training am I not qualified to speak of Godhead—I retire in humility where such great

*5-4-44.

questions are involved—but it appears to me that there is a way of studying the Ramayana with reverence, with adoration of the great qualities of the hero and heroine and with full appreciation of the unparalleled influence that it has exerted in ages past and will exert for ages to come on the lives and character of our people. Every day that I read that epic my opinion gains strength that it is one of the greatest epics that ever were composed by man. I should call it the greatest epic, but I just shrink from that statement because I have no acquaintance with the originals of epics comparable to it in date and extent. There is no doubt, however, that it is one among the books that have influenced the hearts and the thoughts of whole peoples, not those only that have been able to read it in the original or in translations but those unlettered millions of our country who have always been there, even during the palmiest days of our culture, and who have merely heard the story told them either at home by father or mother or in the streets on public occasions by those expositors who seem in some ways to be peculiar to our sacred land.

A story spread so wide amongst the people, known even to children, cannot be retold with any embellishment or with any hope of drawing unusual attention. I have no such ambition. But, am I being too much of a pessimist, am I being a hopeless misreader of things around me, when I say—with a good deal of grief and sorrow—that, perhaps, the Ramayana is not quite as familiar to the younger generations that are coming up as it was to us of an older day? Is it not true, alas, that great numbers of our youth at school and college are being brought up without adequate knowledge of the very springs of our civilization and culture? Would it be an exaggeration if one expressed a fear that the young were not sufficiently familiar with the details of the story, with the high nature of the characters that have played parts in it, and with the greatness and splendour of the narrative which has come down to us in every vernacular of India as well as in Sanskrit? Is it an exaggeration to say that a student of the Ramayana not out of touch with its sanctity and its unequalled importance to the study of our civilization can talk to an audience largely composed of the younger generation with some hope of profiting them? I believe there is, and in the coming years there is going to be, a greater need than ever of our going back with reverent hearts to this most beautiful and moving of all stories in literature. No one would be mis-spending his time or the time of those that listen to him if he and they together dwell with fondness and with affection on the lives of Sri Rama and Sita and try to understand the circumstances in which Dasaratha came to play the part which is the beginning, the starting point, of this great story.

Today, I intend only to touch on the light in which I regard this beautiful poem and shall speak to you about it. My idea in subsequent talks, if I have the good fortune to go here again and address this audience or audiences similar to this, is to review the character of the great men and women that have played conspicuous parts in the story, taking up Sri Rama himself first. I do not know how long he will hold me, not in bondage—that he will hold me for ever, but, I mean, I do not know how many lectures I should give to the full unfolding of the manifold excellences of his character, of the various aspects of his life that we should dwell upon and never cease to dwell upon and of how as the years went on he prepared himself for the unique part he had to play, and how around him there were ranged characters of scarcely less importance, which sometimes heightened his character, sometimes illustrated it and sometimes, if you will allow me to say so, glorified his character. Afterwards, I shall take up the life of that unparalleled heroine of all literature, Sita herself, whose name is a synonym for all the virtues of women in any land and of any time, a character which sometimes, I grieve to think is not, even amongst us, fully valued under the malign influence of a thought that however great she might have been in origin, she took a place in a degraded sex and was, therefore, liable to the small imputations to which that sex is by a certain section of 'superior man' amongst us condemned. Then we shall deal with the next one in importance, Hanuman, and so on. It is now too early for me even to prescribe the order in which I shall take up these characters.

I do not believe for one moment, let me repeat it, I do not for one moment think that I shall tell you anything that you do not know or that you have not thought of before or that somebody has not suggested before to you. I much wonder, unless a man wishes to condemn himself as being original for the sake of being original, whether an Indian taking up this kind of task can really say anything or suggest anything which has not been discussed threadbare already. Once more, then, I shall by way of concluding this preface merely say that my willingness to expose my thoughts to your examination must, I specially entreat you, be met on your part with a desire to listen to one who is no better than you in any way but means just to engage you for a while on this occupation, than which it is difficult to imagine one that is more profitable either to the mind or to the soul. Moreover, often as you have heard these things before, you like to hear them again. I may tell you nothing special, but you may perhaps tell yourself at the end, "Well, this gentleman is a good chap though he seems to know pretty little. He need not have called us together just to listen to this. But it does not matter. After all we have heard about our Rama and no time is said to be lost if spent that way." Look at me and receive what I say in that genuine spirit of charity. You all know the familiar saying that if you drop a vessel into a huge body of water, the vessel can only take up its own measure. I can do no more, nor can you for that matter. We are all alike. Some people are very wise. When they study big books of this kind, the thoughts that occur to them and the ideas that inspire them are of the most elevated character, having their roots in the Sastras and in the sacred laws and make them more or less on a par with those original thinkers who laid the foundations in ancient times of our culture. From that grade to the grade of the ordinary student who brings only his own ignorance to the task, there is every grade of equipment and every grade of preparation. To each according to his capacity.

Sometime ago, writing of my diffidence to a friend, I seemed to have said something like this: 'Suppose you go to the Marina. There is the illimitable ocean spread out before us, witness to the majesty and incomprehensibility of Nature. On the shore you may have a poet thinking in rhapsodies of what he sees and the splendours that meet his vision. You may have a philosopher who will muse and, perhaps, reconstruct the very structure of the great thought that put those things together in space. You may have a pious man who simply takes his mind to the contemplation of the Great Being who made the ocean. the sky and all things that revolve in eternal Samsara. At the same time with these people of high quality, you may have children who merely take up the sands and throw them at each other. Each does his part.' I am like a child, just throwing a little sand at you—perfectly natural—and so, give me my place; I am entitled to do what is according to my own nature. Can I see the ocean? Do not pity me, do not scorn me; I just do what I can; no one can do more. All alike pay homage to the ocean,—the illimitable ocean—and I pay my homage too.

Now, then, for a word to indicate my attitude in these talks. Those of you—and I know you are amongst the majority—who believe in the origin of this story, i.e., who think that owing to the great oppression practised by Ravana on the Universe—not only on this earth but on the whole Universe—the Gods felt compelled to seek help of the Almighty and the Almighty taking pity on the Universe came down in human form to put an end to the misery of the Universe, are fully entitled to believe it. Nothing that I shall say, believe me, nothing will disturb you in that faith. That faith is not yours alone; it is there, taught in the book; throughout the story Valmiki himself represents Sri Rama as an Avatar of God, and his great assistants in the story as, in a way subordinate to him, Avatars too. I do not believe, however often I read the story, that it is possible to effect a separation between the parts where the poet alludes to Rama merely in his human character with human limitations, from those parts where he speaks of him as a God descended among men. Those who think that to the kernel of the story representing Sri Rama as a man subsequent ages added elements of divinity are only guessing, while the story itself, as it is told by Valmiki, has its foundation on this faith, and there is no mistake about it. I dare not question it; it is there in so many places. Valmiki says in so many words that Sri Rama was God but limited himself and came down amongst men to function for a certain purpose in order to bring deliverance to a suffering Universe.

But, what is the real significance to the understanding of the epic of this foundation of faith? You all know that as in all literary criticism, in India too, the fundamental postulate is that an epic is a great work of art which is intended expressly for the edification of man. If God took shape amongst us as one of us, He did so for the purpose of giving us instruction how to live, how to prepare for our parts in life, how to go through it. The epic is to be read with a view to benefit by its teaching, to draw at every turn lessons of supreme value for the conduct and regulation of ourselves. That much is clear. God as Rama was born in the royal family of Ayodhya in order that He and those associated with Him in various capacities may in their various ways exemplify and vindicate to us the very nature of earthly existence. If we do not read the poem with that object in view, we gain nothing by it, nothing whatever. Ladies, whether highly educated or absolutely illiterate, all take lessons from Sita's story. How can they help it? "Sita did so and so. Although I may not do exactly alike, although I may fail most miserably, I must keep that ideal in view. I must never lose sight of what is right and proper as it is exemplified in that great life, specially for my benefit. For me, Sita and Rama lived and struggled and suffered so that I may be a better person than I was born," each one of them says to herself. If that is the case, it is worth our while to pay attention to the way in which these great characters grew up in the hands of the poet almost from the very birth until, during their long lives, they go through a variety of circumstances and experiences on a scale vastly greater than what happens to us here. It seems to me that if a person read the poet in order that his soul may be edified, he would find,—just give me your best attention—that that object would be best gained by fixing attention on the main characters as human beings that played their parts like human beings in circumstances that assail and confront human beings at every turn. If at any time or any part in the story you say to yourself, knowing the fundamental fact and never being able to get away from it, "Oh! but he was a god; he could do anything; she was a goddess and she could do anything; all that has no application to me", then, you miss the entire point of the story. Every single thing they did, every single thing they said, aye, every joy and every grief they experienced, they did, said and experienced in order that it may throw light upon your own life and give you strong, steady, firm, trustworthy guidance in the trials that await you. If at any time you say, "This is an impossible thing. God may do anything He pleased; He is omnipotent, omniscient, omnipresent, omni-penetrative; how does it affect me who am so unlike in every respect?" If a person says that, he misses the whole story; he reads for nothing, he listens for nothing at all.

It appears to me, furthermore, that it is no act of impiety to study the Ramayana as an epic poem concerning human beings. It is an act, on the other hand, which gives to Valmiki his own due, establishes him as a man who held in his mind—assuming that he was the one that wrote the story—a clear, fully-formed, full-blooded conception of men and women of superior ability and superior value to us, of superior moral stature. I would exhort you all to read the poem from this point of view.

What would you say, for instance, of a most captivating drama being played on the stage, characters dressed, everything perfectly fitting each other and portraying the intended parts beautifully and the whole drama being played on the highest level so as to make you forget everything else and throw your whole being into a study of the story and to make you identify yourself for the moment with the hero or the heroine, if all of a sudden, the hero flared up on the stage and shouted, "Do not believe a word of what I am saying. I am only Subbu of the last house!" What would you say of characters that suddenly break out in the midst of the most exciting part of the story and disenchant you like that, disturb the tenor of your thoughts and tell you, "You are merely listening here to a part and witnessing a drama on the stage; it is not real life. Do not vex yourself, therefore. Do not be bothered; it is only a play and the fellow who plays the hero is the cook in so-and-so's house!" Suppose somebody throws you off your mind in that way or the characters themselves say to one another what they would say in ordinary life,—then, you think that somebody has deprived you by main force of a great spiritual possession at the time when you were watching a great event taking shape before you and identifying yourself with it, forgetting everything that actually will be when you go home, that actually was before you went to the play. While you are there, you expect the illusion to be perfectly maintained. Anything in the nature of a jar irritates you beyond endurance. I do not say that you would be irritated by the commentators who say very often, "Well, Sri Rama over-plays his part as a mourner for his wife from whom he is separated. Do not believe all this. He was only playing a part." The commentator now and then says that. Occasionally, too, gods and goddesses come down and witness the great scenes that are being played. Let us say Sita is being carried away by Ravana. Supposing one of the gods said, "That is right! The whole thing is developing according to plan. We want this thing to happen. And it has happened", what would you say?

The Ramayana has been told to us times without number. Every line of it has been scanned and commented upon minutely, not hundreds, not thousands but millions of times over. We have all conned every little thing in it. Nevertheless, somehow or other, in our mixed human nature, there is a tendency which we nourish to come again and yet again to the story, whether before breakfast or after siesta in the afternoon or midnight and it is. time to be sleeping. At whatever time we go, to whatever place, whoever the expounder may be, somehow or other there is that in us which helps us to put aside all disturbing illusions, all the things that are calculated to take us away from the environment of the story itself even while our circumstances are such as to cause distraction for the time. A child crying or somebody falling asleep on you and all the other things may be calling attention to the wretched world around you; but even so, somehow, there is in all of us—provided we are Hindus by training and in spirit, an ability, what shall I call it, an almost non-human ability to put aside those distractions and to remain under the influence of that illusion as though the whole thing were being enacted on the stage by men fully trained for the purpose amidst appointments of a first-class character which will produce and maintain the illusion at its greatest. We have that amongst us. Everyone of us has it and it is a marvel how we retain it.

I should ask you always to put yourselves in that condition and remain in it whenever you read this great epic. The whole thing is done before you with a set purpose and unless you help that purpose to fulfil itself in you, you read it for nothing. Everything, therefore depends on the way in which you open the book and read it. I take up the book anywhere and read it. To me Sri Rama is not divine. Nevertheless, the illusion is always there, in full force. I can throw myself heart and soul into the very essence of the story. When I read the book, I read that book and do nothing else; my whole mind is devoted to it. A hard-hearted man like me, I read it, and, strange to say, there is not a page which does not bring tears into my eyes! Any fine sentiment, any tender feeling, any affection between brother and brother, any re-union of beings that have been separated for a time, aye, any homage paid to friendship, to gratitude or to any of those eternal abiding virtues of human character, brings tears into my eyes! I stop; I cannot go on, I have to wait and wipe my eyes and then go on. Why do I do that? A hardened man of the world, why do I do that? Why has it that effect on me? I suppose it is because deep down in my nature, going to strata which perhaps in my waking life I shall never touch, there is a spirit of the utmost reverence and affection for those great characters. Why? Even if Rama and Sita were not of this land but were the hero and heroine in an alien poem, I should feel probably not so very much affected but nearly as deeply. Human nature is human nature; whether nurtured here or in another land, it is just the same.

And that brings me to the main point of the lecture which I should like you to take away with you, viz., that the divinity of Sri Rama need not be questioned for a moment, no, I wish I can bring myself to believe it—but, I find as a matter of fact, that it is not essential to the understanding of the story or to profiting by the story. And, I can tell you without boasting that, perhaps, robbed as I am of that faith, I am able to get for the building up of my own nature more from the Ramayana than many another student of that book who believes in the divinity of the character but is not able for some reason or other to take in the real spirit in which the lives were lived. After all, when you come to look at it, it seems to be this way. There is the great vault of the heaven above. We are all under it. We function under it. Our lives are ordered under it. We quarrel and fight, we kill each other, acquire and lose. We do so many things under this over-arching heaven. If thus the over-arching heaven enters into our lives, our doings and sayings, shapes our character and regulates the details of our lives, it does so and who can question it? Whether I say that it does so or not, the fact is that it does. My belief does not affect it; my non-belief cannot abolish it. It is there, immutable, eternal, unalterable by the thought of the individual. I may be a man of science, I may be a man of logic, I may be a naturalist-minded man, this, that or something else; but, if there is the influence of heaven on my life, though I may be ignorant of it, I cannot get away from it. It is there always, affecting everyone of my thoughts, giving shape to everyone of my doings, however big or however small, however significant to other people or however devoid of value to others. That which is done by me is subject to this eternal, immutable influence. So, if Rama and Sita and Hanuman had divinity in them, they had it. Everywhere, everywhere in the story, that influence is there and will be there. It is not possible, it is not scientific, it is not accurate, it is not sensible to say that Rama was divine in some of his acts and not divine in others, that Sita behaved only in some parts of her life like Lakshmi but that in some others she got out of her Lakshmi-hood by some strange device. If divinity appertained to these characters, it did appertain, aye, and for ever. To try and separate some things in the Ramayana from other things in the same book for the quality of being especially marked by the divine influence or of being especially the symptom of divinity is, it seems to me, to show ignorance of the very fundamentals of the poem. The thought of divinity need not, therefore, affect your understanding of the poem. You may read the poem as an epic, as a great epic, that has influenced the whole lives of millions of people for generations upon generations.

One word more. You all know—I need not elaborate it to an audience of this kind, but I will just remind you, I need only remind you—that even the theory of avatar philosophically stated applies to all humanity in one sense, remote it may be and comprehended only by great students of our literature. In one sense, every single creature in this planet or elsewhere is merely an emanation from the one and only source of all life and the one and only cause of the Universe. In that wise, we are all avatars; only, in us the divine element is not nearly so prominent as in the case of some others. It is a question only of degree, a question, as it were, only of the proportion of time and proportion of events in which the divinity plays its part. That, really and properly considered, is what distinguishes one man from another. In a great man, the divine or super-human element manifests itself oftener, more clearly and to better purpose than in the case of a comparatively ill-developed man. That is why they speak sometimes of the evolution of souls. Some souls are developed more than others on a higher plane and, therefore, in them it is possible for us to see and in their writings and speeches it is possible for us to hear more often the note of divinity than in the case of other people not so fortunate or so far advanced in evolution as they. Sri Rama, if you will allow me for a moment to talk of him,—I cannot pretend to keep Rama from you any longer—was an embodiment of the great virtues of human character. Hear him speak, see him do things, have anything to do with him, come under his influence; you cannot escape the touch of divinity. That is why a study of his life is more profitable to us from the point of view of the soul than the study of the life of other heroes.

Lives of other peoples are not without instruction too. Less evolved characters there always have been. For instance, it is the function of poets and novelists and others of sorts to create for our benefit, out of their superior knowledge and superior creative power, characters whom it is worth our while to study, to make them function upon a stage where human circumstances prevail, so that from these imperfect characters living in very imperfect conditions and created so as to dwell in our imagination by men of imperfect development in authorship,—even these characters, I say, we do not read of without some profit. You take the novels of our greatest writers. They are not without benefit to us unless we read them as we play cards. But to those that study these great and moving books, with their hearts working on them, with their minds playing on them, and deriving at every stage something of value to their own building up, to them, all these books, like Jean Valjean, for instance, are of immense educational and spiritual value. I am mentioning this just for the purpose of enforcing this point that even if a hard-hearted man, intellectually well-trained and merely prepared to learn and improve,—even if such a man came to study the Ramayana and took it up only as a great poem written with a great purpose by a great man,—even if one did that one would profit immensely. We all do much more; we all value the Ramayana not merely as an epic poem but as a poem that has gone to the shaping of the whole of India's history. It is that which charges that epic and the Mahabharata and other books of that nature with the deepest instructional value to us and we shall do well, therefore, with our minds attuned to the gathering of these spiritual lessons, to pay attention to the great characters, Sri Rama, Sita, Hanuman and the others, as they slowly evolve. For, it is possible for us to see a certain evolution even of these characters. It is not as if they were born so. Sri Rama was no doubt God. But he came into the world like a child, was brought up like a child; a great teacher took him in hand, taught him everything, taught him archery, taught him fighting, taught him the things of the world, taught him the great meaning and the purpose of the rivers and mountains and sacred places and the inner meaning of sacrifices. So it was that Rama grew under Visvamitra. Visvamitra is no small man though I have never ceased to blame Valmiki for dismissing him so abruptly at the end never to meet him again. What a part Visvamitra played! Just think of that! A man who had the making of the whole of Sri Rama's character, who taught him not merely tapas, yajna, the daily sacrifices, prayers and all that but, the very art of war; a man who made Sri Rama what he was, who took Rama in hand in his plastic childhood, gave him shape and fitted him for the greatest part played by anyone,—a man of that type to be dismissed so summarily! Was it fair I ask, of the poet? I think it is a sudden exit, not to be tolerated.

So Rama grew in family life, under father and mother and under, like any of us, a step-mother, who had human frailties, unfortunately. He had his difficulties of a joint family. You see how he went through them all in a story full of the tenderest pathos and the most moving emotions. You must study the character of Rama.

Generally speaking, when there is a very highly developed character in a book, when you have a Sri Rama, critics of the modern day tell us: "Oh, Sri Rama? He is an uninspiring character. What is there in him? He is a monster of perfection. Before you turn the hundredth page, you can say exactly what he will say or what he will do next. He will do the right thing, the proper thing, and what must be done. He is not like us; he does not belong to us." When in any book, a character is painted and portrayed almost perfect, the critic is very impatient. He says, "I want a man of flesh and blood like me, a fellow who is subject to the same temptations, who wants to eat well, who must have first-class coffee in the morning, a human being like me, who goes through life struggling like me, pinched, pressed, tortured, as most of us are. I want to know how a great man comes out of that all. That is a great man, who, going through the mill, undergoing my experiences, suffering my sufferings, enjoying my joys, still comes out top, overcoming all those handicaps and limitations, showing in his fullest development the grandeur of human character, approaching the divinity from which he came and I came and you came, too. That is what we want," such critics say. "We want a man who is not a superman; that has no value to us. We want a man essentially human in his feelings, in his outlook on life, in his struggles and triumphs. We want him to be human, and being human, to triumph over his human limitations, develop his divinity, and in the end establish himself in the throne of human hearts as King, unsurpassed." Sri Ramachandra than whom there is no better as husband, as son, as king, as man, we see him growing up. That is the beauty of the Ramayana. The man who reads the Ramayana thinking that from the beginning he is dealing with God, will get nothing out of it. You must read the story as a human story, lived among human beings by a human being, and, then, Oh, what rich treasures there are of wisdom in it!

I do not know how long I will take over Sri Rama. But however often we dwell on him, however long we deal with him, in whatever way we understand him, his life comprehending all other lives, playing its part in the shaping of every other incident, will be full of lessons. By way of preparation, as it were, I may tell you that I shall beg you to deal with Rama not as a man in whom there was all knowledge, all propriety, all virtue, from the very beginning, unfailing till the very end—that is not the way to read his life—but, as a man who struggled, who was tempted, who had his weaknesses—do not be surprised; I am not committing any defamation or any blasphemy; he had his weaknesses—who put them down, overcame them, surpassed them all. It is only as we shall study Rama in that light that we shall get the richest treasure of wisdom from this great epic which I shall venture to study with you in our future talks.

SECOND LECTURE*

With deep salutations to the audience. Ladies and gentlemen! For a man like me who wishes to keep close to Valmiki's text, it is a disadvantage not to be able to quote from memory. In my experience, I have scarcely met an expositor of the Ramayana who is unable to reel off verses without any help. In that respect, as in others, I am unusual. If I want to refer to any verses, I shall be obliged to read.

The four brothers were born within a few hours of one another and there was not, therefore, any occasion for making differences between them on account of age. But in the Ramayana, seniority is established carefully and as between Bharata and Lakshmana it also becomes a matter of some little dispute. Valmiki even says that they were all alike except that Rama had a different complexion from the rest. Sometimes he uses the same adjective with reference to them. But, from the beginning the superiority of Sri Rama is placed beyond all doubt. In all respects, he was unapproached even by his brothers.

In the beginning, the great qualities of the family are described under heads of appearance, learning, conduct, skill of various kinds and so on. I need not refer to them. They were, except for small differences among each other, without rivals in the rest of the world. The poet specially refers to their character. He speaks of their devotion to the truth and to the interests of the subjects. He, especially, speaks of their feelings, their unaffected feelings, of reverence towards elders, mentioning the parents by pre-eminence. That, of course, confers a unique distinction on this family. But I think, as students of Indian history and of history in general and as students who are aware of the fortunes of royal families, we must take it as a very special good fortune of this Ikshvaku family that, although there were four brothers, there were no rivalries among them, no attempts to pass one another, no feeling at any time of close competition in any respect. If we think for a moment of the children of even wealthy families well known to us, we can appreciate the unique character of this particular family.

---

*12-4-44.

The poet plunges at once into the attempts of the old King to get the boys married, although they were just fifteen or over. And as he was consulting his ministers and preceptors, there enters the famous Rishi, Visvamitra. King Dasaratha seems to have had a fatal defect of promising in haste and repenting at leisure. He did that in this case. When Visvamitra appeared on the scene, he greeted him with the warmest of welcomes and offered to do anything he wanted in an excess of devotion, leaving no loophole for himself. Visvamitra fixed him down and was not slow to state his demand. He said he was performing a yajna which was threatened by two rakshasas and their followers, Maricha and Subahu. The two rakshasas themselves, the rishi was careful to explain, were the instruments of King Ravana of Lanka. When King Ravana was unable to do mischief himself, he must have been deputing these two men under him. Dasaratha at once offered his own services and said, "I am not unfamiliar with tactics of war. I will come and stand by you instead of my son." When the name of Ravana was mentioned, Dasaratha trembled all over; the poor man drew back. He said, "He is not the sort of chap whom I would care to meet." And then,—I ought to point out that the poet shows one of his great qualities here,—he puts into the mouth of the King, under the influence, no doubt, of fear and hesitation, passages of great rhetorical merit. You know one of the devices of ancient and modern rhetoricians is repetition of phrases that are either high-sounding or happy in their making-up. There are two expressions which Dasaratha uses freely: न रामं नेतु मर्हसि[1], नैव दास्यामि पुत्रकम्[2]. These he repeats five or six times in a manner which impresses us as coming from the poor man's distressed heart. Visvamitra, no doubt like himself, got thoroughly excited and said he would go away. He uses an ironical expression: "You remain in this place ruling your kingdom with your wellknown capacity to fulfil promises." With that slightly sarcastic cut he is about to depart, when Vasishtha intervenes with his great authority and, instructing Dasaratha in the special characteristics of the visitor advises the King most earnestly to fall in with his wishes. Dasaratha agrees and by way of complying with the demand, says the poet, sends for Sri Rama and Lakshmana. We have got to notice that Visvamitra did not ask for Lakshmana. He hardly men-

1. I. 20. 4, 6, 9, 11, 12. 2. I. 20. 25, 26.

tioned the name. But, apparently, in that family it was impossible to think of Sri Rama without at the same time thinking of Lakshmana too. That was no subtle thought in the case of Dasaratha. When he thought of sending Sri Rama, he knew Lakshmana would go too; so, he sends for both of them.

At this point it would be well if I drew your attention to a phrase which for its beauty and expressiveness is hardly equalled. This is the way in which the poet describes the relation between Sri Rama and Lakshmana. He says 'Lakshmana is like a second life to Sri Rama, only he functions outside Sri Rama's body.' Sometimes he uses the two phrases together and that is extraordinary. The poet seems to be very fond of it himself and he uses it frequently.

बाल्यात्प्रभृति सुस्निग्धो लक्ष्मणो लक्ष्मिवर्धनः ।
रामस्य लोकरामस्य भ्रातुर्ज्येष्ठस्य नित्यशः ॥
सर्वप्रियकरस्तस्य रामस्यापि शरीरतः ।
लक्ष्मणो लक्ष्मिसम्पन्नो बहिः प्राण इवापरः ॥
न च तेन विना निद्रां लभते पुरुषोत्तमः ।
मृष्टमन्नमुपानीतमश्नाति न हि तं विना ॥ I. 18. 27-9

'Sri Rama cannot sleep without Lakshmana nor would he eat anything sweet unless Lakshmana partook of it too.'

यदा हि हयमारूढो मृगयां याति राघवः ।
तदैनं पृष्ठतोऽभ्येति सधनुः परिपालयन् ॥ I. 18. 30

'If ever Sri Rama went out hunting, Lakshmana would be at his back with drawn bow.' In the Aranyakanda, Surpanakha, in describing her adventure with the brothers to Ravana, uses that expression. In fact, Surpanakha's behaviour is extraordinary. Though when she was with them she was not particularly truthful or respectful, when she describes the brothers and the wife to her master and brother, she is exceedingly truthful. She describes them in language of genuine appreciation, gives them their true character without any deduction. Even Sita she describes as of extraordinary charm, though she offered when talking to Sri Rama to take the place of 'that deformed woman'. About Lakshmana she says

"रामस्य दक्षिणो बाहुः" III. 34. 13

In the Yuddhakanda, when one of Ravana's informers Suka, describes Lakshmana to him, he uses the same expression:

'रामस्य दक्षिणो बाहुः नित्यं प्राणो बहिश्चरः' VI. 28. 25

When Lakshmana lies on the ground rendered breathless by Ravana's sakti and Sri Rama laments over his body, the poet says:

राघवो भ्रातरं दृष्ट्वा प्रियं प्राणं बहिश्चरम्।
दुःखेन महताविष्टो ध्यानशोकपरायणः॥ VI. 102. 9

I am mentioning these various uses of the expression only to show that Valmiki, like other poets, is fond of repeating expressions that have been given a happy form.

In another place, Sri Rama himself says to Lakshmana when his crowning as the Yuvarajah yet seemed probable:

लक्ष्मण मां मया सार्धम् प्रशाधि त्वं वसुन्धराम्।
द्वितीयं मेऽन्तरात्मानं त्वामियं श्रीरुपस्थिता॥ II. 4. 43

"This great access of fortune that has come to me," he says, "I am going to share with you. It is not for me exclusively. It is yours as well. For, to me, you are द्वितीयः अन्तरात्मा. Again, Sri Rama says:

सौमित्रे भुङ्क्ष्व भोगांस्त्वमिष्टान् राज्यफलानि च।
जीवितं च हि राज्यं च त्वदर्थमभिकामये॥ II. 4. 44

'If I wish these things at any time, it is not so much on my own account as that you may share them with me'. Identification of that kind between brothers in a royal family, who may be either proclaimed or covert rivals in ordinary life, is something out of the common. In fact, the affection and the bond between these two brothers parallelled only by the affection and the bond between the other two brothers is so unique in story or in fable that it would be necessary for us to dwell on it exclusively at one of our meetings. Today I do not mean to do more than just to say that it is unique and that for several reasons it is worth our while to pursue this relationship as it was displayed time after time in the most wonderful manner in the story. At present, you will, perhaps, allow me to pass on to another point that is noteworthy. As I am keeping close to Valmiki's text, you will allow me now and then to refer to the poet's peculiarities when they rise above the page, as it were, and strike your notice.

Lakshmana was so much a part of Sri Rama and the fact, apparently, was so well known to everybody that, as the story develops from sarga to sarga and Sri Rama and Lakshmana under the guidance of Visvamitra go through various adventures, observing great vows and learning great things and adding to their knowledge of everything, we find, curiously enough, that Visvamitra, who did not invite Lakshmana, takes notice of him only very rarely. If he talks to them, he only says, 'Rama, Raghava' addressing the elder brother. It would be uncharitable to assume that he did not like the presence of Lakshmana or that he wished intentionally to ignore him. I suppose in his mind too, as in the minds of everybody else, to speak to Rama was to speak to the other brother too. You need not specially have a form of address for it. As he gives them instruction in various matters, he mentions Rama and not Lakshmana except once or twice and that when he uses the dual number. Even when he taught them the great twin-mantras of Bala and Atibala, he taught them to Sri Rama. The commentator, hard put to it to explain the matter, says that Lakshmana is also included in the word Rama by Upalakshana, the Sanskritic equivalent for one of the forms of the English figure of speech, synecdoche. When Sri Rama is mentioned, Lakshmana is also included in it. Another commentator giving this explanation adds as an alternative, if some of you should be displeased with it, perhaps, that having learnt it directly from Visvamitra, Sri Rama taught it to Lakshmana later on privately. But, one way or another, it is noteworthy how Lakshmana, by himself no small or mean person, is in the story treated as if he were in physical body as in functions and characteristics only a part of Sri Rama.

Now, I come to another point in the development of the story as to Rama's character. On this point I shall have to dwell at some little length and quote from the text. Sri Rama and Lakshmana received their first baptism in bloody war when they met Tataka in her own forest known as Tatakavana. Here again it is noteworthy that Visvamitra, when he stated his troubles to the old King, mentioned only Maricha and Subahu as his tormentors. He carefully omitted the name of Tataka. Why he did is a guess to which we may give a moment's attention but it is a guess only. Not that she was not disturbing the yajna, for one of the epithets that Visvamitra applies to her later on is यज्ञविघ्नकरी I. 26. 22. She was also tormenting. Nevertheless, if he did not mention her to King Dasaratha when he applied for help, it can be accounted for in this way: Visvamitra knew that the King would not readily consent to give Sri Rama and that he would have to state his case as attended with as little danger as possible. To go and tell Dasaratha at once, 'Besides these two people, there is the she-devil, Tataka, whom also Sri Rama will have to dispose of' would be, perhaps, to have added to his difficulties. For, in those days as in these, even a case-hardened warrior hesitated to take the life of a woman. Visvamitra knew that there was no putting this woman out of action except by the extreme step of taking her life. To have told the old King, 'Well, I am taking your son and asking him the first thing in his military career to kill a woman' would perhaps be to have made his application in an impossible court. I guess, therefore, that that was why he kept this fact from Dasaratha although it must have been coming up to his own consciousness every minute he was talking to the old King.

Before he meets Tataka, Visvamitra warns Sri Rama. 'This is a tricky woman,' Visvamitra tells him, 'Do not show any softness to her. Kill her: that is the only thing to do with her. And, do not hesitate. Do not be squeamish because she is of the wrong sex.' Visvamitra further says, 'People like you, who are Princes and have the first duty to protect your subjects from harm, cannot afford to have these small scruples conflicting with it. If it is necessary to kill a woman, kill a woman, and this is one such. I warn you beforehand. Do not show *Ghrina* to her.

नृशंसमनृशंसं वा प्रजारक्षणकारणात् ।
पावनं वा सदोषं वा कर्तव्यं रक्षता सता ॥
राज्यभारनियुक्तानामेष धर्मः सनातनः ।
अधर्म्यां जहि काकुत्स्थ धर्मो ह्यस्या न विद्यते ॥ I. 25. 18-19

Sri Rama takes this injunction in good part. For, the Rishi had taken care to quote precedents also. He had said, 'Do not suppose I am asking you to be the first king in the world to go and kill a woman. Great beings have done it before you. Indra killed Manthara, while Maha Vishnu himself killed the wife of Bhrigu. And, then, take this man Parasurama; he killed his mother. With these precedents and others, you ought to have no scruple'. We have got to take note of the fact that at the first flush, Sri Rama took it in good part. 'My father when he gave me to you', he said, 'enjoined me to follow you and to obey you, to do whatever you bade do without hesitation. My father is a great King and you are a great Rishi and my preceptor. Why am I going to say 'No'? '

सोऽहं पितुर्वचः श्रुत्वा शासनाद् ब्रह्मवादिनः ।
करिष्यामि न संदेहस्ताटकावधमुत्तमम् ॥ I. 26. 4

Sri Rama says it is a great duty and he will kill Tataka: न संदेहः । Having said that, a few moments later, when Tataka appeared before him, somehow, his conscience smote him. His inborn instincts re-appeared. He says to Lakshmana, 'Look at this terrible woman. Weak people who see her merely will die. But, look here, she is a woman. I am not going to forget that fact. The only thing that is wanted is that Visvamitra should be free of her trouble. I will take care that she is (in our modern military language) immobilised. I will prevent her from doing him harm. Let us take off her hand, the lobes of her ears, deform her and send her away: she will be harmless.' So, by an arrow he cut off her arms. Lakshmana, not wishing to be behindhand, sent another arrow and cut off her ears and the tip of her nose. But the woman assumed protean forms and showered stones on them without end. She could not be seen and she did great mischief by her power of assuming various forms and also of remaining concealed from view. So, the poor brothers were much harassed. They sent their arrows in the direction whence the sounds came but their attempts were not wholly successful. The woman had still great mischief in her. Visvamitra seeing the trouble they were in reminded him, 'I told you so. She is not a woman to whom you ought to show any mercy. She is not fit for that sort of treatment. I told you, "kill her." The sun is going down. If you let five minutes pass, it will be too late, for after sun-down, these rakshasas become ten times more powerful than during day. Despatch her now.' So Rama did: he killed her.

We have got to look at this matter from the strictly disciplinal point of view. It is worth while spending a few minutes discussing this matter. Why did Sri Rama of whose straight thinking and straight acting none of us have any doubt, why did he, having passed his word, न संदेह: , in a few minutes disobey the sage and not kill Tataka at once? Why did he delay and say to Lakshmana that he would try merely to render her impotent for mischief? It is here we have to be a little bit careful how we judge Sri Rama in this matter at the very beginning of our discussions about him. Although there is no help from the commentators—and I have not had any from previous expositors—I think I should put it this way: In all big matters, Sri Rama trusted his own judgment and would not follow others' unless their deliverances coincided with his own judgment. Where he still had a lingering doubt he preferred to follow his own instincts. He had without thinking of it promised Visvamitra that he would take Tataka's life at once. But, at the last moment, when it came to the actual test,—as it happens to us sometimes when the real moment for action comes, whatever our resolution, hesitation creeps in,—he said, 'If I can in spirit obey Visvamitra, it is enough. Why should I follow him to the very letter? I will make her absolutely powerless.' I think I would not have the smallest hesitation in acquitting Sri Rama of any intention either to disobey the sage or to go back on his own plighted word. These hesitations and doubts assail men at every turn, whatever your mind may be and however firmly you might have made it up, when the actual moment for action comes; and there is no saying that some feeling that you had put down for the moment when things were far away might not reappear in full force and ask that you should pay respect to it. That is how I would put it. As for the duty of sparing the other sex, I think Visvamitra enunciated a good rule and a sound law. To a king, the highest duty, the most sovereign requirement, is protection of those who deserve protection; the other duties fall into the background. However great, therefore, may be the consideration that you give to woman, it must give place, as the old Rishi said, to this supreme necessity,—duty of protection. You cannot allow a great yajna and all the consequences that flow from it to be marred by this scruple.

I think that is the lesson that we have to take from this little episode.

I would now come to an important landmark in the Balakanda. We come to the context where Visvamitra and the rishis propose to Sri Rama and Lakshmana that they should go to Mithila and the attraction in Mithila, as they put it, is twofold. King Janaka is performing a great sacrifice and it is worth watching it. Another thing is that in that King's possession there is a great divine bow, the one which Siva used when he destroyed the Tripuras. That bow has come into Janaka's possession. The exact way, the stages through which it passed are not uniformly described in the poem nor is it necessary for us to go into that controversy and fix it. One way or another, Janaka at that time possessed the bow. So, these Rishis including Visvamitra told Sri Rama and Lakshmana, 'We go to Mithila in order that we may be present at that great sacrifice and in order also that you may see this famous bow which was handled by the great god in a great action and which subsequently has attracted the notice of all kinds of people because they came and tried to lift it and draw it. They could do neither. So you had better go and see it.' I want you to notice here one thing. Valmiki's omissions are very striking. At that very time, it was well known that Janaka had ordered it to be known that his daughter Sita was to be given as bride to that person who would take the bow and string it. She was, therefore, to be *Virya-sulka*. Visvamitra and the rishis should have known it. Visvamitra could not have been innocent of the matter. Nevertheless, they did not mention it to Sri Rama. They only mentioned to Rama what the bow was. I think that is one of those significant reticences which even our elders practise in daily life. They want young ones not to know everything. They like to keep some things from them so that they may be surprised or that they may not by anticipation disable themselves in any way from the performing of the great duty. Whichever the intention may be—it may differ in different cases—Visvamitra must have thought to himself 'I will not tell Rama about his having to try his hand on the bow.' When they go there and King Janaka asks 'Who are these Princes who look so handsome', he says who they are and that they have come to see the bow. Then Janaka says for the first time, 'Oh, the bow! You know I have made a promise that whoever is able to manipulate it should be the husband of my daughter Sita? If Rama is lucky, he will be my son-in-law'. Of course, you must know the decorous way in which Rama would behave. He said never a word. The bow was brought. It would appear five thousand men had to drag the carriage which had eight wheels. When the bow was brought, Janaka was saying by way of encouragement how many fellows had come and been unable even to lift it. As this fifteen year old boy stood in front of the thing, apparently hesitantly and coyly, the audience must have felt 'He is going to be another failure.' Visvamitra only said 'Show it to these boys. Let them see it.' The great box came over and he lifted the lid and looked at the bow. And, in a tone of apparent humility, he asked, 'May I touch it?' They both said, 'Yes, certainly'. Rama again asked, 'May I take it and try to work it?' and they said, 'Oh yes.' Without any obvious effort, he took the bow and bending it, strung the instrument but it broke in his hands in twain. As it broke, the poet says, the world shook, everybody dropped in fear, birds and beasts alike were seized with a great fright; only King Janaka, the two brothers, and Visvamitra were able to maintain their posture. The rest of the world was thrown out of balance. As the bow broke, amidst such demonstrations, Janaka at once said, 'My heart's wish is fulfilled. I have found the suitable bridegroom. Now, I will send people, trusted messengers, to Dasaratha and ask him to come and bless the couple as they become husband and wife.'

In narrating this story subsequently to Anasuya, Sita gives a slightly different account. That is one of the characteristics of the poem. An episode is not always repeated in the same language or in the same order of its details. Some little discrepancy is to be generally found. In this case, however, as it is one of the principles of exegesis, I do not think it necessary to say that there is any inconsistency. What Sita says is "As soon as the bow was broken and I became the victor's property, my father took water in a vessel and was about to give me away on the spot to Sri Rama but Sri Rama said 'No, I cannot accept a wife whom my father has not approved of'." So, King Janaka had to send messengers. That is the way Sita puts it. Her recollection must be correct, I take it. There are also other discrepancies between the two accounts but we are not at the moment concerned with the rest. This, however, is of some significance as I shall refer to it later.

दीयमानां न तु तदा प्रतिजग्राह राघवः ।
अविज्ञाय पितुश्छन्दमयोध्याधिपतेः प्रभोः ॥ II. 118. 51

'He was not willing to take me on the spot as one conquered, because he wanted to know his father's wish in the matter.'

You know as soon as Dasaratha received the message of Janaka, he rejoiced and set out to Mithila with his great preceptors and the army too. Now, there is a point here worth mentioning. As you read the text, you find Sita stood on a footing somewhat different from the footing occupied by her sister Urmila and her cousins Mandavi and Srutakirti. She had been conquered already. She had fallen to the lot of Sri Rama. But, as you know, three other weddings also took place at the same time. How did they take place? That is a thing worth seeing from the text. Janaka did not offer Urmila to Lakshmana—that is the great point—nor were Mandavi and Srutakirti offered to Bharata and Satrughna respectively. The poet, apparently following the Brahma-vivaha system, said that in form. Vasiṣhtha, having given the long pedigree of the Ikshvaku family, concluded his oration—a catalogue of names—with these words: 'And now, Oh King, I solicit the hand of Sita for Sri Rama and the hand of Urmila for Lakshmana.' For the first time, the thing is mentioned then. It is not as if Janaka had a large number of horoscopes that had been examined, had run about offering the girl to this man and that, had enquired, 'Do you want Rs. 20,000 or more?' The old prescribed thing was for the bridegroom's men appointed for the purpose,—Vaidiks, learned men,—to go about and find out a suitable bride. That was what was done. Vasishtha soliciting the hand of Urmila for Lakshmana, the other wedding being taken as a matter of course, was in conformity with the usage. Then Visvamitra took up the story. He says, 'Now a rare thing in human history has happened. Whoever heard of two kings like Janaka and Dasaratha coming at one place! Satananda here and Vasishtha there, the Ikshvakus and the Videhas, now that we are all here, I request you, King Janaka, to give your brother's daughters also to the other two sons of the Ayodhya monarch.' The proposal came from the bridegroom's side;

the solicitation was all the other way. When the ceremony actually takes place, the famous verse which can never be repeated too often on auspicious occasions was spoken by Janaka. He held his daughter Sita by the hand and fixing her before Sri Rama within sight of the Agni he said:

> इयं सीता मम सुता सहधर्मचरी तव ।
> प्रतीच्छ चैनां भद्रं ते पाणिं गृह्णीष्व पाणिना ॥
> पतिव्रता महाभागा छायेवानुगता सदा ।
> इत्युक्त्वा प्राक्षिपद्राजा मन्त्रपूतं जलं तदा ॥ I. 73. 27-28

'Here is my daughter who is going to be your partner in all the prescribed duties. Take her and be blessed. Take her right hand in your right hand. She will be faithful unto you and bring you the best of luck and she will follow you like your shadow, for ever and for ever.' So was that marriage concluded. The other pairs were also united in holy wedlock.

Passing over the dread episode of Parasurama, I will, with your permission, come to the concluding part of the Balakanda where the poet describes the condition of transcendental bliss in which these four couples lived together under Dasaratha's roof. The poet has no words good enough to describe the closeness of the union of the ways in which husband pleased wife and wife pleased husband. Especially does he refer to the couple, Rama and Sita, for, as it will happen in this fateful story, Bharata and Satrughna were early taken away by Yudhajit. Whether Mandavi and Srutakirti followed them to Kekaya, the poet does not mention. Our poet is peculiar; he cares only for Sita. He has work enough describing her, detailing her deeds and bringing before the reader her great qualities. The other three brides are not mentioned. In fact, Mandavi and Srutakirti have their names mentioned only once. Whether they went to Kekaya is not known to us. Even when Bharata returned—he returned only after Dasaratha's death of which he did not know at the time—Mandavi and Srutakirti are not mentioned. If the poet did not think it necessary to say anything about them, I suppose it is reasonable on our part to pay no attention to them. We cannot help it. Let us suppose that everything was all right with them.

But, there is one little point that has lent itself to some controversy. As the poet describes the love of Sita to Rama and of Rama to Sita, he uses highly poetical and suggestive language. He says, 'They read each other's thoughts readily; in fact these told each other what they wanted. The tongue and the lips did not play any part, nor perhaps did the eyes; heart spoke to heart. Hridaya and Hridaya commingled. The desire of each was known to the other. It is difficult to say who loved whom the more'. And, then, in a verse the poet says:

प्रिया तु सीता रामस्य दाराः पितृकृता इति ॥ I. 77. 27

That expression was expounded here once by a highly esteemed authority, Sahiti Vallabha T. Sundaracharyar. Sri Rama cherished Sita, the poet says, thinking that or for the reason that she was given to him or chosen for him by his father. It is astonishing that the poet should say this in particular not of Mandavi, Urmila, or Srutakirti who got their husbands by choice of their fathers, but of Sri Rama who did not get his wife through the choice of his father. He won her by his own prowess, भुजबल The skilled poet mentions this point, perhaps, because he remembered at the time what Sita says later on that Sri Rama was unwilling to conclude the marriage without his father's consent. The father had to come and say 'Yes' before Sri Rama would take her. Perhaps, to emphasise a little point the poet has specially used it in that case. I have not seen the curious commentary in which it is also said that the word पितृ here does not refer to Dasaratha but to Janaka, पितृकृता being taken to mean पितृदत्ता. Because, although it might have been a genuine *svayamvara,* the Brahma form was gone through and Janaka gave her into the hands of Sri Rama. But, whatever it is, it is worth noting that in the case of Sri Rama, whether it was the choice of the father or his mere consent, it was one of the reasons which augmented the love of the couple for each other. 'My wife has, no doubt, come to me because I was strong and could bend that bow. But, my father has heartily consented to this alliance. She is, therefore, for that reason also dear to me'—I think it is best to take it that way and ascribe to Sri Rama in this connection another great virtue, that he did not at any time forget or underweigh the importance of doing great things in his life only with the full consent and approval of his father. The choice of a wife is one of those vital matters, according to Hindu notions—they are fast passing away—in which the father of the bridegroom takes an important part. In this case, although Dasaratha comes into the story late, still the very fact that he was present at the marriage and gave his full consent was as good to Rama as it was to his brothers in whose cases the old Hindu law was in full operation.

THIRD LECTURE*

Ladies and Gentlemen,—I said the other day that among human relationships, that between the brothers Rama and Lakshmana was unique. Of that there is express evidence in the Poem. Affection is not measurable, and it is only by personal experience that we can realize the difference in depth between one affection and another. We have seen already that the love that drew Rama and Sita together was most remarkable. When she was lost to him there was no limit to the grief that he bore, no limit to the exertion that he made to recover,—in fact the whole poem deals with that topic. He could not find any rest being away from her. He nearly went mad. He wandered from place to place in the forest. He raved. He implored the trees and hills and rivers. He threatened the gods with destruction of the world. He threatened to take his own life. Lakshmana was hard put to it to comfort him in this extreme sorrow. That the unparalleled exertions which Rama was putting forth were however not for *Sita's* own sake, but for *Honour,* there is no hint till the climax, till we come to the killing of Ravana and the summoning of Sita to his great presence. We have no indication whatever of the feeling that overcome him at that supreme moment, the feeling that Sita had a stain, or might be supposed to have a stain, on her character, and that to take her back as Queen of Ayodhya would be tarnishing the honour of his family and of himself. Every moment, before the death of Ravana, he seems to have regarded her as his very life. Often he found that it was impossible to live without her. Then when he saw her, in the presence of his friends, this black suspicion arose in his mind, and he uttered words of cruelty which today make hard reading for us and bring tears to the eyes of every one.

And yet, this great love which Rama put aside so firmly at that moment, and which has found beautiful expression in many places in the poem, this romantic love, was exceeded by the love he bore to Lakshmana. That was in its own class. There are three places where Sri Rama declared in so many words that Sita was not so high in his affection as

*19-4-44.

Lakshmana. I will just read two or three striking passages in which this comparison is made by himself, passages of striking beauty and pathos. In Yuddhakanda, when Rama and Lakshmana were both prostrated by the effect of the 'naga-bana', serpent arrows, of Indrajit, Rama came to himself a little before his brother, and seeing him look as though without life, he expresses his grief in many slokas of surpassing appeal from which I shall read three.

> किं नु मे सीतया कार्यं किं कार्यं जीवितेन वा ।
> शयानं योऽद्य पश्यामि भ्रातरं युधि निर्जितम् ॥ VI. 49. 5

Here is one of those express comparisons—"what would it matter to me if my brother was dead and lost to me, even if I got back Sita?"

> शक्या सीतासमा नारी मर्त्यलोके विचिन्वता ।
> न लक्ष्मणसमो भ्राता सचिवः साम्परायिकः ॥ VI. 49. 6

"A wife quite the equal of Sita may be found if we make a thorough search in the earth, but a brother like Lakshmana, supreme in war, it will be very difficult to find."

> परित्यक्ष्याम्यहं प्राणान् वानराणां तु पश्यताम् ।
> यदि पञ्चत्वमापन्नः सुमित्रानन्दवर्धनः ॥ VI. 49. 7

"If Lakshmana is really gone, I shall myself take my own life in the presence of these allies of mine (vanaras)."

Then another time, when Lakshmana had been struck a shrewd blow by Ravana's 'sakti', he lay, too, apparently dead; and then,

> राघवो भ्रातरं दृष्ट्वा प्रियं प्राणं बहिश्चरम् ।
> दुःखेन महताविष्टो ध्यानशोकपरायणः ॥ VI. 102. 9

Rama cried out in great affliction:

> यथैव मां वनं यान्तमनुयातो महाद्युति. ।
> अहमप्यनुयास्यामि तथैवैनं यमक्षयम् ॥ VI 49. 17*

*In the BOMBAY Ed. from which the Lecturer was quoting, this verse occurs both in this context and in the 'Nagapasabandha' scene; in the M. L. J. Ed., followed in this Volume it occurs only in the latter.

"Even as Lakshmana followed me into the hardships and terrors of the forest, so will I after him follow him into the abode of Yama."

देशे देशे कलत्राणि देशे देशे च बान्धवाः ।
तं तु देशं न पश्यामि यत्र भ्राता सहोदरः ॥ VI. 102. 12-13

This is practically a repetition of the former idea. "Wives are easy to get in many parts of the world. Dear relations may be seen almost anywhere. But I do not know any region of the earth where a brother like Lakshmana can be had." In the same place you read:

इहैव मरणं श्रेयो न तु बन्धुविगर्हणम् ।

"It is better to die at this place," and then you have this somewhat remarkable saying from Sri Rama

किं मया दुष्कृतं कर्म कृतमन्यत्र जन्मनि ॥

(Bombay Ed.) VI. 101. 18*

This allusion to a *previous birth* is not easy to find in the case of Sri Rama. I came across it only in this passage; I am not aware of any other passage**. Sri Rama, according to the Poet, being an incarnation of Vishnu, a previous birth is unimaginable; and that he should ascribe his misfortunes to misdeeds in a previous birth passes our comprehension.

To proceed, when Lakshmana was revived by Sushena with the aid of the 'oshadhis,' sovereign herbs fetched specially for the purpose by Hanuman, Sri Rama embracing his brother uttered this sentiment to him:

न हि मे जीवितेनार्थः सीतया चापि लक्ष्मण ।
को हि मे विजयेनार्थस्त्वयि पञ्चत्वमागते ॥ VI. 102. 40-41

Then we have testimony to this disparity in the affection Sri Rama bore to Lakshmana and that he bore to Sita. It is to be found in Sundarakanda, where Sita herself in a

*These two half verses are not in the M. L. J. Ed.
**Publishers' Note. Reference may be made to III. 63.

पूर्वं मया नूनमभीप्सितानि पापानि कर्माण्यसकृत्कृतानि ।
तत्रायमद्यापतितो विपाको दुःखेन दुःखं यदहं विशामि ॥

passage of rare charm which describes the character of Lakshmana says this to Hanuman:—

मत्तः प्रियतरो नित्यं भ्राता रामस्य लक्ष्मणः ॥ V. 38. 62

Hanuman, who had seen how Rama suffered agonies by thoughts of Sita, must have thought that the man who could survive separation from Sita must be a hard-hearted person. To Hanuman whose opinions of Rama and Sita were so high, Sita herself says:—'you don't know! Lakshmana is dearer to my husband than I am.' Women know this by instinct, they can weigh love in the truest of scales—their innate perception! I wish to add, ladies and gentlemen, that this must have been uttered by Sita without the slightest shadow of jealousy. She herself stood so high in Lakshmana's affection for the sake of Rama, and when she made this assertion about the love of Rama to her we may take it to be beyond doubt.

But at this point it is worth remembering that Rama was the most unique character, and therefore it is necessary to remember that, according to the Poet, these merely human attachments, these personal affections all yielded place in his heart to an even greater passion. And what was that? The passion for righteousness, the passion for high honour, the passion for Dharma! It was an active element in his nature, and we find that put to a supreme test more than once and Rama coming out triumphantly as an eternal claimant to truth. This is what he says to Kaikeyi when with great misgiving as to his attitude she breaks the news to him and asks him to abandon his coronation as 'yuvaraj'; Sri Rama says to her—this is remarkable—,"Why was I not told that before? Don't you know my nature?"

अहं हि सीतां राज्यं च प्राणानिष्टान् धनानि च।

हृष्टो भ्रात्रे स्वयं दद्यां भरतायाप्रचोदितः ॥ II. 19. 7

"What would I not have given to him if it were right and proper that I should do so, wealth and kingdom and" (I blush to add) "Sita? I would have given everything to Bharata. Why was I not told quickly and in time?"

Then there is the famous scene where Sita assumes the character of his confidential adviser. You remember the famous scene where Sri Rama made a pact with the Rishis to punish the Rakshasas. "Why do you agree to make war against them?" she says. विना वैरं च रौद्रता (III. 9. 4). To make war without righteous cause is one of the things you should avoid." Let those who will judge Sita in their small minds for this daring of hers, but truly considered, she only did her duty, a duty which we don't allow our wives to perform, and which, alas, they are not qualified to perform. There is no sphere of life in which a wife is not entitled to give counsel. Let us take example from the way Sri Rama did it. "You have a claim," he says, "to be heard in all these matters, and I honour you for this confidence of yours," and he adds in striking words,

> अप्यहं जीवितं जह्यां त्वां वा सीते सलक्ष्मणाम् ।
> न तु प्रतिज्ञां संश्रुत्य ब्राह्मणेभ्यो विशेषतः ॥ III. 10. 19

"I may abandon my life, I may abandon you, I may abandon Lakshmana, I may abandon everything, but not my promise once made and particularly to Brahmans." A promise made must be carried out, no matter what tribulations and trials there may be. It is supreme. There then is Sri Rama's character shining out as a beacon to all humanity. Not that this is stated for the first time. But it is worth remembering that many a man among us will keep a promise so long as it suits him, but there is no one who will risk all and lose all rather than break his promise.

Look at Lakshmana, what a contrast! While Rama proclaimed that Dharma was above everything, Lakshmana, when he declared his doctrine, said only, "To me Rama sums up everything; he is all in all; I do not look behind him, and beyond him my goal is his approbation, my goal is his happiness.' Occasionally Rama speaks of Dharma and so on, but that does not appeal to Lakshmana. 'Your good, your prosperity, sums up all that I see; if you give up the kingdom, I don't see that you are doing good, that you are doing the right thing. What is there higher than you?' says Lakshmana, 'your interest is everything; I don't put any thing higher.'

When Sumantra returns to Dasaratha to report how he left the trinity in the forest, and the family sits together, this question is addressed to Sumantra: "What did Rama, Lakshmana, and Sita say?"; and they were all ears listening to their message. Rama said: "May my mother ever follow her Dharma and honour my father; may she be good to Kaikeyi:

may she never forget her duty to the king (meaning Bharata) !" But what did Lakshmana say? When Rama's message was given in those terms Lakshmana did not follow suit. He says to the old man:—

> असमीक्ष्य समारब्धं विरुद्धं बुद्धिलाघवात् ।
> जनयिष्यति संक्रोशं राघवस्य विवासनम् ॥ II. 58. 30

"Your banishment of Rama is wrong, radically wrong and blameworthy; I don't approve."

> अहं तावन्महाराजे पितृत्वं नोपलक्षये ।
> भ्राता भर्ता च बन्धुश्च पिता च मम राघवः ॥ II. 58. 31

There is the *summum bonum* of all his existence. He repudiates his father without qualification. "I do not consider Dasaratha my father. To me Rama is brother, he is my protector, he is my relation, and he is my father," and he adds, "Rama takes in my heart the place which I would have given to Dasaratha if he had behaved properly." You see at a glance how Lakshmana makes his life one of utter devotion to RAMA, whereas Rama's greatest love was the love of an abstraction called RIGHT. What a tremendous difference between Rama and Lakshmana !

Lakshmana was, as you know, characterized as the very embodiment of the principle of 'kainkarya'; his 'Lakshmi' was 'Kainkaryalakshmi,' that is to say, 'kainkarya' or service was the badge or distinguishing 'lakshana' or mark of Lakshmana. What are the chief points in his character? He has a dog's qualities, a slave's virtues. As a watchful guard, if there is a stranger or even a friend in apparent enmity, he barks; he suspects, but as a faithful slave will suspect. This is kainkarya in the extreme sense, utter devotion and nothing else. You see these characteristics in him displayed throughout. Twice at the post of duty his vigilance is tried hard, once when Sita at Panchavati contrary to Rama's orders urges him to leave her and go to Rama's aid and threatens to take her life if he will not, and again when Durvasas against Rama's orders demands admission to his presence and threatens a comprehensive curse for neglect. He suspects Bharata of hostile designs when he comes to Chitrakuta followed by his army and by all Ayodhya, and Rama has gently to reprove him. His efficiency in work is attested by Rama as well as by Sita. Reticence is a marked quality of such a character. He lets Sugriva speak for him in the council of war about Vibhishana; at Sita's ordeal by fire he never raises his voice. Angry and violent he can be, but at bottom he is a simple and unsophisticated nature. You see him quick to repent, generous, nay magnanimous, in owning to his fault. Shy of women, he has a high respect for the sex. Simple as he is then, you will allow that Lakshmana possesses many lovable qualities, all springing from his uttermost devotion to Rama.

What did Sumitra say when Lakshmana set out for the forest with Rama and Sita?

> रामं दशरथं विद्धि मां विद्धि जनकात्मजाम् ।
> अयोध्यामटवीं विद्धि गच्छ तात यथासुखम् ॥ II. 40. 9

"Rama is your father. Sita is your mother. The forest is Ayodhya where you were born. Go now and be happy." This is not a mere wish, it is a statement of the fullest hope, "Go, so would you attain happiness !" Sumitra here, as a little farther on when she comforts Kausalya in her extreme grief, shows her superiority to the elder queen in perception and ideals.

Sumitra's injunction to her son to look on Rama as his father and on Sita as his mother was superfluous. Witness Sita's testimony to his behaviour :

> पितृवद्वर्तते रामे मातृवन्मां समाचरन् ।
> ह्रियमाणां तदा वीरो न तु मां वेद लक्ष्मणः ॥ V. 38. 60-61

She told Hanuman, "Rama was his father and I his mother all these years." We may regard this in the light of Sita's apology for the harsh words that she had used to Lakshmana when she lost her self-control upon hearing the counterfeit cries uttered by the dying Maricha. When we consider the cheap and hackneyed expressions of gratefulness or regret, current among us, we see that Sita's expression of regret for her conduct towards Lakshmana conveyed in these words was the best and most genuine possible.

Testimony we also have from Rama when he expressed his gratitude and love to Lakshmana for the lovely hermitage that he erected at Panchavati. In his joy he embraces Lakshmana and says:—

सुसंहृष्टः परिष्वज्य बाहुभ्यां लक्ष्मणं तदा ।
अतिस्निग्धं च गाढं च वचनं चेदमब्रवीत् ॥
प्रीतोऽस्मि ते महत्कर्म त्वया कृतमिदं प्रभो ।
प्रदेयो यन्निमित्तं ते परिष्वङ्गो मया कृतः ॥
भावज्ञेन कृतज्ञेन धर्मज्ञेन च लक्ष्मण ।
त्वया पुत्रेण धर्मात्मा न संवृत्तः पिता मम ॥ III. 15. 27-29

We have a curious reversal of fatherhood here. Says Rama, "When Dasaratha died he really did not leave me a loser,"—this is a poetical conceit—"he left an image of him in you. I find in you what I should have found in my father if he had lived,"—a strange statement about a *younger* brother—"he is not dead, he is alive because *you* are here," meaning by that the great services performed by our father while we are young. That Lakshmana took the place of a father to Rama in the forest is a strange and unusual poetical conceit of Valmiki, which has no parallel anywhere else.

To the same effect, however, is Sita's testimony contained in the passage in which she gives a beautiful description of Lakshmana's character to Hanuman in the asoka grove.

यं दृष्ट्वा राघवो नैव वृत्तमार्यमनुस्मरेत् ॥ V. 38. 63

"If Lakshmana is by my husband, my husband never thinks of his dead father, because Lakshmana stands to him in that place."

Besides the scene at Panchavati hermitage we have another notable instance of Rama's display of affection to Lakshmana, when after Indrajit's death he eulogises Lakshmana, hugs him and fondles him. The fight with Indrajit was the second greatest battle in the war. In the scheme of the Ramayana, Vishnu having divided himself among all the four sons of Dasaratha, each of Rama's brothers is represented as accounting on his own for one mighty rakshasa; and Indrajit was in some ways the most puissant of these oppressors of the world. As you know from the opening sarga of the Uttarakanda, Agastya and the great rishis rated his destruction higher than that of Ravana himself because of his magic arts which rendered him invisible and well nigh invincible in battle. His death at the hands of Lakshmana struck them with amazement, and the world's rejoicings at that event were unmatched even by the rejoicings over Ravana's death. Rama and Vibhishana showed great confidence in Lakshmana when they trusted his arm to overpower Indrajit.

Before I describe Rama's joy at Lakshmana's victory, let me refer briefly to how Indrajit met his end. I shall not linger over the gruelling fight that went on between him and Lakshmana for three days on end. They pounded each other hard, and who dare affirm which of them pounded the harder? When the battle had lasted long enough, Lakshmana called to mind Rama's injunction जहि, 'kill', and discharged the fatal missile calling upon it to do that office, invoking the name and fame and prowess of Rama in a celebrated verse:—

> धर्मात्मा सत्यसन्धश्च रामो दाशरथिर्यदि ।
> पौरुषे चाप्रतिद्वन्द्वः शरैनं जहि रावणिम् ॥ VI. 91. 73

I once heard an interpretation of this 'abhimantrana' by a learned and popular reciter of the Ramayana at Bangalore which I may mention here though some of you may know it already. Lakshmana invoked Rama first as a 'dharmatma', but the arrow did not respond, because there might be some doubt as to the righteousness of his act in killing Tataka. Then he called him a 'satyasandha', but the dart stayed fixed, because Rama did not keep his promise to kill Vali at sight. Lakshmana then called upon Rama as 'Dasarathi', still the arrow wouldn't budge, as after all Rama was born out of a divine 'payasa'. Finally he said, "पौरुषे चाप्रतिद्वन्द्वः" and directly he uttered those words the arrow flew and carried off the head of Indrajit. That was because it was an incontestable fact that in prowess Rama had no equal. The exposition as one heard it looked rather clever, but on reflection one dismissed it as unconvincing.

When Indrajit had fallen, Lakshmana, his body drenched with blood, went to Rama supported by Hanuman and Vibhishana. Having made obeisance to Rama he stood respectfully by his side and in broken accents told him that dread Indrajit had been slain. Rama was transported with joy and praised Lakshmana for the wonderful deed he had performed. Then the poet goes on to describe the display of Rama's affection in all its depth and intensity.

स तं शिरस्युपाघ्राय लक्ष्मणं लक्ष्मिवर्धनम् ।
लज्जमानं बलात्स्नेहादङ्कमारोप्य वीर्यवान् ॥
उपवेश्य तमुत्सङ्गे परिष्वज्यावपीडितम् ।
भ्रातरं लक्ष्मणं स्निग्धं पुनः पुनरुदैक्षत ॥
शल्यसंपीडितं शस्तं निःश्वसन्तं तु लक्ष्मणम् ।
रामस्तु दुःखसंतप्तस्तदा निःश्वसितो भृशम् ॥
मूर्ध्नि चैनमुपाघ्राय भूयः संस्पृश्य च त्वरन् ।
उवाच लक्ष्मणं वाक्यमाश्वास्य पुरुषर्षभः ॥
अद्याहं विजयी शत्रौ हते तस्मिन् दुरात्मनि ।
रावणस्य नृशंसस्य दिष्ट्या वीर त्वया रणे ॥
छिन्नो हि दक्षिणो बाहुः स हि तस्य व्यपाश्रयः ।

VI. 92. 9-12, 14, 15

Rama smelt his head and pulling the bashful young hero on to his lap, hugged him, riddled as he was with wounds, and looked at him with tender feeling. He turned Lakshmana's face this way and that, a very strange thing, but he did this again and again as if he could never have his fill of gaze at it. Seeing Lakshmana smarting from his many wounds and fetching deep sighs, Rama was powerfully affected and could not help heaving a sigh himself. Smelling his head once more he passed his hand all over Lakshmana's body to alleviate the pain, and spoke soothing words to him. "Now my task is more than half finished," he said to Lakshmana. "The battle is all but won. When you struck down Indrajit, you struck down the right arm of Ravana. What is he hereafter? Indrajit was his mainstay. You disposed of him." Well, ladies and gentlemen, what is that affection? Only osculation was lacking.

I spoke of Lakshmana's shyness of woman. At any rate he did not feel at ease before women. Sugriva knew this, so when Lakshmana came to his palace in a frenzy of anger to convey Rama's displeasure at his supposed failure of duty and to deliver his threat, Sugriva asked Tara to soften him first.

अथवा स्वयमेवैनं द्रष्टुमर्हसि भामिनि ।
वचनैः सान्त्वयुक्तैश्च प्रसादयितुमर्हसि ॥

त्वद्दर्शनविशुद्धात्मा न स कोपं करिष्यति ।
न हि स्त्रीषु महात्मानः क्वचित्कुर्वन्ति दारुणम् ॥
त्वया सान्त्वैरुपक्रान्तं प्रसन्नेन्द्रियमानसम् ।
ततः कमलपत्राक्षं द्रक्ष्याम्यहमरिंदमम् ॥ IV. 33. 35-37

"When you have spoken to him in your sweet way he will no longer be angry, for great men will not do anything cruel to women. I will not see him till you have first conquered him by your honeyed words."

When the upper garment and ornaments which Sita had contrived to cast off when passing over Risyamuka hill were shown by Sugriva, Rama cried out in great grief, "Look, Lakshmana, look well at this garment and the jewels; they must have fallen on soft green grass, they look exactly as they used to when they were on Sita's body." Lakshmana's answer to this appeal for confirmation is well known:—

नाहं जानामि केयूरे नाहं जानामि कुण्डले ।
नूपुरे त्वभिजानामि नित्यं पादाभिवन्दनात् ॥ IV. 6. 22

"I know some only. I have never raised my eyes and looked her in the face. I always saw her feet to which I bowed in reverence. You'd better judge. I can't identify the armlet or the ear-rings. I can see the *nupura.*"

Then in the scene in Uttarakanda in which Rama abandons Sita finally and Lakshmana conducts her to the vicinity of the Poet's hermitage, she learns from Lakshmana's lips for the first time of the cruel decree which Rama had passed against her to please a suspicious world. She begs poor Lakshmana to *see her* and be witness to her pregnancy.

निरीक्ष्य माद्य गच्छ त्वमृतुकालातिवर्तिनीम् । VII. 48. 19

"You will have to bear witness to my character when it is assailed in future. Look at me, I have promise of Rama's love in me."

Agony is piled on agony. Lakshmana is dumbfounded at the request, and makes this beautiful reply to Sita:—

दृष्टपूर्वं न ते रूपं पादौ दृष्टौ तवानघे ॥
कथमत्र हि पश्यामि रामेण रहितां वने ।
इत्युक्त्वा तां नमस्कृत्य पुनर्नावमुपारुहत् ॥ VII. 48. 21-22

"I have never seen you before. I have had only a glimpse. *Now you ask me to look at you and Rama is not here, the man who suspected you before and who may suspect again!"*

There I will leave this distressful scene*—with this thought, ladies and gentlemen. To suffer greatly—that is the privilege and portion of the great and good of the earth. Theirs are the sufferings which have no tongue. What in comparison to them are the sufferings of meaner mortals like us who rail at the gods and beat our breasts at every stroke of ill luck?

*Publishers' note:—The Lecturer was visibly moved when he read Sita's words and Lakshmana's reply.

FOURTH LECTURE*

Ladies and Gentlemen,—I said last time that the 38th Sarga of Sundara Kanda contained in a few slokas a handy description of Lakshmana by Sita. Some of you might have made a reference to it. If not, I would only say it is not too late. I intend to start off to-day with half a verse from that passage.

वृद्धोपसेवी लक्ष्मीवान् शक्तो न बहु भाषिता। V. 38. 61

One who waits respectfully on elders, one who is full of the Lakshmi, as the commentators say, of Kainkarya, one who is strong and one who does not speak much, "न बहु भाषिता". That is the expression to which I wish to ask your attention. Moderation in speech, that is one of the qualities of a devoted servant. A servant, like a woman in the family or like a child, must be seen but not heard. That is the rule to be observed by those who have to wait on the convenience of others. Lakshmana had that quality. But we have, placed before you by the Poet, the adjective शक्तः. It almost seems as if it furnished the original of the ordinary English saying "strong but silent man." Nowadays, strong men are very vocal too. It seems as though Sita had in her mind the utter devotedness of her brother-in-law, how he quietly and observantly fulfilled her wants and those of her husband while at the same time being fully competent and fully efficient in the discharge of all the duties of a body-attendant. That however, though a fitting description, must be understood with the ordinary qualifications; for Lakshmana could talk and talk vigorously too when there was occasion. While he had the quality of curbing his tongue when there was no occasion, there were however times when he could not suppress himself. Then either his impatience or his anger put him forward oblivious of restraint, and then the Poet makes him say things which only a commonly silent man could be expected to say. Those who do not speak often, when they explode, explode violently. Lakshmana had strong feelings, especially where his brother's or sister-in-law's interests were concerned. When they seemed in peril, nothing could restrain

*26—4—'44

the proctective activity of Lakshmana. In the Ayodhya Kanda when the question was being decided whether or not Rama was to undergo banishment, when the matter was still in dispute over a long period between Dasaratha and his favourite wife, Lakshmana said never a word. But when everything had been settled and he was burning with anger, he waited until the conversation started between the hero and his mother, Kausalya. Then indeed the pathetic situation of the poor mother overpowered Lakshmana and he could not brook to be silent any more. So he burst out. And then we have a conversation in which Lakshmana assumes the offensive and says harsh things and Rama is on the defensive, calms him, begs him to be quiet. "Be reasonable," he says. "I am only obeying my father's commands. To obey our parents, is it a sin? On the other hand, it is a great virtue. And in obeying them I am not merely rendering up literal obedience. My object is to save our father from the ignominy and the penalty that attends it in the other world, of breaking one's vows. Failure to fulfil a promise is the greatest shame that can befall a monarch. Our father will have to serve a period in hell if I allowed him to break his word. I will not. I am going to see him safe in the other world also. That is my object. Understand it please." And then of course he breaks in with an encomium on the virtue of Dharma. That is Lakshmana's opportunity. He pours scorn upon the Dharma. "I don't understand it," he says. "It is nothing but weakness. It will land you in trouble." And it is then that we have Lakshmana enunciating doctrines which are astonishing in the brother of Sri Rama. He says, "I am a strong man and I am your protector. I am the guardian of your interests. I cannot see you deprived of what is emphatically yours. If Bharata stands in the way, he and his partisans shall know what it is.

भरतस्याथ पक्ष्यो वा यो वास्य हितमिच्छति।
सर्वानेव हनिष्यामि मृदुर्हि परिभूयते॥ II. 21. 11

A soft man like you will be continually humiliated. I'll finish this Bharata and any man who calls himself his partisan."

प्रोत्साहितोऽयं कैकेय्या स दुष्टो यदि नः पिता।
अमित्रभूतो निस्सङ्गं वध्यतां वध्यतामपि॥ II. 21.12

Here Lakshmana shows by a hint that he suspects an actual plot between Dasaratha and Kaikeyi. He says, "These two have arranged matters between them already. The old man is to pretend that he is unwilling and the young lady is to push him on and so between them they have a plot. I sec. But we will frustrate it all. Let the old man be bound. If necessary, we shall take his life and not hesitate." Then follows the famous verse which the Poet puts into the mouth of Lakshmana.

गुरोरप्यवलिप्तस्य कार्याकार्यमजानतः ।
उत्पथं प्रतिपन्नस्य कार्यं भवति शासनम् ॥ II. 21. 13

Some persons read the last quarter आर्यं भवति शासनम् । Whichever it is, it comes to this: Let it be your father; let it be your Guru. It does not matter. If he does not know what is right and what is wrong, if he is determined on going the wrong way, there is nothing for it but to deprive him of his liberty, nothing for it but to punish him. This famous verse occurs in the Mahabharata,* where Bhishma speaks it, when he has to contend against his master, Parasurama. But I am concerned now to point out to you one of the peculiarities of our Poet. Valmiki has a great sense of the appropriate as we should say. This very sentiment he puts into the mouth of the twin brother, Satrughna, a little later on in the same Kanda. Lakshmana and Satrughna being so much alike, it stands to reason that when Satrughna applies his mind to the same subject, he should think the same thoughts. The Poet puts very nearly the same words also into his mouth. This is what Satrughna says: "Why didn't our brother Lakshmana restrain the old man's liberty, if necessary, and give Rama the kingdom that was his? I don't mind. Old people occasionally behave in a silly way. They cannot be allowed to be free."

पूर्वमेव तु निग्राह्यः समवेक्ष्य नयानयौ ।
उत्पथं यस्यमारूढो नार्या राजा वशं गतः ॥ II. 78. 4

"The old man having placed himself at the mercy of this woman should already have been deprived of his liberty." The verses that I before read from Lakshmana are uttered before Kausalya, and in the presence of Rama he speaks to

* Udyogaparva, 178. 48

her and says, "You don't know how I feel now at this moment."

अनुरक्तोऽस्मि भावेन भ्रातरं देवि तत्त्वतः ।
सत्येन धनुषा चैव दत्तेनेष्टेन ते शपे ॥ II. 21. 16

He swears that he is devoted to his brother. He swears by several things, and what is it that he wants to confirm by these strong and many-sided oaths?

दीप्तमग्निमरण्यं वा यदि रामः प्रवेक्ष्यति ।
प्रविष्टं तत्र मां देवि त्वं पूर्वमवधारय ॥ II. 21. 17

What a sentiment! How violent! Fine sentiment, honourable in the extreme, such as should be put down in golden characters. But how strong! "दीप्तमग्नि ......" "If Rama intends to take out his life by falling into the fire or by entering the dreaded forest, mother mine, I assure you that before he does it, I shall have done it. I shall have fallen into the fire. He will have to come after me." Rama, as is his way, understands the nature of his brother, and speaks soft words to him.

तदेनां विसृजानार्यां क्षत्रधर्माश्रितां मतिम् ।
धर्ममाश्रय मा तैक्ष्ण्यं मद्बुद्धिरनुगम्यताम् ॥ II. 21. 44

I want particularly to draw attention to the words 'Kshatra-dharma.' Rama is a Kshatriya just as much as Lakshmana. They are proud of their birth. Nevertheless Rama says that the Kshatriya Dharma which is always to fight, with or without provocation, must be abandoned. He says, "You must not act that way." "धर्ममाश्रय". "Don't be cruel; don't be harsh. Follow Dharma." And other verses follow in similar strain. But Lakshmana could not stand it. He thinks it is untimely preaching.

येनेयमागता द्वैधं तव बुद्धिर्महामते ।
स हि धर्मो मम द्वेष्यः प्रसङ्गाद्यस्य मुह्यसि ॥ II. 23. 11-12

"That Dharma by contemplating which you are lost, that Dharma I hate." Fancy the contrast between the attitudes of the brothers. What difficulty Rama must have had in restraining Lakshmana! Rama had said like any ordinary man, "What am I to do? It is not the old man that is to blame; it is not the lady that is to blame. It is not I. It is all the doing of Fate, "दैवस्य कर्म". Whoever withstood Fate? Whoever can withstand Fate? You and I and all of us must submit. Take it quietly, Lakshmana." No. Lakshmana is far from convinced. He says, "That is the doctrine of weakness. It is the weak man, it is the foolish man that throws himself on Destiny. Destiny, Fate! We make our Destiny. What is this strong arm for? What are these broad shoulders for? Why is this bow and why are these arrows? To submit to Fate? We should scorn our Fate."

न शोभार्थाविमौ बाहू न धनुर्भूषणाय मे ।
नासिराबन्धनार्थाय न शराः स्तम्भहेतवः ॥ II. 23. 31

Then he appeals to his brother, "Tell me, tell me, I cannot keep myself under control. Tell me which the person is whom I am to attack and slay for your sake. Name him. Give me the order."

ब्रवीहि कोऽद्यैव मया वियुज्यतां तवासुहृत्प्राणयशस्सुहृज्जनैः ।
यथा तवेयं वसुधा वशे भवेत् तथैव मां शाधि तवास्मि किंकरः ॥

II. 23. 41

That is a point to which I wish to draw attention. In spite of his uncontrollable fury, the frenzy of anger, in spite of that, Lakshmana is not willing to take the field and apply violence—he is so ready to actually apply violence—unless he, Rama, gives the order. He waits for his consent. Impatient, angry, uncontrolled, nevertheless he would not take a step without his brother's sanction. So final is his dependence on Rama, so ultimate is the authority that he gives to Rama that however much he differs, he will not take his own line unless it is previously sanctioned. Well, that marks a devotion such as is rarely seen in life and but occasionally in story. Then Rama of course puts it down in his own way quietly. He persuades Lakshmana to put aside all his weapons and assume a gentle manner. Lakshmana yields, but mind you, he does not yield his heart. His opinion is his opinion. He won't yield that. He still thinks that Rama is wrong. He still thinks that everything should be obtained by the application of force. But the time is gone. He won't take the field without orders. So when after the great altercation between Rama and Sita, it is settled that she also is to follow him,

Lakshmana thinks that the time is come for him to say what he will do. He takes it for granted almost that he will accompany Rama and says, "I am also going to make preparations for departure." Rama says, "No, you shall not follow me. You've got business here. You've got to look after my mother. You've got to look after your mother. See what is being done in the palace. Kaikeyi has assumed the ascendant. The old man is nowhere. Your mother and my mother require the tenderest care. Remain behind and look after them." Thus Rama goes on saying till Lakshmana turns upon him and says

> अनुज्ञातश्च भवता पूर्वमेव यदस्म्यहम् ।
> किमिदानीं पुनरिदं क्रियते मे निवारणम् ॥ II. 31. 7

"You have already given me leave to follow you. What is the use of withdrawing now?" As a matter of fact, in the poem there are no verses clearly indicating that previous permission had been given. It only marks the wishful straining by Lakshmana of the words that had fallen from Rama's lips. Rama had said certain things which Lakshmana over-interprets in his own favour. It is difficult to find out what they are. Commentators after some research have discovered two or three passages. One of them is worth quoting, and I shall ask your leave while I read it to you. In asking Sita also to remain behind, that is, in the process of the dispute between husband and wife, Sri Rama had told her,

> भ्रातृपुत्रसमौ चापि द्रष्टव्यौ च विशेषतः ।
> त्वया भरतशत्रुघ्नौ प्राणैः प्रियतरौ मम ॥ II. 26. 33

Bharata and Satrughna are dear to me as my own life. I want you to stay behind in order to look after them. He had said that to Sita. Now, Lakshmana who was full of anger but had eyes to see and ears to hear, said "Oh yes I am not of these to be protected by Sita. He means to take me." He had marked the words down then. "You didn't mention me as the third person for Sita to take care of. Certainly you intended to take me. Take me," he says.

Now you might have been struck by the strong denunciation of the dharma ideal by Lakshmana. That however is no mere accident. Later on in the poem in a grave context, when Indrajit had brought the counterfeit figure of Sita and killed her before Hanuman and Hanuman had rushed up to

Rama's presence and reported this tragedy, Rama lost heart. He fell into a swoon and was unable to control his feelings. He says, "Let us beat a retreat. All is over. What is there to do here any more?" And then in order to comfort him, as it was Lakshmana's duty on many other occasions to minister comfort to his brother who is thrown on his mercy, by way of administering the necessary consolation, Lakshmana speaks through the best part of a sarga. And there, strange to say, he repeats in unmistakable terms this antipathy of his to the doctrine of dharma. He says, "Didn't I tell you before when we started this misery, when you surrendered the kingdom at the instance of Kaikeyi, didn't I tell you that dharma was futile? There you are. See where you have come to now. Faithfully following the doctrine of dharma, obeying your father, you have been landed in this trouble." Then he contrasts dharma with artha. "Artha", he commends, "that is the thing to work for, worldly gains, advantages, things which are ours. You ought to be after these. You have done wrong. You pursued the wrong course and landed yourself in terrible misery." Strange position to take up and yet—that is what Lakshmana says through many slokas written in Valmiki's best style. Three or four verses from this context are often quoted, and have become famous. This first one

शुभे वर्त्मनि तिष्ठन्तं त्वामार्य विजितेन्द्रियम् ।
अनर्थेभ्यो न शक्नोति त्रातुं धर्मो निरर्थकः ॥ VI. 83. 14

"Your worthless dharma, your good-for-nothing dharma is not competent to protect you from all difficulties."

यस्यार्थास्तस्य मित्राणि यस्यार्थास्तस्य बान्धवाः ।
यस्यार्थाः स पुमान् लोके यस्यार्थाः स च पण्डितः ॥
यस्यार्थाः स च विक्रान्तो यस्यार्थाः स च बुद्धिमान् ।
यस्यार्थाः स महाभागो यस्यार्थाः स गुणाधिकः ॥ VI. 83. 35. 36

"Obey your father by all means, but yield up your wife to a Rakshasa, that is the thing."

त्वयि प्रव्राजिते वीर गुरोश्च वचने स्थिते ।
रक्षसापहृता भार्या प्राणैः प्रियतरा तव ॥ VI. 83. 41

Not that this is a doctrine foreign to the nature of Lakshmana. Commentators may say so but it is not true as pointed out.

It is compatible wholly, it is consistent wholly, with what at an earlier period he had enunciated as the doctrine for strong men to follow. I mean only to remind you of what I said before, that here above all things the Poet intends to enforce the contrast between Rama and Lakshmana, how Rama in the midst of the direst calamities could not be made to deviate even by a hair's breadth from the highest duty of all as he saw it but how Lakshmana, only next to him in rank, as we should say, in the story, could not rise to the height of that theme.

I must now describe another quality of Lakshmana to which I have alluded. But I must bring it to prominence now. He was one of those great natures which are highly susceptible, which could be excited to a pitch of excitement easily (always the mark of a generous nature, of a noble nature), made angry quickly, but at the same time liable to lose that anger quickly too and become generous and even magnanimous afterwards. The two qualities follow, आशुकोप:, आशुतोष । Get angry quickly and get gentle quickly too—mark of a noble nature. And Lakshmana, as I told you before, was very suspicious when there was any trouble to his brother that he anticipated. Any one fell under his suspicion. As I told you before, he suspected his father of having colluded with Kaikeyi. Now you remember the advent of Bharata near Chitrakuta, how he came there with his army, all the ministers and nearly the whole city of Ayodhya, in order to persuade his brother to return to what was in his opinion his kingdom. There was a cloud of dust to be seen from where the brothers were. Rama asked his brother to ascend the top of a tree and find out what it was. Lakshmana went up the tree, saw the army coming. He had no trouble in identifying that the army came from Ayodhya and that Bharata was there at the head of the whole movement. So without coming down from the tree, he cries out, "Here is that precious brother of yours. He is not content to leave us here in peace. He wants to be sure that we should never return even after fourteen years and bother him. He wants to come and kill us here. But before he can take the field, I know what to do." Of course he bursts out

सम्प्राप्तोऽयमरिर्वीर भरतो वध्य एव मे ।
भरतस्य वधे दोषं नाहं पश्यामि राघव ॥ II. 96. 23

"I see nothing in killing our brother."

एतस्मिन् निहते कृत्स्नामनुशाधि वसुंधराम् ।
अद्य पुत्रं हतं संख्ये कैकेयी राज्यकामुका ॥
मया पश्येत् सुदुःखार्ता हस्तिभग्नमिव द्रुमम् ॥
कैकेयीं च वधिष्यामि सानुबन्धां सबान्धवाम् ॥ *II. 96. 25-26*

See how far he is transported into the region of anger. "I will kill Bharata, and to be sure of things, I will kill the mother too. And I will kill all her partisans, her relations and all who call themselves hers." That was Lakshmana's way and Rama knew it. He says to him, "Don't be so hasty, brother. Bharata has no bad intentions, I assure you. He comes here with the friendly idea of requesting me to take the kingdom back for myself. Be calm." And then Rama goes forward in argument; finding that Lakshmana has been impressed a little and was on the way to come down, he praised Lakshmana's victim. He says, "You don't know Bharata at all. Are you anxious to take the kingdom? Lakshmana, do you want the kingdom? Nothing easier. I have only to tell Bharata, 'Here is Lakshmana anxious for the kingdom. Give it to him.' And he will make it over." He knew his Bharata. Lakshmana, so single-minded was he in guarding the interests of his brother, so like a faithful dog, he can only suspect everybody. What made him suspect is not his interest, is not any small idea, but the desire to protect what he conceived were the imperilled interests of Sri Rama. When we think of the high motive actuating him, we see how though it was suspicion, it was not an unworthy suspicion. It was not a suspicion which we should put in the category of wickedness or of shameful misbehaviour. As soon as Rama pointed out that he had overshot the mark of vigilance in the protection of his interests, poor Lakshmana is shamefaced, is stricken with repentance, comes down and crawling reluctantly to the side of his brother, he says in a soft voice, "Do you think our father also is there? Please see." Now mark how natural the transition is. Most touching in the extreme. Finding that he had been thoroughly mistaken and being ashamed of himself, he goes forward and expresses almost his wish that with the army should come the old man himself, and Sri Rama falling in with that repentant mood of his brother and anxious to confirm it, says, "No wonder if father also comes in and asks me to take back the kingdom. Probable. I see his elephant, I see the horses. But father's renowned white umbrella? I do not see it. Just look. And so he takes him down gently. He knows that the father is not there. But just humouring the brother's repentant mood, he says. "I don't think he is there though I should not wonder if he was."

Now it was half playfully that Sri Rama said to Lakshmana, "If really you are after the kingdom, why don't you tell me? I will ask Bharata to transfer it. He would do it in a moment." What he said playfully had to come true in a way later on. When the time for his own abhisheka had come after the war and he had been crowned, there was the question who was to be made the yuvaraja. Perhaps remembering this scene that we have been going through, perhaps thinking that it was in the end a proper thing to do, Sri Rama says to Lakshmana, "You be the Yuvaraja." Now Bharata was the elder of the two by a few hours. Besides Bharata had been practically king for fourteen years. To take the yauvarajya away from him and to offer it to Lakshmana was a departure from what would be ordinarily expected. Yet Sri Rama does it partly to show Lakshmana that he was not speaking in fun then. "If it comes to your really desiring to take it, Bharata won't make the slightest hesitation. Here you are. Do you want it?" And as if to confirm this position Bharata seems to say repeatedly, "Yes, Lakshmana, take it, take it, take it please."

सर्वात्मना पर्यनुनीयमानो यदा न सौमित्रिरुपैति योगम् ।

When Lakshmana perhaps also remembering that scene but believing that to wear a coronet on his head might interfere with his kainkarya dharma, believing that his Lakshmi was the kainkarya lakshmi and no other Lakshmi, he was firm in the refusal. And so in the end,

नियुज्यमानोऽपि च यौवराज्ये ततोऽभ्यषिञ्चद् भरतं महात्मा ॥

VI. 131. 93

Now having pointed out one occasion on which the magnanimity of Lakshmana's nature was transparent, I now come to another scene of equal importance in which this quality of Lakshmana, this quality of generosity always attending an outburst of indignation, was also manifested. In Sugriva's palace it was. Sri Rama stricken with grief at his separation from his beloved, had counted the days carefully when Sugriva was to discharge the promise that he had made.

And then he had asked Lakshmana to go and convey his disapprobation of Sugriva's conduct to him. He had worked himself up to a pitch of anger. And he had charged Lakshmana to go forward and tell Sugriva, "Tell him this from me,

न च संकुचितः पन्था येन वाली हतो गतः ।
समये तिष्ठ सुग्रीव मा वालिपथमन्वगाः ॥ IV. 30. 81

"That deadly portal through which Vali was sent by me is still open for you. Nobody can close it. Nobody has closed it. It is there awaiting you if you fail to do this. Fulfil your promise; else, you will follow where your brother had to go." Hearing these words, Lakshmana felt that his brother had been enraged and so determined to kill Sugriva, enthrone Angada and get his office performed by Angada. He bursts out in anger and says, "I'll go and finish all these." Then Rama realised the mistake he had made. To have excited this excitable creature was very wrong. So he said to him, "Brother Lakshmana, don't take things literally. I was in a temper. I spoke roughly. Don't go and communicate these things to Sugriva. Speak gently, manage it all properly." Lakshmana says, "Yes". But he had been made so angry by the tortures that he witnessed of Rama's grief, he had been excited so highly by them that what Rama said by way of pacification was quickly forgotten. And so he goes. And here the Poet is in one of his humorous moods. Lakshmana in anger is a fit subject for him to show the beauty of his writings. So he says,

शक्रबाणासनप्रख्यं धनुः कालान्तकोपमम् ।
प्रगृह्य गिरिशृङ्गाभं मन्दरः सानुमानिव ॥ IV. 31. 11

Lakshmana strode forward, took long steps in his anger and as he went forward, his destructive energy had to be somehow satisfied. So he pulled a branch here, a branch there, broke them into pieces, and put his feet every now and then on some hard rock and pounded it. He went forward in that style, impatient, and shook his head now and then as if he asked himself, "What am I to say?" Having lost his balance, he had often to remind himself. So he seems to say "What did Rama ask me to say? I am to say this. Then that fellow will reply. He must give a reply to that." So there was put a statement first on Rama's authority, then a rejoinder, then a surrejoinder and so on. So arranging all this in his mind, he went forward.

कामक्रोधसमुत्थेन भ्रातुः कोपाग्निना वृतः ।
प्रभञ्जन इवाप्रीतः प्रययौ लक्ष्मणस्तदा ॥ IV. 31. 13

So he goes. You should remember my saying that Sugriva was vigilant and that he asked Tara first of all to pacify Lakshmana's anger*. A little time elapses. Some things happen. Finally the monkeys guarding the palace make a little fuss and that makes Lakshmana still more angry. But in the end Tara comes forward and after saying a few things by way of preparation of Lakshmana's heart, she asks him, "Come in please, come in." Of course Lakshmana was unwilling at first to go where ladies might be found for he knew Sugriva was in one of his self-indulging moods. He was not willing to go there. But Tara persuades him, "Never mind. You are a brother. Come", as only Tara could say. Then as Lakshmana went forward,

कूजितं नूपुराणां च काञ्चीनां निनदं तथा ।
स निशम्य ततः श्रीमान् सौमित्रिर्लज्जितोऽभवत् ॥ IV. 33. 25

He had never gone into the company of women. There were a good many of them, there was a bevy of ladies and he heard the clink of their jewels. Then he hung down his head and would not look up. But she spoke to him gently and drew him as it were.

स तां समीक्ष्यैव हरीशपत्नीं तस्थावुदासीनतया महात्मा ।

So the poet concludes

अवाङ्मुखोऽभून्मनुजेन्द्रपुत्रः स्त्रीसंनिकर्षाद्विनिनिवृत्तकोपः ॥
IV. 33. 39

By that time his anger had gone and he was half pleased at the soft surroundings, and the mellifluous speech made by Tara. So he quieted down. Finally this was how he behaved. Tara in her last spell of speaking had conclusively proved to him that Rama and Lakshmana had been a little hasty in condemning Sugriva, that already before the time had fully expired, he had taken the necessary steps for the gathering

* Lect. III, pp. 37-8.

in of his vast army. And then Tara made so bold as to say, "Hark, already I hear the noise of the monkeys that are coming. Why this excitement? Why this anger?" And so Lakshmana saw that he had been perhaps a little hasty and then he bursts out. He says to Sugriva who had by that time recovered his full consciousness and was speaking as he should speak and had also said in extenuation of his fault (if fault it was—it was not one) the famous saying which Sita later on herself enunciates:

न कश्चिन्नापराध्यति । IV. 36. 11

A beautiful sentiment. It ought to be on everybody's lips. But, no, it ought to be in everybody's heart. We who are so apt to get angry with others, to become impatient at others' shortcomings, we ought to remember

न कश्चिन्नापराध्यति ।

In this world there is no man above error. The best of us will go wrong and all have need therefore of mercy and compassion. When Sugriva said that, Lakshmana's heart was softened quite, and as Sugriva potested he was going to do his duty all right, that nothing was left undone, and they had been a little too harsh with him, Lakshmana used these noble sentiments:

दोषज्ञः सति सामर्थ्ये कोऽन्यो भाषितुमर्हति ।
वर्जयित्वा मम ज्येष्ठं त्वां च वानरसत्तम ॥ IV. 36. 17

"There is nobody besides my brother, Rama, and yourself, there is no third soul in the world, who can see wrong when it occurs and who can speak the appropriate words." Well, what can be a greater honour than to be placed by Lakshmana himself alongside of Sri Rama who, if anybody knew on earth, knew how to speak and what to speak. To Sugriva

सदृशश्चासि रामस्य विक्रमेण बलेन च ।
सहायो दैवतैर्दत्तश्चिराय हरिपुंगव ॥ IV. 36. 18

"You are my brother's equal in vikrama and bala. You have become our ally because the gods are pleased that that should be the case. It is Heaven's gift, your alliance. You know why I lost my temper and said harsh words to you. It is because I saw my brother in distress. How could I see my brother in distress? That made me angry and I lost my temper. I came and said harsh things. Forgive me.

किं तु शीघ्रमितो वीर निष्काम त्वं मया सह ।
सान्त्वयस्व वयस्यं त्वं भार्याहरणकर्शितम् ॥ IV. 36. 19

Don't tarry any more. Come away with me and come to my brother. See in what condition he is. Administer comfort to him. Tell him all is ready and everything has started. Having seen him in sorrow I came and spoke harshly."

यच्च शोकाभिभूतस्य श्रुत्वा रामस्य भाषितम् ।
मयां त्वं परुषाण्युक्तस्तच्च त्वं क्षन्तुमर्हसि ॥ IV. 36. 20

He actually apologized. Now, you know, ladies and gentlemen, what magnanimity of soul is required for a person to apologize to another. We who are so apt to offend knowingly and unknowingly, we hesitate to apologize. Sometimes I too apologize. For Lakshmana to apologize and apologize in those handsome terms, praising Sugriva as the very equal of his brother, is to go the whole way that generosity of nature can take a man. Here is therefore one of the noblest of souls.

Now I am coming to the last part of this discourse. It will take a little time but it is worth doing. I am coming now to exhibit Sri Rama as a martinet, a stern disciplinarian. He could not else be the generalissimo of a vast army of monkeys, notoriously unstable and hard to keep to one straight course. He was the martinet. When he gave the order, the order must be obeyed and Lakshmana being his kinkara, his willing kinkara, had often to obey difficult orders. Twice he was driven to an impossible position. Lakshmana was the very soul of obedience, of literal obedience. And yet in order perhaps to show how life is full of difficulties to us all, how the man who commands is placed oftentimes in a difficult position and how a man who is the very soul of obedience is also placed in a very difficult position, how this world, even when we have the highest characters, one way or another puts us all in difficult situations, let me refer to this. We have got Sri Rama putting Lakshmana as it were through a hard test. Going away in search of the golden deer, he had told Lakshmana, "Be careful. This is a forest full of perils and dangers. I am going away to bring what Sita desires with her whole heart. Mind you, you have to take care of her. Don't stir.

Watch keenly, watch with all your skill." So many words were not necessary for Lakshmana. He knew his business and he took every care of Sita. You all know what happened. When Maricha at the end cried in imitation of Rama's voice, poor Sita was maddened with grief and she ordered Lakshmana to go up and see. He was not willing. He tried to tell her all about her husband as if she did not know. "Don't you know your husband? Is there any danger to him? What is likely to happen to him? And if anything is to happen to him, am I going to save him? Don't fear. I am here to protect you. I am under strict orders. Your husband is a bad man to disobey." She would not listen. You know what things she says. Horrible things to repeat. Having said them all and finding that even that most harsh imputation was not quite able to dislodge him from his post of duty, Sita adds

समक्षं तव सौमित्रे प्राणांस्त्यक्ष्ये न संशयः ॥ III. 45. 26

"While you are looking on I am going to die at your feet." What was the poor fellow to do? And the woman will do it. She was all too near doing it. She was a Rajput woman. She threatened to do it. Lakshmana thought therefore that he was in the last extremity. What was he to do? Was he to see her die at his feet? Was he to obey his brother or was he to forget at the last moment his brother's order and go and save the life of this poor woman? She was mad. She abused him. He abused her and abused her sex. "You women are horrible creatures. Yes, I will go. I can't see you die. You have driven me to choose between one horrible alternative, that of disobeying my brother, and the other alternative which I consider still more horrible, to see you kill yourself before me. Well, I will go. That seems to be the lesser evil. Well, I will go." Having gone, when he reported this fact to his brother, I do not know what he expected. Lakshmana could not have expected any mercy from his brother. He did not ask for it at all. That was not his nature. But you and I pleading for Lakshmana at that moment would have said, "What was this poor fellow to do? You gave him an order. He obeyed it as long as he humanly could. But if that woman would drive him away under threat of killing herself, do you mean to say he should still have stayed?" We might have pleaded with Sri Rama. Not that Rama did anything. But he passed a solemn censure. What more was needed for a sensitive person? Rama passed a solemn censure. He said, "A woman is a woman after all. That poor girl, she loves me so much. I am her very life, what would be left to her without me? She thought I was in danger. You must expect, you must be prepared for her saying all sorts of things, like a mad woman. She might have said anything, she might have threatened to do anything. You ought not to have come away. You ought to have stayed and protected her." Would you be in Sita's place, would you be in Rama's place, would you be in Lakshmana's place? All the three the Poet contrives to put in a desperate situation and all reach the limits of their endurance, every one of them. Here it was Rama says,

नाकरोः शासनं मम ॥ III. 59. 24

"You have disobeyed me." That means, "I am displeased with you. You have earned my displeasure." Poor Lakshmana! After all, he did what was best in the harsh circumstances. That was his reward. A more generous man, one who was less of a disciplinarian, might have said, "Yes, you were in a terrible trial, Lakshmana. I think you did right. I might have done the same." Well, Rama could have risen to that magnanimous height and spoken in that strain. But Rama was the embodiment of Dharma. For him duty is duty. You are posted in a place from which you should not stir, a soldier's post of duty. To turn away is to desert, to incur the penalty of being shot immediately, out of hand.

Now another time yet, in worse circumstances—if worse circumstances could be possible—Lakshmana was put to a severe trial. In the Uttara Kanda, the concluding stage of this series of transactions which we call the Ramayana, Fate or Kala came to summon Sri Rama back to Heaven where he was wanted. He and Rama were closeted together in conversation. The hermit whose disguise Kala had taken stipulated beforehand, "Now, post your best man as sentry at the gate. I don't want anybody to come and either see or hear what takes place between you and me. This is absolutely strictly between you and me. Let me not have the apprehension that somebody will rush in or stay and hear." And so Rama says to Lakshmana, "Dismiss the ordinary sentry and you take the place yourself and remain there. And did you hear what this hermit has stated? If you come in, if you hear, the penalty is death." "All right", says Lakshmana. He posted himself at the gate. The conversation inside went on. It grew to a climax. It was nearly ended. Fate is harsh. If things had waited another minute, everything would have been over and all would have ended well. But the wheel of Fate goes round. While yet Rama and the hermit were together, who should appear but Durvasas, the ever-hungry, the ever-angry man. He came to the gate and asked to be let in. See how foolish that man was. He only wanted to be fed. Lakshmana could have ordered it and ordered twenty other people's food. Durvasas says, "No, I must see Rama now, this instant, or I curse you, I curse Ayodhya, I curse everybody." What was Lakshmana to do? He had been charged not to stir from his post under penalty of death. Here was this man able to enforce his threat, who threatened to kill Lakshmana, to kill Rama, to kill everybody, and he would have done it. What was Lakshmana to do? What would you have done? What would I have done? What would Rama himself have done? See how impossible positions are created. He went in. He said, "Never mind, let me die. The death of one in such a crisis is better than universal destruction."

एकस्य मरणं मेऽस्तु मा भूत् सर्वविनाशनम् ॥ VII. 105. 9

So saying once more he chose the lesser of the two evils. Everything was over as he went in. Perhaps he saw, perhaps he heard the last word. Rama pacified Durvasas, fed him and dismissed him. Only after having done that duty to that most exacting of all mortals did he return to Lakshmana and say, "Well, Lakshmana." "Well Rama," he he says, "I know what you want me to do. Kill me, kill me, I am ready. I knew it. Take my life. It is at your disposal." Then burst out Vasishtha at that moment. Says Vasishtha, "That is the decree of Fate. You said that you would kill him. He incurred the penalty. The penalty must be executed. I know that in circumstances like these banishment is considered as the equivalent of death." So it is that the decree of death was changed into one of transportation. That is where the story ends.

But we see here, ladies and gentlemen, in these high epic poems what is called the hand of inexorable Fate. Fate creates all sorts of difficult situations for us. We are in the hands of a power far higher, far higher than any human being. Rama was not bad, Lakshmana was not bad. However conscientious we may be, however clearly we may see our duty at the moment, however perfect our behaviour might have been, ,you still see how Fate transcending all human happiness can create desperate situations where the man intending to obey must disobey and where the man who is given an order and means to execute it, must hesitate twenty times before carrying it out. Such situations do not often beset us. You and I have no such high ideals that we should be tested. These great human beings who were born to exemplify the course of proper conduct, marching under the lash of Fate, are put in extreme situations where it is difficult to turn this way or that, where you cannot perform one duty without failing in another, where you are as it were in a dreadful *Dharmasankata,* where turn which side you will, you must fall into error and the choice has to be made. But even though the best choice is made, the lesson that the Poet means to enforce on us all is that *the penalty of a wrong must be paid.*

FIFTH LECTURE*

Brothers and Sisters,—It may be of advantage to recall certain sentiments with which I opened this series of talks. Lakshmana, as I ventured to point out, is a simple character, easy to understand, without contradictions in itself, cast in a mould which is very familiar to people of the world. Sri Rama whom I propose to discuss to-day is somewhat different. He has a somewhat complex character. Certain qualities may seem to be in conflict in his nature with certain other qualities. Some of his doings have been subjects of constant dispute and controversy. And some of us who are Rama's devotees, under the guidance of senior critics, even venture to criticise certain of the measures ascribed to him. Perhaps you will allow me to say a few words about how characters in history or in fiction are handled. Authors who make it their business to study human nature and present it in concrete instances to their readers, authors who bestow attention on their work are of different calibre; not all are experts in their line. When they draw characters, there is no fairness about them; there is no coherence. And if they are not well-practised it may be that as we read about them we pronounce the judgment that they are not in conformity with what the author intended them to be. Other authors however describe their characters as their constant companions. They dwell with them in their inmost thoughts. They turn them over and over again in their minds and when they delineate them, they are therefore able to make them conform in every particular with their own intentions of what they should be. They are the great authors of the world, men who are able to bring into perfect accord their own conceptions of their heroes and heroines and their descriptions of them, their doings and their sayings. Valmiki was not perhaps the creator of either Sri Rama or his story. He only presents him to us as he had him presented to himself. Nor is it possible to maintain that he invented or devised many of the incidents and episodes which illustrate the character of his hero and his heroine. They too must have come to him from ages before. I am considering Valmiki

* 3—5—'44.

and his story in the ordinary human light. Of course tradition has it that he was Sri Rama's contemporary and composed the poem in Rama's own day. Whether that be exactly true or not, it is certain that Valmiki's imagination was not brought into play in portraying Sri Rama or in detailing the narrative. To us Valmiki was perhaps responsible for the arrangement of the subject-matter. He was perhaps responsible for the sentiments ascribed to the hero and heroine and other characters. Certainly the language, the framing of the language, the figures of speech, are all his own work. So much being premised, is it allowable to go further and to say that the description that Rama has been given in various portions of the great epic, that that description exactly accords with the received character of the hero? I think it is and I have not much doubt in my own mind that that was the case.

Then we come to the next point in the argument. Did Valmiki for his materials make a selection of the legends and stories that had gathered round Sri Rama or were certain of these so well-known in his day that he could not venture to discard any of them even if they did not accord with his own idea? It is a matter purely of guessing, and we may have occasionally to think, when we discuss Sri Rama as a fully-developed character and examine the compatibility of part with part, that the Poet was not perhaps free to choose; it may be that here and there when the correspondence is not complete or falls short of the standard that would satisfy us, we may have to fall back on the theory—I merely venture to put it forth as my own guess—we may have to fall back on the theory that perhaps the particular episode which offends against the standard of consistency was not of his choice and he was not able to put it aside because the tradition connecting him with the episode was so strong that he could not venture to put it aside. May be we shall have to say that once or twice. But when such conditions occur, I shall not presume to think that I carry your judgment with me. I shall merely leave it to you and not mind one way or the other if my view meets or does not meet with general acceptance.

Now then, if Rama, as I venture to think, was a real character of flesh and blood like ourselves, if he lived like us amidst surroundings of his day and his part of the world, if he was subject to the ordinary human feelings which we find daily at work amongst ourselves, if so, we must be prepared to find every now and then that he sometimes moved on one level and sometimes on another level and we shall have to judge his conduct or his sayings according to our belief as to the sphere in which at the moment he had his being. For we all know from experience that neither the best nor the lowest amongst us, neither men or women, neither Westerners nor Easterners, none who is human, is able to occupy one level of thought, one level of action, and one level of function; we go up sometimes when we are in good moods, receptive of ethical notions, conscious of our duties, comparatively strong to resist temptations, in noble surroundings, amidst noble people, thinking noble thoughts and capable of doing noble deeds. Alas! such moments are not always available. It is only rarely that there is a combination of circumstances conductive to our being kept on our own highest level. Often, too often indeed, there are circumstances that drag us down, bad examples, sordid inducements, sordid considerations. Temptations of one kind or another beset us all round and even the men amongst us who have received the most careful training and who have trained themselves most carefully and conscientiously, even we find that there is a certain environment of high quality necessary if we are to be ourselves at our highest. Too commonly we fall, we do improper things, we do things that we would not have done otherwise or in other circumstances, we do things that we wish we hadn't done; and we do them consciously, knowingly, hoping that others will not detect our fault, or if they did detect it, would forgive us on account of this or that other consideration. Sri Rama had the extraordinary merit,—I say merely extraordinary—what I mean is unequalled and unmatched merit, of remaining most often at his own highest level. He seldom fell below it. If at any time he did, we could easily spot the conditions that determined the decline; perhaps the decline was conscious, perhaps it was not, perhaps it was entirely excusable. Occasionally perhaps the excuses are difficult to find for us, men of limited vision. But the point, ladies and gentlemen, is and don't be afraid of this thought, there is nothing wrong about it, nothing blasphemous,—that occasionally we do find that Sri Rama did and said things which perhaps his own higher nature would not approve. It is not easy for us to say why he did these things, how he came to do them and how far they must be ascribed to defects in his character. I do not mean to go over the whole catalogue but before I begin the discussion actually, I wish to tell you finally, that in my judgment they do not take away even by a small particle from the sublimity of Rama's character. The man must be thoroughly ignorant of human character, must be perversely blind and deaf to all that happens round him, who thinks because now and then Sri Rama showed the common qualities of human nature, that therefore he was of the common clay. No, I wish to say without any reservation that, considered as a human being should be considered, Rama stands almost immaculate. Almost immaculate I say. Why I use the word *almost* I wish with your permission to make clear to-day, by trying to understand certain episodes that are narrated in the poem. But before I do so it is necessary to make a rapid survey of what Rama stands for to-day, and of how we hold him as unapproachable, as a man, as a husband, as a friend, as an ally in peace and war, as a king. No greater testimony is required to prove this than the fact that while he was only still twenty-five or twenty-six according to Sita, but thirty-seven or thirty-eight by ordinary calculation, while he was only of that age, without any advantage of a kingdom to rule, of estates to distribute, of honours to give, of wealth to give away, without any of these advantages, he established himself, as I say at that young age, as the supreme crown and glory of his age. All alike who came into contact with him, whether senior to him in age or junior, whether kings with crowned heads or ordinary persons, whether great warriors, saints or sages, all alike bowed to him in reverence. His own brothers, scarcely junior to him as we reckon ages amongst ourselves, even his brothers, considered that he was by head and shoulders above them, far away in reach of character and entitled to their most obeisance. Whether in the Ayodhya kanda where he moved among people comparatively his equals, kings, queens and sages, or in the next two kandas where he was practically alone with his own brother and his wife, or in the Kishkinda kanda where again he had a few people who looked up to him as ordinary people look up to each other, or in the Yuddha kanda where he did great deeds, commanded great armies, conducted significant campaigns, did doughty deeds of war, every one who came into contact with him put him in a class of his own and durst not compare himself or herself with him. Of this the most striking proof is to be found in the concluding scene of the Yuddha kanda—I call it concluding, excluding the Abhisheka part in Ayodhya itself—where just after the battle when he summoned to his great presence her who was the cause of the great war, her for whom he had incurred unparalleled sacrifices, whom he loved like his own life, and without whom he often threatened to take out his own life, summoning her to his great presence he gave expession to sentiments that shocked every single hearer, not her only, not Lakshmana only, not Vibhishana only, but the whole host of monkeys and any surviving Rakshasas there might have been. They all listened to him, they all saw him when he sat apparently in state, all by himself, lost in serious awe, may I say, in gloomy thought, giving expression to sentiments of harsh, unfeeling, cruel import. All stood or sat in their places. What was Sri Rama after all? He was not the Emperor of India at that time; he was no great sage as we count sages. Why, why did no one, monkey or man, murmur a word of protest? Perfectly clear, not one approved. Everybody thought that he was doing something that they could not explain, that they could not justify to themselves. But not a voice was heard, not a hand raised in disapprobation. The man had imposed himself so irrevocably on all that came near him that what he said was law unto every one, what he decreed was to be obeyed in every particular without question and without demur. If he said something they could not approve, it was the doom of Fate that descended on them all. To it they must submit. They durst not protest. Now I want you to realise, ladies and gentlemen, how great must have been the man who could become so unquestionably supreme in his kind. That Sri Rama was and he could not be that unless he were what he professed often to be, *the guardian and the embodiment in himself of Dharma.* Time after time, under the most difficult circumstances, when all about him pulled him down, gave him advice which was of a worldly nature, when everything pointed to what we might call ordinary conduct, he adopted courses of action which astonished people by their complete rectitude, by the high altitude of moral excellence that they rose to. Not to mention the ordinary things like renunciation of power and the abandonment of kingdom, which must occur to you all, let us come to the crowning episodes in the

Yuddha kanda itself. Take the occasion when Vibhishana sought asylum with him. He held, as you know, a great council of war, he had eminent counsellors. But excepting Hanuman who seemed rather weak in the advice that he gave, excepting him, every one including his own brother, Lakshmana, would have had him reject Vibhishana, while one or two would have him order his killing; almost alone therefore, alone, in spite of the advice of everybody, rejecting it all as beneath him, he rose to his own topmost level and said the famous words:—"No man shall seek my protection in vain. He may be wicked, he may be undeserving, he may even be my bitterest enemy, Ravana himself. But if he comes to me in a friendly and submissive spirit, I will not turn him back." Fancy, ladies and gentlemen, what tremendous consciousness of his own moral power he must have had when he announced these great sentiments and carried them out without any qualification or reservation.

Take again the moment when, locked in mortal battle with Ravana himself, he gained some advantage and Ravana was driven to come down from his chariot—it was destroyed and he lost his great bow—Sri Rama drew himself up to full dignity and told his enemy whom he had made so many arrangements not only to vanquish but to kill, instead of seizing that moment to press his advantage and remove him altogether, he tells him, "Now, Ravana, you are at a great disadvantage. To-day I have seen you at your best. You have fought bravely; you have fought nobly; you have accounted for many a warrior on my side. Still you are tired. You are obliged to come down and stand like me on your feet, you've lost your great bow, I give you time. Go home now. Come to-morrow, refreshed and strong in your chariot and with a new bow and new arrows. You shall then see how I can give you battle." Whoever heard of such a thing? Whichever hero did such a thing?

Yet again, when having killed Ravana, he listened to Vibhishana who was stuggling between two sentiments and finally Vibhishana came to him with tears and said, "True he was my elder brother; true he was my king; true he protected me often; but he was a bad. He ruined many women. He made light of life. He made unjust wars. Altogether I do not think I shall perform his obsequies. It may not be right of me to do so." I say it was quite easy for an ordinary man to say, "Yes, throw his body into the sea and be done with him." But we are dealing with Sri Rama. He said to Vibhishana at that supreme moment—you have heard of people who exhumed bodies that have been buried under the ground and threw them subsequently into the water or into the fire—what did Sri Rama do at that moment when even Vibhishana would not do the last rites by his brother? He said, "No Vibhishana, you are wrong. I did not kill an ignoble man in battle. Ravana was a great warrior; he was a great man; he was a great king and greatly he died. Perform his obsequies according to the prescribed Sastra." And, "you will attain merit," he added.

Well, ladies and gentlemen, if there was a human being who could reach those unimaginable heights of moral purity and grandeur, is it any wonder that all the world bowed to him, accepted his smallest wish as the decree of Heaven? That he was. And yet, thanks be to human nature which we all have, as the poets say, as the world says, one nature is common to us all. Full of dread and awe as we are, as we contemplate Sri Rama, it fills us now and then with pride that he too, he too thought very much as we should have thought. Trouble depressed him; sorrow struck him hard; he had his moments of anguish. Alas, the Poet says he cried and wept bitter tears now and then! He grew angry sometimes, he was in despair sometimes; he was about to commit suicide now and then. He said harsh things of people. He suspected just as you and I would suspect. He did everything that we with flesh and blood do. Don't think that we bring him down from his high level; we raise ourselves to kinship with him as we notice these incidents. If being like us with flesh and blood, actuated by our motives now and then, feeling angry, feeling depressed, feeling sorry, if being like us, it was still possible for him to rise to those great altitudes, though we may not soar so high, may we not rise half an inch above ourselves? May we not subdue our nature to some extent? It won't turn all to gold, this base lead of which we are made. No, it won't. Nevertheless we could clean that lead, make it shine according to its own nature and then, ladies and gentlemen, we shall have read of Sri Rama to some purpose. We shall have heard the Ramayana with some advantage, and upon our lives and our character some influence of a very exalted and almost divine nature will have been exerted so that we shall all be somewhat the better for having come under the influence of this great epic of Valmiki. Now then, to my task to-day.

I have brought together here certain incidents and episodes in which Sri Rama shows his human qualities, not his superhuman virtue but his human qualities. First, I think it best to go along in some order as I hope, after I have spoken, some amongst you, I hope with all my heart, some amongst you will go back to the poem itself and see whether I have given you trustworthy guidance or whether I have been trying to mislead you. First of all when Dasaratha and Kaikeyi having sat together, or rather she having sat with him in order to deflect the course upon which the king had previously determined, when under her bidding he sent for Sri Rama to announce the dread news, what was Sri Rama doing? He was then in his own place with Sita. As on the last occasion when he saw his father, he had been told he was going to be crowned Yuvaraja, he says to her in full expectation of the coming honour, says to her as you or I would have said in similar circumstances contemplating the advance in life that is going to come to us through the blessing of God. He said to her, that is, to Sita:

देवि देवश्च देवी च समागम्य मदन्तरे।
मन्त्रयेते ध्रुवं किञ्चिदभिषेचनसंहितम्॥ II. 16. 15

His mind was pure, his heart was unsuspicious. So he says to her, "Doubtless my father and Kaikeyi are planning some nice things by way of preparation. Great things are in store for me and therefore for you."

लक्षयित्वा ह्यभिप्रायं प्रियकामा सुदक्षिणा।
सञ्चोदयति राजानं मदर्थं मदिरेक्षणे॥ II. 16. 16

You remember how Kaikeyi and he were great friends. He says, "No doubt, Kaikeyi being so fond of me and hearing the great intention he has towards me, wants the king to be quick about it and nice about it."

सा प्रहृष्टा महाराजं हितकामानुवर्तिनी।
जननी चार्थकामा मे केकयाधिपतेः सुता॥ II. 16. 17

"Quite certain. I am being summoned to be put in the second place in the kingdom," he says to Sita.

हन्त शीघ्रमितो गत्वा द्रक्ष्यामि च महीपतिम् ।
सह त्वं परिवारेण सुखमास्व रमस्व च ॥ II. 16. 20

"While I go and have the great ceremony performed, you rest awhile here in happiness with your own people and spend the time in happy contemplation of the prospect." Well, the Poet puts these sentiments into the mouth of the great person whom we are studying. And it appears to me that that shows above all things how very human Sri Rama was. It was a great thing that was happening to him and he looked forward not only to his father but to his step-mother who had shown him such marked affection, he looked forward to their plans together for his prosperity.

Then when the worst was known and he came back, he goes to tell his mother of the reverse, for the mother was also rising aloft on hope. She had to be told. When he goes to her, the Poet gives a touch which is quite contrary to what he has been saying before. Before that, as soon as Rama heard that he was to renounce the kingdom, that his brother was to take it, that he was to go to forest for fourteen years, the Poet has said, "Not a muscle moved on the noble countenance. It shone in full lustre as it always did. Nobody could see that a lightning stroke had fallen. For all that Rama appeared, he was still on the high tide of prosperity and power. He did not show the slightest unhappiness or disappointment." That was what the Poet had said. When Rama went to his mother to tell her what had happened, this is what the Poet says:

"धारयन् मनसा दुःखम्" II. 19. 35

"Controlling his unhappiness within his own heart." That shows you that there was unhappiness and that he merely conquered it. It was not as if there was no trouble in his mind, no grief or thought. Having to break bad news he went dejected to her.

धारयन्मनसा दुःखमिन्द्रियाणि निगृह्य च ।
प्रविवेशात्मवान् वेश्म मातुरप्रियशंसिवान् ॥ II. 19. 35

Now that shows again that Rama, great as he was, sublime as his development had been on the ethical side, could not help the depressing character of the circumstances.

Then when he went before Sita, it was still worse. Natural. We like to feel that Rama behaved as you and I would have behaved in similar circumstances. Probably we should have wept and rolled on the floor. Rama too was susceptible to some extent.

प्रविवेशाथ रामस्तु स्वं वेश्म सुविभूषितम्।
प्रहृष्टजनसम्पूर्णं ह्रिया किञ्चिदवाङ्मुखः॥ II. 26. 5

It had all been decreed for the great event—

प्रहृष्टजनसम्पूर्णम्

All people were eagerly looking forward for the great news to come. As he went in, there was a little grief in his face and he put his head down.

अथ सीता समुत्पत्य वेपमाना च तं पतिम्।
अपश्यच्छोकसन्तप्तं चिन्ताव्याकुलितेन्द्रियम्॥ II. 26. 6

Instead of coming back rejoicing and jumping, he wore a sad and thoughtful countenance, and Sita was struck with grief to see him. Till now he had subdued his feelings and did not allow them to interfere with his speech or to appear in his face. But when he went to her who was so full of expectation and expected to receive him in quite another style, he was unable to control his grief.

तां दृष्ट्वा स हि धर्मात्मा न शशाक मनोगतम्।
तं शोकं राघवस्सोढुं ततो विवृततां गतः॥
विवर्णवदनं दृष्ट्वा तं प्रस्विन्नममर्षणम्। II. 26. 7-8

His face had changed. The colour on his face had become a little pale. He was perspiring. There was some feeling which he could not control.

आह दुःखाभिसंतप्ता किमिदानीमिदं प्रभो॥ II. 26. 8

What is this? What has happened? Why all this excitement and stir?

Now I come to another passage in which the Poet makes Rama speak to Lakshmana. Lakshmana wants to accompany him and for one brief moment Rama tries to keep him back. You know for what reason. That shows his human weakness better than anything else.

स्निग्धो धर्मरतो वीरः सततं सत्पथे स्थितः ।
प्रियः प्राणसमो वश्यो भ्राता चापि सखा च मे ॥ II. 31. 10

He says this to Lakshmana, "You are all this to me." All this is preparation for leaving him, for asking him to remain behind.

मयाऽद्य सह सौमित्रे त्वयि गच्छति तद्वनम् ।
को भरिष्यति कौसल्यां सुमित्रां वा यशस्विनीम् ॥ II. 31. 11

When Sita and I are away in the forest who is there to look after my mother and your mother?

अभिवर्षति कामैर्यः पर्जन्यः पृथिवीमिव ।
स कामपाशपर्यस्तो महातेजा महीपतिः ॥ II. 31. 12

Our father is infatuated and as to our step-mother who has won this round, she is not likely to relent towards her rivals,

सा हि राज्यमिदं प्राप्य नृपस्याश्वपतेः सुता ।
दुःखितानां सपत्नीनां न करिष्यति शोभनम् ॥ II. 31. 13

will not do them any good. At this particular moment Rama's grief almost overpowers him. He says, "Kaikeyi will not take care of them and Bharata may be too much under his mother's influence."

एवं कुरुष्व सौमित्रे मत्कृते रघुनन्दन ।
अस्माभिर्विप्रहीणाया मातुर्नो न भवेत्सुखम् ॥ II. 31. 17

He means both of them. "Neither my mother nor your mother without us to protect them can be happy." Now you will see how later on when anybody else speaks of Kaikeyi, Rama springs to her side and says, "Do not abuse her." He may suspect her; he may not think very well of her. Perhaps his belief is that knowing her weakness he will be able to make full allowance for it. He will be able to realise how she is not acting for herself but for her dear son under pardonable circumstances and how perhaps she too is in the hands of Fate, working out Fate's cruel decrees. These allowances he would make even when he censures her conduct but other people may not able to do so. So when Lakshmana at any time tells him "Ah, how I hate Kaikeyi," he would say, "No, no, not that thing, Lakshmana, never say such a thing." So too when anybody accuses Bharata in his hearing, he would speak in the highest terms of him. But when he talks to himself as it were—for Lakshmana is not different from him—when he talks to himself, his real feelings find vent to some extent and he gives expression to the deepest emotions at the moment.

Then I shall mention one other thing and stop for the day. We see now how under a stroke of adversity he felt more or less like a human being, as other human beings would have felt. He suspected people; he suspected Kaikeyi and he suspected Bharata too to some extent. That was like us. Here we see him in this particular incident that I am now going to relate, here we see him trying to enjoy a little innocent fun at other people's expense. Just a little innocent fun. You remember that poor Brahman named Trijata who as Rama was giving away his property right and left to his people, was, like Kuchela in the other story, under pressure from his wife, making a pilgrimage to Sri Rama to ask for his help. He says to Rama, "You are giving away so much. I am a very poor man with many children and one of the means of subsistence that I have is to pick the grains of paddy left behind by the reaper. That is my way of life. I find it very hard to get along. I have a large family. Will you look with pity on me?" And then you remember how Sri Rama asks him, "That stick of yours, take it; stand there and throw it as far as you can with your full strength. My cows stand all between. All the cows that are between this spot and the spot which your stick reaches shall be yours." And then Rama was amused to see how this Brahman, suddenly seized with a little bit of greed as it were, exerted all his strength, waved the stick twice or thrice round his head and threw it. It went to the other bank of the Sarayu. So he had an immense wealth of cattle at once at his disposal. Rama gave it all to him. And then he says, "I was perhaps rather unfeeling to you. I should have done this thing perhaps in another way but I wanted to know how a Brahman like you could use the strength that he had in order to get something. I wanted to know that you could use all your strength. That was not quite proper. I should have relieved you without this trouble. Just excuse me. I wanted to have a little amusement."

उवाच च ततो रामस्तं गार्ग्यमभिसान्त्वयन् ।
मन्युर्न खलु कर्तव्यः परिहासो ह्ययं मम ॥
इदं हि तेजस्तव यद्दुरत्ययं तदेव जिज्ञासितुमिच्छता मया
इमं भवानर्थमभिप्रचोदितो वृणीष्व किंचेदपरं व्यवस्यति ॥

II. 32. 40-1

"I only wanted to know your strength and how far you would exert it, whether it was always at your disposal. Now having done so, I am so pleased. Will you ask me if you want to have anything more? I shall be happy to give you." But Trijata was of the family of Garga. He was, like a Brahman, contented and he had this immense wealth all at once. He did not ask for anything more. He said, "I am pleased for the time."

Well, let me handle one more point. We now saw that Rama was not above a little merriment. Now we come to a quality of a slightly different nature. He was leaving the palace. There was great mourning, as you know, within the palace and outside. He and Lakshmana and Sita had got into the chariot. Sumantra was driving. They were going at some distance and Dasaratha, Kausalya and other people had come out of the palace to see them, to have a last look at them. And the old man cried out to Sumantra, "Stop, stop." But Rama said:

तिष्ठेति राजा चुक्रोश याहि याहीति राघवः ।
सुमन्त्रस्य बभूवात्मा चक्रयोरिव चान्तरा ॥ II. 40. 46

"Go on, drive on." Not knowing what to do, the Poet says, Sumantra was like a man caught between the front and back wheels of a chariot. He did not know what to do and looked up to Rama, "I am asked by your father to do one thing and you ask me to do just the opposite thing." Then says Rama, "Perhaps you are afraid that when you go back after leaving me in the forest, the old man will be angry with you for not having obeyed him.

नाश्रौषमिति राजानमुपालब्धोऽपि वक्ष्यसि ।
चिरं दुःखस्य पापिष्ठमिति रामस्तमब्रवीत् ॥ II. 40. 47

If my father on your return should take you to task for disobedience, you know what to do. Just say that in the bustle and noise you did not hear him." And Sri Rama says in defence of this departure from truth:

चिरं दुःखस्य पापिष्ठम् ।

"The justification for telling this white lie is that it is foolish to prolong the wail. It is absolutely foolish and disastrous to prolong the wail of grief. So go on," he says. Apparently Sri Rama was a little fond of this thought,

चिरं दुःखस्य पापिष्ठम्

for a few sargas later we find him saying the same thing when he found that the people of the rural parts were following in great numbers and would not be stayed. He says to Sumantra again, "Run on" and as they cry out, he says:

चिरं दुःखस्य पापीयः । II. 50. 5

putting the comparative degree instead of the superlative.

Then again there are things, little peccadillos which we have got to remember in order to see that Rama was just like us when in trouble, apt to choose the easiest way out. There were a number of Brahmans of great sanctity following him obstinately. They went as far as the river Tamasa, when he crossed over to the other side. These people slept on this side. As they were asleep, Rama says to Sumantra, "Now, you had better take this chariot and drive northward as if you were trying to return to Ayodhya. And when they are off their guard as it were, come back from that side by another way. I'll come and join you and then we can drive away without their knowing anything." So he adopts this ruse in order to throw them off the scent, these people whom it was difficult to shake off, who in their loyalty and adoration were determined to follow him until he yielded to their request and returned. That was their hope. Simple people! Their whole lives were wrapped up in him. Hoping to keep him back, they followed him obstinately. So it was necessary to get rid of them by some little trick. This was what he taught Sumantra.

Now with that, gentlemen, I will stop for the day and take up this subject again. Rama is inexhaustible. He will keep me to himself for a long time. But I will try and shake him off as he shook off these pursuing Brahmans. I am trying to gather together the instances in which Valmiki presents Rama to us in a way we can understand him. If he was always on the highest level and never came down, if he was always unapproachably great, what good is he going to be to us? In some respects he must be like us. There are other instances in which we perceive the kinship between Rama and ourselves, and as an adoring study of the great epic is only of value in proportion as it raises our nature, as it enables us to conquer our lower selves and live as long as possible and as firmly as possible on our own higher level, since our business is, if possible, to get from this epic that which will enable us from bad to get to good, we shall do well to dwell on the next occasion on some of the other episodes where Rama shows his human qualities in a degree which so far from interfering with our adoration and worship of him, only make us love him the more dearly, regard him as closely bound with us, as also one through whose example we may be enabled in ever so humble a measure to rise above ourselves, as they say, from our lower to our higher selves. For so man improves. Not that he ever is above weakness, but when weakness assails him, he remembers these mighty examples and tries to rise above it. He may not succeed but even the trial is good for something. One trial may fail; two trials may fail, may often fail. The third may meet with partial success. The fourth, fifth and so on. Our lives may be short; our lives may be bounded on every side by things that are coarse and sordid, nevertheless they are lives, let us remember, similar in quality to the life that Sri Rama had; and if, when we grapple with our weaknesses, we try to remember him, may be, as I said before, in some humble measure we shall improve our own nature and learn to live our better selves more often, more firmly and to better puropse.

SIXTH LECTURE*

When we separated last time, I was mentioning a certain guileless trick played by Sri Rama on his subjects, how he made a feint as it were of returning to the city so that those who wished to follow him lost the track. To-day my first point would be the substance of a message which he gave to Sumantra as he was giving him leave. Sumantra, faithful charioteer of the Ikshvakus and minister of old time, was unwilling to leave Rama and Lakshmana and Sita and begged hard to be permitted to remain with them in attendance upon them and doing such service as might be vouchsafed to him. Sri Rama gave several reasons why he could not accept that position, and sending back Sumantra to the old place at Ayodhya, conveyed to him one very good reason. It shows that Sri Rama was able to read other people's hearts even when those other people resembled him least. In other words, even of bad persons, even of persons out of sympathy with him, he could read the hearts. Nothing was hidden from him. Usually people are able to understand those who are like themselves, who have passed through experiences similar to theirs, and whose mental make-up is more or less like their own. Where outward circumstances differ greatly, the understanding, unless a person is of exceptionally shrewd character, is difficult. So we say in Tamil, "பாம்பின் கால் பாம்புக்குத்தான் தெரியும்." This is a familiar doctrine. Carried into the exalted sphere of Vedanta it is often described in abstract language as an approximation of subject and object. In some cases it is described even as an identity of subject and object. The point however is that a straightforward simple person, not fully acquainted with the ways of the world, will find some difficulty in understanding points of view alien to his own character. When Sumantra objected to going back, Rama says to him, very shrewdly as you may see at once, "You know, Sumantra, why I send you back. I have several reasons but the principal reason is this. My step-mother, Kaikeyi, is a hard-natured, hard-hearted woman. She will want to be sure that I have really come to the forest. If

* 10-5-'44.

she suspects anything, woe be to my father! The penalty will all fall on him. If you go back without me and explain what has been happening here, all will be safe. She will understand that the old man has kept his word and that I have obeyed him. Your presence in Ayodhya without us is therefore essential for the safety of my father." I mention this just to show that while Rama rose high above other persons in the world and his head was far up in the clouds at the summit of human excellence almost approaching divinity, his feet were firmly planted on the ground. In the fifty-third sarga when the three exiles had crossed the Ganges and taken up their temporary abode under the shade of a big tree, left alone without Sumantra, Sri Rama for the moment threw off all restraint. Till then he had passed through very exciting moments. His feelings had been worked up to the highest pitch. The eyes of the world were upon him. Temptations set hard on him. Father and preceptor and mother and everybody had tried to tempt him from the path that he had marked out for himself as one of righteousness. Whatever he felt, he had to keep down. In the eyes of the world the one thing he had to maintain was that he was a filial son, that he was anxious to maintain the character of his father. He risked everything, lost everything, in order to maintain his father's honour and he further had, as I have mentioned before, to show that whatever the change in the outward circumstances that had come over him and his fortunes, he was not dejected or depressed, and that adversity had failed to disturb his equanimity. He showed that the worst fortune would find him unmoved, anchored, strong and sure in his own pure nature. What affected him, if anything, was the highest. The small things of the earth like kingdoms, honour, he did not mind. By honour, I mean position. That then had been the part he played during all the trying hours that he passed in Ayodhya and on the way when Sumantra drove him as far as the Ganges. When he was left with Sita and Lakshmana and there was nobody else, the restraints that he had put upon himself fell away, and for a moment he was left free to commune with himself as it were. For you will understand that Lakshmana and Sita made no difference whatever to his solitude. He had, as it were, time for a soliloquy. And then the best part of that sarga is devoted to a description of how he gave vent to his own inner feelings and spoke without any restraint whatsoever, without any regard to outward appearances, to Lakshmana, Sita being an interested listener. The words were addressed to Lakshmana. But Lakshmana being more than figuratively a part of himself, we may take it that it was a speech made to himself. I have noted several slokas, all of them of the deepest import, quite necessary for the understanding of one aspect of the great character that we are studying, showing above everything else that he felt in his heart like ordinary people, that he had a deep community of emotion with us all, and that ordinary things affected him in the ordinary way, though when it came to action, the course taken was exactly the opposite to that any other person in his circumstances would have taken.

कृतकामा तु कैकेयी तुष्टा भवितुमर्हति ॥
सा हि देवी महाराजं कैकेयी राज्यकारणात् ।
अपि न च्यावयेत्प्राणान् दृष्ट्वा भरतमागतम् ॥ II. 53. 6-7

"She will be glad now. Yes, Kaikeyi will be happy. But seeing that her son has come to Ayodhya, her ambition may rise. Instead of making her son a mere Yuvaraja, the idea of making him king may occur to her and she may practise on the life of my father." That is the meaning of this sloka. "I hope she will not deprive him of his life."

अनाथश्च हि वृद्धश्च मया चैव विनाकृतः ।
किं करिष्यति कामात्मा कैकेय्या वशमागतः ॥ II 53. 8

"This old, imbecile, helpless man, left without me to guard him, having fallen into the hands of Kaikeyi, infatuated with love of her, what will be his fate?"

इदं व्यसनमालोक्य राज्ञश्च मतिविभ्रमम् ।
काम एवार्थधर्माभ्यां गरीयानिति मे मतिः ॥ II. 53. 9

"Of the three purusharthas, Dharma, Artha and Kama, I now see, watching my father and his behaviour, that Artha and Dharma take their place below Kama (काम एव गरीयान्) for,

को ह्यविद्वानपि पुमान् प्रमदायाः कृते त्यजेत् ।
छन्दानुवर्तिनं पुत्रं ततो मामिव लक्ष्मण ॥ II. 53. 10

"I am a son out of the common. I am an obedient son, a son whom any father would like to keep about him. And yet under the pressure of the woman on whom he dotes he sends me away."

सुखी बत सभार्यश्च भरतः कैकयीसुतः ।
मुदितान् कोसलानेको यो भोक्ष्यत्यधिराजवत् ॥ II. 53. 11

Now he thinks of Bharata. He contrasts himself with Bharata. "I have lost everything. I have come away to the forest with my wife and with my dear brother. He, Bharata, is enthroned, is going to rule over the Kosalas and he is going to do it with his wife. He is going to have his queen by his side." Notice this please. This is the one place in which the wife of any of the brothers is alluded to, not by name but merely as bharya. In no other place does the Poet allude to the other persons.

स हि सर्वस्य राज्यस्य सुखमेकं* भविष्यति ।
ताते च वयसातीते मयि चारण्यमास्थिते ॥ II. 53. 12

"Father is old and can take no part in affairs. I am away. So Bharata will be sole monarch of the whole place. Yes. He will determine the fortunes of all the peoples in Ayodhya."

अर्थधर्मौ परित्यज्य यः काममनुवर्तते ।
एवमापद्यते क्षिप्रं राजा दशरथो यथा ॥ II. 53. 13

This is a word very hostile to Bharata. "If Bharata is going to be enjoying his fortune, very well. Very well. The fate awaits him that has befallen my father."

अपीदानीं न कैकेयी सौभाग्यमदमोहिता ।
कौसल्यां च सुमित्रां च संप्रबाधेत मत्कृते ॥ II. 53. 15

Having said a word about the father and the brother, he now turns to the step-mother. "On my account, remembering that they were attached to me, that they were very reluctant to part from me, remembering how they stood by me and fought for me and contended with the old king for me, she is not going to let them alone. She is going to give them hell."

* In II. 53. 12 Govindaraja's reading is मुखमेकम्.

क्षुद्रकर्मा हि कैकेयी द्वेषादन्याय्यमाचरेत्।
*परिदद्या हि धर्मज्ञे भरते मम मातरम्॥ II. 53. 18

"She is a wicked woman, not scrupulous at all. She may do bad things. She may give poison to your mother and mine." See how long-repressed feelings find strange vent. This is not in accordance with Rama's real nature. Having been forced these many hours to play a high part to keep up appearances, to put on a brave countenance in the face of adversity, to remember the highest duty to all and to follow it, having been under this great pressure, moral pressure of a most unbearable kind, when he finds all that removed, he throws off all the outward disguise that he wore till now and then a strain in his real nature, a strain which makes him common with us all, breaks out and it makes him say these extraordinary things and when I have read these, I wish to make an observation. I shall make that observation with your kind permission.

एको ह्यहमयोध्यां च पृथिवीं चापि लक्ष्मण।
तरेयमिषुभिः क्रुद्धो ननु वीर्यमकारणम्॥ II. 53. 25

"What do you take me to be? You know my strength; you know my valour; you know my prowess. By means of my arrows I can reconquer the whole world if only I care. I am strong enough to bring under my umbrella the whole of this girdled earth; but I won't." But he is reminded of his strength; he is reminded of what he could accomplish if he wished. That means that he has by sheer force of will subdued all his desire, conquered the baser and more selfish part of his nature and come away to the forest, not doing the thing which he might have done, not grasping the thing which he might have grasped if he had only cared. "ननु वीर्यमकारणम्" means "Strength is given me not to do unjust and improper things but to do just things. If I use my force to get Ayodhya back under me, I should be doing something very improper. That is why I don't do it. Don't think I am impotent." He reminds himself as it were.

अधर्मभयभीतश्च परलोकस्य चानघ।
तेन लक्ष्मण नाद्याहमात्मानमभिषेचये॥ II. 53. 26

*The Lecturer follows the Bombay Ed. which reads:—
परिदद्याद्धि धर्मज्ञ गरं ते मम मातरम्॥

"I could have anointed myself, putting aside Dasaratha and everybody else. Why didn't I? I have a fear of wrong-doing. I don't want to do that which is ignoble or improper just for gain." Very well. The good man, the true man, the righteous man, has this sort of faith.

एतदन्यच्च करुणं विलप्य विजने वने।
अश्रुपूर्णमुखो रामो निशि तूष्णीमुपाविशत्॥ II. 53. 27

"Having exhausted himself by expressions like these, by shedding bitter tears, he spent the night quietly and silently." Having discharged, as it were, the smaller and the lower part of his nature, he wisely resumed his silence. He spent the rest of the night in meditation.

Now to some of you an idea may occur which I must dispose of at this point. Just bear with me for a few minutes. It is a point of casuistry. Nevertheless, most of you are men and women of the world and trained in the ways of men and women and some of you perhaps are very sophisticated in your arguments. It may occur to you if really, as I put it, there was a higher and a lower nature even in Sri Rama. While the higher nature triumphed and held him aloft, above the reach of common humanity, an object of admiration and worship for all, yes, in his time and after, while that higher nature expressed itself in astonishingly fertile ways for the education and edification of mankind, any of you might ask, "Was there a lower part in his nature? Was there also in his composition an element similar to ours?" Yes. That is true and that is the point I have been trying to make since the commencement of these discourses. And if anything, I have shown you how in Valmiki's text there is a clear unmistakable reference to what we may describe as the common human element in Sri Rama's nature too. Now you may ask—I put the question that occurs to you in this way, and I shall try to answer it. Take it for what it is worth and I am sure in my heart that I see the truth.

What do we say of persons who have a lower and a higher nature, who keep the lower nature to themselves, hide it as it were from the observation of their fellows and only show the better part of their nature? We call them hypocrites, don't we? That is the common name that we apply to such people, those bad in their hearts, low and mean in their attitudes, who appear to the outside world as if they were generous and noble-hearted and capable of great sacrifices and so on, people who present a better appearance to the world than the reality which they conceal. Such persons we call hypocrites. Now what I have said, what the Poet has said, about Sri Rama might bring him under this odious heading of hypocrite; for, his lower nature, his selfish nature, he keeps down, does not show it to anybody, keeps it to himself. The better part of his nature he shows outside. Now, ladies and gentlemen, the fact is Rama's character is exactly the reverse of a hypocrite's nature. I wish you to grasp it so that if there is this mixed element in him it is without the slightest element of poison. In the ordinary hypocrite's case the better part which is manifested outside is foreign to his nature, it is put on, it is merely pretended, it is borrowed for the occasion. It is just an outer cloak for the express deception of the world. The real nature, the wickedness of the nature, is practised, is brought into play for the benefit of the individual. The hypocrite benefits himself by working his lower nature, but secretly. His higher nature which is foreign to him, which is merely put on, is just for the deception of others, in order that he may practise his lower nature, in order that he may do bad and mean things, in order that he may pursue a selfish career. See what it was in the case of Sri Rama. The lower nature was not only hidden, it was put down. It was conquered. He did nothing in pursuit of his selfish desire, did nothing whatever, considered it Adharma, put it down by main moral force, rose above it. And what he did, what he actually practised, what the world saw in reality, was his higher nature. The promptings of his greater self, the divine elements, come into play every time. The merely human element is suppressed. Well that is exactly opposite to what a hypocrite should do, would do. So that while we have this outward similarity, the reality points to the fact that the higher element was Rama's real nature. The lower element was that which adhered to him loosely because he came among men and was a man among men and moved like a man among men. He had a small point of affinity with us. The little things that affect us and govern us, affected him also; only they did not govern him, he governed them. That is the important difference, the all-important difference which makes a whole universe of evolution stand between Sri Rama and any other person like ourselves.

Now having said that much, let me pass on to an incident of a slightly different character which will show that Sri Rama had another quality in common with us, a quality which we have no reason whatever to condemn, a quality which I have already mentioned, a desire to enjoy himself for a little when there is occasion as when he did in the case of Trijata. He had a little fun at the old man but at the same time when everything was over, he repented of it, told that man, "Well, I was only jesting, playing. I hope I have done you no harm. If there is anything else you desire, please ask me." Only the Brahman being the very soul of contentment, would not ask for anything else.

Now I will come to the Aranya Kanda where he encounters Surpanakha. Surpanakha coming in causes a little flutter in that world of three persons. She appears before the three as a monstrous, ill-looking, frightening creature and then there occurs a scene full of humour and enjoyment. The Poet himself apparently enjoys this scene, and you and I then may be pardoned if we extract a little merriment out of it. The Poet's enjoyment is best shown by the unnecessarily detailed contrast he makes between Sri Rama and Surpanakha as she sat before Sri Rama. The Poet is amused at the contrast between the two, Rama and Surpanakha and the humour is heightened by the fact that Surpanakha makes love to Rama. What a fine pair to make love! I shall just read the passage without spoiling the thing by any translation of mine.

सुमुखं दुर्मुखी रामं वृत्तमध्यं महोदरी ।
विशालाक्षं विरूपाक्षी सुकेशं ताम्रमूर्धजा ॥
प्रीतिरूपं विरूपा सा सुस्वरं भैरवस्वरा ।
तरुणं दारुणा वृद्धा दक्षिणं वामभाषिणी ॥ III. 17. 10-11

Here I want to show the felicity which the Poet has reached almost unconsciously. "दक्षिणं वामभाषिणी" I should expect he uses them in the literal sense, दक्षिण magnanimous, obliging by temperament; वाम wicked, bad by nature. Dakshina and Vama are not contrasted so much in their figurative meanings as in their literal meanings.

न्यायवृत्तं सुदुर्वृत्ता प्रियमप्रियदर्शना। III. 17. 12

Nobody would wish to see Rama and Surpanakha contrasted. No point of similarity would ever occur to us. Nevertheless the Poet, apparently in full enjoyment of the juxtaposition, has brought the contrast before us by a series of very clever expressions. Now when Surpanakha appeared there, she asked him, "Who are you to be here in our region? This is the jurisdiction of my brother. Who are you here?" And then the Poet starts off on a note of high praise for Sri Rama.

ऋजुबुद्धितया सर्वमाख्यातुमुपचक्रमे।
अनृतं न हि रामस्य कदाचिदपि सम्मतम्॥ III. 17. 15

Sri Rama was a straightforward person. Nothing crooked or subtle would occur to him though he could understand anybody else's tricks. Naturally, left to himself, he was straightforward. And he began to tell her who he was, why he and his brother and Sita were in the forest by themselves. he and his brother and Sita were in the forest by themselves. He completed his story. But here the Poet adds अनृतं न हि रामस्य कदाचिदपि सम्मतम्. The Poet pays a homage to Sri Rama's truthfulness. Sri Rama was a truthful character with a high regard for things in their exact nature; and then he was in an Asram where falsehood could not enter. Besides, there was a woman in the case. Surpanakha, whatever else she was, was a woman. So he gave a straightforward answer. That is how the Poet introduces us to Surpanakha's advances. Horrid advances they were. She started by saying who she was and finally finished by saying, "You are so handsome a man. I am struck with your beauty and wish to have you for husband. Come along. I will make you a free man. You are apparently encumbered here. I will make you a free man. I will gobble up Lakshmana by one mouthful and I will gobble up Sita by another. So your impediments being removed, you and I can wander forth in the forest and enjoy ourselves to our heart's content." Then it occurred to Rama that the thing was taking a funny turn. He apparently makes up his mind to have a little pleasure. But at this point I must draw your attention to Rama's characterization of himself which comes into question in this context. Rama says twice in the course of the Kishkindha Kanda to Sugriva, twice to him he says:

अनृतं नोक्तपूर्वं मे वीर कृच्छ्रेऽपि तिष्ठता।
धर्मलोभपरीतेन न च वक्ष्ये कथंचन ॥ IV. 14. 14-15

"I am a truthful person. I never speak any untruth. Here I pass my word, I give an undertaking," he says to Sugriva. Therefore understanding this literally we must be thrown into some sort of surprise when we find that he is trying to take some pleasure out of this stupid woman, Surpanakha. To Surpanakha he says:

अनुजस्त्वेष मे भ्राता शीलवान् प्रियदर्शनः।
श्रीमानकृतदारश्च लक्ष्मणो नाम वीर्यवान् ॥
अपूर्वी भार्यया चार्थी तरुणः प्रियदर्शनः।
अनुरूपश्च ते भर्ता रूपस्यास्य भविष्यति ॥ III. 18. 3-4

These are the words used by Rama to Surpanakha. See how he puts it, just a little: अनुजः is junior to me, शीलवान् a good fellow, प्रियदर्शनः good-looking, अकृतदारः unmarried. He has not taken a wife yet; he has not had much commerce with women before and he desires it अपूर्वी भार्यया चार्थी. "You are a handsome, beautiful woman. You will match each other. He will be a fitting husband for such a one as you."

एनं भज विशालाक्षि भर्तारं भ्रातरं मम। III. 18. 5

"Take to him. Don't bother me. I have a wife already." Now these words seem to me to leave no doubt whatever that Rama was making fun of this stupid woman. No doubt whatever. He uses the word भर्ता twice and he says to her, "Take him. He is a fitting husband." There is no doubt whatever. Only some commentators fasten upon the word अकृतदारः. I am afraid there is a certain class of Rama worshippers who are unwilling that we should discover him in a jesting mood. Would Rama too make a jest? Is he capable of laughter? He must be a solemn man, the embodiment of Dharma. Here he is holding things up always. To find him come down to the level of other persons, cutting jokes and all that sort of thing, is absurd. Therefore they are at pains to interpret away the words अकृतदारः. They say, in fact, one says, "Every root in the Sanskrit language can have any meaning, any *dhatu* can have meaning. अकृतदार: means a man who having married, has not brought his wife with him. They give that meaning to the verse and they think they so save the truthful character of Sri Rama. Now what can you do with the words भार्या, भर्ता? Commentators, however, are ingenious enough to say अनुरूपश्च ते भर्ता—ते अभर्ता. Take the word like that. The final result would be that we should make Rama talk nonsense. If really what Rama meant was that Lakshmana had not brought his wife, was he unable to put it in straight language to poor Surpanakha? Should he say अकृतदार: and lead her to understand that he was unmarried, and have this other meaning in his own bosom just to satisfy himself? Now what is the point in giving that other meaning to it? What is the point? What do commentators gain by it? And yet a large number of us being clever, ingenious people, loving an argument and thinking how we can floor the other side just for the love of playing upon words, solemnly interpret this passage like this: अकृतदार: was meant by Sri Rama to mean a man who has not his wife at the moment with him.* Now the whole point is, what did Rama want Surpanakha to understand? What he had in his own mind is not material. If, by using the words अकृतदार:, though he might have meant the other meaning, he did deceive Surpanakha, he was guilty all the same. Now in English there is a word 'equivocation,' which means using words which have two meanings, which can be interpreted in two ways, one really intended for the benefit of the other party and the other intended for one's own self. Now what matters is what you make the other party understand. If the other party takes the ordinary sense, which alone is possible, then that party is deceived. You have been guilty of deceit. That the word is capable of another meaning which you may produce in a court of law if somebody accuses you having told a lie, is nothing to the point, nothing at all to the point. And yet our people spend time and

---

* Govindaraja's comment referred to is as follows:

अकृतदार: असहकृतदार इत्यर्थः। "न वितथा परिहासकथास्वपि" इत्युक्तेः। "अनृतं नोक्तपूर्वं मे न च वक्ष्ये कदाचन" इत्युक्तेश्च अकृतदार इति नार्थः॥ IV. 7. 22. Ed.

energy and all their knowledge of Sanskrit grammar to split words as they please, to break them, take them out of their context and to produce a passage which taken in the plain way yields fine good common sense, but interpreted according to themselves, would produce an extraordinary meaning and would not save in the end the character of the party. Now there is in every language a thing of this kind—puns, you know. I think there is hardly a language, eastern, or western, which has not got it. Perhaps Sanskrit is richest in the facilities it affords to people for concocting passages which can be made to mean two things. The French language is peculiarly rich in this kind of thing. A pun there is described as a *double entendre* but that word has an implication that the second or the subtler meaning is somewhat obscene, not fit for the drawing-room. I think all ethicists will agree that equivocation is worse than a lie. In our own literature there is a form of speech in which a word or phrase or sentence has two meanings, one meant for the context, another, a deeper meaning, perhaps allegorical, perhaps referring to a future time when it will be realised in another sense altogether. You have words there either by accident or by the Poet's design so formed that while one meaning is applicable to the context and entirely satisfies the case, there is a farther meaning which can also be put upon the passage which does not interfere with this meaning but which perhaps indicates a coming state of things. They say a great Poet, a great sage or some one who, in the sphere of self-conquest has attained great merit, may sometimes say things which mean one thing but which have another meaning to be realised yet. Some power within you, or some outside power operating on you, makes you use such words as are charged with quite another meaning. That however is a very different thing from saying that words like अकृतदार: should be interpreted in such a way that they will save Rama from speaking untruth, that is to say, that they are capable of a certain sense which Rama alone knows but which is not present to the mind of the hearer. What matters really is that which enters the mind of the listener. If the mind of the listener is misled, then the blame does rest upon the speaker. The speaker cannot be acquitted. I have therefore no hesitation in believing that this passage was intended merely as a joke; and then I wish to read to you what a great commentator, Nagoji Bhatta, says in Tilaka on this subject. His testimony is worth having because he wrote after Govindaraja and with full knowledge of what that orthodox commentator has said on this point. This is what he says* "Some commentators wish to make out that अकृतदारः means 'a person who having married has not brought his wife with him and does not have her as his companion at the moment.' But really it seems to me that the passage is to be understood ordinarily, and we are to remember that the poet wishes us to understand that when a person is making a joke or *parihasa* a little deviation from the truth is no great harm or sin." And then here is the point. To show that Sri Rama could not have had as his plain straightforward meaning anything like what is usually ascribed to him by commentators, we have unequivocal testimony from what Lakshmana was saying. Lakshmana was making a joke which was meant to be regarded as nothing but a joke. Here no commentator can show his ingenuity.

एनां विरूपामसतीं करालां निर्णतोदरीम्।
भार्यां वृद्धां परित्यज्य त्वामेवैष भजिष्यति॥ III. 18. 11

Lakshmana describes Sita in this way using the words that Surpanakha had already applied to her, in order to show that Rama was the fitter husband. He said to her, "That gentleman is my master. I am his servant and if you marry me, you will have to be the servant of a servant and you will have to be Sita's servant also. How would you like it? No, that would not do at all. So marry him. He is the proper person. Why should he be tied down to that awkward looking woman? You cannot even see her stomach. She seems to have nothing (alluding playfully to her having a slender waist), she seems to be an old rotten creature. He will dismiss her, discard her and take you." Now there are many other slokas uttered by Lakshmana which clearly show that he was jesting, making fun of Surpanakha. But that silly creature was unable to understand that they were

* The Tilaka commentary referred to runs as follows:

अकृतदारोऽकृतपरदारपरिग्रह इति, धातूनामनेकार्थत्वादसन्निहितदार इति वा हृदिस्थोऽर्थः। न हि रामो मिथ्या ब्रूते। परिहासादौ मिथ्याभाषणे न दोष इत्यनेन सूच्यते इति वयम्। एवमुत्तरत्रापि॥ Ed.

making fun of her. She took everything literally. From Rama she was thrown on to Lakshmana and Lakshmana threw her back on Rama. She was quite willing to be tossed this way and that and finally, coming to Rama, she says, "Now look here. I am going to marry you. If you think Sita is an obstacle, I shall simply eat her up now, this moment." So saying, she moves forward towards Sita.

इति सा लक्ष्मणेनोक्ता कराला निर्णतोदरी ।

She took it as literal truth,

मन्यते तद्वचस्तथ्यं परिहासाविचक्षणा ॥ III. 18. 13

not being able to understand that it was a joke. She took the words in their ordinary meaning. That shows you therefore that both Rama and Lakshmana took part in this little joke. Now you know the sequel, how when she actually went to Sita's side in order to molest her, Rama said, "No more joking. You have carried it too far, my dear brother."

तां मृत्युपाशप्रतिमामापतन्तीं महाबलः ।
निगृह्य रामः कुपितस्ततो लक्ष्मणमब्रवीत् ॥ III. 18. 18

Then he became angry for the first time. The Poet uses the word निगृह्य which gives rise to little scruple. Some would understand the word to mean merely preventing Surpanakha by a threat or by making the sound 'Hm' or by showing his hand. I do not know why it is necessary to restrict it that way. It may even be that Rama pulled her back, no harm in saying so. But apparently in the eyes of these people it is not right to show Rama as having touched that wretched creature. So Rama says

क्रूरैरनार्यैः सौमित्रे परिहासः कथंचन ।
न कार्यः पश्य वैदेहीं कथंचित्सौम्य जीवतीम् ॥ III. 18. 19

Sita is nearly gone, is just saved in time. So when we make a joke hereafter, we must know with whom to make it. You must not make it with people of this kind, gross stupid creatures who live only in the flesh and do not understand anything of the mind.

इमां विरूपामसतीमतिमत्तां महोदरीम् ।
राक्षसीं पुरुषव्याघ्र विरूपयितुमर्हसि ॥ III. 18. 20

The next point will keep us a little. It is somewhat elaborate. So I will stop here for the day, requesting you only to remember that on a plain reading of this portion it appears that Sri Rama was only indulging in an innocent joke, that he was having a little fun. Poor man, he and his wife and Lakshmana were in the forest, all thrown on themselves and had only each other's company. What do you know of a railway journey of two or three days? You get sick of the whole thing. You want something to relieve you. Here were three people constantly in each other's company, wanting some little relief. Surpanakha came and afforded them scope for a little jest. What is there wrong in supposing that Sri Rama partook of it when he himself uses words like परिहास, भर्ता, भार्या ! No harm. We do not save him at all by saying that he equivocated with the word अकृतदारः. If he did, he was even more guilty as if he lied. He neither lied nor equivocated; he was only joking.

SEVENTH LECTURE*

When I last spoke, I was on the Surpanakha episode. The poet, I pointed out, treats it as a proper subject for the display of his humour. But its humorous aspect is overshadowed by the consequences that followed from it. It may be described in a way as the seed-plot for the whole story; for it was Surpanakha, unable to reconcile herself to her humiliation, that set up the brothers Khara and Dushana, and later on, after their death, went to Ravana and stirred him up also. That this aspect of it is really important appears from the latter part of the poem. After the promiscuous battle in Lanka, in which large hosts of monkeys and Rakshasas met, and the monkeys, hard pressed in the fight, went to Rama and besought him to help them out of the difficulty, he took part in this great battle; and it was then that he played one of his marvellous tricks. He assumed myriad forms; one Rama appeared before each combatant. Sometimes he appeared in his own form, single; sometimes he was not visible at all, so confounding the enemy, it is said, that he made a great holocaust, destroyed lakhs upon lakhs of people, thus creating in the city of Lanka bereavement and grief upon an unexampled scale. In the next sarga the poet describes a very remarkable scene; you get a very large number of these Rakshasa women, some that had lost their husbands and been widowed, some that had lost their fathers and protectors, some their brothers, some their sons. All these women met together and, holding one another in their arms, made a huge cry of lamentation, much as our women used to do in our time, but, I suppose on a considerably larger scale. And then, fancy, a remarkable scene occurs. Here again the poet's sense of humour and his profound knowledge of human nature come out in bright display. These women, as is their nature in any great calamity, threw the blame for their great misfortune upon a person of their own sex. "Some woman is at the bottom of this," they said, "and who can it be but Surpanakha who went and defied Rama himself"? They ascribed the whole of the misfortune that came upon Lanka and its people to the mischief originated by Surpanakha in her meeting with Sri Rama. Once more

---

* 25-5-'44.

the poet is amused. He cannot think of Surpanakha and Rama meeting each other without being excited. This is the lamentation of these Rakshasa women, deprived of their sons, brothers, fathers, husbands.

कथं शूर्पणखा वृद्धा कराला निर्णतोदरी ।
आससाद वने रामं कन्दर्पमिव रूपिणम् ॥
सुकुमारं महासत्त्वं सर्वभूतहिते रतम् ।
तं दृष्ट्वा लोकवध्या सा हीनरूपा प्रकामिता ॥
कथं सर्वगुणैर्हीना गुणवन्तं महौजसम् ।
सुमुखं दुर्मुखी रामं कामयामास राक्षसी ॥
जनस्यास्याल्पभाग्यत्वाद्वलिनी श्वेतमूर्धजा ।
अकार्यमपहास्यं च सर्वलोकविगर्हितम् ॥
राक्षसानां विनाशाय दूषणस्य खरस्य च ।
चकाराप्रतिरूपा सा राघवस्य प्रधर्षणम् ॥
तन्निमित्तमिदं वैरं रावणेन कृतं महत् ।
वधाय सीता सानीता दशग्रीवेण रक्षसा ॥ VI. 95. 6-11

"Why should this woman provoke him? What chance had she with him, this woman who is fit for nothing but destruction at the hands of the world? Rama swore vengeance because of this. Ravana will bring about his own destruction and the destruction of everybody connected with him, and there will be an end to all soon." So said the women. That is the significance of the Surpanakha episode.

Now we come to the scene in the Aranyakanda, where Sri Rama, not being able to bear the thought that Sita had been taken away from his protection when he was away, and not being able to bear the pangs of grief, loses his balance of mind, and becomes unhinged. Through passage after passage he says the most excruciating things. There is no end to his agony. The poet surpasses himself in these scenes. The real truth is that Rama is beside himself and does not know what he says. We have occasionally heard of people who fall into such fits of grief and are unhinged in mind, but they are comparatively rare in these days. I shall speak later on of some characteristics of the poet and his descriptions, when it will be my duty to point out that in those old days men and women gave way to their emotions without any attempt at self-control, and not even a hero of the stature of Rama was free from it. I have picked out just a few passages. Here Rama has excited himself into an abnormal fit of impatience with the whole world, and is angry with everybody. He has been addressing the waters, the trees, the ground, the beasts and the birds, but nothing responds. Then he thinks of the gods. They at least must know everything. "They have concealed her from me, and I shall now use all the force at my command. I will destroy everything if they will not give her back to me." Fancy the paroxysm of grief that overcomes him, the greatest man of the world, one who teaches *dharma* at every stage. He, losing his wife, is thrown into this most extraordinary fit. Then, in his anger, he forces out of Lakshmana's hands the great bow and says,

> लक्ष्मणादथ चादाय रामो निष्पीड्य कार्मुकम् ।
> शरमादाय संदीप्त घोरमाशीविषोपमम् ॥
> सन्दधे धनुषि श्रीमान् रामः परपुरञ्जयः ।
> युगान्ताग्निरिव क्रुद्ध इदं वचनमब्रवीत् ॥
> यथा जरा यथा मृत्युर्यथा कालो यथा विधिः ।
> नित्यं न प्रतिहन्यन्ते सर्वभूतेषु लक्ष्मण ॥
> तथाहं क्रोधसंयुक्तो न निवार्योऽस्म्यसंशयम् ।
> पुरेव मे चारुदतीमनिन्दितां दिशन्ति सीतां यदि नाद्य मैथिलीम् ।
> सदेवगन्धर्वमनुष्यपन्नगं जगत्सशैलं परिवर्तयाम्यहम् ॥ III. 64. 75-78

"No scourge will be so fierce as I am going to be. I am up now and nothing shall stop me. I am going to take full toll of this universe." And he includes सदेवपन्नग. Not that he means it; he does not know what he says. That is the condition to which his grief has brought him. You cannot suppose that Rama in full command of his senses would say such things, and yet that is the condition to which he has been brought by the transport of his emotion. Then it falls to the lot of Lakshmana to comfort him. That is somewhat unusual, for Lakshmana is the angry man, and Rama the soft one. The position is now reversed. Lakshmana says nice things.

पुरा भूत्वा मृदुर्दान्तः सर्वभूतहिते रतः ।
न क्रोधवशमापन्नः प्रकृतिं हातुमर्हसि ॥
चन्द्रे लक्ष्मीः प्रभा सूर्ये गतिर्वायौ भुवि क्षमा ।
एतच्च नियतं सर्वं त्वयि चानुत्तमं यशः ।
एकस्य नापराधेन लोकान् हन्तुं त्वमर्हसि ॥
त्वमेव हि पुरा राम मामेवं बहुशोऽन्वशाः ।
अनुशिष्याद्धि को नु त्वामपि साक्षाद् बृहस्पतिः ॥
बुद्धिश्च ते महाप्राज्ञ देवैरपि दुरन्वया ।
शोकेनाभिप्रसुप्तं ते ज्ञानं संबोधयाम्यहम् ॥

III. 65. 4-6; 66. 18-19

"You were gentle to all, with your emotions in strict control and actuated by benevolence to all life. Just because you are angry, can you run away from your nature? No, just as it is impossible to separate the moon from his splendour, impossible to separate the effulgence of *surya* from him, impossible to take away movement from *vayu*, just as all these things are natural and you cannot take these qualities away from where they inhere, so from you, your great character for a gentle nature and a benevolent mind cannot be taken away. Do not become a stranger to your own nature. That wicked creature Ravana has taken away your wife and why do you propose to punish the whole universe of life? Is it so impossible to find him out and punish him and recover the lost jewel? Give up this enterprise, and let us make a search and find her out. If I lost my temper and said such foolish things, I would be reprimanded and put right by you. If you are going to play this part, who is going to fulfil your pledge? I am not trying to be your teacher. Only, I find that, unable to bear your grief, you have allowed your usual good sense to go to sleep. I am just trying to awaken that good sense, that is all." A little later they meet the body of Jatayus on the way, lying in his last gasp, just waiting, before he gave up the ghost, to meet Sri Rama and tell him what had happened to his wife. Learning the truth from him, they do the last thing to him, as a pious son would do to his father; they burn his body, and Sri Rama, in his infinite mercy, sends the soul of Jatayus to its final abode. Then Rama says, "Fourfold is my calamity. This bird, who tried to do me a little service, he is gone too. This my calamity is worse than fire. It is so great that it will destory *agni himself*." You see therefore how when great misfortunes occur, even great ones lose their balance and say things that they should not say, and put themselves in a most pitiable condition, when we can only get hold of them, wipe their tears, ask them to sit down, throw water on their faces if possible, and wait until the fit of grief passes away. I am trying to show you that Sri Rama was not above this.

Now I come to another feature of his character which is also a great proof, on the one hand, that he was a human being and, on the other, that our poet was a great student, an unsurpassed student, of human nature. In the Kishkindha kanda one side of Rama's character is depicted with that degree of subtleness by our poet which readers often miss. I shall try, with your good leave, to bring it out. You remember how, having made Sugriva king instead of Vali, he was invited to come into the kingdom and take part in the festivities. But Rama says, "I am under a vow (he did not take the vow when he left Ayodhya) not to enter a township and I cannot come into Kishkindha where you are going to be anointed. I shall stay out here. You may get the ceremony of coronation performed there." So he chooses his abode on the Prasravana hill and settles down there immediately after the coronation. Sugriva gives himself up at once to the enjoyment of his extraordinary fortune, and he becomes a slave of wine, woman and music and really indulges in an orgy of sensual passion. But this is the very beginning. Rama has taken his abode outside. See how the poet works Sri Rama up. Rama hears the riotous noise in the city. No malice in this, but he notices it. Things which he would not ordinarily notice now strike him because he is in such a condition himself. He thinks, "I am the cause of it all. Sugriva has recovered his kingdom and his wife, and it is all through me." Then Lakshmana has once more to play the part of a comforter. He tells Rama, "Please wait patiently until *sarad* comes. We have got to wait four months, and you are already getting impatient." Then he comforts himself with the thought:

> उपकारेण वीरस्तु प्रतिकारेण युज्यते ।
> अकृतशोऽप्रतिकृतो हन्ति सत्त्ववतां मनः ॥ IV. 27. 45

"This world will be an unfit place to live in, and people will lose faith in each other, if persons like Sugriva, being in the position of one who has received immeasurable benefit, turned ungrateful and forgot how much they have got to return. Else the peace of mind of people like me will be destroyed. No, that calamity will not happen." But soon the other thought comes to him. Lakshmana says finally to him:

नियम्य कोपं प्रतिपाल्यतां शरत् क्षमस्व मासांश्चतुरो मया सह ।
वसाचलेऽस्मिन् मृगराजसेविते संवर्धयन् शत्रुवधे समुद्यमम् ॥ IV. 27. 48

"Wait till autumn comes. Listen to me and wait patiently for the expiry of these four months. You are not an impatient person; you are strong enough by yourself to get all you want in this world; and you are competent by your own unaided strength to conquer. You have now got Sugriva and there is no need to lose your patience."

Another characteristic of the poet which I shall have the privilege to point out, if I get so far, is his great mastery, the unequalled mastery, of comparisons and similes. They pour out of his mouth helter-skelter. Most of them are apt, striking, beautiful, yielding the utmost literary pleasure to the sensitive critic. Here is a great succession of similes too. Notice how able the poet is, how keen a student of human nature. Rama being in this state of mind and full of the thoughts of his wife and unable to bear the separation, the similes take a curious form.

एषा घर्मपरिक्लिष्टा नववारिपरिप्लुता ।
सीतेव शोकसंतप्ता मही बाष्पं विमुञ्चति ॥
एष फुल्लार्जुनः शैलः केतकैरधिवासितः ।
सुग्रीव इव शान्तारिर्धाराभिरभिषिच्यते ॥ IV. 28. 7, 9

See how the natural order of things is reversed. Instead of comparing Sita to the natural objects he describes the natural objects and mentions Sita as the standard of comparison; that is to say, while observing the extraordinary things of nature, his mind is full of her, and he cannot but think of her.

नीलमेघाश्रिता विद्युत्स्फुरन्ती प्रतिभाति मे ।
स्फुरन्ती रावणस्याङ्के वैदेहीव तपस्विनी ॥ IV. 28. 12

You see clearly what this means. Now the rainy season is at its height, and the severity of the rain makes it difficult for Rama to bear his grief.

इमाः स्फीतगुणा वर्षाः सुग्रीवः सुखमश्नुते ।
विजितारिः सदारश्च राज्ये महति च स्थितः ॥
अहं तु हृतदारश्च राज्याच्च महतश्च्युतः ।
नदीकूलमिव क्लिन्नमवसीदामि लक्ष्मण ॥ IV. 28. 57-58

"Having regained his wife and obtained his kingdom, Sugriva is happy. But I pine here while he is enjoying himself."

अयात्रां चैव दृष्ट्वेमां मार्गांश्च भृशदुर्गमान् ।
प्रणते चैव सुग्रीवे न मया किंचिदीरितम् ॥
अपि चातिपरिक्लिष्टं चिराद्दारैः समागतम् ।
आत्मकार्यगरीयस्त्वाद्वक्तुं नेच्छामि वानरम् ॥
स्वयमेव हि विश्रम्य ज्ञात्वा कालमुपागतम् ।
उपकारं च सुग्रीवो वेत्स्यते नात्र संशयः ॥ IV. 28. 60-62

"When Sugriva was at my feet, just before the coronation, I could have commanded him to do anything. But I did not wish to say a word about what his duty was to me. I treated him with so much consideration. I took pity on him, I said I would not make trouble for him, and I forbore."

Now we come to another little scene to understand the sequel. Sugriva has amongst his ministers a person of unsurpassed foresight and wisdom, Hanuman. Knowing that the time had nearly expired, he goes to Sugriva and calls him out of the harem and expostulates with him. "You have received so much from Rama, but you have forgotten him and are annoying him by your indulgence. The time is up. Please wake up and do your duty." Sugriva gives orders to his commander-in-chief to bring all the monkeys from every quarter of the kingdom, so that they may all assemble together, and says to Hanuman, "when the monkeys assemble here or while they are assembling, do everything yourself and do not wait for me to give the orders."

सुग्रीवः सत्त्वसंपन्नश्चकार मतिमुत्तमाम् ।
संदिदेशातिमतिमान् नीलं नित्यकृतोद्यमम् ॥
दिक्षु सर्वासु सर्वेषां सैन्यानामुपसंग्रहे ।
यथा सेना समग्रा मे यूथपालाश्च सर्वशः ॥
समागच्छन्त्यसङ्गेन सेनाग्राणि तथा कुरु ।

* * *

स्वयं चानन्तरं सैन्यं भवानेवानुपश्यतु ॥
त्रिपञ्चरात्रादूर्ध्वं यः प्राप्नुयान्नेह वानरः ।
तस्य प्राणान्तिको दण्डो नात्र कार्या विचारणा ॥
हरींश्च वृद्धानुपयातु साङ्गदो भवान्ममाज्ञामधिकृत्य निश्चिताम् ।
इति व्यवस्थां हरिपुंगवेश्वरो विधाय वेश्म प्रविवेश वीर्यवान् ॥

IV. 29. 29-34

This is an instance of Sugriva-ajna. The order must be implicitly obeyed. Any departure from his order will be at once visited with extreme punishment, nothing less. "If anyone comes here after the fifteenth day, his life is forfeit." Having given this order for the mobilisation of his army, he goes back to his harem. He ought to have remembered that he was dealing with a very human being. Rama loses his balance once more. He does not know what Sugriva has done within the margin of time allowed to him. He makes no inquiry. In his ignorance therefore his anger mounts up. He loses once more all respect for his ally, and gives vent to his anger in many *slokas* which I have no time to quote. But I am going to read, not translate, three *slokas*. I do not know what the poet meant by putting them in here. They are first class poetry, but they have sentiments and words which are not proper in the mouth of Sri Rama. One would have thought that the poet wanted to say these things in his own capacity, but having made Sri Rama the describer, puts these verses into his mouth. But why should Valmiki himself go into these things? It is characteristic of the later poets to whom decency of speech is not always a binding rule.

चञ्चच्चन्द्रकरस्पर्शहर्षोन्मीलिततारका ।
अहो रागवती सन्ध्या जहाति स्वयमम्बरम् ॥
दर्शयन्ति शरन्नद्यः पुलिनानि शनैश्शनैः ।
नवसङ्गमसव्रीडा जघनानीव योषितः ॥

मीनोपसंदर्शितमेखलानां नदीवधूनां गतयोऽद्य मन्दाः ।
कान्तोपभुक्तालसगामिनीनां प्रभातकालेष्विव कामिनीनाम् ॥

IV. 30. 45. 46. 55

It is blasphemy to put this into Sri Rama's mouth. Either it shows that Rama's mind for the time being dwelt in these images, or, being at the business himself of describing the *sarad* and having to say these things, the poet put them into the mouth of that person.

I read to you Rama's severe order against Sugriva.* I told you also how Lakshmana took it and how he magnified it in his own excitable mind, and where he was only to communicate a threat, threatened to execute; and then Sri Rama was horrified at the effect of his own threat. Rama said, "That is not what I meant. Speak softly and gently." But Lakshmana forgets everything. I then read to you this *sloka*:

न च संकुचितः पन्था येन वाली हतो गतः ।
समये तिष्ठ सुग्रीव मा वालिपथमन्वगाः ॥ IV. 30. 81

This is what Sri Rama says to Lakshmana in order that he may communicate it to Sugriva. But there is another place where again Sri Rama, it seems to me, falls below his own level, and it gives you at once the state of mind in which he was.

एक एव रणे वाली शरेण निहतो मया ।
त्वां तु सत्यादतिक्रान्तं हनिष्यामि सबान्धवम् ॥ IV. 30. 82

"I killed Vali, but let him die all alone. In your case my anger is so great that I shall not be satisfied with killing you; I shall kill all your kith and kin." Then you remember how Tara pacifies Lakshmana. It is worth while at this stage to read some of her beautiful *slokas* to show you what an ancient Portia she was. Many of our advocates may learn lessons from this speech of Tara, where she addresses serious arguments to Lakshmana, and finding that they had produced an effect on him, tells him what will finally clinch the matter.

* Vide pp. 50-51.

नैवं लक्ष्मण वक्तव्यो नायं परुषमर्हति।
हरीणामीश्वरः श्रोतुं तव वक्त्राद्विशेषतः॥
नैवाकृतज्ञः सुग्रीवो न शठो नापि दारुणः।
नैवानृतकथो वीर न जिह्मश्च कपीश्वरः॥
उपकारं कृतं वीरो नाप्ययं विस्मृतः कपिः।
रामेण वीर सुग्रीवो यदन्यैर्दुष्करं रणे॥
रामप्रसादात्कीर्तिं च कपिराज्यं च शाश्वतम्।
प्राप्तवानिह सुग्रीवो रुमां मां च परंतप॥
रुमां मां कपिराज्यं च धनधान्यवसूनि च।
रामप्रियार्थं सुग्रीवस्त्यजेदिति मतिर्मम॥ IV. 35. 2-5, 13

"My husband is the lord of monkeys, and he is a great king. Do not forget that. You treat him as if he were worse than a schoolboy. He is not ungrateful, and he does not deserve that. He has not forgotten what great benefits, what matchless good he has received at your brother's hands. My husband is so good a man and he has done his duty. I tell you, if you know his nature, you will admire it. There is nothing that Sugriva will not give up to please Rama."

त्वत्सहायनिमित्तं वै प्रेषिता हरिपुङ्गवाः।
आनेतुं वानरान् युद्धे सुबहून् हरियूथपान्॥
तांश्च प्रतीक्षमाणोऽयं विक्रान्तान् सुमहाबलान्।
राघवस्यार्थसिद्ध्यर्थं न निर्याति हरीश्वरः॥
कृतात्र संस्था सौमित्रे सुग्रीवेण यथा पुरा।
अद्य तैर्वानरैः सर्वैरागन्तव्यं महाबलैः॥
ऋक्षकोटिसहस्राणि गोलांगूलशतानि च।
अद्य त्वामुपयास्यन्ति जहि कोपमरिंदम॥ IV. 35. 19-22

Tara discovers that Lakshmana's anger has nearly evaporated. She says, "My husband has already given the necessary orders. He wants to come and tell you that everything is ready. The monkeys are all due to come on the fifteenth day, and you will see them in their crores upon crores." Then, being completely pacified, Lakshmana forgets his anger, is thoroughly satisfied that his anger has been misplaced and tells Sugriva, "I am sorry. Please forgive me. I lost my temper because I could not bear my brother pining there. Please go to him and tell him a word of consolation." As soon as Rama hears everything, his magnanimity once more asserts itself. In the joy of his heart he embraces Sugriva.

> इति ब्रुवाणं सुग्रीवं रामो धर्मभृतां वरः।
> बाहुभ्यां संपरिष्वज्य प्रत्युवाच कृताञ्जलिम्॥
> यदिन्द्रो वर्षते वर्षं न तच्चित्रं भवेद् भुवि।
> आदित्यो वा सहस्रांशुः कुर्याद्वितिमिरं नभः॥
> चन्द्रमा रश्मिभिः कुर्यात्पृथिवीं सौम्य निर्मलाम्।
> त्वद्विधो वापि मित्राणां प्रतिकुर्यात्परंतप॥ IV. 39. 1-3

"Is it a wonder if the lord of Heaven sends down rain on the parched earth? It is his nature. If the sun drives out all darkness from sky, is it a thing to be wondered at? Just as it is natural for Indra to pour down rain, for the moon to drive out warmth and unpleasantness from the world, just as it is his very nature for the sun to abolish darkness, so it is in the very nature of things for you to do." It is the very person who in the preceding sarga spoke so much against Sugriva. That means only this, that his real nature re-asserts itself here and he speaks his proper feeling.

Hitherto I was dwelling on those passages and episodes in the story where the human element in Rama's character comes out and comes out in intensity, just as, if you and I were worked up to a high pitch of anger, or impatience, or jealousy, we would work ourselves down to a very low state of mind. I shall be obliged to traverse the whole of the Ramayana up and down to pick out passages wherein either through his own lapse or through the weakness of others concerned with him, we may see how far he presented human nature. It is really unnecessary for me to dwell on these again and again, but lest there should be any doubt, I shall say a word. *In our human nature there are a higher and a lower nature, a superior good and a less good.* In those who are well trained and have obtained some mastery over their own will, the lower nature just appears, makes its appearance felt, but is soon put down, and the higher nature has full play and the man behaves properly. But if, as I said, through bad training, through evil example and through the wickedness of surrounding people, if through these various causes, good advice is not given at the proper time, we fall and go to pieces, we cause trouble to ourselves and to all about us. But in the case of great ones, what happens is not that there is no evil force, that there is no suggestion of wrong-doing, but that the moment they appear, as soon as this human nature asserts itself, the higher nature comes down with full force, crushes it and then has its own free play. So should we in our lives learn, as soon as some unworthy motive seems to prevail, to pull ourselves together firmly and strongly, remember the great ones who have gone before us, call to our aid their great moral precepts and tell ourselves that we must not give room to it. And then our higher nature will assert itself. There is a famous verse in which the higher and the lower natures join issue. It is a beautiful sloka. It is commonly applied to Dushyanta* when not remembering the episode of love between him and Sakuntala owing to a curse, he still is charmed with her beauty and struggles hard within himself, "Why should I renounce her? Why not take her?" The thought contends for mastery for a while. It is something before which saints lose their souls. What will great people say? What effect would it have on the reputation, on the fame of my *kula*?"

क्वाकार्यं शशलक्ष्मणः क्व च कुलम्, भूयोऽपि दृश्येत सा
दोषानां प्रशमाय नः श्रुतमहो, कोपेऽपि कान्तं मुखम्।
किं वक्ष्यन्त्यपकल्मषाः कृतधियः, स्वप्नेऽपि सा दुर्लभा
चेतः स्वास्थ्यमुपैहि, कः खलु युवा धन्योऽधरं धास्यति ॥

Give a chance for the higher nature to work its way, otherwise we are gone. Time after time Sri Rama curses his lower self and continually moves in action on the higher.

* Ed.'s Note: It is more commonly applied to Pururavas in Kalidasa's Vikramorvasiya, but really it is a verse spoken by king Yayati in a lost drama on Yayati and Sarmistha.

EIGHTH LECTURE*

Ladies and Gentlemen,—The point that I was speaking about when we last parted was that Sri Rama with characteristic generosity made amends in expressive language for his somewhat hasty displeasure with Sugriva. I am taking the point a little further today as it has some significance. In two or three more places later on in the epic Rama makes similar amends to Sugriva, and those occasions are worth a little study at our hands. I shall take up the earliest occasion, and, being tempted by the suggestiveness of the Poet's language, shall linger a while although it may seem I am irrelevant. The sloka occurs in the eighteenth sarga of Yuddha kanda. A word about the context. Vibhishana has come seeking earnestly the protection of Rama. Rama holds a Council of War as it were, asking his comrades and chief advisers which course to adopt. Nobody except Hanuman advises acceptance of Vibhishana's request. That is somewhat strange. The chief ground of the objection is that Vibhishana is a rakshasa, that he comes as an emissary of Ravana, perhaps to kill Rama when he is not on his guard. For, as Sugriva shrewdly says:

> ईदृशं व्यसनं प्राप्तं भ्रातरं यः परित्यजेत् ।
> को नाम स भवेत्तस्य यमेष न परित्यजेत् ॥ VI. 18. 5-6

"A brother who deserts his brother's side in the midst of such calamities—who may hope to find faith in him? Whom indeed will he not traitorously forsake?" Also, they say, 'he comes here to fulfil his ambition of becoming king of Lanka.' Sri Rama sets aside all these considerations. I shall read some verses containing sound common sense.

> उद्योगं तव संप्रेक्ष्य मिथ्यावृत्तं च रावणम् ।
> वालिनश्च वधं श्रुत्वा सुग्रीवं चाभिषेचितम् ॥
> राज्यं प्रार्थयमानश्च बुद्धिपूर्वमिहागतः ।
> एतावत्तु पुरस्कृत्य युज्यते त्वस्य संग्रहः ॥ VI. 17. 66-67

I call it common sense. "Seeing how able and watchful you are and knowing how wicked his brother is, hearing this

* 31-5-'44.

further fact that you killed Vali in order to instal Sugriva, and desiring to be king in the country—which is a natural ambition of those who are in the position of a younger brother, he has purposely come here; I think these considerations make it advisable to take him." That was Hanuman's straight advice. But notwithstanding Sri Rama's own opinion, now and then Sugriva, with Lakshmana behind him, took strong objection. Referring to Sugriva's remonstrance that Vibhishana had been faithless to his brother, Rama says:

> न सर्वे भ्रातरस्तात भवन्ति भरतोपमाः ।
> मद्विधा वा पितुः पुत्राः सुहृदो वा भवद्विधाः ॥ VI. 18. 15-16

This is a famous sloka, and it bears a lot of meaning. I am going to dwell on it today on all sides. The last point is the one relevant to the point which I am on; सुहृदो वा भवद्विधाः indicates the repentance of Sri Rama for former harshness to Sugriva. "In the world there are few allies and friends so trustworthy as you are," says Rama to Sugriva. It gives a complete acquittance to Sugriva—'no ally like you' says Rama to him—and why is it so? The comment is significant. 'When in my impatience I imagined that you had forgotten your promise and undertaking, I charged Lakshmana with a harsh message, and he in his own way did not mitigate its severity. Forgetting the injustice done to you on that occasion you have given me valiant assistance.' So explain the commentators; Rama's words are a full appreciation of Sugriva's services. The Poet seems here and in this case to be teaching us this great lesson in human relationship, viz., that when a friendship or understanding or a bond of love is created, one way, a certain way, of strengthening it is for the parties to fall out and then become reconciled. That is a great fact which novelists and story-tellers employ,—to create a division and then a reconciliation. The affection is strengthened then. So it seems to be between Sri Rama and Sugriva. It is possible where you have a noble and generous nature on both sides; where you have exalted characters, once good faith is established between them, differences only go to fortify the good will.

In this world certain people are taken as examples of excellence in certain relationships. He who is an ideal brother may not be an ideal son, an ideal friend may not be an ideal brother, and so on. So Sri Rama takes different people as examples for different relationships. Of the ideal brother Bharata is the outstanding example, Vibhishana was not so. Sri Rama might have well said so. Bharata was, you all know why. Of course, what occurs to you immediately is that when the kingdom of Ayodhya fell to Bharata by every right, Rama having relinquished it and betaken himself to the forest, and Kaikeyi having obtained it from Dasaratha as a boon for him, when the kingdom came to him, he surrenders it to his elder brother in an extraordinary way. He goes to the forest attended by all his people and he begs them all to back his own request. And yet Sri Rama refuses. But the high quality of Bharata's character comes out here.

तदानुपूर्व्यां युक्तं च युक्तं चात्मनि मानद ।
राज्यं प्राप्नुहि धर्मेण सकामान् सुहृदः कुरु ॥ II. 104. 10

'In our family of Ikshvaku, the eldest son has the claim to this throne; you are pre-eminently fitted to wear the crown,' says he. But Sri Rama's point of view is quite different. It is not a matter of succession. To him the great thing is to save the honour of his father, to redeem his solemn promise and ensure his passage into heaven. He must vindicate the honour of his father. So said the Gandharvas and others who came to the place where Rama and Bharata pitted their wits against each other. The whole of the conversation was conducted on quite a high level. It was so elevated that the very gods descended and drank in every word of the conversation reported by the Poet with skill in verses remarkable for beauty and simplicity of diction. I have mentioned the principal points in the conversation of the brothers. At one stage when the arguments advanced by Bharata had all been met by Rama, the celestial witnesses intervene, and they speak to Bharata and give their verdict as it were. They say with one voice.

भरतं राजशार्दूलमित्यूचुः संगता वचः ॥
कुले जात महाप्राज्ञ महावृत्त महायशः ।
ग्राह्यं रामस्य वाक्यं ते पितरं यद्यवेक्षसे ॥ II. 112. 4-5

Of deep import are these vocatives addressed to Bharata by these inhabitants of the other world, who counsel him 'Sri

Rama speaks the truth in this matter; he hits the nail on the head.'

सदानृणमिमं रामं वयमिच्छामहे पितुः ।
अनृणत्वाच्च कैकेय्याः स्वर्गं दशरथो गतः ॥ II. 112. 6

'Your father made a great promise to Kaikeyi and there he is in debt to her. From that he must be redeemed. The only course is what your brother does. Otherwise it would have oppressed your father's soul. If he had acted contrary to your father's order before by crowning himself yuvaraj and you acquiesced in it, or if he accepts the kingdom now and carries out your father's command by proxy as besought by you, the immediate result will be that Dasaratha would go to hell." That was the unanimous verdict of the Gandharvas, Siddhas, Paramarishis, and Rajarishis. It was not therefore once that Sri Rama renounced the kingdom. When it fell back to him for a second time he stood faithful to his father and refused it again. So it was twice that he renounced the kingdom, properly speaking. Therefore he was fully justified when he says to Sugriva मद्विधा वा पितुः पुत्राः। I should read to you one or two statements of Sri Rama in the course of his argument with **Bharata.**

सोऽहं वनमिदं प्राप्तो निर्जनं लक्ष्मणान्वितः ।
सीतया चाप्रतिद्वन्द्वः सत्यवादे स्थितः पितुः ॥
भवानपि तथेत्येव पितरं सत्यवादिनम् ।
कर्तुमर्हति राजेन्द्र क्षिप्रमेवाभिषेचनात् ॥ II. 107. 8-9

"Standing on our father's promise I have come to the great forest with Sita and Lakshmana. Our father laid a command on you and me. The part resting on me I have fulfilled. The other you must fulfil. While my part requires me to go to the forest, your part requires you to be in the kingdom."

ऋणान्मोचय राजानं मत्कृते भरत प्रभुम् ।
पितरं त्राहि धर्मज्ञ मातरं चाभिनन्दय ॥ II. 107. 10

"You must do this for my sake, I enjoin you. Protect your father and please your mother,"—all proper things to do and a duty resting on Bharata. And then he adds—

लक्ष्मीश्चन्द्रादपेयाद्वा हिमवान् वा हिमं त्यजेत् ।
अतीयात्सागरो वेलां न प्रतिज्ञामहं पितुः ॥ II. 112. 18

"It is impossible that I should neglect father's promise," he says, and he ranks the impossibility among these natural impossibilities.

कामाद्वा तात लोभाद्वा मात्रा तुभ्यमिदं कृतम् ।
न तन्मनसि कर्तव्यं वर्तितव्यं च मातृवत् ॥ II. 112. 19

When Bharata is alone he thinks ill of his mother. His idea of the gross inequity of Kaikeyi is so strong that he cannot mention her without some vile adjective.

धर्मबन्धेन बद्धोऽस्मि तेनेमां नेह मातरम् ।
हन्मि तीव्रेण दण्डेन दण्डार्हां पापकारिणीम् ॥ II. 106. 9-10

"I will kill her but for my brother" he told Satrughna.

हन्यामहमिमां पापां कैकेयीं दुष्टचारिणीम् ।
यदि मां धार्मिको रामो नासूयेन्मातृघातकम् ॥ II. 78. 22

A strange and romantic lover of Dharma! Rama knows this unfilial trait in Bharata and thinks it is wrong. So at the time of taking leave he enjoins on him this:—

मातरं रक्ष कैकेयीं मा रोषं कुरु तां प्रति ।
मया च सीतया चैव शप्तोऽसि रघुसत्तम ॥ II. 112. 27-28

"I charge you and swear to you by me and by my wife Sita, treat Kaikeyi with respect and with consideration."

Now I come to a point, ladies and gentlemen, where I go on my own a bit as it were. While for every single relationship one man can be taken as a pattern, for brotherliness, for filial duty, and for faithful friendship, there is one person, Sri Rama, who was a model in respect of all these relationships. In him Valmiki gives us an ideal son, an ideal brother, an ideal friend and an ideal enemy too. We have spoken of him as an ideal son, and when he himself speaks of himself as an ideal son, according to Dandin and others, it is not a boast but a true statement.* We shall speak of him next as a brother, how much better brother, Rama was. Perhaps the Poet means 'younger brother,' when he refers to Bharata as a pattern brother. To see how Rama behaved

*स्वगुणाविष्क्रिया दोषो नात्र भूतार्थशंसिनः ॥ Kavyadarsa I. 24

to Bharata we must go back a little. You remember how in the latter half of Ayodhya kanda, in the conversation between the brothers, finding Bharata somewhat obstinate, Rama said, "You say Father was a fool, was in his dotage. Long before, there was a promise which our father had made when he married Kaikeyi.

पुरा भ्रातः पिता नः स मातरं ते समुद्वहन्।
मातामहे समाश्रौषीद्राज्यशुल्कमनुत्तमम्॥ II. 107. 3

That promise is still binding. Don't set aside that." Unfortunately there is no other allusion to this promise. Why did not Kaikeyi herself mention it? Why did not her monitress mention it? Why did not Sumantra mention it? Nobody mentions it, we are left wondering why. Various explanations are offered. The important point is that there was one man who had an uneasy consciousness of it. He was King Dasaratha. Apparently he remembered it, but then as the brothers grew up, Sri Rama outshone the others so decisively that he was the universal favourite. The other brothers were far, far behind him, so that even Kaikeyi's father apparently forgot it, or thought it prudent not to press it. When Dasaratha desired to make Sri Rama yuvaraja, he thought it was a favourable circumstance that Bharata was absent in his maternal uncle's country with Satrughna. He omitted to send invitations to Asvapati and Janaka, ostensibly on account of the great distance. The real reason was that he remembered the promise he had made to Asvapati! So he says to Sri Rama—

विप्रोषितश्च भरतो यावदेव पुरादितः।
तावदेवाभिषेकस्ते प्राप्तकालो मतो मम॥ II. 4. 25

"While Bharata is away, that is the time most opportune to crown you. No doubt Bharata is a good chap; he goes the way in which the righteous persons go; still—

किं तु चित्तं मनुष्याणामनित्यमिति मे मतिः। II. 4. 27

I know that men's minds are not constant." The meaning is not clear from the text, but apparently he means that even in the case of persons like Bharata, the *fait accompli* is the best course for avoiding difficulties. One point occurs to me here. Why did not Sri Rama contradict his father knowing as he did Bharata's character? He did not. Not that he endorsed what Dasaratha said, but he did not gainsay him. And, ladies and gentlemen, let me say this. Like father, like son! This element of suspicion was not wholly off Sri Rama's heart! When on returning to Ayodhya after the conquest of Lanka he passes Bharadvaja's hermitage, he revolves in his mind what might happen, calls Hanuman and says to him: "I trust your judgment. Fly at once in advance, and return to me with a bit of knowledge. Go to Bharata and tell him the story, and watch his face, note his gestures and each change of look and attitude, and find out how he stands relatively to me so that I may regulate my behaviour." Here comes the magnificent love of truth, fidelity to human nature in the Poet's depiction of character. He wants us to understand that in royal families when something great is at stake it is the commonest thing in the best friends to distrust best friends. Rama inherited this.

एतच्छ्रुत्वा यमाकारं भजते भरतस्तदा ॥
स च ते वेदितव्यः स्यात् सर्वं यच्चापि मां प्रति ।
ज्ञेयाश्च सर्वे वृत्तान्ता भरतस्येङ्गितानि च ॥
तत्त्वेन मुखवर्णेन दृष्टया व्याभाषणेन च ।
सर्वकामसमृद्धं हि हस्त्यश्वरथसंकुलम् ॥
पितृपैतामहं राज्यं कस्य नावर्तयेन्मनः ।
सङ्गत्या भरतः श्रीमान् राज्यार्थी चेत्स्वयं भवेत् ॥
प्रशास्तु वसुधां कृत्स्नामखिलां रघुनन्दनः ।
तस्य बुद्धिं च विज्ञाय व्यवसायं च वानर ॥
यावन्न दूरं याताः स्म क्षिप्रमागन्तुमर्हसि ॥ IV. 128. 12-17

"Who will not cling to an ancient, hereditary, and prosperous kingdom, strongly protected by its four-fold army, which has fallen into his lap? Should Bharata administering it day by day during these fourteen years have grown attached to it by use and wont, it would be perfectly natural. Let him fill the throne and rule all the earth, why not?" "So," says Rama to Hanuman—and this is the most important point—"go and learn where his feelings lie and which way his real mind tends." Ladies and gentlemen, it is not my purpose at all to hint that there is any sinister motive behind this probing into Bharata's mind and the direction of his thoughts or desires. His father's feeling was a real, malignant suspicion. This suspicion of Rama's is sublimated. That thought which in Dasaratha's case savours of some, even if only slight, hostility, is in Sri Rama's case sublimated. "If it is Bharata's desire to cotinue to hold the reins of the kingdom, I am not going to stand in the way. Let me go back to Dandaka." That is Sri Rama! *The Ideal Brother*—methinks it is *Sri Rama*, not even Bharata. If there is a greater proof of brotherliness, I don't know it.

I want to say a word to you about Rama as an enemy. For, even to the enemy he was considerate. His treatment of Vali after having killed him on the field of battle is righteous. Ravana desired to kill Hanuman when he posed as the ambassador of Sugriva. When well-known spies of Ravana, Suka and Sarana, were discovered by Vibhishana's keen eyes, Sri Rama's treatment of them was considerate. He not only pardoned them but gave them liberty to see everything and learn all they wanted from Vibhishana. But for Rama's mercy they would have been killed by the monkeys. Look at the way he fought the enemy. When Garuda comes announcing himself as Sri Rama's dear friend and external self who has come to help him and Lakshmana—

अहं सखा ते काकुत्स्थ प्रियः प्राणो बहिश्चरः ।
गरुत्मानिह संप्राप्तो युवयोः साह्यकारणात् ॥ VI. 50. 46

he uses an extraordinary expression—

सखे राघव धर्मज्ञ रिपूणामपि वत्सल । VI. 50. 56

"You who love even your enemies!"—a remarkable description of one of the chief qualities of Sri Rama.

One last point. When Vibhishana, recollecting that no love was lost between him and Ravana, is overcome by a scruple whether it would be right and proper for him to perform his brother's obsequies, it is left to Rama to recognise his enemy's greatness.

अवश्यं तु क्षमं वाच्यो मया त्वं राक्षसेश्वर ।
अधर्मानृतसंयुक्तः कामं त्वेष निशाचरः ॥
तेजस्वी बलवान् शूरः संयुगेषु च नित्यशः ।
शतक्रतुमुखैर्देवैः श्रूयते न पराजितः ॥
महात्मा बलसंपन्नो रावणो लोकरावणः । VI. 114. 99-101

Among warriors skill and abilities are considered the primary virtues. If one warrior is strong and valiant, it is enough to win the admiration of another warrior. So Sri Rama tells Vibhishana, "True enough, Ravana was false and wedded to unrighteousness. But it behoves you to remember what a great man he was. A man of infinite might and dauntless valour, he did not suffer defeat even at the hands of Indra and the gods.

मरणान्तानि वैराणि निर्वृत्तं नः प्रयोजनम् ॥
क्रियतामस्य संस्कारो ममाप्येष यथा तव । VI. 114. 101-102

"Hatred and strife cease when death has claimed the foe. Therefore let the last rites be duly paid by you to your brother." Fancy how far the notion of magnanimity can be carried when Sri Rama adds, "to me he stands in the same relation as you!" The commentators add, rightly, that the real meaning of ममाप्येष यथा तव is, "I regard him after his death in the relation of a brother to me. If you fail to perform his obsequies, I am prepared to do them." That is not an exaggerated meaning.

NINTH LECTURE*

The editors regret that no report of this Lecture exists. It dealt with the exile of Rama, with special reference to *him,* up to the coming of Bharata to Chitrakuta. The main heads compiled from the Lecturer's notes of the talk and the slokas read by him are given below.†

Rama devoted to Dharma—II. 2. 29, 31, 40-41.

रामः सत्पुरुषो लोके सत्यः सत्यपरायणः ।
साक्षाद्रामाद्विनिर्वृत्तो धर्मश्चापि श्रिया सह ॥
धर्मज्ञः सत्यसन्धश्च शीलवाननसूयकः ।
शान्तः सान्त्वयिता श्लक्ष्णः कृतज्ञो विजितेन्द्रियः ॥
व्यसनेषु मनुष्याणां भृशं भवति दुःखितः ।
उत्सवेषु च सर्वेषु पितेव परितुष्यति ॥

Rama's physical charm—II. 3. 28-30.

गन्धर्वराजप्रतिमं लोके विख्यातपौरुषम् ।
दीर्घबाहुं महासत्त्वं मत्तमातङ्गगामिनम् ॥
चन्द्रकान्ताननं राममतीव प्रियदर्शनम् ।
रूपौदार्यगुणैः पुंसां दृष्टिचित्तापहारिणम् ॥
घर्माभितप्ताः पर्जन्यं ह्लादयन्तमिव प्रजाः ।
न ततर्प समायान्तं पश्यमानो नराधिपः ॥

Kaikeyi to Manthara about Rama—II. 8. 14, 15, 18, 19.

धर्मज्ञो गुणवान्दान्तः कृतज्ञः सत्यवाञ्छुचिः ।
रामो राजसुतो ज्येष्ठो यौवराज्यमतोऽर्हति ॥
भ्रातॄन्भृत्यांश्च दीर्घायुः पितृवत्पालयिष्यति ।
यथा वै भरतो मान्यस्तथा भूयोऽपि राघवः ॥
कौसल्यातोऽतिरिक्तं च मम शुश्रूषते बहु ।
राज्यं यदि हि रामस्य भरतस्यापि तत्तदा ।
मन्यते हि यथात्मानं तथा भ्रातॄंस्तु राघवः ॥

---

* 7-6-'44.

† The readings being of the Bombay edition.

Dasaratha to Kaikeyi about Rama—II. 12. 85-86.

नालं द्वितीयं वचनं पुत्रो मां प्रतिभाषितुम् ।
स वनं प्रव्रजेत्युक्तो बाढमित्येव वक्ष्यति ॥
यदि मे राघवः कुर्याद्वनं गच्छेति चोदितः ।
प्रतिकूलं प्रियं मे स्यान्न तु वत्सः करिष्यति ॥
शुद्धभावो हि भावं मे न तु ज्ञास्यति राघवः ॥

Rama's indifference—People waited to see him anointed—II. 17. 10-15.

अलमद्य हि भुक्तेन परमार्थैरलं च नः ।
यदि पश्याम निर्यान्तं रामं राज्ये प्रतिष्ठितम् ॥
ततो हि नः प्रियतरं नान्यत्किंचिद्भविष्यति ।
यथाभिषेको रामस्य राज्येनामिततेजसः ॥
एताश्चान्याश्च सुहृदामुदासीनः शुभाः कथाः ।
आत्मसम्पूजनीः शृण्वन्ययौ रामो महापथम् ॥
न हि तस्मान्मनः कश्चिच्चक्षुषी वा नरोत्तमात् ।
नरः शक्नोत्यपाक्रष्टुमतिक्रान्तेऽपि राघवे ॥
यश्च रामं न पश्येत्तु यं च रामो न पश्यति ।
निन्दितः सर्वलोकेषु स्वात्माप्येनं विगर्हते ॥

Rama swears *obedience*—II. 18. 15-16.

अतोषयन्महाराजमकुर्वन्वा पितुर्वचः ।
मुहूर्तमपि नेच्छेयं जीवितुं कुपिते नृपे ॥
यतोमूलं नरः पश्येत्प्रादुर्भावमिहात्मनः ।
कथं तस्मिन्न वर्तेत प्रत्यक्षे सति दैवते ॥

Rama declares his heart—II. 18. 28-30.

अहो धिङ् नार्हसे देवि वक्तुं मामीदृशं वचः ।
अहं हि वचनाद्राज्ञः पतेयमपि पावके ॥
भक्षयेयं विषं तीक्ष्णं पतेयमपि चार्णवे ।
नियुक्तो गुरुणा पित्रा नृपेण च हितेन च ॥
तद् ब्रूहि वचनं देवि राज्ञो यदभिकाङ्क्षितम् ।
करिष्ये प्रतिजाने च रामो द्विर्नाभिभाषते ॥

Kaikeyi holds him down—II. 18. 34-35, 40.

यदि सत्यप्रतिज्ञं त्वं पितरं कर्तुमिच्छसि ।
आत्मानं च नरश्रेष्ठ मम वाक्यमिदं शृणु ॥
संनिदेशे पितुस्तिष्ठ यथानेन प्रतिश्रुतम् ।
एतत्कुरु नरेन्द्रस्य वचनं रघुनन्दन ।
सत्येन महता राम तारयस्व नरेश्वरम् ॥

'But why didn't Father tell me himself?'—II. 19. 6.

अलीकं मानसं त्वेकं हृदयं दहतीव मे ।
स्वयं यन्नाह मां राजा भरतस्याभिषेचनम् ॥

Kaikeyi pleaded—II. 19. 15.

व्रीडान्वितः स्वयं यच्च नृपस्त्वां नाभिभाषते ।
नैतत् किंचिन्नरश्रेष्ठ मन्युरेषोऽपनीयताम् ॥

Rama undertakes to go *at once* and makes a solemn protest; he sounds a high note—II. 19. 20, 22, 23, 25, 26.

नाहमर्थपरो देवि लोकमावस्तुमुत्सहे ।
विद्धि मामृषिभिस्तुल्यं विमलं धर्ममास्थितम् ॥
न ह्यतो धर्मचरणं किंचिदस्ति महत्तरम् ।
यथा पितरि शुश्रूषा तस्य वा वचनक्रिया ॥
अनुक्तोऽप्यत्रभवता भवत्या वचनादहम् ।
वने वत्स्यामि विजने वर्षाणीह चतुर्दश ॥
यावन्मातरमापृच्छे सीतां चानुनयाम्यहम् ।
ततोऽद्यैव गमिष्यामि दण्डकानां महद्वनम् ॥
भरतः पालयेद्राज्यं शुश्रूषेच्च पितुर्यथा ।
तथा भवत्या कर्तव्यं स हि धर्मः सनातनः ॥

Sita's account of this transaction to Ravana—III. 47. 14-18.

कैकेयी मम भर्तारमित्युवाच द्रुतं वचः ।
तव पित्रा समाज्ञप्तं ममेदं शृणु राघव ॥
भरताय प्रदातव्यमिदं राज्यमकण्टकम् ।
त्वया तु खलु वस्तव्यं नव वर्षाणि पञ्च च ॥

वने प्रव्रज काकुत्स्थ पितरं मोचयानृतात् ।
दद्यान्न प्रतिगृह्णीयात् सत्यं ब्रूयान्न चानृतम् ।
एतद् ब्राह्मण रामस्य व्रतं धृतमनुत्तमम् ॥

To Hanuman—V, 33. 23-26.

ततस्तं स्थविरो राजा सत्यधर्मे व्यवस्थितः ।
ज्येष्ठं यशस्विनं पुत्रं रुदन् राज्यमयाचत ॥
स पितुर्वचनं श्रीमानभिषेकात्परं प्रियम् ।
मनसा पूर्वमासाद्य वाचा प्रतिगृहीतवान् ॥
दद्यान्न प्रतिगृह्णीयात्सत्यं ब्रूयान्न चानृतम् ।
अपि जीवितहेतोर्हि रामः सत्यपराक्रमः ॥

A bold attempt at reconciliation of the discrepancy—by crying Dasaratha begged! Then what becomes of पितुर्वचनम् (वचनम् wish or order)?

Rama's equanimity—II. 18. 41; II. 19. 1, 32-33, 35-37.

इतीव रामं परुषं वदन्त्यां न चैव रामः प्रविवेश शोकम् ।
प्रविव्यथे चापि महानुभावो राजा च पुत्रव्यसनाभितप्तः ॥
तदप्रियममित्रघ्नो वचनं मरणोपमम् ।
श्रुत्वा न विव्यथे रामः कैकेयीं चेदमब्रवीत् ॥
न चास्य महतीं लक्ष्मीं राज्यनाशोऽपकर्षति ।
लोककान्तस्य कान्तत्वाच्छीतरश्मेरिव क्षयः ॥
न वनं गन्तुकामस्य त्यजतश्च वसुन्धराम् ।
सर्वलोकातिगस्येव लक्ष्यते चित्तविक्रिया ॥
धारयन्मनसा दुःखमिन्द्रियाणि निगृह्य च ।*
प्रविवेशात्मवान्वेश्म मातुरप्रियशंसिवान् ॥
सर्वोऽप्यभिजनः श्रीमान् श्रीमतः सत्यवादिनः ।
नालक्षयत रामस्य कंचिदाकारमानने ॥
उचितं च महाबाहुर्न जहौ हर्षमात्मवान् ।
शारदः समुदीर्णांशुः चन्द्रस्तेज इवात्मजम् ॥

*Cf. Lect. V, p. 66 above.

Compare Lakshmana's behaviour—II. 19. 30.

तं बाष्पपरिपूर्णाक्षः पृष्ठतोऽनुजगाम ह ।
लक्ष्मणः परमक्रुद्धः सुमित्रानन्दवर्धनः ॥

Rama's Lone Glory—II. 21. 55-58.

स मातरं चैव विसंज्ञकल्प-
मार्तं च सौमित्रिमभिप्रतप्तम् ।
धर्मे स्थितो धर्म्यमुवाच वाक्यं
यथा स एवार्हति तत्र वक्तुम् ॥
अहं हि ते लक्ष्मण नित्यमेव
जानामि भक्तिं च पराक्रमं च ।
मम त्वभिप्रायमसन्निरीक्ष्य
मात्रा सहाभ्यर्दसि मां सुदुःखम् ॥
धर्मार्थकामाः खलु जीवलोके
समीक्षिता धर्मफलोदयेषु ।
ये तत्र सर्वे स्युरसंशयं मे
भार्येव वश्याभिमता सपुत्रा ॥
यस्मिंस्तु सर्वे स्युरसन्निविष्टा
धर्मो यतः स्यात्तदुपक्रमेत ।
द्वेष्यो भवत्यर्थपरो हि लोके
कामात्मता खल्वति न प्रशस्ता ॥

Rama's advice to Mother*—II. 24. 20-31.

तां तथा रुदतीं रामोऽरुदन्वचनमब्रवीत् ॥
जीवन्त्या हि स्त्रिया भर्ता दैवतं प्रभुरेव च ।
भवत्या मम चैवाद्य राजा प्रभवति प्रभुः ॥
न ह्यनाथा वयं राज्ञा लोकनाथेन धीमता ।
भरतश्चापि धर्मात्मा सर्वभूतप्रियंवदः ॥
भवतीमनुवर्तेत स हि धर्मरतः सदा ।
यथा मयि तु निष्क्रान्ते पुत्रशोकेन पार्थिवः ॥

*Cf. Lect. XXIX below.

श्रमं नावाप्नुयात् किंचिदप्रमत्ता तथा कुरु ।
दारुणश्चाप्ययं शोको यथैनं न विनाशयेत् ॥
राज्ञो वृद्धस्य सततं हितं चर समाहिता ।
व्रतोपवासनिरता या नारी परमोत्तमा ॥
भर्तारं नानुवर्तेत सा च पापगतिर्भवेत् ।
भर्तुः शुश्रूषया नारी लभते स्वर्गमुत्तमम् ॥
अपि या निर्नमस्कारा निवृत्ता देवपूजनात् ।
शुश्रूषामेव कुर्वीत भर्तुः प्रियहिते रता ॥
एष धर्मः स्त्रिया नित्यो लोके वेदे श्रुतः स्मृतः ।
अग्निकार्येषु च सदा सुमनोभिश्च देवताः ॥
पूज्यांस्ते मत्कृते देवि ब्राह्मणाश्चैव सत्कृताः ।
एवं कालं प्रतीक्षस्व ममागमनकाङ्क्षिणी ॥
नियता नियताहारा भर्तृशुश्रूषणे रता ।
प्राप्स्यसे परमं कामं मयि पर्यागते सति ॥
यदि धर्मभृतां श्रेष्ठो धारयिष्यति जीवितम् ।

Rama's advice to Sita—II. 26. 24, 25, 33-36.

भरतस्य समीपे ते नाहं कत्थ्यः कदाचन ॥
ऋद्धियुक्ता हि पुरुषा न सहन्ते परस्तवम् ।
तस्मान्न ते गुणाः कत्थ्याः भरतस्याग्रतो मम ॥*
भ्रातृपुत्रसमौ चापि द्रष्टव्यौ च विशेषतः ।
त्वया भरतशत्रुघ्नौ प्राणैः प्रियतरौ मम ॥†
विप्रियं च न कर्तव्यं भरतस्य कदाचन ।
स हि राजा च वैदेहि देशस्य च कुलस्य च ॥
आराधिता हि शीलेन प्रयत्नैश्चोपसेविताः ।
राजानः संप्रसीदन्ति प्रकुप्यन्ति विपर्यये ॥
औरसानपि पुत्रान् हि त्यजन्त्यहितकारिणः ।
समर्थान्संप्रगृह्णन्ति जनानपि नराधिपाः ॥

Rama begs his father to be kind to Kausalya, and asks forgiveness of his mothers for unintended slights.

---

*Cf. Lect. XXV below.
†Cf. Lect. IV, p. 45 above.

Rama and Guha—Guha's hospitality declined—II. 50. 43-45; 48-49.

यत्त्विदं भवता किंचित् प्रीत्या समुपकल्पितम्।
सर्वं तदनुजानामि न हि वर्ते प्रतिग्रहे ॥
कुशचीराजिनधरं फलमूलाशनं च माम्।
विद्धि प्रणिहितं धर्मे तापसं वनगोचरम् ॥
अश्वानां खादनेनाहमर्थी नान्येन केनचित्।
ततश्चीरोत्तरासङ्गः सन्ध्यामन्वास्य पश्चिमाम्।
जलमेवाददे भोज्यं लक्ष्मणेनाहृतं स्वयम् ॥

Guha narrates to Bharata later on—II. 87. 15-18.

तत्सर्वं प्रत्यनुज्ञासीत् रामः सत्यपराक्रमः।
न हि तत्प्रत्यगृह्णात्स क्षत्रधर्ममनुस्मरन् ॥
न ह्यस्माभिः प्रतिग्राह्यं सखे देयं तु सर्वदा।
इति तेन वयं सर्वे अनुनीता महात्मना।
लक्ष्मणेन यदानीतं पीतं वारि महात्मना।
औपवास्यं तदाऽकार्षीद्राघवः सह सीतया ॥
ततस्तु जलशेषेण लक्ष्मणोऽप्यकरोत्तदा।

One of Rama's "contradictions"—refusal of Guha's hospitality, acceptance of Bharadvaja's and Sabari's. Govindaraja's comment on—II. 87. 16.

इत्यनुनीता वयमित्यनेन स्वाङ्घ्रिभक्ताग्रेसरगुहसमर्पितफलादेः भक्तिपूतत्वेन शबरीविदुरादिन्यायेन परमभागवततया स्वीकार्यत्वेऽपि स्वप्रियतमपितृप्रमुखबहुजन-विश्लेषजनितवैमनस्येन पुण्यनदीतीरे उपवासचिकीर्षया च गुहसमर्पितं न प्रतिजग्राह रामः इति च गुहेनापि विदितमिति गम्यते।

Tilaka comment—

(1) Bharadvaja had the necessary qualification for giving Madhuparka. Guha was not of the right caste.
(2) He was not a subject of Ayodhya and therefore not liable to give *tribute* to royalty.
(3) Still as Guha was a Tattvajna exception might have been made.

But Rama was on Vrata—course of religious restriction.

The rule need not have been extended to the relation between guest and host. Rama put the matter on a high level of principle. Other reasons were mixed up, but no one is bound to make a full statement of all the motives and reasons of his action.

A most startling comment by Govindaraja on II. 87. 23—what *can* be its meaning?

ततस्त्वहं चोत्तमबाणचापभृत्
स्थितोऽभवं तत्र स यत्र लक्ष्मणः ।
अतन्द्रितैर्ज्ञातिभिरात्तकार्मुकैः
महेन्द्रकल्पं परिपालयंस्तदा ॥

एको भ्राता नगराद् वनानि निरगमयत् । अयमपरः सुषुप्तिदशायां किमपि कुर्यादिति शङ्कया सज्जायुधः सन् यत्र यत्र स लक्ष्मणः स्थितः तत्र तत्र स्थितोऽभवम् । प्रतिपदं तमनुसृतवानभवमित्यर्थः । अतन्द्रिभिः ज्ञातिभिः आत्तकार्मुकैः । मम परिकराश्च अयं वनचरो निषादजातीयः रामे किंचित्करिष्यति चेद् एनं च प्रहराम इति सावधाना मां प्रतिपदमन्वसरन् इत्यर्थः । एवमस्थाने भयशङ्किभिः कृतम् । वस्तुतः स न केनचित्परिभाव्य इत्याह—महेन्द्रकल्पमिति ।

Hear *my* comment on this comment: A rare treasure guarded by several persons, each naturally watching the others narrowly and considering himself the only faithful keeper!

Rama's high principles—II. 97. 3-8.

पितुः सत्यं प्रतिश्रुत्य हत्वा भरतमाहवे ।
किं करिष्यामि राज्येन सापवादेन लक्ष्मण ॥
यद्द्रव्यं बान्धवानां वा मित्राणां वा क्षये भवेत् ।
नाहं तत्प्रतिगृह्णीयां भक्ष्यान्विषकृतानिव ॥
धर्ममर्थं च कामं च पृथिवीं चापि लक्ष्मण ।
इच्छामि भवतामर्थे एतत्प्रतिशृणोमि ते ॥
भ्रातॄणां संग्रहार्थं च सुखार्थं चापि लक्ष्मण ।
राज्यमप्यहमिच्छामि सत्येनायुधमालभे ॥
नेयं मम मही सौम्य दुर्लभा सागरांबरा ।
न हीच्छेयमधर्मेण शक्रत्वमपि लक्ष्मण ॥

यद्विना भरतं त्वां च शत्रुघ्नं वापि मानद।
भवेन्मम सुखं किंचिद्भस्म तत्कुरुतां शिखी ॥

*Rama to Bharata—II. 112. 18, 19, 27-28.

लक्ष्मीश्चन्द्रादपेयाद्वा हिमवान्वा हिमं त्यजेत्।
अतीयात्सागरो वेलां न प्रतिज्ञामहं पितुः ॥
कामाद्वा तात लोभाद्वा मात्रा तुभ्यमिदं कृतम्।
न तन्मनसि कर्तव्यं वर्तितव्यं च मातृवत् ॥
मातरं रक्ष कैकेयीं मा रोषं कुरु तां प्रति।
मया च सीतया चैव शप्तोऽसि रघुनन्दन ॥

Going back to Dasaratha's non-utterance of the order of banishment, Rama did not think of taking advantage. Anyhow Dasaratha acquiesced, however much he deplored it and would have liked Rama to repudiate and disown him, cf. II. 12. 85, 86.†

नालं द्वितीयं वचनं पुत्रो मां प्रतिभाषितुम्।
स वनं प्रव्रजेत्युक्तो बाढमित्येव वक्ष्यति ॥
यदि मे राघवः कुर्याद्वनं गच्छेति चोदितः।
प्रतिकूलं प्रियं मे स्यान्न तु वत्सः करिष्यति ॥
शुद्धभावो हि भावं मे न तु ज्ञास्यति राघवः ॥

Not that Rama could not read his thoughts. But he would have preferred his father's honour to his wish. Dasaratha did openly convey his wish at the end.

At the final leave-taking—

Dasaratha—II. 34. 26—

अहं राघव कैकेय्या वरदानेन मोहितः।
अयोध्यायां त्वमेवाद्य भव राजा निगृह्य माम् ॥

Secret signal from Kaikeyi—II. 34. 30-31.

रुदन्नार्तः प्रियं पुत्रं सत्यपाशेन संयुतः।
कैकेय्या चोद्यमानस्तु मिथो राजा तमब्रवीत् ॥

*Cf. Lect. VIII, pp. 103-104 above and Lect. X, pp. 140-141 below.
†Cf. Lect. XXVIII below.

श्रेयसे वृद्धये तात पुनरागमनाय च।
गच्छस्वारिष्टमव्यग्रः पन्थानमकुतोभयम् ॥

But the old man again rebels and breaks out—II. 34. 36-38.

न चैतन्मे प्रियं पुत्र शपे सत्येन राघव।
छन्नया चलितस्त्वस्मि स्त्रिया भस्माग्निकल्पया ॥
वञ्चना या तु लब्धा मे तां त्वं निस्तर्तुमिच्छसि।
अनया वृत्तसादिन्या कैकेय्याभिप्रचोदितः ॥
न चैतदाश्चर्यतमं यत्त्वं ज्येष्ठः सुतो मम।
अपानृतकथं पुत्र पितरं कर्तुमिच्छसि ॥

Final reply of Rama—II. 34. 42, 43, 45, 47-49.

यस्तु युद्धे वरो दत्तः कैकेय्यै वरद त्वया।
दीयतां निखिलेनैव सत्यस्त्वं भव पार्थिव।
न हि मे काङ्क्षितं राज्यं सुखमात्मनि वा प्रियम्।
नैवाहं राज्यमिच्छामि न सुखं न च मेदिनीम्।
नैव सर्वानिमान्कामान् न स्वर्गं न च जीवितम् ॥
त्वामहं सत्यमिच्छामि नानृतं पुरुषर्षभ।
प्रत्यक्षं तव सत्येन सुकृतेन च ते शपे ॥
न हि शक्यं मया तात स्थातुं क्षणमपि प्रभो ॥

Dasaratha implores him 'stay this one night!'—II. 34. 33, 34.

अद्य त्विदानीं रजनीं पुत्र मा गच्छ सर्वथा।
एकाहं दर्शनेनापि साधु तावच्चराम्यहम् ॥
मातरं मां च संपश्यन् वसेमामद्य शर्वरीम्।
तर्पितः सर्वकामैस्त्वं श्वः काल्ये साधयिष्यसि ॥

Rama's refusal—'No! I am off tonight'—II. 34. 40, 50.

प्राप्स्यामि यानद्य गुणान्को मे श्वस्तान्प्रदास्यति।
अपक्रमणमेवातः सर्वकामैरहं वृणे ॥
अर्थितो ह्यस्मि कैकेय्या वनं गच्छेति राघव।
मया चोक्तं व्रजामीति तत्सत्यमनुपालये ॥

'We shall be happy in the forest'—II. 34. 51, 59.

मा चोत्कण्ठां कृथा देव वने रंस्यामहे वयम्।
प्रशान्तहरिणाकीर्णे नानाशकुनिनादिते ॥
फलानि मूलानि च भक्षयन्वने
गिरींश्च पश्यन्सरितः सरांसि च।
वनं प्रविश्यैव विचित्रपादपं
सुखी भविष्यामि तवास्तु निर्वृतिः ॥

"वनवासो महोदयः!" II. 22. 29.

Sumantra's testimony to the happiness of the exiles; his report to Kausalya—II. 60. 5-11, 21, 22.

त्यज शोकं च मोहं च सम्भ्रमं दुःखजं तथा।
व्यवधूय च सन्तापं वने वत्स्यति राघवः ॥
लक्ष्मणश्चापि रामस्य पादौ परिचरन्वने।
आराधयति धर्मज्ञः परलोकं जितेन्द्रियः ॥
विजनेऽपि वने सीता वासं प्राप्य गृहेष्विव।
विस्रम्भं लभतेऽभीता रामे विन्यस्तमानसा ॥
नास्या दैन्यं कृतं किंचित् सुसूक्ष्ममपि लक्ष्यते।
उचितेव प्रवासानां वैदेही प्रतिभाति मे ॥
नगरोपवनं गत्वा यथा स्म रमते पुरा।
तथैव रमते सीता निर्जनेषु वनेष्वपि ॥
बालेव रमते सीताऽबालचन्द्रनिभानना।
रामा रामे ह्यदीनात्मा विजनेऽपि वने सती ॥
तद्गतं हृदयं यस्याः तदधीनं च जीवितम्।
अयोध्या हि भवेदस्या रामहीना तथा वनम् ॥
न शोच्यास्ते न चात्मा ते शोच्यो नापि जनाधिपः।
इदं हि चरितं लोके प्रतिष्ठास्यति शाश्वतम् ॥

विधूय शोकं परिहृष्टमानसा
महर्षियाते पथि सुव्यवस्थिताः।
वने रता वन्यफलाशनाः पितुः
शुभां प्रतिज्ञां प्रतिपालयन्ति ते ॥

Rama's perfect happiness in Chitrakuta—II. 94. 14-16, 19.

गुहासमीरणो गन्धान् नानापुष्पभवान्बहून् ।
घ्राणतर्पणमभ्येत्य कं नरं न प्रहर्षयेत् ॥
यदीह शरदोऽनेकाः त्वया सार्धमनिन्दिते ।
लक्ष्मणेन च वत्स्यामि न मां शोकः प्रधर्षति ॥
बहुपुष्पफले रम्ये नानाद्विजगणायुते ।
विचित्रशिखरे ह्यस्मिन् रतवानस्मि भामिनि ॥
इदमेवामृतं प्राहुः राज्ञि राजर्षयः परे ।
वनवासं भवार्थाय प्रेत्य मे प्रपितामहाः ॥

Rama to Sita—II. 95. 12, 13, 15-18.

दर्शनं चित्रकूटस्य मन्दाकिन्याश्च शोभने ।
अधिकं पुरवासाच्च मन्ये तव च दर्शनात् ॥
विधूतकल्मषैः सिद्धैः तपोदमशमान्वितैः ।
नित्यविक्षोभितजलां विगाहस्व मया सह ॥
त्वं पौरजनवद्व्यालान् अयोध्यामिव पर्वतम् ।
मन्यस्व वनिते नित्यं सरयूवदिमां नदीम् ॥
लक्ष्मणश्चैव धर्मात्मा मन्निदेशे व्यवस्थितः ।
त्वं चानुकूला वैदेहि प्रीतिं जनयती मम ॥
उपस्पृशंस्त्रिषवणं मधुमूलफलाशनः ।
नायोध्यायै न राज्याय स्पृहये च त्वया सह ॥
इमां हि रम्यां गजयूथलोडितां निपीततोयां गजसिंहवानरैः ।
सुपुष्पितां पुष्पभरैरलंकृतां न सोऽस्ति यः स्यान्न गतक्लमः सुखी ॥

TENTH LECTURE*

Ladies and Gentlemen,—Departing from my practice somewhat I propose today to deal in detail with one of the famous passages in the great epic. The topic will be the debate between Sri Rama and Bharata in Chitrakuta. That debate listened to by the celestials with a sense of edification stands as a monument of the Poet's skill. May be such detailed study may draw somewhat upon your patience. But I hope you will feel that I have not done so out of any spirit of wantonness. The character of Sri Rama comes out in the conversation in high colours. It is worth our while at the risk of a little attention to detail to read some of these momentous sargas in the Poem. The meeting between the two brothers is fully described in Sargas nos. 100 to 112 in the Ayodhya Kanda. But of these the first four do not refer to the actual subject-matter of the debate. So I shall skip over them, referring only to one rather interesting feature. At the end of the 103rd Sarga the Poet describes the meeting and then, curiously enough, he mentions only Rama, Lakshmana and Bharata. For some reason Satrughna is wholly omitted. It may remind you somewhat of the omission of Lakshmana in many passages in the Bala Kanda, to which I referred in my opening talks. This is how it goes:

स राघवः सत्यधृतिश्च लक्ष्मणो महानुभावो भरतश्च धार्मिकः ।
वृताः सुहृद्भिश्च विरेजुरध्वरे यथा सदस्यैः सहितास्त्रयोऽग्नयः ॥

II. 103. 32

The simile too takes in only three, the three Agnis. Satrughna must have been regarded by the Poet at the time as somewhat too insignificant to mention in this great context. It is rather curious. It cannot be entirely an oversight because the Poet makes a great sloka here and brings in a simile with the three Agnis. This is the first meeting between the brothers. The subject is opened after the famous 'kaccit' Sarga (100) and after the Sarga in which the funeral ceremonies are described (102). Then Sri Rama asks his brother "what brings you here now to the forest with all this paraphernalia?"—for he had brought his subjects, ministers,

*14-6-'44.

the wives of the king, also the great merchants and so on. "Why this enormous crowd and this great army?" Then Bharata opens the battle, as it were, with this skirmish. He makes three points worth remembering and he does not make many others. In the first place, he emphasises the tradition in the Ikshvaku family, which is unbroken, that the eldest son succeeds to the throne. Then he says that he is very unwilling, in fact he is very annoyed, that his mother's improper proceedings should have succeeded at all. He says, "My mother's attempt should be completely foiled; I do not wish to profit by it." And the third point he makes is that it is the unanimous wish of the people of the kingdom that Rama should return and take charge of the great office. Let me read a few slokas.

> स्त्रिया नियुक्तः कैकेय्या मम मात्रा परंतप ।
> चकार सुमहत्पापमिदमात्मयशोहरम् ॥ II. 104. 6

"My father was induced to this ill-proceeding by Kaikeyi. She has ruined her great name through history and she has committed a great sin."

> सा राज्यफलमप्राप्य विधवा शोककर्शिता ।
> पतिष्यति महाघोरे निरये जननी मम ॥ II. 104. 7

This is not language which should be used by a dutiful son. But the circumstances were particularly aggravating as you know and poor Bharata loses his patience. Whenever he thinks of his mother, he says, "How has she ruined the family and its name, ruined her name, ruined my name and brought devastation on the whole kingdom!" He cannot forget it. Every time he thinks of her he loses his temper and uses abusive language. Then Bharata says to Rama,

> एभिश्च सचिवैः सार्धं शिरसा याचितो मया ।
> भ्रातुः शिष्यस्य दासस्य प्रसादं कर्तुमर्हसि ॥ II. 104. 12

No entreaty can be more earnest, more humble in tone. But Sri Rama was not to be won by such means. First of all, he protests that Kaikeyi should not be mishandled by the son. As we have seen, Sri Rama himself did not approve of Kaikeyi's conduct. But that is nothing. A son's minute examination of a mother's proceedings would never be proper and in this case Sri Rama thought it was particularly ungracious on Bharata's part to denounce his mother in such unlimited language. So he says,

न चापि जननीं बाल्यात्त्वं विगर्हितुमर्हसि ॥ II. 104. 17

"You are a boy, cannot keep your temper." Then he says, "Why do you think that your mother has no right to command you? Why do you dispute her authority? The mother is as good as the father." That is a sentiment which we must remember.

यावत्पितरि धर्मज्ञे गौरवं लोकसत्कृते ।
तावद्धर्मभृतां श्रेष्ठ जनन्यामपि गौरवम् ॥ II. 104. 21

Such authority resides in the mother's wish as in the father's.

एताभ्यां धर्मशीलाभ्यां वनं गच्छेति राघव ।
मातापितृभ्यामुक्तोऽहं कथमन्यत्समाचरे ॥ II. 104. 22

I have been ordered by both father and mother to go and live in the forest for fourteen years. The great man adds the word धर्मशीलाभ्याम्, Dharmasila as an epithet to Dasaratha and Kaikeyi who were held up to odium so much. He calls them Dharmasila. In another passage he is going to say also that they have done no* wrong. It is an extraordinary thing for a son to say at that time but Sri Rama feels that something is due to be said on behalf of even Kaikeyi. After all what has Kaikeyi done? She has exercised her right. She had in her possession boons granted by the husband, long kept in suspense no doubt, but suddenly revived for a sinister purpose. She had a legal right to those boons and she demanded them. Where was the harm? And after all let us remember, as I have told you before, that forest life, deprivation of the pomp and circumstance of kingly office, these forfeitures and penalties never appeared to Rama in the light in which they appeared to other people either of that time or of this time. He took them as he would take any other turns in life. They did not hurt his soul. So he says purposely धर्मशीलाभ्याम्. "I do not object to this. Kaikeyi exercised her right and in the direction of natural affection towards an only son. Where is the harm? And our father held himself down by the promise that he had made." So ends the skirmish. As I told you, it was at night.

---

*II. 111. 29.

Next morning after the usual ablutions, the brothers and all others who had come there, people deeply interested in the proceedings and anxious that Bharata's will should succeed all right, met together in solemn conclave, all full of the idea that a great event was going to take place and that they were going to be witnesses to it. Bharata begins by saying "Well, you say, brother, that the kingdom has been given away. The father has given the kingdom to be presented to the son by the mother, Kaikeyi took it from Dasaratha; Kaikeyi gave it to me. Very well, let it be so, if you want. In formal law I have taken the kingdom. It is mine and I dispose of it now, by offering it to you. Take it." That is how he puts it.

सान्त्विता मामिका माता दत्तं राज्यमिदं मम। II. 105. 4

She has been satisfied. That is your trouble. It has been given to me.

तद्ददामि तवैवाहं भुङ्क्ष्व राज्यमकण्टकम्॥ II. 105. 4

Take the thing. There is no flaw. Now there is no flaw in the legal situation.

In reply Rama begins by a dissertation on Fate, which you know is one of the eternal topics of our literature. Kala, Vidhi—that is accountable for everything. We are destined to behave in particular ways. All is pre-determined. What is the use of our resisting or trying to take our own line? Then there follow sixteen slokas. These sixteen slokas contain great aphorisms, familiar in our ancient literature. Some of them may appear even platitudinous. But remember we regard them in this light after having heard these things millions of times and after these things have been written about in all books, spoken, lectured upon by good men and by bad men always and become current coin, debased and outworn. But at the time of the Ramayana, they could not have been so. These verses embodying great truths must still have been charged with fresh import and in the mouth of Sri Rama they could not have been the trite, unmeaning things they might appear to us. I take leave to think that it will not be waste of time to read the sixteen verses and give their translation then and there, poor translation as it may be, in my own language. You must have heard many of these verses.

सर्वे क्षयान्ता निचयाः पतनान्ताः समुच्छ्रयाः।
संयोगा विप्रयोगान्ता मरणान्तं च जीवितम्॥ II. 105. 16

All accumulations come to an end by depletion. Elevations end by crumbling and falling. Unions end by separation. Life ends by death.

> यथा फलानां पक्कानां नान्यत्र पतनाद्भयम् ।
> एवं नरस्य जातस्य नान्यत्र मरणाद्भयम् ॥ II. 105. 17

As ripe fruits must inevitably fall to the ground, so must a born man inevitably perish.

> यथागारं दृढस्थूणं जीर्णं भूत्वावसीदति ।
> तथावसीदन्ति नरा जरामृत्युवशं गताः ॥ II. 105. 18

Just as a building supported by strong pillars decays in time and comes down, so do men pass away, victims of age and death.

> अत्येति रजनी या तु सा न प्रतिनिवर्तते ।
> यात्येव यमुना पूर्णा समुद्रं लवणार्णवम् ॥ II. 105. 19

The night, when it passes away, never returns. The Yamuna discharges her waters into the great ocean but never turns back in her course.

> अहोरात्राणि गच्छन्ति सर्वेषां प्राणिनामिह ।
> आयूंषि क्षपयन्त्याशु ग्रीष्मे जलमिवांशवः ॥ II. 105. 20

Days and nights pass over the heads of all creatures on earth, and soon consume their lives as the sun's rays dry up the water in summer.

> आत्मानमनुशोच त्वं किमन्यमनुशोचसि ।
> आयुस्ते हीयते यस्य स्थितस्य च गतस्य च ॥ II. 105. 21

Whether you stand still or move, your days diminish. Grieve then for yourself. Why grieve for aught else?

> सहैव मृत्युर्व्रजति सह मृत्युर्निषीदति ।
> गत्वा सुदीर्घमध्वानं सह मृत्युर्निवर्तते ॥ II. 106. 22

Death travels with one; death rests with one. However far one goes, one cannot leave death behind but it returns too.

> गात्रेषु वलयः प्राप्ताः श्वेताश्चैव शिरोरुहाः ।
> जरया पुरुषो जीर्णः किं हि कृत्वा प्रभावयेत् ॥ II. 105. 23

The skin is wrapt in folds and wrinkles. The hairs turn white. Age destroys a man. What can he do to avoid this?

नन्दन्त्युदित आदित्ये नन्दन्त्यस्तमिते रवौ ।
आत्मनो नावबुध्यन्ते मनुष्या जीवितक्षयम् ॥ II. 105. 24

At sunrise men rejoice thinking they may work and earn. At sundown they rejoice also thinking they can enjoy themselves. But they do not realise that their lives are shrinking.

हृष्यन्त्यृतुमुखं दृष्ट्वा नवं नवमिहागतम् ।
ऋतूनां परिवर्तेन प्राणिनां प्राणसंक्षयः ॥ II. 105. 25

As the seasons come round, men fancy they are ever fresh and feel happy. But with each cycle of the seasons our lives are shortened.

यथा काष्ठं च काष्ठं च समेयातां महार्णवे ।
समेत्य च व्यपेयातां कालमासाद्य कंचन ॥
एवं भार्याश्च पुत्राश्च ज्ञातयश्च धनानि च ।
समेत्य व्यवधावन्ति ध्रुवो ह्येषां विनाभवः ॥ II. 105. 26-27

These two slokas must be taken together. As logs of wood come together on the wide ocean, and having drifted together for a time, part from each other, so do wives, sons, kinsmen and possessions come together, and separate. This separation is unavoidable.

नात्र कश्चिद्यथाभावं प्राणी समभिवर्तते ।
तेन तस्मिन्न सामर्थ्यं प्रेतस्यास्त्यनुशोचतः ॥ II. 105. 28

No one on earth ever escapes the course of nature. So mourning for the dead cannot avail one when one's turn comes.

यथा हि सार्थं गच्छन्तं ब्रूयात्कश्चित्पथि स्थितः ।
अहमप्यागमिष्यामि पृष्ठतो भवतामिति ॥
एवं पूर्वैर्गतो मार्गः पितृपैतामहो ध्रुवः ।
तमापन्नः कथं शोचेद्यस्य नास्ति व्यतिक्रमः ॥ II. 105. 29-30

As a man, falling in with a caravan on the move, says to those there, "I too will accompany you," so is the journey of life, which has been already performed by our fathers and grandfathers. When one joins the journey, which knows no change, how can one complain?

वयसः पतमानस्य स्रोतसो वानिवर्तिनः ।
आत्मा सुखे नियोक्तव्यः सुखभाजः प्रजाः स्मृताः ॥ II. 105. 31

Like a stream that never reverses its course, so one's life ever lessens in duration. One must therefore strive for happiness, through righteousness, for it is well known that all men seek happiness.

That ends the 105th Sarga. The 106th Sarga opens with Bharata. Between these brothers, as between other disputants in the great Poem, there is an exchange of courtesies. Each one begins with a formal word "How nicely you have spoken! You are clever in speech." And then follows the refutation. That is usual. Bharata praises Rama's teaching and professes to be edified but his heart is untouched. He will not relent, as you will see, towards Kaikeyi.

प्रोषिते मयि यत्पापं मात्रा मत्कारणात्कृतम् ॥
क्षुद्रया तदनिष्टं मे प्रसीदतु भवान् मम । II. 106. 8-9

"Have pity on me. It was when I was away that Kaikeyi behaved in this fashion, fancying that it would please me."

धर्मबन्धेन बद्धोऽस्मि तेनेमां नेह मातरम् ॥
हन्मि तीव्रेण दण्डेन दण्डार्हां पापकारिणीम् । II. 106. 9-10

"She deserves to be severely punished but I don't punish her because I am afraid of violating the rule of Dharma,"—and as he said once before—"I am also afraid of your serious displeasure. As for my father, Dasaratha, he was an old man and a dotard. He was in the hands of my mother." Then he breaks out into a general observation, which many might have always to remember.

अन्तकाले हि भूतानि मुह्यन्तीति पुरा श्रुतिः ॥ II. 106. 13

"The old saying has it that people weaken in their age, become somewhat senile.

राज्ञैवं कुर्वता लोके प्रत्यक्षं सा श्रुतिः कृता । II. 106. 14

This old saying has been abundantly testified to by our father." Then Bharata ventures on advising his own elder brother.

You know the word 'Apatya' means 'son'. It is neuter in gender but it means 'son'. It comes from a peculiar belief that the son saves the father from falling, that is, from perdition as we say. That is why he is called 'Apatyam'. He prevents the father's fall. Bharata uses the word in that literal sense and ventures to instruct his brother in the truth.

साध्वर्थमभिसन्धाय क्रोधान्मोहाच्च साहसात् ॥
तातस्य यदतिक्रान्तं प्रत्याहरतु तद्भवान्। II. 106. 14-15

"Thinking that he was under some obligation, our father whether it was by the anger—perhaps it was in fear of the anger—of the wife that played upon him, whatever it was, through some mistake, passed an unjust order. The transgression of our father, that unjust order passed by our father, you had better undo it. Put it right. Father did wrong through some mistake, may be he was a fool.

पितुर्हि समतिक्रान्तं पुत्रो यः साधु मन्यते ॥ II. 106. 15

He is called a *son* in this world who when the father has gone wrong, puts the matter right."

तदपत्यं मतं लोके विपरीतमतोऽन्यथा ॥ II. 106. 16

"If a son does not do it but obeys his father in the wrong course, then he must not be called Apatya; he helps his father's fall, brings it about. You had better be an Apatya."

मा भवान् दुष्कृतं पितुः ॥ II. 106. 16

"Do not go and carry out the wrong order passed by the father. Do not confirm him in the error of his ways and thus bring down Heaven's punishment upon him. Do the right thing and save him." See how a clever man can twist things to his own purpose.

Now I have got to tell you of something which people do not ordinarily notice in the Poem, do not ordinarily notice, I do not say I have discovered something which is hidden from other people. Early in this Kanda the question arises whether really Rama carried out the father's promise properly. Those that believed that he was doing wrong contested that position earnestly and sincerely. This was the way they argued. Just listen. In the Ayodhya Kanda, as you know, the commencement marks the determination of the king to create a Yauvarajya in his kingdom and elevate Sri Rama thereto. So first he calls Rama and promises that he would do so. Then, in order to give it the broad basis of popular approval, he sends for the surrounding magnates, all the rich men in the kingdom, merchants, poets, philosophers and so on and to that meeting assembled he makes his proposal. Of course they all welcome it unanimously and think that the king never did a better thing in his life than when he transferred the responsibility to the son who so deserved to bear it. It was after this that under the influence of Manthara, Kaikeyi played upon the old man's feelings and bound him down to carry out promises which had been forgotten. So this was a second promise. Just think of that. The earlier promise was made to the people, to Sri Rama himself. It was the second promise made to Kaikeyi that prevailed with the king. Lakshmana and Bharata and all the other people quarrelled with this preference given to the second promise. Why was that considered the more binding on the old king? He had made this promise before. Now, as a matter of fact, it is rather a stretch of language to call the first thing a promise made to anybody. It was an arrangement that the king proposed to make for the benefit of his subjects. Nobody had a right to demand it from him. He, thinking that the time had come for him to relieve himself of part of his kingly burdens, wished to transfer them to his son. It was a wise measure no doubt, but it was a measure in the interests of himself and of the kingdom. It was not to be elevated into the dignity of a solemn undertaking made to others which those others had a right to exact from him. That was not the view that people could ordinarily take. But seeing that the real advantage was given by the king to this other promise to Kaikeyi, which they did not like, they chose for purposes of argument to clothe the first proceeding also with all the air and authority of a solemn promise. Between these two promises the other promise should, in their opinion, have prevailed. Now let us for one moment consider how the matter appeared to Sri Rama. It is not clearly stated in the Poem but I am fairly sure, and I am seldom sure of things,—I am fairly sure that if Sri Rama had been put through a catechism upon this subject, he would have argued it out like this:—

"Let us assume for a moment that the other was a promise and that the two were co-ordinate promises. Nevertheless, it is demeaning to carry it out. I have got to make a choice between these two promises of our father. If I carry out the first promise, will not people say I preferred it because it was full of advantage to me? It was a gainful preference that Rama was asked to exercise, they would say. My conception of Dharma is very different. Where two duties demand my obedience I prefer without hesitation the one which calls for sacrifice on my part, which imposes sufferings on me. I am not going to be tempted to make a preference which could be brought up against me as having been dictated by purely selfish and unworthy considerations." That is how, you may be perfectly certain, cent per cent certain, Sri Rama would have argued the matter. Now why do I make such a stress upon this? Bharata, you know the born brother of Sri Rama, although he lived sometimes away from him, knew his heart very well, being like-minded, like himself most magnanimous and generous in spirit, wishing always to see the right and then to follow it. Now see how he puts it. "My brother, I know your ways. You always like to do a thing which brings you trouble. You are an inviter of suffering. You like to sacrifice yourself. I will show you how to make the sacrifice. Look at this.

अथ क्लेशजमेव त्वं धर्मं चरितुमिच्छसि ॥ II. 106. 21

If it is in your nature to prefer a painful duty, here it is.

धर्मेण चतुरो वर्णान् पालयन् क्लेशमाप्नुहि । II. 106. 22

Do you suppose keeping all the four Varnas in their proper jurisdictional duties is an easy thing? It is an arduous duty, comes upon your patience. It will exercise your greatest wisdom, it will give you sleepless nights. Come on, come and take that.

चतुर्णामाश्रमाणां हि गार्हस्थ्यं श्रेष्ठमाश्रमम् ॥
प्राहुर्धर्मज्ञ धर्मज्ञास्तं कथं त्यक्तुमर्हसि । II. 106. 22-23

Of all the Asramas Grihasthasrama has been put at the head. How can you knowing Dharma get away from it? Come." And then he adds, "I am only a boy. Don't put too much on my unripe shoulders.

श्रुतेन बालः स्थानेन जन्मना भवतो ह्यहम् ॥ II. 106. 23

In comparison with you what am I but a poor, undeveloped, immature juvenile?

हीनबुद्धिगुणो बालो हीनः स्थानेन चाप्यहम्। II. 106. 24

(Of course he was born a few hours later).

स कथं पालयिष्यामि भूमिं भवति तिष्ठति ॥

भवता च विनाभूतो न वर्तयितुमुत्सहे। II. 106. 24-25

When you are here, what will people say? How can I go and take upon myself all this burden? I have brought everything from the capital, I have brought all the women of the land; I have brought all the gurus; Vasishtha is here; I have brought all the *samagris* necessary for the abhisheka; the army is here, minstrels—all things are here; all the musical accompaniments are here. It is my intention to have you crowned here. Take it. Let me anoint you here.

इहैव त्वाभिषिञ्चन्तु सर्वाः प्रकृतयः सह ॥

ऋत्विजः सवसिष्ठाश्च मन्त्रवन्मन्त्रकोविदाः। II. 106. 26-27

Whom else do you want? All the priests are here; the men who know the Vedas from end to end are here. Let them anoint you."

But Rama was absolutely firm. He never showed the slightest sign of yielding. Then the great audience assembled there, who watched the proceedings with the most tremendous anxiety, for they were anxious that Bharata should prevail in the contest, they, the Poet says, had mixed feelings. They had never thought of it before in that light, as Sri Rama put it. They said, "We should have liked that Bharata prevailed and Sri Rama went back to be king over us. But then, see Rama's arguments and see how firm he is in his Dharma." So between the satisfaction of Rama's steadfastness under the rule of Dharma on the one hand and grief on the other that they were not to have him to be their ruler, the crowd swayed this way and that. Sometimes they rejoiced; sometimes they lamented their fate. The Poet put it this way. I will just read.

तदद्भुतं स्थैर्यमवेक्ष्य राघवे समं जनो हर्षमवाप दुःखितः।

At the same time

न यात्ययोध्यामिति दुःखितोऽभवत्स्थिरप्रतिज्ञत्वमवेक्ष्य हर्षितः ॥

II. 106. 34

How firm he is in carrying out his promise, his father's promise though it be. But outwardly they seconded Bharata's prayers.

Then Sri Rama says in the next sarga. "You think that I, being the eldest son, must obey father and that you need not. Is that your opinion? Father has laid on me one duty, going to the forest. He has laid on you another duty, being king at Ayodhya and ruling the kingdom. You forget that that is your duty.

भवानपि तथेत्येव पितरं सत्यवादिनम् ।
कर्तुमर्हति राजेन्द्र क्षिप्रमेवाभिषेचनात् ॥ II. 107. 9

Go and get yourself crowned. Do not waste time here. Carry out your father's wish as I am carrying out his wish.

ऋणान्मोचय राजानं मत्कृते भरत प्रभुम् ।
पितरं त्राहि धर्मज्ञ मातरं चाभिनन्दय ॥ II. 107. 10

Please your mother by carrying out your father's wish." Then, I told you before that Bharata used the word 'Apatya' to persuade Rama. Now Rama knows the trick just as well. He says

श्रूयते हि पुरा तात श्रुतिर्गीता यशस्विना ।
गयेन यजमानेन गयेष्वेव पितॄन् प्रति ॥ II. 107. 11

There was once a great man named Gaya who in the place called Gaya performed a great Yajna and saved his Pitris. That man having saved his Pitris has laid it down for posterity

पुन्नाम्नो नरकाद्यस्मात्पितरं त्रायते सुतः ।
तस्मात्पुत्र इति प्रोक्तः पितॄन् यः पाति सर्वतः ॥ II. 107. 12

Because a son saves the father from the Naraka called 'Put' by performing what is called Ishtapurta, be it in wealth, in temples and so on, he is called Putra. A son who performs these benevolent offices and dedicates them for the benefit of his father is called a Putra. Now Rama says to Bharata, "You had better be a Putra: You asked me to be an Apatyam, I ask you to be a Putra."

Then this is a very common saying.

एष्टव्या बहवः पुत्रा गुणवन्तो बहुश्रुताः ।
तेषां वै समवेतानामपि कश्चिद्गयां व्रजेत् ॥ II. 107. 13

The prescription is that the man should bear many sons. One won't do, no, not even two; for life is subject to so many mutations and vicissitudes. We want one son at least to go to Gaya and perform Sraddha. Now, ladies and gentlemen, how famous must this Gaya have been for it to get this sanctified flavour even in the time of Sri Rama! What an ancient place it must have been! One must wish to get many sons of whom some one fellow may go to Gaya and perform Sraddha.

एवं राजर्षयः सर्वे प्रतीता राजनन्दन ।
तस्मात्त्राहि नरश्रेष्ठ पितरं नरकात्प्रभो ॥ II. 107. 14

Then Bharata was constantly saying to Sri Rama, "Now, you are a great man, born to a great and noble life, born to enjoy the luxuries and the honours of the kingdom, for you to go away and suffer in the forest is a thing intolerable." Rama says, "Nothing of the kind." I told you towards the end of the last talk that Sri Rama did not feel he was banished when he was in the forest.* He took so kindly to the life of the forest that he seemed to fit in there. Sita too seemed to think that she was living only in Ayodhya. To them attuned as their hearts were to life anywhere provided it was high and pure, to them life in the forest did not matter. So Sri Rama says, "Don't you go and pity me, my dear young brother. Don't think that I am going to suffer. You think you are going to enjoy and I am going to suffer. Nothing of the kind. I am no worse than you. There is perfect parity between us," and he brings it out very clearly thus.

त्वं राजा भरत भव स्वयं नराणां वन्यानामहमपि राजराण्मृगाणाम् ।
गच्छ त्वं पुरवरमद्य संप्रहृष्टः संहृष्टस्त्वहमपि दण्डकान् प्रवेक्ष्ये ॥
II. 107. 17

"You go and be king over men. I am going to be king of the wild beasts in the forest. Go in your joy to Ayodhya. I am also going to the forest in the fullness of happiness. Don't think I am going to suffer.

छायां ते दिनकरभाः प्रबाधमानं वर्षत्रं भरत करोतु मूर्ध्नि शीताम् ।
II. 107. 18

Well, you go and take shelter from the heat of the sun under the famous umbrella. I shall also protect myself from the

* See Lect. IX, pp. 119-120 above.

heat of the sun by this excellent umbrella of trees. I am not going to suffer.

> एतेषामहमपि काननद्रुमाणां छायां तामतिशयिनीं सुखी श्रयिष्ये ॥
>
> II. 107. 18

No doubt Satrughna will be your attendant. Well then, do you suppose I am going to be unattended?

> शत्रुघ्नः कुशलमतिस्तु ते सहायः सौमित्रिर्मम विदितः प्रधानमित्रम् ।
> चत्वारस्तनयवरा वयं नरेन्द्रं सत्यस्थं भरत चराम मा विषीद ॥
>
> II. 107. 19

Don't repine. I am going to be as good and as happy as you will be. Go back."

Then follow two sargas, ladies and gentlemen, which I am going to ignore for purposes of this talk. In the first of these two sargas Jabali teaches Sri Rama the false doctrine of materialism. In the next sarga Rama of course chastises him for it in proper language. Some people consider that both these sargas are spurious and have been put in by later writers. Whether it is so or not, we are not concerned. They do not affect the argument, nor do they affect the story. At the end Vasishtha comes between Sri Rama and Jabali. Finding that Rama has been administering a severe rebuke to this Brahman, the sage Vasishtha comes and uses his good offices to protect the Brahman. He says to Rama, "Jabali only argued for a purpose. He does not mean it. He wanted to find out if you are somewhat incautious and he could persuade you to go back to the kingdom. But you are a wakeful chap. Never mind Jabali, leave him alone." Then he begins a long narrative. He says

> इक्ष्वाकूणां हि सर्वेषां राजा भवति पूर्वजः ।
> पूर्वजे नावरः पुत्रो ज्येष्ठो राज्येऽभिषिच्यते ॥ II. 110. 35

You know Ikshvaku in the family; of course he was Manu's own son, and so on. Vasishtha had been preceptor to all of them and he knows all of them and mentions them all and adds that in every single case a dead king had been succeeded by the eldest son. So he says to Rama, "You had better come and take the kingdom." He seconds Bharata now and advises Sri Rama to go back. When there is an elder son, a younger son cannot succeed.

Then Vasishtha, thinking that Rama was perfectly docile and would take everything quietly, pushes his advantage a little. He says, "You want to obey your father. He is an old man. I am your Guru, greater than your father. Obey." But Sri Rama puts him also in his place.

यन्मातापितरौ वृत्तं तनये कुरुतः सदा ।
न सुप्रतिकरं तत्तु मात्रा पित्रा च यत्कृतम् ॥ II. 111. 9

He says, "No son can ever adequately repay what he takes from his father and from his mother. Don't tell me that the guru is greater than a parent. I won't take it from you."

यथाशक्ति प्रदानेन स्नापनाच्छादनेन च ।
नित्यं च प्रियवादेन तथा संवर्धनेन च ॥ II. 111. 10

"A hundred things the father and mother do to the son, as the English poet says, "little nameless unremembered acts of kindness and of love." Who can tell, who can measure, who can ever describe, who can ever repay the million kindly acts received from one's father and mother?"

स हि राजा जनयिता पिता दशरथो मम ।
आज्ञातं यन्मया तस्य न तन्मिथ्या भविष्यति ॥ II. 111. 11

"I will not fail to do that which my father bade me do." I want to say a word about Vasishtha here. It may be considered highly improper but I am fully justified by the text of Valmiki. Vasishtha plays a curious part. He does not play the conspicuous and commanding part that his great name could justify. He was the very fountain of Dharma. All knowledge came from him. No part of the Veda or anything that had authority was unknown to him. There was no tapas that he had not performed and he was an old, old man who had seen all things and yet he plays a curious part in the whole story. When Sri Rama fights a lone hand against the combined opposition of everybody, he might have looked for some assistance from this great source and fountain of Dharma. Why was he left alone? Why didn't Vasishtha say, "This chap was quite right, he must have carried out his father's command?" If he had said so, how things would have progressed! But he did not. He took sides with the other people, and mind you, having done that, when Bharata came from his uncle's house, Vasishtha persuaded him solemnly in the name of all the gurus, Vedas and so on, to take the kingdom and become king. "Father has gone; brother is absent; the kingdom cannot be kept in anarchy." That was what Vasishtha advised then. But Bharata refuses. The poet says of Bharata*

विललाप सभामध्ये जगर्हे च पुरोहितम् ॥ II. 82. 10

This tiny dot of Bharata chides him and says, "How can you ask me, you old repository of the honour of the Ikshvaku family, how can you ask me? No, not proper on your part to ask me to be king when Sri Rama is there. Absurd." जगर्हे च पुरोहितम्. Now Vasishtha plays therefore this ineffective part in the story.

Bharata is a man of resource. He has got one or two tricks up his sleeve always. He now says, "I am going to perform Prayopavesa since my brother is not willing quietly to yield to me. I will apply this moral process of coercion. I will lie down on the kusa grass. I refuse to eat, I refuse to sleep until my brother yields." Now you who are so familiar with the Satyagraha method will be interested to know how the thing fares in the Ramayana. Bharata calls Sumantra and tells him. "You go and bring the grass." Sumantra is a very old chap, as old as Vasishtha. He won't at once obey this young chap. So he looks at Sri Rama. Sri Rama does not countenance it. So he does not stir. Then Bharata says, "I will go and bring the grass myself." He goes and brings the grass himself and lies down. And then he says, "Now brother, what are you going to say?" Rama says, "This is quite wrong. What are you doing? You are a funny chap, Prayopavesa is not our province. We Kshatriyas ought not to do it. It is only Brahmans who have got to obtain some debt or other thing from some fellows, some over-due debt, it is they that have got to do this. We ought not to do this.

ब्राह्मणो ह्येकपार्श्वेन नरान् रोद्धुमिहार्हति ।

न तु मूर्धाभिषिक्तानां विधिः प्रत्युपवेशने ॥ II. 111. 17

We never should resort to this coercive practice. It is not for a Kshatriya to do this." But when the famous bridge had to be constructed and the monkey host had to be carried across the water and Samudra was not very pliant, what did Sri Rama himself do? Did he forget at that time that he was a Kshatriya? He seems to have. But you see, ladies and gentle-

* See Lect. XIII below.

men, there seems to be some appropriateness working out in all these matters. Bharata did not succeed in his attempt. Rama who unlike a Kshatriya went and did it, did not succeed. He lay down for three days and three nights, fasted, kept vigil, suffered anxiety. But Samudra did not appear. So he says, "I am going to give it up." And then when he threatened, when he took up his bow and arrow and said "I will dry up this ocean", it was then that the Ocean God chose to make his appearance. Then, mind you, force prevailed. No mild measures answered. Another time in the story of the Ramayana the monkeys, finding that they could not meet Sugriva after the stipulated month, thought that nothing was left to them but to go and meet certain death at the hands of Sugriva. Led by Angada they all lay down. They also entered upon this Prayopavesa, wishing to end their lives by this means. Angada seems to have been very fond of this Prayopavesa. He came again and again to it, three different times. But there was an old eagle, elder brother of Jatayu, called Sampati. That chap found out that there was going to be a lot of death near him. He was a disabled bird who had hunger gnawing his body. He was not able to move out very much and get at his prey. So he thought, "If these monkeys should die, what a grand time I am going to have", and as he was patting himself on his back for this stroke of good luck articulately, these monkeys heard him speak and then suddenly Prayopavesa came to an end.

Now to complete this picture is rather irrelevant but interesting. Hanuman too in the Sundara Kanda did not practise it but thought of it. It shows you how Prayopavesa was considered a proper thing in those days. Hanuman, not finding Sita in all his rambles, just says this

> अदृष्ट्वा किं प्रवक्ष्यामि तामहं जनकात्मजाम् ।
> ध्रुवं प्रायमुपैष्यन्ति कालस्य व्यतिवर्तने ॥ V. 12. 8

Now if the Ramayana shows us anything about this Prayopavesa, it is that it is futile.

Finding that Sri Rama disapproved of it, Bharata did not at once get up from the Upavesa, did not at once get up. He appealed to all the people whom he had brought from Ayodhya and said, "Why don't you say a word to my brother? See how obstinate he is. Speak to him." Having heard both sides, all these people, although they wished Rama to return, had not the courage to say so to him. So they said, "What are we to do? Your brother seems to be right." Then Rama says to Bharata, "You see, your own men desert you. This Prayopavesa is wrong. Get up, you fellow. You have done this wrong. You must do Prayaschitta. Go and perform Achamana, come and touch me. That will purify you."

So Bharata did. He gave up Prayopavesa. But, as I told you, he had another trick up his sleeve. Another step in the debate opens. Bharata says to Rama, "You say that our father has ordered one son to be king and another son to be a hermit. That is so. You want to obey father. Very well, you go and be a king; I will go and be a hermit. You be my proxy and I will be your proxy. Let us reverse our parts."

यदि त्ववश्यं वस्तव्यं कर्तव्यं च पितुर्वचः ।
अहमेव निवर्त्स्यामि चतुर्दश समा वने ॥ II. 111. 26

Fourteen years I shall pass here. Why should you?" Rama now says to the assembled people. "Look at the man who has brought you here. See how foolishly he talks. Can I, being ordered to go to the forest and live there for fourteen years like a hermit, pass it on to another? Am I justified, is there anything that will justify me, in passing it on to another? Can I have this done by proxy (Upadhi)?" You may vote at a bank meeting by proxy. You cannot do this thing. Rama appeals to the assembly. He says to them, not to Bharata

विक्रीतमाहितं क्रीतं यत्पित्रा जीवता मम ।
न तल्लोपयितुं शक्यं मया वा भरतेन वा ॥ II. 111. 28

"When father has entered into great transactions, when he has bought some things, when he has mortgaged some things, when he has sold some things, am I (like a modern minor) to go and sue in the law courts? Neither Bharata nor I can change that in the least degree. We are bound by what our father had done. It will bring shame on me if I do it."

उपधिर्न मया कार्यो वनवासे जुगुप्सितः । II. 111. 29

k here,"—this is the word (Upadhi) that I me
e—

युक्तमुक्तं च कैकेय्या पित्रा मे सुकृतं कृतम् ॥ II. 111. 29

he is carried away by the vehemence of his argument so far that instead of merely acquiescing in Kaikeyi's course, he now begins to justify it—"she had the right to do it."

> वृतो राजा हि कैकेय्या मया तद्वचनं कृतम् ।
> अनृतान्मोचयानेन पितरं तं महीपतिम् ॥ II. 111. 32

"I have saved father, tried to save father for my part; you do it for your part."

Then it was that the Maharshis and Devas who had assembled to witness the scene gave the verdict to which I have already referred. "This day Sri Rama has done the right thing. It is his action that has saved Dasaratha from going to Naraka. He is in Svarga because the debt that he owed to Kaikeyi, the tremendous moral debt that he owed to her, however arduous, has been paid to the full by Rama. Dasaratha has his place in Heaven. Now you cancel it and ask him to go back to Ayodhya. The old man must come down." Bharata is not yet beaten. His resources are there still. He falls at Rama's feet and holds them tightly by the arm and says, "Brother, all right, you think you have beaten me in argument. Perhaps you have. But I am a fool. I cannot go and govern. Who will obey me? All people say, 'We want Rama, we want Rama.' What can I do? I cannot govern. I have no capacity. What shall I do?

> रक्षितुं सुमहद्राज्यमहमेकस्तु नोत्सहे ।
> पौरजानपदांश्चापि रक्तान् रञ्जयितुं तथा ॥ II. 112. 11

As in a dry season when the rains are late, the peasants lift up their hands and ask Indra to shower rain upon them, so are all the people, our relations, friends, poor subjects, ministers and all—they all want you and you alone to be king."

> त्वामेव हि प्रतीक्षन्ते पर्जन्यमिव कर्षकाः ॥ II. 112. 12

And then he says:

> इदं राज्यं महाप्राज्ञ स्थापय प्रतिपद्य हि ।
> शक्तिमानसि काकुत्स्थ लोकस्य परिपालने ॥ II. 112. 13

This sloka is somewhat obscure. I prefer to interpret it in the light of one commentator. I think the sloka is intended to mean this. As a last resource Bharata says, "Brother, this kingdom is yours. You accept it and then appoint a regent if you want. He whom you choose and appoint must by that very process become competent to govern. You therefore take the kingdom as yours and appoint somebody to rule on your behalf and in your name and under your authority." Rama is pleased to hear this. He says,

आगता त्वामियं बुद्धिः स्वजा वैनयिकी च या।
भृशमुत्सहसे तात रक्षितुं पृथिवीमपि॥ II. 112. 16

My brother, now that you have shown this extraordinary humility, by that very thing you have proved to me your complete competence to govern this kingdom.

अमात्यैश्च सुहृद्भिश्च बुद्धिमद्भिश्च मन्त्रिभिः।
सर्वकार्याणि संमन्त्र्य सुमहान्त्यपि कारय॥ II. 112. 17

If you have any doubts anywhere, you have plenty of people to advise you, old ministers, people who have already governed parts of the kingdom. Take their advice and go on. But if you still think there is some hope of my returning, dismiss it all from your mind. It cannot be.

लक्ष्मीश्चन्द्रादपेयाद्वा हिमवान् वा हिमं त्यजेत्।
अतीयात्सागरो वेलां न प्रतिज्ञामहं पितुः॥ II. 112. 18

Unnatural things may happen. Things may part from their most innate attributes. Not I. I won't leave my promise or my dharma." I have already quoted this sloka to you.* So I wont't go into it. Then his last word is that Bharata should forget Kaikeyi's misdeeds and treat her as a mother should be treated. That shows you, ladies and gentlemen, how even in the heat of argument or in the extremity of a situation Rama will not forget his duty, especially to those who consider him in some ways their enemy. Kaikeyi looked upon him as a rival to her son, to be got rid of by banishment and as the commentators say, by hoped-for death. Whatever it was

कामाद्वा तात लोभाद्वा मात्रा तुभ्यमिदं कृतम्।
न तन्मनसि कर्तव्यं वर्तितव्यं च मातृवत्॥ II. 112. 19

she did wrong owing to bad motives it is true. But don't remember it against her. That would be wrong.

* Lect. VIII, p. 103.

Don't retain it; don't let it rankle in your mind. You must behave to her as an ordinary son should behave to his mother.

मातरं रक्ष कैकेयीं मा रोषं कुरु तां प्रति ॥
मया च सीतया चैव शप्तोऽसि रघुसत्तम ॥ II. 112. 27-28

Then it is that the last scene occurs in this most edifying drama. Suddenly as if by magic Bharata produces a pair of sandals ornamented with gold. Apparently they were part of the things that they had brought and thought of using if Rama could be persuaded to have the ceremony of abhisheka. They were there. So he took them and Vasishtha prompted him to take the sandals. The sandals were taken. Then Bharata says, "Here are the sandals, brother. Do me this favour. Once stand on these sandals and then get down. People say that as he stood on the sandals, his greatness by some mystic process was transferred to the sandals, and Bharata carried the sandals home, installed them and regarded them as he would regard his elder brother; from those sandals he would get the necessary moral authority, the inspiration from time to time to behave as a true king. In other words, he could be in some ways Rama's regent in the kingdom. It is said that when they had been once used by Sri Rama, Bharata took them reverently and put them on his head. In what light Bharata regarded the whole of these proceedings appears in the 115th Sarga.

एतद्राज्यं मम भ्रात्रा दत्तं सन्न्यासवत्स्वयम् ।
योगक्षेमवहे तस्य पादुके हेमभूषिते ॥ II. 115. 14

Bharata says, "Rama is still king. He has only deposited the kingdom with me as a trust. He is the king. I am only a king for him. I am only a trustee. The ownership is there. सन्न्यासवत्स्वयम् is not used in the ordinary sense, but in the sense of a firm and emphatic 'Nyasa'. These sandals that I am carrying, they are king.

भरतः शिरसा कृत्वा सन्न्यासं पादुके ततः ।
अब्रवीद्दुःखसंतप्तः सर्वं प्रकृतिमण्डलम् ॥ II. 115. 15

When the subjects assembled before him, he tells them all, with grief oppressing his heart

छत्रं धारयत क्षिप्रमार्यपादाविमौ मतौ ।
आभ्यां राज्ये स्थितो धर्मः पादुकाभ्यां गुरोर्मम ॥ II. 115. 16

Dharma stays in this kingdom not because of me but because of those sandals. He did the anointing ceremony to the sandals.

ततस्तु भरतः श्रीमानभिषिच्यार्यपादुके ।
तदधीनस्तदा राज्यं कारयामास सर्वदा ॥ II. 115. 26

Whenever something had to be done, when a valuable present or tribute was brought,

यदा हि यत्कार्यमुपैति किंचिदुपायनं चोपहृतं महार्हम् ।
स पादुकाभ्यां प्रथमं निवेद्य चकार पश्चाद्भरतो यथावत् ॥
II. 115. 27

having first dedicated it to the sandals, announced every thing to the sandals, he did the proper things subsequently.

You see then the point is settled easily for us as to who won in this mighty debate between Rama and Bharata. Both won and both lost. That was the funny thing. Outwardly of course Bharata lost. He had to go back without taking back his brother. But he won in this sense. Kaikeyi's wish was, Dasaratha's idea was, everybody's idea was, that when Rama was banished and when he went away, when Sita and Lakshmana went away, the coast was perfectly clear for Bharata and Bharata was to be yuvaraja and subsequently king, not as regent but in his own right. And Manthara's hope communicated very loyally to Kaikeyi was that during this period of fourteen years of compulsory banishment Rama would be forgotten. Sita, the handsomest beauty on earth, the rarest jewel of womanhood, somebody would come and do violence to her; Rama would have to fight, or who knows he may lose her and losing her, Rama is certain to die and with him Lakshmana too. This thing is pretty certain to happen,—ninety-nine per cent will happen—so everybody thought. Bharata therefore was to be king. The kingdom of Ayodhya was to pass into his hands. That was the original idea. Bharata by his obstinacy, by his bringing up resource upon resource, modified this position to some extent. He got Sri Rama to admit, though not in words, by his actions, that though exiled he still owned the kingdom and was king and that

Bharata ruled it by means of Rama's sandals to which was communicated this rare moral elevation. So we are justified in thinking that the honours of the battle were about equally divided, Sri Rama winning in fact and Bharata winning in law and in form and at the same time also deriving, so the Poet says, so everybody believes, deriving his power to govern, his courage, his wisdom, his all-round vigilance, deriving all these qualities from Sri Rama's sandals.

So ends this famous passage. It is full of edification. Those who have time may be exhorted every time to read those beautiful verses. Ordinarily, in other places, the Poet uses expletives and vocatives somewhat loosely and in profusion. Here the thought is concentrated, there is plenty of matter to say, matter of a most exalted and educative kind. So even the language is free from unnecessary verbiage as we say. Here language and matter are married together to give you a passage of rare beauty, of rare charm and of rare virtue to purify the heart and purify our lives.

ELEVENTH LECTURE*

Ladies and Gentlemen,

Before I take leave of the character of Sri Rama I must deal with two points of absorbing interest which have engaged not only the attention but the warm feelings of disputants for many many centuries. Two episodes have given rise to controversy. Authorities which cannot be questioned are found on either side of the dispute and it will not do for me to lay down any precise judgment as though it were beyond question. But it would be helpful to students of the Ramayana if I brought together the issues raised over these problems.

Today I will deal only with the Vali episode, leaving the other great bone of contention, the conduct of Sri Rama with regard to Sita at the end of the Yuddhakanda to another occasion. Perhaps it would be well to state at the outset what the main points are which will engage our attention. It is brought up by critics against Sri Rama that he killed Vali from a concealed position. That he killed him at all is also brought up against him as something against the course of natural justice. Incidentally questions of smaller importance are mixed up with the main issues. I will first mention them. I know some of my friends who are imbued with the modern spirit, as we should say, in internationalism, regard imperialism of any kind as a vice among kings and those invested with kingly authority. We are a subject people and, therefore, to us every form of control by another people is odious, especially in these days when as a result of this great war, great expectations of liberty and freedom and self-expression all over the world among nations great and small have been raised. At a time like this it is no wonder that the claim of one people to dominate over a whole continent or the claim of one king to tribute and homage from all kings over a large area is regarded with no sympathy. We think it a vulgar form of self-assertion. Among kings especially we scarcely distinguish it from inordinate ambition and a desire to tyrannise over weaker peoples. Sri Rama in defending himself asserts this imperialism in strong terms, almost without any qualification. To us therefore of the modern day that claim appears a little

* 21-6-'44.

out of the character of Sri Rama. I am however bound to point out to you who are studying an ancient Poem and the character of a great king who functioned centuries ago, I am bound to point out to you that we have no right to judge of Sri Rama's ideas by the light of modern aspiration. Let us especially remember that contentment was a virtue of the Brahmnan caste. In Kshatriyas it was not regarded as a virtue. It was often held up as a sign of weakness. That Kshatriya was worthy of honour of all who night and day strove to extend the limits of his kingdom, who desired to extend his sway over the whole continent. Yagas were performed for the purpose of extending the area over which a king's authority was acknowledged. It was not a virtue in those days for a king to be contented with what he inherited. But he was considered unworthy of the throne if he did not increase its glory, if he did not add to its dominion, if in fact, he did not bring alien peoples under his own umbrella. If therefore Sri Rama asserted this principle in somewhat unequivocal terms, we are not justified in judging him by other standards. That then must be taken out of the indictment against Sri Rama.

Then he asserted that in killing Vali he was acting as a deputy or delegate of his brother, Bharata. Bharata was king of Ayodhya and therefore had the whole of Bharatavarsha under him and if in Kishkindha the king misbehaved, it was right of Bharata to punish him, and if Bharata was not available on the spot, it was the right of Bharata's brother, of any one of his kinsmen, in fact, who claimed that he belonged to the royal family, it was the right of such a person to inflict the deserved punishment. That was the extension of the imperialistic doctrine which Sri Rama enunciated without reserve. Then the question is—another point that brings in modern notions—if Sri Rama had jurisdiction to take up Vali's misdeeds and to inflict proper penalties upon him, was the jurisprudence of the times such that the penalty of death could be inflicted upon a person who had been guilty of appropriating his younger brother's wife? You may be reminded of a passage in Indian history where Nuncomar who forged a document was punished with death and historians have regarded that it was essentially unjust as the Indian Penal Code did not include forgery among the capital crimes. But in those days the East India Company and its representatives in Calcutta were not restrained by any such notions. If a man was inconvenient and had been caught and it was necessary to dispose of him so that he may be no more trouble, they were not very scrupulous as to what they did with him. I am afraid that in punishing Vali with death Sri Rama was guilty of some such extension. I shall point that out later.

Then the question is raised thus. The main object of Rama was that his wife should be recovered. Why did he not choose Vali as his ally, who could have done it for him in no time? For, it was generally acknowledged that Vali was a monkey of immense prowess and that he had already conquered Ravana and almost treated him with contumely. Why was not Vali taken as an ally instead of his weaker brother? Another small question that is raised is, why did Sri Rama not kill Vali at the first encounter? Why did he at that time let him go and ask Sugriva to come again and summon him to a single combat? The reason given by Sri Rama is generally believed to be unsatisfactory, and commentators and readers of the Ramayana generally have been at pains to discover why Sri Rama did this apparently weak thing. Another question that I shall raise but which to my knowledge has not been raised before is whether Sri Rama was consistent with his own action when he regarded the capture of Ruma, Sugriva's wife, by the brother as a crime that deserved extreme punishment. Now these several questions I will attempt to deal with. But let me explain as before in previous discussions that I shall confine myself as far as possible to the text of Valmiki, that I shall not travel beyond his words, that I shall not call to my aid the authority of any other Purana or any other version of the Ramayana that may be current amongst us. It is necessary for us to fix our eyes exclusively on what Valmiki has said and to ground ourselves on his words. It will not do to travel outside and get into trouble with questions of Sastra or Sastraic exegesis.

There are those who in defiance of the express words of the Poet himself claim that Sri Rama was not concealed when he aimed his arrow at Vali. They allow that Vali did not know that there was somebody aiming at him. Vali was not aware of it. But though he was not aware, they are not disposed to think ill of Rama's action in killing him; for they contend that he did so openly and not from any covert position. That however is against the express text. The words in the text are:

सर्वे ते त्वरितं गत्वा किष्किन्धां वालिनः पुरीम्।
वृक्षैरात्मानमावृत्य व्यतिष्ठन् गहने वने ॥ IV. 12. 14

'Hiding their bodies behind the trees'; 'stayed in a dark forest'. Now the words वृक्षैः...गहने वने can have no other meaning. And when Vali accuses Rama of having been hidden when he aimed his arrow, it is conclusive that Rama makes no answer to it. He does not deny it. On the other hand, he admits it and defends his action. He only says, "Yes, I did so. But who are you? You are only a monkey, an object of the chase. Kings like me, kingly people like me, are entitled to hunt you and the chase allows the huntsman to be hidden or to prepare traps or to do anything of the kind which may be called 'kuta'. I am not bound to fight you as though you were a worthy combatant. I am not bound to give you notice or to call you to measure your prowess against mine." That is Sri Rama's defence. Obviously, therefore, it was a fact that he killed Vali not in open fight, not face to face in a straight encounter, but in a fashion which as between ordinary warriors would be considered highly improper or dishonourable. To throw some light upon this I will read to you two of the comments of the greater exegetists. Govindaraja himself—no man can claim to be a greater Ramabhakta than he—does not mince his words over the question. He says

"प्रतिज्ञातं च रामेण तथा वालिवधं प्रतीति प्रतिज्ञानिर्वाहाय छद्मनाऽपि वालिवधः कृतः" IV. 16. 37-38

Vali was killed by Rama although by a fraud just because he had made a promise to Sugriva. Then, exercising a little freedom with the matter of the text, in another place he says "यदि रामो वालिनः पुरतस्तिष्ठेत्", that is, if Rama had stood in front of Vali,

"तदा विदिततदीयप्रभावतया वाली प्रह्वो भवेत्, तदा तद्वधो न युक्तः, प्रतिज्ञा च व्याहन्येत, तद्द्वारा तन्मित्रं रावणोऽपि शरणं व्रजेत्, देवकार्यं च लुप्येत्, अतः प्रच्छन्नो वालिनमवधीत्। IV. 18. 45

that is, Vali, knowing the great skill in battle of his antagonist, might have made his submission and when submission is made Rama was not the man to go forward with a battle. He must at once grant protection to the saranagata. In that case the promise that he had made would be frustrated. Also, Ravana who was the sworn friend of Vali would also come and say, "I will fall at your feet. Excuse me." Then his mission would not be fulfilled. It was therefore necessary for Sri Rama to lie hidden when he aimed his arrow. Now was this right, was this in accordance with the law of chivalry as it was acknowledged at the time? Even in those days, as is obvious from the difficulty that these people feel, such fight was not considered proper. No true warrior would attack another when he was not aware of the combatant. I will give you an extraordinary illustration of it from the Ramayana itself. Now, let me ask your minds for a while to dwell on a very dramatic incident in the great battle. In one of the incidents of the battle several of the most eminent persons on both sides are engaged. Rama is on the scene; Lakshmana is on the scene; Hanuman, Sugriva and Neela and everybody on the one side, and on the other you have got Ravana himself besides others. Now the battle is about to open and as the great warriors face each other, Ravana knowing his old antagonist, Hanuman, by face, gives him a blow on the chest with his palm. Hanuman reels under the blow but quickly recovering, lands a blow himself on the chest of Ravana with the palm. Ravana in turn swayed this way and that but he said, "Now, look here. You are a strong person. You have given me a blow which has caused me to be unsteady." Well, that is a noble warrior's characteristic, to praise the strength and skill of the enemy. But do you know what Hanuman says in reply? He says, "Well, it is all very well for you to praise me. But I am ashamed, I am ashamed that even after that blow you should be alive to compliment me." This infuriated Ravana and then instead of a straight blow with the palm, he clenches his right fist and strikes with that as hard as he could at Hanuman's chest. Hanuman could not stand it. His eyes became dim and he was not aware of what was happening. For the moment he was put out of action. Then Ravana thinking that for the moment Hanuman was disabled, turned to Neela who was the commander-in-chief on the spot and he was engaged with him. Meantime, Hanuman recovered and wishing to pay back what he had got, if possible, with interest, came to where Ravana stood. But finding that he was engaged with Neela, he did not like to take advantage of it but told Ravana

विप्रेक्षमाणो युद्धेप्सुः सरोषमिदमब्रवीत् ॥
नीलेन सह संयुक्तं रावणं राक्षसेश्वरम् ।
अन्येन युध्यमानस्य न युक्तमभिधावनम् ॥ VI. 59. 73-74

"When a man is engaged with another, it is not honourable to attack him.*" So said Hanuman and kept back. He nursed his vengeance and went for Ravana when Ravana was all alone and could pay him full attention. Now that incident in which Hanuman enunciated this chivalrous doctrine that you must not take advantage of a foe when he is otherwise engaged, when he could not deal directly with you, is of particular application when we review Sri Rama's conduct. It is not alone that Vali was not able to deal with Sri Rama. He was not aware of Rama's existence on the spot. So it is a greatly aggravated form of unworthy combat.

Now I will postpone for a little while the consideration of why Sri Rama did this. It is necessary now to follow the text of Valmiki through some sargas in order to find out what might have been at the bottom of Sri Rama's action, what could have made him think of this. The text seems to help us a little—I will not say it does, I dare not make that assertion. But as we read the passages and dwell on the individual words here and there something like a dim light is thrown upon the subject. In the first place I want to ask your attention to a matter not germane to our issue now but which will become important later. Sugriva had two grievances against Vali; one of them was real, the other fanciful. Sugriva told Hanuman and Hanuman in turn told Sri Rama and Lakshmana that Vali had done two wrongs to his brother. One wrong of course was that he had appropriated his wife, Ruma. The other wrong, represented as wrong curiously enough, was that he drove Sugriva out of his kingdom. The fact was that it was Vali's kingdom and he merely took it back when Sugriva had unknowingly become king. He only took it back but Sugriva represents it and Hanuman represents it as though he had been unlawfully deprived of what was his.

स हि राज्यात्परिभ्रष्टः कृतवैरश्च वालिना ।
हृतदारो वने त्यक्तो भ्रात्रा विनिकृतो भृशम् ॥ IV. 4. 27

* See Lect. XIX below.

He has been driven out of the kingdom, his kingdom, and he has been deprived of his wife and the brother has betrayed him. Now Sugriva is very careful. Sugriva says to Sri Rama

वालिना निकृतो भ्रात्रा कृतवैरश्च राघव।
वालिनो मे महाभाग भयार्तस्याभयं कुरु॥
कर्तुमर्हसि काकुत्स्थ भयं मे न भवेद्यथा। IV. 5. 24-25

"I am afraid of my brother. He is much stronger than I. He has driven me out and he has humiliated me. I want you to give me protection from him so that I need not fear him." That is all he says; there is no suggestion of Vali's being killed but Sri Rama in replying and giving him encouragement says

वालिनं तं वधिष्यामि तव भार्यापहारिणम्। IV. 5. 27

He mentions it first himself. "I will kill your brother because he has taken away your wife."

अमोघाः सूर्यसंकाशा ममैते निशिताः शराः॥ IV. 5. 27

Notice that he now uses the plural number. Obviously he intends to use many arrows in killing Vali. They will never fail of action. अमोघाः, सूर्यसंकाशाः, निशिताः. They are keen arrows that will never fail of effect. Now notice once more:

तमद्य वालिनं पश्य क्रूरैराशीविषोपमैः॥
शरैर्विनिहतं भूमौ विकीर्णमिव पर्वतम्। IV. 5. 29-30

I will fell him down with my arrows, with my keen arrows, with my well-directed arrows and I will do it today," says Sri Rama. आशीविषोपमैः As keen as serpents.

Now it appears therefore that at this point Rama was thinking only of a straight encounter, of an open battle with Vali, for otherwise why should he think of many arrows? Then Rama says to Sugriva once more

उपकारफलं मित्रमपकारोऽरिलक्षणम्।
अद्यैव तं हनिष्यामि तव भार्यापहारिणम्॥ IV. 8. 21

Once again he swears, "I will kill him and that too today." Sugriva then enunciates his demand.

पुराहं वालिना राम राज्यात्स्वादवरोपितः ॥
परुषाणि च संश्राव्य निर्धूतोऽस्मि बलीयसा ॥
हृता भार्या च मे तेन प्राणेभ्योऽपि गरीयसी । IV. 8. 32-33

He has deprived me of my kingdom and he says, "Ruma is dearer to me than my own life; her he has made his own."

In another place Rama repeats what he had stated about his "arrows" (plural) and says:

अमोघाः सूर्यसंकाशा ममैते निशिताः शराः ।
तस्मिन् वालिनि दुर्वृत्ते निपतिष्यन्ति वेगिताः ॥
यावत्तं नाभिपश्यामि तव भार्यापहारिणम् ।
तावत्स जीवेत्पापात्मा वाली चारित्रदूषकः ॥ IV. 10. 32-33

"That Vali of yours, your enemy who has done you harm, will be alive only so long as my eye does not fall upon him. When my eye falls upon him, when he comes within the range of my vision, he dies." You see how Rama looks upon it. I want your attention to be concentrated on this point. Rama thinks that he should slay Vali at once, that very day. There should be no doubt about it. Then he thinks, at the moment no doubt, of having a straight fight and of having to use therefore many of his arrows. Then when he come to the twelfth sarga Sugriva who misdoubts the personal strength of Sri Rama, who fancies that Vali was a giant in comparison with this human being, just asks him for some proof or test by which he could be sure in his own mind that his ally, Sri Rama, would really be a helpful ally, an efficient ally. So he proposes to him two tests with one of which we are not concerned at the moment. The other was this. There were seven sala trees standing in a row. Sugriva says, "My brother Vali is so strong that if he shook one of the trees, the whole tree would be bare at once. All the leaves would fall and he could do it with all the other trees as well, so strong is he personally. Sri Rama was somewhat piqued that this should be mentioned as something against which he must prove and measure his own strength. So, as if carelessly, he took an arrow and directed it at the sala trees. It pierced all of them. Then it went on to the earth beyond, pierced the earth, came back to its resting place. Sugriva was taken aback. I suppose he half regretted he had proposed the test to such a man. Then he actually falls at his feet and says to him, "How strong you are! I never dreamt of this. So you can kill all the Devas if you will. You are extraordinary. I am proud of you. I am glad I have got you for my ally in this contest."

येन सप्त महासाला गिरिर्भूमिश्च दारिताः ।
बाणेनैकेन काकुत्स्थ स्थाता ते को रणाग्रतः ॥ IV. 12. 9

"Who is the man that can stand in front of you and fight you? There is no man who can do it, because you have done all this, destroyed so many things with a single arrow." The single arrow idea comes in now, as between them in conversation. I want you just to lay hold of these little points. They are not little because we are puzzled to find out the mentality of Sri Rama and we cannot go and ascribe to him all sorts of dishonourable motives. Let us therefore remember that now for the first time the idea of a single arrow comes in, the idea of how much can be done by one arrow, how much might can be exercised by a single arrow when it is directed properly by Sri Rama.

तमद्यैव प्रियार्थं मे वैरिणं भ्रातृरूपिणम् ।
वालिनं जहि काकुत्स्थ मया बद्धोऽयमञ्जलिः ॥ IV. 12. 11

"I bow to you in reverence. You are the greatest and mightiest warrior I have seen. Oblige me by liquidating my brother today." Then they went to Kishkindha, and you know Sugriva challenges Vali to a single combat. Lakshmana and Sri Rama and Hanuman stand hidden in a thick grove behind trees. Vali being much the stronger of the brothers beats him almost to a pulp. And Sugriva looks round to where Rama could be seen. In the meantime, the Poet says Rama, seeing his ally in serious risk, took out his arrow and knowing that he was in great danger of life, desired to aim at Vali. But apparently Vali and Sugriva when locked together in single combat, were so alike in size, in complexion, in movement and quickness and so on, that he was unable to distinguish which was Vali and which was Sugriva. He therefore shrank from taking the fatal aim. He would not send his arrow lest he should kill the wrong person and bring his own mission into serious risk.

यन्नावगच्छत्सुग्रीवं वालिनं वापि राघवः ।

As he was not able to say which was Vali and which was Sugriva,

ततो न कृतवान् बुद्धिं मोक्तुमन्तकरं शरम् ॥ IV. 12. 20

and as that one arrow was going to prove fatal, it would take away life and therefore he could not aim it. Then Sugriva flees for life; he goes to his own place, Risyamuka, where quickly the brothers join him with Hanuman. Then Sugriva gently upbraids Sri Rama. "My dear friend, if you had told me before that you would not kill Vali, I would never have gone out to challenge Vali to a combat. Look at me, in what condition he has left me. I am ashamed of myself. Why didn't you tell me before that you were not willing to kill Vali?" Then Rama pleads, 'I was confounded."

ततोऽहं रूपसादृश्यान्मोहितो वानरोत्तम ।
नोत्सृजामि महावेगं शरं शत्रुनिबर्हणम् ॥ IV. 12. 32

"With the terrible arrow I had in my hand I could have disposed of one of you. But suppose you had been struck, what would have happened to me, what would have happened to Lakshmana, to Sita in Lanka? Think of that. By killing you who is my ally, I should be practically destroying the whole of my life and my life's mission.

जीवितान्तकरं घोरं सादृश्यात्तु विशङ्कितः ।
मूलघातो न नौ स्याद्धि द्वयोरपि कृतो मया ॥ IV. 12. 33

That was my thought and therefore I refrained from killing Vali. Now you had better put on something to show that you are Sugriva, something to distinguish you from your brother and then go and challenge him again to combat. I will fulfil my promise."

तस्माद्युध्यस्व भूयस्त्वं मा मा शङ्कीश्च वानर ॥ IV. 12. 36

"No more doubt about me."

अस्मिन् मुहूर्ते सुग्रीव पश्य वालिनमाहवे ।
निरस्तमिषुणैकेन वेष्टमानं महीतले ॥ IV. 12. 37

"If you go and draw him out, challenge him to fight, then I will with a single arrow kill him at once." That was his promise.

Then

सर्वे ते त्वरितं गत्वा किष्किन्धां वालिपालिताम् ।
वृक्षैरात्मानमावृत्य व्यतिष्ठन् गहने वने ॥ IV. 14. 1

the same thing the Poet repeats. In a dense grove they stood hidden behind trees. Then Rama assures Sugriva once more,

अद्य वालिसमुत्थं ते भयं वैरं च वानर।
एकेनाहं प्रमोक्ष्यामि बाणमोक्षेण संयुगे॥ IV. 14. 10-11

"I will release you at once from the dread that your brother has caused, by one arrow, with one arrow and today." See how the idea of having a straight fight and the necessity of using many arrows has gone from Sri Rama's mind. He had repeatedly made a promise to Sugriva that as soon as he saw Vali he should be disposed of and with one arrow. This one arrow idea got hold of him apparently. It possessed him. Not to use more than one arrow to kill Vali. And repeatedly in the poem as we go on, we find the Poet mentioning this fact that he killed Vali with a single arrow as a great proof of Rama's might. Now, ladies and gentlemen, whatever we may think, we are not entitled to assume that that was a mere oversight or accident. It was something deliberate and it could not have been undertaken if it was incompatible with notions of honour. Let us go on a little. Of course you know that before Vali accepts the second challenge, his able wife, Tara, tries to dissuade him. Tara uses all her rhetoric upon him. From her own son, Angada, who was in touch with some spies she has heard that Sugriva has come a second time because he has secured the assistance of some mighty person, of some irresistible man. She has heard all that and Angada has told her everything about Sri Rama. So among other things she tells him, finding that he was not willing to be easily dissuaded, she tells him everything she knows. She asks him. "Do you know whom you are going to fight with? Not Sugriva. That fellow is only the combatant to be put forward. But you will have to fight Sri Rama

रामः परबलामर्दी युगान्ताग्निरिवोत्थितः।
निवासवृक्षः साधूनामापन्नानां परा गतिः॥ IV. 15. 19

a good gentleman willing to help the poor and distressed, the friend of all those who need help. He however is like the Fire at the Yuga's end. You cannot go and resist him."

आर्तानां संश्रयश्चैव यशसश्चैकभाजनम्।
ज्ञानविज्ञानसंपन्नो निदेशे निरतः पितुः॥

धातूनामिव शैलेन्द्रो गुणानामाकरो महान्।
तत्क्षमो न विरोधस्ते सह तेन महात्मना॥ IV. 15. 20-21

"You shall not go and fight him. Don't make an enemy of this Sri Rama. He has this, that and a third thing." I read these slokas only to show in what light Sri Rama appeared even to a person like Tara who had never seen him or heard of him except perhaps now. So she advises her husband to make peace with his brother. "Don't go and punish Sugriva; make peace with him." And then she says. "Appoint him Yuvaraja." Apparently therefore he has not been Yuvaraja before though he had been king himself in the supposed absence of Vali. He had not been Yuvaraja. She says for the first time, "You appoint him Yuvaraja." But there is one thing she does not advise him. I want to ask your attention to that. You remember how when Ravana consults Vibhishana, Kumbhakarna and other people, they advise him to give back Sita to her proper husband. Tara, who was advising Vali in a similar situation, might have added, "Give back to Sugriva Ruma also because he makes a great grievance of it. The kingdom is one source of vexation to him. But this Ruma business is also a great trouble. If you want to pacify Sugriva fully, you must not only instal him as Yuvaraja but you must also restore his wife to him." The last one was one of the grounds of quarrel between the brothers. Why didn't Tara, so wise, so circumspect, why didn't she advise him then to do so? I cannot make it out.

Now in this fight also Sugriva soon loses ground. Then seeing that he was reduced to extremities, Sri Rama killed Vali with a single arrow.

ततो धनुषि संधाय शरमाशीविषोपमम्।
पूरयामास तच्चापं कालचक्रमिवान्तकः॥
ततस्तेन महातेजा वीर्योत्सिक्तः कपीश्वरः।
वेगेनाभिहतो वाली निपपात महीतले॥ IV. 16. 33, 36

Now in that way Vali was disposed of. I have tried to show you that some extraordinary importance was attached to this idea of killing Vali by a single arrow. Also extraordinary importance was attached to his being killed that very day. "अद्यैव" is repeated several times. Sugriva was getting impatient and felt many misgivings as to what was going to happen and when on the first occasion Rama did not aim the arrow, he went back somewhat reassured by Rama's solemn assurances but I suppose with a little doubt also still. So the thing had got to be done. It was not as if Rama could postpone the end or draw the struggle out that Sugriva may be filled with dismay, vexation and doubt. That was, it seems to me, perhaps the direction in which we should look for the reason. I would not be too sure of anything at this distance of time but it appears to me that some little light might be obtained if we paid attention to these considerations. Now who was this Vali? Let us think about that a little. I do not say for a moment that Rama was diffident. As regards the relative strength of Vali and Rama, I do not wish to suggest for a moment that Rama was afraid of meeting Vali in single combat. Far be it from me to make such a suggestion. But the point is that Rama was not able as we know later on, to kill even Ravana very easily. It appears that at the last stage of the struggle things were so evenly balanced that the issue was really in doubt. The gods and the Maharishis who came to witness the battle were in serious dismay as to what was going to happen. They actually told Indra, "You see the unequal combat between the two. Ravana fights seated in his chariot. Poor Rama stands on his feet on the ground. So you had better give him your chariot." And Indra did so. Matali himself brought it and he was the charioteer. Rama was given not only a chariot but a shield and a bow and new arrows—all these were supplied anew. Then, as you know, still the struggle was even and it was not certain that Rama would win. So once more the Maharishis and others inspired Agastya to go to Rama's help. He came and in the ear of Sri Rama taught Adityahridaya. That had to be taught to him. Moreover at the last moment it was still doubtful and Matali once more told him, "I don't want to tell you much, but believe me, this is the moment for you to use the extreme, the most powerful weapon. Don't hesitate. Use the Brahmastra." You see, ladies and gentlemen, how even in fighting with Ravana Rama often found his full strength tested to breaking point and it came to his receiving miraculous help. Now Vali was so much stronger than Ravana that in the Uttara Kanda it is related how when Ravana was about to go and challenge him to combat, he discovered him in the southern ocean doing part of his sandhya rites. Then it would appear that Vali knowing that somebody was behind him and not with a friendly intention, kept as it were the back of his eye upon him and as soon as he came sufficiently near with wicked intent he caught hold of him and put him in his arm-pit and so carried him to all the other oceans and finally took him to his own home and deposited him on the ground, a thoroughly humbled and broken-down chap. Then Ravana burst out in admiration of Vali's strength.

अहो बलमहो वीर्यमहो गाम्भीर्यमेव च ।
येनाहं पशुवद्गृह्य भ्रामितश्चतुरोऽर्णवान् ।। VII. 34. 37
त्रयाणामेव भूतानां गतिरेषा प्लवङ्गम ।
मनोऽनिलसुपर्णानां तव चात्र न संशयः ।। VII. 34. 39

"Hitherto I have known only three people who could do this mighty thing that you have done, namely, the Mind, Vayu and Garuda. Now I have had a fourth and that is, yourself, to be added to this category."

Hereafter Hanuman has also to be added.

त्वया सह चिरं सख्यं सुस्निग्धं पावकाग्रतः ।।
दाराः पुत्राः पुरं राष्ट्रं भोगाच्छादनभोजनम् । VII. 34. 40-41

"Come, let us go to the sacred fire and before that fire let us swear eternal friendship to each other. Between us let all these things be shared alike. Now let us be such friends that we shall have no difference in all these matters. Let us be one for all practical purposes." The extraordinary thing is that he puts in there दाराः पुत्राः. That shows how in those days the wife was only considered an important item of the property. Then on that occasion Ravana lived in the house of Vali as though he was another Sugriva.

स तत्र मासमुषितः सुग्रीव इव रावणः ।। VII. 34. 44

That is, he was treated by Vali as a younger brother, fondled and taken care of.

Now what do you think would have been Rama's fate if he had actually entered upon a straight face to face fight with Vali? I do not say that he would have lost. No. That is not my point. But let us remember that the fight between

Ravana and Sri Rama is described by the poet as having lasted for seven days, that there was no remission or relaxation of the struggle, that it continued to be of the same intensity all those days and nights, that there was no moment when either combatant failed in his vigilance or in the exercise of his greatest strength.

> देवदानवयक्षाणां पिशाचोरगरक्षसाम् ।
> पश्यतां तन्महद्युद्धं सर्वरात्रमवर्तत ॥ VI. 110. 37

The battle lasted seven days when all these people were spectators.

> नैव रात्रं न दिवसं न मुहूर्तं न च क्षणम् ।
> रामरावणयोर्युद्धं विराममुपगच्छति ॥ VI. 110. 38

Now if that was the case later on with Ravana, with Vali the fight would have lasted at least for seven or eight days. Sugriva's patience would have been lost. He would have been stricken with fear and Rama's promise to dispose of Vali that day would not have been carried out. And you know in the style of the battles of those days, when you have a straight fight, you do not kill your enemy straightway. The first arrow never succeeds. Your arrow is resisted by the other man's arrows and you try a second time, a third time, a fourth time, etc. It is only after the enemy is exhausted and you too are getting nearly exhausted, that the issue is finally decided. That would have been the result of a straight encounter between Vali and Rama. Never doubting for a moment that Rama would have come out victorious, it is at the same time clear that he would have to be carrying on for many days this well-maintained struggle and that perhaps by that time Sugriva would have lost his patience completely.

Then our commentators go beyond the text a little and bring in other stories. I do not know whether I am justified in referring to them but one of much importance I must mention because there is some foundation for it in Valmiki's text. You know Indra gave a gold garland to be worn by Vali always, especially when he went to meet the enemy in battle. This was believed to have some mystic power to make Vali strong and to assure him of victory. But whether it had anything more than that is not mentioned by our Poet. But somewhere else it is narrated and Govindaraja brings it up.

एतत्काञ्चनमालाधारणकाले यः पुरो युद्धायागच्छति
तस्य बलं सर्वं तवैव भविष्यतीति महेन्द्रेण दत्तामित्यर्थः

IV. 11. 39 commentary.

'You will acquire all the strength of your enemy if he comes in front for battle.' I do not know what truth there was in this or whether Sri Rama knew about it. But it is mentioned there as perhaps one of the reasons why it was necessary to adopt a manifest trick or fraud in this battle.

Then the question is asked, as I said, why instead of making a compact with Vali, Rama should have chosen the weaker of the brothers. As a matter of fact, ladies and gentlemen, you know how before Sri Rama met Kabandha and disposed of him, he knew nothing about Sugriva. It was this Kabandha who for the first time informed him that if he went to Sugriva in Risyamuka, he would help him. Kabandha said, "There is no one who knows the entire world, its geography and topography and other things so well as Sugriva. He knows all about this Ravana. You had better ask him." And he further said, "Sugriva is a straight chap. He has been in trouble like you. He also has lost his wife. Therefore he would sympathise with you. You need his help; he needs your help. You are proper allies of each other. Go and strike a pact with him." That is why Sri Rama came in search of Sugriva. Between people in similar circumstances there is a subtle bond of sympathy. The fact that he had lost his wife endeared him to Sugriva. Rama thought, "That is the proper man who will understand my trouble." So each promised help to the other. What was Vali? He was in the very height of his power, in supreme strength. There was no occasion for him therefore to sympathise with Sri Rama. I do not suppose that is a serious question though Vali puts it to him after his fall. He asks Rama, "Why did you not apply to me? I could have asked Ravana to bring your wife here. That fellow would have run up here." But as I just now read to you he and Ravana had made such a close alliance, they held so many things in common, that it is very doubtful if Vali would have done it then. Now when everything was over it was very easy for him to say so.

Why did not Sri Rama kill Vali at once, the first time they met? I told you of Sri Rama's difficulty. But you see nobody is willing to believe that Sri Rama was really in doubt as to how to distinguish between brothers. As a matter of fact, no commentator believes it. Both the commentators say, "Oh, no no! Sri Rama could certainly have drawn a distinction between the two." For one thing, when the fight was over and Sugriva was returning a humbled and defeated individual, he could easily have seen which was Vali. Besides, Hanuman was there and why not ask him? He would have told him easily. And besides, do you suppose for a moment that Rama could not distinguish his enemy? So you go and find all sorts of other reasons. One man says in his ingenuity, "You see there is such a thing as a man's life fixed beforehand. Vali had a few more hours to live and so Rama kept quiet at that time and did not aim that fatal arrow." Then I told you how Govindaraja explains it. Govindaraja really says that Rama certainly could have known who was Vali and who was Sugriva but he did not care for the moment to do so.

"ईदृशे विषय एवंविधानृतवचनं न दोषायेत्यप्यनेन ध्वनितम्।"

Tilaka, IV. 12. 32

So says a great commentator. Rama had some other thing in his mind. We do not know exactly what. We are unable to define it. But he gave this excuse, that he was unable to distinguish the brothers. It was a false excuse. So say both the commentators and it was an extraordinary thing that that should be done. As a matter of fact, to ascribe to Sri Rama this inability to distinguish the two brothers one of whom was so much stronger that he always beat the other hard is difficult no doubt. But at the same time, ladies and gentlemen, I have a suggestion to make. It is bold of me to make it but I believe it is supported by the words of the Poet. When the brothers were first locked in combat, Rama had not finally made up his mind whether he would go out and have a straight fight with Vali or whether he would from his place of covert position attack. Perhaps he hesitated at the last moment. "Am I going to do this wrong thing, this unchivalrous thing?" He might have hesitated thus. But he then quickly made up his mind remembering that he had made a promise to kill him at once, that he should not have the fight prolonged for seven or eight days and leave everything in doubt. For here is a famous passage which is of some importance in probing the mind of Sri Rama. Sri Rama himself, you remember, says to Vibhishana at the last moment from his greater experience. "When you go to a battle with another, don't suppose that either party is sure of victory. Always a battle is a doubtful thing. You never know which party will be successful.

नैकान्तविजयो युद्धे भूतपूर्वः कदाचन ।
परैर्वा हन्यते वीरः परान् वा हन्ति संयुगे ॥ VI. 112. 18

One side has not always won till now. May be your warrior is stricken by his enemies. It is only to be expected that he would come out victorious. In a battle victory cannot be predicted as certain for either party." Sri Rama himself made this great enunciation. Why not ascribe to him a moment's doubt? There is no harm in it. I should think therefore that on the first occasion when he did not aim his arrow at Vali, he hesitated for a moment as to whether he would not go forward and challenge Vali himself. But then probably he thought that that was not the proper time. May be therefore that there was a moment of indecision. Not at all unlikely.

Well, I should say, ladies and gentlemen, while I have suggested a possible explanation, I myself do not see why we should not believe that Sri Rama did not at that time distinguish between the brothers. His word we have no right to doubt. But if we must doubt it and run after some explanation, perhaps mine is as worthy of your thought as any other.

I told you of the naked imperialism of Sri Rama's doctrine. This is how he enunciates it:

इक्ष्वाकूणामियं भूमिः सशैलवनकानना ।
मृगपक्षिमनुष्याणां निग्रहप्रग्रहावपि ॥
तां पालयति धर्मात्मा भरतः सत्यवानृजुः ।
धर्मकामार्थतत्त्वज्ञो निग्रहानुग्रहे रतः ॥
तस्य धर्मकृतादेशा वयमन्ये च पार्थिवाः ।
चरामो वसुधां कृत्स्नां धर्मसंतानमिच्छवः ॥
ते वयं धर्मविभ्रष्टं स्वधर्मे परमे स्थिताः ।
भरताज्ञां पुरस्कृत्य निगृह्णीमो यथाविधि ॥ IV. 18. 6-7, 9, 11

This whole earth belongs to the Ikshvakus. He calls himself a Parthiva not in the sense that he was a ruling king but that he was a kinsman of a ruling king, and therefore entitled, he says, to constitute himself deputy whenever occasion arose and whenever some wrong was done. "As I belong to the Royal House of Ayodhya, I have jurisdiction everywhere and I may myself inflict the penalty on the wrong-doer." That, you will say, is an assumption of power and authority which nothing can justify. Bharata did not appoint Rama as his deputy. But this is the comment that Govindaraja makes:

"यद्यपि भरतेन नादेशः कृतः तथाऽपि नेदमसत्यम् ।"

We must not call this a lie.

"यथाकथंचिद्भरतेन राज्यभरणस्य स्वीकृतत्वात्तदन्येषां
तत्कुलीनानां तदादिष्टत्वं सिद्धमिति हृदयम् ।"

It follows, he says, from the very fact that Bharata has assumed sovereignty that all his kinsmen had a share of that sovereignty. They could and should go and do in his absence what he would have done if he had been on the spot.

The comment in Tilaka is a little more clever. He anticipates some of the points that we would make. He says as follows:—First of all, Sri Rama says that he has got power from Bharata to do this. Therefore, although to our knowledge Bharata did not give such authority, we may infer from it the existence of such a commission. Secondly, he says, "When Bharata was king, some of the power of the king also spread out to all his relations. So Rama had a share of it and he could have dont it." Thirdly, he says what I pointed out before on one occasion, *viz.*, that Rama had appointed Bharata Regent, and therefore might take power. As a matter of fact, when Bharata and Rama concluded their debate it was arranged that Rama should, in reality, that is in law, be king and that Bharata should be only regent. Therefore, Bharata held delegated authority and the man who delegated it certainly could act for him. You cannot dispute his right. Rama being himself the delegating authority could on occasion resume it whenever he liked.

Now I will come to my last point, about Ruma.

ज्येष्ठो भ्राता पिता चैव यश्च विद्यां प्रयच्छति । IV. 18. 13

Rama says to Vali, "Your brother, Sugriva, is junior to you. You must regard him as your son. When you appropriated his wife, therefore, you were really doing the wrong thing with your own daughter-in-law."

औरसीं भगिनीं वापि भार्यां वाप्यनुजस्य यः ॥ IV. 18. 22

I mention this prominently in the last part of my talk today because there is a point really in this. You remember, ladies and gentlemen,—not that I told you—but you remember in the story of the Ramayana, later on when Sita has to be taken back, Rama assumes a terrible mien, sends for her in the presence of the world and then solemnly addresses to her words of repudiation, all because the world may think and say something bad of her. He says to her, "Who will say that you are pure, having been under the control of that wicked, remorseless man for one whole year, who will believe it if I told it? No, I cannot therefore accept you as my wife, to be queen when I am king, to be accepted as the head of your sex." He had the most abundant clear and sacred evidence from Hanuman himself as to the condition in which she was, how she struggled against Ravana. He had all that evidence in his possession. Nevertheless, he mistrusted her for a minute and on the strength of that thin, indistinct twilight suspicion he had the hard-heartedness to reject her and tell her cruelly, "Go anywhere over the world. I have no more use for you. Do what you like with yourself." Now remember he tells Vali repeatedly that he is a भ्रातृभार्यापहारक. "You have taken away your brother's wife; you have taken away your daughter-in-law; you are living in unlawful union with her. You are a wicked man. I must punish you and death is the punishment for you." Well, Sugriva what must that fellow have had in his mind as to the honour of his wife, when having known that she was living with Vali, willingly or unwillingly never mind, having known that she was living with him as his wife, he begged Rama to kill his brother and give his wife back to him? What do you think of that wife and what do you think of that husband? Rama himself, mind you, says this to Vali, "You are living with her." So there is no doubt that her purity had been destroyed. But what did Sugriva actually do? He did not make her go through the fire ordeal; he did not wait a day or two. No prayaschitta, nothing. He simply took her back and when Lakshmana goes laden with a terrible message from Sri Rama, he finds that Sugriva was locked up with Ruma. This was what he saw.

रुमां तु वीरः परिरभ्य गाढं वरासनस्थो वरहेमवर्णः ।
ददर्श सौमित्रिमदीनसत्त्वं विशालनेत्रः सुविशालनेत्रम् ॥ IV. 33. 66

He was in that condition. He was embracing Ruma tight. Then Lakshmana enters and sees him in that edifying posture! Here the Poet draws the following contrast with his great sense of humour. Both were *Visalanetra.* Only Lakshmana's eyes were wide open because he saw this extraordinary sight, something thoroughly unfamiliar to him. And the other fellow also opened his eyes wide because Lakshmana discovered him. Sugriva therefore was not very scrupulous about this matter. A wife who had gone from him and lived with the brother in concubinage is brought back to him and he takes her back. I do not say such things do not happen. They do happen, alas. But no one who has so lost his wife would go and make such a terrible complaint of it to another person and ask him to kill the other fellow in order to give the wife back to him. Was it merely a jewel, was it merely some article that another man had taken away for the moment? It was a wife, dearer than one's own life. I do not mind Sugriva's conduct so very much. I want to draw your attention to Rama's apparent inconsistency. For him to have restored Ruma, who had lived with Vali, to her original husband and known that that husband took her back and lived with her again as her husband, for a man who knew that and killed Vali in the process, what was his own attitude to his wife and when, in fact, all that he knew was that she had been helpless as a captive in the control of a most wicked man, one who was known all over the world for the way he had raped other women, for the cruel manner in which he had behaved to others. Rama was so considerate to Ruma and to Sugriva but he had not an iota of compassion when he came to consider his own wife whose innocence was blazoned forth to all the world.

TWELFTH LECTURE*

Friends,—We have to consider today the episode of Rama's repudiation of Sita after the war with Ravana ended. Like the Vali episode this particular part of the Ramayana is also the subject of keen controversy. Some authorities hold that Rama need not have repudiated Sita as he did. Others believing that Rama could do no wrong try to make out that his conduct in this matter as in others was above reproach. It is difficult at this distance of time for us to decide the question and nobody will have the presumption to believe that any remarks that he offers will be considered to conclude a matter which ages have disputed. Still, as intelligent persons studying the Ramayana with reverence and with attention, we may traverse the familiar ground, not in any hope of receiving new enlightenment but with the idea that we may know what could be said on both sides.

Let me at the outset dispose of two points raised by students entitled to reverence. One is somewhat extraordinary, not justified by Valmiki's text at all but based on other works of lesser authority, claiming however to interpret the incidents of the Ramayana faithfully. The story according to them is that when Ravana appeared in Janasthana to carry away Sita, the real Sita disappeared entering Agni and the Sita who figures in the subsequent kandas right up to this repudiation by Sri Rama and the ordeal by fire, was a Maya Sita. This has been vouched for by great authorities and there are larger numbers of people among us who like to believe this story. But it deprives the Epic of all interest. We cannot be interested seriously in the adventures of a mere Maya Sita. I think it is very difficult for us to persuade ourselves that when Rama and Lakshmana bemoan their separation from Sita, when they threaten Sugriva with death for not carrying out his promise to search for Sita, and when subsequently, not finding her, they weep and weep, all the time it is only Maya Sita that they are bothering about. I think it is extraordinary that any people should believe that the Sita of the greater part of the tragedy was a counterfeit Sita and should still interest themselves deeply in her fortunes, elated

*28-6-'44.

when she rejoices and grieved when she suffers. That, I think, is an impossible position. I therefore discard the Maya Sita story as entirely unfounded and calculated to take away our interest in the whole of this drama.

There is another little point also worth mentioning in the beginning in order that we may follow the text without being diverted. That is perhaps a point upon which I may not command your assent even to the extent that I perhaps do over this Maya Sita story. But whatever it is, I had better clearly indicate my preference. I do not think I shall read the actual words but the point is that there is a certain set of orthodox people among us, who venture to think that the disparity between the sexes in respect of character and title to human sympathy, that the disparity between the sexes in these respects and similar respects is very very great indeed, and that to a woman however exalted and pure, separate protest is not allowed, courageous speech is not allowed, independence of judgment is not allowed. They go so far as to think that even Sita, being after all a woman, must be treated as subordinate to man and not entitled to take her own ground upon matters of importance. She may be right or she may be wrong in particular spheres. But wrong or right is not the question that people would consider. They will say, "She is not entitled to independent judgment." They point out that when Maricha seduced Rama away and Lakshmana hesitated to go after him even after the most pitiable counterfeit cries were heard, Sita forgot herself to such an extent that she ventured to use harsh language to Lakshmana, ascribed very very bad motives to him, assailed his character, began to beat her breast and so compelled him to forsake his duty to watch over her and go after Rama, abandoning the person who required protection and going to the protection of a man who certainly did not need any protection. To that extent Sita drove Lakshmana and our great supporters of the theory that one sex is so much superior to the other, go to the length of saying that by disrespect, by improper ascription of motive to Lakshmana, Sita incurred such a heavy sin that all the misfortunes that came to her subsequently were punishments for this *Apachara.**

---

*Govindaraja on VI. 119. 34-35.

"रावणागमनमारभ्य एतावत्पर्यन्तं सीतायाः
परभागवतभूतलक्ष्मणापचारफलमुपपादितम् ।"

Well, I think, ladies and gentlemen, that theory is not entitled to so much respect at our hands. When I deal with the character of Sita upon a later occasion, I shall venture to say a word or two in defence of her in this particular context and in other contexts as well where her conduct has been criticised. For the moment, however, we may dismiss this story too, that the Poet intended the woes of Sita to be read by students as so many different ways in which she was punished for the extravagance of her behaviour.

Now we shall follow the text a bit, not quite to the extent that we did on previous occasions but just enough to indicate the state of mind of Rama and Sita during this scene of tragic distress. Even before Sita appears before him, the trouble in Rama's mind seems to have begun. In telling Vibhishana to go and bring Sita, Rama expressly says, "Ask her to bathe and perfume herself. Let her put on scents and come to me bedecked with all the jewels she has." Vibhishana tells her this message. Sita is perplexed. She says, "I would rather see him at first as I am, soiled, grief-stricken, tear-bedewed, miserable. Don't ask me to bathe and put on my jewels and appear as though I have been leading a gay life. Let me see him as I am, that is, as I have been here." Vibhishana perhaps thinking that he had already seen signs of trouble on Rama's face, tells her, "I think you had better follow your husband's order." Perhaps admonished, Sita does as she was bidden and when she appears before Rama, she is carried in a palanquin. You know the usual noises of people on such occasions,—some armed with clubs and sticks going before and asking people to move this side and that and perhaps letting the clubs fall on one or two persons' shoulders, thus raising a hue and cry. Somehow or other that displeased Rama. Says he, "Don't molest these people. They are my people. Let them see Sita. There is no harm. A woman is protected by her conduct and by her character. These things, the signs of royalty, the pomp and circumstance of a royal household, they won't help. Screens do not help; enclosures do not help. The best protection of a woman is her conduct and here now when there is distress and misery and the end of a cruel war, let her come. There is no harm. After all she appears where I am. That is certainly not blameworthy." So saying Rama shows great agitation. Though he speaks sternly, his head is bent and turned in one direction. And as he speaks apparently against the institution of purdah but irritated that Sita should be hidden at all from people, everybody there including the allies, Sugriva and Vibhishana, and Lakshmana himself—all are seized with fear. They think that there is electricity in the air, as they say. Rama is not easy in his mind. There apparently is some trouble. Sita approaches him. She is taken down from the palanquin and at Rama's bidding walks a few steps and approaches him. Standing as she was just in front, you can well conceive her eagerness to look at his face and read her fate. As she looks at his face, something alarms her as it has already alarmed all the people there. She sees that she is not coming back to the warm bosom of a loving husband from whom she has been separated for a long time. But she is apparently moving into a court of high judgment in order to hear sentence against a criminal. The speech with which Rama opens the interview, if you may so call it, is not calculated to compose her agitation. The speech divides into two parts. In the first part he makes it out that he has done his duty, that he has vindicated the honour of the Ikshvaku family, that he has established his prowess, that he has destroyed the man with his followers who ventured to insult him by carrying away his wife. The disgrace is wiped out. "But," he says to her, "remember I didn't do all this for your sake. No." When he comes to that passage Sita at once sees that a tragic fate awaits her. So the Poet says she looked up and her eyes seemed to indicate the kind of mortal dread which a stag or hind shows when the huntsman has sent his fatal arrow. Then Rama intensifies his hostile attitude. He knits his brows with the severity of a magistrate

स बद्ध्वा भ्रुकुटीं वक्त्रे तिर्यक्प्रेक्षितलोचनः ।
अब्रवीत् परुषं सीतां मध्ये वानररक्षसाम् ॥ VI. 118. 12

and then his heart burst in twain.

जनवादभयाद्राज्ञो बभूव हृदयं द्विधा ॥ (The Bombay Edition)

Then follow words which it is hard even to read at this distance of time.

प्राप्तचारित्रसन्देहा मम प्रतिमुखे स्थिता ।
दीपो नेत्रातुरस्येव प्रतिकूलासि मे दृढम् ॥ VI. 118. 17

"There is a stain on your character." Fancy his saying that himself. "There is a cloud resting upon your conduct. As you stand before me, my eyes are pained to see you, as a man whose eyes are sore cannot stand a bright light." Here a commentator shrewdly remarks that by this very simile Rama condemns himself. It shows that there is nothing wrong with the light. The light is all right; it has done no harm. It is this man whose eyes are sore. Why blame her? But that is only a grim joke. It does not help at all.

तद्गच्छ ह्यभ्यनुज्ञाता यथेष्टं जनकात्मजे।

Go where you like and as you like.

एता दश दिशो भद्रे कार्यमस्ति न मे त्वया॥ VI. 118. 18

There are ten directions in one of which you may go.

"कार्यमस्ति न मे त्वया"

I have no more use for you.

कः पुमान् हि कुले जातः स्त्रियं परगृहोषिताम्।
तेजस्वी पुनरादद्यात् सुहृल्लेख्येन चेतसा॥ VI. 118. 19

Which man descended from a great family can take back with confidence and with longing a wife who has gone and lived for about a year in another man's house?

रावणाङ्कपरिभ्रष्टां दृष्टां दुष्टेन चक्षुषा।
कथं त्वां पुनरादद्यां कुलं व्यपदिशन् महत्॥ VI. 118. 20

I boast of having descended from the Solar family; I am born of Dasaratha; I am born of the race of Raghu. I boast of it. How can I take you who have been seen on Ravana's lap for a time?

तदर्थं निर्जिता मे त्वं यशः प्रत्याहृतं मया।
नास्ति मे त्वय्यभिष्वङ्गो यथेष्टं गम्यतामितः॥ VI. 118. 21

I have recovered you by my valour from your captor, that wicked Rakshasa. I have re-established my fame. I have cleared off the stain which had for a time clouded my name.

"नास्ति मे त्वय्यभिष्वङ्गो"

I have no attachment, I have no desire for you.

"यथेष्टं गम्यतामितः"

You may now take your final leave of me and go where you like.

इति प्रव्याहृतं भद्रे मयैतत् कृतबुद्धिना।

I have carefully considered this matter and this is my resolution. So he shuts out any remonstrance or any protest on her part.

लक्ष्मणे भरते वा त्वं कुरु बुद्धिं यथासुखम्॥
सुग्रीवे वानरेन्द्रे वा राक्षसेन्द्रे विभीषणे।
निवेशय मनः सीते यथा वा सुखमात्मनः॥ VI. 118. 22-23

He mentions four people and says to Sita, "Well, you may fix your affections on any one of these four people.* I do not mind. Choose one or other of these if you like." See what the freedom that he gives her is. Here, outraged by the unsparing language, commentators are anxious that we should not put a sinister construction upon the passage. So they say that here Rama can only have meant that Sita should choose one of these people as the giver to her of a maintenance allowance, that she might go and reside under the protection of one of these people. "That is what Rama meant", says the commentator.† Ladies and gentlemen, my opinion is that there is no need to soften the language here. Rama meant harsh things. He was angry. He was dissatisfied. There was trouble in his breast. He suspected her fidelity without a doubt and he therefore says to her, "You come to me with a stain. How can I take you? I give you perfect freedom. You are no good to me." And when a man speaks in anger, he says anything. We have all known angry people say absurd things. Haven't we seen how even a fond mother who combs the hair of her daughter every morning with the greatest pain, using the best oil she could get and the softest comb,

*Five persons according to the Bombay Edition including Satrughna.

"शत्रुघ्ने वाथ सुग्रीवे राक्षसे वा विभीषणे।"

†Govindaraja's comment referred to runs thus.

"अत्र लक्ष्मणादौ मनःकरणं नाम अनाथाया रक्षकत्वेन तत्तद्गृहे वर्तनम्। भर्त्रा परित्यक्तायाः स्त्रिया बन्धुगृहे वासविधानात्। "न स्त्री स्वातन्त्र्यमर्हति" इति स्मृतेः (Cf. Manu, 5. 148). न त्वत्रान्यथा ग्रहीतुं युक्तम्। महापुरुषेण तादृशोक्त्ययोगात्॥"

dwelling with pride on the way the hair grows from day to day and speaking with pride of it and its regular growth to her neighbours, haven't we heard a woman of that kind when she is in anger saying, "When am I going to see this lock of hair on fire?" Such things are not foreign to our experience. When a father is angry, when a mother is angry, when a husband is angry, there is no limit, there is no limit to the language used. You may say, "Can we ascribe such things to Sri Rama?" But my whole point if you have followed me these days is that Sri Rama was just a human being and when he was angry he said foolish things. When he was sorry he wept bitter tears. There is no doubt about it. There is no need to soften the language, for see what follows. This is the final word he says:

न हि त्वां रावणो दृष्ट्वा दिव्यरूपां मनोरमाम्।
मर्षयेत चिरं सीते स्वगृहे परिवर्तिनीम्॥ VI. 118. 24

"You know what an angel you are, the most beautiful woman on earth, the most captivating. Ravana is a fellow without any restraint whatever. He is just a beast. Do you mean to say you could have lived in his house for a year under his protection and at his mercy without his having defiled you? Is there a possibility of it?" He puts her this sharp question. न हि त्वां रावण: etc. "He cannot control himself for a whole year, absurd." And then स्वगृहे etc., "when every minute you are at his disposal!" Now mind you, Rama has received the most unimpeachable testimony to her conduct in the Asokavana; his own trusted messenger, Hanuman, had seen her and brought him reports how she resisted Ravana and his advances, how she defied him and how she always took his (Rama's) name in reverence and begged Hanuman to tell him of her. "Tell him," she says, "tell him of me. I am constantly thinking of him. I have no other thought. I am living just for his sake. Tell him I have taken a promise from Ravana that he should not touch me for a year and I hope that before the year is out, I shall be rescued." Therefore, there is no reason for believing that Ravana could have touched her. He has given her a year's respite. Even supposing that Rama has not heard that Ravana lay under a curse that if he attempts to rape a woman against her will, his head would burst to pieces, he certainly heard from Hanuman what sort of life she lived surrounded by those Rakshasis, living only on the hope of being rescued by Rama and living in the hope that the rescue would come before the year of respite was out. He had all this testimony before him and still he chose to employ that language. Later on, when after the fire ordeal was over and in the presence of the great gods Agni himself handed her over to him saying, "Here, take back your wife. She is pure, pure in every sense of the word. She has not sinned; she has done nothing which could be called infidelity to you. Take her, Rama," and he takes her, then amongst other things he says, "I didn't suspect her. I never had a doubt about her conduct. Do I not know that by the fire of her own conduct she could have burnt that chap if he had attempted violence? Do I not know that Ravana would have risked his very life if he had attempted to do wrong to her?" He says all these brave things afterwards when she has been handed back to him on the highest possible authority. If you give cent per cent value to these subsequent protestations, you must convict him of some insincerity and pretended harshness in this speech when he actually repudiated her. The two things are certainly inconsistent, that is to say, on first appearance. But, believe me, ladies and gentlemen, the true way of interpreting is that Rama swayed this way and that. Examine your own hearts and suppose you were in similar circumstances. You would have hesitated too. On the one side he felt that all was right and that he was not behaving properly when he accused her. But, on the other side, as he thought of the possibilities, as he thought of the unscrupulous wickedness of Ravana whose harem was full of these women taken from all the world over, as he thought of that and as he thought of the beautiful woman that stood there before him, his anger overpowered him. He swayed between these two feelings and at first the worse feeling prevailed. He lent himself entirely to these sinister thoughts and under their influence insulted Sita beyond endurance and repudiated her in the presence of the world. That repudiation was sincere. There is no doubt about it. The subsequent repentance was also sincere. Now once more examine your own hearts. When you have been wronged and are in doubt, when subsequently everything turns out well and all people smile round about you and you are inclined also to pat yourself on the back for having been a fine fellow, would you not say, "I knew this from the beginning, didn't I? There was something in me that told me that she was all right and that I had no business to suspect her." That is to say, one feeling prevailed at first. The contrary feeling prevailed when the sun shone bright and the world was again all right. There is no reason for us to suppose that when he first spoke he was insincere or that when he spoke afterwards he was insincere. Both times he was sincere. Only at one time one feeling prevailed and at another time the other feeling prevailed. Perfectly natural. That is the only way of interpreting it and I have practically no doubt in my mind that the Poet intended to show us that Rama was just like other people in such terrible and trying times. The worse feeling prevails for a time. But subsequently when the evidence is overwhelming and the whole world turns upon you and says, "what a grand fool you have been," you begin to say, "I never was a fool, I knew this from the beginning." Let us also remember that in Rama's first speech to Sita there were these harsh sentiments piled one upon another but there was not an order that she was to undergo any test or give any proof. The proof he had already constructed for himself and he acted upon it. He condemned her and asked her to go wherever she liked. He said, "I have no use for you," as good as saying, "If you die, I am not going to care. Whatever may happen to you, I do not care." Having said that, he left it to Sita entirely to defend herself. She says after protesting that that was not the language to be used by a noble husband to a noble wife, after protesting that she was not her own mistress when Ravana touched her,

> यद्यहं गात्रसंस्पर्शं गतास्मि विवशा प्रभो ।
> कामकारो न मे तत्र दैवं तत्रापराध्यति ॥ VI. 119. 8

"It was not because I wanted to touch him and see how he felt, that I came into contact with him. It was forced upon me. Don't you see? And yet you say these things to me as if I was a common woman and you were a common husband." She upbraids him in strong language and then this is how she begins:

> न तथास्मि महाबाहो यथा त्वमवगच्छसि ।
> प्रत्ययं गच्छ मे येन चारित्रेणैव ते शपे ॥ VI. 119. 6

She does not use the language of an unfaithful wife.

पृथक्स्त्रीणां प्रचारेण जातिं तां परिशङ्कसे।
परित्यजेमां शङ्कां तु यदि तेऽहं परीक्षिता॥ VI. 119. 7

Well, all her pleadings did not avail with Rama. Then finding that on his face there was no relaxation, no abatement of severity, she turns to Lakshmana and says, "Now there is no course other than the ordeal by fire. Go on, let Agni blaze. I will find refuge in him. That is the only remedy for this kind of misery."

चितां मे कुरु सौमित्रे व्यसनस्यास्य भेषजम्।
मिथ्योपघातोपहता नाहं जीवितुमुत्सहे॥ VI. 119. 18

"Set up a pyre, let it blaze. That is the only remedy." Then says the Poet, although a hush of the deepest misery and the greatest awe fell upon the whole audience, Lakshmana and Vibhishana and Sugriva and Hanuman and Jambavan, the old bear of eternal wisdom, not a voice was raised in protest. Nobody dared to say a word against Rama's conduct. This is what the Poet says:

न हि रामं तदा कश्चित्कालान्तकयमोपमम्।
अनुनेतुमथो वक्तुं द्रष्टुं वाप्यशकत्सुहृत्॥*

Everybody turned his face in another direction. They did not even look at his face. Even to look at his face they were so afraid. Everybody quaked. I told you this before as proof that Sri Rama had established his moral supremacy over the whole world to such an extent that he could do anything he pleased. Even against the most wrong thing nobody dared to say a word. This kind of thing happens again in the Uttarakanda which I shall presently refer to. As if to show that after the whole tragic scene had been gone through, everybody's heart relented and all persons were anxious for a reconciliation, the Poet says that at the end of it all, amongst the gods, the old father Dasaratha himself appears and he speaks to Rama and afterwards he turns his attention to Sita and then—he calls her daughter, not daughter-in-law—he calls her daughter and says to her, as if this plea was required.

कर्तव्यो न तु वैदेहि मन्युस्त्यागमिमं प्रति।

*VI. 119. 22 according to some Mss.

Don't you be displeased, don't you be angry with Sri Rama because he abandoned you.

रामेण त्वद्विशुद्ध्यर्थं कृतमेतद्धितैषिणा ॥ VI. 122. 34

Rama was anxious to do you good, to clear your character before the eyes of the world and therefore he abandoned you and he was made to say, "Go your way, you are no good to me. Don't take it literally and don't be displeased with Rama on that account." That again only follows Sri Rama's change. This too is all after the event. When the tragedy had been gone through, when Sita's heart had been wrung once with despair and all things have turned out well, then of course each person is anxious to put the best face upon it and to say all things have turned out well. "Don't entertain any more ill-feeling this way or that. All persons must have meant well." Well, upon this occasion Rama's conduct has to be explained by his suspicion of infidelity. Unfounded as it was, it was still there rankling in his bosom.

In the later incident there was no such heavy justification. It was all because of certain slanderous tongues that were busy in the streets of Ayodhya. Reports came to Sri Rama that his subjects were discussing his conduct pretty freely and that they were saying things like this to each other.

शृणु राजन् यथा पौराः कथयन्ति शुभाशुभम् ।
चत्वरापणरथ्यासु वनेषूपवनेषु च ॥ VII. 43. 13

These sons and daughters of purity venturing to discuss Rama and Sita say to themselves—little tongues wag, don't they?—they say to themselves, "What sort of happiness can he have sleeping with that woman who has lived for a time in Ravana's house? How can he enjoy?

कीदृशं हृदये तस्य सीतासंभोगजं सुखम् ।
अङ्कमारोप्य तु पुरा रावणेन बलाद्धृताम् ॥ VII. 43. 17

How does he not shrink from a woman who has been taken to Lanka by a Rakshasa and who has lived among Rakshasis?" And then this is the way the Poet shows his consummate knowledge of human nature in this passage.

अस्माकमपि दारेषु सहनीयं भविष्यति ।

"Tomorrow or the day after when our women misbehave, we must also put up with it."

यथा हि कुरुते राजा प्रजा तमनुवर्तते ॥ VII. 43. 19

एवं बहुविधा वाचो वदन्ति पुरवासिनः ।

नगरेषु च सर्वेषु राजञ्जनपदेषु च ॥ VII. 43. 20

"Whether you go into the streets of the city or whether you walk into the rural parts, this is the kind of thing that people say." When this was reported to Sri Rama, of course he naturally hesitated. What nonsense can this be? I myself had a little suspicion. But Sita underwent the fire ordeal when the whole world was looking on and all the gods came and testified to the purity of her character. I took her as she was delivered to me by Mahendra himself (instead of Agni he now becomes Mahendra).

लङ्काद्वीपे महेन्द्रेण मम हस्ते निवेशिता ।

अन्तरात्मा च मे वेत्ति सीतां शुद्धां यशस्विनीम् ॥ VII. 45. 10

My heart tells me that she is pure. There is such a thing as a good name and a bad name.

पौरापवादः सुमहांस्तथा जनपदस्य च ।

अकीर्तिर्यस्य गीयेत लोके भूतस्य कस्यचित् । VII. 45. 12

This is extraordinary, difficult to believe. It would appear, according to Sri Rama, that if only certain persons made up their minds that one individual was behaving disgracefully and spoke ill of him, such a man is damned in the other world also, whether justly or unjustly, the Poet does not say. You have only to be slandered by a certain number of people who may be persistently spreading infamy against you, that is quite enough apparently.

पतत्येवाधमाँल्लोकान् यावच्छब्दः प्रकीर्त्यते ॥

So long as that ill-fame lasts,

अकीर्तिर्निन्द्यते देवैः कीर्तिर्लोकेषु पूज्यते ॥ VII. 45. 13

a man who has lost his fame on earth is abandoned by the gods. They also slander him. All people exert themselves in order to get Kirti."

कीर्त्यर्थं तु समारम्भः सर्वेषां सुमहात्मनाम् ।

अप्यहं जीवितं जह्यां युष्मान् वा पुरुषर्षभाः ॥ VII. 45. 14

This is spoken by Rama to his three brothers. He has summoned them as soon as he heard these slanders. "I shall abandon my own life, take my life "युष्मान् वा पुरुषर्षभाः" and I should be glad to kill you all. "अपवादभयाद्भीतः" I shrink so much from ill-fame that I shall kill myself if necessary."

"किं पुनर्जनकात्मजाम्" VII. 45. 15

See the place assigned to Sita in the gradation. "I should kill you, I should kill myself in order to rescue my name from infamy." What about Sita? Sacrificing her is not so big as sacrificing the brothers because as I told you, the theory was in the old days that any woman was only the private property of the husband, completely at his disposal. The thing goes to this extent. If she is treated roughly by a fellow like Ravana, if her character is spoiled, it is not she who is hurt, it is not she whose name is damaged, it is her husband's. His name is marred, his reputation is gone, his family is traduced. So he is bound to take revenge. That is the old theory. You and I must recognise it when we deal with these old stories, these heroic fables, where under the influence of jealousy crimes of a very black type are perpetrated. In judging of these people you must remember that the independent existence of a woman was not recognised. Now in order to show you that that is the proper way of interpreting Rama's conduct towards Sita upon this occasion, I will give you the testimony of another great poet Kalidasa, not that I place Kalidasa above Valmiki in these respects but that we are on safe ground in interpreting Valmiki as proved by the fact that such a great interpreter also as Kalidasa himself says

निश्चित्य चानन्यनिवृत्ति वाच्यं त्यागेन पत्न्याः परिमार्ष्टुमैच्छत् ।

Having found that this stain on his reputation could not be removed by any other means, अनन्यनिवृत्ति irremovable by other means except by abandoning his wife, Rama desires to re-establish himself and his great name by abandoning his wife. Then follow some words of the Poet.

अपि स्वदेहात्किमुतेन्द्रियार्थाद्यशोधनानां हि यशो गरीयः ॥

Raghuvamsa 14. 35

These Kshatriyas, whose sense of honour is fantastic, carry it to a romantic extent, dwelling in regions where it is difficult even to breathe for ordinary human beings; for the Kshatriya's sense of honour is extraordinarily drawn out to fine length until it becomes so tenuous that you and I cannot appreciate it. That is their way. They are people who think that their whole wealth consists of *yasas*. To them *yasas* is greater than their bodies. They are prepared to go and fight anywhere in order to maintain their honour. Let there be a whole army; a single man may often be found to fight it for the sake of honour. Stories are often told in Rajput annals of how men braved the greatest possible dangers in order to establish their character as heroes. Just a common feature where a whole race is bred up to believe that honour, personal valour, distinction on the field of battle, is above all things. The Japs in all the world today have really that feeling, not that they count it bravery but they count it a kind of loyalty to their Mikado. If a general loses a battle, if a Jap turns back from defeat, then he does something which is high treason against the Mikado, and the Mikado is not only the Emperor of Japan but he is the Moon-God himself. That is their belief. Therefore these British tommies and American soldiers often say, "These Japs are terrible fellows because when we are in trouble we run away. You cannot make a Jap run away, he is there, prepared to die but not flee." Why, the story is told of how in Port Arthur during the Russo-Japanese War it became necessary to block the port so that it might not be available for the sailing of men-of-war and the port could be blocked only by two large ships being sunk there. And the sinking was not possible unless on each boat there were a hundred people prepared to get everything ready and then sink themselves also with the boats. It seems the admiral asked for two hundred volunteers, and five thousand came forward and they all wrote their names promising to do this with their blood. That is the valour of the Jap. Well, in ancient stories, our Rajputs and their ancestors were famous for this sort of thing. To them honour was everything. There was nothing from which they shrank. When a man is prepared to give up his whole life, what else would he care for? Sita was only a means of gratifying the sexual passion. When I am prepared to sacrifice so much else!—I mean, that is the way in which when it comes to an argument, when it comes to your being really in mental anguish, when grief overpowers you and you are paralysed, you are unable to think clearly;

in such a situation a woman whom you otherwise honour and love and adore and hang all your jewels upon and allow to dominate your whole life—well, a woman whom you treat with all this consideration, when however she is weighed in the balance of real values in a crisis like this, she sinks into the position of इन्द्रियार्थ, a means of gratifying our senses, no more. Now Rama decrees that Sita should be banished. This time Rama sinks lower and lower. Not only does he, against the testimony of his own conscience, agree to banish Sita but he does it secretly. He does not tell her. He asks Lakshmana to take her away to the forest because, being pregnant she had asked herself to be allowed to live one night among the Rishis and Rishi-patnis and he had already agreed that that should be done. He secretly instructs Lakshmana, "tell her that this is the ostensible reason, but when you have taken her to that place, leave her there and come away."

I am coming now to an interesting point.

न चास्मिन् प्रतिवक्तव्यः सीतां प्रति कथंचन ॥ VII. 45. 19

He says to his brothers and other people there, "Don't you talk to me about this matter, don't contradict me. I have made up my mind." He says in many words in this context what he has already said by the one word "कृतबुद्धिना" "नात्र कार्या विचारणा" Don't hesitate.

अप्रीतिर्हि परा मह्यं त्वय्येतत् प्रतिवारिते ॥ VII. 45. 20

If you don't do this, if you obstruct this, if you protest against this, I shall be very displeased with you.

शापिता च मया यूयं भुजाभ्यां जीवितेन च । VII. 45. 21

I bind you down by an oath upon my legs, he says. That is extraordinary, swearing by the legs. This occurs in two or three places in the Ramayana. I have not seen it often but it does occur when a senior asks a junior to perform an act and he somehow or other suspects that that fellow will be reluctant. This kind of thing happens to Sri Rama once when Khara and Dushana and their fourteen thousand followers threaten the brothers and Sita. Rama asked Lakshmana to go into a cave with Sita and remain there, ready-armed with bow and arrow. "But don't come out. Let me fight all these chaps myself. I have taken an oath that their lives are forfeit to me individually. I don't want to share the glory with anybody else." He put Lakshmana there in the cave to guard Sita and then he says

तस्माद्गृहीत्वा वैदेहीं शरपाणिर्धनुर्धरः ।
गुहामाश्रय शैलस्य दुर्गां पादपसंकुलाम् ॥ III. 24. 12

I don't want you to oppose this order, to object to it. I bind you by an oath upon my legs.

शापितो मम पादाभ्यां गम्यतां वत्स मा चिरम् ॥ III. 24. 13

Then again, when Vali tells his younger brother Sugriva, "You stay behind at the mouth of the cave while I go inside and kill Dundubhi. You had better stay here. Don't stir, let me go all alone.

इह त्वं तिष्ठ सुग्रीव बिलद्वारि समाहितः ।
यावदत्र प्रविश्याहं निहन्मि सहसा रिपुम् ॥ IV. 9. 13

While I enter the cave and kill my enemy, you stop here."

मया त्वेतद्वचः श्रुत्वा याचितः स परंतपः ।
शापयित्वा च मां पद्भ्यां प्रविवेश बिलं महत् ॥ IV. 9. 14

Having bound him down by an oath on his feet, he left him. This swearing by the feet is rather extraordinary. I think however that this is due to the fact that a senior's feet being often touched by the hands and by the head of a junior in making namaskaras to him, the senior's feet are therefore objects of very special veneration to the junior. Therefore only the senior should administer such an oath to the junior. That is a somewhat strange thing which I thought I might share with you.

Ladies and Gentlemen, I have been speaking to you today of a violent human passion. Of all feelings that agitate our mind, of all feelings that make them forget themselves and become beasts in carrying out its dictates, jealousy is the worst, jealousy where your wife's honour is concerned and you suspect that something wrong has happened. Then you forget all decency. No notion of any kind can deter you from taking the last step of vengeance. Jealousy is one of the worst passions known to men and it is the worst of all when a man has genuine greatness, when he comes of a high family, when he cares for his honour, when he thinks that his wife is handsome and, though faithful, might be coveted by others. Then it is that a true and noble nature descends to the most violent action. Sri Rama therefore under the influence of this jealousy decreed the complete abandonment of Sita and told her, "I have no more use for you. What happens to you I do not care. Your conduct I will not examine; I will not be responsible for you. The ends of the earth are open to you. You may go anywhere you like." When he said these words he meant them. It is the noblest man, it is the man who cares most for his honour, it is the man whose personal dignity is of the highest kind, it is he who, when he is torn by these feelings and suspicious against his wife, is capable of doing the worst things.

It is extraordinary how great poets have treated this subject of jealousy nearly the same way as they analyse the progress of this feeling and study it, as it advances from step to step corrupting the soul and making it capable of black thoughts, black plots and black deeds. The progress of this jealousy in the human heart is the same, and great poets not only have shown the same sentiments but they have sometimes used the same language. I just want you to see how another Dhiratidhira character in tragedy feels. What if he comes from the West and from English literature? All first class literature is human literature and belongs to the whole of mankind. In the great play of *Othello* where Shakespeare depicts this passion of jealousy in its worst form, he shows how it degrades the great character of Othello, for he was a big fellow, brave on the field of battle, unsuspicious generally speaking. This is from the soliloquy of Iago. Iago has played on the heart of Othello, has put suspicion, confirmed it by various tricks, fanned the flame until it burns violently and threatens to consume everybody. Then speaking of jealousy he says himself,

> "Trifles light as air
> Are to the jealous confirmations strong
> As proofs of holy writ."

(*Othello, III. iii.* 322-4)

When we deal with this great passion of jealousy as worked out by Valmiki in this great epic, it would be useful, it would be helpful, in fact, it would facilitate a better understanding of our nature if we see how in another great man's character similar things have happened. Then he goes on to say what is true of Sri Rama himself. Othello at least had something, a handkerchief; he had heard something, seen something. Rama had nothing at all. All that he could say is, "You are an angel and Ravana is a wicked person. When you were in his control, how is it possible for things to have been right?" That was all he could say, a kind of negative suspicious attitude. In the case of Othello,

> "Dangerous conceits are, in their natures, poisons,
> Which at the first are scarce found to distaste,
> But with a little act upon the blood,
> Burn like the mines of sulphur."
>
> (*Othello, III. iii.* 326-9)

Then Lodovico asks Othello at the last moment when everything is over and Desdemona has been choked and all is found out and the truth has come out, "What shall be said to thee?" and listen to the answer. How true, how natural, how exactly a parallel to what Sri Rama says.

Othello:—

> "Why, any thing:
> An honourable murderer, if you will;
> For nought I did in hate, but all in honour."
>
> (*Othello, V. ii.* 293-5)

Then at the end, at the very end Othello says taking leave as it were not only of Lodovico but of the others also, of the world, instructing the world as it were, as to the havoc wrought by jealousy,

> "Speak of me as I am; nothing extenuate,
> Nor set down aught in malice: then must you speak
> Of one that loved not wisely but too well;
> Of one not easily jealous, but being wrought
> Perplex'd in the extreme; of one whose hand
> Like the base Indian, threw a pearl away
> Richer than all his tribe; of one whose subdued eyes,
> Albeit unused to the melting mood,
> Drop tears as fast as the Arabian trees
> Their medicinal gum."
>
> (*Othello, V. ii.* 342-351)

Othello, the great warrior, a stern man, who has seen men falling round him and yet not moved an inch, that man says, "I have never cried in my life. I do not know what tears are."

".........of one whose subdued eyes
Albeit unused to the melting mood,
Drop tears as fast as the Arabian trees
Their medicinal gum."

Now I must take your leave—I hope it is not too late,—to show you the reverse side of human character. We have just now seen, ladies and gentlemen, how jealousy corrupts our nature, makes us see things that are not there, shuts our eyes to clear evidence, makes beasts of us—yes, that is what it does. There is another great hero in Tennyson's poem, *King Arthur of the Round Table,* a man, as you know, who stood for personal honour, personal valour, widespread benevolence, universal love, no hate, readiness to succour distress, sternness in punishing wrong-doers, a man who stood for all these qualities and founded an order of knights so that from savagery and barbarism of the worst kind England may be brought up to be a country where high ideals prevailed and high culture could be established. That was Prince Arthur. You know too how in his origin a certain unearthly element was believed in by the people, thus bringing him into a closer parallel with Sri Rama himself who, we all believe, is somewhat unearthly in origin. In the case of King Arthur the whole of his work was ruined by a subtle poison which spread over the whole of the State and corrupted its polity, and that was the misconduct of his wife, Guinevere, another famous beauty of fiction, one who erred with Lancelot, the most famous of the Round Table after King Arthur, perhaps stronger than he and more valorous. But between him and Guinevere, there grew up an amour which was carried to wicked lengths until it led, as the Poet says, to "red ruin, and the breaking up of laws" (*Guinevere,* 423) and the disbanding of the great Round Table and a great heroic life had to close in shame and humiliations seeing the mighty work that it had begun only half accomplished. But when Guinevere found out how she had undone her husband's work, feeling repentance she went to a nunnery and when she was there, returning from one of his most sanguinary battles, Arthur, knowing that his end was near and unwilling though mortally wounded that he should leave this earth without a final interview with her whom he had loved and adored but who had ruined him, his name and all the work for which he came into life, desiring to see her and take leave of her, he comes into this nunnery. In this final scene the Poet is seen at his very best. King Arthur being a Christian, instead of pronouncing harsh judgment upon his wife, tells her how wicked she has been. But unlike Rama, unlike Othello, he tries to forgive her. If there was jealousy in him, it was there only in the germ. He had outlived it. Now that is a most extraordinary thing. I do not think it is a thing which you can find commonly in life. When a man is jealous, when a man has been betrayed by his wife, he seldom forgives her, as you know, unless he is one of those craven creatures who wishes to profit by the shame of his wife. Such people we know too. But commonly a man of spirit resents that. It was left to Prince Arthur who was more than an ordinary man, who, I told you, partook of divinity to some extent, it was left to him to speak in language which almost seems to be above the common reach of humanity. The passage is somewhat long and perhaps it is familiar to a great many amongst you. But believe me, ladies and gentlemen, it is a mistake to suppose that because a passage is familiar, it has no use. A passage of deep import, written in beautiful touching language and conveying the highest sentiment, can never become too familiar. If you know it by heart, so much the better, for you can sometimes run over the whole of the lines yourself. Every time that you read it, every time that you repeat it, you feel elevated and unless you are hopelessly gone, you are certainly likely to be the better after reading the passage than before. I will just read it. This is Arthur to Guinevere who lies low at his feet asking to be forgiven:—

> "'For think not, tho' thou wouldst not love thy lord,
> Thy lord has wholly lost his love for thee.
> I am not made of so slight elements.
> Yet must I leave thee, woman, to thy shame.
> I hold that man the worst of public foes
> Who either for his own or children's sake,
> To save his blood from scandal, lets the wife
> Whom he knows false, abide and rule the house:
> For being thro' his cowardice allow'd
> Her station, taken everywhere for pure,
> She like a new disease, unknown to men,
> Creeps, no precaution used, among the crowd.
> Makes wicked lightnings of her eyes, and saps

The fealty of our friends, and stirs the pulse
With devil's leaps, and poisons half the young.
Worst of the worst were that man he that reigns!
Better the King's waste hearth and aching heart
Than thou reseated in thy place of light,
The mockery of my people, and their bane.'
He paused, and in the pause she crept an inch
Nearer, and laid her hands about his feet.
Far off a solitary trumpet blew.
Then waiting by the doors the warhorse neigh'd
As at a friend's voice, and he spake again:
'Yet think not that I urge thy crimes,
I did not come to curse thee, Guinevere,
I, whose vast pity almost makes me die
To see thee, laying there thy golden head,
My pride in happier summers, at my feet.
The wrath which forced my thoughts on that fierce law,
The doom of treason and the flaming death,
(When first I learnt thee hidden here) is past.
The pang—which while I weigh'd thy heart with one
Too wholly true to dream untruth in thee,
Made my tears burn—is also past—in part.
And all is past, the sin is sinn'd, and I,
Lo! I forgive thee, as Eternal God
Forgives: do thou for thine own soul the rest.
But how to take last leave of all I loved?
O golden hair, with which I used to play
Not knowing! O imperial-moulded form,
And beauty such as never woman wore,
Until it came a kingdom's curse with thee—
I cannot touch thy lips, they are not mine,
But Lancelot's: nay, they never were the King's.
I cannot take thy hand; that too is flesh,
And in the flesh thou hast sinn'd; and mine own flesh,
Here looking down on thine polluted, cries
'I loathe thee:' yet not less, O Guinevere,
For I was ever virgin save for thee.' "

Just like Sri Rama, he knew only one woman.

"...............I love thee still.
Let no man dream but that I love thee still.
Perchance, and so thou purify thy soul,
And so thou lean on our fair Father Christ,

Hereafter in that world where all are pure
We two may meet before high God, and thou
Wilt spring to me, and claim me thine, and know
I am thine husband—not a smaller soul,
Nor Lancelot, nor another.' "

(*Guinevere*, 504-563)

Now, ladies and gentlemen, just to impress upon you one word. Though this forgiveness of a woman whose crime had been black and had led to tremendous ruin, though this forgiveness seems super-human, our story, the Ramayana itself, has a parallel to it. Ahalya, who according to Valmiki, is no saint, ruined a great life besides her own, viz., Gautama. Now what did Gautama do? By Valmiki's measurements all things are exaggerated. Time also is drawn out to portentous length. After a thousand years during which they remained separate, Gautama returns, finds Ahalya who through the touch of Rama and Lakshmana, becomes purified, takes her back to his bosom. That was the noble life of our ancients when it was still simple and unsophisticated and uncorrupted. Sin there is. Who does not sin? No one who is not liable to err. To err is human; to forgive is divine. Forgiveness is among the greatest virtues of our character, *Kshama* is every time extolled in all poetry and of this Kshama great instances surely, where private feelings have been hurt, are Gautama who forgave Ahalya and Prince Arthur who says to Guinevere when she has been purified by going to the other world, "Hereafter in that world" etc.

So end these great stories with eternal lessons for us. Because I have said jealousy is human, that it is natural, that it is commonly found, it does not mean that it is a virtue. It means that it is a human passion leading to violent crime and must if possible be conquered or at least kept down within stern limits and when the sin has been sinned, as King Arthur says, there is a time for forgiveness. True repentance followed by a pure life must lead to forgiveness. Forgiveness though practised by a human mind, is divine in its quality. When we are jealous and punish others, we are only human. But when remembering these great examples we forgive those who do wrong to us, for the moment we are not human but we are drawn up to the full dignity and height of divinity.

THIRTEENTH LECTURE*

Ladies and Gentlemen,—Several of my talks were taken up with the character of Sri Rama. I now take leave of him but we shall meet him every now and then while discussing the other figures in the great epic. It is impossible to get away from him either far or long. Students of the great epic like to pay their homage to the character of some one person or another and call him their favourite or their ideal. There is such a variety of great men and great women that play their parts in the epic that it is no wonder that one man's favourite is not another's. Who your favourite is depends very much upon the kind of ideals you have in life, upon the way in which individual characteristics strike you, upon your general education and training, upon the way great people have presented the different characters to you, upon your temperament and your own individuality, I have heard some describe Bharata as the noblest figure in the pages of the Ramayana. I have heard others similarly put Lakshmana at the top. I have heard some people say that to them Hanuman is the most attractive figure. Of course as you know Vibhishana is reckoned amongst the greatest Bhaktas, by some placed alongside Lakshmana, by some placed even above him. For my own part, I do not like to yield my heart to any one except the hero himself. Others are great, are meritorious, are great examples to us of one virtue or another or the combination of some of them. But I find it difficult to say, omitting Rama himself, that any one commands my homage a great deal more than others. I study them all alike with reverence, with a desire to understand their real nature as expounded by the Poet and as exhibited in their various deeds and in their various sayings. In our Poem there are three great kingdoms, those of Ayodhya, Kishkindha and Lanka. In the pages of the Ramayana all these kingdoms change hands. Curiously enough, in every case it is the eldest brother that loses the kingdom and the younger brother gets it. In the case of Ayodhya the eldest brother does not lose it by any fault of his. He gladly surrenders it to the brother. In the other two cases there is a struggle and the elder brother loses his life before his kingdom, the younger

---

* 5-7-'44.

brothers in both these cases desiring the death of their elder brothers. In the case of Ayodhya the study reveals another great circumstance. Not only does Rama cheerfully give the kingdom up in favour of Bharata but Bharata in his turn shows the same self-denial and would have given it back to Sri Rama if Sri Rama had yielded. That is extraordinary, each brother vying with the other in not desiring the kingdom but making it over to the other party. In some ways it is the case of the rotten pumpkin amongst children. "I do not want this," says one and pushes it off. The other just touches it and says, "I don't want it either," and pushes it back. That was the case of Ayodhya. Only they do not regard it as a rotten pumpkin but as a great prize which it was not proper for them to annex to themselves but which it was noble to give away to the other party. In that respect the difference is striking. But I would not have you think, and I would not have you suppose that I think, that Sugriva and Vibhishana were necessarily greedy people or that they were carried away by overweening ambition or that they were in any way bad people. No. They were good people too, very good people at that. Nevertheless they were not averse to getting the kingdom from their brothers. Of course they thought that their brothers were great sinners and that they were doing wrong to the kingdom and that in their hands the kingdom would perhaps prosper better. But there is no doubt that they desired the kingdoms eagerly and that they were not unwilling that their brothers should be killed in order that they might succeed to them. I have some slokas here about Sugriva,* but I need not trouble you with them. We have only recently been dealing with them. You cannot have forgotten how Sugriva desired Sri Rama to kill Vali as soon as possible in order that he might get his wife back and the kingdom. He never forgot the kingdom. In the case of Vibhishana I have to cite this fact that when he came for protection from his brother to Sri Rama, Sri Rama's principal advisers guessed rightly enough that Vibhishana's ambition was to become king of Lanka after Ravana. There was no mistaking that, for Sri Rama himself admits it as it were. He himself says,

"राज्यकाङ्क्षी च राक्षसः" VI. 18. 13

he does not doubt it.

* IV. 10. 10-11, 30; 8. 39.

"There is no doubt that this Rakshasa Vibhishana is desirous of getting the kingdom." At a critical stage in the war when it had just begun and the fortunes of Sri Rama and his side seemed very very low, Rama went so far as to say that if Lakshmana was not going to revive but pass away on the field of battle, he would much like to finish his career there and then. Then he took leave of the people there, so near to the end he was in his imagination. But one thought troubled him, namely, that when Vibhishana came for protection he was in a great hurry to give symbolical coronation to him. The real coronation had not yet taken place and did not seem likely at all to come off. So Sri Rama says,

तच्च मिथ्याप्रलप्तं मां प्रधक्ष्यति न संशयः ।

"Without doubt what worries me is that unredeemed promise I made to Vibhishana—

यन्मया न कृतो राजा राक्षसानां विभीषणः ॥ VI. 49. 22

that I have not been able to make Vibhishana king of the Rakshasas as I had promised." And Vibhishana himself finding that the game was nearly up bemoans his own lot and amongst other things says जीवन्नद्य विपन्नोऽस्मि "I am in great extremity,—although I am alive." प्राप्तप्रतिज्ञश्च रिपुः I despair of over becoming king as I had hoped."

प्राप्तप्रतिज्ञश्च रिपुः सकामो रावणः कृतः ॥ VI. 50. 19

That was the worst of it. "Ravana has had his desires fulfilled, every one of them."

Then there is a remarkable passage in the Yuddhakanda which is worthy of our attention at this point. You remember my saying that Bharata took the kingdom of Ayodhya as a trust on behalf of Sri Rama and that he ruled it for fourteen years under the guidance, mystic guidance, of the sandals of the hero. It was a sacred trust with him. When Sri Rama returned at the end of the exile, Bharata of course welcomes him, declaring that his greatest desires have been fulfilled, that the great restoration would take place and that above all, he could hand back the trust that he had taken and administered. The first thing he did was to ask Sri Rama to put the sandals on again.

पादुके ते तु रामस्य गृहीत्वा भरतः स्वयम् ॥
चरणाभ्यां नरेन्द्रस्य योजयमास धर्मवित् । VI. 130. 52-53

He himself put them under Sri Rama's feet.

अब्रवीच्च तदा रामं भरतः स कृताञ्जलिः ॥
एतत्ते रक्षितं राजन् राज्यं निर्यातितं मया । VI. 130. 53-54

"I am now returning the trust to you, the whole of it which you delivered to me as a deposit.

अद्य जन्म कृतार्थं मे संवृत्तश्च मनोरथः ॥ VI. 130. 54

My birth has now fulfilled its purpose. My desire is accomplished.

यस्त्वां पश्यामि राजानमयोध्यां पुनरागतम् । VI. 130. 55

I tried to make you king fourteen years ago. You would not come and take it. Well, this long period has gone and you have come back and I live to see what greater happiness is possible.

अवेक्षतां भवान् कोशं कोष्ठागारं पुरं बलम् ॥ VI. 130. 55

Please come and inspect the treasury, the granary and the munitions.

भवतस्तेजसा सर्वं कृतं दशगुणं मया । VI. 130. 56

Owing to the mystic properties of these sandals and the inspiration they gave me I have been enabled during this period to enhance everything, treasury, granary and munitions, everything tenfold."

Then takes place a most wonderful incident. Sugriva and Vibhishana and all the big monkeys stand about and watch this conversation between the brothers with great concern,—the one brother having returned from a glorious campaign after recovering his wife and his honour to take back the kingdom, the other yielding it back out of the gladness of his heart enhanced tenfold in value all round. This was a sight too strong for them to bear, too strong not to evoke the tenderest emotions. So the Poet says they all wept to see the most wonderful thing take place.

तथा ब्रुवाणं भरतं दृष्ट्वा तं भ्रातृवत्सलम् ॥
मुमुचुर्वानरा बाष्पं राक्षसश्च विभीषणः । VI. 130. 56-57

Whether it was the monkey spirit or the rakshasa spirit, it melted at this sight. They all wept. I would much like to know exactly what passed through the minds of Vibhishana and Sugriva. How they dreaded their brothers, what feelings they entertained towards them, how they schemed and intrigued and fought and prayed to have them despatched! How they were glad to take the kingdom after them! Contrasting this with what they saw, is it any wonder that they wept? It was a range of feeling far beyond them. They could not imagine that it was possible for any two brothers to love and respect each other so much.

My intention, ladies and gentlemen, is to deal at some length with the character of Bharata. Then I shall deal with Sugriva and Vibhishana in turn.

Of the three whom I have contrasted, certainly Bharata stands on a pedestal of his own. Reading over his speeches and noting the way in which he behaved one might think that he had a great deal of persistence and strength of will. Of these we have had already some proof in the way in which he matched them or tried to match them against his own brother's. It was only his elder brother, Rama, who could surpass him in resolution, in determined pursuit of the highest. Only to him had Bharata to yield a little. Otherwise he would have held his ground firmly against anybody else as we see. His utterances are all strong, decided and unequivocal. There is no hesitation about them, nothing of the tentative, nothing of the dim, none at all. One might almost think that his long residence with his grandfather and his uncle had made him a spoilt child as it were, for he does not seem to have been afraid of anybody unless it was Sri Rama himself. And why should he be afraid of anybody? We might even describe him as an untamed youth. How differently Lakshmana would have behaved in similar circumstances, it is just interesting to speculate a little. What a great contrast between the two brothers! Alike noble and high-minded and self-sacrificing, they nevertheless differed so much that you would never mistake the one for the other. Lakshmana would have collapsed and surrendered at once if Sri Rama had said. "Do this or that." He might think differently, his feeling may be that Rama was doing something wrong or harsh, he may not approve of it; nevertheless even if he attempted to say one word of protest, Rama had only to put his foot down, there would be an end of all opposition. Lakshmana delighted to eliminate himself where his brother was concerned. He was just a servant, an instrument for the carrying out of the great man's purpose and nothing more. Only he was an animated instrument and sometimes had his own ideas. But they were there just buried. Bharata was quite different. When he differed from Sri Rama, he would say, "Please, my brother, allow me to put in a word." He would begin modestly but he would say what he felt without hesitation. One might almost say that he had an individuality, a strong individuality and expressed it so that you felt great respect for Bharata. You admired the magnanimity with which he conducted himself before his brother. You admired the resoluteness of his purpose, you admired his resourcefulness in changing tactics in order to persuade his brother to his view. You might do all this. But I wonder if you would love him to the same extent as you would love Lakshmana. Lakshmana you would grasp to your whole heart, but Bharata you would bow to, you would salaam to him and say, "Yes, you are a great man, you are a good man." Respect and admiration are the feelings that he draws from me, while Lakshmana draws the whole of my love. I do not know whether it is the same with you or with many of you. But that is my feeling towards these great heroes. For let us see. When Vasishtha asked Bharata to take the kingdom after having performed the obsequies to the father and be crowned king, Bharata says, "No, I don't want to do it." And the poet says*

विललाप सभामध्ये जगर्हे च पुरोहितम् । II. 82. 10

In the presence of the whole audience he wept and at the same time in that great assembly he ventured to censure his old preceptor. He censured him. He said, "I am surprised that a wise man and an old man like you should try to persuade me to take the kingdom which belongs to my brother by the traditions of the Ikshvaku family.

How can you ask me to take it? I won't take it. I would go and offer it to him." Now for a young fellow like Bharata to censure the old man in the midst of an assembly takes a deal of courage, a deal of self-confidence. But he was except

* See Lect. X, p. 136 above.

on this one subject, a very good man. When he was sent for by Kausalya and appeared before her, that lady very naturally imagined that Kaikeyi's intrigue was agreeable to her son. So as soon as he came, she burst out.*

इदं ते राज्यकामस्य राज्यं प्राप्तमकण्टकम्। II. 75. 11

She used unfortunately the very word which would have been like a stab to Bharata. Bharata did not like to take the kingdom at all. He wanted to give it back. He thought his mother had done wrong. But Kausalya just uses the epithet राज्यकाम to him. She says, "You are evidently anxious to take the kingdom from my son."

विव्यथे भरतस्तीव्रं व्रणे तुद्येव सूचिना॥ II. 75. 17

It seemed to him as though a lancet had been thrust into the wound and was being turned. And then as if that was not enough, Kausalya adds still more harsh sentiments. Perhaps before we understand this it is necessary to remember that when Dasaratha learnt how the kingdom was to be taken from Rama and given to Bharata, he said a great many things in his misery and one of them was, "If really that chap Bharata desires to take advantage of his mother's misconduct and take the kingdom, if really his heart inclines in that direction, then I will renounce him. I do not want that after my death he should do anything to gratify my spirit." That is very often what we say in our great anger, when we get very angry with any of our relations, "If I die, you needn't even bathe, my dear chap." "You need not do anything" as if it is possible for a son to avoid that, however bad the relations may be between father and son. The son has got to do it. But it is usual with us to say that when we dislike a son. We do not want him to do anything. Even to intimate relations we say, "If I die you need not even bathe." So Dasaratha had said

भरतश्चेत्प्रतीतः स्याद्राज्यं प्राप्येदमव्ययम्।
यन्मे स दद्यात्पित्रर्थं मां मा तद्दत्तमागमत्॥ II. 42. 9

"That which he offers to me, that gift need not come to me, I do not wish it to come to me." In other words, "I do not want him to perform any funeral ceremonies for me." He had said that. Kausalya remembered it. And not content with having

* Cf. Lect. XXIX below.

said to Bharata that he was राज्यकाम, she proceeded to the next step and said, "Now please Bharata, let Sumitra and me go away from this place to where Rama is. We would go to Chitrakuta. Only I will take away the Agnihotra with me," so that the obsequies may not be properly performed*. She being the eldest queen, one who had been anointed by her king beside him, the Agnihotra was in her charge. So she threatened to take it away.

अथवा स्वयमेवाहं सुमित्रानुचरा सुखम् ।
अग्निहोत्रं पुरस्कृत्य प्रस्थास्ये यत्र राघवः ॥ II. 75. 14

The belief that the efficacy of the offerings to our departed ancestors depends very much upon the love that prevailed between the dead and the living, that belief is alluded to in the Ramayana itself. Bharata says when he meets Sri Rama in the forest, "Our father is dead. I have performed everything myself. But you have got to do something. Do it. In fact, what you offer to our father's soul or spirit would be much more welcome to him than anything that I have done," He says so.

प्रियेण किल दत्तं हि पितृलोकेषु राघव । II. 101. 8

"They say that would be without any diminution,

अक्षय्यं भवतीत्याहुर्भवांश्चैव पितुः प्रियः ॥ II. 101. 8

and you were the favourite of our father, weren't you?

त्वामेव शोचंस्तव दर्शनेप्सुस्त्वय्येव सक्तामनिवर्त्य बुद्धिम् ।
त्वया विहीनस्तव शोकरुग्णस्त्वां संस्मरन् स्वर्गमवाप राजा ॥
II. 101. 9

Dasaratha has gone away. The last thought in his heart was you. He waited for you. He longed to see you. His whole desire was fixed upon you. When you went away, the grief in his heart knew no assuagement and he always remembered you. So he is gone and what you offer will be much more welcome than what I have offered."

* Publishers' Note: Or rather that they may be properly performed, that is, by Rama, for, as both the great commentators point out,

"अग्निहोत्रमिति राजदेहस्याप्युपलक्षणम् ।"

It is at this point when Kausalya had accused Bharata of desiring the kingdom and threatened to go away with the Agnihotra depriving him of the means of performing the obsequies, it is then that Bharata's heart as it were broke. There was no end to his grief and sorrow and he gave expression to that in a succession of slokas which have become famous. Through the whole of one sarga he swears that he did not desire Rama to go away at all without the kingdom, and he invokes curses upon himself in case he should have so desired it. And the whole of the sarga is taken up with slokas ending with यस्यार्योऽनुमते गतः. It is repeated a great many times, it is not possible to read them all. As a matter of fact, it is quite clear that Bharata could not have spoken them at that moment. It was the poet's intention to describe the round of a man's duties and virtues. The whole of that lot he brings in here in these verses. He puts them into the mouth of Bharata. Bharata is made to say "May I have the sin of that man who omits this duty or who performs this wrong" and so on. In fact, the commentators say that it was the Poet's intention to put into the mouth of Bharata a full description of a man's duties and virtues in life. And there is a combination of sounds in two slokas which are somewhat remarkable. I suppose the poet intended that some who begin Sanskrit should try them as a means of testing their powers of distinct utterance.

अधर्मो योऽस्य सोऽस्यास्तु यस्यार्योऽनुमते गतः ॥ II. 75. 23, 25

It is a simple thing but there is a profusion of sibilants there that people are apt to stumble in uttering them. When this course of abjuration was over, Kausalya's heart was softened. She said, "No, no, I am very sorry I said this to you.

दिष्ट्या न चलितो धर्मादात्मा ते सहलक्ष्मणः* ।
वत्स सत्यप्रतिज्ञो मे सतां लोकानवाप्स्यसि ॥ II. 75. 62

You are just like Lakshmana. I did not realise it at all. You are a good boy. सत्यप्रतिज्ञः. You will fulfil your purpose to the very letter. You will certainly attain to the salvation which is the lot of all good people."

*Govindaraja's reading.

इत्युक्त्वा चाङ्कमानीय भरतं भ्रातृवत्सलम्।
परिष्वज्य महाबाहुं रुरोद भृशदु:खिता॥ II. 75. 63

For his part he did this.

लालप्यमानस्य विचेतनस्य प्रणष्टबुद्धेः पतितस्य भूमौ।
मुहुर्मुहुर्निःश्वसतश्च दीर्घं सा तस्य शोकेन जगाम रात्रिः॥ II. 75. 65

The whole night he rolled on the ground and cried, sobbing and calling the name of Rama, sometimes consciously, sometimes unconsciously. Then he makes up his mind after the obsequies to go to where Sri Rama was and bring him back. You remember his saying to Sri Rama when he actually met him, you remember we dealt with it at some length—I am not going to describe that scene at all today for we have had it under Sri Rama's description—you remember how he said to Sri Rama, "Look here. If somebody in the family must be in the forest, let it be me. You go back. I will take your place." And then Sri Rama said, "This is not a matter to be arranged by proxy. Each man must do his part by himself." This idea that he would go to the forest instead of Sri Rama occurs in the Poem very early. It was not at Chitrakuta, suddenly, that it occurred to him. Earlier, in the course of the distressful interview with his mother, he seems to have thought of it. To begin with he told her that he would thwart her intentions by going to the forest, fetching his brother back, and with contented mind serving him as a slave—this not to spite her, but really for his own sake.

निवर्तयित्वा रामं च तस्याहं दीप्ततेजसः।
दासभूतो भविष्यामि सुस्थितेनान्तरात्मना॥ II. 73. 27

Then he went further and said that he would make atonement for Rama by taking his place in the forest.

आनाय्य च महाबाहुं कौसल्याया महाबलम्।
स्वयमेव प्रवेक्ष्यामि वनं मुनिनिषेवितम्॥ II. 74. 31

"I will myself go to the forest and live with Munis having brought my brother back and installed him as king."

रामः पूर्वो हि नो भ्राता भविष्यति महीपतिः।
अहं त्वरण्ये वत्स्यामि वर्षाणि नव पञ्च च॥ II. 79. 8

"The fourteen years that he has to stay in the forest, I will stay instead of him." The object seems to be this. "My mother shall not attain her purpose, she who is only a mother to me in name."

न सकामां करिष्यामि स्वामिमां मातृगन्धिनीम् ।
वने वत्स्याम्यहं दुर्गे रामो राजा भविष्यति ॥ II. 79. 12

"I will live in the forest." That is how he would have his vengeance fall on that lady. "You wanted me to be king and him to be in the forest. To punish you most we shall reverse our parts. I will go to the forest and make you as miserable as possible." That is his meaning. You know that when he goes to the forest he meets Guha on this side of the Ganges and Guha first of all distrusts him. He is a great friend of Sri Rama and he wonders why this chap goes there so soon after his banishment with such an army and the whole palace moving. What is the object? Cannot be anything very good. So he puts it to Bharata straight. "Tell me what your purpose is" and as soon as Bharata says what his object is, Guha is completely satisfied and he says,

धन्यस्त्वं न त्वया तुल्यं पश्यामि जगतीतले ।
अयत्नादागतं राज्यं यस्त्वं त्यक्तुमिहेच्छसि ॥ II. 85. 12

"What a great man you are! I shall not meet your equal on earth. Without any effort on your part you got a great kingdom you could take with all honour. Nobody will blame you if you did it and yet you renounce it in pursuit of what you consider to be a great duty. You are so great that I am afraid I cannot see your equal anywhere." And then hearing that Rama and his party stayed there one night on the bank, Bharata is full of anguish and says to Guha, "This is the spot where my brother and my brother's wife gave up the luxuries to which they were entitled. Here they lay on the grass, here they stripped themselves of all pomp. Just human beings they were here. Now tell me exactly where my brother slept, where she slept, tell me exactly what they did." And no description could be full enough to satisfy him. All night he heard the story and Guha described how Rama refused to eat any food and was content with the water that Lakshmana brought him. Then Guha moves about to his place and Bharata placing his hand on his struggling heart goes about inspecting the spots as they were as sacred to him as to Guha, and then going to where Sita was stated to have slept he says,

मन्ये साभरणा सुप्ता सीतास्मिन् शयने शुभा ।

"I guess she must have slept with her jewels on, she did not take them off when she went to bed."

तत्र तत्र हि दृश्यन्ते सक्ताः कनकबिन्दवः ॥ II. 88. 14

"I see here and there beads of gold." The idea is that the jewels were rubbed against the hard bed and some little gold particles had fallen off. Not many days had passed. Therefore the marks were still left there. "I can see the gold particles here and there sticking still."

उत्तरीयमिहासक्तं सुव्यक्तं सीतया तदा ।

"Oh, yes, her Uttariya, the upper garment of silk, must have rolled about here."

तथा ह्येते प्रकाशन्ते सक्ताः कौशेयतन्तवः ॥ II. 88. 15

"A few threads are left here." It seems to me that if gold particles could have come off the jewels and they could remain there so long, the jeweller's art in those times could not have been highly developed. Then on that spot seeing how Rama and Sita and Lakshmana had dropped all their pomp and reduced themselves to the barest of lives, he says,

अद्यप्रभृति भूमौ तु शयिष्येऽहं तृणेषु वा ।

"I am going to do the same. I am not going to sleep on a soft bed any more. No more couch for me. I will sleep on the bare floor or on a grass bed."

फलमूलाशनो नित्यं जटाचीराणि धारयन् ॥ II. 88. 26

"I will eat only fruits, roots, and I will wear on the body only the bark of the tree and skin of the deer, and I will also clot my hair.

तस्यार्थमुत्तरं कालं निवत्स्यामि सुखं वने ।

तं प्रतिश्रवमामुच्य नास्य मिथ्या भविष्यति ॥ II. 88. 27

"What my brother has sworn that shall be fulfilled. I am not going to destroy his vow. His vow is that there should be somebody living in the forest. Let it be me. The vow is fulfilled."

वसन्तं भ्रातुरर्थाय शत्रुघ्नो मानुवत्स्यति ।

"When I live here in the forest instead of my brother, Satrughna will live with me. Lakshmana will go with Rama and rule in Ayodhya.

लक्ष्मणेन सह त्वार्यो ह्ययोध्यां पालयिष्यति ॥ II. 88. 28

"Let them go and let the Brahmins there anoint them and make them the rulers and may the high gods enable me to fulfil this vow of mine."

अभिषेक्ष्यन्ति काकुत्स्थमयोध्यायां द्विजातयः ।
अपि मे देवताः कुर्युरिमं सत्यं मनोरथम् ॥ II. 88. 29

As a matter of fact, though Bharata said so, he did not change his dress immediately. Next morning he goes to Bharadvaja's Asrama and there the Poet says वसानो वाससी क्षौमे (II. 90. 2) he had for under and upper garments two pieces of silk. I suppose when we go to sacred places it is usual for us to wear silk. So he wore silk that day. He did not wear the chira and the valkala. About dress you know how people are particular. If a man is fond of some dress, you can dress in order to please him. But when he went to see Sri Rama he wore the rugged valkala and he had clotted his hair.

जटिलं चीरवसनं प्राञ्जलिं पतितं भुवि । II. 100. 1

That was how he went to see Rama himself. Before he approached Rama he had to mount up a good distance and as he goes up he pours out his heart to Satrughna who went along with him and there again he makes a rhetorical appeal. He says न मे शान्तिर्भविष्यति. Slokas end with that expression. "My soul will know no rest until this thing takes place."

यावन्न रामं द्रक्ष्यामि लक्ष्मणं वा महाबलम् ।
वैदेहीं वा महाभागां न मे शान्तिर्भविष्यति ॥ II. 98. 6

"Till I see them each one, Rama and Lakshmana and Vaidehi, I cannot rest.

यावन्न चन्द्रसंकाशं द्रक्ष्यामि शुभमाननम् ।
भ्रातुः पद्मपलाशाक्षं न मे शान्तिर्भविष्यति ॥ II. 98. 7

"Till I see my brother's radiant face shining like the fullmoon or like the lotus in bloom."

सिद्धार्थः खलु सौमित्रिर्यश्चन्द्रविमलोपमम् ।
मुखं पश्यति रामस्य राजीवाक्षं महाद्युति ॥ II. 98. 10

That is, Lakshmana is the lucky man. "How I envy him!" he says, "He is always with my brother. He always looks up to him and is inspired by the glory of that countenance.

यावन्न चरणौ भ्रातुः पार्थिवव्यञ्जनान्वितौ ।
प्रग्रहीष्यामि शिरसा न मे शान्तिर्भविष्यति ॥ II. 98. 8

"Till I see my brother, fall at his feet and hold his feet with my hands, and then see there, see on the feet the natural marks of a Parthiva, till I see all those things, my soul won't rest."

यावन्न राज्ये राज्यार्हः पितृपैतामहे स्थितः ।
अभिषेकजलक्लिन्नो न मे शान्तिर्भविष्यति ॥ II. 98. 9

"Till he goes to Ayodhya, till the waters of the different oceans and the different holy rivers are poured on his head and he takes his rank and dignity as king, I won't rest."

As for Sri Rama, his confidence in Bharata is unbounded. When the subjects follow him out of the city as he is going to the forest and the subjects cry out, "You are our only refuge, come back. Don't abandon us to another person," and so on, he turns back and says to them

या प्रीतिर्बहुमानश्च मय्ययोध्यानिवासिनाम् ।
मत्प्रियार्थं विशेषेण भरते सा विधीयताम् ॥ II. 45. 6

"The love that you bear me, the affection that you extend to me, increase it and give it all to my brother Bharata.

स हि कल्याणचारित्रः कैकेय्यानन्दवर्धनः ।
करिष्यति यथावद्वः प्रियाणि च हितानि च ॥ II. 45. 8

"He is a very good man, a man of pure conduct. He will do every thing in proper style. He will do what pleases you and what is good for you."

Did you ever hear of a departing king saying so much about his successor?

ज्ञानवृद्धो वयोबालो मृदुर्वीर्यगुणान्वितः ।

"By knowledge of the world he is an old person, only he is young in age." It is extraordinary that Rama who is only old by a day should speak of him as 'Bala'.

अनुरूपः स वो भर्ता भविष्यति भयापहः । II. 45. 8

"He will remove all your perils and dangers." And then when he speaks to Lakshmana he says, "Do you suppose that our father and our mother whom we have left behind are going to have a hard time? Nothing. Bharata is too good a chap.

भरतः खलु धर्मात्मा पितरं मातरं च मे ।
धर्मार्थकामसहितैर्वाक्यैराश्वासयिष्यति ॥ II. 46. 7

"He will convert them by sweet words. Lakshmana, don't grieve. I do not grieve for father and mother. They are in very safe hands.

भरतस्यानृशंसत्वं विचिन्त्याहं पुनः पुनः ।
नानुशोचामि पितरं मातरं चापि लक्ष्मण ॥ II. 46. 8

Bharata will look after them just as though I were there and you were there." And in the Aranya Kanda when Lakshmana says something harsh about Kaikeyi, Rama stops him at once and says, "Why are you talking of Kaikeyi? There is Bharata. Talk about him."

न तेऽम्बा मध्यमा तात गर्हितव्या कथंचन ।
तामेवेक्ष्वाकुनाथस्य भरतस्य कथां कुरु ॥ III. 16. 37

"Let us speak of him, the good man. Why speak about Kaikeyi and make yourself unhappy?

निश्चितापि हि मे बुद्धिर्वनवासे दृढव्रता । III. 16. 38

My resolution is strong and unshakable to live here in the forest for fourteen years. But when I think of our dear brother, even that strong resolution grows weak a little. I want to go to him and see him.

भरतस्नेहसंतप्ता बालिशीक्रियते पुनः ॥ III. 16. 38

Remember when we were in that parnakuti, do you remember what sweet things he said, what loving things? I remember all those utterances of his." He says, "I cannot forget them."

संस्मराम्यस्य वाक्यानि प्रियाणि मधुराणि च ।
हृद्यान्यमृतकल्पानि मनःप्रह्लादनानि च ॥ III. 16. 39

What are these epithets?

कदा न्वहं समेष्यामि भरतेन महात्मना ।
शत्रुघ्नेन च वीरेण त्वया च रघुनन्दन ॥ III. 16. 40

"Well, are these fourteen years ever going to end and shall we all be together once more rejoined as a family?"

Then let us go to the Yuddhakanda. Ravana has been killed. Vibhishana has been crowned and the final scenes with Sita are all over. Rama makes preparations for the return. Vibhishana then begs him to stay on for a day or two. "Having come all this way and helped me to this great kingdom, are you going back without giving me the pleasure of being your host for at least a few hours? That is not fair," says Vibhishana.

पूजितोऽहं त्वया सौम्य साचिव्येन परन्तप ॥
सर्वात्मना च चेष्टाभिः सौहृदेनोत्तमेन च । VI. 124. 17-18

"You have honoured me enough. You have paid me enough homage by your first-class alliance with me, by the assistance you gave me in all matters with your whole heart, and by all your valorous deeds. That is enough for me. I do not want any more hospitality."

न खल्वेतन्न कुर्यां ते वचनं राक्षसेश्वर ॥ VI. 124. 18

"Why do I say so? Do you think, O, chief of the Rakshasas, I have no desire to be nice to you and to be kind? Your invitation I should gladly accept. Do not think I am rustic enough to decline it. Only I cannot tarry here."

तं तु मे भ्रातरं द्रष्टुं भरतं त्वरते मनः ।
मां निवर्तयितुं योऽसौ चित्रकूटमुपागतः ॥ VI. 124. 19

"The poor fellow ran after me with the whole palace and all his subjects, and with the army, and there he begged me as hard as he could. In the hardness of my heart, in the sternness of my resolution I said 'No' to him. That bothers me now."

शिरसा याचतो यस्य वचनं न कृतं मया । . VI. 124. 20

Now, I come, ladies and gentlemen, to a part of Bharata's character which may not be omitted in any consideration of him as the brother of Sri Rama. There is one aspect which is not pleasing to dwell upon. I will mention it not by way of criticism or by way of taking away from the greatness of a truly great character but just to show how there are some people in whose minds the sense of wrong or evil done excites so much hatred that it disturbs the harmony of their character. Bharata lacked the quality which we associate with a dutiful son. To his father he was all loyalty and respect. Only he did not like the way how in his senility he gave way to Kaikeyi and he stated it in harsh enough language. But I am thinking of his relations with his mother. Let us remember that Kaikeyi has been visited with the dislike and odium of generations upon generations of Hindus. She has paid heavily enough for her sins. Even during her lifetime there was no end to the curses that were heaped upon her. But let us remember that court intrigues are by no means uncommon. For a woman to plot to get the kingdom for her own son is nothing extraordinary. It is a pity that it should have happened in the Ikshvaku family and where Rama was the principal character. But you know how she was a good woman at first, very fond of Rama, as fond of him as of Bharata, but how she was persuaded by a very clever intriguer. Bharata, however even before he knew anything of the doings in the royal family of Ayodhya, while still he was with his uncle, says to the messengers who come to him—remember the messengers don't tell him the truth; they merely say, "Please come, there is business for you," and he starts—but before he starts, as soon as he sees them all, he makes enquiries of the family, of Kausalya, of Rama, of Lakshmana and so on. Of each he has something nice to say. Of Kausalya and Sumitra he says, "धर्मज्ञा" (II. 70. 8-9) "both of them very good; they know Dharma." But when he comes to speak of his mother—he knows no harm as yet of her—still this is the way he puts it.

> आत्मकामा सदा चण्डी क्रोधना प्राज्ञमानिनी ।
> अरोगा चापि मे माता कैकेयी किमुवाच ह ॥ II. 70. 10

"very fond of herself," that is, extremely selfish; "apt to become angry on slight occasions, had a high opinion of herself. What did she say?", he asks. Now I would ask of you all, however bad your mother may be, though you may have a poor opinion of her character, would you speak in that way to messengers coming from her? Surely you would not address them in that fashion. Nobody is under an obligation to speak the truth about others. There is no obligation to speak the truth to them about your mother and without any solicitation on their part. Well, that is a lapse that I cannot forgive. However wicked the mother may be, that is not the spirit in which a son should behave to her. I do not ask him to go and praise her unnecessarily and in a false spirit. He need not do so. If other people abuse her, let him be quiet, not say a word. But for him to launch out a crusade is scandalous.

Then through two sargas after he returns home and hears what she has done for him, he abuses her in the most unpardonable language. I will select a few verses which seem to me to be particularly noteworthy.

त्वत्कृते मे पिता वृत्तो रामश्चारण्यमाश्रितः ।
अयशो जीवलोके च त्वयाहं प्रतिपादितः ॥ II. 74. 6

"Through you my father is gone. Rama too has been exiled to the forest and you have handed my name down to infamy through the generations. Don't talk to me any more, murderer of your husband.

मातृरूपे ममामित्रे नृशंसे राज्यकामुके ।
न तेऽहमभिभाष्योऽस्मि दुर्वृत्ते पतिघातिनि ॥ II. 74. 7

You are not the daughter of Asvapati. You have ruined the good name of your father's family.

न त्वमश्वपतेः कन्या धर्मराजस्य धीमतः ।

You are a Rakshasi, born by mistake in that family.

राक्षसी तत्र जातासि कुलप्रध्वंसिनी पितुः ॥ II. 74. 9

Why don't you fall into the fire and take yourself away?

सा त्वमग्निं प्रविश वा स्वयं वा दण्डकान् विश ।

Where you have sent my brother and his wife, you go.

रज्जुं बधान वा कण्ठे न हि तेऽन्यत्परायणम् ॥ II. 74. 33

Or tie a rope round your neck. No other fate is fitting for you.

अहमप्यवनिं प्राप्ते रामे सत्यपराक्रमे ।
कृतकृत्यो भविष्यामि विप्रवासितकल्मषः ॥ II. 74. 34

When I have brought back Rama and given his kingdom to him I shall have fulfilled my duty; that is the one way in which I am going to wipe off the stain that you have put upon me, on my good name." Then a little later occurs one of the most funny scenes. Manthara—who had been rewarded by Kaikeyi for her services with all kinds of jewels worn on every part of her body—so the Poet says—appears. The most fashionable jewels which are fit for the noblest queens were all put on her body and she looked like an ornamented monkey. She appeared in a place in the palace where Satrughna was. Somebody saw her there and reported her presence to him. Here is the bad woman flourishing her jewels, the reward of her wickedness. Then occurred the savage scene—it won't occur in these days—when passions were strong and men did not know how to restrain them. Satrughna himself goes, seizes her by the hair and drags her upon the ground.

तस्या ह्याकृष्यमाणाया मन्थरायास्ततस्ततः ।
चित्रं बहुविधं भाण्डं पृथिव्यां तद्व्यशीर्यत ॥ II. 78. 17

The jewels that she wore were rubbed against the hard ground and then marks of gold were left all over the place. I am quoting this just to show how in those days goldsmiths had not yet developed their art fully.

तेन भाण्डेन संकीर्णं श्रीमद्राजनिवेशनम् ।
अशोभत तदा भूयः शारदं गगनं यथा ॥ II. 78. 18

She seems to have worn quite a hundred or two hundred of these on her body. Otherwise even if they fall on the floor you cannot describe that part as though it were a piece of sky fallen on the ground with all the stars together. Then in order to rescue her, her friends go about and appeal to Kaikeyi. Kaikeyi comes upon the scene and intercedes. Bharata does not notice her at all and says to Satrughna,— Just listen to this:

अवध्याः सर्वभूतानां प्रमदाः क्षम्यतामिति । II. 78. 21

"Just excuse her, forgive her. Of all beings on earth, women ought not to be molested." Kaikeyi stands by pleading. He says to his brother Satrughna:

हन्यामहमिमां पापां कैकेयीं दुष्टचारिणीम् ।
यदि मां धार्मिको रामो नासूयेन्मातृघातकम् ॥ II. 78. 22

"I would gladly kill her, this wicked woman, if only I were sure that my brother would not hate me for having killed my mother. If I were sure that my brother would not be displeased, then I would kill her on the spot." Surely that is not the language which a faithful son should use to his mother.

इमामपि हतां कुब्जां यदि जानाति राघवः ।

"If Sri Rama should know that you have killed this hunchback,

त्वां च मां च हि धर्मात्मा नाभिभाषिष्यते ध्रुवम् ॥ II. 78. 23

he will never again say a word in his life to you or to me." Then when he comes to Bharadvaja the great sage, what does he do? Bharadvaja also has some doubt about Bharata at first. Bharata reassures him. Bharadvaja is pleased with him and says, "All right. Let me now say good-bye to you all." And the next morning Bharata and Satrughna and the ladies all stand round the Rishi. The ladies make obeisance to Bharadvaja one by one and the Poet specifically mentions this—something that would never happen now—they touched his feet actually. No sage would allow his feet to be touched in these days. Then Bharadvaja says to Bharata, "Will you kindly tell me who is who amongst these ladies?" And then Bharata describes Kausalya; then he describes Sumitra, both of them in highly flattering language. But when he comes to his mother, should he use language like this?

यस्याः कृते नरव्याघ्रौ जीवनाशमितो गतौ ।

"She, on whose account, by whose misconduct Rama and Lakshmana have come very near to death,

राजा पुत्रविहीनश्च स्वर्गं दशरथो गतः ॥ II. 92. 25

father has been deprived of his son and unable to bear the grief, has perished—she on whose account these tragedies, have happened,

क्रोधनामकृतप्रज्ञां दृप्तां सुभगमानिनीम् ।
ऐश्वर्यकामां कैकेयीमनार्यामार्यरूपिणीम् ॥ II. 92. 26

this is my mother.

ममैतां मातरं विद्धि नृशंसां पापनिश्चयाम् ।
यतोमूलं हि पश्यामि व्यसनं महदात्मनः ॥ II. 92. 27

My misery is not going to end, all on her account." Bharadvaja is naturally shocked that the son should speak in this style about the mother. He says with the wisdom of a man who knows the future, "Don't talk ill of her. You do not know what she has done. She has done something good for the universe. We are all going to be the better for what she has done. Talk not in that strain about her." But Bharata does not modify his opinion. And this, mind you, though Kaikeyi has given proof that she has become a reformed character—she no longer is the Kaikeyi of old who brought King Dasaratha from the heights of his pride to the depths of misery. That is not the Kaikeyi now. The very fact that she joined this group and that she came along with Kausalya and Sumitra, in the same carriage as the Poet says, shows that she also desired the return of Sri Rama. Nevertheless, Bharata's heart was not mollified in the least. So when he speaks to Sri Rama afterwards in that great conversation between them he says still:

प्रोषिते मयि यत्पापं मात्रा मत्कारणात्कृतम् ॥
क्षुद्रया तदनिष्टं मे प्रसीदतु भावन् मम। II. 106. 8

"That mean-minded woman wickedly, when I was away, brought about all this trouble. Forgive me. I am not responsible. I am bound by duty, otherwise.

धर्मबन्धेन बद्धोऽस्मि तेनेमां नेह मातरम् ॥*

"I would kill her."

हन्मि तीव्रेण दण्डेन दण्डार्हां पापकारिणीम्। II. 106. 9-10

He says this to Rama himself. After all this, discussing the whole thing over again, he says, "Don't be guided by the doings of my mother. Put that out of your mind, my brother. Mother was wicked; she was sinful. She plotted and ruined everything. I would kill her now. But I am afraid of Dharma." Once more Rama plays a great part. He speaks for Kaikeyi most earnestly. You remember I read some verses at the end when Sri Rama says "Don't do any mischief to her. By Sita and myself I bind you down by solemn oaths that you should not speak ill of her or molest her or dishonour her in any way."

* Cf. Lect. VIII, p. 104.

Then we come to the closing scene when after his half-fruitful mission—I do not like to say it was fruitless*—Bharata returns home. This is the last sloka in the scene:

तं मातरो बाष्पगृहीतकण्ठ्यो दुःखेन नामन्त्रयितुं हि शेकुः ।

The three mothers desired to take leave of Sri Rama having to go back but they were so overcome with grief that the words stuck in their throats. They could not speak, they were unable to take leave of Sri Rama. What about him? Had he more presence of mind?

स त्वेव मातृरभिवाद्य सर्वा रुदन् कुटीं स्वां प्रविवेश रामः ॥

II. 112. 31

He too was unable for his part to say a word. He merely cried and then went into the parnakuti, but not without having made due pranamams to them all.

The commentators specially add the word सर्वाः to मातृः· Why does the Poet specially say that Kaikeyi too received the most devoted pranamams from Sri Rama? Even the commentator goes too far. He need not say

अनेन कैकेय्या दोषराहित्यं सूचितम् ।

For Rama is so exalted a character that even if a little stain had remained in Kaikeyi's case, he would not have omitted the duty of making pranamams to her. She was his mother like the others. He never forgot the duty that he owed to her. He never would have withheld from her the marks of reverence that he showed to Kausalya and to Sumitra. There is no doubt about it. And as I have said she was repenting also. Why does the Poet specially mention सर्वाः and enable the commentator to say that Kaikeyi had been repenting? The meaning is, ladies and gentlemen, as far as I can see,—the commentator does not say it but I do it and I do not think I go out of my way—Rama wanted to give an object-

---

* Publishers' Note: Cf.

ततः शिरसि कृत्वा तु पादुके भरतस्तदा ।
आरुरोह रथं हृष्टः शत्रुघ्नेन समन्वितः ॥

II. 113. 1, where the Poet sets down that Bharata was contented and happy.

lesson to Bharata. Bharata had spoken unrestrainedly about his mother, forgetting entirely his duty to her. By making pranamams to her, the same as to the others, Rama gave practical proof to Bharata as to what the duty of a son was. That was his object. There is one word which the commentator adds, which it seems to me is characteristic of the style of interpretation that we generally have in this country. But it is wholly misguided. Did I not read to you now

"रुदन् कुटीं स्वां प्रविवेश रामः"

"With tears in his eyes Rama went into the Parnakuti," says the Poet. Why not leave it there? It is a beautiful sentiment. It makes us love and adore Rama. But the commentator must add रुदन्निव "pretending to cry" because he was the great one, the divine one and he ought not to cry, but like a human being he cried. But we prefer him to behave like us. That is his value to us. And I think I would take रुदन् to mean literally that Rama, out of the sincerity of his heart, was so overcome with feeling at the last moment at parting from the mothers and from the brother who were so dear to him and from whom he was to remain separated for fourteen long years. God knows what those years would bring, what miseries would fill them day by day. Nothing was clear yet; all was dark at that time. If Rama wept, why should we not believe that he sincerely and truly wept? *He **did**.*

FOURTEENTH LECTURE*

Friends,

Sugriva's career portrayed in the Ramayana divides itself into two halves, a greater and a lesser. The earlier is the lesser half. During this period Sugriva has to attain his position. He has lost what was his, and he was always overshadowed and even overawed by an elder brother who was his superior by far. He has to find his way cautiously. He distrusted people, he had no confidence in himself, and having to seek allies, he was, generally speaking, in a position of disadvantage. When he had got over his difficulties and come into his own, his tone, as it were, became stronger, and we find him both speaking and acting more firmly and more like his own self. It is strange that at first when he saw Rama and Lakshmana, he feared they were the agents of Vali, sent to compass his ruin. He expresses his misgivings to Hanuman. Hanuman does not share them, and he chides him almost in language which seems surprising to one who was only a trusted minister. Hanuman was the most distinguished of them all, but the others also were very considerably able, Nala, Nila and Tara. I want to read a *sloka* in which Hanuman expresses his astonishment at Sugriva's distress in order that we may draw from it a useful lesson.

अहो शाखामृगत्वं ते व्यक्तमेव प्लवङ्गम ।
लघुचित्ततयात्मानं न स्थापयसि यो मतौ ॥ IV. 2. 17

"By showing this weakness you have really shown that you are a monkey." We have to remember that Sugriva and Hanuman were two of the greatest members of their tribe. Ordinarily they would not account themselves as greatly inferior to men. At any rate, when they talk to each other, they will not speak disparagingly of their own tribe. *Kapitva* should not be to them a term of reproach, though it might be amongst men. It is surprising that Hanuman should say that, as though he were deriding the very stock from which he came and of which he was so distinguished a specimen. That it was a man that wrote the poem is the secret that

* 12-7-'44.

we should learn from it. He ascribes to the speaker, forgetting for the moment that he was a monkey, sentiments not likely to have been uttered by Hanuman and Sugriva.

Rama and Sugriva, as soon as they made up their alliance, began to repose complete confidence in each other. At any rate in the beginning, complete confidence was expressed in each by the other.

> ततोऽग्निं दीप्यमानं तौ चक्रतुश्च प्रदक्षिणम् ॥
> सुग्रीवो राघवश्चैव वयस्यत्वमुपागतौ ।
> ततः सुप्रीतमनसौ तावुभौ हरिराघवौ ॥
> अन्योन्यमभिवीक्षन्तौ न तृप्तिमुपजग्मतुः ।
> त्वं वयस्योऽसि मे हृद्यो ह्येकं दुःखं सुखं च नौ ॥ IV. 5. 16-18

Having gone round the fire, held each other's hands and sworn mutual fidelity, they looked at each other steadily for a while, and were satisfied, each thinking that he had chosen the proper ally. They said "We share our sorrows and our joys alike." Please remember what Ravana said to Vali when they became friends.* If you have forgotten it, let me remind you. Ravana says

> दाराः पुत्राः पुरं राष्ट्रं भोगाच्छादनभोजनम् ।
> सर्वमेवाविभक्तं नौ भविष्यति हरीश्वर ॥ VII. 34. 41

Some of you may think that this, from the Uttarakanda, is not of the same degree of authority. But our commentators have a way of quoting the Uttarakanda when it suits them, and not minding it when it does not go in their favour. But it strikes me as strange that Ravana should include दाराः. I suppose this is only an extravagance of language, perhaps, showing us in what regard Ravana held the numerous members of the harem.

Then we find a simple thing which has led to a strange comment in some enlightened circles. You will see that as they enter upon their friendship, Sugriva puts searching questions to Rama, and Rama does not answer them himself, but bids his brother Lakshmana answer them. This is in observance of a regular rule of etiquette in palaces. A king should address only kings of his degree of importance, and

* Vide Lect. XI, p. 157.

ministers should address ministers. This is somewhat disconcerting, and so it has led people to think that Sugriva really offered an affront to the greatness of Rama, and that some of the misfortunes that came to him later were the result of this disrespect on his part. There is no reason for thinking in this way at all, for we find Sugriva plucking the branch of a tree in order that he and Rama may sit together, while immediately after, Hanuman does the same and bids Lakshmana take his seat with him. There is nothing to show that that was intended as any disrespect to the majesty of Rama, and I am not willing to believe that this natural pairing off should have led anybody to suppose that Sugriva was in the very beginning of his friendship guilty of a piece of insult, either deliberate or unintended.

Then, Sugriva is considered guilty of a piece of concealment when, being asked to say where Ravana could be found and what sort of strength he had, he says

न जाने निलयं तस्य सर्वथा पापरक्षसः ।
सामर्थ्यं विक्रमं वापि दौष्कुलेयस्य वा कुलम् ॥ IV. 7. 2

Sugriva says that he is not in full possession of details regarding Ravana. He puts the statement rather widely and it is not sufficient to convict him of anything like wilful concealment. I myself think that the terms are a little too wide, for Sugriva could not have been so ignorant as these words seem to hint. He certainly knew much, but not sufficient to induce confidence at the moment in Rama's mind. Of course, if the Uttarakanda be taken into account, this is a very clear violation of conscience. There it is distinctly stated that Ravana stayed for one whole month in Vali's place, just like Sugriva, as a member of the family. Then it would be incredibly wrong. But I would hesitate a lot before I brought a charge against Sugriva of infidelity in the beginning of his contract, because in the very passage he says

एवमुक्तस्तु सुग्रीवो रामेणार्तेन वानरः ।
अब्रवीत्प्राञ्जलिर्वाक्यं सबाष्पं बाष्पगद्गदः ॥ IV. 7. 1

Sugriva is unable to talk clearly. So he is not likely to launch at once into a piece of falsehood, and Rama had no suspicion whatever that anything had been kept from him.

मधुरं सान्त्वितस्तेन सुग्रीवेण स राघवः ।
मुखमश्रुपरिक्लिन्नं वस्त्रान्तेन प्रमार्जयन् ॥ IV. 7. 15

Rama wept, it seems, and took his upper garment and by the end of it wiped his tears.

एष च प्रकृतिस्थोऽहमनुनीतस्त्वया सखे ।
दुर्लभो हीदृशो बन्धुरस्मिन् काले विशेषतः ॥ IV. 7. 18

This is clear proof that there was not on the part of Sugriva any subterfuge and that there was complete understanding between Sugriva and Rama, and that each had perfect confidence in the other. No reserve of any kind could be traced.

Then, you remember my pointing out, perhaps contrary to the current belief of superficial readers, how from the text it is clear that Sugriva gave orders in good time for the search to be started. He wanted his monkey forces to be summoned in good time. Then I did not point out, as it was not necessary at that time, what he had actually done. Not only did he give orders that the monkeys should be assembled in a fortnight, but, furthermore, he bade Hanuman, or Nila Commander-in-Chief, or perhaps both together, to attend to the rest of the business without intermission; and there was no need to refer anything to him again. I think that clears him of all charges of neglect; and I did mention before how Lakshmana, having learnt the truth from the lips of Tara herself, apologises in full measure for having used rough language and for having been discourteous.

*हरींश्च वृद्धानुपयातु साङ्गदो भवान् ममाज्ञामधिकृत्य निश्चिताम् ।
इति व्यवस्थां हरिपुंगवेश्वरो विधाय वेश्म प्रविवेश वीर्यवान् ॥

IV. 29. 30

Believing that in this business everything would be proceeded with all right, Sugriva retired into his palace. Of course, his mistake was that he lived his riotous life a little too ostentatiously for the comfort of Rama, which he should not have done. If he was a considerate person, he would have realised that his benefactor was most unhappy yet, and that therefore his enjoyment of his new-found happiness should be a little less noisy.

Sugriva was a person, therefore, in the first part of his career, of great caution and would not praise people readily.

* Cf. Lect. VII, p. 95.

This appears also a little later, when, along with Lakshmana, he expresses his desire that Vibhishana should not be taken into the confederacy. He did not like that a man coming straight from the arms of Ravana should, without further trial of a very stringent character, be treated with confidence, thereby showing the utter contrast between his nature and Rama's. In fact, Rama had the good fortune to be surrounded by extremely good people; great characters were all around him. Nevertheless, in many respects they served as foils for his own character to shine even more splendidly. We must remember that perhaps Valmiki did it on set purpose, to show how no man is great, but there is a greater, and there is a far greater. You can have a Sugriva, you can have a Vibhishana, a Bharata or a Lakshmana, and yet, over and above them all and without their deficiencies, you can have a character which reaches very perfection. It is just to show that that the Poet has brought round Rama these great characters. It is a part of the Poet's design. This is how Rama enunciates his doctrine which none of these people were able to understand at all.

सकृदेव प्रपन्नाय तवास्मीति च याचते ॥
अभयं सर्वभूतेभ्यो ददाम्येतद्व्रतं मम । VI. 18. 33-34

Here is a man who has lost his kingdom and is going to a strange country with monkeys, and he says, I am going to offer protection without reserve to anyone who just comes and says 'please', I do not want anything more. From all dangers, from all enemies, I grant such persons full protection. It is the height of benevolence, almost unimaginable. Then as if that was not enough, he implements it in this sloka.

आनयैनं हरिश्रेष्ठ दत्तमस्याभयं मया ।
*विभीषणो वा सुग्रीव यदि वा रावणः स्वयम् ॥ VI. 18. 34-35

"Bring him here. I have given him abhaya already. My principle is much more thorough than this, much more drastic. Even if Ravana himself came and asked me protection, I shall embrace him and give him all protection." Lakshmana, being a man of few words and not always ready with his tongue in the presence of Rama, especially by way of contradiction, allowed Sugriva to speak for him. Sugriva was surprised

* Cf. Lect. XVII below.

beyond measure, but seeing the extreme confidence with which Rama spoke and not being able to resist the grandeur of the sentiment, he was struck dumb.

> किमत्र चित्रं धर्मज्ञ लोकनाथ सुखावह ॥
> यत्त्वमार्यं प्रभाषेथाः सत्त्ववान् सत्पथे स्थितः । VI. 18. 36-37

"Is this a wonder? You are of all princes the ideal, the strongest and the best. If you should speak thus, it is no wonder." Then he proceeds,—here the good nature of Sugriva comes out—

> मम चाप्यन्तरात्मायं शुद्धं वेत्ति विभीषणम् ।
> अनुमानाच्च भावाच्च सर्वतः सुपरीक्षितः ॥
> तस्मात्क्षिप्रं सहास्माभिस्तुल्यो भवतु राघव ।
> विभीषणो महाप्राज्ञः सखित्वं चाभ्युपैतु नः ॥ VI. 18. 37-38

"My own inner feeling says that Vibhishana is all right. So recommended, we are not going to resist him. Let him join us, and you will find that we treat him exactly like one of us." No more difference, no more distrust, no more lack of willingness to help or be helped.

When all this about his excessive caution has been stated, please remember Sugriva's greatness of soul. So soon as they came to the sea-side, before yet the bridge was constructed, he says

> तां दृष्ट्वा तु पुरीं लङ्कां त्रिकूटशिखरे स्थिताम् ॥
> हतं च रावणं युद्धे दर्शनादुपधारय । VI. 2. 10-11

He gives a promise to Rama. Being a great chieftain conscious of his own prowess and with full trust in his own strength, he assures Rama. "Now that we have come to this place, wait till we see Lanka. Let us only see that man Ravana and I will bring his corpse to you. The moment he becomes visible to us, remember he is a dead man." That was the confidence with which Sugriva spoke. Then a little later, Ravana sends the messenger Suka to perform the third of the four expedients. Ravana bade Suka to draw Sugriva away from Rama's side. So Suka comes and says something to Sugriva by way of inducing him. Even the poet does not refer to what passed.* Sugriva sends a spirited answer. He would not be turned aside from his duty by a friendly, but wicked person.

न मेऽसि मित्रं न तथानुकम्प्यो न चोपकर्तासि न मे प्रियोऽसि।
अरिश्च रामस्य सहानुबन्धः न मेऽसि वालीव वधार्ह वध्यः ॥
निहन्म्यहं त्वां ससुतं सबन्धुं सज्ञातिवर्गं रजनीचरेश।
लङ्कां च सर्वां महता बलेन क्षिप्रं करिष्यामि समेत्य भस्म ॥

VI. 20. 23-24

"You have been no good. You are Rama's enemy and therefore my attitude to you is that you ought to be sent to destruction even as Vali was. You deserve no better. I am going to kill you. I will make a bonfire of this Lanka and reduce it entirely to ashes."

I will next take you to a consideration of a remarkable exploit by Sugriva. While yet the general battle was not joined, when they had gone only to Suvela and could see Lanka and all its defences, when the moon shone full in the sky, all went up and from there took a survey of Lanka. Strangely enough, Ravana appeared there, giving orders, perfectly at ease, but, in his turn, surveying the hostile army that had established itself. Suddenly it struck Sugriva that he must redeem the promise that he had made. Being a hero of true mettle, without further thought or taking leave of people, up he jumped to where Ravana was and challenged him to single combat. Compared to this, all the boxing matches that we see pale into insignificance. In fact, throughout the Yuddhakanda we see how Valmiki—for he must have been a warrior perhaps in spirit—is able to describe innumerable battles in innumerable different ways. There is no doubt a family likeness, but the variety of combats on the one side and the way he matches strength with strength is astonishing. Here the battle between Sugriva and Ravana is described through a long sarga in very fine and spirited language. Sugriva says,

लोकनाथस्य रामस्य सखा दासोऽस्मि राक्षस। VI. 40. 10

---

* Publishers' Note:—The Poet says :

"सर्वमुक्तं यथादिष्टं रावणेन दुरात्मना।" VI. 20. 15

and the words of the 'duratma's' message are given in verses 10—12 preceding.

"You know who I am. Rama and I are allies. I have come here to assist him in his cause. He regards me as an ally, as if I were a co-ordinate part. Really I am his *dasa.* Though in his judgment an ally, I am truly at heart his *dasa.*" When they came together in Kishkindha, they embraced each other, and between them there was only equality. Sugriva himself tested Rama more than once. See what time has effected. He has seen Rama, his character, his prowess, and has sunk relatively to a position of attendance. He no longer regards himself as an ally. In the combat he plucked Ravana's diadem. Ravana became angry and not being able to overcome Sugriva, he adopted his *maya* tactics. Sugriva knew that Rama deprecated that kind of trickery, and so he must not meet *maya* by *maya.* Thinking that he had done enough to humble Ravana, he jumped back to where Rama was and took his position on Rama's side. The commentator takes advantage of रामपार्श्वम् VI. 40. 29, and says "he was ashamed to come and stand in front of Rama, but went to his side." Clever, but by no means convincing. Then Rama remonstrates with him. "How reckless you are! You are second in command. After me you are the chief. You go and risk your life like this for just a little scrap. You have done wrong to do this without taking counsel of any of your colleagues. You have exposed us all to serious danger. When you were there still struggling and had not returned and everything was in doubt and no one knew what would happen, while I looked on, this was the conclusion that I was coming to. 'Supposing the worst happened to Sugriva, I am not going to retreat from here. I am going to do my mission here. I will kill Ravana, recover Sita, make Vibhishana king in Ravana's stead. And then I will go back and, instead of anointing myself king of Ayodhya, I will anoint Bharata king and end my career'." Sugriva, utterly confused, could only say in defence

तव भार्यापहर्तारं दृष्ट्वा राघव रावणम् ।
मर्षयामि कथं वीर जानन् पौरुषमात्मनः ॥ VI. 41. 9

"When I saw the person who took your wife away by force, how could I keep quiet? A strong fighter like me, I could not help it."

Then we come to another scene in which Sugriva figures, I do not know whether to say in glory or in a dubious light.

Kumbhakarna had come into the field of battle, almost like a hill in appearance, rugged like a hill too, by no means an easy customer even for Hanuman or Sugriva. When he came, what he did was to open his mouth, catch hold of monkeys and put them in. There are two or three sargas in which Kumbhakarna and his extraordinary size and strength are spoken of, and his deeds, almost crude in conception, are given in very interesting detail. But somehow or other, nothing surprises these warriors. The ordinary captain comes and matches himself against the renowned warrior. When Kumbhakarna came into the field, Sugriva matched himself against him. Though Sugriva was himself a big monkey, he was nothing by the side of Kumbhakarna. Kumbhakarna simply put him in his arm-pit and, knowing that he was Sugriva the commander-in-chief, he said "I have finished this host. I may go back and proclaim my triumph." And walking back in comparative ease and security, he just pressed his arm and was crushing Sugriva. Hanuman, who was much the stronger of the two, saw this from a distance. For a moment he struggled within himself. "Here is my master caught. Am I to look on and not help him? That would be wrong. But Sugriva is a mighty monkey, he knows how to escape, some expedient will occur to him. If I go and rescue him, he will never forgive me afterwards. This will also be published abroad that Hanuman had to get him out of some scrape." And as Hanuman had predicted, Sugriva knew how to escape. What he did was to struggle hard and just reach the nose of Kumbhakarna. He bit it off, and having done this, as he had sharp nails, tore off his ears so hard that Kumbhakarna had to drop him in sheer annoyance. Up he jumped and came back to where Rama was.

Sugriva had many exploits to his credit. He killed three of the biggest giants of the other side. The Poet gives three Rakshasas to Hanuman, three to Sugriva and three to Angada. The Rakshasas whom Sugriva brought down were Kumbha, Virupaksha and Mahodara. Hanuman had better heroes. The Poet himself is in a joyous mood in describing the slaying of Mahodara. Instead of saying *harsha,* he says *harusha,* VI. 98. 38. It is not alone the metre that compelled it, but some spirit of enjoyment in describing this hilarious scene.

Now I come to point out one of Sugriva's greatest characteristics. From the very beginning they had all ascribed to him great severity, cruelty of punishment. The smallest fault will be visited with capital punishment. Curiously enough, in the whole of Ramayana, Sugriva is not mentioned as having removed anybody in this way. But everybody was afraid of him. There was a case when he might have lost his temper and ordered the destruction of hundreds of monkeys, when they all went to the Madhuvana and destroyed it. When Hanuman had returned in triumph and narrated his story, the monkeys lost their heads, went into the Madhuvana where Sugriva had appointed expert gardeners, ate all the fruits, destroyed the trees and drank all the honey away. The warden of the park who was at the head of the guards, Dadhimukha, seeing that Hanuman and the host of monkeys let themselves loose, remonstrated with them, but they had no ears to hear. The Poet says that in order to show their utter contempt for these guardians, they exhibited their backs to them. It was reported to Sugriva, but hearing the extent of the damage and the participators in the work of hooliganism, he said to Rama and Lakshmana, "Please be easy. These monkeys would not have let themselves loose like this unless they had seen Sita. Though they may be guilty, I am not going to punish them, for they have done a great deed which it was our desire that they should do."

Now I come to describe one of the shadows, as it were, in so brilliant a character as Sugriva's. Here I am going to point out how in spite of his great qualities, there was something in Sugriva calculated to show that he was at one time a somewhat weak character, apt to give way to weakness. Before Hanuman jumped across the sea, before even the monkeys had come across Sampati and he had given them a hint as to where Sita was to be found, when they had just come out of Svayamprabha's cave garden, the monkeys, not being able yet to know how to get to Lanka nor being sure that Sita was there, found that they had exceeded the time limit, and imagining that their heads would all be off, made up their minds that they would enter on a fast unto death. And Angada was the one who recommended this course of self-immolation as the most honourable. Then it occurs to Tara, maternal uncle of the young prince, that they need not do so, and he suggests that they may all go back to the cave. Angada seemed to lend an ear. But Hanuman, who was the minister of Sugriva, took alarm at this state of things, and wishing to dissuade Angada from such a course, holds out all sorts of inducements to him. So he says to Angada, "Sugriva has done so many things to you. After him you are going to be king. He will do you no harm. Therefore let us all go back." Angada remonstrates.

स्थैर्यं सत्त्वं मनःशौचमानृशंस्यमथार्जवम् ।
विक्रमश्चैव धैर्यं च सुग्रीवे नोपपद्यते ॥
भ्रातुर्ज्येष्ठस्य यो भार्यां जीवतो महिषीं प्रियाम् ।
धर्मेण मातरं यस्तु स्वीकरोति जुगुप्सितः ॥
कथं स धर्मं जानीते येन भ्रात्रा महात्मना ।
युद्धायाभिनियुक्तेन बिलस्य पिहितं मुखम् ॥ IV. 55. 2-4

"Is he a hero and dutiful brother, who knowing that his brother was inside the cave, closes the cave by means of a huge rock and walks away to become king and the husband of his wife?" No doubt Sugriva thought at the time that it was not Mayavi that had been killed by Vali, but that it was Vali that had been killed by Mayavi. What grounds he had to think so, the Poet does not say; nor does Sugriva himself say. He saw blood come out after one year of waiting. It might be the Asura's blood or not. Sugriva imagined that it was Vali's and hoping to shut the evil Rakshasa in, he put a huge rock. But we cannot forget that people might ask, "If he was not sure, why not make sure by walking in? Why did he not take his monkeys?" People must have put that question and come to their own conclusion. Only we know that the Poet does not make an open censure of Sugriva's conduct, but gives a charitable construction and says that he was by no means anxious to become king, but that his ministers forced him to do so. He allowed himself to be hustled into the kingship.

I want to tell you that at this stage of his career he was a little weak, and undeveloped yet. When two courses are open, each plausible, each capable of being presented in an agreeable way, the tendency is to choose the easier and more advantageous course. Sugriva fell into that tendency. Angada, a *Dayada* and the son of a man who had been killed, took the more sinister view. How can we blame him? Sugriva was certainly hasty and chose the easier course always which gave him advantage.

Angada denounced Sugriva not only for base treachery to his brother Vali, but for black ingratitude to his sworn ally Rama.

सत्यात्पाणिगृहीतश्च कृतकर्मा महायशाः ।

विस्मृतो राघवो येन स कस्य तु कृतं स्मरेत् ॥ IV. 55. 5

Here, Angada was wrong, as we have seen*, Rama and Lakshmana came to know the truth about what Sugriva had done to assemble the monkey hosts and apologised to Sugriva. But Angada was not willing so to excuse him and he was quite wrong. The facts were within his knowledge; nevertheless he accuses Sugriva of having forgotten Rama and what was due to Rama.

Again, Angada asks: "Was it the fear that he would be ungrateful and unrighteous if he did not send an army, or was it the fear of Lakshmana's arrow?"

लक्ष्मणस्य भयाद्येन नाधर्मभयभीरुणा ।

आदिष्टा मार्गितुं सीता धर्मस्तस्मिन् कथं भवेत् ॥ IV. 55. 6

'Fear dictated this course, not dharma,' says Angada. Even here he was unjust to Sugriva.

Angada adds,

न चाहं यौवराज्येन सुग्रीवेणाभिषेचितः ॥

नरेन्द्रेणाभिषिक्तोऽस्मि रामेणाक्लिष्टकर्मणा । IV. 53. 30-31

"I do not believe that Sugriva made me yuvaraja. It was Sri Rama." That was true. Angada is justified once more in this statement that it was Rama who made him yuvaraja.

'I have also done a wrong,' says Angada and

स पूर्वं बद्धवैरो मां राजा दृष्ट्वा व्यतिक्रमम् ॥

घातयिष्यति दण्डेन तीक्ष्णेन कृतनिश्चयः । IV. 53. 31-32

"If I go back, Sugriva will remember that I am his *Dayada,* that I am waiting to become king after him. So he will give me the severest punishment." Then the Poet says something very significant. When Angada says all these things to Hanuman and the other monkeys, he tells them, "You are free to choose. Though, for my part, I think I must enter on this

* Lect. VII, p. 95.

fast unto death, I am willing to abide by your decision." He places himself at the disposal of his men, of their more mature decision. This readiness to own immaturity of thought pleased them so much that the monkeys took his side.

विवेश चाङ्गदो भूमौ रुदन् दर्भेषु दुर्मनाः ।
तस्य संविशतस्तत्र रुदन्तो वानरर्षभाः ॥
नयनेभ्यः प्रमुमुचुरुष्णं वै वारि दुःखिताः ।
सुग्रीवं चैव निन्दन्तः प्रशंसन्तश्च वालिनम् ॥ IV. 55. 17-18

They all said Sugriva was a usurper, and Vali was a good king. I am inclined to think that in saying this the monkeys gave expression to some story that must have been fairly believed in at that time.

Then is given an estimate of Sugriva's great might, of the enormous forces he enjoyed and brought into the field for the help of Rama. It is most amusing. Having killed Vali, Rama bestowed all this on Sugriva. He became mighty at once through the help of Rama. He who commands such forces cannot be defeated in battle.

FIFTEENTH LECTURE*

Sisters and brothers,

In the opening days of 1907—thirty-seven years ago—there occurred an event in the political world of India, which will serve as a suitable introduction to my talk today. The famous Dadabhai Naoroji Congress had concluded, and the feeling of Congressmen generally was that the threatened split had for the time been averted and that our efforts should all be directed to its prevention next year. That, however, as you know, was not to be. After the 1906 Congress concluded, Mr. Gokhale, who had taken a prominent part in the proceedings, thought that the good work should be completed by a series of public talks in various parts of India, showing young people how wild talk about the severance of the British connection and about a thorough-going boycott of everything British might end in disaster. He toured through Upper India, and his first lectures had a very great effect, producing anguish in the hearts of those whose efforts to weaken the Congress had caused all the trouble. At that time Bengal was served by a famous daily newspaper called 'Bande Mataram.' Its editor was A.G. The first lectures had appeared in the press and they were reported in full. We were all astonished one morning to read the editorial headed "Exit Vibhishana". The idea was that Gokhale, by declaring himself on the side of the British power and against the surging national movement, had played the part, the odious part, that Vibhishana played when deserting his brother and going over to join Sri Rama on the other side of the water. I was naturally hurt very much by the reference to my master Gokhale, but I was still more hurt by the use of the name Vibhishana to signify a traitor. I had been brought up to believe that Vibhishana was a Bhakta of the first order, that he was a noble character who might be held up to pious people as an example of devotion to Dharma and to those who practised it with sincerity. Was Vibhishana to be held up to public execration as a man who had abandoned a noble cause and exposed his kinsmen and his land to the perils of a foreign invasion? That, anyhow, was not the light in which I was trained to understand

* 19-7-'44.

that character. And on enquiry I was much pained to learn that the name Vibhishana was used, generally speaking, in Upper India to mean a traitor, a betrayer of his national cause. That opened up a great difference between North India and South India in the understanding of this great epic, the Ramayana. But I am glad my enquiries since then have proved that there is not that very great difference that I thought at that time was prevalent. There are many in South India who, for some reason, inflamed by the political feeling of the day, regard Vibhishana as a character to be held up to contempt and to odium; and there are in other parts of India many who hold the contrary opinion. Nevertheless, I think, if we were to take a census today, we should find more people inimical to the reputation of Vibhishana in Upper India than here. It appears to me a misfortune that a character in our greatest epic whom the Poet himself has held in the highest esteem and whom for centuries upon centuries India has regarded as an ideal devotee, a man who exemplified by whatever he did, according to the Visishtadvaitins, in faithful reproduction, the various attributes and stages, one after another, of the progress of a *prapanna*, that a character of that high order should by any means be regarded by the politically inflamed people of the time as a character to be avoided, to be mentioned only with disapprobation. It seems to me to be a melancholy fact, and I cannot reconcile myself to it. I wish today, talking to an audience in sympathy with Valmiki and his general ideas, in sympathy with our great traditions, that Vibhishana should be possibly saved from his detractors, and presented to you in what I consider to be a correct light. I hold that Vibhishana was a good man according to the standards of his time, and is a good man according to the standards of our time too. Let me make my meaning clear by devoting a part of the time this evening to an illustration of the chief elements of Vibhishana's nature. The first question that occurs to me is, who is a traitor? In common parlance today, a traitor would be one who betrays his country or his nation to the enemy who has invaded the country and makes war upon it. By extension, of course, it would apply to any politician or public worker who sets himself deliberately for private profit, or who, for the sake of title or for some such purely worldly considerations, sets himself against the efforts made by patriots for the liberation of their country. Unfortunately, I am not in sympathy with the deep hatred that political parties bear today to each other. Politics are just on the surface of human affairs. They do not go deep down into the heart of things or into the profundities of our real nature. They have small connection with our relations to the other world or to our being able to secure the grace of the Almighty. Why should people who hold one political opinion execrate men on the other side to such an extent that whatever their private character may be, however great their usefulness to the public may be in other directions, however exemplary their conduct may be, why should people hold them up to be the enemies of the future of the nation? All parties, it seems to me, have their place in politics. No one party has the monopoly of truth or of political wisdom. Each party requires the assistance of the others, if only we knew that political wisdom and political truth are to be found in the doctrines of every organised political party. We ought all to regard one another as allies in the task of serving the country. Perhaps the exigencies of the day may throw us even into some rivalry of actual work, and we may be found on opposite sides of the camp, each trying to negative the work of the other. But we need not traduce the character of the great men on the other side. Well, that is the preliminary remark that I wish to make, that more than property, more than the honour of your wives, more than the affairs of litigation which cast off fellow-feeling, more than all these, political differences seem to call forth from our people the vilest language to be applied to one another. It is a thing that I cannot understand, and it is a thing which I wish were eliminated from the education of our boys if possible, for ever and for ever. No young man ought to be taught to think that a leader of high reputation, just because he happens to be on the other side, is a vile man to be abused and to be spoken of as one who had to die, or if he will not die, to be destroyed if the good of India has to be served. I think that that man would be the greatest benefactor of his day who could teach the young in our colleges and schools to think that private merit, the beauties of human character, the dignities of human conduct, are to be found in all political parties, and that it is wrong for a young man to narrow his sympathies and his heart. That, however, is a desire which is not going to be fulfilled in my time. Young men delight in throwing mud at older people. I have suffered a great deal myself. I have known other people who have a title to real greatness and to the gratitude of our country suffer undeservedly at the hands of young men. This is a very special feature of democratic politics. It was not the case at a time when politics had not become democratised. It is much more prevalent in America and England, where politics have established themselves over a good many generations and where at the moment, if you will ask my honest opinion, the converse of democracy is far more in evidence than the good it has done or the good it is likely to do for some time. Democracy is certainly the best form of human governance that has yet been devised, but it wants to be served by brave men, by true men, by first class men. It stands liable ever to the greatest abuse at the hands of untried men who think that abuse is the staple of politics and hatred is the hall-mark of patriotism. This sermon has been drawn out of me partly because I think it is an evil of the day, which in India is of foreign origin and may well be eradicated, and partly because it accounts for the degradation to which the great name of Vibhishana has been unfortunately subjected. If our politics were not what they are, if the word 'patriotism' has not been applied in the modern way, Vibhishana's name would well have been pure and unsullied in our estimation. For, what is meant by patriotism? I ought to be very careful in the words I use, for people who bring political bias in the listening of a leader interpret it in their own way, according to their predilections, not necessarily according to the words of the speaker or his real sense. Pray, let me be understood to say what I wish to say, not what you think I am saying. I was going to say that patriotism is not necessarily a virtue of human character. It is an emotion. It is a high feeling, an inclination of the heart of a noble order, of an exalted character. But whether it works well or ill, whether the consequences of patriotism are good or bad, whether the country is served well by the patriot in the end, depends upon how the emotion is directed. Take the love of the child in the mother. The mother would spill her blood, give her life for the child. What is there in the world which she would not do for the welfare of the child? But we all know how often mothers untrained to their task, not knowing the nature of children do not bring them up properly and even spoil their general health completely. However sincere, however loving, however devoted, however sacrificing she may be, the ignorant mother cannot bring up a child in proper ways. She herself, out of the excess of her love, becomes a source of the child's weakness, perhaps of its wickedness. We see to what bad uses love may be put, and we know too how in times of famine and acute trouble, women, burdened with two or three children and not knowing how to find the day's bread for them, and thinking that they should put an end to their own lives, think that the necessary preliminary for that is that they should kill their own children. See where it leads. I am trying to point out that this noblest of all feelings, the love of her child, can lead a woman to the commission of deeds the very mention of which fills us with horror. On the other hand, take a wise father or a wise mother who has read books on how the young should be protected and guarded from evil practices, who can teach them to love the noble and the sincere, and avoid what is likely to degrade. Think how strong a power for good in the life of our nation becomes the possession of a mother or father of that character. So now you will see how I am justified in saying that even our strongest passions, our noblest emotions, are only to be welcomed to the extent that they are used for uplifting purposes by those in whose hearts they play a prominent part. Patriotism thus may be good, or it may be bad in its effects, however honourable a man's intentions may be. No man is born with all these good qualities. If we want to examine their origin in human affairs, we shall find perhaps that they had a very simple physical origin, and from that physical origin, by gradual perfection of their associations, by gradual exaltation of the uses to which they are put, these moral ideas have become purer and purer, until now we think that the chief end and aim of education is to inculcate them in the young.

Allow me a few minutes to show how patriotism arose in human history. Patriotism is not today what it meant at first. At first patriotism was largely confined to tribes and communities. From being strictly limited to families and to little villages, it gradually extended and came to mean a kindly feeling, a love of our kinsmen, a love of our people. In our history we have the Kosalas, the Vaidehas and communities of that kind. No one had a country or land or district of his own. He belonged to a certain tribe or community, whose welfare was to him a prime concern. Originally this community migrated in the land. People moved rapidly from one part of the land to another, and gradually this feeling was transferred to the land itself, until now, by long usage, the word 'patriotism' is applied much more commonly to a feeling concerning the country where we were born rather than to a feeling concerning the people to whom we belong. Now, that is the change that has come over the word 'patriotism'. From being communal or tribal, it gradually transferred itself to the country where these communities or divisions settled down permanently. And the feeling now is that the highest patriotism is that which includes all India and all the people living in India. Men who call themselves Bombayites or Bengalis we regard as men not yet fully developed (*apakva*). The unit of patriotism has become the whole country of India. If anybody says he is a Bengali and does not care for anything else, we put him down as one whose ideas are still very crude. If a man calls himself a Muslim entirely, or a Hindu or a Sikh entirely, and says that India comes next in his affection or not at all, we regard him as unpatriotic, or patriotic in a very limited and narrow sense. Formerly, about twenty years ago, everyone in this country was proud of saying "I am an Indian first, and then a Hindu or Muslim or Sikh." I remember, when I was young, that was the hall-mark of a true patriot. Alas, how our politics have become degraded and debased! Today there are Muslims who cry from the hill-tops "I am a Muslim first, second and third, and no Indian." The Hindu is often heard in retaliation to say the same thing. What a change has happened within a few years! Few people think of the whole of the Indian people as one people. That, however, is the creation of the last few generations.

There is more I have got to say. While we in this land have gone back and shrunk to lower and lower ideals, what are the other people in the world doing, the noblest minds and the best trained hearts? They are thinking not only of their national politics as the best in the world, but they are thinking of international politics as the best in the world. They think the whole of the world, the entire earth and the people of the different communities and countries are one, one family, one human family. That we ought to have one patriotism, the highest world patriotism, is the great idea now working itself in the minds and hearts of the wisest men of the day. Fancy what a melancholy idea it is that we should be going back to communal politics while the best men are thinking of this earth itself as entitled to their patriotism. There are people who think that we should bring up the young in our schools and colleges imbued with this patriotism.

If Vibhishana, seeing Rama, knowing his nature, knowing how he was the exemplar of human virtue in the world and how he was there to save humanity, and realising the majesty of such a character, was drawn to the service of that superlative person and took himself away from his narrow and crude and wicked surroundings, is that to be regarded as a sign of human depravity? I really fail to understand. That was what Vibhishana did, no less. That is the point I wish to impress upon you. Unlike other people who thought that Rama was only a good man, Vibhishana thought that he was an ideal man, the best man of his time, the greatest hero from whom he should not only take an example, but whom he should serve and obey. If, listening to that divine voice, you do not feel drawn to it, if, confronting such a great man before you, you do not feel impelled to bow down before him, a man whom you ought to follow to the ends of the earth, for God's sake do not blame the man who does that. Deplore your own weakness, bewail your backwardness, but do not blame the man who rises far above the feeling of his time. I am perhaps stressing this point much too much. You may ask me, "Did Vibhishana really think of this world patriotism, this citizenship of the entire earth you are thinking of?" No, I do not claim that. What I say is that while Vibhishana perhaps did not understand this universal patriotism as we do, did not envisage even Lanka as the very goal of his efforts, he watched Rama and Ravana, found the one to be base metal though a kinsman and a brother, who attracted him with good food and clothing and an honourable place in the royalty of the land. But what was all that beside Rama? Ravana combines all the wickedness of the worst kind with actions that degrade mankind utterly.

There are some who say "If Vibhishana thought that Ravana was not a good man to serve and live with, let him get out of Lanka and live somewhere else in India and be a quiet person. Why should he help Rama?" That is what Indrajit said to his uncle. This question has been answered already. A man must be either good or bad. One has no right to be neutral, unless one thinks that both sides are equally good. But the whole difference is between good and bad, between Dharma and Adharma. A man who hesitates when a supreme crisis is upon him, when the forces of good are contending against the forces of evil, when the world's fate is hanging in the balance, when he can serve the cause of the good, can he instead of choosing the right place and the right sphere of action, simply fold his hands and give up his claim to individual life? I have not known many people act in that way. And that could not have been Vibhishana's attitude as between Rama and Ravana. I think it is not right to suggest that neutrality might have been the best attitude of Vibhishana. As I said, neutrality is understandable if it serves the purpose of the time and the place itself. If the forces of good and evil are about equally balanced and you are unable to decide on which side you should throw your weight in order to make the good prevail against the evil, you must decide. Join the fray you must; keeping out of things is impossible. I have never known, even in fiction, if a great character has been that of a neutral. In one of Lytton's novels, there is in one of the closing chapters, reference to a great figure of the time, a nobleman who might have played an honourable part in the affairs of the day, who, however, not feeling that he was drawn decisively to one side or the other, remained neutral. Perhaps that is the only instance which even the writer of stories has imagined. Those who say therefore that when he decided to abandon Ravana, Vibhishana should at least have tied up his things and remained neutral, do not understand the dignity of human nature, do not understand the purpose for which mankind lives on this planet.

There are those who say, "Let him join Rama, but why did he make himself so active and stand by the side of Rama and point out Kumbhakarna, Indrajit, Prahasta, etc., and expose all the secrets of Lanka and its defences at critical moments of the war, and give his highly valued advice and assistance to Rama? That is only a question which sounds well in the asking. Joining Rama, he was quite right in doing the best on that side. He was there to ensure the victory of Dharma over Adharma, of virtue over wickedness, the triumph to the side into which he threw himself.

Then another question is put. Here too my answer is straight. People say, "Let him have thrown all his energies and abilities to bring about the success of that enemy and the destruction of his own brother. But why should he make himself king? Why not say that he did not want to be king?" Because in the text of the poem there are references to the rajya as having inspired the efforts of Vibhishana, and Vibhishana himself is made to say once or twice that the fortunes of the war were on the side of Ravana, I shall make only one large observation now, in the light of which we may study the text. How could Vibhishana renounce the kingdom? He was the sole man alive. In that island of Lanka besides the young people and the very old people and widows and orphans, all the fighting men had been killed, and there was no member of the royal family except himself, and the four ministers with him. And what was Lanka? Would it have attracted anyone as a kingdom to rule over? After that terrible war in which everything of value would have been destroyed, what was there to make a man desire to be king? When all the monkeys who had been luckily on the side of victory went in the Pushpaka Vimana to see Rama and Sita crowned, from Lanka only Vibhishana went; there was nobody else to go. What can be a more vivid proof of the utter desolation that had come to that land? To say that Vibhishana was a very ambitious, grasping man to take Lanka greedily is wrong. If he took Lanka, it was in the highest sense of duty and service, it was because a stricken land wanted a wise, honest, and straightforward ruler. This is how I prefer to understand it. It may have been a desire to rule over Lanka, but he desired it only because there was no other fortune for that island except to come under the influence of a man who knew how to distinguish between good and evil and desired to further the interests of his people. Even that desire to take the kingdom was a proof of the unselfishness of Vibhishana, not of his selfishness. That is the character to which I shall draw your attention in my next address. I shall read the relevant portions of the text, so that you may see that what I have said here was entirely in illustration of the text. You will probably see that I have not been very wide of the mark, that I have not whitewashed his character more than I should have done or that I have depicted his character as one of transcendental quality. I really believe that I shall invite you to do justice to Vibhishana's character and nothing more. For that great character to be called that of a traitor, a betrayer of his country, an ambitious, greedy man who was prepared to sacrifice his kinsmen and the brother to whom he owed everything is to misunderstand it. He did not betray his kingdom so that it might become the property of the enemy. Rama was going to leave it in the hands of a Lanka man, so that there was not the idea of a betrayal of one's own country in order that it might be the slave of another country, subject to the political ills of foreign domination.

SIXTEENTH LECTURE*

Fellow-students of the Ramayana,—A friend for whom I have the highest respect for his great learning once propounded the problem, why did Rama cause a token *Abhisheka* to be made in the case of Vibhishana before even the war began seriously, while he did nothing of the sort in the case of Sugriva. His own answer was highly learned, but did not convince me. I propose to-day, at the beginning to say a few words to bring before you clearly the contrast between the two characters, and trust that in the end the problem may find an appropriate answer. Let us remember that Vibhishana is accepted as the embodiment of *bhakti* in its pronounced form of *prapatti*, i.e., seeking refuge with Rama. Vibhishana-saranagati is a frequent theme for those that expound the great epic. He sought asylum with Rama, rebelling against the authority and escaping from the threatened punishment of his brother. On the other hand, it is very interesting to see how at the very first talk between Rama and Sugriva, Lakshmana says to Hanuman on behalf of his brother:

अहं चैव हि रामश्च सुग्रीवं शरणं गतौ ॥
एष दत्त्वा च वित्तानि प्राप्य चानुत्तमं यशः ।
लोकनाथः पुरा भूत्वा सुग्रीवं नाथमिच्छति ॥
पिता यस्य पुरा ह्यासीत् शरण्यो धर्मवत्सलः ।
तस्य पुत्रः शरण्यश्च सुग्रीवं शरणं गतः ॥
सर्वलोकस्य धर्मात्मा शरण्यः शरणं पुरा ।
गुरुर्मे राघवः सोऽयं सुग्रीवं शरणं गतः ॥
यस्य प्रसादे सततं प्रसीदेयुरिमाः प्रजाः ।
स रामो वानरेन्द्रस्य प्रसादमभिकाङ्क्षते ॥ IV. 4. 17-21

"My brother and I are seeking asylum at the hands of Sugriva. My brother, having been a very wealthy man, distributed all his wealth before he left Ayodhya, and he attained great fame. Having been himself the protector of the world, he now seeks the protection of Sugriva. Rama, on whose

* 26-7-'44.

favour the world used to wait, has now come to the very door of Sugriva asking for his favour or *prasada*." Many other *slokas* may be quoted. It shows the perfect contrast between the attitude of Sugriva and the attitude of Vibhishana when they approached Rama. Rama sought the protection of Sugriva and Vibhishana sought the protection of Rama. That settles everything. In every respect therefore Sugriva was the equal of Rama, and each needed assistance from the other. They were therefore on a similar or co-ordinate footing. To show how this position remained almost undisturbed till the very end, let us see how when Rama returned home after the exile and just before the *pattabhisheka,* they both met Bharata and how he welcomed them. It is not perhaps to be noticed so very minutely, but the contrast is instructive, and it is my belief that the poet intended it.

अथाब्रवीद्राजपुत्रः सुग्रीवं वानरर्षभम् ॥
परिष्वज्य महातेजा भरतो धर्मिणां वरः ।
त्वमस्माकं चतुर्णां तु भ्राता सुग्रीव पञ्चमः ॥
सौहृदाज्जायते मित्रमपकारोऽरिलक्षणम् । VI. 130. 44-46

"As soon as Bharata met Sugriva, he embraced him and spoke as follows. (The latter half of the second verse seems to be a proverb of the time quoted more than once in that very form.) We are four brothers already. We welcome you into the family as the fifth brother." See how close that affinity is. When Vibhishana approached him, he spoke gently.

विभीषणं च भरतः सान्त्ववाक्यमथाब्रवीत् ॥
दिष्ट्या त्वया सहायेन कृतं कर्म सुदुष्करम् । VI. 130. 46-47

"Being my brother's ally, you seem to have done great and difficult things for him." There ends the greeting for Vibhishana. This is the way in which the two people stand contrasted. Sugriva, to fulfil his part of the contract, brought into the field a mighty army, mighty not only on account of its enormous and unimaginable size, but also because it included such persons as Hanuman, Jambavan, Angada, Nala. Vibhishana when he came, came almost alone. He was attended by four ministers, even whose names the poet forgets to mention.* Vibhishana brought himself; that was a great thing to bring.

Then, those that read the Ramayana and know the story will see at once that Sugriva was indispensable to the conquest of Lanka, whereas Vibhishana was not expected at all. He comes there just before the bridge is constructed, and we almost think that while he came there on his own account and was highly useful, it could not be said that Rama found him absolutely essential for the campaign. He gave great assistance. In fact his assistance was of the highest importance in particular difficulties but it could not be said that it was indispensable and was as great as in the case of Sugriva.

Then, Sugriva was unaware of Rama's greatness. He did not know who he was at first. When Rama said, "I shall assist you," Sugriva seemed sceptical of Rama's ability to assist him. He was not sure that Rama could stand before his brother Vali. Therefore he asked him to prove his strength and his skill in war. He was not satisfied until the first and second proof were given. In the case of Vibhishana, he had full knowledge of Rama's greatness, his prowess and his moral worth.

Then in the case of Sugriva, there was not much to do before the coronation. Vali was killed on the very day the test was completed,'अद्यैव'. The whole thing was so swift and sudden, they became friends, Rama proved his skill in war, Sugriva challenged his brother, Rama killed him and the coronation took place as a matter of course. There was no great war as in the case of Ravana. The bridge had to be constructed and several days were spent before Ravana's army was dispersed and destroyed, and his brothers and his sons and great generals were disposed of, and he himself was the last man to disappear from the scene. In the case of Vibhishana therefore there was a considerable interval and a good deal of time for doubt and misgiving, and Vibhishana would have to live on promises. That is why Rama said, "I make you this promise. Do not think that because there are difficulties, I may not carry out my promise. It may take time.

* They are named in VI. 37. 7:

अनलः शरभश्चैव संपातिः प्रघसस्तथा ।
गत्वा लङ्कां ममामात्याः पुरीं पुनरिहागताः ॥ Ed.

Great trouble has to be undergone before you will become king. Still, in order to show that I am in earnest, I will make this token *abhisheka* and convert it into a real one as soon as your brother is destroyed." In the case of Sugriva there was no need at all to live on promises. The promise was made and at once fulfilled. That, I think, is sufficient to explain why in one case there was a token coronation and in the other there was not.

Also look at the part played by the coronation itself. In the case of Sugriva, all his services to Rama, that is, all his duties by the pact between him and Rama, came to be fulfilled after the coronation. The search for Janaki takes place after it. But in the case of Vibhishana there was nothing to be done after the coronation.

Only one word more about this contrast which is instructive. While I have said so much which might seem to imply that Sugriva stood higher than Vibhishana, I will conclude with this observation which, I think, is abundantly justified. Maybe, Sugriva had a higher status, and he was considered to be of the same rank as Rama, though he himself, you may remember, calls himself a *dasa* of Rama. He says, "Rama treats me as if I were his ally, but I am only his *dasa*." * That only shows that Sugriva had a proper sense of modesty about him. In the case of Vibhishana, perhaps the status might have been not so much on the same footing, but I am fully persuaded by the language used and by their relationship, that he enjoyed the greater love, the greater confidence at the hands of the Ayodhya brothers. It is only in the Uttarakanda that mention is made of the award that Vibhishana had, of an unusual character, by his association with Rama, that he became a *chiranjivi*. That is one of our universal beliefs among Hindus, that he is one of the great *chiranjivis*.

Another point about Vibhishana which I should like to make is that Rama, when he received Vibhishana's request to be taken, seemed to be unaware of the identity of Vibhishana. But there are here and there passages which indicate that he could not have been unaware, although at the moment itself, in the very context, mention is not made of it. For instance, in the Aranyakanda, Surpanakha is asked about her family. She says to Rama, "I am sister to three brothers.

* VI. 40. 10. See Lect. XIV at p. 216 above.

One is Ravana, the great king of Lanka, conqueror of the world. Then there is Kumbhakarna, the strong, mighty warrior." And then she mentions Vibhishana, but mentions him as a *dharmatma,* one who belongs to the order that obeys the *dharma* of the world. Surpanakha herself testifies to the goodness of Vibhishana. So Rama could not have been unaware of him. Secondly, in the Sundarakanda, when Sita talks to Hanuman about Ravana and his obstinacy, she says, 'I have heard from Vibhishana's daughter, whom the mother had sent to me for confidential talk, that Ravana once consulted a great astrologer, an old man who knew the three *kalas* and whose prognostications generally came true. He said, "This Sita is going to be a terrible burden. Give her back and make peace with Rama. That advice was given to Ravana, but Ravana did not heed it. His heart is still wickedly bent upon me." We fancy that Hanuman must have communicated it to Rama. Then you remember in the Sundarakanda itself the scene where Hanuman appears before Ravana, and, angered by Hanuman's misdeeds, as he understands them, to the city of Lanka, Ravana orders his men to kill the monkey. Of course it was impossible for anybody to kill Hanuman. Nevertheless, that was the order that Ravana passed. At that time Vibhishana protested and said it was not right. "Nobody kills a messenger that comes from a brother king. If you are displeased with him, there are ways of punishing him, but death is not the penalty prescribed. You will be discredited in the high circles where you have now a great name." Ravana accepts this advice for once. So he says, "Very well, as you say there are alternative punishments open to me, I will think of a punishment appropriate in this case. I will set fire to the monkey's tail, so that among his own kinsmen he will have to appear without that appendage which they all value highly." What happens you know. This is another thing which Hanuman could not have forgotten. Only the astonishing thing is that when Vibhishana appears high up with his four ministers asking that he should be introduced to Rama and Rama consults the important people, Lakshmana, Jambavan, Hanuman and Sugriva, Sugriva, along with Lakshmana, dissuades him. Hanuman is the one person to recognise the acceptance of Vibhishana but even he omits to mention how Vibhishana had assisted him actually in Lanka when he was there and how he was the means of saving his life and giving him the occasion to set fire to the greater part of Lanka. He might have mentioned it; perhaps he had already mentioned it.* But that was the time, when the pros and cons of Vibhishana's acceptance were considered, to mention this. It does not appear that Hanuman brought it to the notice of Rama, or that Rama remembered it as one of the considerations in favour of acceptance. When I come to Hanuman, I shall have to mention this as one of the three or four occasions upon which Hanuman's memory seems to have failed. I am going to advance this proposition that when Hanuman, on account of his boyish pranks amongst the Rishis, drew on himself their curse that he would not remember his prowess or his greatness unless continually reminded of it, it seems to have been a little more comprehensive than the word implied. The curse was that he would not only not remember his strength, but that he would not remember vital points when they were necessary. That seems to have been the meaning, as I shall show when we come to discuss Hanuman.

About Vibhishana, it seems necessary to mention that while he was praised in Rama's camp for his being a *dharmatma* and not a Rakshasa in spirit, the greatest antipathy seems to have existed between him and Indrajit. Two passages occur in the Ramayana where they swore at each other in the bitterest possible language. To read Indrajit's language, you might be listening to one of those people amongst modern politicians whom I described the other day, full of the feeling that patriotism was the highest virtue, that fidelity to your kinsmen is the highest virtue, and that even where the sovereign needs of *dharma* were in jeopardy, you are required to choose your patriotism in preference to *dharma*. That theory Indrajit enunciates in very proper language, which you would all greatly appreciate. Indrajit says—he especially hates Vibhishana because he is a *dharmatma*—

सत्त्वेन वीर्येण पराक्रमेण शौर्येण धैर्येण च तेजसा च।
एकः कुलेऽस्मिन् पुरुषो विमुक्तो विभीषणस्तात कनिष्ठ एषः॥
ऐरावतो विस्वरमुन्नदन् स निपातितो भूमितले मया तु।
विकृष्य दन्तौ तु मया प्रसह्य वित्रासिता देवगणाः समग्राः॥
सोऽहं सुराणामपि दर्पहन्ता दैत्योत्तमानामपि शोकदाता।
कथं नरेन्द्रात्मजयोर्न शक्तो मनुष्ययोः प्राकृतयोः सुवीर्यः॥ VI. 15. 3, 6, 7

* See V. 58. 145-9.

"What a younger brother you have", says he to his father. "This man has not got any of the great qualities of the family. As for me, in my fight with Indra, I once felled the great elephant Airavata and he rolled on the ground. I pulled out his tusks at that time. Having done this, I used them on the Devas who ran away. That was me. And look at this uncle of mine. Am I going to draw back in battle when these people come to fight? They are only two men." Then says Vibhishana in reply—he is somewhat annoyed with the young man's speech to him, a senior and uncle.

न तात मन्त्रे तव निश्चयोऽस्ति बालस्त्वमद्याप्यविपक्वबुद्धिः ।
तस्मात्त्वया ह्यात्मविनाशनाय वचोऽर्थहीनं बहु विप्रलप्तम् ॥
त्वमेव वध्यश्च सुदुर्मतिश्च स चापि वध्यो य इहानयत्त्वाम् ।
बालं दृढं साहसिकं च योऽद्य प्रावेशयन्मन्त्रकृतां समीपम् ॥
धनानि रत्नानि विभूषणाणि वासांसि दिव्यानि मणींश्च चित्रान् ।
सीतां च रामाय निवेद्य देवीं वसेम राजन्निह वीतशोकाः ॥

VI. 15. 9, 11, 14

"You are young and unripe. Why are you brought into this great council where the elders meet and exchange high thoughts? It is a mistake. You say many unmeaning and foolish things without knowing the consequences. Pray have a thought." And then turning to Ravana, he says, "If you want to remain in Lanka free from care and trouble and with honour and safety, go and fall at Rama's feet, restore Sita to him and take also costly presents as tribute. Otherwise there will be great danger for us." Then says Ravana in reply—words which have become famous in literature—

वसेत्सह सपत्नेन क्रुद्धेनाशीविषेण वा ।
न तु मित्रप्रवादेन संवसेच्छत्रुसेविना ॥
जानामि शीलं ज्ञातीनां सर्वलोकेषु राक्षस ।
हृष्यन्ति व्यसनेष्वेते ज्ञातीनां ज्ञातयः सदा ॥
नित्यमन्योन्यसंहृष्टा व्यसनेष्वाततायिनः ।
प्रच्छन्नहृदया घोरा ज्ञातयस्तु भयावहाः ॥ VI. 16. 2, 3, 5

"Vibhishana, you are my *jnati*, a *dayada*. A *dayada* is always to be mistrusted. A *dayada* is the very soul of envy, jealousy, hostility in heart. You may go and dwell by the side of your neighbour who is inimical; you may even play with a serpent having made him excited; but you cannot dwell, if you are wise, with a *jnati*, for a *jnati* talks sweetly, but his heart is with the enemy. He is a real ally of the enemy. When a man is in trouble, his *jnatis* rejoice. Never trust a *jnati*. He will always bring you some danger. He will smile with hatred in his heart." Then after several *slokas* ending with तथानार्येषु सौहृदम् (16. 11-14), Ravana renounces him in these words:—"If any other person not being you, my younger brother, had spoken so to me, I would liquidate him this instant. But as you are my brother, but the enemy of the family, I abandon you. Run away from this place." Vibhishna bids him farewell. He says, "You are a victim of death, and you cannot escape it. That is why you do not heed the words of caution and safety which I say. Be happy, if you can, without me. These words of mine which would warn you against evil courses do not reach your heart. That is the world's way. When a man is destined to perish friends' admonitions are thrown away upon him." Then he comes away and says to the monkeys who are round Rama from on high, "I have come to seek Rama's asylum, I have left my wife and my children behind. I come here because my brother has spoken ungently to me and he has despised me and put scorn and contumely upon me as if I were his man-servant." Then you know the consultation that takes place. Rama in the end says, "Even if it be Ravana's own self, I will not abandon him." Vibhishana says, "I have abandoned all my previous glories, given up Lanka, my wealth and my relations. I am your man entirely and wholly, every inch of me." Then says Rama on oath

> अहं हत्वा दशग्रीवं सप्रहस्तं सहानुजम् ।
> राजानं त्वां करिष्यामि सत्यमेतद् ब्रवीमि ते ॥
> अहत्वा रावणं संख्ये सपुत्रबलबान्धवम् ।
> अयोध्यां न प्रवेक्ष्यामि त्रिभिस्तैर्भ्रातृभिः शपे ॥ VI. 19. 19, 21

"In the hearing of all I make this pledge, that after killing Ravana with his mantris Prahasta and others, I will make you king. I swear (in those days this seems to be very common, almost the marks of high being) by my three brothers that I will not return to Ayodhya until I have destroyed your brother and made you king."

Then, later on, we come to a remarkable passage in which Indrajit and Vibhishana play a great part. I am going to dwell somewhat on this because it is one of the most interesting parts of the poem which is full of the most exciting, the most brilliant passages of description and of a high order of poetic fancy. When Indrajit first enters the field against the brothers and the monkey army, he employs his usual sorcery. He hit upon the expedient of sending the serpent arrows. These arrows, burning and fuming, struck all over the bodies of the brothers, and there was not one inch of space in their bodies which was not pierced by one of these consuming arrows of serpents. So bad was the effect that everybody thought that they were dead and there was consternation in the camp. The great ones, mighty monkeys too, could do nothing and think of nothing. But Vibhishana had a gift of seeing Indrajit while nobody else could see him. Sugriva was disconsolate as all the other monkeys were. Vibhishana, however, knew that these arrows were not fatal. While they caused a kind of giddiness in the head, they could not take away the lives of the brothers. He conciliates especially Sugriva who was most in grief. "Do not cry. This is the very nature of war. Once you win, once the other man wins. At the moment Indrajit has got the upper hand. These, who are our dear ones, are going to be free from this *moha*. Do not discredit yourself and me." Vibhishana brings consolation to his friends. "You and I have chosen the right side in this war, the side on which *dharma* dwells. How can we suffer? What troubles you is the excess of fear for these brothers. There is such a thing as too much affection, too much fondness. Instead of doing what is right, you droop, you hang down your head, you cry, and you do nothing. That is why even an excess of affection may bring about death." This idea of *ati* being fatal is very common in Sanskrit poetry. अतिस्नेहः पापशङ्की (Sakuntala, IV. 19-20). Now when Lakshmana had to comfort Rama in the Aranyakanda, he says, "Do not give way to this absorbing love. Where you have a wick which has been wet in water, even such a wick, if placed where there is plenty of oil, will absorb the oil and burn itself out. Even if your heart is *prasanta*, if only you take in too much of this *sneha*, then a great deal of harm would be done." That was the comfort that Vibhishana gave to Sugriva when the great arrows of Indrajit had only thrown the brothers into a swoon and had not deprived them of life.

Then took place a most remarkable scene. When Indrajit went back to his father, he reported how he had thrown the two brothers to the ground, so that the whole army had been paralysed and the two brothers had been killed. Ravana was in great exultation and high spirits, and there was on this side a corresponding depression. Desperate counsels began to be heard. Then it occurred to Ravana that he ought to choose that moment for causing the greatest possible misery to Sita, so that she may abandon all hope of rescue by her husband and then fall an easy prey to his own scheming designs. So he tells the Rakshasis around Sita to put her into the Pushpaka-vimana, take her to the battlefield and let her see the two brothers from whom she expected rescue. Then, having lost all hope, she would come to him. Sita is brought to the battlefield, where she breaks out into a loud wail. But she is consoled by Trijata, who says, "Do not give way to despair. Look at their faces. They do not look like corpses. They are not going to die." But the monkeys themselves are not satisfied, and they cry. At that time Rama comes to consciousness, being the stronger of the two brothers, more quickly, and seeing how Lakshmana lies prostrate before him, he sets up a loud wail. I have mentioned this before while speaking of Rama.* Then he says, full of despair, to the allies Sugriva and others, "Sugriva, you have done your duty by me. You are a prince of allies. From you and each one of these monkeys I have received every assistance that you could give me. You have discharged your duty and you may all go back. I am going to die here." See to what state Rama has reduced himself. And then, as the whole scene is in great misery, nobody being able to lift up his head, the poet himself is oppressed with the tremendous desolation that he has caused, and so he relieves the tension of feeling by a little episode. You all know how often in the tragic poems this kind of thing occurs. At that moment there entered, as if on important business, a strange, black, shrouded figure, and the figure struck, without turning this side or that towards where the brothers were. All people thought that it was Indrajit himself who had caused this desolation, come back to finish the brothers. The whole lot

* Lect. III at p. 29, above.

of the monkeys, instead of falling upon this Indrajit, as if in one mind, ran away and fled from the scene. Then Sugriva saw that dark, shrouded figure greet him. It was Vibhishana himself. Then the monkeys rallied, and then Vibhishana in his turn sets up a wail, "This nephew of mine has caused this distress. All my hopes are frustrated, and, what is worst of all, Ravana will win. His words will come true when he struck his breast and said to me, 'I am going to kill Rama and Lakshmana.'" Then, as he gave way to despair, it was Sugriva's turn now. He comforts Vibhishana: "These two people are not dead. They are going to kill Ravana." But then his heart is not satisfied with the comfort that he utters. He says to Sushena, "You had better take these two people away to Kishkindha. I will finish this Ravana and rescue Sita and bring her there." All this is, on the part of the poet, a skilful contrivance to show how these people were not clear in their minds.

Then occurs a famous scene a few *sargas* later on, when I shall bring before you the important passages in which Vibhishana plays a creditable part. Both Kumbhakarna and Prahasta were against Ravana's designs and did not approve of the capture of Sita. Their advice was submission to Rama and the return of Sita. But Prahasta says, "When you called us in council, we came to this conclusion. I advise you, as the most honourable course, the return of Sita. As you are determined not to give her up, there is no doubt we must fight now. You are bent upon this obstinate course. You have honoured me time and again by presents and by various titles. Why will I not do you good? You are my benefactor. You are pursuing a wrong course. Nevertheless, I am prepared to go into the fight. I shall give up everything. I will make a *homa* of my life." Kumbhakarna says a similar thing. "A person who, not knowing his own strength and the enemy's strength, adopts a wrong course, is going to face difficulties of various kinds and be pulled down from his high position. We gave you this advice long before but you did not listen to us. That is the proper course, but you are impossible, you do what you like." Ravana made an appeal. "Yes, you gave me that advice and, perhaps, owing to my folly, perhaps owing to my pride of valour, I did not care to listen to you. All that advice is now lost. Why repeat it now? Think what is proper to do now. What is past, nobody is going to bewail. What is gone, is gone. If you are Kumbhakarna the great, the powerful, the strong, then put right what I have done wrong. He is a brother who comes to the rescue of the distressed." Then says Kumbhakarna, "Being a close relation of yours, also your brother, I gave you advice which I thought proper. Now you will see my prowess. I will kill Rama and his brother and make the monkeys run," and so on—Kumbhakarna repeats four slokas. See how even in those days, being faced with the same conflict of duties, the dilemma as to the existence of all duties which appeal to us, the choice is made differently by different people. I do not blame Kumbhakarna or Prahasta; nor can we blame Bhishma in the Mahabharata. Two mighty duties make an appeal to your heart. Then you decide in favour of one after due deliberation, not recklessly nor momentarily. But as we are all of different minds and of different training, let not the one side abuse the other side as traitors or cowards. Our great men have chosen this course. Both apparently are honourable. Let us see for a moment, how, after this great Kumbhakarna, performing exploits of an unparalleled kind on the field of battle, had been killed by Rama, Ravana hears the fatal news. He says, "My right arm is gone." Then follows an exclamation of repentance on his part. "What troubles me now is that that good man (Vibhishana), having given me proper, wise, brotherly advice, was thrown out. It recoils on me. Not knowing the real merit of Rama, who he is and what he is come here for, not knowing his strength and my strength, here I am. I am ashamed of myself. I flung him away." Ravana was thinking like this only for a moment.

Then follows a remarkable passage where Vibhishana renders great assistance. Indrajit was about to perform a great witchery. If he had done that properly, all would have been lost. He would not only have been invisible, but invincible. But at the proper time, when the crisis came, Vibhishana pointed out all this danger to the brothers and asked Lakshmana to kill Indrajit before he gets under the *nyagrodha* tree. Lakshmana challenges Indrajit before he gets under the tree. Indrajit turns out in despair, and sees his uncle Vibhishana. Says Indrajit, "You were born and brought up here under the care of my father. How could you do me harm? You are a *dharma dushana*. You are a disgrace, we are all ashamed of you. You have become the servant of the other side. You do not perceive the immense difference between the one duty and the other. Where is this and where is that?" You could not wish for a better statement of the patriotic point of view.

इह त्वं जातसंवृद्धः साक्षाद्भ्राता पितुर्मम ।
कथं द्रुह्यसि पुत्रस्य पितृव्यो मम राक्षस ॥
न ज्ञातित्वं न सौहार्दं न जातिस्तव दुर्मते ।
प्रमाणं न च सोदर्यं न धर्मो धर्मदूषण ॥
शोच्यस्त्वमसि दुर्बुद्धे निन्दनीयश्च साधुभिः ।
यस्त्वं स्वजनमुत्सृज्य परभृत्यत्वमागतः ॥
नैतच्छिथिलया बुद्धया त्वं वेत्सि महदन्तरम् ।
क्व च स्वजनसंवासः क्व च नीचपराश्रयः ॥
गुणवान् वा परजनः स्वजनो निर्गुणोऽपि वा ।
निर्गुणः स्वजनः श्रेयान् यः परः पर एव सः ॥
यः स्वपक्षं परित्यज्य परपक्षं निषेवते ।
स स्वपक्षे क्षयं प्राप्ते पश्चात्तैरेव हन्यते ॥ VI. 87. 11-16

"Your brother may be all that you say and more. Preferable is your own man, however wicked. He who is an alien is an alien. You may now prove treacherous to us and join the other side. The other side, having made full use of you, will finish you also along with us." Vibhishana puts forward a defence for himself. As in all cases, the abuse and the denouncement are stronger than the defence, just as in the case of Vali, where his accusations against Rama seem stronger than the defence, Vibhishana says, "You abuse me now, but you must have known that I was not a Rakshasa at all in spirit. I was born in your family. I am among you, but not of you. Why should not a brother be abandoned, if he is wicked? If a man takes away the property of another or abducts another man's wife, one may give him up, as one would give up a burning house. On account of these doshas, I have abandoned your father. You are in the hands of Yama. You may prate and say what you like."

अयुक्तं निधनं कर्तुं पुत्रस्य जनितुर्मम।
घृणामपास्य रामार्थे निहन्यां भ्रातुरात्मजम्॥
हन्तुकामस्य मे बाष्पं चक्षुश्चैव निरुध्यति।
तमेवैष महाबाहुः लक्ष्मणः शमयिष्यति॥ VI. 90. 17-18

"Here is my brother's son in battle. I ought to kill him. It is not right to kill one's own brother's son. But I must give up this feeling of tenderness for relationship, and on account of Rama, I shall kill this Indrajit. But as I take my bow and arrow and aim at him, tears fall from my eyes and I cannot take proper aim. Let Lakshmana do it." See how *dharmasankata* preys on the heart of the man.

SEVENTEENTH LECTURE *

Vibhishana was specially skilled in seeing through the wiles of his kinsmen. The *maya* that Indrajit and others practised he pierced. Also when spirits on Rama's side drooped and fears threatened to prevail, Vibhishana brought them up with encouragement and helpful suggestions. Time and again during the war that was the service he rendered, timely warnings, timely suggestions, regardless of the harm that might be done to those whom he had denounced as the enemies of righteousness. At the point that we have now reached in the story I have to refer to an incident already mentioned in these lectures † when Indrajit brought a counterfeit Sita into the field and there killed her. This was done while he was engaged in a fight with Hanuman and a large number of his followers. Hanuman tried to prevent the killing, but just as he jumped to the rescue, the Rakshasas crowded round him; and seeing them do so, the Vanaras crowded also and there was a melee and poor Hanuman was unable to penetrate to the very centre of the catastrophe. He loudly exclaimed against Indrajit, and Indragit in turn said, "In war there is nothing like a scruple. Whatever injures the enemy must be done." It sounds Hitlerian, but Meghanada anticipated him many centuries ago. After this encounter and when Indrajit had run his sword through Maya Sita (yajnopavita-margena), Hanuman continued to fight for a while before he could come out. But he was not successful. This was one of the occasions when a failure against the enemy has to be recorded. Not only was Hanuman unable to rescue Sita who, he thought, was the victim, but he was unable even to fight the forces against him successfully. Then, the poet says, he drew the forces back in regular order. That was the utmost he could do. Then, when a little later he reported the fact to Rama, Rama fell down in a swoon and he had to be taken care of by Lakshmana and others. You may remember how Lakshmana took the occasion, most unnecessarily as we thought, at any rate as I tried to make you think, to rail against *dharma* and Rama's devotion to it.

* 2-8-'44.

† Lect. IV at p. 45 above.

"This is the effect," he said, "of your devotion to *dharma*. *Artha* is the thing." After a while, Vibhishana comes to the scene, and learning how things stood, he bade Rama take heart. "This is absurd. Sita has not been killed. Hanuman had been deceived. The Sita was killed was a counterfeit Sita." And Vibhishana gives his reasons in a few slokas.*

मनुजेन्द्रार्तरूपेण यदुक्तं च हनूमता ।
तदयुक्तमहं मन्ये सागरस्येव शोषणम् ॥
अभिप्रायं तु जानामि रावणस्य दुरात्मनः ।
सीतां प्रति महाबाहो न च घातं करिष्यति ॥
याच्यमानस्तु बहुशो मया हितचिकीर्षुणा ।
वैदेहीमुत्सृजस्वेति न च तत् कृतवान् वचः ॥
नैव साम्ना न दानेन न भेदेन कुतो युधा ।
सा द्रष्टुमपि शक्येत नैव चान्येन केनचित् ॥
वानरान् मोहयित्वा तु प्रतियातः स राक्षसः । VI. 84. 9-13

"Hanuman who is distressed beyond measure has come and told you something which cannot have happened. It is as impossible as the drying up of the ocean. I know the ways of my brother, and I know his heart. Whatever he may do to Sita, he never will kill her. He is so devoted to her that he cannot bear the thought of an injury to her. I have often requested him in his own interest to surrender her back to you, but he would not listen. Do not be frightened. My nephew is a crafty person. He has deceived all your followers." Then Rama was consoled and he resumed the battle. So mighty was his strength and the prowess that he displayed on that occasion that the poet says that Ravana in sore distress was obliged to flee from the field.

I am only concerned with Vibhishana's devotion, and so I pass on to the next point. This is when Rama and Ravana were locked in their last encounter. Vibhishana was not only great in counsel, he not only exposed the defects of his kinsmen and offered advice and consolation, but he did mighty deeds of prowess in battle. In this last encounter Ravana was sorely pressed by the brothers Rama and Lakshmana and also his own brother Vibhishana who usually wielded the *gada*. On this occasion it is said that he brought it heavily

* Cf. Lect. XXV below.

down on the horses of Ravana's chariot and killed them so that Ravana was unchariοted and got very angry with his brother who had done this great harm to him. In his anger Ravana took his *sakti*, which is a kind of spear, I suppose, and hurled it straight at his brother, saying that it would finish him. Lakshmana watched this fatal stroke and sent his arrows in good time for them to destroy this *sakti*. Ravana got wild, took another *sakti* and hurled it once more at his brother, when Lakshmana came and stood between the two and said, "I shall take it, it shall not touch Vibhishana." Mighty kind of thing to do in battle! The result was that the spear did really strike Lakshmana who fell down in a swoon which appeared to be fatal. This was what Ravana said:

मोक्षितस्ते बलश्लाघिन् यस्मादेवं विभीषणः ।
विमुच्य राक्षसं शक्तिस्त्वयीयं विनिपात्यते ॥ VI. 101. 28

"This shall strike at you straight. *Sakti* is accustomed to draw blood from the enemies, and it will not go without your life." As a matter of fact, I have already told you, when dealing with Lakshmana, the sequel to this incident.* Being concerned solely with Vibhishana for the moment, let us pass on. Thus saved by Lakshmana, Vibhishana lived to do greater services to his great ally.

Finally we come to the last scene of the war when Ravana has been laid low and the gods and men and all other creatures rejoiced. All nature rejoiced that a great enemy of human kind was dead. This is one of Valmiki's practices, *viz.*, that he makes kinsmen, however great they may be as enemies, straightway be stricken with grief when they see that the very things that they have always expected and helped had been brought about. The moment Ravana is slain, Vibhishana is seized with remorse. He comes straight to the corpse and gives vent to his lamentation:

तदिदं वीर संप्राप्तं मया पूर्वं समीरितम् ।
काममोहपरीतस्य यत्ते न रुचितं वचः ॥
यन्न दर्पात्प्रहस्तो वा नेन्द्रजिन्नापरे जनाः ।
न कुम्भकर्णोऽतिरथो नातिकायो नरान्तकः ॥
न स्वयं त्वममन्येथास्तस्योदर्कोऽयमागतः । VI. 112. 4-6

---

* Lect. III at p. 29 above.

words which would be highly inappropriate and undignified if the victim were alive. But when a man is down and you are face to face with his armies, it is only a melancholy reminder of a warning that had been neglected, of wise counsels that had been set aside in contempt. "What has happened is the very thing that I predicted. You were then infatuated, were proud and would not listen to me. Great people would have kept you back from this fatal course if only you had listened. You have now reaped the bitter fruit of it all."

At first Vibhishana thought that it was his duty as the only surviving kinsman of the deceased to perform the obsequies himself. So he requests Rama to allow him to set fire to the remains of his brother. "Here is my brother who was in life a mighty person characterised by great qualities of bounty, valour and strength. To beggars he gave freely. What luxuries has he not enjoyed? Servants and attendants he had to look after him. To his friends and associates he gave in abundance of his wealth. To those who were his enemies he has been a terror and a scourge. Besides all this he was a man who performed great austerities, and knew how to perform all the rites prescribed. Pray let me do what to his corpse has now to be done." Rama thus being requested by Vibhishana, says, "Death pays all debts. All enmities cease at death. Nobody should carry hatred beyond the grave. Why should we hate Ravana any more? Our object has been attained. You and I have become one by a sacred alliance, and therefore what he is to you, he is to me, an elder brother. I am also both entitled and under an obligation to perform the obsequies. If you do not do them, I shall do them."

I come to another thing which seems to be much more tender and is somewhat out of the way. I bring this to your notice as it is somewhat characteristic of the style of our great commentators.*

मरणान्तानि वैराणि निर्वृत्तं नः प्रयोजनम् ।
क्रियतामस्य संस्कारो ममाप्येष यथा तव ॥ VI. 112. 26

The commentator says, "Ravana cannot do me any harm now. He carried away my wife and he killed my dear friend

* Lect. VIII at p. 108 above.

Jatayu, but now he can do me no harm. Now it seems as if Rama reminds himself that once before when Vibhishana had not yet been accepted, he had said,

विभीषणो वा सुग्रीव यदि वा रावणः स्वयम्। VI. 18. 35

"Supposing it were Ravana himself come to me, I would take him all right. Do you think I used those words lightly? I really wished in my heart of hearts that Ravana should come to me and I should accept him and forgive him. I intended to do him some good but he was obstinate. The perversity of his nature triumphed. So he cried out

द्विधा भज्येयमप्येवं न नमेयं तु कस्यचित्।

एष मे सहजो दोषः स्वभावो दुरतिक्रमः॥ VI. 36. 11

'I may break in two, but I won't bend to anybody. It may be that it is a vice in me, but it is inborn. Who can change his own nature?'" It struck me that I should mention this to you, as it is in accordance with the great attitude which Rama's nature had reached. If he had used these words in the sense that I have now described. there would have been nothing unusual about it. It would be Sri Rama all over. Unfortunately, a little later Vibhishana is visited by a compunction. You have heard me refer to a belief, amongst people,* a belief which is now prevalent as strongly as before, contrary, however, to our usual practice and the Sastras, that however dear a man may be to you by ties of blood, you need not do him any *samskara*, you need not observe pollution. We say to our people when we are angry, 'You need not even bathe if I die.' And a man. who is angry, says, 'I am going to drink milk when I hear you are dead.' We have also seen Bharata say to Rama, "No doubt I performed the obsequies to our father, being on the spot. But father's soul would not have been so pleased, and all those rites would not have been so effective as if you had been there. They say that obsequies are most efficacious only when performed by the dear ones. Father died thinking of you, unable to bear the grief of your separation. Your performance of the last rites would really help the departed

*Lect. XIII at p. 193 above.

one." That sort of grief oppresses Vibhishana at the moment. He now remembers how they hated each other and asks himself whether it would be right for him to do the last rites to his brother. Would it be any good? He says, "He was a very bad man and there was no end to his wickedness. How many good women has he ruined in his life! The man delighted in doing wicked things to people. He had the shape of my brother, but was my enemy. If I do not do these rites, people may now say I am a wicked, heartless man. But when they have first passed judgment against me as a miscreant, as one who failed his brother even after death, when they themselves remember how many wickednesses my brother has been responsible for, how many women he has outraged, they will say Vibhishana was right. But you may remember how Rama counsels against it.* He reminds him of the greatness of his brother, of his austerities, of how by the might of his sword he warred against the very gods and overcame them all. He did it all by virtue of his great austerities, by means of which he obtained tremendous boons from the gods. Great things stood to his credit.

I have tried to review Vibhishana's deeds in order to show that there is nothing in them which may appear to be selfish or low, nothing mean or poor about him. The charge was brought against him that he betrayed his kinsmen, proved false to those who had brought him up and allowed him to grow in strength. That charge is brought, I think, through a failure to distinguish between great things and greater things. There are things in the world much greater than fidelity to your kinsmen. We do not, we cannot, praise a judge who gives judgment from a court of law in favour of his kinsmen, simply because he is a kinsman. On the other hand, we praise kings who have punished their sons because they were guilty. And yet, when we judge Vibhishana, why should we say he ought to have stood by his brother, however inimical he was to humanity? The sooner we dismiss it and restore Vibhishana to his place among the *chiranjivis*,† the better for us all.

---

* Lect. V at pp. 63-4 above.

† This is in keeping with Kalidasa, according to whom Vibhishana has a secure place as one of the two monumental columns of the Ramayana, the other being Hanuman, 'कीर्तिस्तम्भद्वयमिव,' Raghuvamsa, XV. 103.

HANUMAN

Many things in his character attract one. I do not wonder that people yield their hearts so thoroughly to him. He was great nearly in every sense of the word. And if we take the deeds performed by him and put them in a heap, I doubt whether the heap that stands to the credit of any other character would come up to it in mere bulk. He performed great deeds of valour, of physical strength which no other living creature of the time could have performed. Deeds which required the greatest strength, the greatest will power, fell to his lot and he performed them with admirable thoroughness and execution. Yes, nobody was as great as Hanuman through the whole pages of the poem if we except Rama and, in a contrary sense, Ravana himself. As in the case of Rama, I propose to deal with some points in Hanuman's story which may seem to take away from his greatness, and having dealt with them at what I consider to be adequate length, I shall then proceed to the deeds that stand to his credit and try to show that they were done on the highest level of devotion, rectitude and sense of duty. Superlatives crowd round Hanuman, as you contemplate him. He is the strongest person in the poem, not even inferior to Vali or Kumbhakarna, the character who was most devoted to Rama and allowed no man to come near him in his love for Rama and his desire to perform all the things, whether he ordered them or not, which would have brought him good. Wise, moderate in counsel, always ready to see things while yet they are only coming, few can approach Hanuman in sheer greatness, in weight of achievement. Nevertheless, mistake me not, and mistake not Valmiki for whom I wish to say a word. Fancy my impudence! Excuse me, because there is no use being indiscriminate. We must take account of the good and things that are not really so good. When I described Rama to you, I ventured to say in how many ways he was like any other human being, in how many ways he showed his own nature as being on a level with ours and yet how he triumphed over it all and mounted up to the highest peaks of virtue and righteousness. We seem near to Rama when we contemplate his weakness, and we look up to him as an example, as an inspiration, as an uplifting force, when we see how, putting this weakness down, he lifted up his own nature until it came to divinity, so much so that we now do not distinguish him from the celestials. That is the virtue of character. Valmiki, in my opinion, has realised this point. So indeed in the case of Hanuman. Hanuman belonged to the Vanara race, somewhat inferior to the Naras. It is therefore from the nature of a monkey that Hanuman has risen. Your appreciation of his greatness will be enhanced when you remember the fact that by nature, by constitution, he was a monkey. We associate certain qualities with that race. Well, Hanuman had them, and more than once in the pages of Valmiki he shows how even when he became a great person, a great ally and a great friend of Rama, an unrivalled performer of glorious deeds, there were traces, now and then to be seen of his humble origin. There is nothing wrong about them. We stand as God made us and allowed us to grow.

It would appear that when he was still young, Hanuman tried his strength against the sun himself. The sun-god struck him and he fell down on a hill and his left cheek was run in, so that he was called Hanuman. Then having been blessed with different boons by the gods on account of his father's advocacy, amongst them immunity from death by reason of *astra* or *sastra,* he was, even while a child, gifted with strength to such an extent that he would go to the hermitages of Rishis and there mar the performance of their *yagas.* He would throw the *havis* about, and although his father and mother came and begged him, he continued to perform these boyish tricks. The Rishis, knowing how greatly favoured he was in the celestial world, bore it all for a long time. But Hanuman took advantage of their goodness. When he became intolerable, they threw on him a disability, *viz.,* that he would not remember his strength until somebody reminded him. At the right moment when his strength should be brought into play, he would forget it, and if the thing was of supreme importance and must be done, somebody should come and goad him.

The question is asked by Rama himself when Agastya was conversing with him. Rama asked him, "I have heard it said that Hanuman was greater than Vali and Sugriva. Why, then, when he was on the side of Sugriva, did he not use his superior strength and finish Vali? This might have been done long ago." Then Agastya tells the story of how Hanuman did not know his strength. But it is not a perfectly satisfactory answer. Did not Sugriva know it? Why did he not praise him? From boyhood they were great friends, as fire and wind. It is only through this disability imposed on him that he did not remember his strength. When Vali and Sugriva fell out and became enemies, the reason why Hanuman did not show his full strength and kill Vali was that he did not know that he was the greater of the two. Sugriva did not know it and Hanuman did not know it. Hanuman had this failure of memory. Nowadays we call it amnesia. Usually we forget words and names. The poem refers only to the failure of Hanuman with regard to the failure to remember his strength. But there are three or four other things where that weakness seems to have come upon him. I have no doubt in my mind that the poet means them to be so understood. I dare not lay it down as a proposition beyond doubt. I only know in my heart that in several other instances Hanuman's weakness seems to show itself. One comes to my mind in prominence. That is about this very matter. When Vali, incensed with his brother's misconduct, drove him from pillar to post, from country to country, all through the world and chased him about, Sugriva was followed by four of his ministers, Hanuman, Nala Nila and Tara. Vali, with his enormous strength, able to jump from one ocean to another, was not able to overtake him. Sugriva says that he came to know the whole geography in such detail during this flight. Then it would appear that suddenly Hanuman remembered something that he might have remembered long ago and saved all this trouble. He remembered that there was a hill just opposite Kishkindha, Risyamuka by name, where, owing to a curse of a certain Rishi, Vali or anybody sent by him would have his head burst into a thousand pieces if he ventured. Hanuman forgot this at first. Sugriva says to Rama that fortunately Hanuman remembered it and saved them all.

There was another occasion when he failed. You remember how when we studied the character of Lakshmana,* we came upon the scene where Tara speaks to Lakshmana and says to him, "Do not be so angry. My husband is a good man, and true to his friends. He will sacrifice me, Kishkindha, and anything to please you and your brother." Having brought down Lakshmana's anger,

* Lect. IV at pp. 51-52 above.

she then says to him, "My husband has not neglected his duty. He has already given the order for the monkeys to assemble." When Lakshmana heard that, he felt that he had spoken in haste, and he afterwards showed that he had been rather hasty in reprimanding Sugriva. When Sugriva gave the original order for his innumerable hosts to assemble on the fifteenth day, Hanuman was asked to see that nothing went wrong. Having devolved the burden of these duties on Hanuman and having placed the entire responsibility on him, Sugriva left for the inner apartments.* When the angry Lakshmana came to the gate and there was great consternation, Sugriva protests to Hanuman that he had done this before. Hanuman says, mounting on a high platform and speaking of moral duty and so on, "The time for work has come, and that you are careless is clear. Rama has no doubt sent harsh words, but you have brought them on yourself. Fold your hands in humble homage, and beg of Rama to excuse you, as a wife would stand within the limits set by the husband." Hanuman forgot that Sugriva had done his duty, and he forgot the further fact that he himself was the guilty party. If more was not done, the blame rested on Hanuman. What would a faithful servant have done? He ought to have said, "Do not be angry with Sugriva. I am to blame." Hanuman should have gone forward to make this disclosure, which he did not. On the other hand he seconded Lakshmana against his own master. What could this be due to? It may be said that his love of Rama and Lakshmana was so great that when they become angry, he took their side and chid his own master. Another explanation is that he showed the common weakness of our servants who, when the master is angry, become angrier. Neither of these theories would do. It appears to me that the poet meant to show that this was one of the forms in which the curse of the Rishis manifested itself.

Another forgetfulness on his part, also very very important, is when Vali was killed and Tara came to the field of battle and cried. Curiously enough, Vali had not actually expired at the time; he lay seemingly dead. Hanuman came there, not only brave and strong, but wise beyond mortal men's capacity, diplomatic to the very point of the great

* Lect. XIV at p. 213 above.

ambassadors, clever in speech. Nevertheless, when he came to see Tara with Vali's body on her lap, he did not notice that life was not extinct, perhaps not due to forgetfulness, but to insufficient observation (all these things are only various manifestations of that original curse). He tells Tara, "There is no use crying any more. Vali has gone to pay his last debt, where great heroes go. There are things to do hereafter. Think of them. One of them is the crowning of your son Angada. You must see him on the great throne of Kishkindha and rejoice as the mother of the future king." Remember that Hanuman at the very moment he set his eyes on Rama and Lakshmana, was scheming for Sugriva succeeding Vali. His nobler instinct leads him to think of Angada as the natural heir.

सर्वे हि हरिशार्दूलाः पुत्रश्चायं तवाङ्गदः ।
इदं हर्यृक्षराज्यं च त्वत्सनाथमनिन्दिते ॥
ताविमौ शोकसन्तप्तौ शनैः प्रेरय भामिनि ।
त्वया परिगृहीतोऽयमङ्गदः शास्तु मेदिनीम् ॥
संस्कार्यो हरिराजश्च अङ्गदश्चाभिषिच्यताम् ।
सिंहासनगतं पुत्रं पश्यन्ती शान्तिमेष्यसि ॥ IV. 21. 8, 9, 11

"Give these monkeys the proper orders. Get control over Angada. Have Vali cremated and then see your son anointed, and when you observe him seated on the throne, you will rejoice, and forget Vali's death." Do you think that these words could have been used by Sugriva's strongest ally, if that ally had been in his proper senses? This was another case where a strange lapse of memory occurred. Tara, however, was wise and prudent. She excelled Hanuman even in the power of diplomacy. She says to Hanuman, "I do not take your word at its proper value. Angada is nothing to me and seeing him on the throne is no concern to me. Besides, when Vali has passed away, Sugriva succeeds to his authority. Over me, over this kingdom, and over the fortunes of Angada himself Sugriva presides." She firmly rejects Hanuman's advice. This is another case where Hanuman's diplomacy met with a complete failure. Tara goes on, "The mere touch of this corpse is enough to me. It outweighs in satisfaction a hundred Angadas. I am not mistress of this kingdom or of Angada." There is a whole *sarga* in which

Sugriva himself sets up a wail after Vali's death. There is a ring of sincerity all through it, which shows that Sugriva was really stricken with remorse when he thought how great, how powerful, how good on the whole his brother had been and how unfaithful had been his own conduct towards him. He blames himself, curses himself and says: "I have done such wrong and do not deserve to live. I am going to burn myself to death. But since you, Rama, have got a service you expect me to do, Angada will perform that service for you. Let me pass away." You cannot believe that Sugriva was speaking merely in a paroxysm of sorrow at the moment. It comes straight from the heart. When Rama saw what he had done, when he saw the grief of Tara and the grief of Sugriva, and how all the monkeys had fled from the scene in utter desolation and grief, Rama himself was affected. The force of the strange deed performed in the guise of an exploit in war came upon him. Why should we not think that Hanuman too was stricken with remorse, and thought that the proper expiation was to pass the crown on to the lawful heir? I wish to ask how it is possible to explain Hanuman's extraordinary behaviour if he did not do it under the influence of the curse of the Rishis. His natural feeling overcame him, and at the moment he spoke as any observer on the spot would have spoken and not like Hanuman who had been Sugriva's ally from the beginning and ran through the world over and over again with him. But there is no harm in supposing that at the moment he really was under the influence of the natural feelings created by the extraordinary occasion, like Sugriva and Rama. There is no more explanation of this matter in the text, and there is nothing which contradicts this view. I venture to think that the poet intends us to interpret his text in this fashion. I do no dishonour either to the poet or to Hanuman. His greatness is not affected. And from the instances of this disability brought forward, you will perhaps think that there is something in it after all.

EIGHTEENTH LECTURE*

Ladies and Gentlemen,

I have a slight fear that when last time I referred to the incidents of forgetfulness on Hanuman's part, with regard to Sita's matter, some students of the poem might have thought that I was straining the language of the poet too far. To put things beyond doubt, I propose to read a few other *slokas* in the same context. You may remember my contention was that Sugriva had done his duty when Lakshmana thundered at the gate. His great mistake was that he indulged in an orgy of sensual enjoyment greatly to the annoyance and vexation of his famous ally. It was an act of the greatest imprudence on his part, apart from the self-indulgent aspect, but he had taken great care that the matter he had undertaken should be put through. This was made clear by his wife Tara when she defended her husband against the incensed Lakshmana. I told you then, as a specimen of her skill in advocacy, that she began by admitting Sugriva's fault and having tried to make a plea on that footing, subsequently showed that he was not at fault at all and that therefore the whole case against him fell to the ground. Here is the comment by Govindaraja on the subject:

> अपराधमङ्गीकृत्य सान्त्वयित्वा इदानीं विचार्यमाणे अपराध एव नास्तीत्याह। IV. 35. 10-11

Later, Sugriva in the presence of Lakshmana, gives a second instruction to Hanuman.

> प्रेषिताः प्रथमं ये च मया दूता महाजवाः।
> त्वरणार्थं तु भूयस्त्वं हरीन्संप्रेषयापरान्॥
> ये प्रसक्ताश्च कामेषु दीर्घसूत्राश्च वानराः।
> इहानयस्व तान् सर्वान् शीघ्रं तु मम शासनात्॥
> अहोभिर्दशभिर्ये हि नागच्छन्ति ममाज्ञया।
> हन्तव्यास्ते दुरात्मानो राजशासनदूषकाः॥ IV. 37. 10-12

This time, instead of fixing fifteen days as the time of arrival and assembly, Sugriva reduces the period to ten days, and he

* 9-8-'44.

gives the order to Hanuman to see that everybody comes within the specified time. It is Hanuman to whom again this order is directed. "Let the several couriers whom I sent before be instructed to make haste. Give them further orders that more haste is required." The note now is, प्रेषित-दूतत्वरणार्थोक्तिः स्वस्य प्रकृतकार्ये पूर्वमेव सावधानतां लक्ष्मणाय द्योतयितुम्। This second order which shortens the period is made to show to Lakshmana beyond a shadow of doubt that he had already taken the necessary action in the matter, so that it is a case on the part of Hanuman of forgetfulness which it is difficult to explain. Having received two orders in the matter and having had the responsibility thrown upon him, for him to speak on behalf of Lakshmana as though Sugriva had really been at fault was a lapse which it is impossible to explain in the case of Hanuman, except on the supposition that that disease of amnesia had for the moment affected him.

Now I have to come to another case of forgetfulness which, however, did not lead to much harm. This is a famous incident where the poet calls it forgetfulness expressly. I need not therefore be at special pains to establish this point. This is in Sarga 102 of the Yuddhakanda. You remember how when Ravana had hurled his unerring spear at Lakshmana and it got struck in his chest, Lakshmana lost consciousness and fell prone on the ground, causing the most intense grief to all the army and especially to his brother, who thought of desperate things in his sorrow. Then the old monkey, Sushena, whom I described as the second Jambavan, who seems to have known something of medicine, remembers the famous curative herbs on the Sanjivani hill and bids Hanuman repeat his feat which I shall describe in the proper place later. The direction is that particular herbs specified by Sushena and described by him, so that a man who had once seen them may at once recognise them, should be brought. Hanuman does the leap without any trouble, but when he searches on the hill-top he forgets the exact description, and hunting about the place, finds that he is unable to identify the herbs, and he tries to recollect. The poet describes the scene in five or six *slokas*. Hanuman says, "What shall I do now? I have forgotten the very thing for which I have come here. Shall I jump over, ask Sushena and, receiving instructions, come back?" Then he remembers that on a former occasion he lifted the whole hill and carried it away. It is Sushena's business to find the particular herb. So he shakes the hill and it comes off. With it he comes over, Sushena takes the herb and, having extracted the juice, applies it to Lakshmana's nostrils. Then Lakshmana revives. Curiously enough on this occasion the poet does not say that Hanuman took the hill-top back to its proper place, apparently because he himself forgot.

Then there are two other points, not so important nor having any particular significance in the story, but which I think are intended by the poet to be other specimens of Hanuman's forgetfulness. I will just put them to you, to complete the picture. You may remember that when I described Bharata's character to you, I said that, like any ordinary person Rama was seized with some little misgiving at the last moment that his brother might have acquired a sort of excessive fondness for the pomp and circumstance of kingship and therefore he sent Hanuman in advance to find out how things stood. Hanuman was to come back when Rama had gone a little way on the journey to Ayodhya and to report exactly how the land lay.* The fact is that Hanuman does not return at all to the place where he was told to come. He stayed with Bharata and came along with Bharata so that there was no time for any confidential talk. He was to watch Bharata and on narrating the story, observe carefully how he reacted to it, whether he showed an impatience, and how he was inclined to Rama. Why did Hanuman not return? The question has occurred to those who have dealt with the poem before. When he was expressly told that before Rama had gone far he should return from Bharata why did he not do so? He was not a servant who could disobey orders. My theory is that on seeing Bharata and narrating the story, his mind was full with other thoughts. He probably saw many things, and some thing about Bharata might have attracted him, thus dismissing that duty of his from the centre of his mind. This, however, is in accordance with what we have known to be Hanuman's weakness. I am afraid, however, I must add that the great commentator whom we usually follow has on this occasion taken a line which I am unable to follow. He puts upon the text a meaning it cannot bear. When he says that Hanuman had no absolute order to return and make a report, that he had to observe Bharata and his attitude from two alternative

* Lect. VIII, p. 106 above, VI. 128. 12-17.

standpoints and that he was to come and make a report only if one of the alternatives was true. This only shows his great anxiety to show that Hanuman was not guilty of any lapse. He puts this strange meaning on the words of Rama. Instead of Hanuman having to observe whether in Bharata a desire to be king himself had found a place, instead of that being the obvious meaning, Govindaraja says that Rama meant "When I go there and meet Bharata, it is my intention to offer the kingdom and ask him to be king. He may take it or not. I do not know whether, when I make a voluntary offer to Bharata, he will accept it gladly or whether he will refuse it. If he refuses the offer, do not come back. If, however, he intends to accept it, come and tell me." This is how he interprets the words. But it is unnatural and we have no alternative but to reject this interpretation. After all, Hanuman's defence is clear, that he simply forgot in the excitement of the moment and met the brother, of whom he must have heard so much.

Another thing is perhaps more easy to explain. I notice it every time I read the poem. When he met Bharata, Hanuman gave him a plain narrative of all the things that happened after Rama, Sita and Lakshmana parted from Bharata. Bharata wanted to know everything in detail. The story is given as Hanuman told it. There is one very significant omission in the story which is difficult to understand; and the omission is the fire ordeal to which, after Ravana's destruction, poor Sita was subjected. I think it is very significant that a very important matter on which so much turns should be omitted. Why did Hanuman forget to mention that? Was it a case of mere forgetfulness? Perhaps he did not like to tell Bharata what must have started in Bharata's mind a thought not favourable to his brother. In that case we must say that Hanuman was very tender to Bharata, that this shocking story need not reach his ears. Generally we all make that mistake. Nevertheless, the usual practice is for us, instead of making a clean breast of the affair, to go on as if nothing had taken place until it is discovered. We do not like to tell unpleasant things, until they become terribly unpleasant and reveal themselves. If so, it is only just an ordinary weakness that prevents people from telling the whole of a story.

Now, about Hanuman I have dealt with what I consider to be cases of more or less intense forgetfulness. But there are some other things that I may mention. I have already referred to two of his conspicuous failures. Hanuman's ability and his diplomacy and his power of presenting a case to people were all acknowledged. Nevertheless, we had occasion to see that on two important matters he met with failure. One is when he tried to get Tara to countenance Angada's coronation. You remember my reading certain slokas in which he expressly bade her to sit up, console herself and look after Angada, made king. I went about finding out from other sargas how on the same occasion, the same event impressed Sugriva and others, how they all felt perhaps that a terrible blunder had been committed amounting almost to a crime, and that therefore something should be done to upset the consequences which might follow; and the most important of the consequences was certainly the question of succession to Vali. It occurs to him that Sugriva was genuine when he desired that he should not be king after his brother. I read to you also a sloka in which, after seeing these scenes of sorrow with his own eyes, Rama himself felt that there was something in the atmosphere of the consequence of a mistake. He cried with tears streaming from his eyes, like the others, and for a moment was speechless. If that was the case, I argued that Hanuman might have felt that after Vali, not Sugriva but Angada should succeed, and he therefore mentioned the matter to Tara. But notwithstanding the overpowering grief of the lady, her head was tightly screwed on her shoulders. She does not seem to have lost her head at all. She says, "That will not do. In our case, after Vali Sugriva takes everything. (I suppose she meant the kingdom and herself too). He is the lord of the kingdom. Therefore he disposes of Angada, not I." What an extraordinarily able woman! I once called her the ancient Portia.

Another failure of his, also conspicuous, was when he tried to turn Angada away from his resolution of remaining behind when the month that had been given had expired, and Hanuman and everybody had failed and they had spent a little guilty time in Svayamprabha's cave enjoying the fruits and the roots and everything that was to be found there. When they came out, they had all incurred the death penalty prescribed by Sugriva. Then Tara, uncle of Angada, had suggested that they might all stay behind, once more enter Svayamprabha's cave and enjoy the luxuries there. Hanuman read in it something serious. He said to himself, "If Angada stays behind and a great many monkeys behind him, what is there to prevent him from becoming king of this part? Sugriva's kingdom will be partitioned, and it is just likely that Angada may become a source of danger to Sugriva." So he uses all his diplomatic skill and tells Angada that he had better go home. "I have known Sugriva all the time" he says, "He won't do you any harm." Then he adds very skilfully, "Do not trust these monkeys. They are after all monkeys. They won't remain faithful to you. Have they not got wives and children at home?" Of course Angada does not listen to him at all. He says, "On the other hand, I know how my uncle is disposed towards me. He remembers that I am Vali's son. Besides, he never made me yuvaraja. He could not help it." This then is another case in which in spite of his great skill in diplomacy, Hanuman failed in argument, and against this chip of an Angada. This is all from Kishkindhakanda.

I now proceed to the next kanda. I am only mentioning instances where the reputed skill of this great person failed. When he was talking to Sita, she, in her tender, pathetic style which draws tears from the reader, tells him everything she had to go through and occasionally expressed her misgivings whether she was right to live and cause anxiety to the great brothers, whether it would not be best for her to take her life and save trouble to so many. "How are my husband and his brother to cross the sea?" she asks, "and how could the monkey army come over to my succour?" Hanuman could no longer bear it. He had ventured to say to her, "Why do you suffer so much? I am here, strong, mighty, powerful. As I came over, so I can go over. You are such a light creature, and if you get on my back, the next instant you will be with your husband. Dismiss all this trouble and anxiety and sorrow. It is very easy to me." Remember that at that moment he was only of the size of a cat. He had searched the whole of Lanka for her, and, unwilling to be detected by any person, he had reduced himself to that very small size. When he spoke to her offering to take her on his back, it seemed ridiculous to her. Being a nice lady, she gently laughed at him.

हनुमन् दूरमध्वानं कथं मां वोढुमिच्छसि ।
कथं वाल्पशरीरस्त्वं मामितो नेतुमिच्छसि । V. 37. 31-32

Then, having made that jocular remark, she could not help saying, "I am afraid you are what you appear to be."

तदेव खलु ते मन्ये कपित्वं हरियूथप ॥ V. 37. 31

Hanuman felt a little piqued. He felt that for the first time he was insulted grossly. He says to himself, "I must show her that I am not this pitiable little cat." And to induce trust in her, to produce the feeling that he was not professing to be strong and powerful while he was really not so, he began to swell and assume his real form. "What do you take me to be?" he says. "You think you cannot trust your slender body to me. I am strong enough to uproot the whole of this Lanka, take all the hills in it, and the men and women upon it, everybody including Ravana, and put them across the sea." That of course was a little exaggeration on his part. I must tell you that exactly as in modern days, when any person becomes a warrior and steps on the field of battle, he does not know how exactly he could be within the limits of truth; not that warriors mean a word of it, not that the other party ascribes any meaning to any of it. In order to excite themselves to the fight, they have got to say some absurd things, to claim that they were all-powerful, that they were engines of mighty destruction, and that they could bring the enemy down to grief. Hanuman had no enemies, but he had some critics. Therefore, he exaggerated a bit. Sita could not then say he was merely a monkey. She saw how powerful he was. Then she brought forward another argument, being very clever like most ladies. She says, "If you take me across, all these Rakshasas will follow you. While you are over the water, you will have to fight. It is a crazy bit of thing. You may be beaten by these Rakshasas. All war is uncertain—most extraordinary how a woman can make a generalisation about war generally. Even if you can carry me and still elude the pursuers, it is not proper for me, knowingly and wilfully, i.e., with the exercise of my will, to touch any person other than my husband. It will not do for me. You may ask me, 'Did not Ravana touch you?' Yes, he did. But I was not then mistress of myself. He laid violent hands on me. Now you ask me of my own accord to sit on your back. It is a very different thing. After all, is it worthy of my husband that, having lost me to Ravana in that way, he should allow me to be taken back to him by the back-door? He ought to come here, destroy Ravana and his family, and show to the world that nobody dare insult Rama's greatness or glory with impunity. It is then that my rescue should follow. You want to take me merely in the same way as Ravana brought me here. That alone will do him full honour if he should come here, destroy his enemy, especially Ravana, and then take me back home in triumph." Hanuman was then convinced that these things did not strike his intelligence at first. He said, "You have spoken as the wife of Rama should speak. I admire you and approve of you. It is true that you have some misgivings that I am likely to be assailed by the enemies. Is there another woman in this world who, having been brought to this very extremity of danger, would say, 'I am not going with you, but would wait for the proper, delayed but honourable rescue?' You have spoken in such a way that Rama would be delighted and would be proud of you. Trust me, I will narrate every detail to him. I will recite to him every word, exactly as it came from you. It is not a desire that I should violate your feeling, that I should have the honour of having touched the body of a most illustrious person. I wanted to do Rama what would please him, my heart being tender with friendship for him. Lanka is separated from the mainland by a broad piece of water, and it is a very strongly defended fort, and I can assure you that it is a very difficult place to besiege. I know my strength, and that is why I made the offer. Do not think I had any other motive. If you do not like to be carried this way, give me some token, so that I may convince your husband that I have seen and conversed with you." This was another matter in which Hanuman failed, but was in the end glad to have failed for Sita convinced him that that was the right course.

We now come to the end of the poem. After Ravana had been killed and when Vibhishana had been crowned and business was over, in great triumph Rama sent Hanuman to inform Sita that she was no longer a prisoner, that Vibhishana was now king of Lanka and that therefore she was now a free lady. Hanuman takes this news doubly exultant, tells her so exultantly that even Sita who is accustomed to his speech is somewhat taken aback. She says to herself, "This Hanuman is a great talker." "Of all the persons I have known, you are the only one who can speak like this", says Sita in her joy at receiving the news for which she has been living with all her heart. What a beautiful tribute to receive from Sita! What would not other persons have given to get this praise from her? We shall not envy Hanuman. As the great Bacon says, *envy is a feeling that we cherish only towards those who are more or less like us. Tell me whether anyone feels envy of the Emperor of England, or of Roosevelt. Having received this great tribute, so great that the like of it had not been pronounced about any person, his heart is filled with pride and joy, and he is very thankful to Sita. What does he offer? Perhaps some of you will say, there is some mistake here. "These Rakshasis, who are terrible women, who have been all these days frightening you and speaking ill of you and threatening you, what would you advise me to do? I will wreak my will on them. I desire to beat them in as many ways as I can. This is the boon I ask of you in return for that praise I received." I consider that Hanuman fell a great deal below his own level, much below his own standard of propriety, when he offered to exercise not merely his physical strength but his teeth and his nails. His anger was so great, his blood boiled to such an extent when he saw the tormentors of the lady of his ideal. When he saw them, his worst feelings were excited. I almost think that Hanuman used those harsh, unworthy words and expressed these very bad sentences in order that Sita's best nature may be roused in the answer that she gave him. It is one of the noblest pieces.† No plea of forgiveness, tolerance or general benevolence would reach such a great height as the words that she spoke. Sita would not hear of it. She said, "What could these poor women do? They did the bidding of their master." How ready to forgive! I suppose Hanuman was suddenly stricken with a returning sense of propriety. Suddenly he dropped his *Kapitva*. These words struck the right chord in him. He thought that the best thing was to run away.

I should take leave of this scene and this point. But I should relate two other scenes which are similar and to which naturally this takes the reader back. When Sita was bemoaning her lot and asking herself whether there was no escape for her, Trijata was there, and she narrated at that time a beautiful dream of hers, in which she had seen Ravana and Kumbhakarna and their wicked lot in the extremity of shame and

* "Envy is ever joined with the comparing of a man's self; and where there is no comparison, no Envy; and therefore kings are not envied but by kings." Bacon : "OF ENVY"

† For a translation of the passage see Lect. XXVII below.

danger, and Rama and Lakshmana borne on mighty elephants, and she saw Sita amongst them, restored to her glory and taking the place that was her due. She says, "This dream of mine is going to be fulfilled. You wicked Rakshasis that torment her now, you may have to bear the vengeance of Rama when he hears of the way you have behaved to her. Fall at Sita's feet now and make sure of her forgiveness." Trijata had already spoken to the Rakshasis, and Sita heard it. Hanuman also heard it. When, later on, Hanuman comes and offers to inflict these torments and Sita forbids him, we are reminded of this former scene of Trijata's dream. I almost think that the poet meant us to connect the two. The dreams of good persons come true, though may be not in every particular. Dreams are meant to indicate coming events. In this case I have little doubt that the poet meant us to connect these two scenes together in our minds and to produce in us the feeling that this second scene was no doubt the unconscious reproduction by Sita and Hanuman of something that they had heard on a former occasion, but of which the precise outline and details they had lost.

There are one or two things which I wish to say in this connection. They should not detract from the greatness that is Hanuman's. How great he was, how great his achievements were, it is impossible to measure by ordinary standards. I have said before that if anything requiring extraordinary physical strength had to be done, something impossible for others. Hanuman did it. We have got to consider some of the very great exploits that stand to his credit. I may consider Hanuman in a big way. I assemble his forgetfulness together, his failures and his other weaknesses together, and I assemble his great exploits. When I have dealt with these, I still have left to deal with one of the greatest things in the life of Hanuman; and that is the way in which he went through scenes of great tenderness and came out of all of them with credit to himself. I shall therefore conclude my talk on Hanuman with reading a number of extracts from the Sundara Kanda. It makes one proud to think that the poet has conceived the character of Hanuman in that great style and executed it also in grand style. Some may say that the poet has exaggerated Hanuman's character. But we are concerned not with the greatness and size of the thing, but the spirit in which they were done.

NINETEENTH LECTURE*

Sisters and Brothers,

Our subject today is the exploits of Hanuman. They were many, as well as great, and, for a wonder, they began with Hanuman when he came into the world. He himself describes to Sita, in order to assure her of his *bona fides,* his origin, apparently wishing to show how he looked like a monkey, while he called himself the son of Vayu. His origin was somewhat peculiar. His father was a monkey named Kesari. He was the king of a small state on a hill called Sumeru. Once it would appear that at the sacred bathing ghat the pilgrims were molested by an asura called Sambarasura. In order to kill him they deputed this Kesari. He was absent for a short time for that purpose from his home, and during his absence Hanuman was conceived and came into existence. His wife had been born a monkey because of a curse, but once she was a beautiful maiden; and remembering that existence of hers, she put on the appearance of a woman and went about in the gardens near her place. She was so ravishingly beautiful that God Vayu took a fancy for her and, displacing her clothes, touched her all over. She became very angry and looked about. Vayu answered her, "Do not be annoyed. I am not going to do anything wrong to you. Your husband Kesari has done a great service to celestial beings, and to reward him, I am going to bestow a child on you who shall be famous in the three worlds and perform miraculous deeds." So, in a neighbouring cave she was brought to bed of a miraculous child. That child had great hunger, ravaging hunger. There being nothing by way of fruits, he just looked up and saw Surya, a beautiful red fruit as he struck the baby to be. Then the story goes on, narrated in two different ways in the Ramayana itself, once in great detail, another time in somewhat of a summary. Jambavan, wishing to induce Hanuman to undertake the great leap across the water, tells him of the story in the Kishkindha Kanda. It is a nice piece for Hanuman to be reminded of what he did when he was but a baby. He had to be reminded because at the moment he was wanted, he was

* 16-8-'44.

in a fit of great depression and sat by himself. He was probably chewing the cud of his disappointing talk to Angada who had foiled him and also put him down with a high hand. So Hanuman sat away from the rest of the monkeys. Angada held a council to find out whether anyone would be strong and brave enough to undertake the leap to Lanka. There is one whole sarga devoted to this particular council. The monkeys who had previously been very proud of their strength, when they saw the broad piece of water making a terrific noise, took alarm. One of them said he could leap ten yojanas, another said he could do twenty, a third, thirty and so on, until they came to Jambavan who, instead of mentioning the figure to which he was equal, went into a long story of reminiscence. "I once was strong and have gone round the earth twenty-one times. Now I can do only ninety yojanas." Angada said he could do all the hundred, but he could not return. Jambavan, though he had lost his early strength, had not lost his skill in talking and diplomacy, and he says to Angada, "Even if you can return, we are not going to part with you. We cannot do without you. We must look upon you as our *kalatra,* meaning apparently, according to its origin, that which is to be protected. You think you are the head here. It is true, but it is our duty to protect you who are our protector. We cannot let you undertake any risk." He then goes to Hanuman and tells him, "You do not know about yourself. We want your services." The first sarga in the Sundara Kanda describes the entire leap of Hanuman. It cannot be described as a leap, but rather as a flight, for he had many adventures on the way, in one or two of which he was stopped and did a little bit of fighting. I am not going to mention this and other things which I dare say you all remember. But this exploit includes not only the leap, but the great deeds he performed on the island. After an elaborate search for Sita, he discovered her, and after her conversation he said to himself, "I cannot return immediately. There are some more things to do. Being a good servant, I must look about and, if necessary, change my line of work." So he made up his mind to appear before Ravana whom he wished to see and threaten if possible. But how was Ravana to be seen? Hanuman laid a little scheme of his own. "I will do some mischief here", he said to himself. "I will reduce this Asokavana to the ground, and destroy a part of the city, so that they may send somebody to attack me." So you know how he drew the unfavourable attention of the guardians of Lanka, and performed great deeds against them in self-defence. One of the deeds was the killing of one of Ravana's sons who was known to be a great warrior. And then you know how he was caught by Indrajit in the Brahmastra and bound by chains. He was then taken to Ravana's presence, and, when they thought that he had been well bound, the period of the Brahmastra's potency over him being over, he shook himself free and sat before Ravana. Pretending, when he began, to be an humble emissary of Sugriva, he speaks defiantly to him as he goes on. "Sugriva greets you in a friendly manner," he begins, but before he finishes, he has hurled defiance at Ravana. Then, when Ravana desires to kill him, Vibhishana interferes, and Ravana is content to set fire to Hanuman's tail, with which fire Hanuman burned the city itself. That was his first exploit, the leap and the subsequent wonderful achievements in the city of Lanka. This, however, though described by the poet in a long sarga and with greatest skill, and generally believed to be Hanuman's greatest exploit, was by no means his greatest. There were others after this, very much more wonderful.

The next one that we shall deal with was when the first great battle took place in which Ravana himself appeared at the head of his forces. His commander-in-chief Prahasta had been killed by his opposite number Nila, and Ravana says, "I cannot neglect this powerful enemy," and takes the field himself. He assembles his great forces and goes into the field. Hanuman confronts him. They had known each other before somewhat but they had not known each other's strength personally. So Hanuman says, "I ought to tell you that monkeys never use bows and arrows." Their only instruments were trees and branches of trees, which they uprooted easily and used against the enemy, or little hilltops and huge stones which they hurled with wonderful aim. The Rakshasas were good at both. Some could use bows and arrows, and there were also strong men who could deal powerful blows in single combat. Ravana was highly skilled in both. Hanuman showed his fist. Ravana first struck Hanuman with his palm on the chest. Of course Ravana's blows were very powerful and Hanuman reeled. But he quickly recovered and struck Ravana with his palm. Ravana took it, but felt the blow so much that he said, "Ah, you are a worthy enemy." But Hanuman says, "I do not care for your compliment. I am ashamed that after my blow, you are alive. I will deliver another, and then you shall go straight to the abode of Yama." Getting provoked, Ravana aimed a powerful stroke with the fist against Hanuman. Hanuman became unconscious. Having disposed of Hanuman for the time, Ravana turned to Nila and was engaged with him in battle. When Hanuman recovered his consciousness he saw Ravana engaged with Nila. So he says, "It is not right to attack a man when he is engaged with another. So I will wait till you are free."* Then Ravana nearly killed Nila, but though he fell on the ground, almost dead, was not quite dead; his father the great god Agni protected him.

Then Ravana turned to Lakshmana with whom he had a brisk exchange of arrows. At the end, finding that the arrow game was not good, Ravana took out his spear, and being a master of the spear, he hurled it with full force at Lakshmana which took him right over the chest; and Lakshmana, unable to stand the blow, fell prone on the ground like a dead man. Then Ravana made a strange move. Seeing Lakshmana fallen, it occurred to him that he must ensure his death. If left there, it may be that he recovers. So he came there and tried to lift up Lakshmana. He put his arm round the body and exercised all his strength to lift him. But Lakshmana would not rise. The poet says that though fallen to the ground, Lakshmana remembered that the Amsa of Vishnu was in him, and as he remembered it, he became incalculably heavy, and Ravana could not lift him. Otherwise he would have taken him and put him into the sea. Ravana stood confounded. Then Hanuman who had worked himself up into a state of great fury saw how things stood. He goes up to Ravana and delivers a terrific blow at his chest with his fist. Ravana fell on his knees, and it would appear that all his ten mouths poured blood through and poor Ravana was in great extremity. Then Hanuman took the opportunity, went to Lakshmana, lifted him—because Lakshmana, knowing that it was a friend, Hanuman, who was devoted to him, became light for him—and took him to his brother. He remembered again who he was, and threw off his extra weight and allowed Hanuman to carry him to safety. Then it was

* Cf. Lect. XI at p. 149.

that Rama became infuriated with Ravana and made terrific war upon him. The shower of arrows from each side was something that astonished the gods. Then Hanuman said to Rama, "You get upon my back as Vishnu used to do with Garuda when he attacked the enemies of the gods. I will bear you." Rama agreed, and on his famous mount he stood and attacked Ravana. Ravana was not so angry with Rama as he was with Hanuman. So he aimed many arrows at Hanuman specially before he struck at Rama himself. Hanuman who ordinarily struck everybody as a great and distinguished being, when he was struck all over with arrows and they struck into his body, shone with even greater splendour. Ravana performed wonders, but in the end Rama proved too strong for him. His arrows struck at Ravana's crown and took it off. Ravana was greatly humiliated, and notwithstanding mighty efforts that he put forth, lost the battle that day. When he stood helpless, discrowned and disarmed, Rama said to himself, "I will not pursue this advantage. It would be unchivalrous." So he says to Ravana, "Go home and return to-morrow, refreshed." Ravana was glad to have the opportunity and retired that day. You see how in this battle, after Rama himself, the honours of the day go to Hanuman, and that is how we are interested in this great fight.

The next exploit that I should refer to is when Indrajit had aimed the Brahmastra at the whole lot of Rama and his army. The two brothers were hit, and the monkeys had all been hit and they all lay prone on the ground. Indrajit thought that he had finished the army that came over the water, and went to report his great triumph to his father. Then night fell and the place became utterly dark. Some of the monkeys had died and others were struggling with their last breath. The two that were still wide awake and strong were Hanuman and Vibhishana. Hanuman felt it only for a time, and Vibhishana had never been struck at all. They came together, and Hanuman said, "I have a torch in my hand. We shall walk over the field of battle, and let us go and comfort and give what assistance we can." As they went round on this sorrowful task, they came upon Jambavan who was struggling hard. Jambavan says in pitiful tones, 'Is it Vibhishana? I do not see you with my eyes, but I recognise your voice. Now, tell me if in your wanderings on the field, you have seen Hanuman anywhere." And then Hanuman stood near. Vibhishana, not giving information in reply to the question, asks him, "On this terrible day when everybody has been hurt, you do not ask me about Rama or Lakshmana, but about Hanuman. How is it that you have not shown the same affection for Sugriva or Angada?" Says Jambavan, "I have a purpose. If Hanuman is alive, then the whole army will all come back to life. But let him be dead, though we are all alive, we are as good as dead. Without him we are perfectly worthless; with him, though we be dead, we may come to life again. That is the great merit about Hanuman. He is as strong as his father Vayu, and if he is alive, we have hope." Hearing this extraordinary praise by his old friend, Hanuman discloses himself, and falls at his feet and says how good he is to praise him like that. Now Jambavan says to himself, "I am born again. Now it is on you that we all depend. Everything hangs on your effort. This is the time for you to exert your full skill and your full strength. As I look round, I see no one who can come to our assistance. Give joy to all these crowds of people, and also enable Rama and Lakshmana who are down to be free of their arrows which nearly choke them." Then he mentions four herbs of miraculous potency and tells him to bring them. They are on the Himalayas, between the mount Kailasa and Rishabha, the herb which revives the dead, the herb which heals the wounds caused by arrows, the herb which restores the proper colour when the body has been discoloured by approaching death, and the herb which joins the severed parts of the body. The *satayojana* leap which Hanuman did before is nothing compared with this. Then Hanuman realises his full strength, and exerting himself all he can, he jumps and takes the great leap, far greater than the big leap over which the poet waxed so eloquent. Then the poet describes how the celestials watched this wonderful performance. There he searches for the four kinds of herbs. The herbs, however, being endowed with great discerning, found out that somebody was come after them. So they said to themselves, "Let us be hidden", and they became invisible. When he found that they were not to be seen, there was no alternative for him but to shift the whole mountain. He shifts the top of the mountain and, taking the leap, comes down. When he brought the herbs and placed them on the battlefield, Vayu blew the scent about and as it struck the nostrils of the dead monkeys, they slowly revived and sat up. Rama and Lakshmana came to life again and the whole field became animated and lively. Then it would appear they raised a tremendous shout and went to Lanka and made a terrific noise and spread destruction all round. Now comes a small thing. It is very significant. If it was a scene of battle and the Rakshasas and monkeys had engaged one another in combat, the herbs would make no distinction between Vanaras and Rakshasas. But the dead Rakshasas, though they might have been in thousands and lakhs, were not there at all. The poet says, "Whom the gods would destroy, they first make mad." So Ravana had previously given an order that as often as the Rakshasas fell to the ground, they should be thrown into the sea, for fear that if they lay on the ground, the enemy should count them and know how many more were alive. And so they were all saved from the healing breath. Hanuman, knowing that he ought not to make a permanent dislocation in nature, took back the hill and placed it where it was as though it had never been disturbed. Upon the second occasion,* although Hanuman must have done it, the poet forgets to say expressly that the restoration was made. The taking of the hill back to the Himalayas and the return to Rama's side, each has only a quarter of a sloka. I suppose the poet means to give us an idea of the quick work that Hanuman did on the occasion.

I now come to an exploit of a somewhat different character. Hanuman performed extraordinary feats of strength on the field of battle. One we have already mentioned was the destruction of Ravana's son Aksha. Now on this great occasion, he kills several famous Rakshasas. Of the most important Rakshasas whom he killed, there were three whom I should mention, Devantaka, Trisiras and Nikumbha. Nikumbha was the greatest. Curiously enough, whenever he mentions chief ministers, the poet ascribes four to each king. Vali, Sugriva and Ravana had four each. Four were the most prominent. Vali's four are not mentioned by the poet. Ravana had placed, at the top of his list, Durdhara, Prahasta, Mahaparsva and Nikumbha, whom Ravana trusted most and on whose wisdom he relied. Moreover, when he sent for Prahasta and asked him to take the field of battle, he tells Prahasta, "I have lost many able commanders. These monkeys seem to be a terrible lot,

* See Lect. XVIII at p. 261 above.

taking a heavy toll of life from our big men. You are one of my top figures. I hope you will have better success. Besides you, there are only four others in whom I have some confidence, myself, Kumbhakarna, Indrajit and Nikumbha. I cannot see how I can save this town, if any other person goes to the fight." So he sends Prahasta to his doom.

Now we have come to another stage of the fight when Kumbhakarna's two sons, Kumbha and Nikumbha, come into the field. Kumbha had been killed by Sugriva and then, greatly angered and resolved to do his worst amongst the Vanaras, Nikumbha comes into the field, and is encountered by our hero of the day. Nikumbha was just like Hanuman that day. But as Hanuman could not use the bow and arrows, Nikumbha said, "I will fight Hanuman hand to hand." I took it into my head that as a sample of the poet's description of these battles, I might translate for your benefit to-day this sarga (VI. 77) as a whole, the fight between Nikumbha and Hanuman.

VI. 77: *The Killing of Nikumbha.* When Nikumbha saw his brother Kumbha stretched on the ground, he cast angry looks at Sugriva, as if he would burn him to ashes. Then he grasped his imposing mace, stupendous like the crest of the mountain Mandara. A gay garland wreathed it round. Its haft had metal bands wrought like the five fingers of a titan's hand. Round it ran a broad strip of gold, while diamonds and rubies studded it all over. Like the death-dealing rod of Yama it seemed, causing dismay to the monkeys and nerving the Rakshasas with courage. Wielding the weapon, which rivalled in size the flagstaff of Indra, Nikumbha, of terrific aspect, roared with mouth yawning wide. On his chest shone a medal of gold; his arms were held by beautiful bracelets; lustrous pendants depended from his ears; a resplendent garland enfolded his neck. With these ornaments and with his club, Nikumbha assumed the threatening semblance of a vast cloud charged with lightning and thunder and shot with a vivid rainbow. As his giant arm twirled the club, the noise was like the bursting yell of the seven winds of heaven, and the light resembled the Fire-god himself bereft of smoke. The vault above whirled around in the toss of Nikumbha's mace, as though Alaka, the city of the Gandharvas, performed rapid revolutions with her grand mansions and palaces, and the moon and stars and planets joined in the rotatory race. In fact the blazing jewels of the club were rendered the fiercer by his consuming choler, and he struck terror into all hearts like the roaring and raging conflagration which make an end of all created things when one Yuga is succeeded by the next. So paralysing was the fear that the Vanaras and Rakshasas alike were unable to make the slightest movement. Alone among them all stood Hanuman in front of the Rakshasa chieftain with his broad breast bared to the fury of the attack. On that breast fell with fierce force the giant club of Nikumbha hurled by the giant's arm. That very instant, lo and behold! from the monkey hero's rock-like breast there shot into the sky, making it one blinding blaze of a thousand meteors, the shattered fragments of the titanic club. Hanuman bore the shock firm and unmoved, while an earthquake spread ruin all round. Then did Maruti, summoning all his strength, concentrate it into his clenched fist and bring it to bear with the violence of his divine father on Nikumbha's chest. Imagine a black cloud streaked suddenly with fierce lightning and riven with thunder's roar; so shook Nikumbha's huge frame and streamed with red blood in profusion. But the giant recovered soon and, grasping the unwieldy bulk of Hanuman with his powerful arms, lifted him off the ground to the loud roar of exultant joy which rose from the Rakshasa ranks. This joy, however, lasted but for a moment for at once with mighty blows of the fist Anjaneya freed himself, and throwing down the captor with main force, leaped on his prostrate body and pounded it mercilessly. Then with both hands he caught the enemy's neck, twisted it about and smashed his head on the rock, setting up at the same time a reverberating roar of triumph. When it was clear that the Rakshasa had expired, the monkeys shouted with glee, the skies thundered with satisfaction, the earth rocked with joy, heaven rained fresh flowers, and consternation, stark and comfortless, seized the enemy's hosts.

The last exploit that I shall mention is his second flight to the Himalaya mountain. I have already mentioned it to you in connection with my previous account of Hanuman's forgetfulness.* On this occasion Lakshmana lay stricken with Ravana's *sakti* and it was necessary to relieve him with these herbs. Sushena, the great physician monkey, requested Hanuman to repeat his old exploit. Upon this occasion there

* Lect. XVIII at p. 260 above.

is an account, not in our southern edition, but in the Italian edition giving the eastern recension, a thrilling description of how Hanuman met with great obstacles on the way. Ravana knowing that Hanuman was on this quest and might bring the reviving herb, ordered Kalanemi, an asura, to stop him. It is a brave adventure, and Hanuman is delayed a good deal. Kalanemi, like Maricha, assumes the form of a hermit and offers hospitality, and poor Hanuman is taken in for a while. Then he suddenly discovers that this is a ruse to keep him from his task. He kills Kalanemi and goes and brings the herb, for Sushena has described the herbs precisely, saying how they would shine with lustre and would almost thrust themselves into his vision. But in this version of the Ramayana it would appear that owing to this excitement of the fight with Kalanemi and the long conversation that he had, he got a little excited and forgot the exact description of the herbs.* On going back with the mountain, he apologises to Sushena. Sushena pounds the herb and applies it to Lakshmana, who comes back to life.

Now one or two things I might say about Hanuman, adding to this list, and chiefly from his own lips. But I shall reserve them for another day. Next time I propose to pay attention to another aspect of Hanuman's manysided character. We shall see him searching for Sita, and having discovered her, how he makes himself known to her, brings her confidence and exchanges great and moving thoughts with her about Rama and Lakshmana and their future work on her behalf. Sita too, in the Sundara Kanda, shines forth in the glory of her character, and although I mean to devote two lectures separately to her, it is impossible to deal with Hanuman all by himself. I shall have every now and then to bring Sita into prominence too, for beautiful as the Sundara Kanda is, as its very name implies, the beauty is in the nature of the tender sentiments exchanged between Hanuman and Sita and the way in which the inner glory of thier nature shines for all time.

* Cf. **Tilaka** on VI. 102. 25 (Bombay Ed. VI. 101. 32).

" चिन्तामभ्यगमच्छ्रीमानजानंस्तां महौषधिम् "

'पूर्वदृष्टानामप्यपरिचये पुराणान्तरोक्तकालनेमियुद्धकृतचित्तचाञ्चल्यं हेतुरिति बोध्यम् ।'

TWENTIETH LECTURE*

Ladies and Gentlemen,

Like most people employed in tasks of great difficulty, Hanuman swayed between moods of confidence and pessimism. Sometimes he felt he could accomplish what he had undertaken, and even added to the compass of his undertakings. At other times he was disposed to question his capacity to fulfil the obligations. The poet shows him to us occasionally in one and occasionally in the other mood. The great exploit that stands to his credit, as I pointed out, is by no means the greatest of those that he achieved. The leap across the sea was nothing to what he had performed as a baby, and what he was about to perform later, when he jumped right up to the Himalayas and brought away a whole hill-top and then restored it to its proper place. But the leap across the Pamban is the one with which his name is most connected in the poem, because it resulted in the discovery of Sita's whereabouts, and was the prelude to his performing some military exploits of a high order. When he undertook the leap it was generally believed that only his father and Garuda could have undertaken such a thing. Between Hanuman, Sita and Rama, this sentiment is expressed five times in the poem, *viz.*, that of all beings on earth, three Garutman, Vayu and Hanuman, could accomplish this marvellous jump across the water. Though it is repeated five times,† curiously enough, Valmiki himself gives some other names as those of people who could do similar things. That is somewhat in the manner of Valmiki. He often gives more than one version of the matter, leaving some room for those who are inclined to dispute over important details. In the third sarga of the Sundara Kanda, for instance, we are given the names of Kumuda, Angada, Sushena, Mainda, Dvivida, Sugriva, Kusaparva, Ketumala, and Hanuman. In the second sarga we get the names of Angada, Nila, Sugriva and Hanuman. In the Yuddha Kanda, Sarga 3, they are given as Angada, Dvivida, Mainda, Jambavan, Panasa, Nala and Nila. The commentators usually say that this is the *svabhava* of the poet that he repeats himself more

* 23-8-'44.

† IV. 67. 23; V. 39. 26; V. 56. 9 (Bombay Ed.); V. 68. 9 (which is only Hanuman's report of V. 39. 26) and VI. 1. 3.

than once no doubt, but with some modifications more or less important. For instance, in the Sundara Kanda, Sarga 30, you remember that after Hanuman had found Sita and was cogitating how he should make himself known to her, give her the token from Rama and speak words of comfort and encouragement to her, a misgiving arose in his mind that Sita might take fright that he was Ravana himself in disguise and cry out, that the Rakshasas might give the alarm, which would bring Ravana's men on the scene, and that he might have to do some hard fighting with the Rakshasas. If he engaged in this hard fighting, would he retain sufficient strength to do the return leap, or would he be so weakened and perhaps disabled that he should not be able to go back? These questions occurred to him, and he doubted very much the wisdom of provoking conflicts which might either finish him or leave him too weak for the rest of the duties. "No doubt I shall punish them severely. But shall I be able to go back? Supposing I am killed, or if I am not killed, supposing I am caught and imprisoned, then what will become of Rama's business? Is there another in the Vanara hosts to whom the task may be entrusted with hopes of its successful accomplishment?" And he answers the question in the negative here. "I do not see another who could help Rama's business. When once I am gone, there is not another amongst my kinsmen whom we could trust to perform this immense leap. I may have the strength to kill thousands upon thousands of Rakshasas in battle. But having so exhausted my strength in the fight here, the return jump across the sea may be too much for me. All fighting, however confident one may be in the beginning, is attended with uncertainty. I do not think I am entitled to put this matter in jeopardy." And so on. Then as you know after weighing the pros and cons he decided that he would disclose himself to her by uttering the praise of Rama which was bound to soothe her fears and win her confidence.

Then when he speaks to Sita, a little later, he says this. "After our conversation with Sampati, we came to the seashore. Then crores upon crores of monkeys became depressed. When my colleagues caught sight of the sea between them stretching for a hundred yojanas, all sat down in despair. Seeing them so sinking, I gave them courage and undertook to do this; and putting them in good spirits, I made them see that I could do it, and I have done it. None of them ever thought themselves equal to the task of leaping over."

Here comes a passage which will puzzle you a bit. When Hanuman was about to take leave of Sita, she asked him, "How is the monkey army to come over to this side of the water? They may be in enormous numbers. I think my fate is sealed." So concludes Sita in her very natural pessimism. "There is no device known by which their passage across may be accomplished. Rama and Lakshmana are human beings, and they cannot do it either. You can do it; Garuda and Vayu can do it; but there is no fourth person to do it. And at the end of the month, when Ravana comes here, I must either become his wife, or as that is impossible meet my death." Hanuman felt that her spirits must be kept up anyhow. It won't do to let her pass away in that mood. So, in order to comfort her, he does what in common parlance is called drawing the long bow. He tells her a huge lie. "You do not know these monkeys. What grand things they have done! More than once they have done the round of this world with the oceans and the land between them." (That is a first class invention). "Amongst the many millions and billions that follow Sugriva, I have my equals, and there are my superiors, but there is not a fellow who is inferior to me. Even I, the least of them, have done it; the rest will perform it easily. (This is a generalisation which is not true either.) Usually, kings send as their messengers, not the best men in their service, but inferior men. That is their practice. In that way Sugriva has sent me. Do not become cast down. At one leap they will come here, all the monkeys." You see Hanuman did not scruple to say what, to put it moderately, can only be described as an enormous exaggeration, with part of it beyond the truth. But that was necessary. Otherwise, Sita was about to sink and might have killed herself. But the wonder of it is that, exactly as it happens to many of us, Sita knew that Hanuman said all this only to encourage her and not because it was true. Therefore, when after setting fire to the place, Hanuman takes final leave of her, she once more says, "I know you alone can do it or your father or Garuda."*

Now we have to turn back a little and see, again very naturally, what these monkeys themselves thought when they

* The reference here is to V. 56. 9 in the Bombay Ed.; it is not included by Govindaraja and is not in the M.L.J. text.

started from Kishkindha. These monkeys, before they dispersed in their various directions, naturally cast a glance forward as it were. "I am going to do this. I am going to do that. Why should Sugriva send so many? I can finish Ravana in one single engagement. I will uproot all the trees about here, break open all these hills, and bore holes in the earth. And as for the sea, I can dry it up." To Sugriva they all boasted like this. I am only concerned to point out how in our ignorance, we often undertake tasks without knowing their real nature. We think we are equal to anything. What man has done, man can do, is a proverb which we often quote. But it is often that our confidence is misplaced, that events prove us wholly in the wrong, and we come to grief. As for Hanuman, he was not above a little bravado of this kind. When he took leave of Sita and resolved to do a deed or two which the people of Lanka should remember, he cried out in the streets as he went along, "A thousand Rakshasas cannot withstand me in battle. While all these Rakshasas are blinking what to do, I will destroy this city, take leave of Sita once more and leap across." He was indulging in what must be called a war brag. No man who goes into a fight can afford to show any weakness, he must say all kinds of things about himself, and Hanuman did it because he ought to do so.

When he went to Ravana and took his seat before him, he delivered what he averred was a message from Sugriva, —which however was not the case at all,—beginning with a greeting from Sugriva. Then he drops all kinds of courtesy and threatens Ravana. "For so many years you have been at the head of this world, doing what you liked destroying kingdoms, subjecting other princes to your yoke and carrying away women. You have done all this because you have received boons from the gods. That dharma is now worked out. Hereafter the wickedness is going to have its turn in quick succession; those misdeeds of yours are going to bear fruit. In the midst of all the Vanaras and bears, Rama has taken a solemn vow that he would be revenged of his enemies, those who took away Sita. Whom do you take this Sita to be, her whom you have brought across the water and imprisoned in your place? She is *kalaratri*. She is going to finish your city. Remember that she is like a big rope that has been fastened round your neck. In a few days it is going to be drawn tight. Your end is drawing near. If you wish to save yourself, deliver up Sita and beg Rama's protection, for Rama is so great a warrior that nobody can stand in battle against him, neither on earth nor on high. Whether it be Siva himself or whether it be Brahma or Indra, no one is equal to Rama in fight." Here the poet has carefully omitted Vishnu in this sloka. The idea seems to be that it would be absurd that Vishnu cannot stand before Rama, as Rama is only an *avatara* of Vishnu. In the mind of the poet Vishnu and Rama were one. In many other instances God Vishnu is specially omitted. One remarkable instance is when in the great battle Rama employs the *gandharva astra* and stands before every single Rakshasa as a terrible Rama. On that occasion when the *mulabala* had been destroyed completely and the gods rained flowers and the Gandharvas sang victory, Rama himself for a moment felt the glow of victory; and under the influence of that exhilarating feeling, saw Sugriva, Hanuman and Vibhishana standing behind him, wondering and looking at him as a marvel, thinking what a strange friend they were having. And then Rama turns round and says,

एतदस्त्रबलं दिव्यं मम वा त्र्यम्बकस्य वा । VI. 94. 38

It is a wonderful *astra* which makes the owner stand in terrible form before every single combatant on the other side. "I can use it or Siva can use it." Here again, he does not mention Vishnu, showing that in his own mind he was Vishnu and that there was no point in mentioning Vishnu. Such passages occur every now and then.

Now I am going to deal with Hanuman as he was appreciated by Rama. Hanuman's greatness can have no measure, no just and adequate measure, except in the judgment of Rama himself. If Rama accepted him, that is all right. So in order to find out what Rama thought of him, we must go to three or four contexts in the poem where Rama speaks his mind fully about Hanuman. In Kishkindha where Sugriva and his four ministers had taken refuge on that hill, the Risyamuka, the two brothers met Hanuman first. Hanuman went in the guise of a fair and acceptable man. He addresses the brothers and asks them who they are. In making the enquiry, Hanuman shows his command of the Sanskrit language, his command not only of its idiom but his great command of the ancient lore, and of the diplomatic vocabulary, and casts such a spell over the brothers that they were unable to resist.

There is a good rule in court circles. It is proper for a king to speak to a king, a minister to a minister. So although Rama would have replied to Hanuman who questioned them at great length, he asks his brother to do so. And in speaking to Lakshmana in the hearing of Hanuman, Rama says words which are cast in such high terms that you would wonder that in a few minutes' talk anybody could produce in the mind of such a judge as Rama such a tremendous impression. This is what Rama says to Lakshmana:

नानृग्वेदविनीतस्य नायजुर्वेदधारिणः ।
नासामवेदविदुषः शक्यमेवं प्रभाषितुम् ॥
नूनं व्याकरणं कृत्स्नमनेन बहुधा श्रुतम् ।
बहु व्याहरतानेन न किंचिदपशब्दितम् ।
न मुखे नेत्रयोर्वापि ललाटे च भ्रुवोस्तथा ।
अन्येष्वपि च गात्रेषु दोषः संविदितः क्वचित् ॥
अविस्तरमसंदिग्धमविलम्बितमद्रुतम् ।
उरःस्थं कण्ठगं वाक्यं वर्तते मध्यमे स्वरे ॥
संस्कारक्रमसंपन्नामद्रुतामविलम्बिताम् ।
उच्चारयति कल्याणीं वाचं हृदयहारिणीम् ॥
अनया चित्रया वाचा त्रिस्थानव्यञ्जनस्थया ।
कस्य नाराध्यते चित्तमुद्यतासेररेरपि ॥
एवंविधो यस्य दूतो न भवेत्पार्थिवस्य तु ।
सिध्यन्ति हि कथं तस्य कार्याणां गतयोऽनघ ॥
एवंगुणगणैर्युक्ता यस्य स्युः कार्यसाधकाः ।
तस्य सिध्यन्ति सर्वार्था दूतवाक्यप्रचोदिताः ॥ IV. 3. 28-35

"For one to speak as this person has spoken, one must know all the three Vedas and have them at command. (It is possible for a person to get up five or six sentences in correct English, but when we go beyond them, we make slips and commit treason against His Majesty's English.) Hanuman spoke at considerable length. Although he spoke much and spoke long, he has not made a single error. He seems to be a great master of elocution. All the organs that help in the art of elocution are at his perfect command. No one has been mismanaged by him in any particular. His speech wins my heart completely and delights my very soul. If a man can talk like Hanuman, he can bring down to his knees even the worst and most implacable enemy. If there is a ruler among men who wants to accomplish great things, he must have at least one minister like this person. If a man has more than one servant like Hanuman, there is nothing on earth that he cannot accomplish. All things will turn out successful." The very first impression he produces on the brothers, he maintains to the end, not merely by his marvellous skill in manipulating the Sanskrit language, but by his complete devotion to duty and by the confidence that he produced that he was quite equal to the performance of the highest and the most arduous tasks. There is no danger that he will not face, no enemy whom he will not encounter; nothing that he will not face to perform services to his master.

When the monkey expeditionists were sent out to go in the four directions, Tara, Jambavan, Nala, Nila and Hanuman were in the group also. It occurred to Rama that after all, supposing one of these did really see Sita and that person wanted to produce some evidence that he was really his emissary, what should he give? Of these enormous monkeys, to whom should he entrust it? So between Sugriva and Sri Rama it was decided that Hanuman should be chosen for this entrustment. Sugriva sends for Hanuman of all the lot and says to him, 'Hanuman, there is no part of this universe where your progress will meet with any impediment. In point of time there is no one on earth your equal. So, though we have set out this vast army in all the directions, remember that Rama and I lay on you, Hanuman in particular, a very special charge. You alone have a combination of all these qualities, and the ability to bend time and space to your purpose.' Rama too caught this confidence from Sugriva, and he gives him his own signet ring. Having given it to him, he says,

अनेन त्वां हरिश्रेष्ठ चिह्नेन जनकात्मजा ।
मत्सकाशादनुप्राप्तमनुद्विग्नानुपश्यति ॥
व्यवसायश्च ते वीर सत्त्वयुक्तश्च विक्रमः ।
सुग्रीवस्य च संदेशः सिद्धिं कथयतीव मे ॥ IV. 44. 13-14

"If you see Sita with this ring, she will cast off all misgiving, and you will be recognised as my direct messenger. I do want any other assurance, as my Sugriva has chosen you to receive this very special commission and asked me to entrust this ring to you. That is enough warrant for my doing so." That is the mark of the uttermost confidence that Rama had in Hanuman.

Then let us see them together at that supreme moment when Hanuman brings the glad news of Sita's existence in safety, and holding out in the hope of restoration to Rama on this side. The monkeys are all there and they are asked to make a report. Being asked by special naming, Hanuman turns southward before opening his lips and makes on *anjali* in that direction, for Sita is there. Now, what tenderness, what depth of homage, what wonderful recognition of his duty before ever he spoke a word! That shows his divine quality, how far above his original status he rose. Then having gone on a little further with the story, he takes the *chudamani* which Sita had given him. As soon as he saw this *chudamani* Rama burst out in tears. He gives vent to his grief, and unable to bear it, he turns round to Hanuman and asks him:

किमाह सीता वैदेही ब्रूहि सौम्य पुनः पुनः ।
पिपासुमिव तोयेन सिञ्चन्ती वाक्यवारिणा ॥
चिरं जीवति वैदेही यदि मासं धरिष्यति ।
न जीवेयं क्षणमपि विना तामसितेक्षणाम् ॥
किमाह सीता हनुमंस्तत्त्वतः कथयाद्य मे ।
एतेन खलु जीविष्ये भेषजेनातुरो यथा ॥
मधुरा मधुरालापा किमाह मम भामिनी ।
मद्विहीना वरारोहा हनूमन् कथयस्व मे ॥ V. 66. 8, 10, 14-15

"Tell me once, twice, or thrice, what were her words, for it is these words that will revive me. I am like a dead man, and those words rain drops of water that will bring me back to life. Repeat those words. Just as we throw water on the face of a man who is passing away, those words falling on my ear will revive me like water. You said that she had a month more and she wanted to draw her life out for that month in order that before that I might come and release her. If so, she is a long-lived woman. I cannot bear to live without her for so long. What did she say? Do not keep anything back. Like a sick man depending on the medicines of the physician, I depend now for my life only on the words that you give." I have read very few words in the world's literature conveying greater affection or greater grief. Then, in continuation of this same scene, Rama gives more and more praise to Hanuman. What panegyric would be too high for one who had performed this rare good office? So Rama says,

> कृतं हनुमता कार्यं सुमहद्भुवि दुष्करम् ।
> मनसापि यदन्येन न शक्यं धरणीतले ॥ VI. 1. 2

"What another man cannot even think of in his conception, that Hanuman has actually performed for me."

Then there is a famous passage consisting of three slokas, each describing a certain order of messengers or servants or agents whom a master may commission for a duty. Such agents are classified by Rama into three groups. But they are very obscure. The words chosen are not very happy, and do not bring out the meaning clearly in the full manner of Valmiki; but their purport is clear.

> यो हि भृत्यो नियुक्तः सन् भर्त्रा कर्मणि दुष्करे ।
> कुर्यात्तदनुरागेण तमाहुः पुरुषोत्तमम् ॥
> भृत्यस्तु यः परं कार्यं न कुर्यान्नृपतेः प्रियम् ।
> भृत्यो युक्तः समर्थश्च तमाहुर्मध्यमं नरम् ॥
> नियुक्तो नृपतेः कार्यं न कुर्याद्यः समाहितः ।
> भृत्यो युक्तः समर्थश्च तमाहुः पुरुषाधमम् ॥ VI. 1. 8-10

In subsequent literature this classification of servants or agents has become famous, and we must therefore read our knowledge into this passage. The first order of servants is those who, noting their master's expressed intention and also the purposes that they have in mind but have not expressed, perform not only what their master has told them expressly, but also other tasks which will help the accomplishment of the main purpose. They have a brain, they have devotion also which impels them to do all these things for the sake of their master. Those who just do what they are told and do nothing more, belong to the second class. The third class is of those who, entrusted with a sacred duty, return home and say they have not been able to do it. Naturally, Hanuman is placed in the first class and receives the greatest possible encomium. Having praised Hanuman as much as he liked, he says, "What can I do? I have no reward to bestow on you now." Remember we are talking of Rama who was a scion of the noblest princely house of the land flowing with milk and honey, a man whose hands have known how to give and give it soon. Here he was, a guest of Sugriva, unable to call a rupee his own. The great ones of the earth will never fail to give something in token of their pleasure, and if they are displeased, will never fail to make you feel it. Their pleasure is worth having, their displeasure is something to avoid. When a king finds himself unable to reward a person, you must think of his misery. Have you not read of a famous emperor of China who used to have two or three servants heavily laden with bags of gold and silver and other coins? Whenever the king saw something unusual, he would give a handsome present to that person. If anybody said something great or clever, he would give something. This is the true mark of greatness. I have known even in private life many men, whom God has blessed, who feel that their pleasure and their satisfaction must never go unacknowledged for want of means. Rama calls himself a *dina.*

> इदं तु मम दीनस्य मनो भूयः प्रकर्षति ।
> यदिहास्य प्रियाख्यातुर्न कुर्मि सदृशं प्रियम् ॥
> एष सर्वस्वभूतस्तु परिष्वङ्गो हनूमतः ।
> मया कालमिमं प्राप्य दत्तश्चास्तु महात्मनः ॥ VI. 1. 13-14

"I cannot give a suitable reward to you who have given me this heavenly message. But I can give myself; here is my body; I will embrace you tight; I will hug you." What more could Hanuman want? Hanuman had attained his salvation at that moment. There is one other passage in the Ramayana where such a high value must be placed on embrace. I take you back to the Aranyakanda, where Rama returned victorious over Khara, Dushana and the fourteen thousand people. He had put away Sita and Lakshmana in a cave. When they came out, Rama went into the hermitage. Sita was proud of her lord and could not contain her joy. She had asked him why he should quarrel with these Rakshasas. She remembers all that and the poet says,

तं दृष्ट्वा शत्रुहन्तारं महर्षीणां सुखावहम् ।
बभूव हृष्टा वैदेही भर्तारं परिषस्वजे ॥ III. 30. 39-40

In our well bred houses where conduct and manners are regulated according to the highest patterns prescribed, it is a common rule for the husband to embrace his wife first. Very rarely I think does a well-bred wife go and embrace even her husband. On this occasion Sita forgot this good rule and as soon as she met her husband, she went and voluntarily hugged him, the rarest joy that a husband can have.

When Ravana has been killed and Vibhishana crowned in his place, Rama deputes Hanuman to carry the good news to Sita. I recall it for this purpose. When Hanuman mentions the good news to her, the lady who heard the good news wanted to reward the messenger. "I have no reward," says she, "adequate on this occasion to give to you who have brought me this great message. I cannot think of a reward which I could give you and feel satisfied that I have rewarded you adequately. If I had gold in abundance and precious stones, if I had all the kingdoms of the three worlds to give, they would not make an adequate reward for the message you have brought me." So says Sita to Hanuman. She was a lady born and used to royal luxury and therefore accustomed to mark her pleasure with something tangible.

Now I come to the last passage, the coronation and the final farewell. Amongst the guests who have come to witness the coronation are the Vanara hosts, and amongst the Rakshasas, Vibhishaṇa and his four ministers only. At the end of the festivities which extended perhaps to several months, and according to some, to one year, Rama gives leave to the guests to depart. We are concerned now with Hanuman only. In the Ramayana there are two accounts, one at the end of the Yuddha Kanda, and the other in the appropriate portion of the Uttara Kanda. They do not exactly tally, but they agree as to essentials. To Hanuman Rama gave nothing. He gave to Sita a beautiful garland of pearls studded with high class jewels which shone like the moon. She did not appropriate it to herself, but after wearing it for a second, she took it out, and looking round amongst the monkeys, made as if she would give it to Hanuman. She saw Rama again and again and he reading her heart at once, said that she might give it to him with whom she was thoroughly pleased.

प्रदेहि सुभगे हारं यस्य तुष्टासि भामिनि।
तेजो धृतिर्यशो दाक्ष्यं सामर्थ्यं विनयो नयः॥
पौरुषं विक्रमो बुद्धिर्यस्मिन्नेतानि नित्यदा॥ VI. 131. 81-82

"Give it to him in whom these qualities shine in combination." There was only one person who answered to that flowing description, and that was Hanuman. In the Uttara Kanda this is described in greater detail, and Hanuman gets a good deal more than the garland. We all know what else he got. When others have been given leave, Hanuman stands up before Rama and says to him,

स्नेहो मे परमो राजंस्त्वयि तिष्ठतु नित्यदा।
भक्तिश्च नियता वीर भावो नान्यत्र गच्छतु॥
यावद्रामकथा वीर चरिष्यति महीतले।
तावच्छरीरे वत्स्यन्ति प्राणा मम न संशयः॥ VII. 40. 15-16

"Please give me this blessing, that my affection for you should never diminish. Do not allow me to think of anything else, or to divide my affection between you and any other person. I want to live so long as your great name is preserved amongst the sons of men. Let me be for ever and for ever your devotee." Then Rama says to him, "Let it be as you wish. As long as my story is told amongst men, so long shall your *kirti* form part of it. And may your life last also." Then follows a remarkable passage.

एकैकस्योपकारस्य प्राणान् दास्यामि ते कपे।
शेषस्येहोपकाराणां भवाम ऋणिनो वयम्॥ VII. 40. 22

"Hanuman, you have done me numerous services, all of the order of the first eminence. For any one of them, all my life is an adequate return. If my life is pledged in return for one of your numerous services, I shall be in your debt in respect of the others, and I shall be indebted to you in a manner that I can never think of repaying."

मय्येव जीर्णतां यातु यत्त्वयोपकृतं हरे ।

नरः प्रत्युपकारार्थी विपत्तिमभिकांक्षति ॥ VII. 40. 23*

It is not characteristic of the highest person to expect a return, for we do good deeds to others when they are in trouble. When we save others' lives, it is then that the greatest good deeds are performed to another. You must be in trouble to receive such a kindness at the hands of your friends. Therefore, if that friend expects a return of equal value, it means that he must get into trouble. Therefore, Hanuman, do not expect a return for any of the things that you have done for me. I was in trouble and had to fight a tremendous battle. You helped me to mighty good purpose. If you did those things for me and I am to return those things to you, it means some harm must occur to you from which I might rescue you. Therefore it is best that your good deeds rest warm in my bosom. Or the passage may mean also "I do not want to do anything in return for your great favours. A man who wants to do something good is also a प्रत्युपकारार्थी."

* The reading adopted for this famous sloka is that given in Appayya Dikshita's "KUVALAYANANDA," 70, Anujnaprakarana. Govindaraja and the Bombay & M.L.J. Editions read:

मदङ्गे जीर्णतां यातु यत्त्वयोपकृतं कपे ।

नरः प्रत्युपकाराणामापत्स्वायाति पात्रताम् ॥

TWENTYFIRST LECTURE*

Ladies and Gentlemen,

We have already seen that with a view to easy and safe exploration of the city, Hanuman reduced himself to the size of a cat. After much search in the Rakshasa king's palace, he entered the harem expecting to see Sita there. In the harem he saw a good deal that he would rather not have seen. Many of Ravana's women were there in all grades and degrees of dishabille, and with marks upon them which could not be mistaken of revelry and merriment. Amongst these his eye fell by chance on Mandodari, the handsomest of Lanka's queens and most beloved of the king. Seeing her and struck with her beauty and charm, our explorer thought for a moment that it might be Sita herself, and in the joy of discovery, the poet humorously represents him as having done what monkeys might be expected to do when they are overjoyed. This is a famous verse.

आस्फोटयामास चचुम्ब पुच्छं ननन्द चिक्रीड जगौ जगाम ।
स्तम्भानरोहन्निपपात भूमौ निदर्शयन् स्वां प्रकृतिं कपीनाम् ॥

V. 10. 54

He showed clearly to what race he belonged. You will forgive me for occasionally referring to this point that although the poet shows Hanuman to have risen very high in quality of every kind, he does not allow us to forget at any stage the species to which he belonged by nature. "He struck on the ground his tail, kissed his own tail, rejoiced, jumped about, sang, ran about, went up the pillars and fell down, thus showing in many ways that he belonged to the monkey race." But as if to show that he was not a mere monkey, but a being who had plumbed the depths of all the Sastras and Vedas and knew what high moral codes were, we next hear of the great scruples that Hanuman felt in seeing these strange ladies in undress more or less. He said to himself, "What am I to do? Is this right of me?"

---

* 30-8-'44.

निरीक्षमाणश्च तदा ताः स्त्रियः स महाकपिः ।
जगाम महतीं चिन्तां धर्मसाध्वसशङ्कितः ॥
परदारावरोधस्य प्रसुप्तस्य निरीक्षणम् ।
इदं खलु ममात्यर्थं धर्मलोपं करिष्यति ॥
न हि मे परदाराणां दृष्टिर्विषयवर्तिनी ।
अयं चात्र मया दृष्टः परदारपरिग्रहः ॥ V. 11. 38-40

He was transgressing the moral code in feasting his eyes upon these ladies. "My fate has led me to this place where I have to see the women of another person lying about and sleeping, the sight inevitably causing me to think unworthy thoughts. I have not done this before, but I am obliged now to do this improper thing." Then however, another reflection followed.

कामं दृष्टा मया सर्वा विश्वस्ता रावणस्त्रियः ।
न हि मे मनसः किञ्चिद्वैकृत्यमुपपद्यते ॥
मनो हि हेतुः सर्वेषामिन्द्रियाणां प्रवर्तने ।
शुभाशुभास्ववस्थासु तच्च मे सुव्यवस्थितम् ॥
नान्यत्र च मया शक्या वैदेही परिमार्गितुम् ।
स्त्रियो हि स्त्रीषु दृश्यन्ते सर्वथा परिमार्गणे ॥
यस्य सत्त्वस्य या योनिस्तस्यां तत्परिमृग्यते ।
न शक्या प्रमदा नष्टा मृगीषु परिमार्गितुम् ॥
तदिदं मार्गितं तावच्छुद्धेन मनसा मया ।
रावणान्तःपुरं सर्वं दृश्यते न च जानकी ॥
किं नु मां वानराः सर्वे गतं वक्ष्यन्ति संगताः ।
गत्वा तत्र त्वया वीर किं कृतं तद्वदस्व नः ॥
अदृष्ट्वा किं प्रवक्ष्यामि तामहं जनकात्मजाम् ।
ध्रुवं प्रायमुपेष्यन्ति कालस्य व्यतिवर्तने ॥ V. 11. 42-46; 12. 7-8

"What harm is there? Yes, I have seen these women of Ravana, but I can say conscientiously that my mind is not in any way affected. The senses project themselves and fasten upon particular objects only if the *manas* directs them so to do. That *manas*, which directs the senses in right ways and in wrong ways, is under my full control. What am I to do? I have come here to look for Sita. The natural thought is that she might be found amongst these women. You can look for a woman only amongst women. Am I to go and look for Sita amongst deer? I have with a clear mind and a pure heart looked all round this place, but my quest has not been fulfilled. What am I to do? If I get back, all the monkeys will gather round me and will all together put me this question: tell us what you have done there. Not having found Sita, what shall be my answer? Since the time is up, I shall enter *prayopavesa* and so finish my career." So he thought for a minute. Then again another thought struck him and he went about seeing again and leaving no nook, no corner, unexamined. He would not leave a space even of four inches unexamined. Sita could certainly not be hidden in such a space. There was no spot however small, even though it be only four inches, which Hanuman did not examine. So instead of giving way to despair, another thought struck him.

अनिर्वेदः श्रियो मूलमनिर्वेदः परं सुखम् ।
अनिर्वेदो हि सततं सर्वार्थेषु प्रवर्तकः ॥
करोति सफलं जन्तोः कर्म यत्तत्करोति सः ।
तस्मादनिर्वेदकरं यत्नं चेष्टेऽहमुत्तमम् ॥ V. 12. 10-11

"I ought not to give way to despair. I must keep up my hopes still. Where I have not looked about still, I will go now and see. Whatever a being does, he must not abandon hope of success." So at this point Hanuman indulges in a long-drawn-out reflection to which I shall return in a moment. There is a long sarga, the thirteenth, filled with his soliloquy which I shall present to you in English at the end of this talk. Then Hanuman enters the asoka wood, and there, after a while he discovers Sita, and makes her out to be Sita by the marks that Sri Rama had already described fully to him. Sita's beauty and charm had been so fully detailed to Hanuman that he could not be mistaken about it. Having discovered her, he marvels at her beauty, at her attraction and at the condition of sorrow in which she is at the moment. Then the poet tells us what this wonderful being, who has seen all the worlds, thinks at the moment when he saw Sita herself, the world's jewel for loveliness, and for chastity and for wisdom.

प्रणष्टापि सती यस्य मनसो न प्रणश्यति ॥
इयं सा यत्कृते रामश्चतुर्भिः परितप्यते ।
कारुण्येनानृशंस्येन शोकेन मदनेन च ॥

स्त्री प्रणष्टेति कारुण्यादाश्रितेत्यानृशंस्यतः ।
पत्नी नष्टेति शोकेन प्रियेति मदनेन च ॥ V. 15. 48-50

"Here is the Sita whom Rama has lost, but who is not lost to his mind and to his heart. She is always there, she on whose behalf Rama suffers in four different ways." Sri Rama has four feelings which depress him on her account. The poet proceeds to mention them. It is rather unusual. How are these four to be connected with Rama's mind? A woman has been lost. She was his dependant, and trusted him and was under his especial protection. Then she was his wife, and she was his lover. So Rama was stricken with remorse. His feeling was also one of deep sorrow, and it changed into harrowing anguish. So Hanuman says that Rama was stricken by a feeling compounded of these four shades of grief. Having seen Sita, Hanuman naturally thinks of Rama at the time, what he must be feeling now, how he described her and so on. Here comes a very famous sloka.

दुष्करं कृतवान् रामो हीनो यदनया प्रभुः ।
धारयत्यात्मनो देहं न शोकेनावसीदति ॥ V. 15. 53

It is a beautiful verse. "This Rama is a hard-hearted man. He does a thing which other people would find very hard to do. Being separated from this lady, he still lives. He is not dead yet. Must be a hard life his." Then follows a train of tender thoughts.

तुल्यशीलवयोवृत्तां तुल्याभिजनलक्षणाम् ।
राघवोऽर्हति वैदेहीं तं चेयमसितेक्षणा ॥
यदि रामः समुद्रान्तां मेदिनीं परिवर्तयेत् ।
अस्याः कृते जगच्चापि युक्तमित्येव मे मतिः ॥
राज्यं वा त्रिषु लोकेषु सीता वा जनकात्मजा ।
त्रैलोक्यराज्यं सकलं सीताया नाप्नुयात्कलाम् ॥ V. 16. 5, 13-14

"Rama and Sita are well mated," says the monkey who is a confirmed bachelor. "Sita and he are alike. The family is also the same. They deserve each other. Having lost this woman, this prize, this jewel of jewels, if Rama should go and dry all the ocean and destroy the earth, I should not think he was doing anything excessive or extravagant. She is such a prize that anything may be destroyed if she is to be recovered by that means. Put Sita in one scale, and the lordship of the three worlds will not weigh even a fraction of Sita."

Then Hanuman observes Ravana coming there. Several sargas follow in which Hanuman is a mere spectator. I shall pass over them merely saying how he must have suffered the most insufferable anguish when he saw all this tragic scene happening below him. Finally, when all had cleared away and the tired Rakshasis seemed to have gone to sleep, Hanuman resolves to say a word, if possible, to Sita. Then he makes up his mind that he ought to speak in the Kosala dialect. Otherwise she may think it is Ravana in disguise. He will therefore talk to her in her own dialect so that she may not mistake him. Then with a rare wisdom and insight it occurs to him that he ought not suddenly to appear before her. It would be well to catch her ear first. He made up his mind that the best way was to speak a few words of her husband and his family, because to her Rama is everything, all in all, life, light and everything. It is his account, his praise that would sound sweet in her ear. So then he speaks about Sri Rama, and finding that she is still suspicious by the way she looked about, he comes down from the tree and then ventures to ask her. He found out that it was Sita but not liking to say that at once, he questions her in a longish sort of way.

रोदनादतिनिःश्वासाद्भूमिसंस्पर्शनादपि ॥
न त्वां देवीमहं मन्ये राज्ञः संज्ञावधारणात् । V. 33. 10-11

"I do not think you can be a divine creature, for I see you weep, breathe heavily; also that your feet touch the ground. I also think that you might be Sita herself because I hear you say, Rama, Rama. Certainly I must be right in my guess." Then she reveals her identity and at the end says,

द्वौ मासौ तेन मे कालो जीवितानुग्रहः कृतः ॥
ऊर्ध्वं द्वाभ्यां तु मासाभ्यां ततस्त्यक्ष्यामि जीवितम् । V. 33. 31-32

"That awful being has given me two months' respite. If during these two months I be not rescued, then the only alternative is for me to take my life." Then Sita says, slowly making up her mind that this is Hanuman, "I have heard of the famous proverb which has come down to us from all time.

कल्याणी बत गाथेयं लौकिकी प्रतिभाति मे।
एति जीवन्तमानन्दो नरं वर्षशतादपि॥ V. 34. 6

"Provided only life is granted to us, we need not at any time give up hope. After a time at least, prosperity must return to everybody. I thought I was not going to live, but now you come here, sent by Sri Rama."

Passing over some passages, we come to the awful scene where Sita sinks within herself in despair and says, "what is going to happen to me?" She is not confident that although Hanuman has discovered her, Rama could be brought to Lanka with his monkey army, and a battle could be fought on the soil of Ceylon and she be taken back. "Tell me, Hanuman," she says, "all about Sri Rama and his brother. What are they doing? Why do they not come? Am I anything to them? They ought to have come by this time and taken me away. I think I shall have to die here." Then to comfort herself, she puts a series of questions to Hanuman, all in the style in which in the Ayodhya kanda Rama puts questions about the kingdom to Bharata in that famous कच्चित्सर्ग, कच्चित् repeated seventy-three times in seventy-six slokas. Sita addresses to Hanuman twenty-two questions about her husband and Lakshmana and others. Then she says,

न चास्य माता न पिता च नान्यः स्नेहाद्विशिष्टोऽस्ति मया समो वा।
तावत्त्वहं दूत जिजीविषेयं यावत्प्रवृत्तिं शृणुयां प्रियस्य॥
इतीव देवी वचनं महार्थं तं वानरेन्द्रं मधुरार्थमुक्त्वा।
श्रोतुं पुनस्तस्य वचोऽभिरामं रामार्थयुक्तं विरराम रामा॥
V. 36. 30-31

"My lord and husband Rama has none on earth so dear as myself. A dearer person there cannot be, not his mother, not his father, not his brothers, no one. Nor is there one who is of the same degree. I shall live only so long as I hear about him and his movements." The poet cleverly uses the word "Rama" four times. Then Hanuman replies in tender slokas. Of course you must remember that Hanuman makes this gesture always when he addresses Rama or Lakshmana शिरस्यञ्जलिमाधाय. Beautiful verses these in which he describes exactly Rama's feelings towards Sita.

तवादर्शनजेनार्ये शोकेन स परिप्लुतः ।
न शर्म लभते रामः सिंहार्दित इव द्विपः ॥
मलयेन च विन्ध्येन मेरुणा मन्दरेण च ।
दर्दुरेण च ते देवि शपे मूलफलेन च ॥
यथा सुनयनं वल्गु बिम्बोष्ठं चारुकुण्डलम् ।
मुखं द्रक्ष्यसि रामस्य पूर्णचन्द्रमिवोदितम् ॥
क्षिप्रं द्रक्ष्यसि वैदेहि राम प्रस्रवणे गिरौ ।
शतक्रतुमिवासीनं नाकपृष्ठस्य मूर्धनि ॥
न मांसं राघवो भुङ्क्ते न चापि मधु सेवते ।
वन्यं सुविहितं नित्यं भक्तमश्नाति पञ्चमम् ॥
नैव दंशान्न मशकान्न कीटान्न सरीसृपान् ।
राघवोऽपनयेद्गात्रात् त्वद्गतेनान्तरात्मना ॥
नित्यं ध्यानपरो रामो नित्यं शोकपरायणः ।
नान्यच्चिन्तयते किंचित्स तु कामवशं गतः ॥
अनिद्रः सततं रामः सुप्तोऽपि च नरोत्तमः ।
सीतेति मधुरां वाणीं व्याहरन् प्रतिबुध्यते ॥
दृष्ट्वा फलं वा पुष्पं वा यद्वान्यत्सुमनोहरम् ।
बहुशो हा प्रियेत्येवं श्वसंस्त्वामभिभाषते ॥
स देवि नित्यं परितप्यमानस्त्वामेव सीतेत्यभिभाषमाणः ।
धृतव्रतो राजसुतो महात्मा तवैव लाभाय कृतप्रयत्नः ॥
सा रामसंकीर्तनवीतशोका रामस्य शोकेन समानशोका ।
शरन्मुखे साम्बुदशेषचन्द्रा निशेव वैदेहसुता बभूव ॥ V. 36. 37-47

"What an elephant would feel like when harassed, pursued, wounded, hurt, threatened by an angry lion, so feels Rama, the lion in this case being the grief caused by not seeing you." Each person generally makes an oath on the object dearest to him. In the Ayodhya kanda, Kaikeyi swears by Bharata, Dasaratha by Rama, but Hanuman swears by all the hills, the fruits and the herbs he has tasted. "You shall meet your husband. Even as Indra is seen mounted on the great white elephant, so will you see Rama one day very soon. He will be on my back as Indra on the back of the white elephant.* Rama has given up all flesh." In the whole of this poem, there is no support for the popular story that Rama and Sita and Lakshmana were vegetarians. On the other hand, there is plenty of evidence here and there that they did eat meat. That is why Hanuman says, Rama denies himself the eating of meat. "He does not drink honey. What can be obtained on the trees and down below he eats once towards nightfall. His mind is always centred on you, and he cannot think of anything else. He is so lost in your memory that he forgets everything about him. Insects may come and bite him, mosquitoes may bite. No worm is disturbed, not even the long slimy serpent; if these crawl over his body, he does not mind, does not whisk them away, does not know that they are there bothering him, being lost in thoughts of you. Always dwelling upon your memory, he is lost only in thoughts of you and is immersed in grief and has no time for thinking of anything else. Usually he does not sleep at all, but if he does close his eyes, suddenly he wakes up saying, "Sita, Sita". If ever he sees an object dear to the other sex, he thinks only of you, mentions your name and speaks to you as if you were there. He is always making what efforts he can to recover you." The poet here gives a beautiful but very natural simile. Having heard so much about her husband, Sita was filled with comfort in her heart that after all Rama was still thinking of her and sorrowing for her and making efforts to get her back. The poet then compares her to the moon in a cloud at the commencement of *sarad*.

Now I want to read to you an English rendering of Hanuman's biggest soliloquy of all. The poet in Sundarakanda excels himself when he depicts Hanuman following a train of thought. In order to appreciate it fully, we must enter Hanuman's mind. He is possessed, as it were, by it and works it out logically, before he jumps on to another bit of thought. It is most interesting, the way the poet works out the thoughts of Hanuman. I have chosen two different pieces. Here is the thirteenth sarga I referred to.

"Leaving the car and moving along the rampart, Hanuman spoke thus to himself:— 'My efforts have been a complete

*This follows the Tilaka reading नागपुङ्गस्य (sl. 40) and commentary.

failure. I have searched every likely place. Pools, tanks and reservoirs, rivers, canals and waterways, forts, fastnesses and citadels, nothing have I omitted. Surely it was this town Sampati mentioned as the place of Sita's confinement. Can it be that she has yielded herself in despair to Ravana, she born of no mortal womb, brought up by a knower of Brahman, and married into the illustrious Ikshvaku family? Perhaps the Rakshasa, in dread of the arrows of the pursuing husband, let her drop to the ground. May be, looking at the rolling waters below, she was killed by sheer fright. Perchance she could not endure the violence of the flight and the cruel grip of Ravana's arms. Is it likely she just slipped into the deep ocean, as the car* jolted and jerked suddenly? Who knows? the cannibal demon might have eaten her up angrily as she resisted his attempts to violate her? If not he, the women of his harem might in a mad fit of jealousy have made a meal of her. Ah, no! she passed away to the other world with the ravishing vision floating in her mind's eye of Sri Rama, lustrous like the *purnima* moon, and captivating like the red lotus. And as she vanished from the earth, she called in loud and piteous cries on the names of Rama, Lakshmana and Ayodhya. Why, there is a chance too she is alive, kept in a small prison like a parrot in a cage crying Rama, Rama. What a dire fate for the peerless lady, daughter of Janaka and wife of Rama! Must she fall into the hands of a Rakshasa whom nothing can restrain? What shall be my answer to the husband's anxious question? that she is lost? that she is hidden? that she is dead? I do not know and cannot say. Should I tell him or should I not? Either way it does not look proper. Where lies my course? If I go back to Kishkindha and confess my failure, the fruitlessness of my great leap and visit to Lanka, what will Sugriva think of me? and the unhappy brothers? and the assembled and expectant monkeys? As soon as Rama hears the word of negation, he will die of the shock, he cannot live an instant after the news. The sensitive and loving Lakshmana will die too. When Bharata learns what has happened to his two brothers, he will die immediately. Seeing Bharata gone, Satrughna will die at once. Nor will their mothers survive,—Kausalya, Sumitra, Kaikeyi. My royal master Sugriva, remembering what Rama

* Publishers' Note: There is no reference to a 'car' in the text, Sundara, 13. 10-11.

did for him and what he should do to Rama in return, cannot bear the calamity and will die. His darling Ruma, sore-stricken, desolate, unable to bear the grief of sudden widowhood, will die. Tara, the hapless queen, hardly recovered from lamentation for Vali, will surely die. Poor orphaned Angada will die also, how can he survive father, mother and uncle? The monkeys, whom Sugriva has protected with affection, honour and bountiful gifts, will realise their helplessness without him, violently beat their heads with palms and fists and so meet their death. No more will they foregather for merriment or jolly festivity on hills or in wooded dales or in caves or in other recesses. Along with wives and children and under the guidance of ministers, they will die in tens and hundreds of thousands by falling from hill tops on rugged rocks, drinking poison, hanging from high places, throwing themselves into the blazing fire, fasting unto the end, or using sharp weapons on their bodies. My return home will be attended with an endless chain of deaths, the destruction of the royal family of Ayodhya and of the entire race of vanaras. Kishkindha I may not re-enter, Sugriva I may not behold again, not having discovered Sita. If I stay away here, it is just possible that the heroic brothers will sustain themselves with hope, and likewise my brethren the monkeys who have sunny dispositions by nature. Frustrated in my high mission, I had best turn anchorite, living under a tree and subsisting on what may happen to fall on the palm or into the mouth. Or I shall seek a well-wooded spot on the seashore, erect a funeral pyre and burn myself on it. An alternative plan would be to sit stiff and allow birds and beasts to make a meal of my body. But why do I make my own devices? Have not the sages prescribed that a person in my extremity shall drown himself in deep water?

'Alas! how full of promise this night was when it began! I fondly hoped a handsome garland of fame was weaving for me. But with no sight of Sita, it lengthens tediously into disappointment and misery.

'Wretched fool, what a dismal train of thought I have followed! To give way to despair is to incur a series of mishaps. One must exist if one is to prosper. I will hold on to life. That way success is certain.

'Now, where is my courage gone? And where my prowess? I will destroy this proud Ravana. If Sita has been killed, she shall be avenged. Suppose, on the other hand, I take him captive and carry him across the sea to hand him over to Rama, that will be like delivering a human oblation to god Agni.

'But wait. Why do I give way to these unprofitable speculations and forebodings? I ought to look for Sita yet. The quest must be continued till it succeeds. Here is another fanciful idea coming into my distracted head. If, when we heard Sampati's assurance of Sita being here, we had gone back to Kishkindha and brought Rama hither, what then? He might have done great deeds of valour. But if Sita was not found, his anger would have been an unquenchable fire and the monkey hosts would all have been burnt in it. The only thing I can do is to remain here and spend my days in penance and austerities. Then at least the poor monkey-race will not perish on my account.

'Look! Here is an asoka-grove with fine big trees. I have not searched this place, let me do so now. Yes, the thought nerves me to a fresh effort. I will make salutation to the celestials, the Vasus, the Rudras, the Adityas, the Asvins, and the Maruts, and then set out on this adventure. If any demons come in the way, I will make an end of them. Then I hope to discover the wife of Rama and deliver her to him as a god might deliver to an ascetic the goal of his austerities. Let me turn the thought over for a minute. That's it! Up now and on! Rama and Lakshmana, I make obeisance to you. The same to you, Sita of divine origin. And to you, not of this gross earth, to Rudra, Indra, Yama, Vayu, Chandra, Agni and the Maruts, to you all my prostrations again and again. Sugriva, master, I do not forget you, give me your blessing. By the favour of all these great ones, I now enter this well-guarded grove. Vayu, my father, moves gently here. For Rama's sake and to escape observation by Ravana, I am shrunken to a small size. Rama has described Sita so well to me. I could infallibly recognize her, if I saw her. Her face would be like the full-orbed moon, perfect in charm, with nose turned up a bit, teeth white as milk, eyes resembling lotus-petals, all made into a glory by a benign smile. Shall I be so blest as to behold it? That low, cruel, villainous creature of the night, putting on a deceitful garb, has brought her away by force and by craft and hidden her here. Are my eyes destined ever to fall on her radiant form?'

Another essay in the art of catching anxious misgivings and giving them body and form in verse of abiding merit occurs later on in this kanda.

Hanuman marvels at his own handiwork in destroying the city of the Rakshasas by the very fire which they meant for his destruction. Having burnt the entire city, he went to dip his tail into the sea.

Having set fire to Lanka, Hanuman has perforce to think of the consequences. He did not do it at first, being a thoughtless monkey.

तत्र देवाः सगन्धर्वाः सिद्धाश्च परमर्षयः ।
दृष्ट्वा लङ्कां प्रदग्धां तां विस्मयं परमं गताः ॥ V. 54. 50

The poet does not say they rejoiced. It would be unworthy of the Devas if looking on destruction they actually rejoiced. Hanuman began to think.

तस्याभूत् सुहांस्त्रासः कुत्सा चात्मन्यजायत ।
लङ्कां प्रदहता कर्म किंस्वित्कृतमिदं मया ॥ V. 55. 3

"A fear seized Hanuman's heart as he looked at the ruin he had wrought, a feeling of vexation with himself. If a man fills his heart with anger, passion, hatred, then strange things happen to him. He speaks strange things, thinks strange things. The great ones of the earth, if their minds or hearts are invaded by anger and threaten to fall under, pull themselves together, draw on their philosophy, and they conquer it. That is what I should have done. When a man is angry, there is no wrong he will not do. If a man is a slave of his anger, he will murder his parents and his preceptor. Good people, innocent men, he will abuse. An angry man does not distinguish between what ought to be, and what ought not to be, said. To an angry man no action is taboo, no word is taboo. Nothing that he will not do, nothing that he will not utter. A real man is he who when he finds his anger uproused, is able to put it down by summoning all his patience, just as a serpent would put away the slough from his body. He alone ought to be called a man." Then the train of thought proceeds to some length. I have translated this portion also, V. 55. 8-36. "A curse alight on me, foolish, thoughtless and sinful! If the whole of Lanka be burnt, Sita is burnt with it. My master's cause is ruined. Sita's safety is the one aim and purpose of all this enterprise; yet I have failed to protect her when Lanka was burning. How simple, how easy it was to start the fire! But in my transport of anger I have cut off our very root. No doubt Sita has been consumed in the fire, not a spot in all the town has escaped, it is one expanse of ashes. If through my recklessness, the great calamity has occurred, it is best for me too to perish here. Which mode of suicide shall I adopt? Shall I throw myself into this conflagration? Shall I become the prey of the fiery mare of the ocean, the *badava*? Or shall I fall into deep water and give my body as food for the hungry creatures there? How dare I face the monkeys, my brethren, or those two heroes after blasting the hope of their lives? Giving a free rein to my passion, I have caused my monkeyhood to stink in the world's nostrils. Cursed be the guna, the quality known as *rajas*, under the influence of which I omitted to save the noble lady, though I could have easily done so. Hearing of her death, the brothers will drop down dead. Sugriva will follow with his relatives. The news will kill Bharata. How can the good Satrughna survive? When the house of Ikshvaku has thus come to a tragic end, the entire world of human beings will be cast into grief without abatement or relief. And of all these endless miseries I shall be the originating cause,—I, who am accursed, not trained in the straight pursuit of dharma, and unequal to the high duty of curbing the demon of anger."

While these unhappy reflections vexed the mind of Hanuman, the outward omens were favourable. In fact they had been so, though he did not realise it. Now his thoughts assumed a fresh colour.

"No, no, it cannot be so bad as all that. That virtuous lady is well shielded by her own purity. She is meant for prosperity and will not die. Fire cannot extinguish fire. The wife of a man of immeasurable greatness, guarded besides by the rectitude of her own conduct,—how will fire dare to hurt her? Now I think of it, fire did no harm to me. The elemental god forgot his office; it surely was because of Rama's peerless quality and Sita's unsullied chastity. She is the divinity of the three brothers, Bharata, Lakshmana and Satrughna, and the heart's own darling of Rama. Harm cannot come near her. If fire, which consumes everything, spared my tail because I am in her service, how can he so much as touch her? Ah! how did I forget this? The crest of Mainaka rose above the waves of the ocean and offered me hospitality, just because my mission was for the benefit of Rama the Supreme. His beloved and devoted wife, if she would but care to use the power of her purity and of her truth, might burn the divine Agni himself; he surely must be impotent before her. Hark! here are the celestial voices reassuring me. 'This city of the Rakshasas is all consumed to ashes, with its turrets and ramparts and stupendous gates. Janaki alone is unscathed amid this wide ruin. We marvel, we rejoice, we give thanks to the Almighty!' Hanuman could not contain his joy.

ततः कपिः प्राप्तमनोरथार्थस्तामक्षतां राजसुतां विदित्वा ।
प्रत्यक्षतस्तां पुनरेव दृष्ट्वा प्रतिप्रयाणाय मतिं चकार ॥ V. 55. 36

"With a heart elated by his success and being certain that the queenly lady had come to no harm, Hanuman resolved that he should once more feast his eyes with a sight of her, and then undertake the return journey."

Soon he was to know that he owed his own safety in part at least to the prayer that Sita had earnestly addressed to Agni. It is in four slokas all ending शीतो भव हनूमतः. (V. 53. 28-32).*

* See Lect. XXVII below.

TWENTYSECOND LECTURE*

RAVANA

Sisters and brothers,

We have come to the second great character in the poem. Ravana stands contrasted with the hero. He is well matched. Greatness and goodness are different things. They do not always co-exist. In some characters they mix in good proportion. They are the salt of the earth. By example, by achievement, and by influence on history, these rare men who combine greatness and goodness are our saviours and prophets. But they are a few. Ravana belonged to the class in whom greatness does not co-exist with goodness. But greatness has its own attraction. In fact it has a fascination for the mind of humanity which is in many ways a danger. Those who read lurid novels and accounts of crime in America on a colossal scale will have experienced the thrill that accompanies the perusal of a great criminal's doings. Even crime, if performed on a grand scale, attracts the human mind and holds it in thrall. In fact, this is considered one of the great evils of the spread of the cinema. Novels and stories of misdeeds that lead to terrific consequences, murders, burglaries, abductions, kidnappings done on a great scale with ingenuity and careful planning beforehand so as to baffle the police and leave them always in the lurch, stories of these great crimes exercise upon our minds and imagination what is called fascination. However much our conscience may disapprove, the eye refuses to close itself to the spectacle. The mind is held down, and even pure-minded people do not close these books of lurid crime, while they go on cursing the authors. Well, Ravana was a criminal of this abnormal type. But when we say criminal, we do not deny to him qualities of a rare kind which contribute to make for greatness. No man can be a criminal without having qualities of mind and brain of an extraordinary type. We shall study Ravana's character therefore with great interest, although morally speaking it is reprehensible, and then perhaps we shall discover, wherein what we specifically distinguish as his greatness lay. One more prefatory remark.

*6-9-'44.

Ravana and Rama constitute a contrast of a very sharp kind. Rama was a rare type of greatness and goodness combined. Ravana had greatness without goodness. But that is not all. Ravana had reached the peak of his power before Rama came into existence at all. In fact it was after many tens of thousands of years of his career that the gods and sages, unable to bear the violence of his crimes, called upon Vishnu to rescue them from him. It was then that the incarnation took place, the fourfold incarnation, so that you see how Rama was a mere baby when compared with Ravana in point of age. By the most generous reckoning for which the poet gives data, Rama must have been between thirty-nine and forty, when the great battle between him and Ravana took place in Lanka. Ravana had by that time performed his penances and wrung from the gratified deities enormous powers which he used for mischief and made himself such an abhorred criminal that he had to be hunted down. Moreover, another peculiar thing worth noticing is that in our poem, Ravana plays a part only for twelve months. Within that period a great deal of his activity is comprised, and the story hurries forward from crime to crime until the culmination is reached. If Rama was a child in comparison with Ravana, what should Sita have been? She was a tiny tot, nothing more. Yet, it was Ravana's sentiment towards her which constitutes the substance of the poem and makes the whole of the tragedy. A man over fifteen or twenty thousand years of age falls in love with a little girl of about twenty or twenty-five and then the plot begins. What an extraordinary thing! Few people have perhaps thought of the oddity of the crime, and yet we find that when Rama and Sita deal with Ravana, they deal with him almost on an equal footing as though they were people of the same age and of the same calibre. Yes, it is a curious thing. It was perhaps inevitable for the plot that Ravana's misdeeds and cruelties should have reached their climax before his enemy was due to come into existence. But it certainly is worth noticing that the plot turns upon a love which an old man, or if you like, a mature man, conceived for a little girl.

Now we shall see on what grand scale Ravana's character is drawn by the poet. First, I shall deal with the long and arduous penance which Ravana performed to obtain his great powers, which do not seem to have been confined to human beings or to divine Rishis, but seem to have extended to the Devas and subdued nature herself. Here is a reference which might be called funny made by Jatayu when he tried to strike a blow for Sita. Jatayu says to Ravana, "I am an old man, but you are still a youth. (That is strange, but we must remember that Jatayu says that he was sixty thousand years old at the time. If Ravana was only twenty thousand years old, Jatayu might well call him a young man in comparison.)

षष्टिर्वर्षसहस्राणि मम जातस्य रावण ।
पितृपैतामहं राज्यं यथावदनुतिष्ठतः ॥
वृद्धोऽहं त्वं युवा धन्वी सशरः कवची रथी ।
तथाप्यादाय वैदेहीं कुशली न गमिष्यसि ॥
न शक्तस्त्वं बलाद्धर्तुं वैदेहीं मम पश्यतः । III. 50. 20-22

"I have been reigning over this world of birds for the last sixty thousand years, and the kingdom has come to me through generations. I am old. No doubt you have age; the strength of youth is in your favour. You can use the bow and arrow. You are seated in a grand car. I am without these advantages. Nevertheless, I won't let you go with impunity, carrying away Sita. So long as I am alive and look on, this crime shall not be perpetrated without due punishment."

Now, a word about Ravana's penances. It was out of the common, even for these mythical stories. He was born with ten heads, and it would appear that at the end of every thousandth year of penance he sacrificed into the holy fire one of his heads. In this way he sacrificed nine, when nine thousand years were gone. When the ten thousandth year was gone, he was about to cut off his tenth head and put it into the fire, when Brahma was gratified and asked what it was that he wanted. Ravana asked for *amaratva*. Brahma said, "I could not grant you that. Immortality is not for you, but you may ask for invulnerability by sections." And then Ravana asked that nobody should be able to kill him who belonged to the Devas, Asuras, Rakshasas, Yakshas, Kinnaras, Gandharvas, Pannagas and so on. He mentioned a lot of these tribes. Then the story is that he did not mention men, as he thought that men were too contemptible, and it was not necessary even to conceive of them as being capable of killing him. It is not clear, the accounts vary.

There is one account given in the Balakanda, and another in the Uttarakanda, but the difference is very interesting. Whether Ravana mentioned men and said, 'I do not want protection as against them' and excluded them that way, or whether he mentioned the other categories omitting men, is not clear. This is from the Uttarakanda.

सुपर्णनागयक्षाणां दैत्यदानवरक्षसाम् ।
अवध्योऽहं प्रजाध्यक्ष देवतानां च शाश्वत ॥
न हि चिन्ता ममान्येषु प्राणिष्वमरपूजित ।
तृणभूता हि ते मन्ये प्राणिनो मानुषादयः ॥ VII. 10. 19-20

"From these I ask for safety. I do not at all think of other categories, men and others of the sort. (You must pay a little attention to *adayah.*) They appear to me to be so worthless that I do not think I should ask to be free from danger from them." In the Balakanda the story is somewhat differently told.

स हि तेपे तपस्तीव्रं दीर्घकालमरिंदम ।
येन तुष्टोऽभवद् ब्रह्मा लोककृल्लोकपूर्वजः ॥
संतुष्टः प्रददौ तस्मै राक्षसाय वरं प्रभुः ।
नानाविधेभ्यो भूतेभ्यो भयं नान्यत्र मानुषात् ॥
अवज्ञाताः पुरा तेन वरदाने हि मानवाः । I. 16. 4-6

Omitting men only, Brahma gives him *abhaya* from the rest. Ravana treated them with contempt, and therefore did not include them in his *vara.* So when they spoke to Vishnu, the gods said, "He could be killed only by a man, not by any other being." Then the question arises: in the Uttarakanda the word used is मानुषादयः. If Ravana did not think of men at all, is it likely that he would have thought of vanaras? He must have treated them with still greater contempt and omitted them from the scope of the *vara.* There is a little clue; it is full of interest and is worth pursuing. When the battle was well on and the rival armies were ranged against each other for a decisive combat, Hanuman stood before Ravana and challenged him. In challenging him Hanuman used the strange words,

देवदानवगन्धर्वैर्यक्षैश्च सह राक्षसैः ।
अवध्यत्वं त्वया प्राप्तं वानरेभ्यस्तु ते भयम् ॥ VI. 59. 55

"You have obtained safety from all these sections. But you are still in peril from my race. So I can kill you." So begins Hanuman. The question is, could Ravana have asked Brahma about vanaras at all, for according to a *sarga* in the Balakanda, the race was created only in order to assist Rama in the great war. They must have come into existence only later on. They must be younger than Ravana, so that if Ravana did not mention them, it is no wonder. But then the poet leaves us in a kind of insoluble puzzle, as he always does. Vali must have been perhaps much older. So must have been Sugriva, Nala, Nila, Mainda, Dvivida, having drunk *amrita* with the Devas. It is impossible to suppose that all the monkeys were after Ravana. The dates get confused, as all figures do in the Ramayana. Now, that some monkeys were in existence and had become even famous is clear from a certain statement made by Ravana in the Sundarakanda. His messengers bring him news of the terrible havoc that Hanuman did to the city after he had seen Sita. When Ravana hears this strange news, this is what the poet makes him say.

दृष्टा हि हरयः पूर्वं मया विपुलविक्रमाः ।
वाली च सहसुग्रीवो जाम्बवांश्च महाबलः ॥
नीलः सेनापतिश्चैव ये चान्ये द्विविदादयः ।
नैवं तेषां गतिर्भीमा न तेजो न पराक्रमः ॥
न मतिर्न बलोत्साहौ न रूपपरिकल्पनम् ।
महत्सत्त्वमिदं ज्ञेयं कपिरूपं व्यवस्थितम् ॥ V. 46. 10-12

"I have myself seen many powerful monkeys. The accounts that you give of this new monkey are so extraordinary that they seem to transcend these. I have not heard of this monkey. This Hanuman that you speak of is a powerful creature, more powerful than I have heard of any belonging to the monkey race." So the monkey race was in existence at the time apparently, and certainly Ravana had heard of them. However that was so, is it right for Ravana to say that he had not heard of Hanuman? Hanuman must have been quite a strong youth when he came to Lanka in search of Sita; and when he was quite a baby, he ran after Surya when he was in eclipse,* and then Indra had to come to save the sun and the *chayagraha* also. At that time he struck Hanuman on the left cheek, and Vayu became very angry because of the mischief done to his little baby, and he held his breath so that the world came into a position of suffocation; no movement was possible and there was great consternation; a big council was held, they all went to the chief of the gods, and Vayu was pacified. Hanuman became at that time the recipient of a great many boons. Now this story of a little baby running after the sun and causing tremendous fright to all the gods, Vayu holding everybody down without breath and the gods assembling to confer on little Hanuman so many boons is an event of such colossal importance in nature that Ravana must have heard of it, because Ravana was a man that dealt with these gods. The poet says that Ravana was of such greatness that when he came out, all the gods were terrified; the sun moderated his heat, Vayu would not move about violently, the sea stilled its noise, rivers ran slow, mountains forgot to be hard, and so on. Nature was hushed and in a state of mortal terror when Ravana was about. If that was the case and all these gods had been in peril on account of Hanuman, this story must have reached Ravana's ears. For him therefore to say that he had heard of Nala, Nila, etc., but not of Hanuman is something which it is difficult to square with other parts of the story. But there are such incompatibilities in the poem—even worse ones than this.

Now Rama was a mere man, it is true, but early enough in his life he had given great proofs of his superhuman qualities. He had made his mark upon earth, and the entire inhabited part of the earth must have been aware of his greatness, his marvellous skill as a rival, his power even over nature, and his ability to stand strong and unruffled against the embattled world. Still, although there were many who thought Rama even at that time to be an *avatara* and spoke of him habitually in that way, it is curious that throughout the poem Ravana never once recognised that he was anything more than a mere man, and that even among men, he was anything very considerable. Proof after proof came to him; still he would not be convinced that there was anything out of the common in this Rama. Early in the poem, in the Aranyakanda, we have the long Maricha episode, *sargas* of great beauty. Maricha knew all about Rama; he had bitter experience of his great skill and his great strength. He had

* See Lect. XIX at p. 269 above.

also known that Rama was something more than man. His mere virtues as a man struck Maricha, and he mentions them all to Ravana. Nevertheless, Ravana goes on saying things of this kind.

अनुक्त्वा परुषं किंचिच्छरैर्व्यापारितं धनुः ।
चतुर्दश सहस्राणि रक्षसामुग्रतेजसाम् ॥
निहतानि शरैर्दीप्तैः मानुषेण पदातिना ।
खरश्च निहतः संख्ये दूषणश्च निपातितः ॥
हत्वा त्रिशिरसं चापि निर्भया दण्डकाः कृताः ।
पित्रा निरस्तः क्रुद्धेन सभार्यः क्षीणजीवितः ॥
स हन्ता तस्य सैन्यस्य रामः क्षत्रियपांसनः ।
दुःशीलः कर्कशस्तीक्ष्णः मूर्खो लुब्धोऽजितेन्द्रियः ॥
त्यक्तधर्मा त्वधर्मात्मा भूतानामहिते रतः ।
येन वैरं विनारण्ये सत्त्वमास्थाय केवलम् ॥
कर्णनासापहारेण भगिनी मे विरूपिता ।

III. 36. 8-13. (readings as in Bombay Ed.)

"He is only a *manusha* and is an object of contempt in many ways. A mere mortal then, he walks on his bare feet, is unable to bring a chariot or even a horse. I gave him no offence whatever, neither did he to me. While not even a harsh word had passed between us, he drew his bow and aimed arrows at people. He killed fourteen thousands of these Rakshasas. The man has done so much harm. He is an object of enmity to me therefore. The whole of the Dandaka forest where all stood in terror of me has now been made a region of security. My word does not run now. My sister Surpanakha, without any excuse assigned, without any provocation, in cold blood, was disfigured by this man." Then Maricha tells him, "You are utterly misinformed about Rama. He is a good man."

रामो विग्रहवान् धर्मः साधुः सत्यपराक्रमः । III. 37. 13

"He is nothing else than Dharma in human form." But all this makes no impression upon Ravana. Look at the obtuseness of the man in some respects. The poet represents him as having a kind of blind spot. However much other people may speak in praise of Rama and bring his great good qualities to his notice, he simply puts them by.

त्वद्वाक्यैर्न तु मां शक्यं भेत्तुं रामस्य संयुगे।
पापशीलस्य मूर्खस्य मानुषस्य विशेषतः ॥
यस्त्यक्त्वा सुहृदो राज्यं मातरं पितरं तथा।
स्त्रीवाक्य प्राकृतं श्रुत्वा वनमेकपदे गतः ॥ III. 40. 4-5

"Listening to the voice of a woman, at one bound this man rushes away from friends, from the kingdom, leaving his mother and his old father. And you call him a hero and that I must respect him." The word *manusha* occurs frequently whenever he speaks of Rama, a word which he would not even mention in his great request to Brahma. When he speaks to Sita in Janasthana, he asks her to take him for husband. He must have had a very strange idea of what marriage means. He makes an infamous proposal to her and proceeds.

अङ्गुल्या न समो रामो मम युद्धे स मानुषः। III. 48. 19

See how deep-rooted his contempt for that race is. Again in the next *sarga* he says the same thing to Sita.

त्यज्यतां मानुषो भावो मयि भावः प्रणीयताम्।
राज्याच्च्युतमसिद्धार्थं रामं परिमितायुषम् ॥
कैर्गुणैरनुरक्तासि मूढे पण्डितमानिनि।
यः स्त्रियो वचनाद्राज्यं विहाय ससुहृज्जनम् ॥
अस्मिन्व्यालानुचरिते वने वसति दुर्मतिः। III. 49. 13-15

"He is going to die. I am going to kill him in a few days. The man who has lost his kingdom has no means of saving you. Give up what little faith you still have in men. The man who has lost a safe kingdom, a vast fortune, the means of keeping worldly glory, and comes to this forest and lives amongst wild elephants, such a fool has your affection. I cannot understand it." Then when he takes her to his own palace, he takes her round all the apartments, and the great and glorious furniture, the decorated rooms and so on and says to her,

न देवेषु न यक्षेषु न गन्धर्वेषु नर्षिषु।
अहं पश्यामि लोकेषु यो मे वीर्यसमो भवेत् ॥
राज्यभ्रष्टेन दीनेन तापसेन पदातिना।
किं करिष्यसि रामेण मानुषेणाल्पतेजसा ॥

दुष्कृतं यत्पुरा कर्म वनवासेन तद्गतम्।
यश्च ते सुकृतो धर्मस्तस्येह फलमाप्नुहि॥ III. 55. 20-21, 27-28

"Look at all this and look at me. Can you think of Rama after this? Whatever *'papa'* you have done, it has borne its fruit and punished you by your having had to live for thirteen years in this forest with your husband. Now the evil is worked out and the good begins. Now begins your prosperous career, the fruit of whatever virtue you may have." You see how he cannot omit the idea of Rama being a man. Once more,

*स्वधर्मो रक्षसां भीरु सर्वथैव न संशयः।
गमनं वा परस्त्रीणां हरणं संप्रमथ्य वा॥
किं करिष्यसि रामेण सुभगे चीरवासिना॥
निक्षिप्तविजयो रामो गतश्रीर्वनगोचरः।
व्रती स्थण्डिलशायी च शङ्के जीवति वा न वा॥
न हि वैदेहि रामस्त्वां द्रष्टुं वाप्युपलप्स्यते।
न चापि मम हस्तात्त्वां प्राप्तुमर्हति राघवः॥
न रामस्तपसा देवि न बलेन न विक्रमैः।
न धनेन मया तुल्यस्तेजसा यशसापि वा॥ V. 20. 5, 25-28, 34

"It is the privilege and prerogative of the community to which I belong to rape other women and carry them away. I do not know now whether Rama is alive or whether he is dead. He will not be able to come here and be seen even by you. You cannot rest your eyes on him. Even supposing he did come and see you, do you think he will be able to take you away from me?"

Then after this, when Rama had indubitably established his greatness and constructed the bridge and come away and was about to strike at Lanka, there is a council of war which Ravana holds. Then his grand-uncle Malyavan advises him. "Without a question Rama is a divine being. I hold him to be Vishnu come upon earth to save mankind and the gods and all created beings. Therefore the best thing for you is to make peace with him and hand over Sita to him and become his friend." That was of course unacceptable to Ravana,

* Cf. Lect. XXIV below.

who got terribly wild. Although Malyavan was his grand-uncle, he reproves him.

मानुषं कृपणं राममेकं शाखामृगाश्रयम्।
समर्थं मन्यसे केन त्यक्तं पित्रा वनालयम्॥ VI. 36. 4

"Why do you tell me that Rama is anything worth considering? His best friends are monkeys. Even his father has kicked him out of his kingdom. I am going to carry this to the bitter end. I will not give up Sita." It is then that he uses the famous expression द्विधा भज्येयम् (VI. 36. 11).* "I may break in two, but I won't bend to anybody. You think it is a vice in me. Maybe. If it is a vice, I have been born with it. Who can transcend his nature? This persistence, this obstinacy, belongs to me from the moment of my birth. I cannot escape it. Therefore, all your advice I reject summarily."

But facts are hard things. Soon after Ravana had seen strong proofs of Rama's extraordinary strength and skill in war, he had to go through some of his bitterest experiences before he realises that, after all, in this mere human being there was some stuff. The first time that he does so is when at the end of that very severe engagement to which I have already referred, Ravana is sore-stricken, has lost his chariot and his bow and arrows, and stands on the ground. Rama might, if he had pursued the advantage, have killed him with a few more arrows. But out of a feeling of the highest chivalry, not wishing to take advantage of a man who was down and beaten so hard, he gives him a promise that he would not hurt him, asks him to go back, refresh himself by sleep and prepare himself for the fight.

कृतं त्वया कर्म महत्सुभीमं हतप्रवीरश्च कृतस्त्वयाहम्।
तस्मात् परिश्रान्त इति व्यवस्यन्न त्वां शरैर्मृत्युवशं नयामि॥
गच्छानुजानामि रणार्दितस्त्वं प्रविश्य रात्रिंचरराज लङ्काम्।
आश्वास्य निर्याहि रथी च धन्वी तदा बलं द्रक्ष्यसि मे रथस्थः॥

VI. 59. 142-143

These words may have been poison to him, but Rama says it in the plenitude of his generosity. "You have done wonders to-day. You have felled many heroes on my side. Therefore, I see that you have been over-exerting yourself. I will

* See Lect. XVII at p. 251 above for the sloka.

forbear now to send more arrows and finish you. Having thoroughly refreshed yourself, come out with a new chariot. I can stand on the ground. Even then you will see what I am when I face an enemy." For the first time Ravana felt thoroughly humiliated but went back. For the first time *bhaya* came to him.

स प्रविश्य पुरीं लङ्कां रामबाणभयार्दितः ।
भग्नदर्पस्तदा राजा बभूव व्यथितेन्द्रियः ॥
मातङ्ग इव सिंहेन गरुडेनेव पन्नगः ।
अभिभूतोऽभवद्राजा राघवेण महात्मना ॥
ब्रह्मदण्डप्रकाशानां विद्युत्सदृशवर्चसाम् ।
स्मरन् राघवबाणानां विव्यथे राक्षसेश्वरः ॥ VI. 60. 1-3

"As an elephant might be struck down and harassed by a lion, as a serpent would be by Garuda, so Ravana felt thoroughly beaten. As he lay in bed or sat up unable to sleep, he thought of these terrific arrows from Rama. Each one was like a Brahmadanda; like lightning the arrows shone." It is a long passage, but it is worth while listening to, because it is for the first time that Ravana feels that he had met an enemy perfectly his equal in every respect and for the first time too that he admits coming defeat.

स काञ्चनमयं दिव्यमाश्रित्य परमासनम् ।
विप्रेक्षमाणो रक्षांसि रावणो वाक्यमब्रवीत् ॥
सर्वं तत्खलु मे मोघं यत्तप्तं परमं तपः ।
यत्समानो महेन्द्रेण मानुषेणास्मि निर्जितः ॥
इदं तद्ब्रह्मणो घोरं वाक्यं मामभ्युपस्थितम् ।
मानुषेभ्यो विजानीहि भयं त्वमिति तत्तथा ॥
देवदानवगन्धर्वैर्यक्षराक्षसपन्नगैः ।
अवध्यत्वं मया प्राप्तं मानुषेभ्यो न याचितम् ॥ VI. 60. 4-7

"How much tapas I did for thousands of years!" he exclaims to the Rakshasas. "Having been reckoned the equal of Indra himself, I am now beaten by a man." Here is a strange extension of meaning which Ravana gives to the words of Brahma when he gave his boons. He did not put it in this form, but in the diseased, disordered mind of Ravana, he ascribes to Brahma a saying of which he was innocent.

"What Brahma said then has come true. What a terrific thing he said!" Brahma only said, "You are not going to be killed by this, that, etc." Still that is how it strikes Ravana in his distress. It occurs to him that Brahma said, "From man you get danger." This is how in our disordered imagination, things look different. Ravana not only fears Rama's strength, but is also afraid of the ultimate end.

विदितं मानुषं मन्ये रामं दशरथात्मजम्। VI. 60. 8

That was the first occasion when Ravana used the word 'man,' if he used it, without contempt. It struck him that there was something in this man.

इक्ष्वाकुकुलनाथेन अनरण्येन यत्पुरा ॥
उत्पत्स्यते हि मद्वंशे पुरुषो राक्षसाधम।
यस्त्वां सपुत्रं सामात्यं सबलं साश्वसारथिम् ॥
निहनिष्यति संग्रामे त्वां कुलाधम दुर्मते। VI. 60. 8-10

In one of his digvijayas Ravana made war upon Anaranya. Having done much harm to him he gets a curse from Anaranya. "From my race of Ikshvakus a man will be born named Rama, and he will kill you in battle." Ravana remembers that curse as he does many other curses he received in his life.

शप्तोऽहं वेदवत्या च यदा सा धर्षिता पुरा ॥
सेयं सीता महाभागा जाता जनकनन्दिनी। VI. 60. 10-11

"I once ravished a woman, Vedavati, and she said, 'Somehow I am going to be your end.' I think she has been born as Sita and I have brought this danger into my palace and all this trouble upon me in consequence." Then he recalls some of the other curses he had received.

उमा नन्दीश्वरश्चापि रम्भा वरुणकन्यका ॥
यथोक्तास्तन्मया प्राप्तं न मिथ्या ऋषिभाषितम्। VI. 60. 11-12

Uma and Nandi must have cursed him about the same time. Once he went to Kailasa and tried a hand against the sacred hill and displeased Mahadeva himself. At that time he was stopped by Nandi when he went in. Ravana turned round, and looking at his odd face he set up a loud laugh. Nandi got very angry, but not liking to do battle in the palace of

Mahadeva himself and without his sanction, he merely cursed him.

यस्माद्वानररूपं मामवज्ञाय दशानन ॥
अशनीपातसंकाशमुपहासं प्रमुक्तवान् ।
तस्मान्मद्रूपसंपन्ना मद्वीर्यसमतेजसः ॥
उत्पत्स्यन्ति वधार्थं हि कुलस्य तव वानराः ।
नखदंष्ट्रायुधाः क्रूरा मनस्संपातरंहसः ॥
युद्धोन्मत्ता बलोद्रिक्ताः शैला इव विसर्पिणः । VII. 16. 16-19

"As you have set up this laugh as loud as thunder, unable to control your contempt for me who have a sort of face, there will be born in the world a race of monkeys having my look and also having my strength, in order to kill you and your whole family. As big as hills they will be, and they will fight with nails and teeth."

Now I am going to read to you a certain passage of some significance, because this shows that Ravana was amongst his followers supposed to be so mighty that no danger, no disgrace, no humiliation, could conceivably happen to him. But when he had his first repulse at Rama's hands and Rama had, in order to make the disgrace as sharp as possible, sent him back home to re-arm himself for the fight, Ravana's followers were stricken with humiliation. Ravana bethought himself of Kumbhakarna. The way he was roused is full of amusement, but let us pass it all over. Kumbhakarna was roused, and he sat up and enquired what was the matter. "Some great calamity must have happened. Otherwise, Ravana would not have roused me." Yupaksha tells him,

न नो देवकृतं किंचिद्भयमस्ति कदाचन ।
मानुषान्नो भयं राजंस्तुमुलं संप्रबाधते ॥
न दैत्यदानवेभ्यो वा भयमस्ति हि तादृशम् ।
यादृशं मानुषं राजन् भयमस्मानुपस्थितम् । VI. 60. 72-73

"We have no fear of any gods. The present trouble is from a mere man. In battle Rama, whose armies were victorious, finding Ravana at his feet, said to him, 'Go home' instead of killing him. This disgrace has happened and it is worrying us. What worse can happen to us? The disgrace that never could have happened to our master from the *devas* or *danavas* has now happened to him from a man."

The next important crisis which brought out the fact that Ravana had been humbled to the dust is in a curious episode in sarga 106 of the Yuddhakanda. Rama and Ravana are locked in severe battle. Rama has struck home; Ravana is in sore distress; but being drunk with the lust of battle, he does not own that he is nearing a collapse. He still fights. His charioteer, apparently one of the princes of that race, noticed that Ravana was losing his balance. He then took the opportunity which trusted attendants often take, of moving the chariot a little away from the centre of the fight, so that Ravana might be saved from the fury of Rama's attack. Ravana did not notice it at once. He saw, however, that he stood at an angle to Rama, then realised what his charioteer had done and fell foul of him.

त्वयाद्य हि ममानार्य चिरकालसमार्जितम् ।
यशो वीर्यं च तेजश्च प्रत्ययश्च विनाशितः VI. 106. 5

"For thousands and thousands of years I have established my fame as a warrior. I have never drawn back. I have established my great reputation as an unrivalled holder of the bow and arrow, and no man dare stand against me. Why did you push my car a little aside and bring disgrace upon me? The reputation that I have taken long years to win, you have destroyed in a moment. This Rama before me, for whom I had great contempt before, I now realise is a warrior worthy of fighting with me. I want to establish my prowess before him."

शत्रोः प्रख्यातवीर्यस्य रञ्जनीयस्य विक्रमैः ।
पश्यतो युद्धलुब्धोऽहं कृतः कापुरुषस्त्वया ॥ VI. 106. 6

Ravana represents Rama as a person whose respect is worth winning. "Rama is a man who delights in exploits of war. When he sees me perform them, he would be struck with wonder and admiration. I am mad after fight. You have made a coward of me." The charioteer here was a resourceful person. He proved conclusively that he was in the right and Ravana in the wrong. Then Ravana saw the great danger he had been in, and in a fit of generosity which comes to great people, gave him his *hara,* and put it round his charioteer's neck.

TWENTYTHIRD LECTURE*

Ladies and Gentlemen,

During our last meeting I described how Ravana began with despising Rama as a mere man, but after several reverses at his hands, changed his opinion and ended by admitting that Rama was not merely his equal, but his superior. That, however, does not do justice to the great ability of Ravana, and that will be my theme today.

At first Lanka belonged to Kubera, half-brother of Ravana, while Ravana and his associates lived somewhere in *Patala*. After Ravana had achieved merit and become powerful, he was induced to recapture Lanka. He drove out his own brother and obtained from him the great chariot called *Pushpaka*. Thereafter he established himself in Lanka as his capital, and from that place as centre, conducted a series of campaigns in the three worlds (*trilokavijaya*). Nobody of note escaped him. Among his great conquests were the great gods and Rishis. His greatness was not confined in that way. Under him and always at his side were Rakshasas nearly as powerful as he, who had to their credit the conquest of many gods and powerful people on earth. His brother Kumbhakarna was almost his equal in physical strength, and but for the fact that he handicapped himself by prolonged sleep, would have probably been such a power by the side of Ravana that to destroy him even greater efforts might have been required than were actually put out. Ravana's son Meghanada was so skilled in the arts of magic that he was the prince of *kutayodhis,* warriors by craft. He was a great man at throwing oblations into the fire in order to get them to those from whom he expected great boons and periodically great assistance. In that way he became so great that in one of his engagements he captured Indra himself and brought him away as captive to Lanka, from which it was on the earnest solicitations of Brahma that he was released. In consequence he obtained the great name of Indrajit and at the same time other boons as well; so that when we think of Ravana's greatness we have to think of it as vastly multiplied by the greatness, on a slightly smaller scale, of people about

* 13-9-'44.

him. He had a son named Atikaya who was also a very great warrior.

It is difficult to believe that a kingdom could have been brought to such a high pitch of prosperity without Ravana introducing a system of ordered administration. He must have been not only great and powerful, but he must have had conspicuous merits as a ruler. The description that the poet gives of the city, the way it was ordered, how it was a city famous for its learning as well as for its splendour, the way in which Ravana was followed and obeyed implicitly, how he held his councils of war and so on, all these were not merely brute strength, but a great deal of what we must call *rajyatantra,* skill in managing great kingdoms, men and their resources. Then too we must remember that the poet represents him as having been next only to Sri Rama in strength and skill in war. Lakshmana was twice beaten by him with the weapon called *sakti* and brought to death's door, from which both times he was rescued by the *oshadhi.* It is therefore fitting that Ravana should be regarded as next after Rama the greatest and most skilful warrior of the time. While among the vanaras, Sugriva and Hanuman were quite equal to having a scrap with him occasionally, they could scarcely be regarded as having been strong enough either to beat or destroy him. That was left only to Sri Rama, and even he found it by no means easy. He had to be assisted in the last stage by the great *aditya-hridaya,* taught to him at a critical moment by Agastya, that moment synchronising, if you remember, with that very moment when Ravana was moved away in his chariot by his driver. The two protagonists seem to have come to the end of their tether at about the same time. Also Indra had lent Rama his own chariot and his charioteer, his shield and a marvellous bow and arrows, so that we are to regard Ravana as having been nearly equal to Rama until overthrown in the end because of the divinity that was in this warrior.

We have now got to go to the text and see how the poet gives us an idea, sometimes himself and sometimes through the lips of his great heroes, of Ravana's greatness. In the Balakanda we have the gods complaining to Mahavishnu of how Ravana had grown rapidly in power and how he did mischief to high and low without distinction and without intermission.

उद्वेजयति लोकांस्त्रीनुच्छ्रितान् द्वेष्टि दुर्मतिः ।
शक्रं त्रिदशराजानं प्रधर्षयितुमिच्छति ॥
ऋषीन् यक्षान् सगन्धर्वानसुरान् ब्राह्मणांस्तथा ।
अतिक्रामति दुर्धर्षो वरदानेन मोहितः ॥
नैनं सूर्यः प्रतपति पार्श्वे वाति न मारुतः ।
चलोर्मिमाली तं दृष्ट्वा समुद्रोऽपि न कम्पते ॥
तत्र त्वं मानुषो भूत्वा प्रवृद्धं लोककण्टकम् ॥
अवध्यं दैवतैर्विष्णो समरे जहि रावणम् । I. 15. 8-10; 20-21

"His ambition is grown so great that he desires frequently to knock Indra himself on the head. He alienates and throws into enmity all the three worlds, and nobody can rise above a certain level but Ravana grows jealous of him immediately and tries to destroy him. Intoxicated with the boons conferred on him by the gods, he is cppressing everybody. The great gods who are ruling the universe, keeping it in order, are afraid of him. Surya dare not warm him; if Vayu goes near him, he shrinks within himself; even Samudra stills his restless waves if Ravana is near. You must go and assume the form of a man, for if as a god you go to fight him, you cannot prevail against him. We have come to implore you to take man's form and go down and kill him. He has become uncontrollable, and nobody can restrain him. His wickedness and his cruelty exceed description."

When he comes to Sita, he comes in the form of a mild *sanyasi*. Notwithstanding that, nature seems to have recognised him even through his disguise, I suppose because there was something in him of superhuman strength which he could not himself suppress or conceal. For when he came near,

तमुग्रतेजःकर्माणं जनस्थानरुहा द्रुमाः ॥
समीक्ष्य न प्रकम्पन्ते न प्रवाति च मारुतः ।
शीघ्रस्रोताश्च तं दृष्ट्वा वीक्षन्तं रक्तलोचनम् ॥
स्तिमितं गन्तुमारेभे भयाद्गोदावरी नदी । III. 46. 6-8

"Even the trees of the forest were afraid; they stood still; the rapid and mighty Godavari, seeing Ravana near, controlled herself and moved very slowly indeed with her waters." That is an unparallelled tribute to the greatness of any person. The gods and every element of nature stood in awe of him. There is a great drama called Mahanataka in which this awe in which Ravana was held even by nature is given in dramatic form. The author of that play introduces a scene in which Ravana has just seen Sita. Having once caught sight of her, his whole soul was afire with the madness of love. He came home all discomposed and went to bed, uneasy, tossing restless and not being able to go through the day's routine. The day's routine was to him extraordinary. In the morning the gods came to him to pay homage, including Brahma. On this morning the gods have come to pay their usual respects, but the man at the gate, knowing the somewhat uneasy condition of the master, tells them to desist from their daily routine. He says to them in tones of familiarity, if not of contempt,

ब्रह्मन्नध्ययनस्य नैष समयस्तूष्णीं बहिः स्थीयतां
स्वल्पं जल्प बृहस्पते जडमते नैषा सभा वज्रिणः ।
वीणां संहर नारद स्तुतिमुखालापैरलं तुम्बुरो
सीतारल्लकभल्लभग्नहृदयः स्वस्थो न लङ्केश्वरः ॥ Mahanataka

"This is not the time for reciting the Veda here, stand out and stand mum. You, Brihaspati, who are fond of showing eloquence, you must talk very modestly. This is not Indra's court. Narada, do not use your *vina*, put it up today. Ravana is not himself today, so you must not disturb him. He has been struck by an arrow of unusual shrewdness. That arrow is the parting line of Sita's hair. From the moment he saw her, he is not at ease with himself." That was the Ravana to kill whom Vishnu had to take birth amongst men.

Now how did Ravana strike those who saw him, those competent to judge him, men who belonged more or less to his class? The poet gives us a description of how he impressed Hanuman when he first met him in his own court. Seeing him, he exclaims in wonder.

अहो रूपमहो धैर्यमहो सत्त्वमहो द्युतिः ।
अहो राक्षसराजस्य सर्वलक्षणयुक्तता ॥
यद्यधर्मो न बलवान् स्यादयं राक्षसेश्वरः ।
स्यादयं सुरलोकस्य सशक्रस्यापि रक्षिता ॥

अस्य क्रूरैर्नृशंसैश्च कर्मभिर्लोककुत्सितैः ।
तेन बिभ्यति खल्वस्माल्लोकाः सामरदानवाः ॥
अयं ह्युत्सहते क्रुद्धः कर्तुमेकार्णवं जगत् ।
इति चिन्तां बहुविधामकरोन्मतिमान् कपिः ॥
दृष्ट्वा राक्षसराजस्य प्रभावममितौजसः ॥ V. 49. 17-20

Hanuman moralises a little. "This king of the Rakshasas has got all the elements of greatness combined in him. For a person who is so great as Ravana, he ought to be a protector of heaven itself. Indra and other people must be at his feet. What keeps him down to some extent and prevents him from attaining the fullness of power is his *adharma*. He does not employ all his power to push righteous causes to fruition. He knows no restraint, perpetrates all the impropriety. If in this world *adharma* were not a source of weakness, this man would be the master of everybody up and below. By his continued career of cruelty and unscrupulous use of power, he has made everybody his enemy, and all the good people are against him." Hanuman who could judge of real greatness had all this thought passing through his mind when he first cast his glance at Ravana. It would be interesting to know what Ravana thought when he saw Hanuman. He does not keep us waiting long. Hanuman had been reported to Ravana as having destroyed a part of the town, and as having killed a great many Rakshasas, amongst them his own son. So when he looked at Hanuman, he understood the greatness of the person. He says, "At one time when I went to Kailasa, I saw Nandi and laughed at him. Has that Nandi come here in the shape of Hanuman?* Or it may be, he is Banasura come here in this shape." That is how the two great beings looked at each other for the first time.

Then when Ravana had gathered together his vast forces and come to the first encounter with Rama and his army, Vibhishana stands forth pointing out to Rama who was who. At the end he came to Ravana himself.

यत्रैतदिन्दुप्रतिमं विभाति च्छत्रं सितं सूक्ष्मशलाकमग्र्यम् ।
अत्रैष रक्षोधिपतिर्महात्मा भूतैर्वृतो रुद्र इवावभाति ॥
असौ किरीटी चलकुण्डलास्यो नगेन्द्रविन्ध्योपमभीमकायः ।
महेन्द्रवैवस्वतदर्पहन्ता रक्षोधिपः सूर्य इवावभाति ॥ VI. 59. 24-25

* Lect. XXII, pp. 317-8 above.

I want to draw your careful attention to this point. The poet wishes us to regard Ravana as a truly great person, not despicable, not hateful, not worthy of our contempt as it were; and that comes out strongly in his comparisons and similes. He compares Ravana in this sloka to Rudra himself. He compares him to Surya also. When Vibhishana fully pointed out Ravana, Rama took in at a glance the nature of the enemy he had to kill. What did he think?

अहो दीप्तो महातेजा रावणो राक्षसेश्वरः ॥
आदित्य इव दुष्प्रेक्षो रश्मिभिर्भाति रावणः ।
सुव्यक्तं लक्षये ह्यस्य रूपं तेजस्समावृतम् ॥
देवदानववीराणां वपुर्नैवंविधं भवेत् ।
यादृशं राक्षसेन्द्रस्य वपुरेतत्प्रकाशते ॥ VI. 59. 26-28

"You are unable to see the man just as you are unable to see the sun. The eye shrinks. I am not able to see him clearly. It is so surrounded by splendour. Even to the great gods such a resplendent beauty is not vouchsafed." If a man by mere sight could impress Hanuman and Rama in that way, then there is no measure within our poor minds by which we can really have an estimate of the man. After he had been killed, Vibhishana speaks of him.

योऽयं विमर्देषु न भग्नपूर्वः सुरैः समेतैः सह वासवेन ।
भवन्तमासाद्य रणे विभग्नो वेलामिवासाद्य यथा समुद्रः ॥
अनेन दत्तानि सुपूजितानि भुक्ताश्च भोगा निभृताश्च भृत्याः ।
धनानि मित्रेषु समर्पितानि वैराण्यमित्रेषु च यापितानि ॥
एषोऽहिताग्निश्च महातपाश्च वेदान्तगः कर्मसु चाग्र्यवीर्यः ।
एतस्य यत् प्रेतगतस्य कृत्यं तत्कर्तुमिच्छामि तव प्रसादात् ॥

VI. 112. 22-24

"This person who is now dead had no equal hitherto. Wherever he went, whomsoever he engaged in battle, he conquered and killed. Just as the *samudra* rolling the waters stops only when he comes to the shore, so Ravana having met you and encountered you, has been checked and three he lies. This person has done all things in his life which mark real greatness. He has given with both hands bounteously to beggars. He was a man of very generous disposition. There is nothing that he has not enjoyed in his time.

He has protected all those who worked for him, so that he was a good master too. And when he had gathered wealth together, he shared it generously with his friends. All the hatred and power to do harm that he had, he directed against his foes. He was a loyal friend, a good master" and so on. If Vibhishana, who was himself a man of *dharma* and knew all the austerities, says of his brother as an *ahitagni*, you must see how holy he was. "He knew the Vedanta very well. In the performance of the prescribed austerities there was nobody like him. To this brother of mine, who was himself a master of all the prescribed duties, to him, now he is no more, I wish to do the last rites. Will you please allow me?" Then a second thought comes to him and it is Rama's turn to speak well of Ravana and ask Vibhishana not to neglect his last duties to his brother.

अधर्मानृतसंयुक्तः कामं त्वेष निशाचरः ॥
तेजस्वी बलवाञ्छूरः संयुगेषु च नित्यशः।
शतक्रतुमुखैर्देवैः श्रूयते न पराजितः ॥ VI. 114. 99-100

"I do not know if all these things were done by him, but I have heard so much of him. When the great gods met him in battle, it was not he who had to run or to own defeat."

Now I have got here a passage in the original Sanskrit which seems to be of surpassing interest. It is a description of the last battle between Sri Rama and Ravana. It is worth reading. I have forborne from translating it as I might have done, but I shall read the original itself and here and there explain a word or two and leave the rest to produce its impression. This battle between Rama and Ravana is really the climax of this war, and the poet wants us to believe that it was a battle between people who were almost equal, and therefore every device known to the war of that time was employed by both people.

गदानां मुसलानां च परिघाणां च निःस्वनैः।
शराणां पुङ्खपातैश्च क्षुभिताः सप्त सागराः ॥
क्षुब्धानां सागराणां च पातालतलवासिनः।
व्यथिताः पन्नगास्सर्वे दानवाश्च सहस्रशः ॥
चकम्पे मेदिनी कृत्स्ना सशैलवनकानना।
भास्करो निष्प्रभश्चासीन्न ववौ चापि मारुतः ॥

ततो देवाः सगन्धर्वाः सिद्धाश्च परमर्षयः ।
चिन्तामापेदिरे सर्वे सकिन्नरमहोरगाः ॥
स्वस्ति गोब्राह्मणेभ्योऽस्तु लोकास्तिष्ठन्तु शाश्वताः ।
जयतां राघवः संख्ये रावणं राक्षसेश्वरम् ॥
एवं जपन्तोऽपश्यंस्ते देवास्सर्षिगणास्तदा ।
रामरावणयोर्युद्धं सुघोरं रोमहर्षणम् ॥
गन्धर्वाप्सरसां सङ्घा दृष्ट्वा युद्धमनूपमम् ।
गगनं गगनाकारं सागरः सागरोपमः ॥
रामरावणयोर्युद्धं रामरावणयोरिव ।
एवं ब्रुवन्तो ददृशुस्तद्युद्धं रामरावणम् ॥
ततः क्रुद्धो महाबाहू रघूणां कीर्तिवर्धनः ।
सन्धाय धनुषा रामः क्षुरमाशीविषोपमम् ॥
रावणस्य शिरोऽच्छिन्दच्छ्रीमज्ज्वलितकुण्डलम् ।
तच्छिरः पतितं भूमौ दृष्टं लोकैस्त्रिभिस्तदा ॥
तस्यैव सदृशं चान्यद्रावणस्योत्थितं शिरः ।
तत्क्षिप्तं क्षिप्रहस्तेन रामेण क्षिप्रकारिणा ॥
द्वितीयं रावणशिरश्छिन्नं संयति सायकैः ।
छिन्नमात्रं तु तच्छीर्षं पुनरन्यत् स्म दृश्यते ॥
तदप्यशनिसंकाशैश्छिन्नं रामेण सायकैः ।
एवमेकशतं छिन्नं शिरसां तुल्यवर्चसाम् ॥
न चैव रावणस्यान्तो दृश्यते जीवितक्षये ।
ततः सर्वास्त्रविद्वीरः कौसल्यानन्दवर्धनः ॥
मार्गणैर्बहुभिर्युक्तश्चिन्तयामास राघवः । VI. 110. 17-31

The battle was so fierce that the seven oceans were all agitated. Thousands of the denizens of the lower world, the whole of the earth shook. The sun was hidden in clouds. They began to be anxious, and it did not seem as if Ravana would go down, so strong and equal was he to Rama. So they all began to pray, "May Rama win and Ravana go down! The one was similar to the other, and the other was similar to the one. No third could be mentioned." Then Rama bethought himself of an arrow of great power, and sent it straight at Ravana's neck. It put down one of the ten heads.

The poet now wants you to see how all the gods and the Yakshas, Kinnaras and Gandharvas saw the head fall down. In that very place where that head had been, another head rose. By two or three arrows he destroyed that head again, and, no sooner was it thrown down than another came and stuck on his neck. That head too was thrown out by Rama's arrows, but another sprang up. In that way a hundred times the head was put down, but was quickly replaced, and there was no prospect of Ravana being killed. He began to think,

> मारीचो निहतो यैस्तु खरो यैस्तु सदूषणः ॥
>
> क्रौञ्चारण्ये विराधस्तु कबन्धो दण्डकावने ।
>
> यैः साला गिरयो भग्ना वाली च क्षुभितोऽम्बुधिः ॥
>
> त इमे सायकाः सर्वे युद्धे प्रात्ययिका मम ।
>
> किंनु तत्कारणं येन रावणे मन्दतेजसः ॥ VI. 110. 31-33

"Arrows which enabled me to do all these great exploits, to destroy so many powerful people, those same arrows are all *manda* when they approach Ravana. Their edge is blunted when they reach him." Rama rained arrows, Ravana too caused some distress to Rama by arrows, but threw *gadas* and *musalas*. Neither relaxed his efforts for a minute either during the night or during the day for seven days. Then Rama's charioteer Matali, who had been trained under Indra, seeing how Rama was unable to make headway against Ravana, told him quietly in the ear, "Employ the Brahmastra." Rama was so engrossed in the fight that all his wits were not gathered together. He had no time to think what was best for the occasion. Matali bethought himself of that sovereign remedy and suggested it to Rama. So the battle ends and the great enemy of the worlds is destroyed.

Now that concludes the section on Ravana's greatness, the extent of his power and the great heights to which as a warrior he rose. Now I wish to say a word about the way in which he was able to obtain the unreserved and loyal assistance of all his men. That requires great qualities. One must be a generous master in measuring one's words when one wants to appreciate the skilful assistance of one's followers. If you are miserly in your praise, they won't give of their best to you. Ravana knew all these arts. When Kumbhakarna had been roused with superhuman efforts and with strange devices, the first thing he did was to ask Ravana to surrender to Rama. Ravana got very angry and reproached him. Kumbhakarna says, "If you want to go to hell, I cannot prevent you. But I am going to fight on your side. Though I do not approve of what you have done, I am not going to keep back, and I will use all my power, skill and strength on your side." When he heard this encouraging word from his brother, Ravana, in order to make him do the very best that he could, took out one of his own *haras* and put it round his neck.

अथासनात् समुत्पत्य स्रजं मणिकृतान्तराम् ॥
आबबन्ध महातेजाः कुम्भकर्णस्य रावणः ।
अङ्गदान्यङ्गुलीवेष्टान् वराण्याभरणानि च ॥
हारं च शशिसंकाशमाबबन्ध महात्मनः ।
दिव्यानि च सुगन्धीनि माल्यदामानि रावणः ॥
श्रोत्रे चासञ्जयामास श्रीमती चास्य कुण्डले ।
काञ्चनाङ्गदकेयूरनिष्काभरणभूषितः ॥
कुम्भकर्णो बृहत्कर्णः सुहुतोऽग्निरिवाबभौ ।
सर्वाभरणनद्धाङ्गः शूलपाणिः स राक्षसः ।
त्रिविक्रमकृतोत्साहो नारायण इवाबभौ ॥ VI. 65. 25-29, 31

When you have ever been decorated by your general on the battlefield, you know what it is. Kumbhakarna, having been decorated by the flattering hands of Ravana, shone as *agni* who had been well fed with ghee. The poet compares Kumbhakarna with Narayana. In the eyes of the poet these Rakshasa heroes were not contemptible, were not the monsters we commonly believe, only they abused their power. Kumbhakarna died at Rama's hands after a fierce battle. So many others died, Indrajit also.

We now come to the penultimate stage. Having lost all big men, Ravana did not lose heart, and was still for continuing the fight, and when all had been destroyed, he was there himself. That was the extraordinary nature of the man. Knowing that doom was approaching him, that he was losing general after general and warrior after warrior, still he held on undaunted and unbeaten. Kumbhakarna and Indrajit too fell, others' fate was beyond doubt, but they were ready and glad to meet it. So maddening is the lust of battle. When Ravana turned round, his eyes fell upon Mahodara. "Trusted comrade," says he, "in this dire distress all my hope is centered on you. You can turn this defeat into victory. Let the force of your arm smite the enemy hard. If you have gratitude this is the time to show it. Retrieve our fortune and save Lanka yet." I have translated this passage in order to show you how Ravana did not lose his wits although his adversity had reached its climax, and how in that last stage he was to address words of exhortation to a warrior who felt at once that upon him rested the whole burden of the battle. The poor Mahodara went, but he had to contend against Sugriva, who accounted for Mahodara in no time. But Mahodara's heart was high even when he died. That is to show how Ravana was great in this respect also, that upon his followers he exerted such a power that they were ready at all times and in the greatest difficulties to fight for him and to die for him cheerfully. He must have been a great man therefore.

This section is intended to show Ravana exercising his varied skill upon a reluctant follower, Maricha, who contends against him through nine sargas. The struggle between them lasts long and passes through many phases. All through Ravana had his eye on his own point of view. Maricha's clever reasoning did not deflect Ravana. Finally Ravana brought him round and made him do his will. You must remember that Maricha had after a career of unbridled wickedness, having suffered a lot for it, turned a hermit in the end, began to practise *tapas*, and was a really good man. When Ravana started on his mad career, he went to Maricha and said,

आर्तोऽस्मि मम चार्तस्य भवान् हि परमा गतिः ॥ III. 36. 1

"I am in sore distress, and whom am I to seek in distress but you? You are my only resource." Maricha dissuades him. "There is somebody near you who is envious of your prosperity, whom you trust, who however wishes to compass your ruin. Listen to me and reject that advice."[1]

सुलभाः पुरुषा राजन् सततं प्रियवादिनः ।
अप्रियस्य च पथ्यस्य वक्ता श्रोता च दुर्लभः ॥ III. 37. 2

"Kings are very unfortunate. They pay their followers and ministers, but when kings are in trouble and want real advice, these men, instead of speaking bravely what would be of benefit to their master, tell him what would please him. Sincere advice is not given. People who always speak what is pleasing to the ear, such there are by the thousand. The man is rare who will speak the beneficial thing though it is not pleasing. Even if you get a man who will say an unpleasant truth, the man to listen to it is rarer still." Then Maricha tells Ravana his own experience. "I have felt the strength of Rāma's arm when he was a mere boy of fifteen. Visvamitra trained Rama in the art of fighting. He went to Dasaratha and persuaded him to send his son to help him in his *yaga,* and gave him all the *astras.* I was the person against whom Rama was brought, and on me his first arrows were directed." In the whole of that description, Lakshmana is not mentioned at all. Then he says what impression Rama produced upon him, how he quakes even when he thinks of Rama.

> वृक्षे वृक्षे च पश्यामि चीरकृष्णाजिनाम्बरम्।
> गृहीतधनुषं रामं पाशहस्तमिवान्तकम्।
> अपि रामसहस्राणि भीतः पश्यामि रावण ॥
> रामभूतमिदं सर्वमरण्यं प्रतिभाति मे।
> राममेव हि पश्यामि रहिते राक्षसाधिप ॥
> दृष्ट्वा स्वप्नगतं राममुद्भ्रमामि विचेतनः।
> रकारादीनि नामानि रामत्रस्तस्य रावण ॥
> रत्नानि च रथाश्चैव वित्रासं जनयन्ति मे। III. 39. 14-18

Rama appears to him as if he were Yama himself with his rope drawn tight. On every tree he sees a figure of Rama. The whole of the forest seems full of Rama. All words which have their initial as 'R', even though they be *'ratna'* or *'ratha'* gave him terror. Curious that Maricha communicates his dread of 'R' to one whose name also begins with 'R'. Then the poet shows how Ravana feels whenever one of his subordinates speaks candidly to him. He is one of those people who want evidently to be told what would please, not what would help. He says to Maricha,

> दोषं गुणं वा संपृष्टस्त्वमेवं वक्तुमर्हसि।
> अपायं वाप्युपायं वा कार्यस्यास्य विनिश्चये

संपृष्टेन तु वक्तव्य सचिवेन विपश्चिता ।
उद्यताञ्जलिना राज्ञो य इच्छेद्भूतिमात्मनः ॥
वाक्यमप्रतिकूलं तु मृदुपूर्वं हितं शुभम् ।
उपचारेण युक्तं च वक्तव्यो वसुधाधिपः ॥
सावमर्दं तु यद्वाक्य मारीच हितमुच्यते ।
नाभिनन्दति तद्राजा मानार्हो मानवर्जितम् ॥ III. 40. 8-11

"I am not asking you to tell me what is good and what is bad. I am only asking you to do me a certain piece of service. I am not come here to receive judgment at your hands. If a minister is wise, he will keep his tongue in his head unless asked to give advice. No king who has the least bit of pride in him will listen to an advice as you give it to me." We have to remember in the course of the talk with Maricha, Ravana shows his extraordinary skill and his fine perception. He first suggests a plan to him, that Maricha should parade before Sita as a golden deer finely bedecked. Then Rama will be asked to follow him. But in a few minutes Ravana improved upon the plan. When Maricha came before Sita, captured her heart, made her yearn to possess him, he had better run away. Rama would follow him, and having run away, he should set up a cry of "Lakshmana, Sita," simulating the voice of Rama. It shows you how quick he is in revolving his plans. Then, finding that Ravana was deep in his own meditations, Maricha tries to abuse him. "In this world this happens time and again. One man is wicked, does wrong, and a thousand people have to suffer on his account. It is not the wicked man alone that suffers."

अकुर्वन्तोऽपि पापानि शुचयः पापसंश्रयात् ।
परपापैर्विनश्यन्ति मत्स्या नागह्रदे यथा ॥
बहवः साधवो लोके युक्ता धर्ममनुष्ठिताः ।
परेषामपराधेन विनष्टाः सपरिच्छदाः ॥ III. 38. 26; 41. 13

"Just as when in a very big tank where there are cobras and the men want to kill the cobras, a great many poor *matsyas* have also to die in the act, good people by mere contact with wicked people have to suffer." In the Yuddhakanda Rama says,

एको हि कुरुते पाप कालपाशवश गतः
नीचेनात्मापचारेण कुलंतेन विनश्यति ॥ VI. 38. 7

"By his wicked act his whole family, his whole race, has to perish." Because a man is placed in great power and many people follow him and look up to him and do his behests, they have to suffer. When there is a man placed in high authority, morally or physically, it is not only for his wicked deeds that other people have to suffer; it is also for his mistakes, errors of policy or judgment that thousands of other people have got to suffer. We know it daily. You remember my reading Vibhishana's warning as he left Ravana. Exactly the same words are spoken by Maricha. "When a man's fate is near, when his doom is sealed, his best friends may dissuade him, but he turns a deaf ear. Such is the potency of fate."

एवं कृत्वा त्विदं कार्यं यथेष्टं गच्छ राक्षस ।
राज्यस्यार्धं प्रदास्यामि मारीच तवं सुव्रत ॥
प्राप्य सीतामयुद्धेन वञ्चयित्वा तु राघवम् ।
लङ्कां प्रतिगमिष्यामि कृतकार्यः सह त्वया ॥
न चेत्करोषि मारीच हन्मि त्वामहमद्य वै ।
एतत्कार्यमवश्यं मे बलादपि करिष्यसि ॥
राज्ञो हि प्रतिकूलस्थो न जातु सुखमेधते । III. 40. 23, 25-26

"Having done this for me and having cried 'Lakshmana, Sita' and drawn away Lakshmana from Sita and left the field open for me, you can come away. I will give you half my kingdom. If you will not do this service, I will throttle you now. I will make you do this even if I have to employ force. You cannot defy me and yet escape." Maricha makes up his mind to go. "I must die anyhow, but I shall get killed by Rama's arrow." Ravana was pleased.

प्रहृष्टस्त्वभवत्तेन वचनेन स रावणः ।
परिष्वज्य सुसंश्लिष्टमिदं वचनमब्रवीत् ॥
एतच्छौण्डीर्ययुक्तं ते मच्छन्दादिव भाषितम् ।
इदानीमसि मारीचः पूर्वमन्यो निशाचरः ॥ III. 42. 5-6

He embraced Maricha heartily and said, "Now you are really Maricha. Till now you were some other Rakshasa."

TWENTYFOURTH LECTURE*

Sisters and Brothers,

I am to concern myself today with the relations of Ravana to the other sex. It is through them he came to grief. It would be necessary, therefore, to pay full attention to this aspect of his character. We have to go to the Uttarakanda to find out how in early life he was a confirmed sinner, and as often as he could, captured women from their protectors, and if they were not compliant, violated them. He created so many enemies against himself in this way, that the celestial women and the semi-celestial women cursed him.

यस्मादेष परक्यासु रमते राक्षसाधमः ॥
तस्माद्धि स्त्रीकृतेनैव प्राप्स्यते दुर्मतिर्वधम् ।
सतीभिर्वरनारीभिरेवं वाक्येऽभ्युदीरिते ॥
नेदुर्दुन्दुभयः स्वस्थाः पुष्पवृष्टिः पपात च । VII. 24. 20-22

"Because this wicked person does not care for the honour of other women, he will meet his end through his misdeeds to the other sex. When this word was uttered, the *dundubhis* of heaven sounded." There were rejoicings in heaven, when this curse was pronounced on him.

In the same kanda, another anecdote is related about him. It would appear that Kubera's son Nalakubara had an appointment with Rambha the divine damsel, and when she was going to the tryst, Ravana met her on the way and, yielding to her charms, ravished her. She reported the matter to Nalakubara and he pronounced a curse.

अकामा तेन यस्मात्त्वं बलाद्भद्रे प्रधर्षिता
तस्मात् स युवतीमन्यां नाकामामुपयास्यति ॥
यदा ह्यकामां कामार्तो धर्षयिष्यति योषितम् ।
मूर्धा तु सप्तधा तस्य शकलीभविता तदा ॥

* 20-9-'44.

श्रुत्वा तु स दशग्रीवस्तं शापं रोमहर्षणम् ॥ *
नारीषु मैथुने भावं नाकामास्वभ्यरोचयत् ।
तेन नीताः स्त्रियः प्रीतिमापुः सर्वाः पतिव्रताः ॥

VII. 26, 55-56, 59-60

"Because he violated you when you were not agreeable, he shall not do this again to anybody. When he attempts the honour of any other woman against her will, his head shall go into seven pieces." When this curse was known, he abstained from misdeeds of that sort; and as at that time he had a large number of women in his harem, those that were still faithful to their husbands and had not given themselves to him, rejoiced to hear that their honour was safe so long as they did not yield it up themselves. This, however, does not seem to have stopped him in his wicked course. We are told that although Nalakubara's curse was strong and sincere, it did not come into effect owing to the fact that the stock of *tapas* that Ravana had accumulated was so great that he could give up a part of it in order to go on in the same way as before. His own story, which must be taken to be conclusive against him, was given to his council consisting of his brothers, sons and cousins, when Rama was about to cross the waters.

महापार्श्व निबोध त्वं रहस्यं किञ्चिदात्मनः ।
चिरवृत्तं तदाख्यास्ये यदवाप्तं मया पुरा ॥
पितामहस्य भवनं गच्छन्तीं पुञ्जिकस्थलाम् ।
चञ्चूर्यमाणामद्राक्षमाकाशेऽग्निशिखामिव ॥
सा प्रसह्य मया भुक्ता कृता विवसना ततः ।
स्वयंभूभवनं प्राप्ता लोलिता नलिनी यथा ॥
तस्य तच्च तदा मन्ये ज्ञातमासीन्महात्मनः ।
अथ संकुपितो वेधा मामिदं वाक्यमब्रवीत् ॥
अद्यप्रभृति यामन्यां बलान्नारीं गमिष्यसि ।
तदा ते शतधा मूर्धा फलिष्यति न संशयः ॥
इत्यहं तस्य शापस्य भीतः प्रसभमेव ताम् ।
नारोपये बलात्सीतां वैदेहीं शयने स्वके ॥ VI. 13. 10-15

---

* Cf. "नलकूबरशापेन रक्षा चास्याः कृता मया"—Brahma to Rama in Mahabharata, Vanaparva (Ramopakhyana), 292. 34 (Kumb. Ed.).

"I shall tell you something that happened to me. Once the young lady Punjikasthala was going to Brahma's *sabha*. She was so attractive that I lost my heart to her. I forced her and then disrobed her. She went into the presence of Brahma, all tattered and torn. Brahma came to know of this, and becoming angry, said this, 'Surely, hereafter if you do a similar deed with an unwilling woman, your head shall burst into a hundred pieces.' I am in dread of that curse, and from that day I have not been trespassing in this line. Therefore when I brought Sita to my palace I have had to be very gentle with her. I could not be violent towards her and therefore I do not compel her to get into my bed." But this made a change in him. After he had been threatened with this serious curse, he changed his ways apparently and became a gentle and affable lover to the women. Apparently, he was such a skilful lover and captured the hearts of people. When he found that he had no other way, he acquired all the arts, was patient with them, indulged them so far as he had to, and in that way obtained the consent of these women before he had anything wrong to do with them. They became willing tools of his lust. Some women were captured by him in war, their husbands having been overcome; others became enamoured of him and came to join him. When Hanuman saw the women in the harem, this was what he observed.

राजर्षिपितृदैत्यानां गन्धर्वाणां च योषितः ।
राक्षसानां च याः कन्यास्तस्य कामवशं गताः ।
युद्धकामेन ताः सर्वा रावणेन हृताः स्त्रियः ।
समदा मदनेनैव मोहिताः काश्चिदागताः ॥
न तत्र काश्चित्प्रमदाः प्रसह्य वीर्योपपन्नेन गुणेन लब्धाः ।
न चान्यकामापि न चान्यपूर्वा विना वरार्हां जनकात्मजां ताम् ॥
न चाकुलीना न च हीनरूपा नादक्षिणा नानुपचारयुक्ता ।
भार्याभवत्तस्य न हीनसत्त्वा न चापि कान्तस्य न कामनीया ॥

V. 9. 68-71

"Except Sita, all the other women in the harem had agreed to have relations with him. There was not a woman who loved another person, no one who had been another's before." This shows how Ravana changed his ways to women and became to them an attractive lover, a person with whom they were desirous to be associated. In every way, they were his willing companions. Hanuman, who saw all this and had been told of course that Ravana was wicked and that he ill-treated women and handled them badly, exclaimed on seeing this,

बभूव बुद्धिस्तु हरीश्वरस्य यदीदृशी राघवधर्मपत्नी ।
इमा यथा राक्षसराजभार्याः सुजातमस्येति हि साधुबुद्धः ॥ V. 9. 72

Being a plain person, not sophisticated, Hanuman said to himself, "If women become enamoured of Ravana like this and if Sita too should have fallen a victim to his blandishment, then this man should be pronounced very fortunate, very lucky." But having let that thought go through his mind, he checked himself.

पुनश्च सोऽचिन्तयदार्तरूपो ध्रुव विशिष्टा गुणतो हि सीता ।
अथायमस्यां कृतवान् महात्मा लङ्केश्वरः कष्टमनार्यकर्म ॥ V. 9. 73

"But Sita is not like these women; she is not likely to have become his victim. But in taking her away from her natural place, Ravana has really committed an unpardonable excess."

Being under this curse he changed his ways and now became an accomplished lover showing to these women the gentle and attractive side of himself, so that when he was killed in battle, the wail set up by his Rakshasa wives was sincere. They all bemoaned his death sincerely, though they realised that he was a bad person, was wicked by nature and had brought all this trouble on himself by his misbehaviour towards Sita. There was a certain degree of genuineness in their grief while they at the same time realised what a bad man he was.

बहुमानात् परिष्वज्य काचिदेनं रुरोद ह ।
चरणौ काचिदालिङ्ग्य काचित्कण्ठेऽवलम्ब्य च ॥
उद्धृत्य च भुजौ काचिद्भूमौ स्म परिवर्तते ।
हतस्य वदनं दृष्ट्वा काचिन्मोहमुपागमत् ॥
काचिदङ्के शिरः कृत्वा रुरोद मुखमीक्षती ।
स्नापयन्ती मुखं बाष्पैस्तुषारैरिव पङ्कजम् ॥ VI. 113. 19-26

"One of these women came to his corpse and embraced it, another took his legs upon herself, another threw her arms round his neck. They shed genuine tears of grief."

ब्रुवाणोऽपि हितं वाक्यमिष्टो भ्राता विभीषणः ॥
धृष्टं परुषितो मोहात्त्वयात्मवधकाङ्क्षिणा ।
यदि निर्यातिता ते स्यात्सीता रामाय मैथिली ॥

न नः स्याद्व्यसनं घोरमिदं मूलहरं महत्।
त्वया पुनर्नृशंसेन सीतां संरुन्धता बलात्॥
राक्षसा वयमात्मा च त्रयं तुल्यं निपातितम्।
न कामकारः कामं वा तव राक्षसपुङ्गव॥
दैवं चेष्टयते सर्वं हतं दैवेन हन्यते।
नैवार्थेन न कामेन विक्रमेण न चाज्ञया॥
शक्या दैवगतिर्लोके निवर्तयितुमुद्यता। VI. 113. 19-26

"You were bent upon your own ruin, so you would not listen to Vibhishana when he gave you proper advice. If hearkening to Vibhishana's advice you had given back Sita to her lord, we should not be widowed now and weeping over your corpse. At one stroke you have ruined three people, all the Rakshasas, their widows and you too. Who can overcome fate?" This is our way. Whenever you hear any lamentation, you may be sure that both men and women say, at one stage or other, 'who can resist fate? All takes place according to predetermined procedure.' Mandodari, wiser than these other women, has a whole *sarga* to herself. It really reaches heights of eloquence in places.

इन्द्रियाणि पुरा जित्वा जितं त्रिभुवनं त्वया।
स्मरद्भिरिव तद्वैरमिन्द्रियैरेव निर्जितः॥
अप्राप्य चैव तं कामं मैथिलीसंगमे कृतम्॥
पतिव्रतायास्तपसा नूनं दग्धोऽसि मे प्रभो।
तदैव यन्न दग्धस्त्वं धर्षयंस्तनुमध्यमाम्॥
देवा बिभ्यति ते सर्वे सेन्द्राः साग्निपुरोगमाः।
न कुलेन न रूपेण न दाक्षिण्येन मैथिली॥
मयाऽधिका वा तुल्या वा त्वं तु मोहान्न बुध्यसे।
मैथिली सह रामेण विशोका विहरिष्यति।
अल्पपुण्या त्वहं घोरे पतिता शोकसागरे॥
पिता दानवराजो मे भर्ता मे राक्षसेश्वरः।
पुत्रो मे शक्रनिर्जेता इत्येवं गर्विता भृशम्॥
प्रवादः सत्य एवायं त्वां प्रति प्रायशो नृप।
पतिव्रतानां नाकस्मात् पतन्त्यश्रूणि भूतले॥

VI. 114. 18, 23-25, 28-29, 31, 40, 67

"In early life you subdued all your senses, you conquered all your passions, you did not yield to any temptations, you stored up *tapas* and obtained boons from the gods, and you were therefore in full control over your own *indriyas*. These senses or *indriyas* wanted to take vengeance on you. They played havoc with you and your fortunes. You have been burnt really by the *agni* of Sita's chastity. When you took her by force in *Janasthana*, her chastity might at that time have burnt you up. It did not, because your downfall was then only beginning. You had still a stock of *tapas*. A year had to go slowly. All the gods were afraid, they did not come near you, but let you go on until the right moment came. How is this Sita either equal to me or superior to me? In none of these respects should you have preferred her to me. But you were infatuated, mad, and ran after fresh conquests. You brought her here, thinking that she would become yours. But the result is that you and I are separated, while she is reunited to him from whom you took her and is going to be happy. What a proud woman I was at one time! I was the daughter of Maya, the wife of Ravana and mother of Indrajit. My father, my husband and my son, all were of the first order of eminence in the world. I have been punished now. The saying is perfectly true, and has been fulfilled in your case. A tear falling from the eyes of a *pativrata* will not go in vain; it will punish somebody hard. And how many *pativratas* have been obliged to weep by your wickedness!"

Though I have said so far that Ravana changed his ways and was gentle with women and obtained their hearts through legitimate means, through the exercise of his charms over them, you must not conclude therefrom that his character was pure and that he was a good person. His greatness was divorced from goodness. He was still capable of great meanness. He could do cruel things, could plot, tell grand lies, construct long yarns, and deceive people. I shall now go into that part of his character. It is most disgraceful and utterly discreditable to him. We are sorry indeed when we see in human or in Rakshasa nature great gifts prostituted to ignoble purposes by reason of the absence of this good nature. Ravana had it not in any measure. He was a cunning man. Though he was brave and could meet anybody in battle, had often brought Indra down on his knees, would often accomplish his purposes by adopting cunning, instead of having a straight fight, Ravana had so much contempt for Rama at first. Why then did he not stand up to him instead of going in the guise of a *sanyasi?* So strong is the attraction of a little craft or cunning to some natures that Ravana fell a victim to that nature. This was known against him not only to Sita but Rama himself. Other people too often twitted him with this meanness. He had Rama and Lakshmana abducted by craft by Maricha and adopted a wrong guise and tried to play upon the feelings of Sita and employed force to bring her away. She did not yield. Otherwise, he would have tempted her too by his trickery. Sita, whose tongue was sharp, did not leave him alone.

न व्यपत्रपसे नीच कर्मणानेन रावण ।
ज्ञात्वा विरहितां यन्मां चोरयित्वा पलायसे ॥
त्वयैव नूनं दुष्टात्मन् भीरुणा हर्तुमिच्छता ।
ममापवाहितो भर्ता मृगरूपेण मायया ॥
परमं खलु ते वीर्यं दृश्यते राक्षसाधम ।
विश्राव्य नामधेयं हि युद्धे नास्मि जिता त्वया ॥
ईदृशं गर्हितं कर्म कथं कृत्वा न लज्जसे ।
स्त्रियाश्च हरणं नीच रहिते तु परस्य च ॥
धिक् ते शौर्यं च सत्त्वं च यत्त्वं कथितवांस्तदा ।
कुलाक्रोशकरं लोके धिक् ते चारित्रमीदृशम् ॥ III. 53. 3-4, 6, 7, 9

"Aren't you ashamed of this act of yours? Knowing me to be alone and unprotected, you steal me and run away with me. I know this now, you were a coward and did not care to fight my husband and brother-in-law in open battle. You adopted this low trick, had them taken away by Maricha. If you had come there and proclaimed yourself and fought with Rama, that would have been something." Sita often reproaches him like this. In his own dignified way Rama says to him when he met him in the battlefield towards the close,

मया विरहितां दीनां वर्तमानां महावने ।
वैदेहीं प्रसभं हृत्वा शूरोऽहमिति मन्यसे ॥
स्त्रीषु शूर विनाथासु परदाराभिमर्शक ।
कृत्वा कापुरुषं कर्म शूरोऽहमिति मन्यसे ॥
भिन्नमर्याद निर्लज्ज चारित्रेष्वनवस्थित ।
दर्पान्मृत्युमुपादाय शूरोऽहमिति मन्यसे ॥

शूरेण धनदभ्रात्रा बलैः समुदितेन च ।
श्लाघनीयं यशस्यं च कृतं कर्म महत्त्वया ॥
शूरोऽहमिति चात्मानमवगच्छसि दुर्मते ।
नैव लज्जास्ति ते सीतां चोरवद्व्यपकर्षतः ॥ VI. 105. 12-15; 17

"You think you are a hero, having done this mean thing, having procured my absence and taken her away. You think you are a brave man. I know your valour. You are well connected; you are a half-brother of Kubera himself, and yet you are not ashamed to do this. Like a thief you steal her from me."

Then I come to another wicked deed of his. He tried to deceive Sita by a low trick again. Rama had the bridge constructed by the monkeys and crossed over and taken his position right on the north side of Lanka. He was sending round his people to see all about the place and find out all about the defences of the city, and the strength of the enemy. Ravana then ordered Vidyujjihva, who seems to have practised tricks to prepare a counterfeit head of Rama, cut off from the shoulders and complete also with a bow and arrow like Rama's. He himself went to Sita and told her to look at this bleeding head of her husband, with his sword and bow and arrow. He then tells her a long yarn. He hid from her the fact that Rama had crossed over to Lanka. He says, "Last night he lay with his huge hosts on the other side of the water. I sent my commander-in-chief Prahasta, and when they were all asleep, my men slew the monkey army and your husband and his brother." The whole of this is a concoction. Of course Sita was taken in and began to weep. Her first thought was of Kaikeyi. Ravana tells her,

एवं तव हतो भर्ता ससैन्यो मम सेनया ॥
क्षतजार्द्रं रजोध्वस्तमिदं चास्याहृतं शिरः । VI. 31. 36-37

"Your husband's hope was to kill me. Here is his head, bleeding, taken from the earth with all the dust gathered round it." We have to remember that the whole of this was an invention of Ravana, and he narrates this without being ashamed. Even if Prahasta had done all that, it was a shameful thing. While Sita was crying in grief, one of his important ministers came with the story of Rama's landing on this side of the water, and he had to leave in a hurry. Now the poet says,

अन्तर्धानं तु तच्छीर्षं तच्च कार्मुकमुत्तमम् ।
जगाम रावणस्यैव निर्याणसमनन्तरम् ॥ VI. 32. 40

As soon as he left, the counterfeit head of Rama left too, showing that it was the work merely of sorcery. Sita was bewildered. Then comes Vibhishana's wife Sarama who told Sita, "Nothing has happened to your husband and his brother. Ravana has been telling you pure fabrication."

न हतो राघवः श्रीमान् सीते शत्रुनिबर्हणः ॥
अयुक्तबुद्धिकृत्येन सर्वभूतविरोधिना ।
इयं प्रयुक्ता रौद्रेण माया मायाविदा त्वयि ॥ VI. 33. 13-14

"I have seen your husband on this side of the water and in triumph. Why grieve over him?"

When Indrajit had felled Rama and Lakshmana by his Nagastra and gone to his father and reported that they were both killed, Ravana, whose one idea was to get hold of Sita somehow, in his triumph sent for the Rakshasis guarding over Sita and asked them to put Sita into the Pushpakavimana and let her see her husband and brother-in-law lying dead in the battlefield, thinking that now that the game was up, Sita would yield herself up to him. What a calculation! This time it was Trijata who consoled her. She came in the Pushpakavimana and she says, "Look at Rama's face and at Lakshmana's face. The two men are only unconscious, and they will come to consciousness again. This Pushpakavimana is so holy that if really you were a widow, it would not hold you."

Then we come to another act of Ravana which is worse than all these. When his fortunes were low, almost at their lowest ebb,—Indrajit had been killed, and his last great warrior had passed away—, Ravana had lost all presence of mind, became very mean and wanted to behave disgracefully. So he said, "Sita has brought this trouble on me. I will go and kill her." He ran to her with the object of killing her. It shows the depth to which the man fell. "At one time my son Indrajit by his *maya* had a counterfeit Sita killed before Hanuman. This time I am going to do it for a real fact." People there thought it was disgraceful for him to do so. At last, when his sword was drawn, Sita wept, poor lady, seeing Ravana in that fearful posture, and said,

हनूमतोऽपि यद्वाक्यं न कृतं क्षुद्रया मया ॥
यद्यहं तस्य पृष्ठेन तदा यायामनिन्दिता ।
नाद्यैवमनुशोचेयं भर्तुरङ्कगता सती ॥ VI. 93. 54-55

"What a foolish person I was! When Hanuman promised to take me on his back, why did I refuse? I shall not be grieving over my husband now." Then Suparsva told him, "She is a woman after all. You are a man and have been a hero all these years and fought on equal terms with the gods and overthrown them. Come and kill Rama." The slight element of honour left in him was roused.

स्वमेव तु संहास्माभी राघवे क्रोधमुत्सृज ।
अभ्युत्थानं त्वमद्यैव कृष्णपक्षचतुर्दशीम् ॥
कृत्वा निर्याह्यमावास्यां विजयाय बलैर्वृतः ।
शूरो धीमान् रथी खड्गी रथप्रवरमास्थितः ॥
हत्वा दाशरथिं रामं भवान् प्राप्स्यति मैथिलीम् । VI. 93. 65-66

"That way you had better obtain Sita if you want."

Now I come to the last section on Ravana. This brings Ravana and Sita together. You will bear in your minds this fact, that Ravana's end came through Sita, that he brought this trouble upon himself by laying violent hands on this pure lady and in a deceitful, cunning manner. In his passion for her, there must have been an element of what I call infatuation, a kind of madness, something which he could not get over. There was something in Sita that held him down. This infatuation was first started in his mind by a man named Akampana who had been watching the whole of the battle between Khara, Dushana and Trisiras on the one side, and Rama on the other. He saw how mighty Rama was and how he could kill these three persons and their followers, all single-handed. Akampana ran away from the battlefield before everything was over and reported the fact to Ravana. Unfortunately this *sarga,* where Akampana makes his report to Ravana, is considered spurious by most people. It would be a pity to lose it on account of some academic considerations, because it contains some noble passages. It contains a wonderful account of Rama himself by an impartial witness, and it also brings out in an extraordinary way the attractiveness and beauty of Sita and the glorious side of her character. Akampana says, "There is one way in which you can kill Rama. His whole life is centred in Sita. Deprive him of her and he is gone." Ravana goes to Maricha. At that time his mind itself was wavering. Maricha dissuades him. Ravana believed Maricha and went back quietly. But soon, to his misfortune, his sister Surpanakha came with her wonderful story. She said, "I went there and saw Sita, the very jewel of the three worlds, character, beauty, conduct all centred in one. You are a proper husband for her. I was going to take her in order to give her over to you. The two brothers got very angry and treated me very shamefully." Believing this, Ravana makes up his mind that he would try and get hold of Sita.

यदि तस्यामभिप्रायो भार्यार्थे तव जायते ॥
शीघ्रमुध्द्रियतां पादो जयार्थमिह दक्षिणः । III. 34. 22-23

"Put your right foot forward to get victory over Rama." Surpanakha wants Rama and Lakshmana killed in battle. Ravana did not venture so far. He was keen on getting Sita, but not on fighting Rama and Lakshmana. When Rama and Lakshmana had been taken away after Maricha, Ravana goes into Sita's presence in the guise of a *sanyasi.* Then follows a long speech by him, one that would do credit to any gallant in a Parisian boudoir, in some parts very vulgar and too direct. Having described her and her charms, he finally asks her who she is.

कमलानां शुभां मालां पद्मिनीव हि बिभ्रती ।
ह्रीः श्रीः कीर्तिः शुभा लक्ष्मीरप्सरा वा शुभानने ॥
भूतिर्वा त्व वरारोहे रतिर्वा स्वैरचारिणी ।
समाः शिखरिणः स्निग्धाः पाण्डरा दशनास्तव ॥
विशाले विमले नेत्रे रक्तान्ते कृष्णतारके ।
विशालं जघनं पीनमूरू करीकरोपमौ ॥
एतावुपचितौ वृत्तौ संहतौ संप्रवल्गितौ ।
पीनोन्नतमुखौ कान्तौ स्निग्धौ तालफलोपमौ ॥
मणिप्रवेकाभरणौ रुचिरौ ते पयोधरौ ।
चारुस्मिते चारुदति चारुनेत्रे विलासिनि ॥
मनो हरसि मे कान्ते नदी कूलमिवाम्भसा ।
करान्तमितमध्यासि सुकेशी संहतस्तनी ॥
नैव देवी न गन्धर्वी न यक्षी न च किन्नरी ।
नैवंरूपा मया नारी दृष्टपूर्वा महीतले ॥

रूपमग्र्यं च लोकेषु सौकुमार्यं वयश्च ते ।

इह वासश्च कान्तारे चित्तमुन्मादयन्ति मे ॥

कासि कस्य कुतश्च त्वं किंनिमित्तं च दण्डकान् ।

एका चरसि कल्याणि घोरान् राक्षससेवितान् ॥ III. 46. 16-23, 31

What did Sita think when all these fine compliments were paid to her? Was she pleased, as women ordinarily are now when their charms are duly appreciated, it is difficult to say. But there is nothing to show that she was displeased. She does not rebuke him for his reference to her personal charms, but pays him due respect as a *sanyasi*. There is reference to the fact that she was very uneasy. She was looking anxiously for the return of her husband and brother-in-law. She remembered under what circumstances they had gone, and as she had heard the cry of Rama, she thought that some danger had occurred to her husband. She was not able wholly to conceal her anxiety, and showed to him all the hospitality that she could. Then she frankly tells him all about herself, and asks him to tell her who he is. Ravana discloses himself and his passion for her.

त्वां तु काञ्चनवर्णाभां दृष्ट्वा कौशेयवासिनीम् ।

रतिं स्वकेषु दारेषु नाधिगच्छाम्यनिन्दिते ॥

बह्वीनामुत्तमस्त्रीणामाहृतानामितस्ततः ।

सर्वासामेव भद्रं ते ममाग्रमहिषी भव ॥ III. 47. 27-28

He makes a proposal direct to her. We must remember that in those days there was no rule against polygamy. What he offered to Sita was, according to the notions of the time, fair and honourable marriage. Sita's rejection was unreserved. In this place, all I need say is that she provoked Ravana to such an extent by her reproaches that he assumes his ten-headed form and begins to threaten her. This is a rule amongst voluptuous people. If there is real love offered, there ought to be no repudiation. True love ought not to be rejected at all. "As Urvasi rejected Pururavas and afterwards repented, so you will have to be." Ravana takes her to his palace and shows to her all the grand things that were there.

अलं व्रीडेन वैदेहि धर्मलोपकृतेन च ॥

आर्षोऽयं दैवनिष्यन्दो यस्त्वामभिगमिष्यति ।

एतौ पादौ मया स्निग्धौ शिरोभिः परिपीडितौ ॥

प्रसादं कुरु मे क्षिप्रं वश्यो दासोऽहमस्मि ते।
इमाः शून्या मया वाचः शुष्यमाणेन भाषिताः ॥
न चापि रावणः कांचिन्मूर्ध्ना स्त्रीं प्रणमेत हि।
एवमुक्त्वा दशग्रीवो मैथिलीं जनकात्मजाम् ॥
कृतान्तवशमापन्नो ममेयमिति मन्यते ॥ III. 55. 34-37

He grew so abject in his love that he falls at her feet and says, "Never has Ravana fallen at the feet of a woman. You get this rare honour." As he fell at her feet and appealed to her in that soft way, he thought he would capture her; cajolery and threats, all were unavailing, but he did not give up. In the 20th *sarga* of the Sundarakanda we come upon a scene of which Hanuman himself was witness. This is what Ravana says to her,

कामये त्वां विशालाक्षि बहुमन्यस्व मां प्रिये।
सर्वाङ्गगुणसंपन्ने सर्वलोकमनोहरे ॥
*स्वधर्मो रक्षसां भीरु सर्वथैव न संशयः।
गमनं वा परस्त्रीणां हरणं संप्रमथ्य वा ॥
एवं चैतदकामां तु न त्वां स्प्रक्ष्यामि मैथिलि।
कामं कामः शरीरे मे यथाकामं प्रवर्तताम् ॥
एकवेणी धरा शय्या ध्यानं मलिनमम्बरम्।
अस्थानेऽप्युपवासश्च नैतान्यौपयिकानि ते ॥
त्वां कृत्वोपरतो मन्ये रूपकर्ता स विश्वसृट्।
न हि रूपोपमा त्वन्या तवास्ति शुभदर्शने ॥
त्वां समासाद्य वैदेहि रूपयौवनशालिनीम्।
कः पुमानतिवर्तेत साक्षादपि पितामहः ॥ V. 20. 3, 5-6, 8, 13-14

"My tribe, my race is not bound by the ordinary rules of propriety that govern your human kind. But if you do not feel inclined, I won't touch you. Let my love consume me as it might. All the hardships that you are now suffering on behalf of your husband, these do not fit you. When he created you, Brahma did his best."

*Cf. Lecture XXII, p. 314.

TWENTYFIFTH LECTURE*

Ladies and Gentlemen,

Last time we were concerned with the infatuation of Ravana for Sita. It was unlike his feeling for other women in that he could not control it in any way. On the contrary it over-mastered him and led him into many troubles and finally destroyed him.

यद्यत्पश्यामि ते गात्रं शीतांशुसदृशानने ।
तस्मिंस्तस्मिन् पृथुश्रोणि चक्षुर्मम निबध्यते ॥ V. 20. 15

Ravana was saying this to Sita in one of his frequent visits. This one takes place in the Asokavana. "Whichever part of your body I see, O moon-faced one, in that very part my eye is fastened, fixed, and cannot take itself away."

चारुस्मिते चारुदति चारुनेत्रे विलासिनि ।
मनो हरसि मे भीरु सुपर्णः पन्नगं यथा ॥ V. 20. 29

"You smile so sweetly; your teeth are so attractive; your eyes are so winsome; you captivate me utterly, as Garuda does when he meets serpents." Then he makes his final appeal to her, throws wide his net of temptation.

पिब विहर रमस्व भुङ्क्ष्व भोगान्
धननिचयं प्रदिशामि मेदिनीं च ।
मयि लल ललने यथासुखं त्वं
त्वयि च समेत्य ललन्तु बान्धवास्ते ॥ V. 20. 35

"Come, let us drink together, let us sport together, let us enjoy each other's company. I will give you any quantity of wealth; and all this earth too thou shalt rule with me. Only take delight in me, and when you are happy, bring all your relations, old Janaka too, and let them all enjoy themselves at my expense." The poet uses specially a frisky metre to show the temper in which Ravana was at the time he spoke. All this was gall and wormwood to Sita. On the other hand it annoyed and provoked her extremely. She scorned him, but in her reply she threw in a mixture of threat, flattery and

* 27-9-'44.

advice to see whether any of these modes could conquer his wickedness. This is her advice to him, pitched in the highest possible key.

यथा तव तथान्येषां दारा रक्ष्या निशाचर ॥
आत्मानमुपमां कृत्वा स्वेषु दारेषु रम्यताम्। V. 21. 7-8

"You do not understand the sanctity of marriage. When you have got another man's wife in your keeping, you must protect her as you would have your own wife protected from others. Think of yourself; think of everybody like you, and then delight in the company of your own wedded wives." In her surprise she says,

इह सन्तो न वा सन्ति सतो वा नानुवर्तसे ॥
तथा हि विपरीता ते बुद्धिराचारवर्जिता। V. 21. 9-10

"Are there no good people in Lanka, are there no honest men who care for righteous conduct, and would you not be guided by them? It cannot be. Lanka is a big place, the Vedas are chanted here, our religion is followed faithfully. There must be many good people. I suspect that you do not follow them. You do not care for the good people that are here. Seeing that your mind is bent upon evil courses, I gather that although there are good people to give you proper guidance, you do not listen to them."

Now a word by way of improving the occasion. This is a common weakness amongst friends, and I should like to say just a word to those who would, if they could, discharge their duties properly to friends. Sita fears that Ravana does not listen to the good people that advise him. That shows what the duty of good elderly people in a community is. The good elderly people ought not to say to themselves, "That fool is a rogue. I will not go near him. He will not recognise my age or my grey hairs. What is the good of going to him?" That is not the attitude that Sita expects good people in any community to take, and it certainly is not the attitude that good people in any community should take. If you have real friends, whether of your age or senior or a little junior, if you have real friends whose welfare you wish and truly care for, your duty, whatever the other party may say or do, is to give them proper guidance. Advise whenever you can, but do not watch him go down the hill of wickedness, and, when all is over, come and bemoan his fate and say, "I would have warned you at that time, but you would not listen." Whether parties are willing or unwilling to listen, the duty of a friend must be fearlessly discharged, and that is to warn against coming evil, and to see that even if he falls in the end, he does not fall without guidance, but falls knowingly. There are many people who do their wickednesses unknowingly, not suspecting that anybody's eye is on them and that ruin awaits them at the end of the lane. To them a timely warning may be useful. As we read these great books and the sayings of these great people in order that we may profit by them, I venture to reinforce the lesson implied in Sita's words to Ravana. In this crisis of their lives she points out, in very proper language, what good men should do in any community, and what men who still waver should do when they receive such advice.

Here is one stage further. Ravana is still trying to seduce Sita. He talks very sweetly to her, flatters her beauty, praises her wisdom and dispraises her husband proportionately.

यथा यथा सान्त्वयिता वश्यः स्त्रीणां तथा तथा ।
यथा यथा प्रियं वक्ता परिभूतस्तथा तथा ॥
संनियच्छति मे क्रोधं त्वयि कामः समुत्थितः ।
द्रवतोऽमार्गमासाद्य हयानिव सुसारथिः ॥
वामः कामो मनुष्याणां यस्मिन् किल निबध्यते ।
जने तस्मिंस्त्वनुक्रोशः स्नेहश्च किल जायते ॥
एतस्मात्कारणान्न त्वां घातयामि वरानने ।
वधार्हामवमानार्हां मिथ्याप्रव्रजिते रताम् ॥
परुषाणीह वाक्यानि यानि यानि ब्रवीषि माम् ।
तेषु तेषु वधो युक्तस्तव मैथिलि दारुणः ॥
द्वौ मासौ रक्षितव्यौ मे योऽवधिस्ते मया कृतः ।
ततः शयनमारोह मम त्वं वरवर्णिनि ॥
द्वाभ्यामूर्ध्वं तु मासाभ्यां भर्तारं मामनिच्छतीम् ।
मम त्वां प्रातराशार्थमारभन्ते महानसे ॥ V. 22. 2-6, 8-9

"In this world when a man goes out of his way to flatter women, tells them nice things and tries to steal their hearts, he becomes more and more dear to them. That is the way of the world. When a big man comes and says nice things to a little girl, she is flattered and thinks, 'I seem to be lucky in the world.' She is rightly drawn to him. But my luck is very different. In proportion as I try to flatter you and win your heart, in that proportion do you repulse me. I get very angry with you. I am the ten-headed Ravana, the terror of the three worlds. There is nothing that I cannot get. Nature herself is afraid of me. The sun, the moon, the stars and Vayu and Agni, all wait on my pleasure. Still I come and fall at your feet; my ten heads roll at your feet; and still you do not yield. I am between two strong emotions, love to you, infatuation for you, and at the same time, anger, displeasure that there should be a tiny little thing of the other sex defying and insulting me. Every time my anger rises, my love says, 'No, do not punish her. Try your arts upon her still more.' Even as a clever driver will rein in the horses when they get out of control and tend to gallop, so too my love controls my anger. Kama is a wicked thing, love is not a thing to encourage. (But it does not need encouragement when it amounts to infatuation. It is already your master.) Towards the party in whom the love rests, instead of getting angry when anger is proper, tenderness and pity both come and take hold of you. You who deserve death at my hands, you escape because of this. Love conquers anger and prevails over the other feelings. You speak such harsh things to me, say such insolent things to me, that for every one of them you deserve cruel death at my hand, not ordinary death. But this cannot last very long; only two months remain of the twelve months I gave you when I first brought you here. After the two months are over, you must get into my bed. If, by the end of the two months, you do not accept me as your husband, then my cooks will drag you into the kitchen and there cut you and mince you to pieces for my breakfast." Despite this threat, she did not yield; she grew a little more insolent and said harsh things to him.

अवेक्षमाणो वैदेहीं कोपसंरक्तलोचनः ।
उवाच रावणः सीतां भुजङ्ग इव निःश्वसन् ॥
अनयेनाभिसंपन्नमर्थहीनमनुव्रते ।
नाशयाम्यहमद्य त्वां सूर्यः सन्ध्यामिवौजसा ॥ V. 22. 30-31

Getting very angry and hissing like a cobra, he said, 'As the sun disposes of darkness in the morning, so shall I dispose of you.' Then he turned towards the Rakshasis who guarded her. These Rakshasis were different from the ladies of the harem, who were queens and princesses brought away from palaces, whom Ravana had won over by his extraordinary skill in all the arts of love. But these Rakshasis were cruel, heartless and slave-minded, whose very look frightened Sita. Now the poet gets into one of his humorous moods and describes how these Rakshasis looked.

> एकाक्षीमेककर्णां च कर्णप्रावरणां तथा।
> गोकर्णीं हस्तिकर्णीं च लम्बकर्णीमकर्णिकाम्॥
> हस्तिपाद्यश्वपाद्यौ च गोपदीं पादचूलिकाम्।
> एकाक्षीमेकपादीं च पृथुपादीमपादुकाम्॥
> अतिमात्रशिरोग्रीवामतिमात्रकुचोदरीम्।
> अतिमात्रास्यनेत्रां च दीर्घजिह्वामजिह्विकाम्॥'
> अनासिकां सिंहमुखीं गोमुखीं सूकरीमुखीम्।
> यथा मद्वशगा सीता क्षिप्रं भवति जानकी॥
> तथा कुरुत राक्षस्यः सर्वाः क्षिप्रं समेत्य च।
> प्रतिलोमानुलोमैश्च सामदानादिभेदनैः॥
> आवर्जयत वैदेहीं दण्डस्योद्यमनेन च।
> इति प्रतिसमादिश्य राक्षसेन्द्रः पुनः पुनः॥
> काममन्युपरीतात्मा जानकीं पर्यतर्जयत्। V. 22. 33-39

To them Ravana says, "So prevail upon her, so talk to her, so work upon her feelings, describe me in such wise to her, that her heart may turn towards me. Do it severally, individually or collectively." Having said this, he roared at her again and approached her as if to strike her. Then one of his queens, by name Dhanyamalini, who was the mother of the famous son Atikaya, threw herself upon him and drew him off and calmed his ill-temper. Amongst other things she said one thing which I wish to indicate.

> अकामां कामयानस्य शरीरमुपतप्यते॥
> इच्छन्तीं कामयानस्य प्रीतिर्भवति शोभना। V. 22. 42-43

This is one of the secrets of love. She says, "In dealing with women, happiness is multiplied a hundred-fold if the other party is a willing partner. If it is otherwise, then the man is bound to burn, burn, burn."

In the Yuddhakanda Ravana summons a council of war and pretends to take their advice as to what he should do. Seeking advice, on his part, contrasts sharply with the methods of Sri Rama. Rama propounds the question to his friends in neutral style. When Vibhishana appeared, he asked all the people about him to tell him what he should do. Though Rama was determined to accept him, he did not put it to them and does not say so. Ravana tells his ministers how he got hold of Sita and also how he got cursed over other women. "Tell me", he says, "what I am to do, but do not say that I should yield up Sita. I have not put myself to all this trouble, disgraced all my character and lost my reputation, in order to give her back. Advise me so that I may retain her." That is the advice he wanted, an advice subject to that very hard condition.

इयं च दण्डकारण्याद्रामस्य महिषी प्रिया।
रक्षोभिश्चरिताद्देशादानीता जनकात्मजा॥ VI. 12. 12

Here is a point that you should note, if you are particular about reading the text at any time. Ravana says something which comes out of the legal side of his mind. He has gone and caught hold of Sita. His advisers may ask him whether he trespassed. If he did so, he was bound to yield her up. In order apparently to anticipate that point, he says, "I have brought her from a place tenanted by our own people, from Janasthana, which is our out-post. The Rakshasas haunt that place and it is there that she was found. She is therefore my lawful prey." Then he declares his infatuation for Sita in express terms to his own people. Did you ever hear in private life, in the kind of life that we live, anybody go and publish his amours in that fashion? Here is a man who, having done a wicked deed to another man's wife, goes and publishes that fact without shame and says that he has abducted a woman for his enjoyment, and asks them to tell him how to compass his end. It is the business of the ministers to see that his nefarious designs go through. "Apparently she is a sluggish-minded girl. I do not think there is another like her." It is on Sita's feet that his eyes dwell most. He says,

सुलोहिततलौ श्लक्ष्णौ चरणौ सुप्रतिष्ठितौ।
दृष्ट्वा ताम्रनखौ तस्या दीप्यते मे शरीरजः॥ VI. 12. 15

"When I see her feet, it is on them alone my eyes dwell. They are so fashioned that they charm me most. My love is inflamed when I see her feet." Now a word about feet. Many of you who have observed these things will know that the feet of women are not always in accord with their general frame. God makes something or other defective. Usually feet are defective. Either they have too big a gap between the fingers, or one side is higher than the other, or the fingers join together most awkwardly, or they are too far separated. Ravana was a very skilful person in observing the feet of Sita and pronounced that they were of the regular type.

उन्नसं वदनं वल्गु विपुलं चारुलोचनम् ।
पश्यंस्तदा वशस्तस्याः कामस्य वशमेयिवान् ॥
क्रोधहर्षसहायेन दुर्वर्णकरणेन च ।
शोकसन्तापनित्येन कामेन कलुषीकृतः ॥
सा तु संवत्सरं कालं मामयाचत भामिनी ।
प्रतीक्षमाणा भर्तारं राममायतलोचना ॥
तन्मया चारुनेत्रायाः प्रतिज्ञातं वचः शुभम् । VI. 12. 17-20

"The tip of the nose is slightly raised. The feeling that I have is *krodha* and *harsha*. It entirely disfigures and discolours me. She asked of me one year's respite, and I was pleased to give it to her." The commentators take exception to it. Sita did not ask for any time at all. It was he that volunteered twelve months' respite to her. They stress that point because they think that it is unworthy of Sita to ask for any respite, and she would not have asked for it. The condition that Ravana imposed on the ministers whose advice he sought is that he would not give her up.

अदेया च यथा सीता वध्यौ दशरथात्मजौ ॥
भवद्भिर्मन्त्र्यतां मन्त्रः सुनीतिश्चाभिधीयताम् । VI. 12. 25-26

He wants Rama and Lakshmana killed. The ministers should tell him, when they had made up their minds, how these two ends were to be compassed.

This infatuation was known to everybody. He himself was at no pains to conceal it. You remember how when Indrajit made a counterfeit figure of Sita and killed it before the eyes of Hanuman, Hanuman ran up to Rama and reported it to him. At that time Rama believed the story and fell into a swoon, and it was with difficulty that he could be brought to consciousness. Vibhishana comes in a little later and, finding how affairs stood, said that it was that scoundrel nephew of his that must have made a *maya* figure of Sita and killed it before Hanuman. Then he assures Rama that Ravana would never kill Sita.

अभिप्रायं तु जानामि रावणस्य दुरात्मनः ।
सीतां प्रति महाबाहो न च घातं करिष्यति ॥
याच्यमानस्तु बहुशो मया हितचिकीर्षुणा ।
वैदेहीमुत्सृजस्वेति न च तत्कृतवान् वचः ॥
नैव साम्ना न दानेन न भेदेन कुतो युधा ।
सा द्रष्टुमपि शक्येत नैव चान्येन केनचित् ॥ VI. 84. 10-12

"I know my brother's mind; he will not kill her. How often have I told him that he should give up Sita! I have warned him that her being there would be the destruction of everybody in Lanka. He won't do it because he won't lose hope. His infatuation has gone to that extent. He will not let anybody see her. He has not brought her here for killing her." (Perhaps the inner meaning is that she will kill him in the end.) In this, however, Vibhishana was slightly over-drawing the picture, for as I told you last time, when Indrajit having fallen, Ravana's worst feelings were uppermost, he became ten times the beast that ever he was and made up his mind to kill Sita who was at the bottom of all this trouble. Then it was that Sita told herself, "What a wicked fool I was not to have availed of Hanuman's magnanimous offer! I then stood upon a nice point." Ravana did wish to kill Sita then. In saying therefore that Ravana would never wish to kill Sita, Vibhishana was slightly over-shooting his point. But he was also right. Vibhishana's instinct was true, for in the end, even though Ravana tried to kill Sita, he could not. Suparsva came and dissuaded him, by saying that he must kill Rama the husband. That roused Ravana's soldierly qualities. Even when Ravana made up his mind definitely to finish Sita, any little thing was good enough to upset his plan.

SITA

Only one word of general introduction; though I have said it, it is worth repeating. No woman that I have read of, certainly no woman that I have seen, comes near Valmiki's conception of Sita. She is unapproachable. He has conferred on her all the attractions that woman could conceivably have. Beauty, tenderness of heart, compassion of the extreme type, fidelity, wisdom of the truest type, courage of the heart, endurance (what has not Sita endured), all these qualities find in her a harmonious abode. She is a piece of nature like which there was and can be none. Let us dwell a little on the happy period of her life. Then we shall soon have to deal with her as a sorrowing woman with no one around her to comfort her. All that she looked upon was hateful, all that she heard from Ravana was murderous in the extreme. That we shall come to. But we can dwell a little fondly, if a little lingeringly, over the time when she was still happy, happy not in Ayodhya, but happy in the forest, away from the kingdom. For what was the kingdom to her? To her Rama was everything. Where he was that was her *svarga*. If he was not with her, that was the opposite to her. But there is something in Ayodhya too, to which we must pay attention, because there too her great qualities shine in their fullness. But there is a preliminary point concerning more the poet than her, to which I shall draw your attention. It is one of the sad experiences of people who have girls to marry off. Sita was a jewel among brides. No man need have suffered any anxiety as to how to get her married. And why should Janaka have been anxious about her? Nevertheless when we first meet Janaka, the poet does not tell us anything about his troubles. But when Sita recounts the story of her marriage, describing it as a svayamvara, to Anasuya in the forest, she says she was just six years of age. She was so wise that she was पतिसंयोगसुलभा।

पतिसंयोगसुलभं वयो दृष्ट्वा तु मे पिता।
चिन्तामभ्यगमद्दीनो वित्तनाशादिवाधनः॥
सदृशाच्चापकृष्टाच्च लोके कन्यापिता जनात्।
प्रधर्षणमवाप्नोति शक्रेणापि समो भुवि॥
तां धर्षणामदूरस्थां दृष्ट्वा चात्मनि पार्थिवः।
चिन्तार्णवगतः पारं नाससादाप्लवो यथा॥ II. 118. 34-36

How could a girl of six have observed this, and how, often should she have observed it to make this emphatic pronouncement? "The father may be the equal to Indra in every respect, position, power, wealth, honour. Nevertheless, if he has a daughter not yet married, from his equal and from his inferior he gets humiliation, censure of the worst kind." She must have observed Janaka, but Janaka is not described as having been very terribly anxious about her. For, if he was, would he have instituted that terrible test for the bridegroom, that he should bend the bow of Siva, which nobody had done before? Very few people were able even to lift it; it had to be hauled on wheels. Would Janaka have said, "I am going to give my daughter in marriage to the man who manages and manipulates this bow?" It seems incredible. Nevertheless, it was Sita who says to Anasuya, "My father saw that humiliation approaching him." I am astonished. I think that we may safely acquit Sita of having made all these observations and communicated them to Anasuya. The fact of the matter is that in the time of Valmiki it had become extremely difficult to marry off girls suitably. At that time the parents of brides had become really very anxious, and Valmiki puts it back in time and ascribes to Janaka ideas similar to those that prevailed in his time. But that is not the only thing. Valmiki is so fond of the idea that he goes back earlier in time. Before that, when Sumali, *i.e.*, Ravana's maternal grandfather, wanted to marry his daughter Kaikasi, he too seems to have been in a similar difficulty. These were only one or two generations after Brahma himself, and so soon the population would not have grown so rapidly! Sumali takes his daughter and tells her,

पुत्रि प्रदानकालोऽय यौवनं तेऽतिवर्तते।
प्रत्याख्यानाच्च भीतैस्त्वं न वरैः प्रतिगृह्यसे॥
त्वत्कृते च वयं सर्वे यन्त्रिता धर्मबुद्धयः।
त्वं हि सर्वगुणोपेता श्रीः साक्षादिव पुत्रिके॥
कन्यापितृत्वं दुःखं हि सर्वेषां मानकाङ्क्षिणाम्।
न ज्ञायते च कः कन्यां वरयेदिति कन्यके॥
मातुः कुलं पितृकुलं यत्र चैव प्रदीयते।
कुलत्रयं सदा कन्या संशये स्थाप्य तिष्ठति॥ VII. 9. 7-10

"You are so beautiful, so handsome, so able and so learned. And yet I am not able to find you a suitable husband. If people have any regard for their self-respect, the daughter is sure to ruin it." Then, when Maya had a daughter to marry, Mandodari, he walked about in the gardens with her, trying to see if any fish would rise out of the water. Ravana happened to pass that way. He asks him, "Who are you?", and Maya replies, "She is my daughter. I have come to this place to find a suitable husband for her." Evidently the poet is fond of that sentiment and he puts it into the mouth of every father of a bride. As soon as he mentioned it, Ravana jumped and said, "I will take the girl." He took her and relieved the father; and the father, out of gratitude, gave him a handsome dowry. One of the items of the dowry was that famous spear which Ravana used so effectively against Lakshmana* twice during the war and hit him hard.

In the Ayodhyakanda when Rama goes and tells his wife that he is going to the forest, she says, "I am going too." He prevents her and frightens her. But she says no, and Rama says a thousand things to please her. Then Rama describes the horrors of the forest in *slokas*, eighteen in number, ending with तस्माद् दुःखतरं वनम् II. 28. 11, and expressions similar to it. Eighteen times he repeats the warning, and also imparts to her a great deal of worldly wisdom, advises her how to behave towards his father, mother, and towards Bharata. Especially on this he is keen. I will read to you that famous verse in which Rama says how Sita should behave to Bharata. It is natural and human for a person in the position of Sita to be angry with Bharata, to be envious of him and to wish him ill, and, whenever she met him, to say how different he was from her husband, how happy Ayodhya and the whole kingdom would have been if Rama had been in his place. Rama foresaw it. So he tells Sita, "Do not commit the folly which women would ordinarily commit in such situations."

ऋद्धियुक्ता हि पुरुषा न सहन्ते परस्तवम् ।
तस्मान्न ते गुणाः कथ्या भरतस्याग्रतो मम ॥ II. 26. 25

* The reference to Maya's 'sakti' is in VI. 101. 30; the 'sakti' hurled in VI. 59. 107-8 was a gift of Brahma to Ravana. Ed.

One of the most beautiful truths in life if we are going to be happy and wise. When a man has reached a high position, holds authority, wields influence, dispenses patronage, and makes himself the mark of contemporary time, if that is the case with regard to any man, then he is likely to have one serious defect, which we must all take note of. People that go to him must remember that he cannot bear good said of any other person. "Those that have arrived at that stage will not endure the praise of another person. So, if you will be wise when I am gone, do not praise me to Bharata." Fancy how Rama, having got hold of a shrewd bit of wisdom, exercises it even against his own brother, knowing him, and not having the slightest reason to think ill of him! It is human nature. Sita has no ear for all this and she does not listen to it. She says, "You speak of the horrors of the forest, of the wild beasts there. Do you tell me that where you are, the wild beasts will come, or if they come, they will be a source of fear? With you near me I am going to be afraid of nothing. What a strong man you are! When I was a little girl in my father's house, the soothsayers used to come and say, 'This little girl is destined to live in the forest!' From that time I have developed a kind of love of the forest, and I am keen to go to the forest. The good, pious men who can see the future have told the same thing about me. I have myself fixed my heart upon it. I have told you more than once that I want to go to the forest and live there, and you have given me permission to do so. Now a good opportunity has come and let us go cheerfully."

Then come certain sentiments of the noblest kind from the lips of this paragon of her sex.

इह लोके च पितृभिर्या स्त्री यस्य महामते ।
अद्भिर्दत्ता स्वधर्मेण प्रेत्यभावेऽपि तस्य सा ॥
एवमस्मात्स्वकां नारीं सुवृत्तां हि पतिव्रताम् ।
नाभिरोचयसे नेतुं त्वं मां केनेह हेतुना ॥
भक्तां पतिव्रतां दीनां मां समां सुखदुःखयोः ।
नेतुमर्हसि काकुत्स्थ समानसुखदुःखिनीम् ॥
यदि मां दुःखितामेवं वनं नेतुं न चेच्छसि ।
विषमग्निं जलं वाहमास्थास्ये मृत्युकारणात् ॥ II. 29. 18-21

This is true. "A woman given by her father with holy water into the hands of the bridegroom belongs to him and cannot be separated from him in this world or in the other. I am not going to leave you, knowing this *dharma*. Even after death, she is his. Tell me what is the reason if, when I am bound to you in this fashion, you do not wish to take me with you. I am yours, to share your joys and your sorrows alike. If you do not wish to take me, I have no reason to live after that. I may take poison, I may enter the fire, or I will throw myself into the water." Remember that Sita is driven to the last extremity and therefore says this extreme thing too. No doubt women are fond of these excesses a little sooner than we are. Our capacity to bear adversity is slightly stronger. That is because we go about and can manage it. To them we are the only people available. Upon us they must exercise the whole of their influence. They generally say, "Very well then, if you want to go, you can go, but do not expect to see me after that." That is their last argument. It comes readily to them, and some women will do it. Even after that Rama was not moved. Then it was that Sita began to use taunts where she had only used entreaties.

सा तमुत्तमसंविग्ना सीता विपुलवक्षसम् ।
प्रणयाच्चाभिमानाच्च परिचिक्षेप राघवम् ॥
किं त्वामन्यत वैदेहः पिता मे मिथिलाधिपः ।
राम जामातरं प्राप्य स्त्रियं पुरुषविग्रहम् ॥ II. 30. 2-3

"I think of my father. He sought all the world for a bridegroom, and at last he got you. If he thought he got hold of the best man for me, he was a fool. What he had got was a woman, a cowardly woman, dressed like a man." These words are usually brought against Sita as a tremendous transgression of duty on her part,* as a violation of the limits that a woman should observe even in the expression of her

* The reference is to Govindaraja's comment on Sita's words in V. 38. 48—"ममैव दुष्कृतं किंचिन्महदस्ति न संशयः ।" The comment runs:—
'किंचिदनिर्वचनीयम् । महद्दुष्कृतमस्तीत्यनेन "किं त्वामन्यत वैदेहः" इत्यादिनोक्तो भगवदपचारः । उक्तं हि "कीदृशं तु मया पापं पुरा देहान्तरे कृतम्" (V. 25. 18) इति । देहान्तरे बालशरीरे ॥'

most profound grief. I do not agree at all. I tell you most definitely that this proves to me beyond all doubt that Sita was a good, true, brave, Rajput woman.

> अनृतं बत लोकोऽयमज्ञानाद्यद्धि वक्ष्यति ।
> तेजो नास्ति परं रामे तपतीव दिवाकरे ॥
> किं हि कृत्वा विषण्णस्त्वं कुतो वा भयमस्ति ते ।
> यत्परित्यक्तुकामस्त्वं मामनन्यपरायणाम् ॥
> न त्वहं मनसाप्यन्यं द्रष्टास्मि त्वदृतेऽनघ ।
> स्वयं तु भार्यां कौमारीं चिरमध्युषितां सतीम् ।
> शैलूष इव मां राम परेभ्यो दातुमिच्छसि ॥
> यस्य पथ्यं च रामात्थ यस्य चार्थेऽवरुध्यसे ।
> त्वं तस्य भव वश्यश्च विधेयश्च सदानघ ॥ II. 30. 4-5, 7-9

"What are you afraid of? What are the things which you dread that you should reject me who have no other person to rely on earth? I am yours entirely, utterly, and yet you discard me. Where is your moral courage gone? You must have been the doer of some terrible deed in order that you should lose your heart so utterly. I am not going to look at another person. Do not throw me on Bharata." She puts a severe, harsh, interpretation on Rama's words. When Rama said, "You dwell with Bharata", instead of understanding him in the proper sense to which it ought to be limited, she twists the words slightly. "Having brought me up from the time that I was a little creature, and having drawn me to yourself in so many ways, why do you hand me to other people like a *sailusha*, like a man who lives upon the earnings of a woman? When I am with you, I do not want good food; plain fare will be like delicious viands for me. The dust of the forest on which you have trodden will be the sandal after my heart; and grass will be the most luxurious couch. No unseemly sight would offend my eye. Do not be anxious on my account. I shall not be burdensome to you. That place where I can be with you, whatever its name be, and wherever it be, is heaven to me. If you are not there, whatever place it may be, it will be *niraya* to me. Know this for certain. Take me, and I promise you, you will be most happy. I am a kshatriya girl and I will not go under the control of other people, of Kaikeyi or Bharata. When you have abandoned me, I do not want life. If I cannot live without you for a minute, how do you ask me to live that long time?"

I wish to show you the very high quality of Sita's sentiments, the attitude to which she could rise in her sublimest moments. Upon these remonstrances of Sita, the poet has shown his utmost skill; threat, persuasion, entreaty, preaching of duty, exposition of the sanctity of marriage, all these things are brought together in one *sarga* and put into the mouth of Sita. It passes my understanding how any but an arrogant male might take objection to this. These words, harshly spoken, were spoken at a time of great mental anxiety. A proud woman, born in and married into a kshatriya family and owning for her husband the greatest man on earth, was she to be told that she was a coward and could not live in the forest with her husband? When she found that he still repeated the same tale, she could not help it. It does her honour that she said those things, for a woman is entitled to say these things boldly to her husband. Her husband and she are one. Why should the husband resent the bold talk of the wife? This is a wicked thought that enters the mind of narrow-minded little-hearted men. I cannot forgive the people who speak ill of Sita.

The best test of it all is how Rama took it. Rama certainly knew what a wife should be. Was he displeased or annoyed? If he did not say so, who are we, the contemptible little creatures that we are, to say so? The taunts he bore, Rama the great, Rama the invincible, Rama the embodiment of *dharma*. He took them quietly. Let us hear what Rama said.

तां परिष्वज्य बाहुभ्यां विसंज्ञामिव दुःखिताम् ।
उवाच वचनं रामः परिविश्वासयंस्तदा ॥
न देवि तव दुःखेन स्वर्गमप्यभिरोचये ।
न हि मेऽस्ति भयं किञ्चित्स्वयंभोरिव सर्वतः ॥
तव सर्वमभिप्रायमविज्ञाय शुभानने ।
वासं न रोचयेऽरण्ये शक्तिमानपि रक्षणे ॥
यत्सृष्टासि मया सार्धं वनवासाय मैथिलि ।
न विहातुं मया शक्या कीर्तिरात्मवता यथा ॥ II. 30. 26-29

He would not have done that if her words pained him. Restoring her confidence, he said to her, "You need not say that putting you to any trouble, I am going to *svarga* and be happy there. When I described the horrors of the forest, I was not afraid of them. I knew I was competent to protect you; I had the strength, the skill, the vigilance. Nevertheless, you wonder why I said 'no' at first. I did not know what a courageous woman you really were. I thought you might be like ordinary women. Now I see who you are, what you are, and I will obey your instructions. How can I leave you behind? You have been made by Brahma for that purpose. Just as a good man who has conquered all his passions and thinks the whole world, his family, cannot put aside his tenderness which has become an inseparable part of his nature, so are you to me. I go to the forest because Dasaratha and Kaikeyi are bent upon it. I have made up my mind to take you with me. And be with me my partner in all that I have to do in the forest." This is the *sloka* which I want you all to remember.

सर्वथा सदृशं सीते मम स्वस्य कुलस्य च।
व्यवसायमनुक्रान्ता सीते त्वमतिशोभनम्॥ II. 30. 41

At the end of this altercation, Rama was brought round so thoroughly and says this. "My family is honoured by you. Your family is also honoured by you. You have done a thing, you have made me do a thing, which is worthy alike of your house and my house." Then he tells her, "As you and I have agreed heartily that we should go together to the forest, I have given away all my wealth and possession to the Brahmins, and you may also do the same.

ततः प्रहृष्टा परिपूर्णमानसा यशस्विनी भर्तुरवेक्ष्य भाषितम्।
धनानि रत्नानि च दातुमङ्गना प्रचक्रमे धर्मभृतां मनस्विनी॥
II. 30. 47

She began to give away all. She had to strip herself as bare as possible of all pomp and the burden of pomp when she went to the forest, so that she may be as light as possible, as little of an anxiety to her husband as possible, and as serviceable to him as possible.

TWENTYSIXTH LECTURE*

Ladies and Gentlemen,

We left Sita denuding herself of all her possessions, like Sri Rama whom she was to accompany. I said that as her time in the forest during the first twelve or thirteen years was marked by happiness to herself according to her desire, we might do well to linger over those passages in the Aranyakanda. But it will be some time before we reach the forest. There is yet much matter of interest to engage us and to help us to find out how exactly their movements were performed before they went.

They have now gone as far as the Ganges and Guha is about to meet them across the river and has moored his big boats alongside of the northern bank. There is here an interesting passage which gives rise to a little difference in meaning. But it seems to me the passage is perfectly clear and there is no reason to suggest an alternative meaning. I mention this not because it is necessary to illustrate any point in Sita's character, but because it may be necessary to fill in the picture so that we may form a clear idea of how Rama and Sita and Lakshmana lived and moved with each other. The boat is ready and Rama says to Lakshmana,

आरोह त्वं नरव्याघ्र स्थितां नावमिमां शनैः ।
सीतां चारोपयान्वक्षं परिगृह्य मनस्विनीम् ॥ II. 52. 75

The words are perfectly clear. "You get into the boat first. The boat is now steady, hold it firmly and carefully and slowly get into the boat. Afterwards, when you have safely got into the boat, take up a proper position and give a hand to Sita." Here the commentator says, *manasvini* is used in a peculiar sense by the poet. The poet's way, as I shall now and then bring out, is to use words in a half-ironical sense. When he says *manasvini,* he means she is a *bhiru,* not one who is brave of heart, as the word may suggest, but one who is somewhat nervous. "Help her to get into the boat when you have yourself got into it."

स भ्रातुः शासनं श्रुत्वा सर्वमप्रतिकूलयन् ।
आरोप्य मैथिलीं पूर्वमारुरोहात्मवांस्ततः ॥ II. 52. 76

---

* 4-10-'44.

This is what Lakshmana did. It is the very next verse. The poet says nothing, but leaves us to understand why Lakshmana did not literally obey the order. He helped Sita into the boat first and then he got in. He reversed the order suggested by the brother. Apparently he thought that that was certainly better. We may take it that Lakshmana had a more practical sense in these matters. The poet says सर्वमप्रतिकूलयन्. Although the action of Lakshmana suggests a reversal, the poet says "not reversing it," meaning by that, I suppose, carrying out the order in the spirit, though not in the letter, knowing that that would be the better plan, the safer plan. Lakshmana carried out the order, he says, in the spirit, while in the letter, it appears, he did not. This is one of the peculiarities of the poet, that he would use words not to be understood in the full literal way, but with a slight subtraction of the sense. Here the commentator, not, I think, too ingeniously, says to us that the word *manasvini* and the word *atmavan* have both a certain intended significance. We are to understand usually that although Lakshmana and Sita were thrown into such intimate contact, they observed all the forms of reserve to the full between themselves. That is what we are to understand. Now Lakshmana helped Sita into the boat, so that he must have touched her, and touched her perhaps in more places than one and held her firmly. Just to indicate to us that we must not let our imagination run riot and put meanings into all this, the poet uses the word *manasvini* about Sita and the word *atmavan* about Lakshmana, intending to suggest to some of us who might be disposed to be light-hearted, that they were both people whose minds were in perfect control. Rama then got in and then Lakshmana got in as third.

Now we have a glimpse also into Rama's ways.

राघवोऽपि महातेजा नावमारुह्य तां ततः ।

ब्रह्मवत्क्षत्रवच्चैव जजाप हितमात्मनः ॥ II. 52. 78

He performed a little *mantra* in order that they may be favoured of the gods. Then they all performed *achamana* with the sacred water.

I am now coming to another river, the Kalindi or Jamna. Having crossed the Ganges, they now had to cross a smaller, but apparently swifter river. Here the order in which they were to proceed was somewhat changed.

सीतामेवाग्रतः कृत्वा कालिन्दीं जग्मतुर्नदीम् ॥ II. 55. 13

This order was somewhat unusual, because at first Rama says to Lakshmana,

अग्रतो गच्छ सौमित्रे सीता त्वामनुगच्छतु ॥

पृष्ठतोऽहं गमिष्यामि त्वां च सीतां च पालयन्। II. 52. 95-96

"You go first; Sita will follow, and I will follow, protecting you both." But when we come to the Aranyakanda, there the order differs. The order was changed from time to time, according to the necessities of the case. When they cross the Kalindi, the poet gives us a few more glimpses. The river was swift and perhaps deep. There might have been danger in crossing but they were just three people, and everything had to be done by themselves.

तौ काष्ठसङ्घाटमथो चक्रतुस्तु महाप्लवम् ॥ II. 55. 14

I read this *sloka* to you and ask you to note it particularly because some people carry away the impression that Rama was an idle spectator of things, merely supervising things when there was hard labour, which all fell upon poor Lakshmana. Rama took his share too. They made a small raft with logs of wood. Then they cut strong creepers and with them tied the things properly.

शुष्कैर्वंशैः समास्तीर्णमुशीरैश्च समावृतम्।

ततो वेतसशाखाश्च जम्बूशाखाश्च वीर्यवान् ॥

चकार लक्ष्मणश्छित्त्वा सीतायाः सुखमासनम् ॥ II. 55. 15-16

As this wooden raft might not have afforded smooth seating, Lakshmana tried to give Sita a proper seat, so that she might not have any inconvenience. That shows that in spite of all the difficulties of forest life, the brothers still paid special attention to the lady whom they had brought, and paid her the honours of her sex, as it were.

तत्र श्रियमिवाचिन्त्यां रामो दाशरथिः प्रियाम् ॥

ईषत्संलज्जमानां तामध्यारोपयत प्लवम्। II. 55. 16-17

Then they all went on the raft. This time, instead of asking Lakshmana to help Sita, Rama himself did it. I do not know whether it is the practice in all our Tamil districts, but generally speaking, husband and wife observe certain restrictions when in company, that even ordinary services are rendered to ladies by other people. Apparently that was also the case in Valmiki's time, for when Rama helped Sita into the boat, the poet gives her the epithet *lajjamanam*. For her to receive physical help from her husband before Lakshmana was something out of the way.

पार्श्वे तत्र च वैदेह्या वसने भूषणानि च ॥
प्लवे कठिनकाजं च रामश्चक्रे सहायुधैः ।
आरोप्य प्रथमं सीतां सङ्घाटं परिगृह्य च ॥ II. 55. 17-18

Some part of the labour had fallen on Rama this time. I want you to note it, because I myself, when I was young and had not known the text intimately, used to wonder how the luggage was carried, and on whom fell the burden. There must have been plenty of luggage to carry. For above all things, just when they took leave at Ayodhya, Dasaratha decreed that Sita should take away with her enough jewels and enough dresses, silk, etc., to last her all the fourteen years, and it must have been a goodly burden. How it was carried, I always wondered. Apparently the brothers divided the burden between themselves. They had their own burdens to carry, the weapons, spades, poles and baskets too.

Then, when they got off safely and were about to rest, there comes a glimpse of how they enjoyed life in the forest.

यद्यत्फलं प्रार्थयते पुष्पं वा जनकात्मजा ॥
तत्तत्प्रदद्या वैदेह्या यत्रास्या रमते मनः । II. 55. 28-29

This is Rama's injunction to Lakshmana. "If, going through the forest, Sita now and then looks about and fixes her fancy upon a flower or upon a fruit and asks for it, bring it to her straightway."

एकैकं पादपं गुल्मं लतां वा पुष्पशालिनीम् ॥
अदृष्टपूर्वां पश्यन्ती रामं पप्रच्छ साबला । II. 55. 30-31

Sita was apparently well-versed in these creatures of the forest. Whenever she met anything strange or anything that attracted her, she would stop and ask Sri Rama to tell her about it. Rama must have studied a good deal of botany to be able to tell her at once.

रमणीयान् बहुविधान् पादपान् कुसुमोत्करान् ॥
सीतावचनसंरब्ध आनयामास लक्ष्मणः । II. 55. 31-32

Lakshmana would bring it all.

विचित्रवालुकां नीलां हंससारसनादिताम् ॥
रेमे जनकराजस्य सुता प्रेक्ष्य तदा नदीम् । II. 55. 32-33

She saw a great river there and enjoyed it. On the waters there floated *hamsas* and *sarasas*.

क्रोशमात्रं ततो गत्वा भ्रातरौ रामलक्ष्मणौ ॥
बहून् मेध्यान् मृगान् हत्वा चेरतुर्यमुनावने ॥ II. 55. 33

Having gone a few miles from that place in the woods on the Yamuna and having killed many deer pronounced to be fit for eating, they ate. I mention it particularly because this is one of the pieces of evidence to show that they were not by any means abstainers from meat.

विहृत्य ते बर्हिणपूगनादिते शुभे वने वानरवारणायुते ।
समं नदीवप्रमुपेत्य संमतं निवासमाजग्मुरदीनदर्शनाः ॥ II. 55. 34

This is to show that they had in them the capacity to enjoy even forest life, that they did not feel they had been deprived of something which was so essential to their happy existence. Having strolled on the bank for some distance just to enjoy the scenery, they came back to their *nivasa*.

I read the next *sloka* and ask you to note it because there is a popular belief that during all the fourteen years in the forest Lakshmana never slept, but kept vigil the whole time. Here is proof in an undoubted text that that was not the case.

अथ राञ्यां व्यतीतायामवसुप्तमनन्तरम् ।
प्रबोधयामास शनैर्लक्ष्मणं रघुनन्दनः ॥ II. 56. 1

Lakshmana slept beyond the time. Rama tells him, "It is time that we left this place. Get up and prepare." The commentator says एतेन चतुर्दशवर्षपर्यन्तं लक्ष्मणः स्वापहीनः अनाहारश्च इति लोकप्रवादः अपास्तः ।

In Chitrakuta, to which they repaired, they built a commodious hut for themselves, and the poet is at pains to tell us how on entering into occupation, Rama performed the holy rites of purification himself. Being versed in the *mantras*, he did it all himself. Then living there,

सुरम्यमासाद्य तु चित्रकूटं नदीं च तां माल्यवतीं सुतीर्थाम्।
ननन्द रामो मृगपक्षिजुष्टां जहौ च दुःखं पुरविप्रवासात्॥ II. 56. 38

they enjoyed the river and the surroundings so well and so happily that they forgot altogether the city which they had left.

Now I am going to read to you certain passages to show that although Sita was so cultured and had for companion the greatest man of the time, nevertheless she had some of the weaknesses of the other sex. We all know how when there is any trouble or danger or fear in the family, without the knowledge of the husband or the father-in-law, the wife sometimes makes vows to gods and goddesses, and then forgets the thing for many years and reminds us at a most inconvenient time. Sita was apparently not free from that weakness. When they crossed the Ganges, and were nearly mid-stream,

मध्यं तु समनुप्राप्य भागीरथ्यास्त्वनिन्दिता।
वैदेही प्राञ्जलिर्भूत्वा तां नदीमिदमब्रवीत्॥
पुत्रो दशरथस्यायं महाराजस्य धीमतः।
निदेशं पारयित्वेमं गङ्गे त्वदभिरक्षितः॥
सा त्वां देवि नमस्यामि प्रशंसामि च शोभने।
प्राप्तराज्ये नरव्याघ्रे शिवेन पुनरागते॥
गवां शतसहस्राणि वस्त्राण्यन्नं च पेशलम्।
ब्राह्मणेभ्यः प्रदास्यामि तव प्रियचिकीर्षया॥
सुराघटसहस्रेण मांसभूतौदनेन च।
यक्ष्ये त्वां प्रयता देवि पुरीं पुनरुपागता॥
यानि त्वत्तीरवासीनि दैवतानि वसन्ति च।
तानि सर्वाणि यक्ष्यामि तीर्थान्यायतनानि च॥
पुनरेव महाबाहुर्मया भ्रात्रा च संगतः।
अयोध्यां वनवासात्तु प्रविशत्वनघोऽनघे॥ II. 52. 82-83, 87-91

Sita clasped her hands and prayed to the goddess. "You know whom you are bearing. Let him cross safely. He is the very hope of the world. Allow him to cross safely.

I praise you, I bow to you. When my husband (and with him Lakshmana and Sita too) has returned to take the kingdom, you may expect something from me. In your name and in order to please you, I shall give to Brahmins a lakh of cows." Here follows something very interesting. "When I have returned home safely, I shall dedicate to you a thousand pots of wine and huge heaps of *mamsa* to eat." Of course some of you may be aware that if we go to certain places, Brahmins though we be, we have got to pay for the killing of a fowl. "I shall go and pay due worship in all these places, temples and *tirthas*." That is the prayer she makes to the Ganges. In the Kalindi to which we have referred, she does the same thing.

स्वस्ति देवि तरामि त्वां पारयेन्मे पतिर्व्रतम् ।
यक्ष्ये त्वां गोसहस्रेण सुराघटशतेन च ॥
स्वस्ति प्रत्यागते रामे पुरीमिक्ष्वाकुपालिताम् ॥ II. 55. 20-21

In the case of the Ganges it was a lakh of cows. Kalindi is not so big, and she reduces the quantity. The cows are only a thousand and the wine pots a hundred.

Then they pass a famous tree which students of the Ramayana know about. It is called the *syama* tree.

नमस्तेऽस्तु महावृक्ष पारयेन्मे पतिर्व्रतम् ।
कौसल्यां चैव पश्येयं सुमित्रां च यशस्विनीम् ॥
इति सीताञ्जलिं कृत्वा पर्यगच्छद्वनस्पतिम् ॥ II. 55. 25-26

She says, "Let my husband fulfil his vow of fourteen years in the forest. I shall pray to you and do you all the worship necessary." Here there is no vow taken, neither wine pots nor cows. This is just to show that Sita had her own mode of propitiating the gods and goddesses like a woman, ways in which the men did not partake.

Now one last word to show how happy they were there.

तां तथा दर्शयित्वा तु मैथिलीं गिरिनिम्नगाम् ।
निषसाद गिरिप्रस्थे सीतां मांसेन छन्दयन् ॥
इदं मेध्यमिदं स्वादु निष्टप्तमिदमग्निना ।
एवमास्ते स धर्मात्मा सीतया सह राघवः ॥ II. 96. 1-2

Here we get another glimpse of their forest life. Apparently, unless I over-interpret the passage, they were in the habit of eating together. Rama gave her, in order to please her, *mamsa.* "This is pure, this is good, this is well-boiled." That tells us really how they lived together in mutual happiness and mutual helpfulness, forgetting the great city with all its luxuries and attractions.

Now we are well on. I am coming to a passage in which Sita shows her complete self-effacement. They have met Viradha, who threatens the lives of all the three, but of the brothers in particular. He first caught hold of Sita, but afterwards left her and took hold of the brothers. Rama and Lakshmana now played a little trick. They said, "He is going in the direction which we intended to take. Let him carry us some distance and save us the trouble of walking." But they forgot that Sita would be left behind.

ह्रियमाणौ तु तौ दृष्ट्वा वैदेही रामलक्ष्मणौ ।
उच्चैःस्वरेण चुक्रोश प्रगृह्य सुभुजा भुजौ ॥
एष दाशरथी रामः सत्यवान् शीलवान् शुचिः ।
रक्षसा रौद्ररूपेण ह्रियते सहलक्ष्मणः ॥
मां वृका भक्षयिष्यन्ति शार्दूला द्वीपिनस्तथा ।
मां हरोत्सृज्य काकुत्स्थौ नमस्ते राक्षसोत्तम ॥ III. 4. 1-3

When she saw that the demon was carrying away Rama and Lakshmana, she lifted her arms high in the air and cried out to the demon, as though he had ears to listen. She says to him, "O, Viradha, take my homage and worship. I yield them gladly. But do me this favour. Leave them alone, and take me instead, and eat me up. Bears and tigers are going to eat me up. Why should I fall a prey to them? You eat me and release them." She offered herself as a ransom, as it were. This is just to show you how, usually speaking, in the last extremity, even though you are surrounded by your own children, your life being in danger, nature has decreed that the foremost tendency, the strongest temptation, will be to protect your own life and then the lives of others. Here Sita was just the opposite. She was trained such-wise that she preferred that Rama and Lakshmana should live, to her own continued existence. Then when she cried out like that, Rama and Lakshmana looked back, saw that Sita was left alone, and then they assumed the offensive and cut down and finished him.

Then, having stayed in Sarabhanga's place for a day, and in Sutikshna's place for another day, the brothers and Sita left the hermitage early in the morning. Here the poet tells us something which he has not told us before. I suspect myself that there is some significance in his doing it. Early in the morning, as they were about to leave, this thing happened.

> ततः शुभतरे तूणी धनुषी चायतेक्षणा ।
> ददौ सीता तयोर्भ्रात्रोः खड्गौ च विमलौ ततः ॥
> आबध्य च शुभे तूणी चापौ चादाय सस्वनौ ।
> निष्क्रान्तावाश्रमाद्गन्तुमुभौ तौ रामलक्ष्मणौ ॥ III. 8. 18-19

It was left to Sita to bring the bows and arrows from the inside and give them to the brothers who were to wear them. We are not told that it was her daily duty, but she did it now. It has a significance, as I shall show you. Immediately they took leave of the Rishi and started. Starting, Sita posed a problem to her husband. This is the context in which Sita suggests that Rama transgresses the rule of propriety in promising protection to the Rishis who came and fell at his feet and asked him to protect them from the Rakshasas who menaced them. Sita enters an emphatic protest against this proceeding of her husband which was warlike, like a Kshatriya at home, and not like a *yati* or *muni* which Rama was to be in the forest. She takes exception to this, but instead of dreading to say so to her husband, as an ordinary wife does now or is expected to do, she, being a Kshatriya lady with a strong sense of what she owed to her husband, remonstrates openly. "This seems to be wrong. You are transgressing *dharma*." That is why the poet makes her bring these weapons on this occasion, which naturally suggests the idea to her that they are weapons which might have been left behind. That is the thought which strikes her and she begins to put in a word of protest.

> अधर्मस्तु सुसूक्ष्मेण विधिना प्राप्यते महान् ।
> निवृत्तेन तु शक्योऽयं व्यसनात्कामजादिह ॥
> त्रीण्येव व्यसनान्यत्र कामजानि भवन्त्युत ।
> मिथ्यावाक्यं परमकं तस्माद्गुरुतरावुभौ ॥

परदाराभिगमनं विना वैरं च रौद्रता ।
मिथ्यावाक्यं न ते भूतं न भविष्यति राघव ॥
कुतोऽभिलषणं स्त्रीणां परेषां धर्मनाशनम् ।
तव नास्ति मनुष्येन्द्र न चाभूत्ते कदाचन ॥
मनस्यपि तथा राम न चैतद्विद्यते क्वचित् ।
स्वदारनिरतस्त्वं च नित्यमेव नृपात्मज ॥
तृतीयं यदिदं रौद्रं परप्राणाभिहिंसनम् ।
निर्वैरं क्रियते मोहात्तच्च ते समुपस्थितम् ॥
प्रतिज्ञातस्त्वया वीर दण्डकारण्यवासिनाम् ।
ऋषीणां रक्षणार्थाय वधः संयति रक्षसाम् ॥
त्वं हि बाणधनुष्पाणिर्भ्रात्रा सह वनं गतः ।
दृष्ट्वा वनचरान् सर्वान् कच्चित्कुर्याः शरव्ययम् ॥
क्षत्रियाणां च हि धनुर्हुताशस्येन्धनानि च ।
समीपतः स्थितं तेजो बलमुच्छ्रयते भृशम् ॥

III. 9. 2-6, 9-10, 14-15

There are three transgressions to which a man is liable even when he makes a slight departure from propriety. Lying or uttering a falsehood is an important transgression. But the other two, which are worse, are, violating the wife of another, and adopting force towards a person without proper provocation, i.e., without a genuine cause. There should be no war unless there is a proper justification. Now comes a description of Rama by Sita herself, a kind of testimonial which she gives him. "Falsehood you never would utter. I know that for certain. You have not done so in the past, and you won't do so in the future. And no impropriety with another man's wife (high class testimony from a wife. Some of our wives may be as confident of our conduct as Sita was, but they would hesitate to give the credit openly). These two evils will not approach you. But this third one, making war or molesting another person without provocation, is an evil which seems to have approached you now. These sages have told you that they are suffering from the depredations of Rakshasas and sought your protection, and you have extended your protection. What business is it of yours? With your brother equally skilled in the use of the bow and arrow, you go into the forest, and it seems to me there will be abundant exercise for it here. You will take the offensive every time." She makes a general observation of an acute kind, which she follows up with a remarkable story to which I must draw your attention. "When a Kshatriya, trained to fight, finds his weapons ready, or when *agni* finds fuel near, then there is danger. It provokes him to an exhibition of his strength." Then she tells a most remarkable story, charged with the fullest significance for all time, a beautiful story which deserves to be better known than it is; I have mentioned this three or four times during recent days. It is the fall of a Rishi. A Rishi performed severe *tapas*, and the gods, as you know, became jealous. Indra came there in the form of a hunter, and he brought with him a clean, bright sword, which he left with the Rishi saying, "Please take care of this till I come and take it back." Then began a change in the poor Rishi's life.

स तच्छस्त्रमनुप्राप्य न्यासरक्षणतत्परः ।
वने तं विचरत्येव रक्षन् प्रत्ययमात्मनः ॥
यत्र गच्छत्युपादातुं मूलानि च फलानि च ।
न विना याति तं खड्गं न्यासरक्षणतत्परः ॥
नित्यं शस्त्रं परिवहन् क्रमेण स तपोधनः ।
चकार रौद्रीं स्वां बुद्धिं त्यक्त्वा तपसि निश्चयम् ॥
ततः स रौद्रेऽभिरतः प्रमत्तोऽधर्मकर्शितः ।
तस्य शस्त्रस्य संवासाज्जगाम नरकं मुनिः ॥ III. 9. 19-22

Whenever he went about, he took this sword in his hands. Where he went only to take roots or fruits from the trees, he was bent upon protecting what was pledged to him, and kept it in his protection. As it was a bright, sharp sword, the Rishi's eye constantly fell upon it and he began to admire it in an academic way. And admiring it, he would touch it and feel the luxury of it. He thought, "What dire execution this will do if it were in a brave man's hands." The man who always thought of his *tapas* began to divert his mind to a contemplation of the merits of the sword and of what could be performed with it. He began to be careless about his *tapas*, and *adharma* caught hold of him. Having lost his hold on his *tapas* and contemplating this sword and occasionally using it for the purpose of cutting down things, slowly his mind, instead of being soft and gentle and tender, began to dwell on cruel images. When that happened the poor man went to hell. The poet puts it beautifully—rather, Sita puts it beautifully. What did this poor Rishi do? He did not want the sword at all. The thing was left with him just to keep, and by constant association with it, by its mere proximity, the man fell from the eminence of innocence to the depth of cruelty and made his way to hell. Now it seems to me that we must recognise that there is a truth in it, although in poetry it happens that the truth is pressed to the extreme stage. The sight of anything harsh hardens our feeling. Familiarity with cruel deeds, or even the entertainment of cruel thoughts changes our nature. That is why, ladies and gentlemen, I am disposed to disbelieve utterly, wholly and unreservedly, the protestations that are now being made on behalf of the nations about to be victorious in this terrific war. They think that the defeated nations should be disarmed and prevented from being mischievous for generations. They call them the aggressive nations. The aggressive nations must be deprived of their armaments, but those nations which are victorious and describe themselves as peace-loving nations ought to have at their disposal enough forces at any time to crush the insurgents. Now look at that. The whole thing is utterly unscientific, to divide nations into warlike and peace-loving. Most nations that have come up and built some kind of prosperity for themselves have been warlike, and warlike with a vengeance. How long ago was Britain peace-loving, or Russia? All these countries have enormous forces at their disposal and cannot remain in peace. The very possession of these forces will drive them into war. There is no mistaking this at all. This division of war-like and peace-loving is wrong. Self-righteous nations describe themselves in that way in order that they may justify their intention to remain armed and to keep other nations disarmed. The proper thing is for no nation to be armed, and to give the necessary weapons into the hands of an international power. A discussion of that problem will take me far. But I want to tell you this, that this story of Sita is a pointer. Although we may safely build this proposition, that any nation that is armed to the teeth may be peace-loving for some time, for five years or ten years, or it may be for one generation, you cannot guarantee that the next generation or their children's children will also remain peace-loving. Such a state of things is foreign to human nature, foreign certainly to well-armed human nature.

Then Sita, having taken the liberty of warning her husband against the constant possession of arms, proceeds.

स्नेहाच्च बहुमानाच्च स्मारये त्वां न शिक्षये ।
न कथञ्चन सा कार्या गृहीतधनुषा त्वया ॥ III. 9. 24

It is a famous passage, and people constantly use it when they give advice to elders.* "I am not teaching you anything, I only remind you of what you already know. Unfortunately in life some circumstances occur and drive fruitful thoughts away from the mind. They go to the corner, as it were, of your mind, and it is necessary to bring them to the centre. I do that service. That is all I remind you, but not teach you." Sita winds up beautifully.

स्त्रीचापलादेतदुदाहृतं मे धर्मं च वक्तुं तव कः समर्थः ।
विचार्य बुद्ध्या तु सहानुजेन यद्रोचते तत्कुरु मा चिरेण ॥ III. 9. 33

"I submit this thought of mine to you. You may accept it or you may reject it. Consult your brother and then, between you, decide the matter as seems to you best. Being a woman and having my mind constantly fixed on the duties of tenderness, I thought I should press this upon your attention."

Now there is a commentator who misunderstands this expression and gives it a totally different meaning†. There

---

* The reading स्मारये त्वां न शिक्षये is that adopted by Mahesvara Tirtha and by Govindaraja whose commentary is followed. Kataka however reads: स्मारये त्वां तु शिक्षये and the Tilaka commentary (for which see next note) prefers this reading.

† The reference is to the Tilaka commentary which follows Kataka. As stated in the previous note, their reading is totally different. Here is the Tilaka commentary on 'स्मारये त्वां तु शिक्षये':— "स्नेहात् भवद्विषयात्। बहुमानात् त्वत्कर्तृकान्मद्विषयात्। किं च बहुमानो नाम मदीयोऽयं भर्तेत्येवमभिमानः। स्मारये पुरावृत्तमिति शेषः। अत्र स्नेहो हेतुः। बहुमानाच्च त्वां तु शिक्षये इत्यर्थः।

तदेव शिक्षणं करोति—"न कथंचन" इति (III. 9. 24)। यत्तु तीर्थः 'स्मारये त्वां न शिक्षये' इति पठति व्याचष्टे च तत्तु उत्तरवाक्ये करिष्यमाणशिक्षणेन व्याहतमिति कतकः॥"

are, however, other passages in the Ramayana which show that the poet is very fond of this expression स्मारये त्वां न शिक्षये. For instance, in the Yuddhakanda, when Matali comes with Indra's chariot to Rama, he looks about a little and hesitates. Rama asks him to go on. Matali is Indra's charioteer and has been in many battles and knows what to do at what time. Therefore to tell him to do a thing was a bit of a liberty, and Rama apologises.

कामं न त्वं समाधेयः पुरन्दररथोचितः ॥
युयुत्सुरहमेकाग्रः स्मारये त्वां न शिक्षये । VI. 108. 12-13

When Vibhishana speaks to Rama, he also says the same thing.

प्रणयाद्बहुमानाच्च सौहृदेन च राघव ॥
प्रसादयामि प्रेष्योऽहं न खल्वाज्ञापयामि ते । VI. 124. 15-16

"I do not give you an order or an instruction. I am your servant. I only give you a hint, remind you in time." So that the passage on Sita's lips should also have this meaning and no other.

Now as this is a context in which Sita is often blamed by people in their ignorance, I should like to tell you how Rama received it, for that is conclusive on the matter.

किं तु वक्ष्याम्यहं देवि त्वयैवोक्तमिदं वचः ।
क्षत्रियैर्धार्यते चापो नार्तशब्दो भवेदिति ॥ III. 10. 3

"You yourself said to me a little while ago that it was the duty of a Kshatriya to wear the bow and arrow and employ them against evil. Nobody should cry, 'Oh, I am harmed. Somebody has hurt me.' It is the duty of a Kshatriya to rush forward and help." Then follows the famous *sloka*,

अप्यहं जीवितं जह्यां त्वां वा सीते सलक्ष्मणाम् ।
न तु प्रतिज्ञां संश्रुत्य ब्राह्मणेभ्यो विशेषतः ॥ III. 10. 19*

"I value my promise, fidelity to my promise, so highly that there is no sacrifice that I will not make. I will sacrifice Lakshmana, I will sacrifice you, even myself. Nothing is too sacred, if it will enable me to keep a promise especially a promise which I have made to Brahmans." This is how he concludes.

* Cf. Lect. III, p. 32.

मम स्नेहाच्च सौहार्दादिदमुक्तं त्वयानघे ।
परितुष्टोऽस्म्यहं सीते न ह्यनिष्टोऽनुशिष्यते ॥
सदृशं चानुरूपं च कुलस्य तव चात्मनः ।
सधर्मचारिणी मे त्वं प्राणेभ्योऽपि गरीयसी ॥ III. 10. 21-22

Beautiful verses these. Rama says, "You have said this to me because you have a right to do so. It was done in good faith, out of an honest desire to put me on the right path. I am not offended. On the other hand, I praise you. I am pleased that you should have spoken like this and not kept it in your mind without my being able to discover it. Nobody will chide one whom he does not care for. You chide me, because you are interested in me, because you love me, because you think I should do no wrong, incur no sin. You identify yourself with me to such an extent as to desire that no harm should come to me and you warn me. No unfriend, no indifferent person is warned usually in life. Therefore I take everything from you in good faith, though I do not think there is anything in the warning. It is worthy of my *kula* and of your *kula*. You are my *sadharmacharini* and have the liberty to admonish me, to put me right."

A little word here, if I may do so, of exhortation. Do we, men, allow our wives the freedom to warn us when we are set on a wrong course? You may sometimes be so obedient to your wives that you follow even their wrong doings. I am not thinking of that. I am thinking of relations established upon a proper basis between husband and wife, where each respects the other's province, but knows also when a solemn warning may be necessary. Our business in life is not so distinguishable from our wives' business that they should know nothing about it, that we should not consult them and be guided by them at all. Most of you may say on the quiet, "What do these creatures know? When women are not competent, consulting them is out of the question." That may be a very good excuse in many cases though that excuse ought not to be allowed to continue. It is our duty to educate our wives to be our companions, to be our partners in joy and in sorrow. That is their proper function. To keep them ignorant in order to justify our failing to consult them every now and then is not a proper course. There are cases to my knowledge in which a woman ventures boldly to tell her husband that he does wrong. In such a case, perhaps, she gets a beating. In any case, she gets a defiance and a complete neglect. That is not unusual. My point to you is that it is not proper. You may do this and you may not do that. That is left to you. But do not go and justify it upon the ground that a wife is inferior in status, that she is there to do some slave duties. She may keep the dhobi's accounts but nothing more. To say that is not proper. It is certainly not sanctioned by the liberty that Rama gave to Sita. In such an important matter as an alliance with the Rishis of the forest, which was likely to lead him into trouble, how could Rama have said to her, "You do not know these things. Keep quiet." He allowed her to speak, and even though he did not follow her counsel he told her she was right to give him a warning, that it was her duty to do so and that it was fitting when her family and his family were taken into consideration.

There is another important incident in which Sita's conduct is called in question. This is when Maricha appeared in the form of a golden deer and stole her heart. Rama had gone away in pursuit of Maricha, and keeping his promise to Ravana, Maricha cries out 'O Sita, O Lakshmana' simulating Rama's voice. And then Sita takes fright. The alarm seizes her that her husband is really in danger. She asks Lakshmana to proceed to his help. You know how Lakshmana resists the request for a time. He says, "Rama is a strong man and nobody in the world can ever stand before him. No danger can ever occur to him without his being able to ward it off. Don't be alarmed. I cannot leave you alone." But Sita reproaches him, and finding that he was unwilling to go, she was so full of fear for Rama that she lost her self-control. She did not know what she was saying. You must put yourselves in Sita's position for a time. Sita, married to the noblest man on earth, left the kingdom to follow him into the forest, and there she herself has sent him on a mortal errand. Danger has occurred to him, so at least she fancies. Is it or is it not natural for her in that extremity to forget everything? Her own life she would forget. What did she care for Lakshmana at that moment? If she was wiser, she might have refrained from using the harsh expressions that she did. But who is wise in anger, in acute misery of that nature, and whose wisdom is under control at that time and brought into use? When you are in the direst distress, in the greatest calamity, and all your fear is roused, are you likely to weigh your words? Does anybody do so? And yet we expect it of poor Sita. We should all have praised her, applauded her, if she had not used those words. She was a lady accustomed to speak freely. Her tongue was seldom under a curb.

अहं तव प्रियं मन्ये रामस्य व्यसनं महत् ।
रामस्य व्यसनं दृष्ट्वा तेनैतानि प्रभाषसे ॥
नैतच्चित्रं सपत्नेषु पापं लक्ष्मण यद्भवेत् ।
त्वद्विधेषु नृशंसेषु नित्यं प्रच्छन्नचारिषु ॥
सुदुष्टस्त्वं वने राममेकमेकोऽनुगच्छसि ।
मम हेतोः प्रतिच्छन्नः प्रयुक्तो भरतेन वा ॥ III. 45. 22-24

"I fancy you are now pleased that Rama has come into danger. Between brothers, *dayadas*, between those who aim at the same thing, this is no wonder. May be you desire me for yourself, or that other brother Bharata may have asked you to despatch Rama and bring me to him." Before we try to put blame or censure upon Sita once more, think of the extremity in which she finds herself in the forest. There was nobody else to appeal to, only Lakshmana, and he refuses to stir on the extravagant idea that Rama is so strong and so skilled that no danger can ever occur to him. Lakshmana having tested Rama's prowess may have that confidence. But Sita has seldom seen him in battle. Even the Khara-yuddha is to come later.* How is Sita to judge, as Lakshmana does, that no harm can ever come to Rama? Once Sita thought that Lakshmana was to be driven from the place, she thought that the best way was to say harsh things to him. Not that she deliberated, but it just occurred to her.

तन्न सिध्यति सौमित्रे तव वा भरतस्य वा ।
† समक्षं तव सौमित्रे प्राणांस्त्यक्ष्ये न संशयः ॥ III. 45. 25-26

"While you stand there refusing to go, I am going to deprive you and Bharata of what seems to be your desire, by taking my life. I will be drowned in the Godavari; I will tie a rope round my neck; I will fall from a height; I will drink poison or enter fire; I won't touch another." She began to beat her

* The error here is corrected at the beginning of the next Lecture.

† Cf. Lect. IV, p. 54.

stomach. What was poor Lakshmana to do? He tried his best to bring her to reason, but reason had been driven out of her mind by grief and anxiety, when she took that last view. And Lakshmana thought that really something terrible might happen to her. She might do any of these things. She was a strong-minded woman, and she had so many alternatives. We may not blame Sita so very much although we all wish in our hearts that she did not say such harsh things to Lakshmana, knowing them all to be false. Even when she uttered these things, she did not believe them. We say all kinds of things when we are angry. We do not weigh our words, and do not care to keep within the bounds of truth. Sita was not above this. When we remember in what frame of mind she at that time was, we may go far indeed to forgive her, although we may still reserve to ourselves the liberty to remark that it would have been well worthy of her, if she had abstained from saying that last word to him. But more than that I am not prepared to say.

Once more, what was Rama's reaction to all this? For that is the true test. When the whole matter was reported to him and he knew what bitter taunts Lakshmana had had to bear and under what circumstances he left his post of duty and came to Rama, what did Rama say? He could not have been pleased with his wife's conduct. He certainly thought that she behaved improperly. But what was his final verdict? That is what you must see. He loved Sita and Lakshmana about equally. In fact Sita says that Rama loved Lakshmana slightly more than herself. It was not as if Rama had any partiality in reserve or in secret. He said what was just and proper. We may at least allow so much to Rama.

जानन्नपि समर्थं मां रक्षसां विनिवारणे।

अनेन क्रोधवाक्येन मैथिल्या निःसृतो भवान्॥ III. 59. 22

"Certainly you knew that I was quite equal to all these Rakshasas put together. From Maricha and the deer no harm could have occurred to me. You knew that. And yet, you allowed yourself to be driven away because of an angry speech from Sita."

न हि ते परितुष्यामि त्यक्त्वा यदासि मैथिलीम्।

क्रुद्धायाः परुषं वाक्यं श्रुत्वा यत्त्वमिहागतः॥

सर्वथा त्वपनीतं ते सीतया यत्प्रचोदितः ।
क्रोधस्य वशमापन्नो नाकरोः शासनं मम ॥ *III. 59, 23-24

"I cannot forgive you. You left your post of duty and left her unprotected. Sita is there in danger. Why did you come, merely because she was angry? I am not pleased with you, Lakshmana. You have done wrong. When she became angry and said absurd things, you became angry too and came away. You have neglected my order, my command." Rama says Sita was angry. He does not say that she should not have done that. He lays the blame upon Lakshmana. "No blame rests upon Sita. She is mad. You must not get angry with mad people." I think there is sense in a commentator's word which I hesitantly offer to you for acceptance.† The commentator says Rama was certainly right, and Lakshmana ought not to have gone. What then was he to do, if Sita did any one of these things? The suggestion made is that Lakshmana should have left the scene, should have come away a little distance, and hung about in the neighbourhood, letting Sita believe that he had gone after Rama, but not going too far, to be able to protect her in case of harm. That is a very proper suggestion, and I believe that was in Rama's mind too.

* Cf. Lect. IV, p. 55.

† The comment of Govindaraja's referred to runs:—

"कथंचिदसहने बहिरागत्यान्तर्हितो भूत्वा तत्परिपालनं कर्तव्यम् । केवलमागमनं तवापनीतिरेवेति भावः ।"

TWENTYSEVENTH LECTURE*

Ladies and Gentlemen,

I have to begin with an apology today. On the last occasion, without knowing it, I fell into an error. Allow me now to correct it. Speaking of the conversation between Lakshmana and Sita when she drove him after Rama, I happened to say that Rama's prowess had not yet been established and that the battle between Rama and Khara and his forces had not been fought at that moment. That was an obvious error. I must have made other mistakes of the kind in the course of these talks. It speaks worlds for your patience and for your forbearance that you have not pointed these out to me.

Another thing that I wish to say before the lecture is that today my talk may be a little prolonged. I am anxious to take leave of Sita today, however difficult it may be. There is so much to say that it will be necessary to omit some things and to slur over other things. Even doing these savings, it is possible I might make a large draft today upon your patience. I hope you will find it possible to accommodate me. One word more before actually beginning. You may remember that in treating of Hanuman and of Rama, I have had occasion to refer to many important incidents in Sita's life. Them I shall take your leave to omit today.

When Ravana had entered Sita's presence and she had offered him a seat and hospitality, she felt a little uneasiness that the reception of a *sanyasin* and the showing of the necessary respect to him fell upon her. She wished her husband and her brother-in-law had been there, and she hoped that they would arrive. So she was constantly looking out. The poet says, she was looking out, it was true, but the poor lady saw only the forest and not the persons she was looking for. It was not only this anxiety that to a guest of a high order the men of the household should offer hospitality, but you may be sure that it was also mixed with the fear that they had gone on a very dangerous and delicate expedition, and she must have been thinking that she was partially responsible for it, and must have desired in her heart of hearts that they should return unscathed from the adventure.

---

* 11-10-'44.

ततः सुवेषं मृगयागतं पतिं प्रतीक्षमाणा सहलक्ष्मणं तदा।
विवीक्षमाणा हरितं ददर्श तन्महद्वनं नैव तु रामलक्ष्मणौ॥ III. 46. 37

She only saw the wood and not the men she was looking for. That filled her with uneasiness. Then after the first exchange of talk between the two, Ravana asked her who she was; and then in giving an account, she makes a statement to which it is necessary to draw your attention. She describes how Rama was banished and how, when he took leave of Ayodhya, she accompanied him, and Lakshmana too. Of Lakshmana she says this at the moment. Remember that he has just gone away from her after exchanging hot words, and she has just told him things that she regretted having said. Hardly any time had passed between that and this.

रामस्य पुरुषव्याघ्रः सहायः समरेऽरिहा।
स भ्राता लक्ष्मणो नाम धर्मचारी दृढव्रतः॥
अन्वगच्छद्धनुष्पाणिः प्रव्रजन्तं मया सह॥ III. 47. 19-20

"When my husband, throwing away the kingdom, took on a *sanyasi's* garb and came to the forest, I went with him, and Lakshmana too." Here she describes Lakshmana in two epithets which are significant as they come so soon after her having spoken roughly to him. She describes him as a *dharmachari* and a *dridhavrata,* not words that should have been applied to a person who cast wicked eyes upon his own brother's wife. Obviously therefore, she now realises that she had spoken harshly, and you and I must remember that in saying those harsh words, she was not thinking of their meaning at all, but of their possible effect in forcing him to obey her. No more significance should be put upon her words than that.

Then she speaks to Ravana of the lavish hospitality that her husband would show to him. This is how she puts it.

आगमिष्यति मे भर्ता वन्यमादाय पुष्कलम्।
रुरून् गोधान् वराहांश्च हत्वादायामिषान् बहून्॥ III. 47. 23

"My husband will bring you abundant food to eat, food such as one gets in this forest. He will bring you food of various kinds." I am only reading this to show that there was no room for people imagining that they abstained from meat. Though she spoke of the abundance of animal food that they would bring, in point of fact, the poet has told us a little before that on that day Sri Rama, suspecting that some evil was going to happen in the hermitage was making haste to go home. He had no time to gather the usual quantity of food. The poet therefore tells us,

> निहत्य पृषतं चान्यं मांसमादाय राघवः ।
> त्वरमाणो जनस्थानं ससाराभिमुखस्तदा ॥ III. 44. 28

That day Rama brought only one *prishata*.

Now we come to the next part of the scene where Ravana declares himself and announces his evil intention. Then Sita bursts out in a fit of uncontrollable indignation. The passage in which she abuses him is highly rhetorical. The poet makes use of the trick of repetition, the same phrase being used over and over again. Besides, the effect is what you might call jejune. There is no ripeness, no maturity, no profundity of thought about it as you might expect. It was made only to abuse Ravana. I do not think you will contend, upon reading the passage, that Sita actually used those elaborate similes and metaphors and rhetorical repetition. It is the poet's fancy of an angry woman roused to the full height of her eloquence in defending herself. I will not read the Sanskrit text, as it will take time, but I will read my translation.

Stung by Ravana's wicked sentiments, Sita answered without hesitation or doubt. Her words were hot with anger and contempt. "Do you know what kind of person my husband is? He is unshakable like the great mountain Sumeru, he is invincible like the great Indra, he is imperturbable like the great ocean. To him do I belong utterly, body and soul. In Rama all the excellences dwell together; like the banyan tree, he affords a wide sweep of umbrageous protection; his word is a bond; his lustre is fadeless. To him do I belong utterly, body and soul. Strong-armed, strong-chested, he has the tread of a lion, he has the majestic mien of a lion, he is a lion in man's shape. To him do I belong utterly, body and soul. His face has the charm and effulgence of the full moon; with the blood of royalty in his veins, he has complete control of his senses and sense-organs; he has a mighty resplendent soul. To him do I belong utterly, body and soul. Do you realise what you are doing? In desiring me, the devoted and worthy companion of Rama, you are a low jackal desiring a lioness far beyond your reach. You can no more touch me than you can touch the radiance of the sun. I guess you behold trees all bathed in gold, as they say doomed persons do, for you are doomed if you dare to desire the beloved of Rama. You desire to draw the tooth of a famished lion. You desire to draw the fang of a fierce hissing cobra. With a feeble arm you desire to lift the huge Mandara, prince of mountains. You desire to drink the *halahala* poison and escape with your life. You desire to cleanse your eye with a sharp needle. You desire to lick a sword's blade with your tongue. You desire to swim across the sea with a stone round the neck. You desire to snatch the sun with one hand and the moon with the other. You desire to carry a blazing fire in your cloth. You desire to walk on a row of pikes with steel points. What disparity there is between a lion and a jackal in the forest, that disparity there is between Rama and you. What disparity there is between the ocean and a tiny rill, that disparity there is between Rama and you. What disparity there is between nectar and sour gruel, that disparity there is between Rama and you. What disparity there is between gold and lead, that disparity there is between Rama and you. What disparity there is between sandal and mire, that disparity there is between Rama and you. What disparity there is between an elephant and a cat, that disparity there is between Rama and you. What disparity there is between Garuda and a crow that disparity there is between Rama and you. What disparity there is between a peacock and a gull, that disparity there is between Rama and you. What disparity there is between a swan and a vulture, that disparity there is between Rama and you. You may carry me away now; but while Rama, like to Indra in prowess, lives and wields the *kodanda,* you cannot bend me to your purpose, any more than a fly can eat ghee and digest it." (III. 47. 32-48)

You remember how she had the presence of mind, when going over Pampa and seeing five monkeys there, to think that if perchance Rama passed that way, they would tell him of her and the fate that had overtaken her. So she took her upper cloth of silk, put her jewels into it, and dropped it where they were. Then when she was taken to the Asoka garden—I am mentioning these things to show that even in distress she was a strong-minded woman and knew what to do at what time—Ravana gives these instructions to the Rakshasis.

तर्जनैर्घोरैः पुनः सान्त्वैश्च मैथिलीम् ।
आनयध्वं वशं सर्वा वन्यां गजवधूमिव ॥ III. 56. 31

This takes place immediately after she is planted in the Asoka grove. We must imagine that between that time and the time when Hanuman came, which was nearly ten months, Ravana continually visited her and tormented her in all sorts of ways. Only a few scenes are described to us by the poet, which however are enough to give us an idea of the continual torments through which the poor lady had to pass. Unimaginable how the poet describes it, or you and I think of it, who have known only the small incidents, the ups and downs, over which she cried so much. Ravana tells the Rakshasis, "Make her all sorts of promises. One way or another bring her to her senses so that she may yield to my desire."

सा तु शोकपरीताङ्गी मैथिली जनकात्मजा ।
राक्षसीवशमापन्ना व्याघ्रीणां हरिणी यथा ॥
शोकेन महता ग्रस्ता मैथिली जनकात्मजा ।
न शर्म लभते भीरुः पाशबद्धा मृगी यथा ॥ III. 56. 34-35

In the two slokas that I have just read, which are only typical of whole *sargas,* are two similes. Our poet is rich in similes; he never describes a situation without bringing in as many comparisons and illustrations as possible. As I told you, they seem to fall from his mouth. Once when matters had gone very far and Ravana's torments had become indescribable and insufferable, she makes a soliloquy in one long *sarga* of long *slokas* (Sundara, 28). It is a contrast in description between the rhetorical passage that I now read and this one. This reaches a high degree of eloquence, with a mixture of various *rasas,* all no doubt variants of the *karuna rasa;* there is *soka,* there is despair (*nirveda*), there is resignation (*upalambha*); and finally there is the determination to commit suicide. "When Sita heard these cruel words of Ravana, she was plunged in grief and shook with fear as a young she-elephant would shake that had been threatened by a lion. While in fear of him she was surrounded by Rakshasa hags and wept like a tender girl abandoned by parents to her fate in a wild spot. "How true", she cried to herself, "is the saying of goodfolk that death will not come to one before the appointed time! See me answerable for past sins and beset by dangers and still holding on to life. Hard must be my heart that, preyed upon by misery and abandoned by hope, it endures still without being shattered to pieces like the crest of a mountain stricken by Indra's thunderbolt. Can it be a sin for me to commit suicide when this horrid demon is about to kill me because I find myself unable to look upon him with favour just as a Brahmana would find himself unable to impart the Veda to one not a twice-born? If my Rama, the saviour of the world, should fail to come in time, this creature of the night will have me carved to pieces as a babe in the womb is by the sharp knife of a surgeon. I have a respite of two brief months, and these will pass away all too soon as the scanty hours of the early morning pass away to a felon condemned to the gallows. O Rama, O Lakshmana, O Kausalya, O Sumitra, O other mothers of mine,—don't you see me sore bested, like a ship in mid-ocean caught in a stupefying storm? Surely some malignant spirit took a beast's shape and killed the brave brothers lest they should rescue me,—like a lightning stroke that might destroy a pair of mighty lions. I now perceive it was the universal enemy Kala who, in the guise of a deer cast his fatal spell over me, when like a doomed fool, I first sent away from my side the elder brother, and then with biting reproaches drove the younger brother after him. Ah, Rama the true, Rama the strong-armed, Rama the moon-faced, Rama the unfailing protector of the afflicted, don't you know I am in the grip of these wicked and ruthless beings? Like good deeds that are thrown away on ingrates, all my merits have turned barren,—my exclusive worship of you, my patience, my lying on the bare hard earth, my fidelity to my wedded lord. If I am not to look on you again, but must fade away without hope, continually disfigured, and dejected, what good has my unwearied practice of *dharma* done to me, or the steadfast devotion of my soul to my husband? Ah me! I shall perish in this woebegone plight, and then at the end of the fourteenth year, having obeyed the paternal command to the letter and with a mind disburdened and self-complacent, you will take new wives, bedeck them with rich jewels and live with them happy and free from care. My heart surrendered to you while yet a girl and dwelling in you all these years in perfect joy and contentment, what hardships and miseries have I suffered for your sake! Yet, alack and alas, all is in vain, and I must die forlorn and crying for help. Why should I drag out this wretchedness any more? I can end it with a dose of poison or a stab of a knife. But in this place closely guarded by demonesses, who will give me either?" So weeping and bemoaning her lot, with her emaciated frame trembling all over, and her face drawn and haggard, but her mind fixed on Rama unwaveringly and to the exclusion of everything else, she moved on towards a simsupa tree, widespreading and in full blossom. Victim of grief and despair, after repeated deliberation, she fastened her braid of hair into a knot round her throat, and said firmly to herself: "Thus will I go quickly to the abode of Yama." Then as she grasped a branch and relaxed her limbs in preparation for the end, her thoughts went revolving round Rama and Lakshmana and others of her kindred. At that moment, wonder of wonders, many omens occurred to her dispelling her sorrow and putting courage into her heart as if to say 'Happiness is at hand.'

Now I am going to tell you a few tit-bits, but only a few out of the vast store that may be gathered, just a few which are important and sometimes quoted by people. You know there is a belief that the chastity of a good woman is like fire, in fact has the potency of fire, and will burn any person to death who ventures to violate or insult her. That is a belief that has been handed down in our literature. Many people take it literally and go about speaking and writing as if Sita had this fire of chastity and, if she had chosen, could have put an end to her troubles. But this is what Hanuman says to the monkeys on his return from Lanka. He knows of this belief, and has some faith in that sort of thing. He tells the monkeys,

सर्वथातिप्रवृद्धोऽसौ रावणो राक्षसाधिपः ॥
तस्य तां स्पृशतो गात्रं तपसा न विनाशितम् । V. 59. 3-4

"This Ravana must be a great man. He must have enormous punya to his credit for though he touched Sita with wicked intention, he was not destroyed." Then he adds,

नियतः समुदाचारो भक्तिर्भर्तरि चोत्तमा ।
यन्न हन्ति दशग्रीवं स महात्मा दशाननः ॥
निमित्तमात्रं रामस्तु वधे तस्य भविष्यति ॥ V. 59. 34-35

"If this fire of her chastity does not burn him to tinder, he is a Mahatma. Nevertheless, his *tapas* is being eaten into rapidly, and when Rama comes here to take vengeance upon him, he need only aim an arrow and Ravana would be a dead person because he does so much wickedness now and torments Sita so much that his *tapas* is being reduced and he will be only a figure going about when Rama comes here."

But what does Sita herself say? She has a passage about this, which is very interesting.

> असन्देशात्तु रामस्य तपसश्चानुपालनात् ।
> न त्वां कुर्मि दशग्रीव भस्म भस्मार्ह तेजसा ॥ V. 22. 20

"I have so much power in me that if I only care and direct it against you, you would be a mass of ash. But I refrain from doing so because I want to preserve this *tapas* of mine. Besides, I have not received an order from Rama to defend myself. The burden rests upon him, and he himself should come and save me. I ought not to save myself." It shows that she was confident that in the end she would be saved.

Then another trait of Sita comes out. Tender as she was in the extreme, and often full as she was of compassion and pity, untouched by any desire to hurt even a fly, nevertheless suffering in Ravana's custody day after day and hour after hour, harassed by these tormentresses, she one day bursts out,

> यादृशानीह दृश्यन्ते लङ्कायामशुभानि वै ।
> अचिरेणैव कालेन प्राप्स्याम्येव मनोरथम् ॥
> नूनं लङ्का हते पापे रावणे राक्षसाधमे ।
> शोषं यास्यति दुर्धर्षा प्रमदा विधवा यथा ॥
> नूनं राक्षसकन्यानां रुदन्तीनां गृहे गृहे ।
> श्रोष्यामि नचिरादेव दुःखार्तानामिह ध्वनिम् ॥
> सान्धकारा हतद्योता हतराक्षसपुङ्गवा ।
> भविष्यति पुरी लङ्का निर्दग्धा रामसायकैः ॥ V. 26. 26-27, 29-30

"This city which is now stricken by so many omens of evil will in a short time lose her splendour. As a woman reduced to widowhood, so will this Lanka be when her lord Ravana is destroyed. In no long time this city is going to be assailed by piercing streaks of grief from every household, for in every household some Rakshasa will have gone to battle and been killed, and there will be grief all round." In her distress she allowed her mind to dwell on this lurid picture of Lanka's misery. It is perfectly natural, and you and I have no heart to blame her.

Again, have we the heart to blame her when we come to this other passage where Hanuman has just left her after scenes of tender parting in the course of which she begged Hanuman to stay the night, reminding us of the passage in the Ayodhyakanda, where Dasaratha asks Rama to stay one night. Hanuman no more complies with Sita's request than Rama did with Dasaratha's. But as soon as Hanuman goes away, the Rakshasis are roused from their sleep. Just as they were rising, they heard sounds of conversation. They heard something at least that had passed between Hanuman and Sita. So they ask her, "Who is this monkey with whom you have been talking? He seems to be a terrible fellow. He goes about destroying all the trees, doing damage in Ravana's forests." This is Sita's reply.

अथाब्रवीत्तदा साध्वी सीता सर्वाङ्गसुन्दरी ।
रक्षसां भीमरूपाणां विज्ञाने मम का गतिः ॥
यूयमेवाभिजानीत योऽयं यद्वा करिष्यति ।
अहिरेव ह्यहेः पादान् विजानाति न संशयः ॥
अहमप्यस्य भीतास्मि नैनं जानामि को न्वयम् ।
वेद्मि राक्षसमेवैनं कामरूपिणमागतम् ॥ V. 42. 8-10

"How can I pretend to know anything of the ways of these Rakshasas who can assume what forms they please? You know better than I. Only a cobra knows the ways of other cobras—(It was a well-known proverb apparently). I do not know who this person is. I think he is a Rakshasa. I too am afraid of him really." Obviously, on the face of it, it is a concealment of the truth. It has given rise to a great deal of controversy. But I will merely tell you that in their anxiety to defend Sita, people say all sorts of things. One set of people say that in this *sloka* there is a hidden meaning which is truthful, and that is what Sita intended. And they construe the passage most ingeniously, twisting words, suppressing passages and in the end producing a meaning which is neither relevant nor sensible, nor any credit to Sita. Others, however, admit that it was a lie, but they ask, why was Sita bound to tell the truth to these Rakshasis. I do not say that she was bound. But when people ask the question 'why was she bound to tell the truth' they admit that it was an untruth. Others say that she was protected by a great *smrti*, which says that in any of five difficult situations a person may utter a lie and escape sin. Now if we read those five contexts, we shall find that they are so elastic that they would afford protection to all the lies that ever were spoken in the world. I will give you one instance which is relevant to the context.

विवाहकाले रतिसंप्रयोगे प्राणात्यये सर्वधनापहारे।

विप्रस्य चार्थेऽप्यनृतं वदेयुः पञ्चानृतान्याहुरपातकानि ॥

"You may tell a lie if thereby you can save a Brahman (from death, it must have meant, and, subsequently, to suit the good or the welfare of a Brahman). To find a wife for a person or a husband for a girl, you may tell a lie." Of course life is difficult and poses new problems. Sometimes you want to protect a man who is not a Brahman. In such a situation you change the text and read मित्रस्य चार्थे. That is the version given here to save Sita by the commentator. You and I might question whether and where Hanuman was invested with the sacred thread and whether we can call him a Brahman. As a matter of fact Sita was acting like any human being in distress. All the moral codes we have learnt will not avail us if our own life is in danger. Then we do anything. It is the instinct of self-preservation which is stronger than any moral precepts. We try to get out of it by the easiest possible means. That is the law, from which nobody can escape, and from which Valmiki did not intend that his heroes and heroines should escape. He treats them as humans. One word more on this point. Sita was not herself in trouble. It was not herself that she wished to protect. Somehow, as Hanuman had left her at that moment and the Rakshasis had detected their conversing together, she felt instinctively that Hanuman was in danger from Ravana's indignation. Would she, or would she not, in that predicament, have taken the easiest possible course to protect him? It was her bounden duty to protect him who had risked everything to protect her. He was at that moment her own self. What she would have done to protect herself in that moment of extreme distress, she was perfectly justified in doing to protect him who had come to protect her at the risk of his own safety. Unfortunately, as often happens in this life, lies are not spoken only when they are necessary. In this case Sita might have spared herself, and need not have departed from the truth and tried to mislead the Rakshasis, for the person whom she wished to protect did not want to protect himself. Just as she was saying this to the Rakshasis, he went about in the streets of Lanka and shouted, "I am Hanuman, the servant of Sugriva, I am Rama's emissary. I am going to destroy this city. A thousand Ravanas may come against me. I will pound them all." So it was a piece of departure from the truth, entirely unnecessary. But that is life, and it seems to me that the poet has shown here his knowledge of the shadows and the lights of life to the very depths. He is a very keen student of life. He just tells us that the very best of us who reach the peak of morality may fall in a moment of extreme temptation, also that the fall might well have been avoided. Govindaraja quotes the *smrti sloka*, reading, 'मित्रस्य चार्थे', and then says, 'इति स्मरणादसत्योक्तिः'। Nagesa Bhatta writes: 'वैदेह्या वचनमज्ञानप्रतिपादकम्। अनेनात्मत्राणादौ मृषावादो न दोषायेति ध्वनितम्।' It just conveyed her ignorance of Hanuman's identity. Now they seem to me straightforward commentaries and we need not go behind them and discover meaning in the text or construct other excuses which seem to be a little far-fetched.

I told you, when talking about Hanuman setting fire to the city of Lanka,

उपतस्थे विशालाक्षी प्रयता हव्यवाहनम्।
यद्यस्ति पतिशुश्रूषा यद्यस्ति चरितं तपः ॥
यदि वास्त्येकपत्नीत्वं शीतो भव हनूमतः।
यदि कश्चिदनुक्रोशस्तस्य मय्यस्ति धीमतः ॥
यदि वा भाग्यशेषो मे शीतो भव हनूमतः।
यदि मां वृत्तसम्पन्नां तत्समागमलालसाम् ॥
स विजानाति धर्मात्मा शीतो भव हनूमतः।
यदि मां तारयेदार्यः सुग्रीवः सत्यसङ्गरः।
अस्माद्दुःखाम्बुसंरोधाच्छीतो भव हनूमतः ॥ V. 53. 28-32

Sita prayed to Agni, unknown to Hanuman. She heard of what was happening and prayed to Agni to spare her saviour. "If I am true to my husband, if I have performed any austerity in life, if I have been the wife of one man and one man only, be cool to him. If I have any good left, any *punya* left, I risk it all. If my truth and constancy are known to my husband and he remembers them in the least, be cool to Hanuman." These are famous passages and I venture to bring them to your notice in order that it may appear to you that I am not running through the texts, omitting passages on which previous readers have fixed their attention and upon which you would like me to fix your attention in turn.

You may remember my telling you of Trijata's dream. When the Rakshasis were tormenting Sita and she was in dire distress and inconsolable, Trijata tells her of a good dream of hers. She interprets the dream all too favourably and says, "Everything is going to turn out well for Sita, and Ravana and all his hosts are going to perish. Lanka is going to be destroyed. Good is going to be re-established, and then you, Rakshasis, will all have to suffer. Rama, when he gets to know what you have done to Sita, will put you all to like torments. Remember that moment is coming, and I advise you, if you are wise in your time, fall down at the feet of Sita and beg her pardon, so that she may save you, for it will be in her power to save you." Then the poet concludes a beautiful *sarga* with the *sloka*,

ततः सा ह्रीमती बाला भर्तुर्विजयहर्षिता ।
अवोचद्यदि तत्तथ्यं भवेयं शरणं हि वः ॥ V. 27. 53; cf. 58. 90

The words of Trijata had consoled her, and she had began to feel that all would end well. So she tells the Rakshasis, "Without your begging me, before you ever fall at my feet, I will give you the pardon: If ever what Trijata says happens, then be sure that I will protect you all." The occasion came when she was to protect them. You remember Hanuman, after Ravana had been killed and Vibhishana had been crowned, came at Rama's bidding to inform Sita that her good fortune had returned. Having conveyed it to Sita, he adds, "Now if you please, give me the order and I will torture these tormentresses of yours." You remember my reading to you the passage, somewhat lurid in its tenor. He said, "I will bite them. I will tear them with my nails and I will crush them with my feet, and I will do what you please." The poet does not tell us anywhere, but I am perfectly certain that the poet intends us to go back to the scene when Sita promised protection to the Rakshasis. Hanuman heard it also. Instead of Rama, it is Hanuman, next in importance to him, that comes and says it. Now follows the famous reply of Sita when she humbles Hanuman and teaches him a lesson that he could never forget. I have got the Sanskrit passage, but to save time, I propose to read the English translation.

After some deliberation, Sita came to a clear resolution and declared it in firm and persuasive terms:—

"Let us remember these women were not their own mistresses but were acting under the orders of a dreaded monarch. It is not just to be angry with them. They are not the cause of my misery. I have no doubt brought it on myself by former misdeeds. The law of karma is inexorable. Do not, I plead earnestly, blame my misfortune on these poor creatures. It is divine dispensation, the decree of Fate. I pardon these slaves of Ravana. They did his bidding. Now he is no more, they will not torment me hereafter. Let me remind you of a great moral taught of old by a bear. You know the story, I am sure. Once upon a time a hunter, pursued by a tiger, got up a big tree, which was already tenanted by a bear. The tiger, halted in his course at the foot, looked up and advised the bear to throw down the hunter, for was he not their common enemy? The bear refused, saying that a guest must be protected by all means, and he would not break the law of hospitality. With this high thought, the bear closed his eyes, sleeping the sleep of the just. The tiger turned then to the fugitive and asked him to hurl down the sleeping bear. This the man did. The bear, however, being used to such mishaps, caught another branch and saved himself. The tiger saw a fresh opening for his talent of persuasion. 'Look at this human,' says he to the bear, 'is not he a miserable ingrate? Down with him.' Quietly and in accents of benignity, the bear enunciated the eternal code. *A righteous man ought not to be turned from the right by the sin of a sinner. The rule of honour is inviolable. Good men have only one jewel, their unblemished conduct, and they must guard it, come what may. Be they good men or bad, be they deserving of death, still must they be pardoned and treated with mercy by one claiming to be an Arya. For no one is above error.* So then let us give up the idea of retaliation or retribution and abstain from injury even to miscreants and persecutors of mankind." (VI. 116. 37-45).

Did Sita remember the promise of protection she had made? Hanuman too had heard it. And there certainly had been no time for either to forget it. I venture to think the Poet meant us to connect the two incidents.

I now come to the most impressive and solemn scene of all in the six *kandas,* where Rama accuses Sita of infidelity and tells her that he cannot take her back and that she is free to choose a protector anywhere. The world was open to her. Sita's answer I shall give, noble words. A woman driven on her own resources, deprived of the hope she had entertained for twelve long months, accused in cruel fashion, and not knowing what to do, still speaks in complete self-possession, while all the world were looking at her. "How harsh and cruel are the things you have said to me! You are no vulgar man, and I am no vulgar woman. प्राकृतः प्राकृतामिव । (VI. 119. 5). Unworthy sentiments! I assert I am not what you suspect. Have faith, trust. I swear on my honour, and ask you, because some women go wrong, can you suspect the entire sex? Suspect me not. Remember your personal knowledge of me. Do you refer to Ravana touching my body? That was not of my seeking, nor even of my tolerating. That which I can control, my heart, has always been with you. As for my limbs, what could I do when they were overpowered? My honour is in your keeping. Having lived together so long, in fact having grown up together, you should know me through and through. If you give me up, I am indeed lost, ruined beyond redemption. When you sent that hero Hanuman to search for me, why did you not send the fatal message of abandonment? If he had told me, I would have died before his eyes and spared you all this trouble. Why undergo all these risks to your life and those of your friends? All these might have been avoided. You have let your ill-temper run away with your judgment, and like a low-bred man, esteemed me lightly as though I was no better than the ordinary type of woman. Only in name am I of Janaka's family. I come out of the pure ploughed earth. You, who know all, have chosen to ignore that fact. You put my conduct through all these years out of your mind.

You have forgotten, alas, the conjugal pledge of palm on palm in our tender years, which was a pledge of everlasting love. And the utter devotion with which I have followed you, and the pious care with which I have preserved, amidst indescribable trials, my loyalty to you—ah me! all this has not weighed with you so much as a feather before you condemned me and finally discarded me." Here Sita paused and looked up at her lord's face. But there was no relaxation in its cold, stern, pitiless stare. Realising that her doom was sealed, she turned to Lakshmana who stood dumb like one dazed in perplexity, and said, "Build me a pyre, I pray you. Suspected and cast away by my husband, I cannot, I will not, live any longer. Fire, consuming fire, is the only remedy for this woe!"

* चितां मे कुरु सौमित्रे व्यसनस्यास्य भेषजम् ॥ VI. 119. 18

Now I come to the last chapters of the story in the Uttarakanda. About the Abhisheka which is the beginning of their renewed happiness, I shall speak later, when I conclude these lectures. Now we see Rama and Lakshmana and Sita and others in the Asoka garden in the great palace of Ayodhya. There is merriment and there is joy all round, and Rama entertains Sita as much as he could.

अशोकवनिकां स्फीतां प्रविश्य रघुनन्दनः ।
आसने च शुभाकारे पुष्पप्रकरभूषिते ॥
कुथास्तरणसंवीते रामः संनिषसाद ह ।
सीतामादाय हस्तेन मधु मैरेयकं शुचि ॥
पाययामास काकुत्स्थः शचीमिव पुरन्दरः ।
मांसानि च सुमृष्टानि फलानि विविधानि च ॥
रामस्याभ्यवहारार्थं किङ्करास्तूर्णमाहरन् ।
उपानृत्यंश्च राजानं नृत्तगीतविशारदाः ॥
बालाश्च रूपवत्यश्च स्त्रियः पानवशानुगाः ।
उपानृत्यन्त काकुत्स्थं नृत्यगीतविशारदाः ॥
मनोऽभिरामा रामास्ता रामो रमयतां वरः ।
रमयामास धर्मात्मा नित्यं परमभूषितः ॥ VII. 42. 17-22

* Cf. Lect. XII, p. 174.

Sita's days of happiness were few, and we shall not be doing wrong to dwell with fondness on these scenes of mutual love and happiness. Rama entertained her. The poet says that he gave her honey and that he gave her *maireya* which is an intoxicating drink. Then he also handed to her well-chosen and well-cooked meat. It would appear that while they were seated together and regaling themselves with wine and meat, beautiful damsels from all parts of the universe came and entertained them. They were under the sway of drink, they had bedecked themselves in full splendour, and they sang and danced and narrated stories and were making merry. Lest you should suppose that in Rama, as he indulged in these pastimes, there was a touch of the sybaritic, of the love of mere luxury and revelry, the poet says,

स तया सीतया सार्धमासीनो विरराज ह ।
अरुन्धत्या सहासीनो वसिष्ठ इव तेजसा ।। VII. 42. 23

that he sat there looking on, as though he were Vasishtha sitting with Arundhati. Now let us dwell fondly on this passage for a moment.

एवं रामो मुदा युक्तः सीतां सुरसुतोपमाम् ।
रमयामास वैदेहीमहन्यहनि देववत् ।। VII. 42. 24

Now follows the stress which was her lot.

अब्रवीच्च वरारोहां सीतां सुरसुतोपमाम् ।।
अपत्यलाभो वैदेहि त्वयि मे समुपस्थितः ।
किमिच्छसि वरारोहे कामः किं क्रियतां तव ।। VII. 42. 30-31

"You are nearing the period of confinement", says Rama. "Therefore I am bound to ask you what you want and then try to meet your wishes. What is your desire? I will try to fulfil it." Sita smiled because her delicate condition was alluded to.

तपोवनानि पुण्यानि द्रष्टुमिच्छामि राघव ।
गङ्गातीरोपविष्टानामृषीणामुग्रतेजसाम् ।
फलमूलाशिनां देव पादमूलेषु वर्तितुम् ।।
एष मे परमः कामो यन्मूलफलभोजिनाम् ।
अप्येकरात्रं काकुत्स्थ निवसेयं तपोवने ।।
तथेति च प्रतिज्ञातं रामेणाक्लिष्टकर्मणा ।। VII. 42. 32-35

She said, "I wish to spend one day at least with the Rishis, live their simple, frugal unsophisticated life, eat just the fruits and roots, and be happy without a care in the mind, without a thought of all this pomp." Poor woman, she did not know what she was asking for; for in very truth, Rama granted her prayer. Only it was not for a day, but for twelve long years. You know how the story was spread about in the city, and all people began to gossip and say that Rama was setting a bad example to the townspeople, that he had taken back a woman who had lived in another man's house, a wicked man's house, for a whole twelve months. And the men said to each other, "If Sita does this, if Sita behaved in that way, and she had been pardoned, all our women will ask for a similar privilege and we shall be obliged to tolerate it and a great many things hereafter. Bad time for us all." When this was reported to Rama, he sent for his brothers and said to them, "This is a stain that I cannot bear, and I must wipe this out somehow." And he announced to them his dread resolve. So Sita was taken out. It fell to Lakshmana to do this. He takes her to the Ganges bank and there he leaves her alone and cries bitterly. "Why do you cry," asked Sita, and Lakshmana told her the truth. This was not the first time that she had been struck in the most tender spot. She paused for a while, collected her thoughts, brave, resigned woman that she was, not forgetting her dignity at that last moment, and she told Lakshmana, "Hear me, Lakshmana, my last word to you. I was born to be unhappy. The spirit of sorrow is incarnate in me by the will of the Creator. So far as I can see, my conduct has been pure. I have not deserved to be abandoned by my lord and master. It is clear that I have committed some atrocious sin in my previous birth. May be, I cruelly parted a man from his loving wife. When last I lived in hermitages, I was with Rama, and in devoted service to him I did not feel any privation or hardship.. Tell me now how I shall explain my presence here, all alone, to the Rishis. What crime shall I own as the cause of my exile? They will say with one voice, 'Our king Rama is the soul of justice. Why has he discarded you?' Ah, Lakshmana, I have no use for life, and may end it in the waters of the Ganges. But I have in me the proper seed of the royal family and may not kill myself. Well, leave me then to my fate. Only I have something to say still. Take back this message. My prostrations, my humble prostrations, at the feet of my mothers-in-law as well as at the feet of the king. When on my account you have touched their feet with your head, tell him from me, 'You know dharma and practise it at all risks. In your heart you will admit my character is without a stain. I have never been false to you whether in mind or in body. Yet because your subjects suspect my purity, you throw me out. So be it, I submit. You honour and love your people, the same as you honour and love your brothers. If to preserve your good name among them, I must be sacrificed, I am content to be sacrificed. As you serve your subjects, so I serve you, not less but more. This body of mine is nothing. To me, as to any woman, the husband is everything, he is kindred, he is preceptor, he is God. My duty is to be of use to him and in his service to lay down my life if need be.' Only take careful note, Lakshmana, of my body. It bears obvious signs of pregnancy. Rama knows this, yet it is meet that you witness my condition with your own eyes."

One last scene yet, not less tragic than any that has gone before. But it is in its own class. It transcends our experience, it defies our imagination, it leaves us speechless with awe, and with a feeling that we are no longer on earth. You remember how when the little boys Kusa and Lava had been recognised in the king's palace, Rama asked to see Sita, and how into his presence Sita is brought by Valmiki himself. And then Rama asks for a *sapatha,* an oath of purity, from Sita before he takes her back. Before the assembled subjects, tributary kings, ministers, merchants from all parts, he asks her to take an oath again that she is pure. Remember Sita was clad in the orange robes of a hermit. You see how her fate pursues her to the bitter end. Must she take an oath again? With downcast eyes and with face of divine resignation, she said,

यथाहं राघवादन्यं मनसापि न चिन्तये।
तथा मे माधवी देवी विवरं दातुमर्हति॥
मनसा कर्मणा वाचा यथा रामं समर्चये।
तथा मे माधवी देवी विवरं दातुमर्हति॥
यथैतत् सत्यमुक्तं मे वेद्मि रामात् परं न च।
तथा मे माधवी देवी विवरं दातुमर्हति॥

तथा शपन्त्यां वैदेह्यां प्रादुरासीत्तदद्भुतम् ।
भूतलादुत्थितं दिव्यं सिंहासनमनुत्तमम् ॥
ध्रियमाणं शिरोभिस्तु नागैरमितविक्रमैः ।
दिव्यं दिव्येन वपुषा दिव्यरत्नविभूषितैः ॥
तस्मिंस्तु धरणी देवी बाहुभ्यां गृह्य मैथिलीम् ।
स्वागतेनाभिनन्द्यैनामासने चोपवेशयत् ।
तामासनगतां दृष्ट्वा प्रविशन्तीं रसातलम् ॥
पुष्पवृष्टिरविच्छिन्ना दिव्या सीतामवाकिरत् ॥ VII. 97. 15-21

"As I have never let my thought wander away from Rama, so let my mother Earth give me an opening. I will go back to where I came from. This earth is not for me, nor this husband, nor these subjects whom no proof can ever convince." Then as she prayed to her mother to allow her to go back to her place of origin, the earth opened, and, marvellous to relate, a throne came up, all of gold and diamonds, strong Nagas, five-headed cobras, bearing the *simhasana*. In that *Simhasana* there was her Mother, who welcomed her, "My daughter, come back. You have had enough of this earth."

So let us leave Sita, crowned with these flowers from high heaven, for, mind you, while earth did not understand, did not applaud her peerless character, heaven did. She was saved, but not to Rama her pitiless husband, nor to the subjects who continually suspected her in spite of repeated proofs. One word about Rama. Do not think I wish to leave in your minds harsh thoughts about that prince of men. A word must be said in explanation. Rama was not an ordinary man. *While he had many points of contact with us, while he showed* many weaknesses to which we are subject, at the same time he carried the virtues of humanity to the very sublimest peak. Why then was he harsh to his wife, notwithstanding he had proofs beyond question that she had been very faithful? I have tried to explain it before, but I shall repeat it now, for it is necessary to understand Rama's character which goes so far beyond the clouds into divinity that we staggering human beings find it unable quite to understand or to appreciate the motive. Still remotely a suggestion may be made, not beyond what the poet has said, but based upon what repeatedly he has affirmed to us as Rama's character, not understood by

Dasaratha, not understood by Lakshmana or Bharata or by any of his subjects, not understood by anyone of the time except perhaps Sita and Sumitra. They seem to know that he was fulfilling the greatest demand upon human nature. He was carrying out a promise that had been made, and in carrying out the promise no sacrifice ought to be counted. That nobody understood in his time. That was Rama's mistortune. It is Rama's glory that though he was laughed and jeered at, though he was dissuaded by all people about him, father, mother, brothers, subjects and Vasishtha too, in spite of their opposition, against the whole world he stood out and stood alone. This is the highest duty, however harsh it appeared. That is Rama's greatness, that he did not mind sacrificing anything to preserve *dharma*. Dharma had many phases. Sometimes it appeared as his father's promise, sometimes it appeared as the honour of his family, sometimes it appeared as the duty to punish the enemy. But whatever it was, what he thought was his highest *dharma*, that he fulfilled and to that end there was nothing that he would not sacrifice. Wife, give up; brother, give up; life, give up; but dharma, maintain it above all things. There was no other possible way. It is difficult for us to understand this extreme rigour of the law. That is Rama's eternal glory. At the risk of being misunderstood, at the risk of being sometimes condemned as an inhuman being, as a man harsh even to the wife who was typical of all the virtues of womanhood, Rama stood true to the abstract conception of *dharma*. If you do not understand it fully, and if you sometimes feel that Rama might have taken a step or two down, it is your business. So let us not blame him, however tender we may be to sorrow over Sita's plight.

TWENTYEIGHTH LECTURE*

Ladies and Gentlemen,

The name of Kaikeyi has a sinister significance being applied now among us to a woman who obtains influence by improper means and uses it for improper ends. As told in the Poem, there is no doubt that Kaikeyi was a most unlovely character. She had abilities, talents of a kind, but she abused them for self-aggrandisement. She was by temperament disposed to domineer over people; she loved power and whoever came under her shadow regretted it. It is abundantly clear, notwithstanding all this, that she was a great character. She was cruel; she was jealous; she told lies. And even when it was pointed out that her course would involve the death of her husband, she did not hesitate to pursue it. The only thing that redeemed her character was the affection she bore at first for Sri Rama and the affection that she seems to have drawn from him. Which was the cause and which the effect, is not clear. Let us give her the credit of having been able to discern the virtues of Sri Rama and appreciating them sincerely. The Poem says however that Sri Rama made no difference whatever between his mother and her so far as his behaviour was concerned. And furthermore, there is the statement, made more than once, that he was more demonstrative in his affection and in his services to Kaikeyi than was her own son, Bharata.

With this general idea it is best to begin with the story that Sumantra gave,—he was thoroughly vexed with her,—of her origin and the character of her mother. He quoted a proverb of the time and said, "What people say is perfectly true, that men take after their fathers and women take after their mothers." "I have heard a story about your mother," he says to her, when her cruelty was exhibited in very sinister fashion towards Sita. The story is briefly told by himself. It seems her mother, the wife of Asvapati, was a bad woman. Asvapati had himself obtained from some Yōgi the power of overhearing conversations between animals. Once when he was asleep, two ants on his cot were talking together. He heard what they were saying and laughed aloud. This lady who

---

*18-10-'44.

could not control her inquisitiveness, asked what the matter was. He protested he could not tell her. "But you must tell me", she says. "No", he said, to which she rejoined, "If you don't tell me, I am led to infer that you were laughing at me." "I am not laughing at you. You may draw what inference you like. But if I tell you, the consequence will be that I shall die on the spot." Says she, "I don't care whether you live or whether you die. But you shall tell me. If you don't I will take my own life here." He went and asked his master. The master says, "Let the woman go. Don't tell." So he discarded her. So far as the story goes, it does not appear that he married again. He had had enough with one. Sumantra says, "I see you are just like your mother. Don't imitate her in every respect and don't demand what may end in your widowhood." As a matter of fact, she did. She did not desist at all in her course. She proved that his story did apply to her. The Poet says: When Sumantra had finished, he was eagerly expecting that it had made some impression upon her, and studying her face. But there was no change there. Not a muscle moved. She was the same hard woman that she had been before when she made her demand. Well, that is the lady whose doings take a great deal of space and were in fact the origin of the entire trouble.

How she treated—excuse my using the expression—her co-wives, is the first idea to which I am going to refer. It was well-known, it was notorious, the way she abused her power with her husband and reduced these people to a very low status indeed. Manthara herself says:

दर्पान्निराकृता पूर्वं त्वया सौभाग्यवत्तया ।
राममाता सपत्नी ते कथं वैरं न यातयेत् ॥ II. 8. 37

"If you allow Rama to be anointed Yuvaraja, Kausalya will become powerful," says Manthara. "Won't she remember what you have done to her in your palmy days? You will have to take it all back from her, perhaps with interest." And Dasaratha says to Kaikeyi when she had made her demand:

किं मां वक्ष्यति कौसल्या राघवे वनमास्थिते ।
किं चैनां प्रतिवक्ष्यामि कृत्वा विप्रियमीदृशम् ॥
यदा यदा हि कौसल्या दासीवच्च सखीव च ।
भार्यावद्भगिनीवच्च मातृवच्चोपतिष्ठति ॥

सततं प्रियकामा मे प्रियपुत्रा प्रियंवदा ।
न मया सत्कृता देवी सत्कारार्हा कृते तव ॥
इदानीं तत्तपति मां यन्मया सुकृतं त्वयि । II. 12. 67-70

"When I have sent him to the forest, what will Kausalya say to me? What shall I say to her in return, having hit her so hard? A good woman all round she was to me, she has been to me, she is to me; servant, companion, wife, sister, mother—what is she not to me? She is all these things and yet on your account, though she is worthy of all honour and consideration, I have not respected her, I have not shown her the consideration due to her by position and character. I have injured her and I have been very kind to you. Both these things torment my mind."

सुमित्रा प्रेक्ष्य वै भीता कथं मे विश्वसिष्यति ॥ II. 12. 72

The words प्रेक्ष्य वै भीता are expressly used I think. Sumitra is the more submissive wife, a more understanding and on the whole, I think, a better-evolved wife than even Kausalya. So he says, "What shall I say to her? How can I look at her, that quiet gentle lady?"

Then Kausalya says to Rama when he goes and announces the dire order that he has received from his father and from his step mother:

यदि पुत्र न जायेथा मम शोकाय राघव ।
न स्म दुःखमतो भूयः पश्येयमहमप्रजाः ॥ II. 20. 36

"Why were you born at all? If you had not been born, my only sorrow would have been that I was a barren woman."

एक एव हि वन्ध्यायाः शोको भवति मानसः ।

"A barren woman has only one grief."

अप्रजास्मीति संतापो न ह्यन्यः पुत्र विद्यते ॥ II. 20. 37

"She has no other trouble. But having you for my son, you of all people, see what I can come to."

न दृष्टपूर्वं कल्याणं सुखं वा पतिपौरुषे ।

"I have married the greatest king on earth but what have I got for it? I have seen nothing like prosperity with him.

Because he is the greatest king on earth, the most powerful and the most dreaded, what have I got?

अपि पुत्रे तु पश्येयमिति रामास्थितं मया ॥ II. 20. 38

"Hitherto I have been expecting that when you came of age, my grievances would be redressed and I would be a happy queen."

सा बहून्यमनोज्ञानि वाक्यानि हृदयच्छिदाम्।
अहं श्रोष्ये सपत्नीनामवराणां वरा सती ॥ II. 20. 39

"Now I am going to be the most unfortunate of the unfortunate queens in this palace. If my son is banished, what is going to happen to me? I am going to hear much that I should not like to hear."

अतो दुःखतरं किं नु प्रमदानां भविष्यति।
मम शोको विलापश्च यादृशोऽयमनन्तकः ॥ II. 20. 40

"My sorrow and my grief and my lamentation are not going to have any end. You know a woman is considered to be most fortunate if she has a son born to her. But if she loses that son, all the misfortunes that were heaped upon her when she had no son, would now be doubled and trebled."

त्वयि संनिहितेऽप्येवमहमासं निराकृता।
किं पुनः प्रोषिते तात ध्रुवं मरणमेव मे ॥ II. 20. 41

"You are now about twenty-seven years old. Even when you are here, a grown-up son with me, so honoured by your father, so respected all over the world, even with you here, this has been my fate. When you have gone, what will be my fate? Only death."

अत्यन्त निगृहीतास्मि भर्तुर्नित्यमतन्त्रिता।
परिवारेण कैकेय्याः समा वाप्यथवावरा ॥ II. 20. 42

"My husband does not show me the honour due to me and I am considered to be no better, perhaps somewhat worse, than any retainer of Kaikeyi."

नित्यक्रोधतया तस्याः कथं नु खरवादि तत्।
कैकेय्या वदनं द्रष्टुं पुत्र शक्ष्यामि दुर्गता ॥ II. 20. 44

"My dear son, when you have gone, how can I look at her face? Always her speech is harsh."

दश सप्त च वर्षाणि तव जातस्य राघव ।

As if to show I am wrong, I have now read the sloka which says that he is only seventeen years old. There is a dispute about the fact. It cannot be seventeen. There must be some mistake so that people say that he was seventeen plus the age at which his Upanayana took place. That will come to twenty-seven or twenty-eight. "My misery is going to end, so I have been expecting all these years."

आसितानि प्रकाङ्क्षन्त्या मया दुःखपरिक्षयम् ॥ II. 20. 45

"I have borne it long, I cannot bear it any more. I am going to be an unfortunate woman living an unfortunate life."

अपश्यन्ती तव मुखं परिपूर्णशशिप्रभम् ।
कृपणा वर्तयिष्यामि कथं कृपणजीविकाम् ॥ II. 20. 47

This is a thing that generally mothers say, when sons do not satisfy them. "What sufferings have I not undergone to bring you up? I have had to fast, move without proper food, undergo much exertion! All has gone to waste."

उपवासैश्च योगैश्च बहुभिश्च परिश्रमैः ।
दुःखं संवर्धितो मोघं त्वं हि दुर्गतया मया ॥ II. 20. 48

Then you remember my reading to you the characterisation of Bharata himself before he had ever known that anything wrong had happened in Ayodhya.* This is how he describes his mother as he knew her before he went to Kekaya.

आत्मकामा सदा चण्डी क्रोधना प्राज्ञमानिनी ॥ II. 70. 10

This is how he describes her to the messengers from Vasistha who had gone to bring him back. Then when Bharata asks his mother why she has banished Rama, he says:

तथा ज्येष्ठा हि मे माता कौसल्या दीर्घदर्शिनी ।
त्वयि धर्मं समास्थाय भगिन्यामिव वर्तते ॥ II. 73. 10

"Kausalya, my elder step-mother, has been to you like a sister, notwithstanding what you have been to her, because she is a dirghadarsini. That means she is a far-seeing woman, very tactful, knows what is proper. She has not returned unkindness for unkindness."

* Lect. XIII, p. 203 above.

तस्याः पुत्रं कृतात्मानं चीरवल्कलवाससम्।
प्रस्थाप्य वनवासाय कथं पापे न शोचसि॥ II. 73. 11

"I am astonished you don't sit down and cry for having sent to the forest Kausalya's son and compelled him to wear the bark and the hide."

Then, let us look at the hold that Kaikeyi had won over the old king. What was her power over him? Manthara says this to Kaikeyi:

दयिता त्वं सदा भर्तुरत्र मे नास्ति संशयः।
त्वत्कृते स महाराजो विशेदपि हुताशनम्॥ II. 9. 24

"You are the favourite wife. Why should anybody have a doubt about it? If you order him, he will throw himself into the fire. That is the condition you have brought him to."

न त्वां क्रोधयितुं शक्तो न क्रुद्धां प्रत्युदीक्षितुम्।
तव प्रियार्थं राजा हि प्राणानपि परित्यजेत्॥ II. 9. 25

"He will not dare to make you angry. Nor can he bear your anger. To satisfy you he will give up his life if necessary."

न ह्यतिक्रमितुं शक्तस्तव वाक्यं महीपतिः।
मन्दस्वभावे बुद्धयस्व सौभाग्यबलमात्मनः॥ II. 9. 26

"You are a lucky woman. Make sure that you use it all to your advantage. Your husband dare not cross you." And Dasaratha himself says to Kaikeyi when he came into the 'anger house,' the name by which they call it, and saw her lying on the ground with jewels all in confusion, he asks her, "What is the matter? What is the matter? You know your power over me. You can get anything from me. Why do you do all this? When have I ever disobeyed you? Why all this at this time?" Dasaratha says:

कः प्रियं लभतामद्य को वा सुमहदप्रियम्॥ II. 10. 32

This is the justice of the old king. "Tell me who is the man I should ruin? Who is the honest man I should ruin and tell me who is the rogue whom I should advance. I will do both."

मा रोदीर्मा च कार्षीस्त्वं देवि संपरिशोषणम्॥ II. 10. 32

"Don't annoy yourself in any way. Don't cry."

अवध्यो वध्यतां को वा वध्यः को वा विमुच्यताम्।

"Tell me which fellow who has deserved to be hung should be let off and tell me which innocent man should be brought to the gallows. I will readily do it."

दरिद्रः को भवत्वाढयो द्रव्यवान्वाप्यकिंचनः ॥ II. 10. 33

"Whom shall I deprive of his property and to whom shall I give property although he is a poor fellow."

अहं चव मदीयाश्च सर्वे तव वशानुगाः ।

"Not me only but all my men, they are yours to command."

न ते किंचिदभिप्रायं व्याहन्तुमहमुत्सहे ॥ II. 10. 34

"Your slightest wish is a law to me. I dare not transgress it."

आत्मनो जीवितेनापि ब्रूहि यन्मनसेच्छसि ।
बलमात्मनि जानन्ती न मां शाङ्कितुमर्हसि ॥ II. 10. 35

"Knowing your power over me, don't have the least misgiving about whether I shall obey you or not. With my life I shall satisfy your wants," he says.

अवलिप्त न जानासि त्वत्तः प्रियतरो मम ।
मनुजो मनुजव्याघ्राद्रामादन्यो न विद्यते ॥ II. 11. 5

"Then, you know," he says to her, "you are very very dear to me. But there is one man dearer than you."

तेनाजय्येन मुख्येन राघवेण महात्मना ।
शपे ते जीवनार्हेण ब्रूहि यन्मनसेच्छसि ॥ II. 11. 6

"Tell me what is it in your mind that bothers you. By that Rama who is dearer to me than even you and who is dearer than everybody else, I swear by him." He little knew what he was doing, poor man, it was to that very person that the harm was to be done—he thought he was placing Rama far above risk. That is why he spoke to her like that.

यं मुहूर्तमपश्यंस्तु न जीवेयमहं ध्रुवम् ।
तेन रामेण कैकेयि शपे ते वचनक्रियाम् ॥ II. 11. 7

"Him whom I cannot forbear not to see even for a minute."

आत्मना वात्मजैश्चान्यैर्वृणे यं मनुजर्षभम् ।
तेन रामेण कैकेयि शपे ते बचनक्रियाम् ॥ II. 11. 8

"I beg you not only on the life of Rama but on the lives of the other brothers as well." He brings them too.

भद्रे हृदयमप्येतदनुमृश्योद्धरस्व मे।
एतत्समीक्ष्य कैकेयि ब्रूहि यत्साधु मन्यसे॥
बलमात्मनि पश्यन्ती न मां शङ्कितुमर्हसि।
करिष्यामि तव प्रीतिं सुकृतेनापि ते शपे॥ II. 11. 9-10

"All my merit I put on the stake that I will do what you desire. Simply command me." Kaikeyi knew the magnitude and the sinister quality of her request. These things are not enough for her. So she binds him down still further, as you will see, by harsh and stringent vows.

यथा क्रमेण शपसि वरं मम ददासि च।
तच्छृण्वन्तु त्रयस्त्रिंशद्देवाः साग्निपुरोगमाः॥ II. 11. 13

"The promise that you make to me now, may all the thirty-three crores of gods hear."

चन्द्रादित्यौ नभश्चैव ग्रहा रात्र्यहनी दिशः।
जगच्च पृथिवी चेयं सगन्धर्वा सराक्षसा॥ II. 11. 14

"Let all these listen. They are all witnesses to your promise."

निशाचराणि भूतानि गृहेषु गृहदेवताः।
यानि चान्यानि भूतानि जानीयुर्भाषितं तव॥ II. 11. 15

"They have all heard, remember. Don't think you have said something to me and that it is only me that you have got to satisfy. The universe has heard you, every bit of it."

सत्यसन्धो महातेजा धर्मज्ञः सुसमाहितः।
वरं मम ददात्येष तन्मे शृण्वन्तु देवताः॥ II. 11. 16

The devil quotes scripture. The woman was masculine. She quotes examples from previous history of great men who have made difficult promises but have kept them and gone to Heaven. She says, "I have also put you on the path of Dharma because you have got to keep this promise." I hope you all know the story of Sibi, I needn't tell you that.

शैब्यः श्येनकपोतीये स्वमांसं पक्षिणे ददौ।
अलर्कश्चक्षुषी दत्वा जगाम गतिमुत्तमाम्॥ II. 12. 43

There was a king named Alarka who promised to give anybody what he asked. A blind man came to him, a Brahmin skilled in the Vedas, and Alarka said, "Ask what you want." The Brahmin said, "I will give my eyes to you; you give your eyes to me." Alarka said, "All right. I have made my promise." He plucked out his eyes and gave them.

सरितां तु पतिः स्वल्पां मर्यादां सत्यमन्वितः ।
सत्यानुरोधात्समये वेलां स्वां नातिवर्तते ॥ II. 14. 6

"Look at the ocean. Having made a promise that he will never transgress into the land, he keeps within his limit" (notwithstanding that there is no Siegfried line there).

सत्यं समनुवर्तस्व यदि धर्मे धृता मतिः ।
स वरः सफलो मेऽस्तु वरदो ह्यसि सत्तम ॥ II. 14. 8

So she bound him down by harsh vows. Poor Dasaratha protested, implored; he threatened, he cursed, he swore. Nothing availed. Then he said, "I have got a very simple-minded son. I am caught by this wretched scheming woman. I don't want my son to go to the forest. But if I tell him even indistinctly, 'Will you go to the forest,' he will at once say, 'Yes,' so simple-minded, so straightforward. 'All right, father,' he will say."

नालं द्वितीयं वचनं पुत्रो मां प्रतिभाषितुम् ।
स वनं प्रव्रजेत्युक्तो बाढमित्येव वक्ष्यति ॥
यदि मे राघवः कुर्याद्वनं गच्छेति भाषितः ।
प्रतिकूलं प्रियं मे स्यान्न तु वत्सः करिष्यति ॥ II. 12. 85-86

"If, being told to go to the forest, my son disobeys me, that would be my heart's wish. But he won't. He is a perversely honest man."

शुद्धभावो हि भावं मे न तु ज्ञास्यति राघवः ।
राघवे हि वनं प्राप्ते सर्वलोकस्य धिक्कृतम् ॥ II. 12. 87

Then Dasaratha tries another method. He says, "If I die, let not Bharata do me any of the last ceremonies, that is to say, if Bharata agrees to take the crown according to your wish,

प्रियं चेद्भरतस्यैतद्रामप्रव्राजनं भवेत् ॥
मा स्म मे भरतः कार्षीत्प्रेतकृत्यं गतायुषः । II. 12. 92-93

when I am dead and gone, let him not do me any of the last obsequies."

Now I come to a point which is sometimes the subject-matter of dispute, but I think the matter is perfectly clear. Still, as there is a doubt in the Poem itself, the Poet sometimes saying the one thing and sometimes saying the other, I will try and make things as clear as I can. Why did Dasaratha grant these boons and banish Rama? Why did he do this extraordinarily inconsiderate act, something not expected at all? Most people say, and I think that is the general belief among people, that Dasaratha was under the charms and spells of his second wife and therefore yielded. What old man who has married a second wife is not a slave? That every one knows. And this Kaikeyi was a bad woman, extremely clever, got him thoroughly under her control and then made him do what she liked. That is the general belief, that Dasaratha did this because he could not resist the spells of his favourite wife. Not that Kaikeyi was very young at the time. The boons were granted पुरा (II. 11. 18), hundreds of years before, when the Devas and Asuras were still fighting and the gods took the help of earthly potentates. As a matter of fact, however, if we carefully examine the text, it transpires that Dasaratha yielded not to her spells or charms—for, them he put by without any reserve as soon as he discovered how wicked this woman was. He did not allow himself to be influenced by her. He was not afraid of her but he had bound himself by a promise which he could not put aside. And as he was a satyavrata, coming of the race of Ikshvakus who never broke their word, he was caught. He tried to get out but could not. This is what he himself says:

यदा तु बहवो वृद्धा गुणवन्तो बहुश्रुताः ॥
परिप्रक्ष्यन्ति काकुत्स्थं वक्ष्यामि किमहं तदा। II. 12. 65-66

The old man knew what would be said of him. He had an idea of it. Because he was so much under Kaikeyi's influence the world knew it, it was a notorious fact—because of that he knew that that would be said of him on this occasion. So he lamented the fact. "When people come and ask me, 'Where is Rama? Where is Rama?' When old men come and ask me and when wise men come and ask me, that is, men who know everything, what shall I tell them?"

कैकेय्या क्लिश्यमानेन पुत्रः प्रव्राजितो मया ॥ II. 12. 66

If I said, "I had bound myself by a promise to my wife, Kaikeyi. Unable to prove false to my own promise, I have sent him away to the forest", that would be true.

यदि सत्यं ब्रवीम्येतत्तदसत्यं भविष्यति । II. 12. 67

But, if I told them this, nobody would believe me. Everybody would say, "The old fellow is lying." "That is my trouble," he says. "Then the world's censure of Dasaratha could not be avoided. Everybody would accuse me." So he tried another trick. He said to Kaikeyi. "I am an old man. You are a young wife. But I will prostrate myself at your feet. Will you then grant this request of mine?"

न जीवितं मेऽस्ति कुतः पुनः सुखं विनात्मजेनात्मवतः कुतो रतिः ।
ममाहितं देवि न कर्तुमर्हसि स्पृशामि पादावपि ते प्रसीद मे ॥

II. 12. 112

"I will touch your feet with my head and hands. Won't you let Rama off?"

स भूमिपालो विलपन्ननाथवत्स्त्रिया गृहीतो हृदयेऽतिमात्रया ।
पपात देव्याश्चरणौ प्रसारितावुभावसंस्पृश्य यथातुरस्तथा ॥

II. 12. 113

This woman who transgressed all *maryada*, all rules of proper conduct, when, being caught by her, Dasaratha said, "I will touch your feet", she put them forward. She was conscious that she was in the position of a great creditor. Dasaratha was only a poor debtor. But because he was crying, his eyes were not working properly at the time and he could not touch the feet actually, just escaped by the sheerest accident. That shows you the extent to which Kaikeyi allowed herself to go in her wickedness.

एवं प्रचोदितो राजा कैकेय्या निर्विशङ्कया ।
नाशकत्पाशमुन्मोक्तुं बलिरिन्द्रकृतं यथा ॥ II. 14. 11

Tied by the rope of his promise, he could not disentangle himself.

धर्मबन्धेन बद्धोऽस्मि नष्टा च मम चेतना । II. 14. 24

This is how he cries, "My mind is paralysed. I cannot think and I am tied all over with this bond of duty—the fulfilment of my promise." So you see that is what compelled him.

Now we shall come to another feature in this lady's character. I told you she told lies. When Sumantra came on the fateful morning, the king had been harassed by Kaikeyi all night to redeem his promise not to crown Rama but to transfer the elevation to her own son. Early in the morning when Sumantra went there, he found the old man was not able to talk to him. He was dozing with grief and with vigil. Sumantra asks, "What is the matter with my master?" Sumantra was a wise man and he saw very far. Then Kaikeyi said to him,

सुमन्त्र राजा रजनीं रामहर्षसमुत्सुकः ॥
प्रजागरपरिश्रान्तो निद्राया वशमेयिवान् । II. 14. 62-63

"He is just now a bit sleepy. He was awake all night, just fancying the details of the *abhisheka* of his son, Rama. Because he was lost in contemplation of all that happiness, he is just now dozing a little."

तद्गच्छ त्वरितं सूत राजपुत्रं यशस्विनम ॥
राममानय भद्रं ते नात्र कार्या विचारणा । II. 14. 63-64

"Don't doubt what I say." Then when Rama is brought there and he sees the perfect contrast between his expectation and the reality, he asks. "What is the matter with my father? Have you done anything or have I done anything? What is the matter?" She says:

न राजा कुपितो राम व्यसनं नास्य किंचन ।
किंचिन्मनोगतं त्वस्य त्वद्भयान्नाभिभाषते ॥ II. 18. 20

"Some slight misgiving about you, some slight fear as to what you will say. Therefore he does not say it. He has got something in his mind, he is not angry with you."

प्रियं त्वामप्रियं वक्तुं वाणी नास्योपवर्तते ।

"His tongue won't move because he cannot speak anything unjust or unkind to you."

तदवश्यं त्वया कार्यं यदनेनाश्रुतं मम ॥ II. 18. 21

"I will tell you what he promised to me. You must therefore do it."

एष मह्यं वरं दत्त्वा पुरा मामभिपूज्य च ।

"Having honoured me and paid me all respect at that time,

स पश्चात्तप्यते राजा यथान्यः प्राकृतस्तथा ॥ II. 18. 22

just as an ordinary man in the street would do, he now regrets the promise that he made to me solemnly."

अतिसृज्य ददानीति वरं मम विशां पतिः ।

स निरर्थं गतजले सेतुं बन्धितुमिच्छति ॥ II. 18. 23

"He has made a promise which he cannot revoke. The water has flown. There is no more damming it."

धर्ममूलमिद राम विदितं च सतामपि ।

तत्सत्यं न त्यजेद्राजा कुपितस्त्वत्कृते यथा ॥ II. 18. 24

She binds him by a previous promise, the same way as she did her husband. "Good or bad, you may like it or you may not like it, but you must do it."

यदि तद्वक्ष्यते राजा शुभं वा यदि वाशुभम् ।

करिष्यसि ततः सर्वमाख्यास्यामि पुनस्त्वहम् ॥ II. 18. 25

"I will tell everything."

यदि त्वभिहितं राज्ञा त्वयि तन्न विपत्स्यते ।

ततोऽहमभिधास्यामि न ह्येष त्वयि वक्ष्यति ॥ II. 18. 26

"He may not be able to tell you but I know it. I will tell you. But you must tell me beforehand that you will carry it out." Of course Rama, you know, is the very embodiment of magnanimity. He says, "All right. Why do you doubt it for a moment?"

करिष्ये प्रतिजाने च रामो द्विर्नाभिभाषते ॥ II. 18. 30

"I am not a man to speak twice about anything. What I have said, I have said. I will do everything that he desires, whether he says it or not. I do not mind. You had better say."

यदि सत्यप्रतिज्ञं त्वं पितरं कर्तुमिच्छसि ।

आत्मानं च नरश्रेष्ठ मम वाक्यमिदं शृणु ॥ II. 18. 34

"Not only is your father bound to me by solemn promises but you have bound yourself also now. Having just now bound yourself, listen to me," she says. And without hesitating or faltering she made her two demands. "Go to the forest for fourteen years and let Bharata take your role here."

एतेन त्वां नरेन्द्रोऽयं कारुण्येन समाप्लुतः।
शोकसंक्लिष्टवदनो न शक्नोति निरीक्षितुम्॥ II. 18. 39

"He cannot even see you, let alone talk to you."

एतत्कुरु नरेन्द्रस्य वचनं रघुनन्दन।
सत्येन महता राम तारयस्व नराधिपम्॥ II. 18. 40

"Save your father's honour and let him go to his rightful place in Heaven." You see how Kaikeyi caught Rama by the very means by which he should be caught. He was the man to observe all rules of honour with the greatest exactitude and precision. Therefore she knew her man. I told you before in speaking of Rama that Kaikeyi believed in him as a man who would fulfil his father's promise at all costs. Kaikeyi's belief in him was proof, greater than any in the world, of Rama's real greatness. Now Kaikeyi was not slow to follow up the advantage. I have mentioned all this, ladies and gentlemen, in order to make you agree with me that Dasaratha did not yield to the charms of Kaikeyi. He was no longer under that voluptuous influence; he has got over that now. It was merely because he was bound by solemn oaths.

यावत्त्वं न वनं यातः पुरादस्मादभित्वरन्।
पिता तावन्न ते राम स्नास्यते भोक्ष्यतेऽपि वा॥ II. 19. 16

Kaikeyi having caught Rama, goes one step further. "Now, son, you know what you ought to do. You must make haste, leave this town at once. Till you leave I won't let your father bathe or eat." Dasaratha who was not able to speak till now as soon as he heard this, cries out:

धिक्कष्टमिति निश्वस्य राजा शोकपरिप्लुतः।
मूर्च्छितो न्यपतत्तस्मिन् पर्यङ्के हेमभूषिते॥ II. 19. 17

"Look at this wicked woman saying this. What a lie! What a wicked thing to say of me." So saying he lost consciousness and fell down.

You see how I told you it was his promise that Dasaratha kept. It was not the beauty or the charms of Kaikeyi that subdued him. But the world did not believe it. In the family nobody believed it. Lakshmana never believed it till the end. He uses the expression, "This wicked woman and the foolish old dotard of my father." When Rama had gone and informed Kausalya of what had happened and Kausalya was in the extremity of grief, Lakshmana just joins her, making the task of Rama still more difficult. He himself complains,

न रोचते ममाप्येतदार्ये यद्राघवो वनम् ।
त्यक्त्वा राज्यश्रियं गच्छेत्स्त्रिया वाक्यवशंगतः ॥ II. 21. 2

"I don't like this either, mother." That is his description of Rama but really it applied to Dasaratha because what bound Dasaratha also bound Rama in turn.

विपरीतश्च वृद्धश्च विषयैश्च प्रधर्षितः
नृपः किमिव न ब्रूयाच्चोद्यमानः समन्मथः ॥ II. 21. 3

"Being under Kaikeyi's influence, what would not the old dotard do? He will say anything, he will do anything. Is it to be followed and obeyed? He will say anything. Are we, wise people, to follow him?" That was Lakshmana's description. If Lakshmana himself was under the misconception, you may take it that the rest of the world was.

But that is not the whole of the story, ladies and gentlemen. Rama himself believed it to some extent and he says it openly to Lakshmana. When they were both together on the other bank of the Ganges, the first night they were alone, Rama says having reviewed all the things that had taken place—he had had no time to review them before—now he slowly turned them over and puts the value of each upon it and assesses every transaction and event properly. Then it occurred to him to say this:—

कृतकामा तु कैकेयी तुष्टा भवितुमर्हति । II. 53. 6

"She has had her heart's desire; she must now be well pleased."

सा हि देवी महाराजं कैकेयी राज्यकारणात् । II. 53. 7

"When Bharata comes back, this woman, Kaikeyi, will stop short of nothing. I am afraid she won't be content with the Yauvarajya, she may kill the old man and make her son king pucca."

अपि न च्यावयेत्प्राणान् दृष्ट्वा भरतमागतम् ॥
अनाथश्च हि वृद्धश्च मया चैव विनाकृत: ।
किं करिष्यति कामात्मा कैकेय्या वशमागत: ॥ II. 53. 7-8

He calls him कामात्मा. "Nor shall I be there to hold him up a little."

इदं व्यसनमालोक्य राज्ञश्च मतिविभ्रमम् ।
काम एवार्थधर्माभ्यां गरीयानिति मे मति: । II. 53. 9

Fancy Rama coming to this conclusion. It is burnt into him by the experiences of the previous day. Dasaratha knowing what Rama was, has banished him in order to please his wife. धर्म and अर्थ come before काम; that is not correct, he says. He says, Kama must come first according to Dasaratha.

को ह्यविद्वानपि पुमान् प्रमदाया: कृते त्यजेत् ।
छन्दानुवर्तिनं पुत्रं ततो मामिव लक्ष्मण ॥ II. 53. 10

"See what my father has done to me. I am the most obedient son in the world, the most loyal son. Still he has banished me for the sake of a woman. Is there another man like our father who will do it even though he be a fool? Our father is a wise man, a very learned man. Still he has done it. Look at the wiles of a woman. If you want hereafter a warning that you must not neglect dharma and artha and hold up Kama, if you want a warning for this truth, here is your father and mine, an example.

अर्थधर्मौ परित्यज्य य: काममनुवर्तते ।
एवमापद्यते क्षिप्रं राजा दशरथो यथा ॥
मन्ये दशरथान्ताय मम प्रव्राजनाय च ।
कैकेयी सौम्य संप्राप्ता राज्याय भरतस्य च ॥ II. 53. 13-14

"Kaikeyi was married into this family and became queen in order to bring about all these. She is going to kill Dasaratha; I am banished; Bharata will be king." Now that shows what I have before pointed out that even to Sri Rama who is capable of rising to the greatest heights, even in his mind there are moments when the lower view prevails. Not that he would always say this or always thinks so. He would speedily conquer all these thoughts but the thoughts were there and occasionally they found expression.

Now one more proof that Dasaratha was only bound by his vows and was not a slave to Kama as the world believed, Rama believed, Lakshmana believed and everybody believed, and Dasaratha feared it would be believed. As soon as all this happened, Dasaratha said to Kaikeyi, "Don't touch me. I have nothing to do with you."

> न पश्यति रजोऽप्यस्य यदा रामस्य भूमिपः ।
> तदार्तश्च विषण्णश्च पपात धरणीतले ॥ II. 42. 3

He was watching the chariot move off with Rama, Lakshmana and Sita. The dust came up. He saw only the dust for a time. Afterwards the dust subsided, when he ceased to see even the dust. He fell down. Then there were the two wives there, Kausalya and Kaikeyi.

> तस्य दक्षिणमन्वागात्कौसल्या बाहुमङ्गना ।
> वामं चास्यान्वगाद्बाहुं कैकेयी भरतप्रिया ॥ II. 42. 4

The right arm was lifted by Kausalya and the left arm by Kaikeyi.

> तां नयेन च संपन्नो धर्मेण विनयेन च ।
> उवाच राजा कैकेयीं समीक्ष्य व्यथितेन्द्रियः ॥
> कैकेयि मा ममाङ्गानि स्प्राक्षीस्त्वं दुष्टचारिणी ।
> न हि त्वां द्रष्टुमिच्छामि न भार्या न च बान्धवी ॥ II. 42. 5-6

"Don't touch my limbs." त्वं दुष्टचारिणी. "I renounce you. You are no wife at all, no relative of mine at all."

> ये च त्वामनुजीवन्ति नाहं तेषां न ते मम ।

"All bond cut off clean. Whoever is your follower or your retainer or your servant or your friend or your advocate, I am nothing to them."

> केवलार्थपरां हि त्वां त्यक्तधर्मां त्यजाम्यहम् ॥ II. 42. 7

"You have abandoned Dharma. I abandon you."

> अगृह्णां यच्च ते पाणिमग्निं पर्यणयं च यत् ।
> अनुजानामि तत्सर्वमस्मिंल्लोके परत्र च ॥ II. 42. 8

"You may say that you married me. True. The fact that I took your hand in conjugal bond and that I walked round the fire with you, I repudiate, I throw it out. ("अनुजानामि" there is made to mean the contrary of what it would ordinarily mean). It won't bind me any more. I don't want you as my wife either here or where I shall go to."

भरतश्चेत्प्रतीतः स्याद्राज्यं प्राप्येदमव्ययम्।

यन्मे स दद्यात्पित्रर्थं मां मा तद्दत्तमागमत्॥ II. 42. 9*

"If Bharata takes this kingdom which you give him, then when I am dead, if he offers me anything by way of oblation, let it not come to me. I do not want to take it."

Then when this took place, Dasaratha went at once to Kausalya's house. Kaikeyi never went there and he never sent for Kaikeyi, so that he died without meeting her again. All this you must remember is to fortify this fact that he rejected her *in toto* as soon as he found out how wicked she was and how treacherous to the worth of Rama. To say therefore that he did it to please her or under her charm is to state something which the Poet himself does not justify.

Then when the death had taken place and they were all widowed, the three hundred and fifty women came to cry. With them came Kaikeyi, Kausalya being an ordinary woman with the ordinary frailties of a woman, saw Kaikeyi and at once began to tell her:

कौसल्या बाष्पपूर्णाक्षी विविधं शोककर्शिता।

उपगृह्य शिरो राज्ञः कैकेयीं प्रत्यभाषत॥ II. 66. 2

She took the head of the king in her lap lest Kaikeyi should do it.

सकामा भव कैकेयि भुङ्क्ष्व राज्यमकण्टकम्।

त्यक्त्वा राजानमेकाग्रा नृशंसे दुष्टचारिणि॥ II. 66. 3

"You wanted to give the Yauvarajya to your son, the old man being still alive at the time the transaction was to have taken place. But now the old man too is gone. My son is gone. So the Rajya is now for you without the slightest obstacle or hindrance."

विहाय मां गतो रामो भर्ता च स्वर्गतो मम।

विपथे सार्थहीनेव नाहं जीवितुमुत्सहे॥ II. 66. 4

---

* Cf. Lect. XIII, p. 193.

"He too has gone to Heaven. I cannot live any longer."

भर्तारं तं परित्यज्य का स्त्री दैवतमात्मनः ।
इच्छेज्जीवितुमन्यत्र कैकेय्यास्त्यक्तधर्मणः ॥ II. 66. 5

"The only woman on earth who can lose her husband who is a god to her and still live and still wish to live is you."

न लुब्धो बुध्यते दोषान् किंपाकमिव भक्षयन् ।
कुब्जानिमित्तं कैकेय्या राघवाणां कुलं हतम् ॥ II. 66. 6

"The whole house of Raghu is laid in ruins because Kaikeyi listened to a cripple." Then the other queens said the same thing.

कैकेय्या दुष्टभावाया राघवेण वियोजिताः ।
कथं पतिघ्न्या वत्स्यामः समीपे विधवा वयम् ॥ II. 66. 19

"How are we widows going to live here near this woman who has murdered her husband?" In fact the whole city said that.

नराश्च नार्यश्च समेत्य सङ्घशो विगर्हमाणा भरतस्य मातरम् ।
तदा नगर्यां नरदेवसंक्षये बभूवुरार्ता न च शर्म लेभिरे ॥ II. 66. 29

They all condemned Kaikeyi.

Now comes the need for putting a question. When Rama left he told Kaikeyi, "Send for Bharata at once, send quickly messengers to bring him." She said also, "Yes. I will send messengers at once." Then lest they should have forgotten it, when Sumantra came back, Rama had told him, "Tell father and mother to bring Bharata at once and not to delay his coronation." Kaikeyi did not do so. Kaikeyi who was mistress of everything and could have done something, for some reason that is not apparent did not send for Bharata at once. He was sent for only by Vasishtha. Why did she not do so? What was in her mind? That question you might ask. I do not know how to give the answer but each one of you may answer it for himself or herself. It is a question which we cannot escape. It has always occurred to me.

Now comes, ladies and gentlemen, an important passage in the Ramayana of which too I am unable to explain the inner meaning. There is a remarkable interview between

Bharata as soon as he came, and his mother. Bharata as soon as he came back, went to see his mother. He expected to see his father there. He could not see the father but saw the mother. Then there took place a talk between them which I am not able to see was perfectly natural. Was it embarrassment or was it any other cause that made them talk in that fashion to each other? But many of you are probably wiser and can see farther. If you can explain it, I should be pleased. After the first greetings were over and he has prostrated himself before her and she had smelt his head, Kaikeyi begins the conversation by asking, "Is everybody well at Kekaya? Had you a good journey?" Bharata says, "Yes. This is the seventh day of my journey. I have come." He had seen everything wrong in Ayodhya. The city was in complete mourning. He had misgivings. He sees his mother. He does not put the question straight nor does she tell him the fact at once. She beat about the bush. He says, "Yes, this is the seventh day. I have come in advance a little. Where is father? Is he gone to Kausalya's palace? It is unusual for him to do that." Kaikeyi says, "Gone the way of all flesh." Bharata falls on the ground and faints. When he regains consciousness, he asks about Rama. He says, "Rama and others were lucky to have been here and to have performed the obsequies." He asks, "Where is Rama? I will go to see him. Also mother, tell me, didn't father leave me a last message, leave me, who was away—the other sons were with him, they were lucky? Has not father said one word to me?" This is what Kaikeyi says,

> रामेति राजा विलपन् हा सीते लक्ष्मणेति च ।
> स महात्मा परं लोकं गतो गतिमतां वरः ॥
> इमां तु पश्चिमां वाचं व्याजहार पिता तव ।
> कालधर्मपरिक्षिप्तः पाशैरिव महागजः ॥
> सिद्धार्थास्ते नरा राममागतं सीतया सह ।
> लक्ष्मणं च महाबाहुं द्रक्ष्यन्ति पुनरागतम् ॥ II. 72. 36-38

She says to him, "This is the last message he left. Nothing about you." That is the sense of it. He cried out, "Rama, Sita, Lakshmana." His last words were these, "Those persons who see Rama return with Lakshmana and Sita, they must be very lucky people, very lucky people." That is all. No

Bharata. That is the point. She wants to rub it in. Bharata got alarmed. He asks, "Where are they then?" Kaikeyi replies, "gone to Dandaka wearing the garb of hermits." Bharata asks her, "Why? Did Rama rob a Brahmin of his wealth? Did he harass an innocent citizen? Did he cast lustful eyes on another's wife? Why was he banished?" Bharata asks. "No. He did not harm any Brahmin or any citizen, and

न रामः परदारांश्च चक्षुर्भ्यामपि पश्यति। II. 72. 49

That was the testimony she gave him. "Rama won't look at another woman." Then she disclosed the truth to him, what exactly had happened.

तमपश्यन् प्रियं पुत्रं महीपालो महायशाः ॥ II. 72. 51

Having stated what had happened, this is how she finishes.

त्वया त्विदानीं धर्मज्ञ राजत्वमवलम्ब्यताम्।

त्वत्कृते हि मया सर्वमिदमेवंविधं कृतम्॥ II. 72. 52-53

"I have done all this, (I have gone through this wicked drama, I have killed him and banished these people), in order to make you king."

मा शोकं मा च सन्तापं धैर्यमाश्रय पुत्रक।

"My dear son, don't grieve and don't bemoan the lot of people. Be brave."

त्वदधीना हि नगरी राज्यं चैतदनायकम्॥* II. 72. 53-54

"This city is at your feet and this kingdom which knows no danger, no peril, is yours."

तत्पुत्र शीघ्रं विधिना विधिज्ञैर्वसिष्ठमुख्यैः सहितो द्विजेन्द्रैः।

संकाल्य राजानमदीनसत्त्वमात्मानमुर्व्यामभिषेचयस्व॥ II. 72. 54

"Crown yourself king," she says.

I do not know what to think of this dialogue. Is this how the thing would happen if you wrote a drama tomorrow and this news had to be exchanged? I do not know whether you would begin that way and finish that way. These are the last words that Kaikeyi speaks. Perhaps there is an expletive

---

* "अनामयम्" is the reading adopted by Govindaraja and in the Bombay Ed. and in the translation here.

also hereafter but you hear Kaikeyi no more. Apparently finding how Bharata took it, how severely he condemned her, how he repeatedly stated, "I want to kill you. I want to kill you. You have killed my whole race, I know that," she was stunned and paralysed. She did not know what to do. She never expected that it would all end in bitterness so soon. When Manthara tells her that Rama was going to be crowned although she put it badly, Kaikeyi took it well and gave her a *haram* as reward. Then her mind was not easily changed. Manthara had to exercise her devilish ingenuity on her. 'You will have to be a slave to Kausalya. Besides, your son will have to follow Rama and Rama may perhaps banish him. He may perhaps take his life." It is only when she heard that Kaikeyi changed. Also notice this please, the way she thinks of Kausalya, just two glimpses, flash-lights, as it were.

स त्वं धर्मं परित्यज्य रामं राज्येऽभिषेच्य च ।
सह कौसल्यया नित्यं रन्तुमिच्छसि दुर्मते ॥ II. 12. 45

She says this to Dasaratha. "You old man, you are not content with me. Having abandoned dharma and crowned Rama, you apparently go and want to live with Kausalya. You want to enjoy the days with her." (He abandoned Dharma, it seems, in crowning Rama.)

एकाहमपि पश्येयं यद्यहं राममातरम् ।
अञ्जलिं प्रतिगृह्णन्तीं श्रेयो ननु मृतिमम ॥ II. 12. 48

"If I see Kausalya one day receiving prostrations from other people, if anybody should make anjali to her and I see that with my eyes far better that I were dead." That is the light in which she regards Kausalya.

Now the question is, was Kaikeyi after this staggering blow and protest from her son, the same or did she change? There is evidence in the Poem, ladies and gentlemen, that Kaikeyi, hard-natured, hard-fibred, hard-hearted woman she was, did repent and did reform herself, and that is a fact which I would like to bring to your notice as a proof, if I may put it in that way, as a proof of the tremendous power of Rama's moral character. Having known him, having lived with him and having enjoyed his affection and esteem for a time it was impossible even for Kaikeyi to go on in her career of unrighteousness. How does this appear? There are two or three signs. The Poet does not say so but you are led to infer the fact and infer it pretty confidently. When Bharata went out with his whole army of ministers etc. to bring Rama back, the ladies also went with him. If Kaikeyi had so chosen and if she did not like Rama to be brought back, she might have stayed at home. Surely somebody would have taken care of her. But she did not do so. She joined the party. And not only did she join the party,

कैकेयी च सुमित्रा च कौसल्या च यशस्विनी ।
रामानयनसंहृष्टा ययुर्यानेन भास्वता ॥ II. 83. 6

These three are mentioned and therefore the plural is used and the plural therefore catches hold of everybody, will not omit Kaikeyi. She therefore was रामानयनसंहृष्टा, she was pleased that Rama should be brought back. She also rejoiced in that prospect. That is the meaning. The commentators draw our attention to the singular यानेन. Certainly they were queens and each could have a separate chariot for herself. But they all went in one in order that they might keep company and console each other. That is the inference. Kaikeyi joined them and spoke words of affection for Rama and wished him to come back. You may be sure that the reforming process had already begun.

Then this sloka, I have already read,* the one dealing with Sri Rama.

तं मातरो बाष्पगृहीतकण्ठ्यो दुःखेन नामन्त्रयितुं हि शेकुः ।
स त्वेव मातॄरभिवाद्य सर्वा रुदन् कुटीं स्वां प्रविवेश रामः ॥
II. 112. 31

It is said at the end of the talk between Bharata and Sri Rama in Chitrakuta when the whole thing was over and they were all about to depart and Rama had stood firm in his resolve to carry out his father's order, that they were unable to say good-bye to him—the three mothers, Kaikeyi included. Their throats were choked with grief at the parting. Therefore they could not say good-bye to him; nor was he able to say good-bye to them. He caught hold of their feet,

* Lect. XIII, at p. 208 above.

bowed to them and went in. The commentator asks us to note the plural सर्वा मातृः, including Kaikeyi. There is another significant word in the Yuddhakanda when the Pattabhisheka was about to take place formally. Bharata came to Sri Rama and told him, "Take back the kingdom that you gave." He formally made the request to him before all people.

> शिरस्यञ्जलिमाधाय कैकेय्यानन्दवर्धनः ।
> बभाषे भरतो ज्येष्ठं रामं सत्यपराक्रमम् ॥ VI. 131. 1

कैकेय्यानन्दवर्धनः is the epithet that the Poet had used. The Poet does not use that expression at all about Bharata usually. He has used it only once before as I shall show presently. These are the two places where Bharata is described as कैकेय्यानन्दवर्धन. Rama is often called कौसल्यानन्दवर्धन and Lakshmana सुमित्रानन्दवर्धन, but Bharata is seldom described as कैकेय्यानन्दवर्धन. In this place the Poet has used that phrase; it means therefore that what Bharata did at that moment pleased Kaikeyi, delighted her. He tells his elder brother: "When you went to the forest, you did so at the bidding of my mother, did you not? When fourteen years ago it took place, you did her the honour, you paid her the due consideration and giving the kingdom to me, you betook yourself to the forest.

> * पूजिता मामिका माता दत्तं राज्यमिदं मम ।
> तद्ददामि पुनस्तुभ्यं यथा त्वमददा मम ॥ VI. 131. 2

'Because I have told you that it is only taken on trust, I have kept it only for you. I have governed it for you wtih the help of your sandals, reporting everything to the sandals and taking the instructions for every act from the sandals,—the Poet has said that, I do not know what exactly it means—it is trust property and I return it to you the same way as you gave it to me."

Then I told you that I would mention where else this expression ककेय्यानन्दवर्धन is used of Bharata. Once before in the Ayodhyakanda Rama, being followed by the grieving subjects of Ayodhya as he went to the forest, turned back

* Cf. Lect. XXX, below.

to them and said, 'Why are you following, my dear people? Bharata is hereafter your king. Trust him. He will do the same thing that you expect me to do. He will be as good as my father was."

* स हि कल्याणचारित्रः कैकेय्यानन्दवर्धनः ।
करिष्यति यथावद्वः प्रियाणि च हितानि च ॥ II. 45. 7

He says that of his brother. Then he uses the word कैकेय्यानन्दवर्धनः meaning perhaps that Bharata has taken the kingdom which came to him owing to the court intrigue of the mother.

There is only one more remark that I have to make. I told you of Sumantra's description of the mother of Kaikeyi. This is how the Poet finishes the Sarga.

नैव सा क्षुभ्यते देवी न च स्म परिदूयते ।
न चास्या मुखवर्णस्य लक्ष्यते विक्रिया तदा ॥ II. 35. 35

Kaikeyi did not change colour at all. Then the old charioteer Sumantra says to Kaikeyi, "There is a great proverb that women take after their mothers and sons take after their fathers. You have done it. You have taken after your mother."—Very complimentary expression! I want to draw your attention to a passage in the Aranyakanda where a popular belief of that kind is alluded to, this time however by Lakshmana when he speaks to Rama about their brother Bharata. He says,

न पित्र्यमनुवर्तन्ते मातृकं द्विपदा इति ।
ख्यातो लोकप्रवादोऽयं भरतेनान्यथा कृतः ॥ III. 16. 34

He puts the popular saying in just the opposite way. It shows that perhaps in one part of the country, one proverb was prevailing and in another part of the country, the other proverb was prevalent. Or it may be that they were fond of saying the proverb in one way when one set of circumstances required it and in another way when another set of circumstances required it. This is what he says: "In the human race characteristics descend to men not from their fathers but from their mothers. That is the proverb." And Lakshmana says to Rama. "Our brother Bharata is a contradic-

* Cf. Lect. XIII, p. 200.

tion, he is an exception to the general rule. He does not take after the mother. He has taken after the father." That is, ladies and gentlemen, as far as Kaikeyi is concerned.

In the next lecture I will take up Kausalya and Sumitra, for they go together better than Sumitra would have done with Kaikeyi. I do hope to finish Kausalya, although she fills a larger space in the Ayodhyakanda. Only one word I must say now in preparation. You won't find in the character of Kausalya the same salient points that you find in Sumitra. This is a well-developed character that challenges your notice. But Kausalya was a good, ordinary woman, a very good woman in her way, but just a human-minded woman with all the faults of our mothers and our sisters, with all their good qualities. But her greatness consists in her having been the mother of Rama. She is distinct from Sumitra in this one way. Sumitra, although the younger wife and attached to her very much, is of a different character altogether. Her calibre is higher. She seems to have developed spiritually better, and, as I have told you once before, she is the only person in the whole entourage of Sri Rama who really understood his character and appreciated it at the highest. The others thought that he was making some bad mistakes, some blunders, that he was dwelling somewhere in an unpractical sphere, Sumitra is however the only one who understood him thoroughly and just remember this when I read her long speech and utterances for you next day. Remember that some of the finest sayings in the Poem, some of the noblest sentiments, are put in the mouth of Sumitra.

TWENTYNINTH LECTURE*

Sisters and Brothers,

We have seen already how when Rama went to announce the order of banishment to his mother, she burst out into an expression of great grief. It was then that she reviewed her past in the palace of Ayodhya, and complained that since the advent of Kaikeyi, she had never known peace of mind and had never been treated with the honour and consideration due to her primacy amongst the queens. In the continuation of her speech she appealed to her son to take her with him to the forest, for without him she could not live at all. Seeing how distressed she was, Lakshmana who stood by, caught her grief from her, but in his manly nature the grief turned into anger, and he burst out into an exhibition of indignation against his father and his step-mother, and threatened to fight it out. He says to his brother, "without your help I can manage these people. I shall teach the old man a lesson. You shall have what is your due, while these arms are still with me. I can restore to you what you seem for the moment to be losing." And he enlarged upon this theme to such an extent that Kausalya took fright in her heart. She certainly did not desire that there should be a fight for the throne and that her husband and her son should be on opposite sides. But as Lakshmana had the best of intentions in this exhibition of temper, she did not like to cancel his intention by force, but quietly said,

भ्रातुस्ते वदतः पुत्र लक्ष्मणस्य श्रुतं त्वया ।
यदत्रानन्तरं कार्यं कुरुष्व यदि रोचते ॥ II. 21. 21

"You have heard what your brother says. If you think you could do that, do so. But if you would rather not, do not." She left it to him, indicating that in her tender heart, violence was not to be approved of. Then, she said,

यदि त्वं यास्यसि वनं त्यक्त्वा मां शोकलालसाम् ।
अहं प्रायमिहासिष्ये न हि शक्ष्यामि जीवितुम् ॥ II. 21. 27

"If you won't take me with you, stay behind and protect me. I am not safe in this place any more. I do not mind your not

* 1-11-'44.

getting the throne, but remain behind even if you are a beggar. If you will neither take me nor remain behind, all I can do is to undertake a prayopavesa and finish myself. Life would be impossible. According to our Sastras, a mother is as good as the father, a trifle better. She has precedence in many respects. As you are bound to obey him, you are bound to obey me too. I do not permit you to go. I forbid your going." Pushed to a corner in this way Sri Rama did not exactly know what to do. So he merely says,

अनुमन्यस्व मां देवि गमिष्यन्तमितो वनम् ।
शापितासि मम प्राणैः कुरु स्वस्त्ययनानि मे ॥ II. 21. 46

"I charge you upon my life, go in and begin the benedictory rites. Give me leave, and all the ceremonies of godspeed, begin. I take this oath." Kausalya not moved at all, still forbids.

यथैव ते पुत्र पिता तथाहं गुरुः स्वधर्मेण सुहृत्तया च ।
न त्वानुजानामि न मां विहाय सुदुःखितामर्हसि गन्तुमेवम् ॥ II. 21. 52

"You dare not leave me while I am in this condition. I do not give you leave. I charge you, stay." Then, seeing this, Rama and Lakshmana fall into a great altercation. Rama says, "Look at this. Who can withstand fate? Fate orders that I be not crowned, but banished. Nobody dare disobey it. This must be done." Once more Lakshmana upbraids him. "Fate? Whose fate? There is no fate to a hero. You and I are not to be afraid of fate. It is only cowards and weak people that take refuge in fate. We make our own destiny. So I will fight." Finally Kausalya says,

कथं धेनुः स्वकं वत्सं गच्छन्तं नानुगच्छति ।
अहं त्वानुगमिष्यामि पुत्र यत्र गमिष्यसि ॥ II. 24. 9

"Even as when a calf moves, the cow moves too along with it, I will also follow you. Start if you want. Wherever you go, you will find me behind you." Then you remember how I told you that Sri Rama in the plenitude of his faith in *dharma*, seeing how under temptation and under difficulty everybody around him is tempted to fall away from duty, takes upon himself to preach it on a high level. So to his mother, without compunction, he tells her duty.

कैकेय्या वञ्चितो राजा मयि चारण्यमाश्रिते ।
भवत्या च परित्यक्तो न नूनं वर्तयिष्यति ॥
भर्तुः किल परित्यागो नृशंसः केवलं स्त्रियाः ।
स भवत्या न कर्तव्यो मनसापि विगर्हितः ॥
यावज्जीवति काकुत्स्थः पिता मे जगतीपतिः ।
शुश्रूषा क्रियतां तावत्स हि धर्मः सनातनः ॥ II. 24. 11-13

"Father has already been abandoned by Kaikeyi. She won't care for him any more. I am going away. And if you follow me, to whom will the old man look in his trouble? He won't live. Even in your thought you must not entertain this idea of abandoning your husband. It is the last thing a dutiful wife should think of. It is a cruel thing. That is your duty, laid down from ancient times. While he is alive, your place is beside him." So admonished by the son, Kausalya did not take offence, but she is brought to her senses somewhat. "Though the son teaches me, it is good teaching" she says to herself. It is easy to bring her to a sense of what is proper.

एवमुक्ता तु कौसल्या रामेण शुभदर्शना ।
तथेत्युवाच सुप्रीता राममक्लिष्टकारिणम् ॥ II. 24. 14

"Yes, you are right. I will do accordingly. I will stay behind." Then, instead of being content with that, Rama begins to rub it in a little. He proceeds still further to confirm her in that attitude, and as he does so, there is a recoil in her. She says,

आसां राम सपत्नीनां वस्तुं मध्ये न मे क्षमम् ।
नय मामपि काकुत्स्थ वनं वन्यां मृगीं यथा ॥
यदि ते गमने बुद्धिः कृता पितुरपेक्षया ॥ II. 24. 19-20

See how her mind swings this way and that in that distressed condition. It is perfectly natural. This time she says, "I cannot live amidst these co-wives of mine. They will point a finger of scorn at me." At this Rama resumes his long sermon. He is never tired of preaching on the high theme of *dharma*. That is his special province and his special care. He is come down from on high in order to establish *dharma* on earth. Whether it is mother or whether it is father, he does the same thing, tells them all what the right thing is.

व्रतोपवासनिरता या नारी परमोत्तमा ॥
भर्तारं नानुवर्तेत सा तु पापगतिर्भवेत् ।
भर्तुः शुश्रूषया नारी लभते स्वर्गमुत्तमम् ॥
अपि या निर्नमस्कारा निवृत्ता देवपूजनात् ।
शुश्रूषामेव कुर्वीत भर्तुः प्रियहिते रता ॥
एष धर्मः पुरा दृष्टो लोके वेदे श्रुतः स्मृतः ।
अग्निकार्येषु च सदा सुमनोभिश्च देवताः ॥
पूज्यास्ते मत्कृते देवि ब्राह्मणाश्चैव सुव्रताः ।
एवं कालं प्रतीक्षस्व ममागमनकाङ्क्षिणी ॥
नियता नियताहारा भर्तृशुश्रूषणे रता ।
प्राप्स्यसे परमं कामं मयि प्रत्यागते सति ॥ *II. 24. 25-30

"Mother, like you there are many women who are pious, who observe all the prescribed fasts, and go through all the prescribed ceremonies. You perform the rites of a woman properly. But that is not enough. Performance of austerities as prescribed in the texts or handed down by custom is not enough. You must follow your husband. It is only by serving the husband, by waiting upon him, and attending to his wants, that a woman will reach heaven. On the other hand, if a woman does not go to the temple, does not pray to the household gods in time and do the prescribed austerities in time, no matter. So long as she is a proper and dutiful wife to the husband, it does not matter. (Sri Rama has taken up our cause, gentlemen). Perform these duties as prescribed properly, stay beside your husband and take care of him. I shall come back all right at the end of fourteen years and then we shall all be re-united. This, your wish, will be fulfilled. I shall return all right." Thus, once more, Kausalya is admonished and learns her duty at her son's hands. She says,

गमने सुकृतां बुद्धिं न ते शक्नोमि पुत्रक ॥
विनिवर्तयितुं वीर नूनं कालो दुरत्ययः ।
गच्छ पुत्र त्वमेकाग्रो भद्रं तेऽस्तु सदा विभो ॥ II. 24. 32-33

* Cf. Lect. IX, p. 114.

"Fate cannot be set aside. It is decreed that you should go and leave me behind, and I must submit to it. I am not able to dissuade you from this resolution of yours. Yes, you go and prosper.

न शक्यसे वारयितुं गच्छेदानीं रघूत्तम ।
शीघ्रमेव निवर्तस्व वर्तस्व च सतां क्रमे ॥ II. 25. 2

"Follow the path of the wise. Do your duty on all occasions and return quickly." She knows it will be fourteen years, and yet she asks him to return quickly. I suppose she means, 'Let nothing keep you afterwards.'

यं पालयसि धर्मं त्वं धृत्या च नियमेन च ।
स वै राघवशार्दूल धर्मस्त्वामभिरक्षतु ॥ II. 25. 3

This is one of the well known verses in the Ramayana. "That *dharma* which you now practise so cheerfully and so scrupulously, let that *dharma* be your protection in its turn. The forest has many dangers, many snares, many pitfalls. When confronted with them, think of the *dharma* that you are following so religiously, and that *dharma* is bound to protect you. You are a good man, a virtuous man, all the good qualities of human nature find their abode in you. Therefore they are bound to shield you from all harm. You are a loyal son, and obey your father and mother. At the same time, you are bound by *satya*. What more?"

Then she began to perform a great *homa* and all the elaborate ceremonies. Kausalya was apparently versed in these ceremonies and is apparently able to pronounce the mantras herself. When the Brahmans had been amply fed, she began again. This time she pronounced a benediction which occurs in several *slokas*. Wherever there is a situation like this in our old fable or story, wherever a mother, anxious for the welfare of her sons, calls upon the gods to protect them, that is parallel in this case. "May you be protected in similar fashion", she says. The repetition of यन्मङ्गल .... तत्ते भवतु मङ्गलम् (II. 25. 32-36) is made here four times, one of Valmiki's rhetorical tricks. "May you have the same auspicious circumstance that attended Indra when he conquered Vritra. When Vinata bade her son Garuda go to heaven and bring amrita for her, when he undertook that very perilous expedition, may the same auspicious circumstance that attended him, attend you. When during the fight between the devas and asuras for the amrita, Aditi prayed to the gods that her son should come out victorious, so the gods did decree; let their blessings rest on you in similar fashion. When Vamana, Vishnu having taken that form in order to conquer Bali, measured the three worlds as three steps and took them all in, what auspicious circumstance attended him, let it wait upon you. May all these look after you and give you their benedictions." The poet clearly says that she herself chanted the mantras. Then having dwelt on these benedictions, she herself felt elated a little. Though all things would be proper, she did not in her own heart feel happy, but she pretended as though she was. You must think of the solemnity of this farewell. She is bidding her son go to the forest for fourteen years, that son being what he was. Naturally therefore she drew him down and said, "If I am lucky, I hope to live all these fourteen years and see you return, take the kingdom and tread the path of the great ancestors you have had. May I see that all honours return, you having fulfilled the great vow you have undertaken, obeying the command of your father, stern as it was. Yes, go, and when you have returned, you will be the joy of my heart. May all things in the universe shield you from harm. I have prayed to the gods and worshipped them and offered them all kinds of things. May they be pleased to accept the gifts and grant my prayer that you go to the forest, live there in comfort and then return." It is difficult to think of such a mother without emotion. The poet says here, she went round him clockwise. It is extraordinary. But it appears either in the old time or generally speaking, it is not proper to do it to a junior when you wish him well.

Having taken leave of her, Rama now goes to a more trying scene. We next meet Sri Rama taking leave of the father and then, very naturally and properly, he tells the father to take care of his mother. As I told you, he is never tired of teaching everybody his duty. So he tells his father,

इय धार्मिक कौसल्या मम माता यशस्विनी।
वृद्धा चाक्षुद्रशीला च न च त्वां देव गर्हते॥
मया विहीनां वरद प्रपन्नां शोकसागरम्।
अदृष्टपूर्वव्यसना भूयः संमन्तुमर्हसि॥

पुत्रशोकं यथा नर्च्छेत्त्वया पूज्येन पूजिता ।
मां हि सञ्चिन्तयन्तीयं त्वयि जीवेत्तपस्विनी ॥
इमां महेन्द्रोपम जातगर्धिनीं तथा विधातुं जननीं ममार्हसि ।
यथा वनस्थे मयि शोककर्शिता न जीवितं न्यस्य यमक्षयं व्रजेत् ॥

II. 38. 15-18

"Reduced to this miserable condition, she does not blame you. Therefore take care of her in my absence more than ever before. Take care of her so that she does not pass away. Do not let her pass away in grief. I leave her in your charge."

Then when Sita goes to take leave of Kausalya, Kausalya bids her come and says to her some extraordinary things to which I must ask your earnest attention. Kausalya says to Sita, "Now you go to the forest with your husband. You are an extraordinary woman. There is hardly another woman who would follow her husband like this to share his misery and his privation."

असत्यः सर्वलोकेऽस्मिन् सततं सत्कृताः प्रियैः ॥
भर्तारं नानुमन्यन्ते विनिपातगतं स्त्रियः ।
एष स्वभावो नारीणामनुभूय पुरा सुखम् ॥
अल्पामप्यापदं प्राप्य दुष्यन्ति प्रजहत्यपि ।
असत्यशीला विकृता दुर्गा अहृदयाः सदा ॥
असत्यः पापसंकल्पाः क्षणमात्रविरागिणः ।
न कुलं न कृतं विद्या न दत्तं नापि संग्रहः ॥
स्त्रीणां गृह्णाति हृदयमनित्यहृदया हि ताः ।
साध्वीनां तु स्थितानां हि शीले सत्ये श्रुते स्थिते ॥
स्त्रीणां पवित्रं परमं पतिरेको विशिष्यते ।
स त्वया नावमन्तव्यः पुत्रः प्रव्राजितो वनम् ॥
तव देववदस्त्वेष निर्धनः सधनोऽपि वा । II. 39. 20-26

Women get most censure from their own sex. We are not such harsh judges of women as themselves. "Amongst us, women," says Kausalya, "it is very common to find a woman following her husband when he is all right. But the moment he falls or becomes unfortunate or loses wealth, however much they might have been in better times looked after, however well they might have been treated, so soon as something wrong happens, they will begin to abuse him and even abandon him. In one moment they will abandon all their love." Well, I do not endorse all this severe condemnation. But in the old time, our literature is full of such things. Even western literature is not free from this. Woman is always trampled upon and abused and condemned as wholly untrustworthy. Their hearts are never really conquered. "My son is a good man. You must worship him as a god. He is everything to you. What if he loses wealth?" Sita did not need this advice. But still she thanks her for reminding her. This tirade against women occurs frequently. One other thing I must point out to you in this connection. When they go to the forest and are in the *asrama* of Agastya, that great fountain of wisdom, speaks in this wise of woman.

एषा हि प्रकृतिः स्त्रीणामासृष्टे रघुनन्दन ।
समस्थमनुरज्यन्ति विषमस्थं त्यजन्ति च ॥ III. 13. 5

"Ever since creation this is women's nature. They will affectionately follow their husbands who are well established, who are prosperous. The moment they become unfortunate, they will abandon them." I used to think honestly that you, women of to-day, are infinitely superior to the women of the ancient time. You stand by us, however much we fall, though, if we push this argument very far, many things may transpire. But the fact is that woman of the old time had her economic independence. She could go about and look after herself much better than she is able to do now. Confined as she is, bound down by stern rules of etiquette which cannot be transgressed except under the heaviest penalty and under the severest imputation, our modern woman is naturally prevented from using her freedom as woman might have done in the old time.

शतह्रदानां लोलत्वं शस्त्राणां तीक्ष्णतां तथा ।
गरुडानिलयोः शैघ्र्यमनुगच्छन्ति योषितः ॥ III. 13. 6

Women imitate these things. "Like lightning they only last a minute. The good temper and the good character of women are never to be trusted. As instruments are sharp, so is a woman. They can run away as fast as Garuda or Vayu. They won't stick to any particular rule." These uncharitable imputations against women's character occur frequently. I have chosen these two because on the one hand, Kausalya speaks in that strain and on the other Agastya does the same.

Now we come to a more pleasant episode. When Lakshmana takes leave of his mother Sumitra, what does she say?

सृष्टस्त्वं वनवासाय स्वनुरक्तः सुहृज्जने ।
रामे प्रमादं मा कार्षीः पुत्र भ्रातरि गच्छति ॥
व्यसनी वा समृद्धो वा गतिरेष तवानघ ।
एष लोके सतां धर्मो यज्ज्येष्ठवशगो भवेत् ॥
इदं हि वृत्तमुचितं कुलस्यास्य सनातनम् ।
दानं दीक्षा च यज्ञेषु तनुत्यागो मृधेषु च ॥ II. 40. 5-7

To Sumitra Rama's real nature is well-known. So she says to her son, "I knew when you were born you were going to spend a lot of time in the wood. Never for a moment withdraw your attention from Sri Rama. Pay him all the respect and all the reverence due. He is your refuge. *Dana, Diksha in Yajna,* and *fight to death in battle,* these three are the greatest requirements of a good man belonging to our familiy." Lakshmana needed no spurring from her. Now follows the famous verse.

लक्ष्मणं त्वेममुक्त्वा सा संसिद्धं प्रियराघवम् ।
सुमित्रा गच्छ गच्छेति पुनःपुनरुवाच तम् ॥
रामं दशरथं विद्धि मां विद्धि जनकात्मजाम् ।
अयोध्यामटवीं विद्धि गच्छ तात यथासुखम् ॥ II. 40. 8-9

"Lakshmana, your life is going to have a great change. But really there is no change. You are not leaving your father or mother behind, nor your well-beloved city. Rama is your father, Sita is your mother and the forest is Ayodhya to you. Go and prosper."

A few *sargas* later we find Kausalya, unable to bear her grief, sets up a wail, a long miserable wail. The old king, disconsolate at the departure of the three, reclines on a sofa. Kausalya, equally disconsolate, if not more, sat beside him and gave vent to her grief. "Kaikeyi has gratified her heart's wish by the abandonment of Rama. She is a she-cobra. Having cast off her slough, she has just discharged her venom at Rama. But as she still winds her crooked course through the house, I fear she may be looking for more victims. Why was not Rama condemned to beggary, but allowed to remain with us here? I would have reconciled myself even if he had been given away as a slave. Your enormity in ordering the fall of

Rama can be compared only to the sacrilege of a Brahmana who maintains the sacred fire in his home, but gives the oblations meant for gods at New Moon and Full Moon to Rakshasas. What a fate for my son, endowed with powerful arms, bearing his *kodanda,* of elephant-like gait, and of heroic mould, to wander with wife and brother in the wilderness! At Kaikeyi's bidding you have consigned them, used from birth to comfort and plenty and pomp, at the moment when they were about to reach the culmination of joy, to the hardships of forest life. Henceforth the poor exiles must subsist on roots and fruits, the hard fare of ascetics long past their prime. Fourteen years! How I wish they could pass away at once and this very instant I could end my sorrow and behold my dear son returning home with Sita and Lakshmana? When is our far-famed city of Ayodhya to hear the glad tidings of their arrival and become gay again with festive flags and buntings? When is she to swell again with pomp and pride at the sight of the brave brothers, as the sea swells at full moon? When is my son to re-enter the capital in his great chariot along with Sita, like a strong bull with his cow alongside? When are the people in their thousands to welcome the princes in the thoroughfares, scattering handfuls of auspicious fried rice? When shall I see them again coming into the city with jewels hanging from their ears, with bows and swords, like two hills with peaks? When again shall Brahmanas go round the city, the lads distributing fruits, the lasses distributing flowers? When shall my son, the very soul of *dharma,* approach me, ripe in wisdom though only twenty-five, the perpetual age of the gods? I shall rejoice then as the earth rejoices when timely rain comes down on it. To judge from my misery at this time, I must have in a former birth cut down from the mouths of sucking babes the flowing breasts of their mothers. I have been parted from my son by the cruel decree of Kaikeyi, as a cow might be sundered from her tender calf by the ferocious paw of a lion. I cannot live after losing an only son, radiant with all the virtues and the lore of the sastras. Without my darling son and without his brother, life has no use for me. This grief for my son consumes me like a fire." II. 43.

As she was thus pouring out her heart's anguish, Sumitra comforted her with sentiments of high wisdom and instruction in duty. Now we see the great difference between Kausalya and Sumitra. Sumitra is more self-possessed, because she understands things in their true light. Though she loses a son just like Kausalya, she is not so grief-striken because she knows the high mission of Rama and Sita. She realises that they go to the forest at the bidding of *dharma* which cannot be set aside.

Sumitra:— "Your grief, dear sister, is misplaced. Do not pity your son and pray stop weeping. You are the luckiest of all mothers. In your son all merits and virtues abide together. It is for your lasting good he has gone to the forest. He is saving the character of his father by carrying out his promise. No tears, let me tell you, no tears for one who stands rooted in virtue, who treads the path trodden before him by holy men, and who by so doing makes sure of his blessedness through eternity. My son Lakshmana is exceedingly fortunate. Of blameless conduct and ever ready to help the afflicted in all grades of life, he now walks in the supreme path of righteousness. Sita too is not acting hastily, she has taken full account of the trials of the venture; in the pure spirit of duty she accompanies the husband who goes in pursuit of his duty. With the banner of fame waving high over his head, what is there, good or meritorious in this world and in the next, which is beyond Rama's reach? He is *dharma* incarnate. His stainless purity and unequalled greatness are known all over the universe. The sun will not dare to scorch his body. The wind, blowing through the forest, and going near Rama, will be at all times agreeable and of mild temperature. When Rama sleeps free from care at night, the moon will touch him with fatherly tenderness and refresh him with cool and soft rays. Remember also, dear sister, when Rama killed the demon Sambara's son in Dandaka, Brahma himself came down and taught him the use of many *astras*. For him therefore the forest can have no terrors, and he will live in it as in this home of ours. Enemies die the moment they come within the range of his arrows. No doubt the whole of this earth will come under his control. His glory being what it is, his valour being what it is, and his beneficent power being what it is, he will of a surety finish his term in the forest and return in triumph to his kingdom. Of the sun he is the sun, of Agni he is the Agni, of the Supreme he is the Supreme, of Lakshmi he is the Lakshmi, of fame, he is the fame, of patience, he is the patience, of deities he is the deity, of all *bhutas* he is the *bhuta*. To such an One, what can do harm in town or forest? Soon he shall be crowned along with Sita, Earth and Lakshmi. What also can be expected, seeing that, as he departed from Ayodhya, every person was overcome with grief and actually shed tears? What can be unattainable to one, though clad in hide and bark, who was accompanied by Sita and therefore by Lakshmi herself? What can be unattainable to one who is preceded and protected by Lakshmana, fully armed with sword, bow and arrows? Grieve not thus, sister mine, doubt not, weep not. Trust my word, I speak what shall come to pass. Your son shall come back at the end of fourteen years. You shall see him at your feet, touching them with reverent head. You shall see his face illumined with the splendour of the full moon. You shall see him, I promise you, anointed and crowned king of the Kosalas; and then these eyes of yours, which now weep tears of sadness, shall drop tears of sheer joy. Noble lady, good fortune shall wait on you. Rama shall come to no harm; no sorrow, no distress shall touch him. All these people around, who watch you with anxiety, must be heartened by your example and made to look on the future with hope. With Rama for your son, you have no need to grieve or despair. Believe me, there is no one on earth more righteous than he. I shall behold you soon weeping for very joy and then liken you to a wintry cloud dropping copious rain, and your son with Lakshmana and friends shall be like a hill drenched all over with it." (II. 44. 1-29.)

Sumitra is at the very peak of her wisdom. Of all people around Rama, she is almost the one, if we except Lakshmana, to really understand Rama's nature, the purpose for which he went to the forest, and the propriety and righteousness of his action.

Now follows a most distressing scene. Kausalya, Sumitra and some faithful people are in Kausalya's room, Dasaratha reclining. Sumantra enters, having taken leave of Rama and Sita and Lakshmana. He comes and says how they were, what prospects they had, and the farewell messages that Rama and Lakshmana gave him. Then, with all her grief renewed and coming up afresh, Kausalya unable to control herself, upbraids the poor old man.

स तूष्णीमेव तच्छ्रुत्वा राजा विभ्रान्तचेतनः ।

मूर्च्छितो न्यपतद्भूमौ रामशोकाभिपीडितः ॥ II. 57. 26

Having heard what Sumantra said, poor Dasaratha could not control himself. He fell down and lost consciousness. When the king fell on the ground unconscious, all the ladies of the harem put out their arms and cried aloud. Having lifted him and placed him once more on the couch, this is what Kausalya says,

इमं तस्य महाभाग दूतं दुष्करकारिणः ।
वनवासादनुप्राप्तं कस्मान्न प्रतिभाषसे ॥
अद्येममनयं कृत्वा व्यपत्रपसि राघव ।
उत्तिष्ठ सुकृतं तेऽस्तु शोके न स्यात्सहायता ॥
देव यस्या भयाद्रामं नानुपृच्छसि सारथिम् ।
नेह तिष्ठति कैकेयी विस्रब्धं प्रतिभाष्यताम् ॥ II. 57. 29-31

What a question to ask! What could Dasaratha reply, poor man? "Get up", she says, "Sorrow is not going to help you. You have done the thing. (That is rubbing salt into the wound). That woman, of whom you are afraid, thinking of whom you do not want even to talk to Sumantra, is not here. So speak up. Why do you not make enquiries of Rama?" Having spoken thus, Kausalya herself, unable to bear her sorrow, rolled on the ground. What a scene of woe!

ततस्तमन्तःपुरनादमुत्थितं समीक्ष्य वृद्धास्तरुणाश्च मानवाः ।
स्त्रियश्च सर्वा रुरुदुः समन्ततः पुरं तदासीत्पुनरेव सङ्कुलम् ॥ II. 57. 34

"All the others also wept. Not the palace only, but the whole town, hearing of this news, set up a wail, and there was one unrelieved lamentation all over the place."

At another time, with Dasaratha seated by her, Kausalya began her usual story, reproaching him, "Everywhere in the three worlds they extol you with enthusiasm as a man of compassion, generosity in giving and mellifluous speech. How could you exile your sons and that tender daughter-in-law, all brought up in luxury? Surely she cannot bear the extremes of heat and cold; accustomed to rich delicious fare, how will she relish the coarse grain of the jungle? With the music of melodious instruments ringing in her ears, how will she endure the harsh and piercing cries of beasts of prey? My Rama, who gives delight to the worlds like the mighty flag of Indra,—where will he sleep now? His powerful club-like arm, I guess, is his pillow. When shall I see once more his face like the lotus, with his hair fragrant like the lotus, and with eyes charming like a pair of lotuses? My heart is hard like *vajra*, seeing it does not fall in pieces even after Rama's departure. Oh, how heartless you were when you drove the sweet and gentle children into the horrid forest! Should Rama survive the period of exile and come back in the fifteenth year, I doubt that Bharata will make ready rendition of the kingdom and its treasure. Do we not daily observe how in performing the *sraddhas* of *pitris* people assign the positions of profit to their own kinsmen and relegate worthy scholars to the subsequent general feeding? Men of high spirit scorn to join the crowd, as bulls resent the sawing of their horns. If the younger brother has already enjoyed the honours of the kingship, the elder brother will spurn them. No tiger will taste the remainder of another animal. The oblation at a sacrifice, the ghee, the cake, the sacred grass, the posts of *khadira*—these, once used, are never considered fit for a later occasion. Like wine denuded of its essence, like a sacrifice robbed of its *soma*, a kingdom is good for nothing which has been in the hands of a junior. Ignominy of this kind Rama will not brook, any more than a tiger will allow his tail to be trampled upon. If the world were banded together, Rama could overthrow it in battle. If he did not seize the kingdom by force, it was only because he would not stoop to the practice of *adharma*. Could he not otherwise consign to the flames all the land and water in creation by means of his gold-adorned arrows? A son of that supreme calibre who can be compared to a bull, tiger or lion has been reduced to naught by his own father, as a fish eats up its own spawn. In banishing a righteous son without adequate reason, you have violated the law laid down in the ancient code and observed by our forefathers through the ages. To a woman the first protector is the husband, the second is the son, the third is the agnatic kinsman; there is no fourth. You, my husband, are as good as lost to me, my son has been driven out. I do not wish to follow him into the woods. The entire population of the country have been ruined by you as well as the kingdom; we the women of the palace are ruined; the ministers and royal staff are ruined; my son and I are ruined; the townsmen are ruined. Only your wife Kaikeyi and her son are happy." II. 61. 1-29.

Do you not sympathise with the poor woman, distracted with grief, saying all these cruel things to her own husband?

It often takes place when a most premature death has happened in the house, and people lamented standing round, bewailing, one person abusing another. Such is human nature.

The old king was stung to the quick by these reproaches. Grief and remorse overpower him. His mind reviewed the past. A former transgression came into his memory. He fell into a trance of mental agony. Trembling all over with exhaustion of body and mind, he brought his palms together in submission, and said to Kausalya: "रचितोऽयं मयाञ्जलिः". "Hear me, I pray you. You have pity on all persons, even on enemies. I implore it in humble spirit. Saint or sinner, a husband is every thing to his wife, her very god. You are devoted to *dharma*, you dare not go against it, you know good and evil, noble and mean. Don't you see plainly my condition? I am full of contrition and self-reproach. Should you rub salt into my wound? I know you are in acute distress yourself; but may I not ask to be spared?" So pleads the husband. (II. 62. 1-9)

Then comes one of the most melancholy things I have read. When Dasaratha said this with his *anjali*, Kausalya, being a good woman, at once comes back to her senses. What put her out of balance is the thought of her son. The moment duty is taught to her or mentioned, she comes round. She realised how thoughtless she had been, and caught his joined palms and placed them on her head with reverence. She then spoke,

प्रसीद शिरसा याचे भूमौ निपतितास्मि ते ।
याचितास्मि हता देव हन्तव्याहं न हि त्वया ॥
नैषा हि सा स्त्री भवति श्लाघनीयेन धीमता ।
उभयोर्लोकयोर्वीर पत्या या संप्रसाद्यते ॥
जानामि धर्मं धर्मज्ञ त्वां जाने सत्यवादिनम् ।
पुत्रशोकार्तया तत्तु मया किमपि भाषितम् ॥
शोको नाशयते धैर्यं शोको नाशयते श्रुतम् ।
शोको नाशयते सर्वं नास्ति शोकसमो रिपुः ॥
शक्यमापतितः सोढुं प्रहारो रिपुहस्ततः ।
सोढुमापतितः शोकः सुसूक्ष्मोऽपि न शक्यते ॥

वनवासाय रामस्य पञ्चरात्रोऽद्य गण्यते ।
यः शोकहतहर्षाया: पञ्चवर्षोपमो मम ॥
तं हि चिन्तयमानाया: शोकोऽयं हृदि वर्धते ।
नदीनामिव वेगेन समुद्रसलिलं महत् ॥ II. 62. 12-18

"You cannot forgive me. I have done the wickedest thing. That you should have been driven to beg a thing of me, what can be worse than that? A woman who has to be pacified by the joined palms of her husband has no good thing to look for. I know what my duty is, and do I not know that you have only been keeping your promise? But grief for the son overpowers me. I am unable to remember my duty whenever I remember my son. Ah, this *soka,* by which all self-control is lost. All the good things you have heard are gone. If an enemy comes and delivers a blow in your cheek, you could bear it. Five nights have gone since our son left us. To me these five nights have been like five years." When she said that, everybody came to his own and there was some little consolation. Then Dasaratha narrates the misdeed, when, trusting his ear, he sent an arrow and killed an innocent boy, in two *sargas,* a most pathetic description. Then Kausalya and Sumitra fall asleep, and while they are asleep, all unknown to them, Dasaratha passed away. Then you know how Bharata is sent for. We have already seen the unfortunate scene between him and his mother. While he was there, Kausalya hears that Bharata had come, and her blood is up again. She drags Sumitra with her and as she is just starting to go and meet him, Bharata himself enters. Kausalya could not bear her grief and bursts out.

इदं ते राज्यकामस्य राज्यं प्राप्तमकण्टकम् ।
संप्राप्तं बत कैकेय्या शीघ्रं क्रूरेण कर्मणा ॥
प्रस्थाप्य चीरवसनं पुत्रं मे वनवासिनम् ।
कैकेयी कं गुणं तत्र पश्यति क्रूरदर्शिनी ॥
क्षिप्रं मामपि कैकेयी प्रस्थापयितुमर्हति ।
हिरण्यनाभो यत्रास्ते सुतो मे सुमहायशाः ॥
अथवा स्वयमेवाहं सुमित्रानुचरा सुखम् ।
अग्निहोत्रं पुरस्कृत्य प्रस्थास्ये यत्र राघवः ॥

कामं वा स्वयमेवाद्य तत्र मां नेतुमर्हसि।
यत्रासौ पुरुषव्याघ्रः पुत्रो मे तप्यते तपः ॥
इदं हि तव विस्तीर्णं धनधान्यसमाचितम्।
हस्त्यश्वरथसंपूर्णं राज्यं निर्यातितं तया ॥
इत्यादिबहुभिर्वाक्यैः क्रूरैः संभर्त्सितोऽनघः।
विव्यथे भरतस्तीव्रं व्रणे तुद्येव सूचिना ॥ II. 75. 11-17

"You wanted the kingdom. You were after it and you have got it, and nobody to molest you. But why should your mother command my son to wear the bark, and why should she send him to the forest? Where my son is, let her banish me too. I will run away to where he is." Then she makes a kind of threat. "I will take Sumitra with me and take the *agnihotra* with me." Her meaning is that she will prevent him from performing the last rites to his father. That fire must be there for that performance. "As I am the eldest queen, I have got control over it. So, if you please, you yourself take me there." Hearing this bitter taunt, poor Bharata who was absolutely innocent at heart could not bear it. Then a famous passage occurs in the Ramayana. Bharata swears that he is perfectly innocent and that he does not favour the step that his mother took and that if Rama and Lakshmana went to the forest, they went there without his consent and that he would be glad if they returned. There are thirty-six *slokas*, in which he swears this fact and calls upon himself all the wicked deeds and their consequences you can think of, if he is really guilty. "If with my consent my brother has gone, may this misfortune befall me. May I incur this sin." So he goes on through thirty-six *slokas*. Poor Kausalya is once more remorse-stricken.

मम दुःखमिदं पुत्र भूयः समुपजायते।
शपथैः शपमानो हि प्राणानुपरुणत्सि मे ॥ II. 75. 61

That is the last important scene we have got to remember. Thereafter Kausalya is the only one whom we meet speaking. The other queens do not speak. Kausalya, however, takes the privilege as the eldest queen.

When they all come to persuade Rama to go back, the queens come too. They enter the hermitage of Rama last of all. Vasishtha leads them. As they enter, they see the Mandakini river. The banks of the north Indian rivers are very high, and people have to go a long path to reach the water. Lakshmana has gone to fetch water frequently and made a path for himself. Kausalya and the other queens come there and note it, and Kausalya's heart is struck. She says to Sumitra,

> इदं तेषामनाथानां क्लिष्टमक्लिष्टकर्मणाम् ।
> वने प्राक्केवलं तीर्थं ये ते निर्विषयीकृताः ॥
> इतः सुमित्रे पुत्रस्ते सदा जलमतन्द्रितः ।
> स्वयं हरति सौमित्रिर्मम पुत्रस्य कारणात् ॥
> जघन्यमपि ते पुत्रः कृतवान्न तु गर्हितः ।
> भ्रातुर्यदर्थसहितं सर्वं तद्विहितं गुणैः ॥ II. 103. 4-6

"Your son and my son were both born to luxury. They had to do nothing for themselves. Now my son sits there and your son has to go down all this distance with a pot, take water and bring it up again. Do you think Lakshmana degrades himself by these occupations? No, do not think so." Now Kausalya says a beautiful thing. "We have all come to pursuade Rama to go back. Today we will start back." See how sanguine they are. They are perfectly hopeful that after this great demonstration on Bharata's part, Rama would say he would go back. So Kausalya says, "This is the last day on which your son will have to perform this." Then,

> अद्यायमपि ते पुत्रः क्लेशानामतथोचितः ।
> नीचानर्थसमाचारं सज्जं कर्म प्रमुञ्चतु ॥ II. 103. 7

"Let him abandon this menial duty." Why does she say '*api*'? The commentator uses his ingenuity very well. I think he is right. The other son Satrughna has not done anything of this kind. Like him, Lakshmana too will not have to do it hereafter. I think that can be the only meaning. Then they move forward a little and they find that even before they came, Rama and Lakshmana and Sita had already bathed on hearing their father's demise and the *pinda* had been placed. Rama does not use rice, but *ingudi*. Kausalya and the party see this, and she is once more grief-stricken.

> चतुरन्तां महीं भुक्त्वा महेन्द्रसदृशो भुवि ।
> कथमिङ्गुदिपिण्याकं स भुङ्क्ते वसुधाधिपः ॥
> अतो दुःखतरं लोके न किंचित्प्रतिभाति मे ।
> यत्र रामः पितुर्दद्यादिङ्गुदीक्षोदमृद्धिमान् ॥

रामेणेङ्गुदिपिण्याकं पितुर्दत्तं समीक्ष्य मे ।
कथं दुःखेन हृदयं न स्फोटति सहस्रधा ॥
श्रुतिस्तु खल्वियं सत्या लौकिकी प्रतिभाति मे ।
यदन्नः पुरुषो भवति तदन्नास्तस्य देवताः ॥ II. 103. 12-15

"My husband ruled over the three worlds. He was like Mahendra himself. Such a man has to get only *ingudi*. Being what he is, Rama has offered *ingudi* to his father. He is perfectly right. The gods can except from a man only what he has. They cannot expect the fare to which they are entitled by their high station."

One last scene. Kausalya then comes into the picture fully. She sees her son and Lakshmana and Sita besides. Seeing Sita, she says,

विदेहराजस्य सुता स्नुषा दशरथस्य च ।
रामपत्नी कथं दुःखं संप्राप्ता निर्जने वने ॥
पद्ममातपसंतप्तं परिक्लिष्टमिवोत्पलम् ।
काञ्चनं रजसा ध्वस्तं क्लिष्टं चन्द्रमिवाम्बुदैः ॥
मुखं ते प्रेक्ष्य मां शोको दहत्यग्निरिवाश्रयम् ।
भृशं मनसि वैदेहि व्यसनारणिसंभवः ॥ II. 103. 24-26

"You were born in Janaka's family, married into the Ikshvaku family, and you are the wife of Sri Rama himself. Your face is like a lotus that has been burnt by the sun, like a tender lily which has been made to wither, like gold that has been soiled by contact with dust, like the moon shrouded by clouds. Looking at your face, even as a fire would burn anything it touches, so does this sorrow consume me."

After this we take leave of the queens altogether, even of Kausalya. They appear and play a silent part hereafter.

I have gone through the round of the great characters in the Ramayana. Although I have not pursued the orthodox line, having no claim to play that part, I should like to consult the feelings of most of you and my own and end with a short account of the *abhisheka*. That is the customary way in which anybody who deals with the Ramayana winds up. I shall do so also next time.

THIRTIETH LECTURE*

Sisters and Brothers,

In conformity with custom, this last talk will be about the great coronation ceremony of Rama and Sita. Four times in the poem is a coronation ceremony mentioned. The first time is in the Ayodhyakanda, when the ceremony does not take place. The next time we hear of Sugriva being crowned king of Kishkindha. The next important ceremony is the coronation of Vibhishana. This really takes place in two stages as it were, once before the war commenced, on the mainland of India when Sri Rama directs that he should be symbolically crowned, and then the real coronation takes place of course when the throne of Lanka becomes vacant. Then comes the great ceremony in Ayodhya, to which we shall pay particular attention today.

Just a few words about the other occasions, for it is of some significance to contrast the preparations made, the materials gathered, and the actual performance of the bathing or the *abhisheka*. I shall read just one verse in which Vasishtha innocently on the fated morning comes near the palace and announces that all things are ready.

इमे गङ्गोदकघटाः सागरेभ्यश्च काञ्चनाः ॥ II. 14. 34

"The water has been brought from Ganga in gold vessels and from the various seas and oceans too." Then, amongst those in attendance are mentioned eight handsome maidens, also an elephant usually used by the king himself. Then the poet describes more fully the things that have been assembled. They are worth mentioning—काञ्चना जलकुम्भाश्च (II. 15. 4-8). Such was the grand preparation made. We have got to see here one important point, that the water has been brought from all kinds of places. Wherever water was held sacred at all, whether in rivers or in an obscure well, or in a pond, from everywhere water has been brought. I should like you to note here that Dasaratha thought of Rama's coronation and immediately fixed the date, the very next day.

* 8-11-'44.

How the water had been brought from all these places is a question to ask. It must mean that the old king who had a little cunning in him, I think, had had the water already brought. Or we may make the supposition, which I think is a little extravagant, that in all palaces these waters used to be ready. I think this supposition is somewhat untenable. I should like to think that Dasaratha really had thought of this ceremony beforehand and had the water brought from all these sacred spots.

Then we shall go to Kishkindha.

आजग्मुस्तत्र मुदिता वराः कन्यास्तु षोडश ॥ IV. 26. 28

Note this here. When Sugriva was to be crowned, sixteen handsome maidens had been brought. Apparently therefore for the *yauvarajya* eight were quite enough. But as Sugriva's was to be a really good coronation for kingship itself, sixteen maidens had to be brought. Here there was no difficulty. The water was brought at the time because he had these monkeys who could perform extraordinary feats. Even here it is mentioned, that the waters were fetched from rivers, seas and other sacred sources.

नदीनदेभ्यः संहृत्य तीर्थेभ्यश्च समन्ततः ।
आहृत्य च समुद्रेभ्यः सर्वेभ्यो वानरर्षभाः ॥
शास्त्रदृष्टेन विधिना महर्षिविहितेन च ॥ IV. 26. 32-34

The commentary says that some Brahmans had been brought from the neighbouring territory to help on this occasion, for otherwise it is difficult to conceive who the monkeys were that had knowledge of the *sastra*. One commentator actually mentions Bodhayana. I doubt very much. Here it is worth mentioning that the bathing ceremony was by the water being poured by the friends of Sugriva, Hanuman, Jambavan, etc.

One other thing we may notice. The poet does not say that when Sugriva was crowned or anointed, Tara sat along with him, or Ruma. He seems to have enjoyed the honour by himself. Lakshmana plays a great part in the coming *abhisheka* ceremony of Vibhishana. That he did not take part in the ceremony in Kishkindha is not made clear, and he might have been among the friends who poured water on Sugriva. The poet does not say. I think therefore that the ceremony was confined to the tribes of Sugriva.

Vibhishana was bathed symbolically on this side of the strait.

> इति ब्रुवाणं रामस्तु परिष्वज्य विभीषणम् ।
> अब्रवील्लक्ष्मणं प्रीतः समुद्राज्जलमानय ॥
> तेन चेमं महाप्राज्ञमभिषिञ्च विभीषणम् ।
> राजानं रक्षसां क्षिप्रं प्रसन्ने मयि मानद ॥
> एवमुक्तस्तु सौमित्रिरभ्यषिञ्चद्विभीषणम् ।
> मध्ये वानरमुख्यानां राजानं रामशासनात् ॥ VI. 19. 24-26

As the ocean was quite near, it was very easy to bring the water. Here it is mentioned that it was Lakshmana who poured water on Vibhishana's head. The same thing happens when Vibhishana was actually crowned after the death of Ravana.

> ततस्त्वेकं घटं गृह्य संस्थाप्य परमासने ।
> घटेन तेन सौमित्रिरभ्यषिञ्चद्विभीषणम् ॥
> लङ्कायां रक्षसां मध्ये राजानं रामशासनात् ।
> विधिना मन्त्रदृष्टेन सुहृद्गणसमावृतम् ॥
> अभ्यषिञ्चत् स धर्मात्मा शुद्धात्मानं विभीषणम् ॥ VI. 115. 14-16

He had a gold *kumbha* brought. He did it again. Then the Rakshasas followed and then the Vanaras. It must have been somewhat trying for the principal party to sit all the time when the water was being poured on the head. But the difficulty was, I think, greater in the case of Rama, who had by his side Sita. You will see how much water was poured on them and by how many people.

But before we go on to the actual ceremony, let us pay some little attention to a little point. In this *sarga* 131 there are a number of *slokas* in the beginning which are almost the same, word for word, as some *slokas* in the Ayodhya-kanda, 105th *sarga*. Therefore, for the poet to repeat the same *slokas* in two places, there must have been a wonderful parallelism of circumstances. What was it? In the Ayodhya-kanda, Bharata, with the whole of the palace and the army and the important citizens of Ayodhya, came to visit Sri Rama and persuade him to return. Then he makes a speech to Sri Rama inviting him to take the kingdom and the crown. He then explains why he holds himself unfitted to be king and why Sri Rama should take the kingdom. In exactly the same way, when Rama has returned after his great triumph, Bharata offers the kingdom again to him. "I have so far managed it as your representative. Now you are here, I deliver the kingdom back to you." So that you see Bharata offered the kingdom once more as he did it before. And the poet, thinking of the similarity in the condition, uses the same *slokas* again. I shall read the *slokas* first and then my translation.

पूजिता मामिका माता दत्त राज्यमिदं मम।
तद्ददामि पुनस्तुभ्यं यथा त्वमददा मम॥
धुरमेकाकिना न्यस्तामृषभेण बलीयसा।
किशोरीव गुरुं भारं न वोढुमहमुत्सहे॥
वारिवेगेन महता भिन्नः सेतुरिव क्षरन्।
दुर्बन्धनमिदं मन्ये राज्यच्छिद्रमसंवृतम्॥
गतिं खर इवाश्वस्य हंसस्येव च वायसः।
नान्वेतुमुत्सहे राम तव मार्गमरिन्दम॥
यथा चारोपितो वृक्षो जातश्चान्तर्निवेशने।
महांश्च सुदुरारोहो महास्कन्धप्रशाखवान्॥
शीर्येत पुष्पितो भूत्वा न फलानि प्रदर्शयन्।
तस्य नानुभवेदर्थं यस्य हेतोः स रोप्यते॥
एषोपमा महाबाहो त्वदर्थं वेत्तुमर्हसि।
यद्यस्मान्मनुजेन्द्र त्वं भक्तान् भृत्यान्न शाधि हि॥
जगदद्याभिषिक्तं त्वामनुपश्यतु सर्वतः।
प्रतपन्तमिवादित्यं मध्याह्णे दीप्ततेजसम्॥
तूर्यसङ्घातनिर्घोषैः काञ्चीनूपुरनिःस्वनैः।
मधुरैर्गीतशब्दैश्च प्रतिबुध्यस्व राघव॥ VI. 131. 2-10

सान्त्विता मामिका माता दत्तं राज्यमिदं मम।
तद्ददामि तवैवाहं भुङ्क्ष्व राज्यमकण्टकम्॥
महतेवाम्बुवेगेन भिन्नः सेतुर्जलागमे।
दुरावारं त्वदन्येन राज्यखण्डमिदं महत्॥
गतिं खर इवाश्वस्य तार्क्ष्यस्येव पतत्रिणः।
अनुगन्तुं न शक्तिर्मे गतिं तव महीपते॥

सुजीवं नित्यशस्तस्य यः परैरुपजीव्यते ।
राम तेन तु दुर्जीवं यः परानुपजीवति ॥
यथा तु रोपितो वृक्षः पुरुषेण विवर्धितः ।
ह्रस्वकेन दुरारोहो रूढस्कन्धो महाद्रुमः ॥
स यथा पुष्पितो भूत्वा फलानि न निदर्शयेत् ।
स तां नानुभवेत्प्रीतिं यस्य हेतोः प्ररोपितः ॥
एषोपमा महाबाहो तमर्थं वेत्तुमर्हसि ।
यदि त्वमस्मान् वृषभो भर्ता भृत्यान्न शाधि हि ॥
श्रेणयस्त्वां महाराज पश्यन्त्वग्र्याश्च सर्वशः ।
प्रतपन्तमिवादित्यं राज्ये स्थितमरिंदमम् ॥
तवानुयाने काकुत्स्थ मत्ता नर्दन्तु कुञ्जराः ।
अन्तःपुरगता नार्यो नन्दन्तु सुसमाहिताः ॥ II. 105. 4-12

All the words and sentiments fit the two contexts. "As you handed the kingdom over to me, I shall hand the kingdom over to you. After all, my mother who was so anxious has been gratified. My mother has been treated with proper reverence, and her great wish has been gratified. This kingdom has been given to me, and as you gave it me, so I give it back to you. For I cannot carry this crushing burden, being but a puny calf where a mighty bull must bear the yoke. I shrink from the perils of a large State, for once disorders break out, they are not easily quelled, any more than a swift torrent can be brought under control after it has burst its dam. How can I hope to follow where you have gone with your inimitable tread? How can a donkey go through the paces of a horse or a crow show the graceful movements of a swan? Another comparison strikes me as suitable. I shall barely suggest it, you alone can comprehend all its implications. If you disappoint the eager people and do not undertake their protection just when they need and expect it, you will be like a tree grown to gigantic size, striking awe into the breasts of men dwarfed beside it, with enormous branches and imposing foliage, but bearing no fruit at all. Think of the sense of frustration and wasted effort of many long years in the heart of the man who planted and tended it with extraordinary care as he watches its luxuriance and rich promise wither away in barrenness. I pray you let no such calamity befall us. Let the expectant people see you anointed king and wearing the lustrous crown of Ayodhya, as they might behold the sun risen to full meridian resplendence. Assume the dignity and pomp of this high station. Every day henceforth, whenever you rise to the day's labours or retire to seek repose at night, your ears shall be regaled by the sound of drums and the music of melodious instruments and the sweeter music of girdles and anklets as fair damsels trip it gaily for your amusement and relaxation." (VI. 131. 2-10). You see how the sentiments fit in on both occasions. These are Bharata's words making a most impressive and undeniable invitation to take the crown.

Rama has come into Nandigrama and there he is seated. Then he is prepared for the great ceremony. The first thing to do is for him to put on civilisation after fourteen years of forest life. The hair has grown all over his head and face, and so he has to be relieved of all this burden. Satrughna orders a number of barbers to appear on the scene.

ततः शत्रुघ्नवचनान्निपुणाः श्मश्रुवर्धकाः ।
सुखहस्ताः सुशीघ्राश्च राघवं पर्युपासत ॥ VI. 131. 13

How all of them could have worked on his head, I cannot imagine. I suppose a selection was to be made. Each might have asked for a minute's turn. All these persons were then bathed. Here it is worth mentioning that all the three brothers are mentioned, and Sugriva and Vibhishana also as having bathed. But poor Satrughna is not mentioned. Once before, when all the brothers were seated to hold the famous conversation in Chitrakuta, Satrughna was not mentioned at all. The commentators say we have to assume that Satrughna was also seated. Apparently, as having been the master of the ceremony and ordered the people about, he did it last and in double quick time. Sita was also decorated for the occasion. Dasaratha's queens decorated Sita themselves. Usually the decoration is performed by professional maids. This time they wanted to have the honour themselves. The poet expressly says that the monkeys who started the procession from Nandigrama to Ayodhya all assumed human form, perhaps to make themselves a little more presentable. In the Yuddhakanda we are specially told that Rama issued an order on the day before the war began. He told the monkeys,

"I know you can all take human form. But remember, in this fight I do not want you at all to do so. Remain monkeys. Only seven people on our side should assume human form." Now, however, there was no such necessity. Then, water was brought for the occasion by the monkeys. What happened to the waters that were brought by Dasaratha and were not used at all, I do not know.

उवाच च महातेजाः सुग्रीवं राघवानुजः।
अभिषेकाय रामस्य दूतानाज्ञापय प्रभो॥
सौवर्णान् वानरेन्द्राणां चतुर्णां चतुरो घटान्।
ददौ क्षिप्रं स सुग्रीवः सर्वरत्नविभूषितान्॥
यथा प्रत्यूषसमये चतुर्णां सागराम्भसाम्।
पूर्णैर्घटैः प्रतीक्षध्वं तथा कुरुत वानराः॥
एवमुक्ता महात्मानो वानरा वारणोपमाः।
उत्पेतुर्गगनं शीघ्रं गरुडानिलशीघ्रगाः॥
जाम्बवांश्च सुषेणश्च वेगदर्शी च वानरः।
ऋषभश्चैव कलशाञ्जलपूर्णानथानयन्॥
नदीशतानां पञ्चानां जलकुम्भेषु चाहरन्।
पूर्वात् समुद्रात् कलशं जलपूर्णमथानयत्॥
सुषेणः सत्त्वसंपन्नः सर्वरत्नविभूषितम्।
ऋषभो दक्षिणात्तूर्णं समुद्राज्जलमाहरत्॥
रक्तचन्दनशाखाभिः संवृतं काञ्चनं घटम्।
गवयः पश्चिमात्तोयमाजहार महार्णवात्॥
रत्नकुम्भेन महता शीतं मारुतविक्रमः।
उत्तराच्च जलं शीघ्रं गरुडानिलविक्रमः॥
आजहार स धर्मात्मा नलः सर्वगुणान्वितः॥ VI. 131. 48-57

Bharata told Sugriva to order the monkeys to bring water from the four oceans early in the morning, and also from five hundred rivers. I wonder what the northern ocean was which is referred to. Hanuman of course did wonders. He has often gone north to bring the *sanjivani*. But what ocean it was I do not see, unless it was Manasasarovar. This is the first occasion when we see the queen crowned along with the king. Neither in Sugriva's nor in Vibhishana's case do we find it. All the rishis took the lead in pouring water on Rama's head, as the Vasus bathed Indra. Next came the *Ritvigs*. The gods who stood in mid air poured waters. Then there was a crown brought. This crown was the one that had been used for Manu, the first progenitor of the family. Vasishtha put the crown on Rama's head, and the other *Ritvigs* came round and put all the ornaments on the head. Presents were given and received. Indra sent by Vayu a garland of precious stones. Rama gave away a lot; a lakh of horses, bulls and cows, a hundred magnificent bulls and thirty crores of gold coins. The distribution must have taken place in a thousand places all over the town. You remember that Sita got a beautiful garland, which with Rama's permission she gave away to Hanuman.

Then the poet comes to the end. He says all the guests were given leave and they took farewell of Sri Rama. Laden with costly presents, the monkeys were sent back to their home. Vibhishana departed, having obtained his *Kula-dhana*—

विभीषणोऽपि धर्मात्मा सह तैर्नैर्ऋतर्षभैः ।
लब्ध्वा कुलधनं राजा लङ्कां प्रायाद्विभीषणः ॥ VI. 131. 90

meaning that Lanka that was given to him was the *kula-dhana*. One commentator says *kula* means *Ikshvakukula;* if we are to believe the story prevalent, a great image of Ranganatha was in Sri Rama's palace at the time and was given away to Vibhishana. Some people say so. There is no authority at all in the text for it. There is a slight discrepancy between this account in the Yuddhakanda at the end, and the account in the Uttarakanda. As a matter of fact in the Uttarakanda the story is that Vibhishana stayed in Ayodhya either six months by one account or a whole year after the *abhisheka* with Sri Rama, hearing all sorts of stories from Agastya. But one commentator says ingeniously that the farewell that is described in the Yuddhakanda is merely to bring the *kanda* to a decent end, and that this is the real farewell. It changes the story, according to the Yuddhakanda in one particular, and it is not at all a change for the better, as you will see.

ततोऽस्य हारं चन्द्राभं मुच्य कण्ठात् स राघवः ।
वैदूर्यतरलं कण्ठे बबन्ध च हनूमतः ॥ VII. 40. 24

It is said here that Rama took a *hara* from his own neck and placed it round Hanuman's neck. But our own story is that Sri Rama gave it to Sita, and Sita with his express permission gave it to Hanuman as the person most fitted for the present. Rama himself says, "You had better choose the person in whom all these qualities are united" and he mentions some very superb qualities. Of course there is no second choice to be made.

Then there is one expression that I want to draw your attention to. It is from the Uttarakanda.

कृतप्रसादास्तेनैवं राघवेण महात्मना ।
जग्मुः स्वं स्वं गृहं सर्वे देही देहमिव त्यजन् ॥ VII. 40. 39

"Each went to his several home." As usual, there is a simile. This simile is full of significance. Each person, when he took leave of Rama and Sita and those excellent men, was really sad at having to go, just as a body is sorry to part. Very few people are glad to die. Our grief chokes us even if we are conscious at the time. Therefore the poet says, when each person took leave of Sri Rama, he was like a *dehi* leaving his body.

Now, ladies and gentlemen, that is the account we see of the *abhisheka* ceremony. We are all very happy indeed that this series of talks has ended in the *abhisheka*. But I should be false to myself if I close at this point without saying what is uppermost in my heart, that the real coronation is in our hearts. Rama and Sita should be crowned in our hearts, enthroned in our hearts. Let them govern your thoughts and regulate your lives. At all important times remember them, and then you cannot go wrong. This is not a sentimental closing, but I really feel that having studied the Ramayana together these months, we must make up our minds that that study will have its beneficial effect upon our lives and upon our nature. We have not studied this poem as a mere poem. We have studied it as a means of purifying our lives. Rama and Sita, not to speak of the others, are often spoken of as the hero and heroine crowned with the perfection of human quality. It is a beautiful sentiment, but in understanding it, there is a qualification we have got to make. The perfection was not there from the beginning; it grew from stage to stage. We began to know of Rama before he was born, and from the time he was born, we follow him in his career. The great incidents and episodes in his life, his trials and tribulations, the adversities he went through, the great changes of fortune that came over him, is it natural to suppose that all these things had no effect on his character, that he was that at the end which he was at the beginning? Life is not that sort of thing. All humanity learns at every step. Every episode in our life, everything that happens to us, has its effect upon us. Adversities teach us one set of lessons. Prosperity teaches us another set of lessons. Nothing happens to us but leaves its mark on our nature. So let us think of Sri Rama as having marched forward to his perfection step by step. For so shall we profit most by his life and by his advance, and by Sita's life and her advance, if we dwell on each incident and each episode with the desire to see how it affected them and how they reacted to it. Otherwise we shall not learn much from the Poem. It is an essentially human document. Valmiki is a master of human nature. He knew it through and through. That is why he takes us step by step, records all the conversations at length. It is only when we contemplate the hero and heroine as undergoing the trials of life and enjoying all the good things that happened to them, it is only as we watch them through the vicissitudes of their life and make note of the way they profit by these things, that we shall get from the study of the Ramayana the utmost advantage that it is capable of giving. So once more I ask you most devoutly, most earnestly, never to let these, Rama and Sita, be far from your heart. We must make an honest and earnest endeavour always to regard Rama and Sita as a model to follow. Then we shall have spent these Wednesday evenings to good purpose, and the eight months that we have spent together on Wednesdays will have given us a great deal of spiritual as well as intellectual benefit.

INDEX

The Publishers had drawn up a complete alphabetical Index of half-verses quoted in the Lectures, but owing to certain printing difficulties, they had regretfully to give up its inclusion in this volume. In its place is furnished below an Index of all slokas in the Ramayana quoted, translated, or referred to in the Lectures, in order of Kanda and Sarga according to the Madras Law Journal Press Edition, which, it is hoped, may be found serviceable.

VII. UTTARAKANDA

CROSS-REFERENCES

The Lectures being character-studies, some of the illustrative verses occur more than once. Besides cross-references supplied at foot of the pages, the following may be found helpful.

Page	Line	cp. Page	Page	Line	cp. Page
32	12	376	193	5	443
34	12	436	"	12	444
45	26	114	"	32	449
50	5	96	194	9	443
54	16	379	200	25	426
55	14	381	203	32	406
66	34	112	205	36	104
73	25	390	207	19	127
75	14	416	208	4	424
"	23	417	211	20	157
"	28	417	216	35	236
"	34	417	248	9	354
76	21	417	250	36	108
95	10	213	251	4	214
103	24	132	"	11	315
"	31	132	293	25	137
"	36	117, 140	305	24	392
104	9	127, 207	326	16	107
"	12	205	344	33	347
"	17	117, 141	347	14	344
107	34	326	354	8	248
108	9	250	357	36	114
110	2	117, 410	390	18	73
"	30	414	392	27	305
111	2	414	410	22	110, 117
"	5	415	414	25	110
114	10	431	"	29	111
"	18	357	415	7	111
117	15	110, 410	416	30	75
124	13	450	417	2	75
127	17	207	"	6	75
"	21	104, 207	"	13	75
132	10	103	"	24	76
"	14	103	419	7	193
137	32	293	436	20	34
147	1	153	443	29	193
153	35	147	"	35	194
157	19	211	444	6	193
174	9	396	450	28	124

ERRATA

Page	*Line*	*For*	*Read*
16	24	तदनं	तदैनं
147	31	भयेत्	भवेत्
200	26	II. 45. 8	II. 45. 7
303	18	सुहांस्त्वास:	सुमहांस्त्वास:
310-11	Transfer fn. on p. 311 to p. 310.		
337	32	19-26	8-10